Organizational Behavior

CORE CONCEPTS

Fourth Edition

Organizational Behavior

CORE CONCEPTS

Fourth Edition

Robert P. Vecchio

Franklin D. Schurz Professor of Management
University of Notre Dame

The Dryden Press
A Division of Harcourt College Publishers

Fort Worth   Philadelphia   San Diego   New York   Orlando   Austin   San Antonio
Toronto   Montreal   London   Sydney   Tokyo

Publisher	Mike Roche
Acquisitions Editor	John Weimeister
Market Strategist	Lisé Johnson
Developmental Editor	Bobbie Bochenko
Project Editor	Christy Goldfinch
Art Director	Scott Baker
Production Manager	Cindy Young

"Construction Workers at Lunch" cover photo © FPG International

ISBN: 0-03-025856-1

Library of Congress Catalog Card Number: 99-63504

Address for Domestic Orders
The Dryden Press, 6277 Sea Harbor Drive, Orlando, FL 32887-6777
800-782-4479

Address for International Orders
International Customer Service
The Dryden Press, 6277 Sea Harbor Drive, Orlando, FL 32887-6777
407-345-3800
(fax) 407-345-4060
(e-mail) hbintl@harcourtbrace.com

Address for Editorial Correspondence
The Dryden Press, 301 Commerce Street, Suite 3700, Fort Worth, TX 76102

Web Site Address
http://www.harcourtcollege.com
THE DRYDEN PRESS, DRYDEN, and the DP LOGO are registered trademarks of Harcourt, Inc.

Printed in the United States of America

9 0 1 2 3 4 5 6 7 8   032   9 8 7 6 5 4 3 2

The Dryden Press
Harcourt College Publishers

To Betty, Julie, and Mark

The Dryden Press Series in Management

Anthony, Perrewé, and Kacmar
Strategic Human Resource Management
Third Edition

Bereman, Lengnick-Hall, and Mark
Compensation Decision Making: A Computer-Based Approach
Second Edition

Bergmann, Scarpello, and Hills
Compensation Decision Making
Third Edition

Boone and Kurtz
Contemporary Business
Ninth Edition

Bourgeois, Duhaime, and Stimpert
Strategic Management: From Concept to Implementation
Second Edition

Calvasina and Barton
Chopstick Company: A Business Simulation

Carrell, Ebert, and Hatfield
Human Resource Management: Strategies for Managing a Diverse Global Work Force
Sixth Edition

Costin
Readings in Total Quality Management

Costin
Managing in the Global Economy: The European Union

Costin
Economic Reform in Latin America

Costin
Management Development and Training: A TQM Approach

Costin
Readings in Strategy and Strategic Management

Czinkota, Ronkainen, and Moffett
International Business
Fifth Edition

Czinkota, Ronkainen, Moffett, and Moynihan
Global Business
Second Edition

Daft
Leadership: Theory and Practice

Daft
Management
Fifth Edition

Daft and Marcic
Understanding Management
Second Edition

DeSimone and Harris
Human Resource Development
Second Edition

Dilworth
Operations Management
Third Edition

Foegen
Business Plan Guidebook
Revised Edition

Gatewood and Feild
Human Resource Selection
Fourth Edition

Gold
Exploring Organizational Behavior: Readings, Cases, Experiences

About the Author

Robert P. Vecchio (Ph.D., University of Illinois) holds the Franklin D. Schurz Chair in Management at the University of Notre Dame. Since joining the University in 1976, Professor Vecchio has taught and conducted research on organizational behavior and human resources management, with special emphasis on leadership. From 1983 to 1990, Professor Vecchio served as head of the Department of Management and Administrative Sciences at Notre Dame. He has served on the editorial boards of the *Academy of Management Review*, the *Journal of Management*, the *Journal of Managerial Inquiry*, *Employee Responsibilities and Rights Journal*, *International Journal of Applied Quality Management*, and the *International Journal of Organizational Analysis*. From 1995 to 2000, he served as editor-in-chief of the *Journal of Management*. The *Journal* is a broad-gauge outlet that publishes rigorous empirical research in all aspects of management, with emphasis on issues surrounding effective management and leadership, as well as social responsibility.

Professor Vecchio was selected as a Fellow of the Center for Creative Leadership in 1974. Also, he was the recipient of a grant from the U.S. Department of Labor to study the leadership process. He has published numerous articles in such journals as the *Journal of Applied Psychology*, the *Academy of Management Journal*, the *Academy of Management Review*, *Organizational Behavior and Human Performance*, the *Journal of Management*, the *Journal of Organizational Behavior*, *Leadership Quarterly*, and *Human Relations*. He has also published *Leadership: Understanding the Dynamics of Power and Influence in Organizations*, with the University of Notre Dame Press. Professor Vecchio has served as a consultant to both for-profit and not-for-profit organizations. He is listed in *Who's Who in America* and *Who's Who in the World*.

Preface

One of my goals in preparing this textbook was to present the substance of the field of organizational behavior in a manner that conveys my personal fascination with the social dynamics that occur in work settings. I have been excited by this field since my first encounter with a course in organizational behavior, more than a few years ago, as a student. The topic captivated me because I had held a number of different jobs up to that point in my life, and I could see the relevance and value of understanding the interpersonal dynamics that exist in the workplace. I began to read more about human behavior in organizations and ultimately came to teach courses in organizational behavior. In writing this book, I attempted to share some of my interest and enthusiasm by taking the scholarly foundations of the field and translating them into a more understandable and accessible format.

Audience and Coverage

This text is designed to provide an introductory overview of the field. The primary intended audience is students at four-year and two-year undergraduate institutions. Also, the text would be relevant for an introductory course in an MBA program. The text reviews the necessary behavioral science foundations, and hence, no prior course work in psychology or sociology is required of the reader. Also, the text does not require extensive prior work experience in order for the reader to comprehend the concepts. The material that is covered is essentially the core material that defines the field of organizational behavior. While other texts attempt to cover four hundred to five hundred concepts in a single text, I have decided to focus instead on only the key concepts that a student should grasp. Because of this focus on essentials, the text is especially suitable for being supplemented by an instructor's additional selected reading materials. Also, the text would be suitable for a quarter-term course, a course in a summer program, or a course that relies on experiential exercises as a major component. It is my hope, therefore, that this text fills an important niche for those instructors who are seeking something other than a traditional broad-coverage type of textbook.

Organization of the Text

In preparing this edition, I sought to maintain a balanced treatment of theory and practice, while presenting classic and contemporary "cutting edge" concepts. Important organizational behavior terms are covered, along with key elements from human resources management, organizational development, and cross-cultural issues. In addition, several chapters are devoted exclusively to organizational theory.

The chapters are organized and arranged so that the material progresses in traditional fashion from a micro (individual) to a more macro (group and organizational) level. The chapters are grouped into three major sections, reflecting this progression: Part I, Individual Processes; Part II, Interpersonal Processes; Part III, Organizational Structure and Dynamics. Under the heading of Individual Processes (Chapters 1 through 5), topics in perception, personality, and motivation are explored. Interpersonal Processes (Chapters 6 through 11 in Part II), includes treatments of power, leadership, decision making, group dynamics, conflict, and stress. The final section, Organizational Structure and Dynamics (Chapters 12 through 15 in Part III), examines issues in communication, organizational design, environmental and cultural influences, and organizational change and development.

Pedagogy

This textbook includes a number of pedagogical features designed to enhance student learning and comprehension.

Learning Objectives   Seven to ten learning objectives at the beginning of each chapter focus the reader's attention on major issues within the chapter.

Vignettes and Boxes   New short articles, written by G. Bernard Yevin, Fontbonne College, illustrate organizational behavior principles. Chapter-opening vignettes, based on real organizations, give true-to-life flavor to chapter topics. The boxed feature "An Inside Look" provides current examples drawn from a variety of corporations and businesses, emphasizing aspects of ethics, diversity, and international issues as they apply to the field of organizational behavior.

Summaries   At the end of each chapter, a summary recaps chapter learning objectives and highlights critical points.

Key Terms   Each chapter contains a list of key terms for the student to use in sorting out and reviewing important concepts.

Critical Incidents and Experiential Exercises   Each chapter is followed by a Critical Incident, a short case for discussion that applies chapter concepts. An Experiential Exercise is also included for each chapter. Some are designed for individual use and some for group participation.

Glossary   A glossary containing definitions of key terms appears at the end of the book. Key terms are set in boldfaced type where they first appear in the text.

Supplements

A comprehensive set of supplements accompanies the fourth edition of *Organizational Behavior*.

Instructor's Manual   The manual includes extensive chapter outlines; class openers; discussion questions and answers; additional experiential exercises; additional readings lists; examples from the popular press to help illustrate lectures; answers to in-text Critical Incidents and Experiential Exercises; additional cases; transparency masters; and teaching notes for the transparency acetates. The *Instructor's Manual* was prepared by Paul Keaton, University of Wisconsin–La Crosse.

Test Bank   Thoroughly revised and accuracy-tested, the *Test Bank* contains over 2,500 items to help gauge student comprehension. Its unique combination of question types includes true/false, multiple choice, essay, and mini-case questions. Each question is classified according to the level of difficulty. The *Test Bank* was prepared by Robert P. Vecchio, University of Notre Dame, and Earl W. Crisp, University of Texas at Arlington.

Computerized Test Bank   A computerized version of the printed test bank is available for IBM-compatible computers.

Transparency Acetates   Color transparency acetates of key figures and concepts used in teaching organizational behavior and teaching notes for them are available. Teaching notes are included in the *Instructor's Manual*.

Video Package   Closely tied to the text, videos featuring real-world organizations and events focus on such topics as decision making, corporate culture, leadership, motivation, and enhancing employee performance.

Acknowledgements

The current and past editions of this book benefited from the efforts of many people. I must say a very special "thank you" to the many reviewers who made numerous suggestions on how to revise and improve the content of each chapter: Samuel Rabinowitz, Rutgers University; Douglas M. McCabe, Georgetown University; Raymond Read, Baylor University; Joseph C. Rallo, Ferris State University; Shiori Sakamoto, California State Polytechnic–Pomona; Cheryl Wyrick, California State Polytechnic–Pomona; Elizabeth C. Ravlin, University of South Carolina; Edward W. Miles, Georgia State University; Sandra Hartman, University of New Orleans; and Carol Harvey, Assumption College.

I am also indebted to the professionals at The Dryden Press who aided in the book's development, production, and design: John Weimeister, Bobbie Bochenko, Christy Goldfinch, Scott Baker, and Cindy Young. I am also grateful for the support of Donna Frahn, who helped in preparing the final manuscript, and my wife, Betty, who critiqued much of the writing. Without their support, suggestions, patience, and encouragement, and the continuing support of my children, this edition would not have been published.

Robert P. Vecchio
June 1999

Contents in Brief

Contents

PART II   *Interpersonal Processes*   123

PART III   *Organizational Structure and Dynamics*   287

PART ONE
Individual Processes

1

An Introduction
to Organizational Behavior

Management is the art of getting other people to do all
the work.

—Anonymous

Organizational behavior is the
science of predicting how
employees will behave, and
then explaining why they don't.

—A Manager

Learning Objectives

After studying this chapter, you should be able to:

1. Define the purpose and nature of the field of organizational behavior.
2. Tell why organizational behavior is an important field of study for managers.
3. Distinguish organizational behavior from organizational theory, human resources management, and organizational development.
4. Outline the basic principles of scientific management and discuss the shortcomings of this approach for managing employee behavior.
5. Relate the findings of the Hawthorne Studies to the development of the human relations approach.
6. Explain why believers in the contingency approach rarely give a simple answer to a seemingly simple question.
7. Describe the currently dominant perspectives in the field of organizational behavior.
8. Cite several challenges that confront managers in the 21st century.
9. Respond to critics who contend that most principles of organizational behavior are obvious.

A Breakthrough View on Management?

With the advent of the re-engineering of the firm, managers are taking a close look at the factors that are critical to the long-term success of an organization. One "new" approach to competitive success recognizes the value of employees as a fundamental asset of the organization. Building competitive success focuses on the value of employees. This approach requires that organizations modify their view of employees and take the lead in developing a corporate culture that maximizes opportunities for attaining both corporate and employee goals. Employees are no longer seen as expendable commodities that drive up operational costs, but as valued assets and keys to corporate viability and competitiveness.

Today, the most successful firms understand that their sustained advantage in the marketplace depends not only on high technology, proprietary information, physical facilities, or patents, but also on how they manage their workforce. The top five performing companies based on return to stockholders — Plenum Publishing, Circuit City, Tyson Foods, Wal-Mart, and

Southwest Airlines—all place high value on how they manage employees. Here are ten policies and practices to adopt in order to improve the culture and increase employee productivity:

Incentive pay is more than money; alternative compensation, recognition, security and fair treatment also have great value to employees.

Employee ownership creates less conflict between management and labor while putting stock in the hands of people likely to take the long-term view.

Employment security conveys the company's commitment to its workforce.

Selective recruiting allows the company to find the best people in the best way. Rigorous selection lets people feel that they are joining an elite organization where higher expectations are the norm.

Competitive wages convey the message that the company values its employees.

Information sharing gives employees the information necessary to do what is required.

Participation and empowerment enable employees to determine and control their own work process.

Cross-training makes work more interesting and challenging for employees at all levels; builds employment security; and provides a flexible workforce.

Promoting from within shows commitment to employees while perpetuating the culture and values of the organization.

Self-managed teams, in which peers monitor and coordinate work, promote participation and empowerment while reducing demands on management.

One difficulty of attaining competitive advantage via the workforce is the time that it takes. Management must commit to the long view; but it can generate significant rewards. Competitive advantage obtained through proactive employment practices is likely to be significantly more enduring and hard to duplicate by competitors.

Source: Adapted from Jeffrey Pfeffer, "Producing Sustainable Competitive Advantage Through the Effective Management of People," *Academy of Management Executive* 9, no.1 (1995).

What Is Organizational Behavior?

All of us have wondered why some people succeed and others fail in the world of work. Most of us have also marveled at how some people seem to possess a bottomless well of enthusiasm for their work, while others regard their work as something slightly better than torture. Although most of us often do nothing more than speculate on the factors that affect our work lives, behavioral scientists have established a relatively new field of inquiry concerned with the scientific study of the behavioral processes that occur in work settings, the field of *organizational behavior*. The content of this field is quite broad. It encompasses such topics as employee attitudes, motivation, and performance, to name a few. And it extends to larger organizational and societal factors, such as the structure of organizations and environmental pressures, that influence an individual's behavior and attitudes.

The field of organizational behavior borrows many concepts and methods from the behavioral and social sciences, such as psychology, sociology, political science, and anthropology, because all are relevant to understanding people's behavior in organizational settings. As a result, issues and topics touching on many academic disciplines may become the subject of study in the field of organizational behavior. Thus, in this book, we will examine sociological topics, such as the importance of organizational structure; psychological questions, such as the importance of personality factors in explaining employee behavior; anthropological concerns with the influence of culture; and political science topics, such as the distribution and use of power in an organization. In general, however, organizational behavior draws most heavily from the field of psychology. In fact, many of the major contributors to the field are psychologists (for example, Maslow, Herzberg, Hackman, Lawler, and Skinner).

Why Bother? Or, Three Reasons for Studying Organizational Behavior

Practical Applications

There are important practical benefits to understanding the principles of organizational behavior. For example, the development of a personal style of leadership can be guided by knowledge of the results of studies that have attempted to relate leadership style to situational requirements (Chapter 7). The choice of a problem-solving strategy (Chapter 8) can be guided by an understanding of the results of studies in the associated topic areas. Especially in the area of performance enhancement (Chapters 3 to 5), benefits can be gained by applying the knowledge that has been gathered in the field of organizational behavior. Additionally, because the environment in which organizations operate is increasing in complexity (Chapter 14), one must understand how to design effective organization structures (Chapter 13) and how to relate to individuals from diverse, and often international, backgrounds (Chapter 14).

It is difficult to overstate the practical importance of being able to deal effectively with others in organizational settings. Attracting and developing talented individuals are two issues critically important to the survival and prosperity of an organization. Emphasis on the *human element* (instead of on technical, financial, and other tangible resources) often separates competing organizations when it comes to organizational performance. This occurs because all serious competitors in a given industry are likely to have attained nearly the same level of technical sophistication. Thus, other things being equal, organizations that have talented and dedicated employees are likely to be more effective. Furthermore, within a given industry, the variability on human dimensions across organizations is likely to be greater than the variability on technical dimensions. Consequently, we can argue that the element that is most important to an organization's welfare—and the one that may be most neglected because of its less tangible nature—is the behavioral element.

As an illustration of how crucial the human element is to organizational excellence, consider professional football teams. All have much the same equipment and facilities. For example, each team has a stadium, a staff of trainers, practice facilities, state-of-the-art equipment, and the like. In addition, each team has the same number of members and essentially the same structure. Therefore, what distinguishes one team from another in the eyes of sports enthusiasts and on the field is largely traceable to the human element: the talent of the players and coaches, the ability of coaches to develop their players' talents, and the ability of the coaches and players to motivate themselves to high levels of accomplishment.

A similar illustration can be made for the reputations of universities and colleges. Generally speaking, colleges that seek to have prestigious reputations have much the same facilities (for example, classrooms, dormitories, and attractive landscaping). However, those institutions having faculty members who possess strong reputations in their fields and students who are more competitively admitted have more solid reputations. The separation of institutions on the dimension of reputation is based largely on the human element.

Personal Growth

The second reason for studying organizational behavior is the personal fulfillment we gain from understanding our fellow humans. Understanding others may also lead to greater self-knowledge and self-insight. Such personal growth is an aspect of education that is often cited as the greatest benefit of studying the liberal arts and sciences. Some may question the practical value of this feature in the business world. But it can, in fact, make a difference when it comes to advancing beyond an entry-level position. Entry-level hirings are based largely on technical competency, such as certification in a specialized area by a BBA, a CPA, or an MBA. Promotions, however, are often based on more than mere technical competency. They are often based on demonstrated abilities to understand and work effectively with superiors, peers, and subordinates. In short, an understanding of organizational behavior may not be a "union card" that helps you get your first job in any obvious way, but it will be invaluable to you once you have that first job and seek to distinguish yourself.

Students who are taking an introductory organizational behavior (OB) course should understand that the purpose of such a course is to provide a framework into which later personal organizational experiences can be integrated. The course material, therefore, forms a foundation for increasing the extent to which they can learn from experience. In short, *what* one learns in an OB course is not as critical as *how* the course prepares one to learn (and thereby to grow) in an organization. The material in an OB course is relevant to personal growth whether one works for a large, established corporation (such as a General Motors, an IBM, or a Du Pont) or a relatively small, fledgling organization.

In many instances, innovations are made initially within organizations. Later, researchers develop and test explanations as to why the innovations are effective, and under what circumstances these innovations are likely to be particularly effective. A good illustration of how innovation preceded our more basic understanding is given by "mutual goal-setting" that involves a supervisor and an individual subordinate (see Chapter 5).

As a field, organizational behavior is constantly opening new frontiers of knowledge. Most of the scholars in the field are young and recently trained. In fact, it is a fairly safe bet that the vast majority of professionals who have ever claimed affiliation with the field of organizational behavior are still alive today. Many of the journals that publish the findings of OB research are relatively new. As you will notice in reading this text, the studies cited are all fairly recent, covering only the past few decades. Yet the widespread acceptance of organizational behavior as an important subject for future managers is evidenced by the fact that an OB course is included in the curriculum of virtually every business school.

Increased Knowledge

The third goal of organizational behavior is to gather knowledge about people in work settings. At a minimum, the field seeks to gather knowledge for its own sake. As evidenced by the progress of many "pure science" fields, such as physics, space research, and chemistry, the practical use of certain findings may not be apparent for years.

A similar process occurs in the field of organizational behavior. For example, early research on leadership processes identified the major dimensions of leadership (to be discussed fully in Chapter 7). Training specialists who followed this research came to apply the findings in the design of the leadership training programs that are now offered to organizations. Additionally, the study of OB can help one think in a critical fashion about matters that relate to the experience of working. Such critical thinking ability can be useful in analyzing both employee and personal problems.

Organizational Behavior and Its Related Fields

Organizational behavior is the systematic study of the behavior and attitudes of both individuals and groups within organizations. This may be termed a micro-level perspective. At the micro level, an organization's attributes, such as size and structure, are usually taken as givens that have uniform effects on behavior in a particular situation. The focus or unit of analysis for the micro perspective is primarily the individual.

Organizational theory focuses on the organization as the unit of analysis. Organizational attributes, such as goals, technology, and culture, are the objects of study. Organizational theory often uses an across-organizations approach, or macro-level perspective, in gathering new knowledge. Organizational behavior and organizational theory use distinctly different research methods. Organizational behavior usually relies on laboratory and field experimentation for gathering information, while organizational theory tends to rely more on surveys and case studies.

The field of **human resources management** (or personnel management) attempts to apply the principles of the behavioral sciences in the workplace. While organizational behavior is somewhat more concept oriented, human resources management is more concerned with applied techniques and behavioral technology. Human resources management tries to provide a link between the individual and the organization by designing and implementing systems to attract, develop, and motivate individuals within an organization (e.g., via the administration of benefits and compensation programs).

Organizational development is concerned with the introduction of successful changes in organizations. Organizational development specialists sometimes approach the task of change from a macro perspective focusing on the structure and values of the organization. Ultimately, these efforts are intended to enhance organizational effectiveness.

One can distinguish organizational behavior from other closely related fields by its emphasis on the scientific study of behavioral phenomena at the individual and group levels. Organizational theory focuses largely on organizational and environmental phenomena; human resources management focuses on the application of behavioral knowledge in selecting, placing, and training personnel; and organizational development focuses on enhancing organizational performance. A useful but perhaps somewhat oversimplified way of understanding these four fields is to distinguish among them on two dimensions: the micro versus macro level of analysis, and theory versus application. A consideration of the combinations that result from crossing these two dimensions suggests that organizational behavior is a micro/theory-oriented field, human resources management is a micro/application-oriented field, organizational theory is a macro/theory-oriented field, and organizational development is a macro/application-oriented field. (Figure 1.1 summarizes the results of a crossing of these two dimensions.) In this text, you will notice that the related fields of organizational theory, human resources management, and organizational development will also be discussed occasionally.

FIGURE 1.1   *Four Fields in the Organizational Sciences*

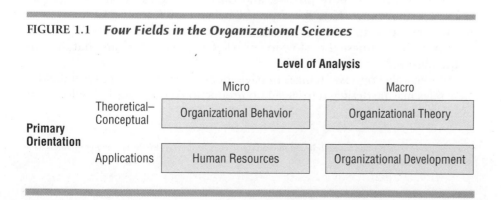

In summary, the field of organizational behavior is characterized by *diversity*, as a consequence of drawing from many different disciplines; *newness*, as evidenced by its relatively recent emergence on the scientific scene; and *vitality*, as demonstrated by the growing number of members in the field, the growth of new publications, and the intensity of scientific debate within the field.

Studying the Behavior of People at Work

Today, organizational behavior is a growing field, rich in its variety of approaches. It is interesting to examine the various ways of viewing worker behavior that have emerged over the years. Taking a historical perspective on attitudes toward worker behavior helps us to both understand where organizational behavior stands today and visualize the directions it may take in the future.

Scientific Management

The Industrial Revolution of the 19th century brought about many radical changes in the management of workers. In contrast to the work of craftspeople of earlier times, work became centrally located in factories. Also, jobs required less skill because machines controlled production processes. Though production increased dramatically, other results of these sweeping changes were not all positive. Some writers, most notably Adam Smith and Karl Marx, pointed out that simplification of work processes beyond a certain point could have diminishing returns and produce feelings of alienation in workers.

Although we recognize the significance of these criticisms of work simplification today, the industrialists of the early 20th century were not yet ready to do so. They preferred an engineering approach to managing worker behavior called **scientific management**. Scientific management, developed by Frederick Taylor, called for the detailed analysis of tasks and time-and-motion studies in conjunction with piece-rate pay schemes in order to improve productivity.[*] Believers in scientific management searched for the "one best way" to perform a task. They introduced standard parts and procedures. In the extreme, the scientific management approach subscribes to the belief that one single best solution exists for a given situation.

The scientific management approach to dealing with worker behavior has been criticized on a number of counts. A major shortcoming is that much time and effort must be devoted to establishing work standards, closely monitoring many aspects of the work process, and calculating rates of pay. The cost of these activities may offset the expected benefits. A further problem lies in worker resistance to attempts to measure effort and productivity. This resistance may be manifested in slowdowns when workers are aware that they are being observed.

Workers also oppose changes in pay schemes because they suspect that the new rates may be designed to speed up production. For example, Taylor advo-

---

[*]In addition to his contributions to time-and-motion study, Fred Taylor was also the U.S. tennis doubles champion in 1881.

cated pay schemes that gave workers a maximum wage increase of only about 60 percent regardless of how much worker productivity increased. Taylor's description of his handling of a worker at the Bethlehem Steel Works provides an illustration of the inequity that can result from such a pay scheme.[1] The job of Schmidt, a pig-iron handler, was to move large, 100-pound slabs ("pigs") of iron from a loading dock onto a railroad car. While employed by Bethlehem Steel as a consultant, Taylor designed an incentive pay scheme (coupled with rest periods) that encouraged Schmidt to haul substantially more iron in a given day. Schmidt responded to the incentive plan by raising his efforts so that his wages increased from $1.15 per day to $1.85 per day. In order to obtain this higher wage, Schmidt hauled 47½ tons of iron per day, whereas he had previously hauled only 12½ tons of iron per day. The inequity that exists in this situation can be understood by calculating and comparing the relative percentage increases in pay and productivity. Schmidt's pay increased 61 percent while his productivity increased 280 percent. Clearly, the company was benefiting more from Schmidt's increased productivity than was Schmidt himself. Taylor's belief that workers should be limited to a 60 percent increase in wages was based on his assumption that greater rewards would make workers more defiant and difficult to manage. This conclusion was based not on scientifically gathered evidence but on untested personal assumptions about human nature. Furthermore, Taylor believed that management was entitled to substantial profits because management bore the responsibility and costs of designing new production techniques.

Taylor's concepts of time-and-motion studies, elemental analysis of tasks, and standards for productivity were partly a reflection of his training as an engineer. A legacy of these concepts is that many jobs are still designed with the goal of maximizing short-run efficiency. The negative implications of workers performing simplified, repetitive tasks did not concern the advocates of scientific management.[†]

Among Taylor's more famous disciples were the husband-and-wife consulting team of Frank and Lillian Gilbreth. Devotees of time-and-motion study, the Gilbreths developed a highly ordered family life that received notoriety in the book *Cheaper by the Dozen*. Following time-and-motion principles, Frank Gilbreth redesigned the manner in which bricklaying was performed so as to greatly improve productivity. The Gilbreths also developed an elaborate system for redesigning jobs based on the notion of an irreducible time-and-motion unit of work task, termed a *therblig* (Gilbreth roughly spelled backward). Along with Taylor, the Gilbreths founded an association to promote scientific management.[‡]

[†]As a counterpoint to these criticisms, some recent writers have argued that Taylor has been much maligned and that his techniques of time study, standardization, goal setting, and monetary incentives may have been based on fundamentally correct concepts for dealing with numerous situations.[2] The validity of one of Taylor's more novel suggestions, that supervisors should learn how to swear in order to motivate others, has not as yet been demonstrated. Scientific management ran into early opposition from labor organizers when it was proposed as an approach to improve efficiency at U.S. military arsenals. A resulting Congressional investigation ruled against the use of scientific management in arsenals and naval shipyards. Labor opponents also claimed that Schmidt, the pig-iron hauler, had actually died from being overworked. With the aid of a detective, Taylor was able to locate Schmidt (whose real name was Henry Knolle), who was alive and well.[3]

[‡]Although Taylor and the Gilbreths initially admired each other's work, they eventually had a falling out. Taylor sought to discredit the Gilbreths, and they criticized his views as well. The Gilbreths had the last word, as Taylor died in 1915.

Human Relations Approach: The Hawthorne Studies

During part of the same period in which scientific management was popular, another school of thought emerged, the **human relations approach**. The human relations approach, which partially grew out of the field of psychology, emphasized the importance of motivation and attitudes in explaining worker behavior. The approach drew much of its strength and following from the results of a series of studies conducted at the Hawthorne plant of the Western Electric Company, located in the western suburbs of Chicago. The **Hawthorne Studies** were important because they demonstrated that in addition to the job itself, certain social factors can influence workers' behavior.[4] Informal social groups, management-employee relations, and the interrelatedness among the many facets of work settings were found to be quite influential.

The Hawthorne Studies represented a major step forward in the attempt to systematically study worker behavior. Although the studies can be grouped into several major efforts or divisions, one is of particular interest: the Relay Assembly Room Study.

In the **Relay Assembly Room Study**, a small group of female employees was taken from its regular workplace and assigned to assemble small telephone relays in an arrangement that was very similar to that of the actual Relay Assembly Department. The decision to separate the women from the remainder of the workforce was based on the researchers' desire to maintain total control over the experimental working environment. Of special interest to the investigators was whether changes in the work setting would influence the women's productivity. Among the changes that the investigators tried were the introduction of rest periods, a free mid-morning lunch, a workday that was a half-hour shorter, a five-day workweek (a novel idea at that time), and variations in methods of payment.

The researchers hoped that their studies would show that the introduction of 10-minute rest periods produced a 12 percent increase in productivity, while a five-day workweek decreased productivity by 16 percent, and so on. But once again, the results were perplexing. Instead of finding that some conditions increased productivity while others decreased it, the researchers found that productivity followed a gradual upward trend over the course of the entire study, regardless of the condition instituted. In addition, when the women were in the test room, their rate of absenteeism was lower than in their original job setting.

These results led the Hawthorne researchers to consider the psychological aspects of the work setting in addition to its more objective features. Careful analysis suggested that the positive outcomes were partially attributable to the fact that the workers enjoyed the attention and recognition that the researchers had been showing them. For example, the workers commented favorably on all the changes that were made, and the workers displayed positive attitudes toward the entire research enterprise. In response to the favorable treatment that they received in the test situations, compared to the usual treatment of workers in that era,[§] the workers reciprocated by providing the results that

[§]In a follow-up interview with one of the women who actually participated in the study, it was reported that it was not uncommon at that time for supervisors to punish a group of operators who failed to meet their assigned standard. One form of this punishment consisted of not permitting the operators to use the elevators.

they thought the researchers wanted. This phenomenon, in which the alteration of social and psychological aspects of a work setting results in enhanced performance largely because the employees realize they are being observed, has been termed the **Hawthorne effect**. The Hawthorne effect explains many instances in which the mere study of people at work, in and of itself, can be responsible for an observed set of results.[**]

Many scholars believe that the Hawthorne Studies show the importance of the social nature of employees. This would seem to contradict the economic or rational approach to employee behavior that is implicit in the principles of scientific management. But just as the scientific management approach possesses problems of application, so does the human relations approach. The greatest difficulties stem from an unproven assumption that is the cornerstone of the human relations approach: the belief that employees who are satisfied with their jobs will feel indebted to their employers and will show their appreciation by being more productive. This suggests a reciprocal relationship between management and labor—that greater concern for improving the condition of employees will pay dividends to employers through greater productivity from happier and more appreciative employees.

Unfortunately, this simple *quid pro quo* relationship has not been firmly established. Studies have not found clear evidence of a relationship between employee satisfaction and productivity. Due to this lack of evidence, it is difficult to endorse the position that managers should worry about their employees' level of contentment in the hope that employees will return the favor. Nonetheless, managers cannot ignore the issue of employee well-being for other solid, defensible reasons, as we shall see in Chapter 11.

Contingency Approach

Following World War II, a new perspective on organizational behavior began to develop. Called the **contingency approach**, it acknowledged the difficulty of offering simple general principles to explain or predict behavior in organizational settings. Nonetheless, the contingency approach did not abandon the search for principles, but instead sought to specify the conditions under which we can expect to find certain relationships. As such, it represented a search for the factors that would aid in predicting and explaining behavior. Organizational behavior researchers who subscribe to the contingency approach believe that employee behavior is too complex to be explained by only a few simple and straightforward principles. Instead, they seek to identify the factors that are jointly necessary for a given principle to hold. Contingency researchers recognize the *interdependency* of personal and situational factors in the determination of employee behavior.

If you ask a contingency researcher for a simple answer to a seemingly simple question, you should expect to be given a fairly complex and highly

---

**Recently, there has been much debate over whether the actual results of the Hawthorne Studies in fact showed substantial and incontrovertible evidence of improved performance due to the workers' being observed.[5] The criticisms stem partly from the lack of extremely tight controls in the study (e.g., some of the workers who were studied initially were replaced by other workers for various reasons during the long course of the study). Nonetheless, the vast majority of scholars who study organizational behavior accept the general conclusion of the Hawthorne researchers and acknowledge the likely existence of such a phenomenon as the Hawthorne effect.

qualified answer. Because human behavior is itself complex, a statement of behavioral principles must also be complex.

For example, consider this seemingly simple question: Which is the better way to behave as a manager, autocratically or democratically? Contingency researchers would not simply pick one alternative over the other, but would try to identify a set of conditions in which one style of supervision could be expected to yield superior results compared to the other style. They would consider such issues as subordinates' expectations and preferences for different styles of leadership. To be sure, if you are in charge of a band of fascists, your subordinates might well expect and desire that you rule with an iron fist.

Cultural differences would also be taken into account in choosing a style of supervision. For example, in North America, democratic and participative supervision is endorsed, while an autocratic supervisory style is generally frowned on. But in other countries, a leader who shows empathy and is will-

---

An Inside Look
Building Your Management Vocabulary

To develop your own personal competitive edge and present yourself as an up-and-coming, value-added staffer to top management, you should build your cutting-edge vocabulary and use it appropriately. According to Hal Lancaster in the *Wall Street Journal*, here are ten terms to know.

Paradigm shift. A fundamental change that will affect your company's structure, your work, and your career. Or it may just be a management fad that will pass. Learn to distinguish between the two.

Knowledge worker. *The* career of the future. These people collect, analyze, and make data do tricks that hopefully lead to profits. To be a knowledge worker, you need to have top-notch computer skills.

Mission statement. A statement of the firm's vision and values with which you must closely align yourself to be successful in that organization.

Value-added. Anything you can do to increase profits, cut costs, create new products, win new customers, etc. Always document what you do and how it benefits the company.

Continuous learning. An old but totally true idea that needs no explanation. Remember that the most important training is "on the job."

Adhocracy. This happens when work teams are formed that cross departmental lines to solve problems or capture opportunities. The problem for individuals is to balance team loyalty and department loyalty. Always remember that management fads are transient, but bureaucracy is forever!

Helicoptering. Hover above and observe the economic tides that push firms into new businesses that create opportunities and out of old businesses that eliminate them. If you can't see the big picture, you won't be in it.

Headlighting. Look beyond the range of your headlights into the new and the unknown. The past may no longer be relevant. Find what is new and relevant and use it to your advantage.

(Fill in the blank) leadership. This term describes the new executive, one who nurtures, empowers, and shares the kudos rather than being a dictator. Choices for the blank are "servant," "steward," "new-age," and "post-heroic." Your temperament, the corporate culture, and your situation will mold your style.

Change agent. What every company wants: someone who will find new solutions and "shake things up." Caution: Companies may really not want as much change as they say they do . . . unless it is the last resort for survival.

Buzzwords come and go just like management fads. Use them to be cutting-edge. To create your own (and be really cutting-edge) just add "-izing" to the end of any relevant or interesting word. And as a final word of caution: Beware of Buzzword Abuse!

Source: H. Lancaster, "Managing Your Career," *The Wall Street Journal*, October 3, 1995.

ing to be influenced by subordinates might be viewed as being weak. In addition, the leader's ability to enact a particular supervisory style would be an important consideration, as would the nature of the task to be performed.

In most cases, a contingency researcher's answer to the question of management style can be summarized in two words: "It depends." But this two-word answer is not meant to be evasive, as a contingency researcher will then attempt to identify precisely what the important dependencies are. Contingency researchers assume that the number of important dependencies can be specified. On the basis of this, they then search for a valid representation of employee behavior. Today, most specialists in the field of organizational behavior subscribe to the contingency approach.

Culture-Quality Movement

The last two decades of the 20th century witnessed the rise of two related themes. The themes grew out of the work of organizational consultants and applied researchers that tied the ascent of Japan's industrial power to corporate ability to inspire commitment, while simultaneously maintaining flexibility.[6] Two terms that gained quick interest among managers and organizational researchers were *corporate culture* and *quality improvement*. The authors of several popular books—Peters and Waterman, *In Search of Excellence*; Deal and Kennedy, *Corporate Culture*; and Ouchi, *Theory Z*—focused on how to build a strong set of shared positive values and norms within a corporation (that is, a strong corporate culture) while emphasizing quality, service, high performance, and flexibility.[7] Simultaneously, Western industry developed an interest in designing an effective response to growing global competition. High quality was seen to be the result of high employee commitment and loyalty. High levels of employee commitment and loyalty were believed to result, partially, from greater employee involvement in decision making. In order to establish new mechanisms for employee involvement, changes were seen as being necessary in existing corporate cultures, and the establishment and maintenance of new cultures became the goal. In some organizations, a deliberate focus can be identified that seeks to have employees openly discuss aspects of corporate culture, and suggest techniques for achieving a culture that emphasizes greater teamwork and cooperation.

Advocates of the **culture-quality movement** claim that productivity and financial returns can be significantly enhanced by developing cultures that emphasize key values. The evidence suggests that, properly introduced, there are economic advantages to following principles of the culture-quality movement. However, for every success story there may be at least as many failed attempts. The case for the culture-quality movement will be discussed in further detail in chapters devoted to the enhancement of employee motivation (Chapter 5) and cultural influences (Chapter 14).

It should be noted that the two current views (that is, the contingency approach and the culture-quality movement) did not integrate the previous approaches of scientific management and human relations, but instead replaced them as the clearly dominant perspectives for the study of organizational behavior. The two earlier approaches have not gone the way of the dinosaurs, however. Although the fervor that surrounded them has clearly waned, they still have some advocates. The human relations adherents tend to be associated with a humanistically oriented or altruistic philosophical camp, while the latter-day scientific management advocates are often found in close association with schools of engineering. The smart money is betting on the eventual replacement of the culture-quality movement by a future (as yet unforeseeable) perspective, while the contingency approach, because of its broadness, will likely be a part of the field as long as it retains an empirical basis.

Challenges Confronting Managers in the 21st Century

As we enter the 21st century, there are several continuing and emerging challenges that confront managers within the domain of employee relations. These issues are not easily defined, nor do they fit into a simple framework. Specifically, these issues include: increasing *workforce diversity*, increasing use of *contingent workers*, and increasing *expression of strong emotions* in the workplace.

Workforce Diversity

In recent years, there has been a recognition of a changing demographic mix in the U.S. workforce. The term *workforce diversity* gained popularity following the publication of a study entitled *"Work Force 2000: Work and Workers for the 21st Century"* (commissioned by the U.S. Department of Labor). One major conclusion of the *Work Force 2000* study was that a large proportion of the new entrants to the labor force for the near future will be from demographic categories other than that of white males. Many leading-edge firms have responded to the challenge of an increasingly diverse workforce by seeking to actively manage diversity for competitive advantage. To some managers, this recent concern with the management of diversity reflects the latest stage in the evolution of affirmative action and equal opportunity issues. Other managers view diversity as an opportunity for increased productivity and competitiveness (e.g., via recruiting talented women and minorities, entering new markets, and maximizing each employee's unique ability to contribute). Yet, many managers still face the challenge of how diversity should be specifically "managed."

Although many executives view diversity as an important issue, they also recognize obstacles to implementing diversity initiatives. Chief among these are competition with other issues, belief that forecasted demographic shifts will not impair corporate ability to attract talent, lack of top- and middle-management support, and fear of a backlash from white males. Additionally, it is not clear how one can deliberately use identifiable group or aggregate differences to manage a workforce competitively, given that the historical trend in civil rights legislation has been to mandate equal treatment of individuals rather than distinctive treatment based on group membership. Also, many managers (and researchers) report that they observe far greater differences *within* groups of people than *between* groups of people. As a consequence of these reservations, the rhetoric that emphasizes the *management* of diversity may be in the process of shifting to that of the *valuing* of diversity. Valuing of diversity implies acceptance of other individuals and tolerance of individual differences, with less of an implied emphasis on making (potentially illegal) human resources decisions based on assumptions of group differences.[††]

Contingent Workers

The use of contingent, or temporary, workers is surging. The U.S. Department of Labor estimates that the use of temporary employees has increased over 400 percent during the past 15 years. As a result, "temps" appear to have a permanent future in the workforce. The superficial advantages to employers are greater flexibility and savings on perks. For example, temps earn 40 percent less per hour than full-time employees, and a majority do not have health insurance or pensions. Another potential advantage is that employers sometimes use temporary employment as a screening device for identifying potential full-time employees. However, it is not at all clear that many temps benefit from the supposed "gateway" opportunity that contingent employment may offer. Adding to this concern are the facts that a disproportionate percentage of temps are minorities, people under the age of 25, and women. On the plus side, temporary employment does give people a chance to gain work experience and develop skills that they might otherwise not have. A major concern for managers, however, is how to effectively manage employees who do not have a sense of commitment or loyalty to their employer.

The Expression of Emotions at Work

The later decades of the 20th century witnessed a gradual emergence of the propensity of employees to act on personal impulse when experiencing strong emotions. Evidence of this growing tendency is given by data on the rise of workplace violence. Murder in the workplace is the fastest growing category of homicides.[9] Also, the increase in hate crimes in society in general has been spreading into the workplace.[10] This rising rate of violence has prompted the U.S. Postal Service to introduce a "hot line" for employees to call in reports of threats concerning former or current coworkers. Factors that contribute to greater violence at work include: failure to screen for unstable applicants, mediocre supervision that fails to manage potential conflict, and perceived inequities. Although murder and other extreme forms of violence make the headlines, there are many other subtle forms of aggressive behavior that plague work settings. These more common, indirect forms include: name-calling, types of intimidation, varieties of derogatory humor, and the withholding of support.

The propensity to act on strong *positive* emotion is also an emerging challenge for managers. Strong positive feelings toward others are manifest in workplace romances (a previously neglected topic in OB). Romance in the workplace has begun to draw much attention because of several forces.[11] First, the proportion of women in the workforce is increasing, and the proportion of women found in traditionally male positions is increasing as well. This

---

[††]Evidence on the impact of increasing diversity in work units suggests that for tasks that require a range of abilities, more diverse work units will generate higher-quality solutions. However, the process may take more time. Also, increases in unit diversity are related to increases in member turnover, and also contribute to greater interpersonal conflict.[8]

trend provides greater opportunity for romantic relationships to form.++ Second, there is a growing concern with the misuse of power in the workplace, as manifest in instances of sexual harassment wherein supervisors (and subordinates) may trade intimacy for career advancement, or where hostile work conditions are created to discourage potential competition. Firms are continuing to struggle with defining policies that counter abuse of power, given the tendency of people to also be driven into intimate relationships as part of natural mate-seeking tendencies (e.g., many people, in fact, meet their eventual spouses at work).

In recent years, several highly visible cases of workplace romance and potential harassment involving the military services and political figures have placed the topic in a spotlight. Because coworkers are likely to resent perceived instances of workplace romance (as it provides opportunities for such genuine inequities as favoritism), managers will be forced to develop and enforce policies that respect employees' rights to associate while restricting occasions for potentially improper conduct.

Criticisms of the Field

Although the field of organizational behavior is relatively new, it has created quite a bit of controversy, drawing criticism from scholars in the field itself, as well as from students and managers. The fact that organizational behavior generates such debates is evidence that the field is truly alive and developing.

Perhaps the most frequent criticism of organizational behavior as a field of study is raised by students in introductory courses. They often say that much of what they learn in their organizational behavior course is fairly obvious and could be derived from common sense.

It's So Obvious

The observation that most of the content of organizational behavior is obvious and common-sensical usually arises in response to reading the results of studies that have been conducted in the field. For example, consider the following behavioral principles that have frequently been demonstrated in behavioral studies: "Rewarding employees on the basis of their past performance is likely to improve their subsequent performance," or "An employee will tend to like a coworker who has indicated a liking for him or her."§§ Some people may think that these statements are ridiculously self-evident and that anyone could make these observations without going through the trouble of scientific studies. And since any one of us could predict such principles, why bother to develop a field around such clichés?

To examine the criticism that organizational researchers do little more than restate the obvious, consider the following case. As part of the effort to win World War II, the U.S. Army set up a research branch of the War Department. During the course of the war, the research branch conducted several hundred

---

++In fact, one survey found that 71 percent of respondents have witnessed one or more romantic relationships at work, and 31 percent have personally been involved in a romantic relationship at work.[12]

§§These statements are variations on the "law of effect" and "the reciprocity principle of interpersonal attraction."

studies on such issues as soldiers' attitudes, morale, and feelings of frustration. In the process, over 600,000 soldiers were interviewed. The results of these studies were so extensive that their final summary required four volumes. When these volumes were finally published, they were widely criticized in the popular press. One criticism was that many of the findings were terribly obvious. For example, a major conclusion of the report was that many soldiers were unhappy during the war. This conclusion seemed so self-evident that it raised questions about the legitimacy of investing energy and time in attitude surveys that generate such obvious findings.

In a review of the four-volume work, Paul Lazarsfeld, a sociologist, provided a brief list of typical findings.[13] How would you rate the novelty of each of the following statements taken from his review?

1. As long as the war continued, enlisted men were more desirous of returning home to the United States than they were after the collapse of the Nazi regime. (Would anyone be surprised to find that soldiers do not want to be killed?)

2. Soldiers from the southern states were better able to tolerate the tropical climate in the South Pacific than were soldiers from the northern states. (Given differences in upbringing and adjustment to climate, this too could be easily predicted.)

3. White enlisted men were more desirous of promotions than were black enlisted men. (Given the lack of real opportunities for blacks in the U.S. military at that time, this is not unexpected.)

4. Highly educated men had more difficulty adjusting to army life, especially as manifested by minor psychological disorders, than did men who were less well educated. (The highly cerebral individual might easily be expected to have difficulty adjusting to a situation requiring obedience and unquestioning acceptance of a difficult daily regimen.)

5. Blacks from the southern states preferred to serve under white officers who were also from the southern states, versus officers from the northern states. (Similarity in backgrounds and values could easily explain this result.)

6. Soldiers who had grown up in rural areas were better able to adjust to army life than were soldiers from urban areas. (Sleeping under the stars might be a difficult adjustment for someone who had rarely, if ever, stepped off a slab of concrete.)

If we acknowledge the obvious nature of these findings, we must question the entire enterprise of research on people in organizational settings. If these are the basic data that serve to develop principles in the field, then the average person is already fairly sophisticated about organizational behavior.

These statements would be true except for one important fact. The previous list presents the exact *opposite* of the actual findings. In truth, soldiers preferred to remain overseas until the war was concluded and wanted to return home only afterward. Southerners had no greater tolerance for the heat of the South Pacific, blacks were more desirous of promotion, poorly educated men had more difficulties in adjusting to army life, and so forth. In each instance, we can now generate an explanation that once again is seemingly obvious. For example, the soldiers' desire to remain overseas could be explained by their commitment to completing the war effort and by their patriotism, while homesickness became strong after their mission was complete; blacks were more desirous of promotion because they were relatively deprived of opportunities as a group; and so on. Had the true findings been presented initially, our reaction would be that they too were obvious.

The notion that behavioral phenomena are obvious is therefore something of a delusion. It may well be that when we are presented with a statement concerning human behavior, we engage in a defensive reaction in which we state, "Oh sure, I would have guessed it." This tendency to claim that we would have foreseen the relative inevitability of an outcome is termed **hindsight bias**. This reaction may be very self-satisfying (after all, it suggests we are well in control of our surroundings), but clearly it also can be very much in error. As every manner of human behavior is at least conceivable, we must not fall into the trap of self-deception by relying on intuition and armchair theorizing in place of an empirical search for evidence. Also, we must search for the joint factors, both personal and situational, that are responsible for a particular regularity in human behavior. Healthy skepticism is necessary because nearly every explanation of human behavior, regardless of its truth or falsity, can be dismissed as obvious after we have heard it.[14]

A Framework for Studying Organizational Behavior

In practice, managers and researchers who are interested in organizational behavior tend to group issues and topics within a number of more or less common categories, such as power, compensation, communication, job satisfaction, leadership, and the like. These commonly used categories form the basis for the chapter topics of this book. The order of the chapters follows a logical flow from within-individual issues to between-individual issues, and ultimately to individual–organizational issues. Thus, the chapters flow from micro (smaller) to macro (larger) levels of analysis and discussion.

Figure 1.2 summarizes the organization of these topics by grouping many of the chapter headings within three larger categories. Initially, we will consider individual-level topics, such as perception, personality, learning, and motivation. Afterward, we will examine interpersonal processes, such as leadership and group dynamics. Last, we will consider organizational and environmental forces, such as structural and cultural influences.

In essence, we will start with the upper-left cluster of topics in Figure 1.2 and proceed clockwise through the framework. An important feature of the framework is the interconnectedness of the clusters (as noted by the use of the ever-popular two-headed arrow). These interconnections denote the interplay, or mutual influence, that exists among the topics. That is to say, interpersonal processes are influenced by both individual and organizational factors, and vice versa. For example, the actual design of a compensation system will be partly a product of individual and organizational forces. The compensation system, in turn, will influence both individual-level and organization-wide activities. Behavioral processes do not occur in a vacuum. Instead, they should be thought of as potential causes and consequences of other processes.

FIGURE 1.2   **A Framework for Studying Organizational Behavior**

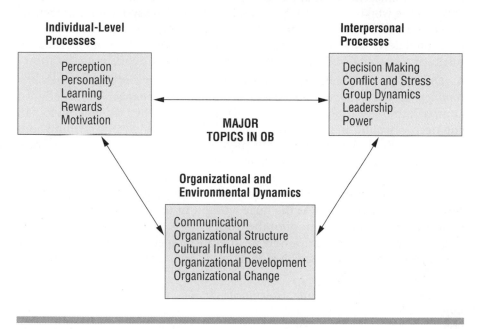

1. *Define the purpose and nature of the field of organizational behavior.* Organizational behavior (OB) is a relatively new field of inquiry concerned with the scientific study of the behavioral processes that occur in work settings. Borrowing many of its concepts and methods from the behavioral and social sciences, OB explores a wide range of subjects that span (1) individually based phenomena, such as perception and personality, (2) interpersonal and work-group processes, such as power and leadership, and (3) organizational and environmental forces, such as structural and cultural influences. Due to its newness, OB is a dynamic and promising field characterized by diversity and vitality.

2. *Tell why organizational behavior is an important field of study for managers.* Understanding OB will help managers in at least three ways. First, through OB, managers can learn to better understand and enhance their subordinates', their superiors', and their own performance. Second, managers will find that studying OB can lead to personal growth. Better understanding of others can be highly fulfilling and contribute to greater self-knowledge and self-insight. Third, OB offers managers knowledge for its own sake. Although some OB findings may not yet have practical applications, they are, nonetheless, valuable additions to the cumulative store of human knowledge.

3. *Distinguish organizational behavior from organizational theory, human resources management, and organizational development.* Strictly speaking, organizational behavior is the systematic study of the behavior of individuals and groups within organizations. In contrast, organizational theory focuses on the organization as the unit of analysis, and organizational attributes such as goals, technology, and culture are the objects of study. The field of human resources management attempts to apply the principles of the behavioral sciences in the workplace by designing and implementing systems for attracting, developing, and motivating individuals within an organization. Finally, organizational development seeks to enhance organizational performance through instituting systematic changes in the structure and values of an organization.

4. *Outline the basic principles of scientific management and discuss the shortcomings of this approach for managing employee behavior.* Essentially an approach to controlling employee behavior developed by Frederick Taylor, an engineer, scientific management used detailed task analysis and time-and-motion studies in conjunction with piece-rate pay schemes to increase productivity. In their search for the single best way to perform a given task, the proponents of scientific management imposed standard parts and standard procedures on manufacturing processes. This approach had many critics. Among its shortcomings was the huge amount of time and effort required to establish work standards, monitor the work process, and calculate rates of pay. Fearing that the new pay rates were an attempt to speed up production, many employees used deliberate slowdowns to resist attempts to measure their effort and productivity.

5. *Relate the findings of the Hawthorne Studies to the development of the human relations approach.* The human relations approach, which partially grew out of the field of psychology, emphasized the importance of motivation and attitudes in explaining employee behavior. This philosophy drew many of its beliefs from the findings of the Hawthorne Studies, a series of studies conducted at a single manufacturing plant. The Hawthorne Studies represented a major step forward in the attempt to systematically study employee behavior and demonstrated that informal social groups, management–employee relations, and the interrelatedness of many other factors all contribute to on-the-job performance.

6. *Explain why believers in the contingency approach rarely give a simple answer to a seemingly simple question.* Proponents of the contingency approach contend that the complexity of employee behavior defies simple explanations. They seek to identify the many personal and situational factors that are jointly necessary to explain and predict behavior. Today, most specialists in the field of OB subscribe to the contingency approach.

7. *Describe the currently dominant perspectives in the field of organizational behavior.* There are presently two dominant perspectives in the field of organizational behavior: the contingency approach and the culture-quality movement. The contingency approach attempts to explain and predict behavior from an analysis of the interdependencies of personal and situational forces. The culture-quality movement focuses on the role of corporate culture in influencing employee performance. Important aspects of corporate culture, such as employee participation in decision making, are seen as underlying employee commitment and loyalty, which in turn affect the quality of employee output.

8. *Cite several challenges confronting managers in the 21st century.* As we enter the new century, managers will be forced to deal with behavioral challenges that result from increasing workforce diversity, the increasing use of contingent (or temporary) workers, and the growing tendency of employees to act on strong negative and positive emotions while at work.

9. *Respond to critics who contend that most principles of organizational behavior are obvious.* Because every manner of human behavior is at least conceivable, we have a tendency to believe that many OB findings appear to be obvious. Such a reaction could lead to a reliance on intuition and armchair theorizing in place of empirical research. No matter how obvious a statement about behavior may be, OB researchers do not accept it as fact until it is scientifically proven.

KEY TERMS

Organizational behavior

Organizational theory

Human resources management

Organizational development

Scientific management

Human relations approach

Hawthorne Studies

Relay Assembly Room Study

Hawthorne effect

Contingency approach

Culture-quality movement

Hindsight bias

CRITICAL INCIDENT

You Just Can't Get Good Help Anymore

The Greenley Corporation's profit over the last five years had increased at an annual rate of 13.5 percent. Most of this increase was a direct result of subcontracts the firm had secured from other companies.

Six months ago, to deal with its 90-day backlog of orders, Greenley introduced an incentive plan to increase output. There were several versions of the plan, each tailored to specific jobs. The one for assemblers and packers offered a bonus of 25 percent for all work over standard. The average assembler-packer was making $9.00 an hour and was expected to assemble and pack 10 units within this period. With time allowed for lunch and rest breaks, people put in seven hours of work and were expected to produce 70 units, resulting in a base of 90¢ per unit.

If the assembler-packer chose to work on Saturday, the rate was time-and-a-half, and management also promised to pay the 25 percent bonus for output over standard. One of the assembler-packers who turned out 82 units a day received a weekly gross pay of $497.25. The calculations were as follows:

Average weekly pay
   (7 hours × $9.00 per hour × 5 days) $315.00

Bonus for 12 extra units per day
   (90¢ per unit × 1.25 percent bonus
   × 12 extra units × 5 days)   67.50

Saturday overtime
   (7 hours × $13.50 [$9.00 per hour × 1.5
   for overtime])   94.50

Saturday bonus for 12 extra units
   (90¢ per unit × 1.5 for overtime × 1.25
   percent for incentive × 12 units)   <u>20.25</u>
                                             $497.25

Last week the production department reported that there was a 100-day backlog of orders. The vice president in charge of production told the president that he would like to start finding subcontractors for some of these orders. The president gave his consent but urged the manager to try to get as much of the work as possible done in-house. "If necessary," he said, "raise the incentive to 35 percent of base pay." The vice president agreed to do so, but pointed out to the president that only 6 percent of the total plant workforce was willing to work on Saturday. "I don't think we're having much success with our incentive program. If you ask me, you just can't get good help anymore."

1. Does the Greenley management think that money motivates people? Explain.
2. Why is the incentive plan not proving effective?
3. Based on the vice president's last comment, how would you characterize his view of human nature?

J. Altman, E. Valenzi, and R. Hodgetts, *Organizational Behavior* (New York: Academic Press, 1985), p. 29.

EXPERIENTIAL EXERCISE

What Do You "Know" about Human Behavior?

Chapter 1 discusses various approaches to the study of organizational behavior. Implicit in the discussion is the point that organizational behavior is an empirically based social science. As such, behavioral researchers must rely on various methods to collect data. Yet much of what we "know" about interacting with others is not derived from data gathering. We develop opinions, hunches, and so forth in our daily lives that help us decide what to do.

The following exercise is designed to give you some feedback about what you think you may "know" about human behavior.

Mark T (true) or F (false) next to each statement to indicate your agreement with it. The correct answers are provided at the end.

_____   1. People are inherently social.

_____   2. People who are often silent are usually deep thinkers.

_____   3. On average, men are better drivers than women.

_____   4. Most managers prefer to use written communication (for example, memos).

_____   5. There are certain aspects of personality that are common to all people.

_____   6. More people who are high achievers come from an upper-middle-class background.

_____ 7. Women apparently have more intuition than men.

_____ 8. Introverts are more sensitive to abstract ideas and feelings than are extroverts.

_____ 9. Most people who are highly intelligent seem to be physically weak.

_____ 10. High-risk takers also seem to be high achievers.

_____ 11. People are more likely to attribute success to luck or "breaks."

_____ 12. Those who smoke appear to take more sick days off from work than nonsmokers.

_____ 13. An appreciation for art or music appears to be inherited.

_____ 14. It appears that most people work primarily for money.

_____ 15. It seems that most great athletes are of below-average intelligence.

_____ 16. Very religious people seem to come mostly from poor backgrounds.

_____ 17. Seventy-five percent of the U.S. population apparently prefers to gather information through intuition.

_____ 18. It appears that most blind people possess excellent hearing.

_____ 19. Most people who go to work for the government are low-risk takers.

_____ 20. University professors have higher self-esteem than do members of any other occupational group.

_____ 21. The best workers in an organization often produce two or three times as much work as the poorest workers.

_____ 22. In social interactions, women look more at the other person than do men.

_____ 23. In the United States, there seems to be a greater emphasis on "fitting in" rather than on "standing out" in social situations.

_____ 24. Good leaders have become quite common in most organizations.

_____ 25. Attempting to influence the behavior of others is a natural human tendency.

_____ 26. Top-level executives appear to have a greater need for money than for power.

_____ 27. History suggests that most famous people were born of poor, hard-working parents.

_____ 28. One's experiences as an infant and child tend to determine behavior in later life.

_____ 29. Work stress is undesirable and should be avoided whenever possible.

_____ 30. Most successful relationships support the notion that opposites attract.

Below are the answers to the statements. Check your answers to see how well you "know" human behavior. Most students get between 16 and 22 right; how did you do?

You may recall that, in introducing this exercise, the point was made that much of what you "know" about human behavior is not based on research. As such, it tends to be in error.

Organizational behavior, however, is based on more than opinion and intuition. It is a science. Therefore, as you begin reading and studying the following chapters, remember that the information is empirically based.

1. T	11. F	21. T
2. F	12. T	22. T
3. F	13. F	23. F
4. F	14. F	24. F
5. T	15. F	25. T
6. T	16. F	26. F
7. F	17. F	27. F
8. T	18. F	28. T
9. F	19. F	29. F
10. F	20. T	30. T

Source: Written by Bruce Kemelgor, University of Louisville; used by permission.

2 Perception and Personality

If I hadn't believed it, I
wouldn't have seen it.

—*Anonymous*

Yon Cassius has a lean and
hungry look;
He thinks too much;
Such men are dangerous.

—*William Shakespeare*

It's not whether you win or
lose, but how you place the
blame.

—*Anonymous*

Learning Objectives

After studying this chapter, you should be able to:

1. Defend the notion that perception is a complex and active process.
2. Explain how facial expressions and other nonverbal cues affect the accuracy of our perceptions.
3. Identify the most common obstacles to accurate perception.
4. Outline the basic principles of attribution theory.
5. Discuss the concept of personality and the factors that affect its development.
6. Describe the most commonly used techniques for measuring personality attributes.
7. Specify and define several dimensions of personality that are especially relevant to organizational behavior.

Your Organization's Cyber-Image

With the rapid growth of corporate and organizational Web sites, cyberspace creates enormous opportunities for a company to broaden its exposure. As the saying goes, "Perception is reality," and it is critical that serious attention be given to how the organization's image in cyberspace is being perceived.

One widely used function of a company Web site is customer service. As a manager fully understands, customer service is one of the fastest ways to influence the public's perception of a company. Yet according to a recent study by Jupiter Communications LLC, an international media research firm with offices in London and New York, 42 percent of the top Web sites do not provide acceptable customer service. On average, they took more than five days to reply to e-mail inquiries; some companies never replied at all. Many companies, even though on the Web, were not accessible by e-mail. Clearly, this can dramatically affect the perception of the nonresponsive organization. Ken Allard, director of the site operations strategies group at Jupiter, noted, "Companies that delay responses to user questions instantly lose a significant degree of credibility and user loyalty, and not responding perpetuates the consumer notion that the Web site is not a reliable method of doing business with that company." Also, an online competitor is often just a mouse click away.

The image of the company is a factor to consider when providing technology to external audiences. Organizations using the Internet and offering Web sites need to be aware that an online customer expects real-time responses and still demands personalized attention. Though automation will never eliminate the human touch, systems can be put in place to modify the customers' expectations. One solution is specialized software to analyze, sort, and forward inquiries to the proper person for response. This requires an in-house mail server or an outsourced server space from an Internet service provider (ISP). Not only does this system create efficiency in managing and responding to inquiries, it can also create a database to track in-bound inquiries, out-bound responses, and requests awaiting attention. Another solution is Auto-Acknowledge software, which analyzes the inquiry and tells the inquirer how long it will take to get a response. It can identify frequently asked questions (FAQ's) and instantly provide answers, while directing complex questions to specialists for immediate attention.

Automating on-line customer service assists companies in responding to inquiries, retaining customers, and improving the response time to inquiries, all of which enhance the perception of customer service—and help the bottom line. Forrester Research reported that an average call-center interaction costs $2.26, but the same interaction handled by automated e-mail response costs 25 cents, a dramatic cost savings.

Source: K.E. Hoffman, "No More Waiting," *Small Business Computing & Communications*, March 1999, 57–58; J. Hodges, "Giving Good Customer Service—Online," *Small Business Computing & Communications*, April 1998, 22.

The ability to accurately perceive and understand others is important for any manager. How we come to know others and understand their behavior are related to perception and personality, two topics that we will consider in this chapter.

The Perception of Others

Although our experience of those around us seems very direct and immediate, careful analysis of what is involved in perceiving others reveals that the process of recognizing and understanding others (that is, **person perception**) is quite complex. For example, imagine that you are looking at a person seated at another desk (in a work or school setting). You will likely notice that the individual is of a certain sex and age, with a particular hair color, and so forth. These attributes all seem to be quite clear and a part of the person being viewed. But an analysis of this episode shows that much more is involved. In truth, cells in the back of your eyes were activated by light waves reflected off the person. These cells triggered neural impulses that traveled via nerves to various parts of the brain. The impulses that reached the higher centers of the brain were then constructed into the experience of viewing the person at the next desk. In considering the chain of events involved in perception, we recognize that we do not have direct and immediate experience with the object, but instead rely on neural transmissions and electrochemical translations of stimuli. In fact, we are only dealing with our own mental activities, not with the actual person.

Most people also erroneously assume that the perceptual process is a largely passive, or receptive, process dictated by attributes of the observed object. Yet the process of viewing a person involves an active focus on the part of the perceiver. For example, when you are viewing another person you are simultaneously being bombarded with other stimuli. The sounds in the room, the weight of your clothes, and the pressure of the chair in which you may be seated are all competing for your attention. However, you actively select and process specific information from your environment. Thus, it is clear that the perceiver is *actively involved* in the construction of his or her experiences. Alluding to this active involvement in selecting, structuring, and interpreting experiences, perception researchers are fond of saying, "There's more to the issue of perception than actually meets the eye."

Accuracy in Perceiving Others

There is great value in being able to accurately assess the emotions and personality characteristics of others. Being able to tell whether others are experiencing a particular emotion enables us to gauge the effects of our words and actions. Knowing something about an individual's personality traits can be highly useful in interpersonal relations. All of us, to some extent, engage in "reading" the emotional styles and personality traits of others. When we approach a new coworker, we are likely to try to accurately assess that person's feelings and traits. The success of salespeople, among others, depends in large part on their ability to accurately assess others.

Facial Expressions   Research findings indicate that most of us are able to identify certain basic emotional states from facial expressions. Several of these facial expressions are universally recognized. For example, smiles and frowns convey the same meaning regardless of an individual's culture.[1]*

Although we can generally read facial expressions in laboratory settings where participants are likely to be fairly honest in their behavior, the "real world" presents many more problems. As anyone who has dealt with a used car salesperson or a politician knows, facial expressions can be very deceiving. Some people are masters of deception, skilled not only in concealing their feelings but also in falsifying their facial expressions.

But such behavior is not foolproof. Based on research, several clues have been identified that can help a viewer determine the sincerity of someone's facial expressions.[3] Researchers have found that if the time between an emotionally arousing event and a person's facial reaction is too great, the reaction is probably dishonest. Also, if all aspects of a person's facial expression do not agree, deceit may be involved. For example, consider a facial reaction in which a person's eyebrows are raised as if in amazement, but his or her mouth is closed. A perceptive viewer might suspect the sincerity of the expression, because in a genuinely amazed reaction, a person's mouth is likely to be open. A third clue is provided by very brief facial expressions that appear on a person's face for a fraction of a second. These microexpressions are likely to convey genuine emotions that emerge just before the person exercises facial control.

Another indication of deception is a subtle shift in the tone or pitch of a person's speaking voice.[4] When someone is lying, there is often a detectable rise in the pitch of his or her voice. **Nonverbal cues,** such as posture shifts, scratching, and frequent licking of the lips, can provide subtle indications of nervousness and, by inference, of possible deceit.[5] Also, increased blinking is associated with psychological stress in that people blink more often when excited or angry.

Other Nonverbal Cues   Nonverbal cues are important in situations in which people are formally evaluated. For example, employment interviews are one important arena in which people attempt to control the impressions they transmit to each other. In a study of the impact of nonverbal cues, undergraduates were hired to conduct employment interviews with a stranger.[6] The interviewee, in fact, was a trained accomplice (confederate) of the researchers,

---

*Charles Darwin was one of the first researchers to study the judgment of emotional states seriously.[2] He contended that the facial expressions associated with emotions were remnants of muscular movements that had functional value in our species' history. As an illustration, consider that the facial posture for displaying disgust is quite similar to the facial expression that occurs during regurgitation. He further argued that certain facial expressions are invariably correlated with specific emotional reactions. For example, a smile would indicate that a person is experiencing a pleasant or happy reaction.

who behaved in one of two possible nonverbal styles. In one condition, the confederate behaved in a style intended to evoke a positive evaluation. Specifically, the interviewee maintained substantial eye contact with the interviewer, sat up straight, smiled a good deal, and frequently leaned toward the interviewer. In the other condition, the confederate's behavior involved slouching in the chair, having little eye contact, smiling not at all, and leaning away from the interviewer. The interviewers' ratings differed significantly as a function of the confederate's nonverbal cues. In particular, they gave the interviewee higher ratings for competence, motivation, and recommendation for hiring when they experienced the nonverbal cues that were deliberately designed to evoke a positive reaction.

A primary implication of these results is that nonverbal cues have powerful effects on our appraisals of each other. Job interviewers are likely to be swayed by such cues when other facets of competing individuals, such as educational qualifications and experience, are equal. Partly because nonverbal cues can be confusing, the actual success rate for interviewers in predicting performance has been fairly poor.[7]

Of all the nonverbal cues used in perceiving and judging others, eye contact is among the most important. Generally, the more eye contact that occurs between two people, the more favorably the relationship is likely to be judged by others.[8] People typically conclude that when others avoid eye contact, it is due to a negative state, such as guilt or depression.[9]

Eye contact that is carried to extremes, however, such as staring, is socially arousing but disruptive. In instances of such staring, the nonverbal message is typically inferred to be that of hatred and potential aggression.[10] Most often, staring has the effect of driving others away (that is, people normally leave a situation when they have been stared at). In organizational settings, staring is sometimes used as a device for extracting compliance from a coworker. For example, if a coworker is having trouble unloading a heavy parcel, he or she may stare at you in order to induce a sense of guilt, which in turn might motivate you to offer your assistance. Given that overt aggression is not socially acceptable in organizations, staring is one of the more powerful social devices for communicating hostility.

Appearance and physical attractiveness also contribute to perceptual judgments. A review of research in this domain shows that physically attractive people are perceived as more sociable, mentally healthy, intelligent, and socially skilled than less attractive people. This tendency exists despite the absence of hard evidence of attractiveness being associated with measures of personality and mental ability. Other evidence does show that more attractive people are socially more popular, less lonely, and more sexually experienced than less attractive people. Physical beauty is also beneficial in generating higher initial salary offers and, surprisingly, is a more powerful influence in the salaries of men than of women. The practical implications of these findings are clear: One should be properly groomed and dressed so as to maximize one's attractiveness, in order to benefit from this common perceiver tendency.[11]

The Perception of Personality Traits

Although much research has been conducted to determine whether some individuals excel in judging others, the efforts have been hampered by several problems. The most notable problem has been the difficulty of determining a specific, unquestionable criterion against which to compare an evaluator's judgment. Many criteria have been proposed (for example, test scores, self-assessments, and peer assessments), but all can be criticized for having possible flaws. For example, test scores do not capture actual behavior, while self-assessments of personality traits may be biased in a favorable direction.[12]

Despite these obstacles, it is nonetheless possible to draw several guarded conclusions about the characteristics of people who are good judges of others. They typically possess high intelligence, esthetic and dramatic interests, good emotional adjustment, and a specialization in the physical sciences rather than in the social sciences.[13] These findings generally make sense, except that we would probably expect specialists in the social sciences to be good judges of personality. One reasonable explanation for the reverse finding is the possible tendency for people who are interested in social relations to be overly sensitive to small differences among people. Sensitivity can lead to overdifferentiation in a judgment task (that is, the tendency to overestimate the importance of small differences). Given that most personal attributes (for example, height, weight, and so on as well as personality traits) follow a bell-shaped, normal distribution, one can be accurate a large percentage of the time when judging others by simply sticking close to the center (or average) of the distribution. Using extreme assessments of others to make judgments can lead to a larger number of errors.

When people try to predict others' behavior from subjective assessments of personality, they are not particularly successful.[14] This has far-reaching ramifications in the workplace, because such predictions are made many times a day by people who are responsible for hiring employees. When other, more objective qualifications, such as experience and education, are equal, assessors often make subjective personality judgments in predicting performance.

Some Obstacles to Accurate Perception

There are many barriers to the precise perception of other's behavior. Each barrier is a possible source of misleading or distorted information.

Stereotyping   **Stereotypes** are judgments of others that are based on group membership. Such attributes as sex, race, ethnic group, and age are the basis of commonly held stereotypes. For example, the beliefs that older workers are not capable of being trained for new tasks and that younger workers cannot handle responsibility are commonly held stereotypes. Occupational groupings also frequently serve as the basis for stereotypes. For example, consider your own views of, say, police officers, top-level corporate executives, and union officials. Even relatively superficial attributes can be the basis of stereotypes, as evidenced by such clichés as "redheads are short-tempered."

This is not to say that stereotypes are totally worthless and inaccurate. In some instances, stereotypes can provide a useful shortcut for quick evaluation. But the potential costs of erroneous evaluations must always be considered.

In the aggregate, stereotypes may, in fact, be based on group characteristics; this is the "kernel of truth" notion of stereotypes.[15] The proposal argues that some stereotypical beliefs are based on an element of truth, in that the beliefs are derived from observations that hold for an entire group but that do not hold with much accuracy for given individuals in the group. While the popular stereotype of, say, police officers may have some accuracy, the variability of the traits of individual police officers is so great that it is extremely difficult to classify an individual officer accurately from the stereotypical information alone.

The Halo Effect The **halo effect** occurs when a perceiver uses a general impression of favorableness or unfavorableness as the basis for judgments about more specific traits. In essence, the perceiver's evaluation is influenced by an overall impression. The halo effect explains why a subordinate who is liked by a superior can do no wrong in the superior's eyes, while a subordinate who is disliked may have difficulty obtaining a favorable review from the same superior.

Most students have witnessed the phenomenon in classroom settings, where an instructor might rate a student highly on participation because of a prior favorable impression of that student, when an actual tally of participation in the class might reveal that the favored student spoke no more frequently than other less highly rated students. One study revealed that U.S. Army officers who were liked were judged to be more intelligent than officers

An Inside Look
Creating the Perception of Being a Leader

It has been said that managers know how to write a business plan, but leaders know how to create change in both companies and people. How does one become a leader? Unfortunately, there is no definitive set of characteristics to use as a model. One creates the perception of being a leader by every decision made, every action initiated, and every risk taken. In other words, one becomes a leader by doing.

So what do leaders do? Leaders think "out of the box," and they look for new and better ways to accomplish the task at hand. Some follow the idea of "if it isn't broken, break it anyway," and they rarely accept the status quo solutions of the past. To merely do what has always been done does not demonstrate one's value. Leaders create excitement within an organization by striving for new approaches, new solutions, and new opportunities. Leaders are valuable because they are willing to leave the past behind and move into new areas, take new risks, and strive to win new rewards for themselves, their employees, and their organizations. Leaders have a passion for growing a business. Often, they find maintenance of operations a boring task.

Leaders are adept at building teams of diversely talented people and instilling a sense of direction.

They provide the motivation and resources to make the attainment of challenging goals a reality. Leaders are capable of making employees feel that they are making a contribution and that they are critical to organizational success. Leaders are driven by their own standard of excellence, and they consistently challenge others to always do their very best. Less than the best is not acceptable, and leaders are very willing to make the hard decisions as required and without reservation.

Risk-taking is a characteristic of leaders and they inspire others to do the same, while reducing fear of punishment for failure. Leaders understand that one resounding success can quickly recover the costs of failures. In conjunction with this, leaders also understand that failure can be a significant motivator that can result in success.

Though there is no formula for becoming a leader, managers who incorporate these traits into their behavior can create the perception that they are a leader.

Source: C. Hymowitz, "Some Managers Are More Than Bosses—They're Leaders, Too," IN THE LEAD, *The Wall Street Journal* (December 8, 1998).

who were disliked, while an examination of scores on intelligence tests revealed no differences between the two groups of officers.[16]

It has also been observed that judges tend to link certain traits.[17] For example, when a person is judged to be aggressive, he or she is also likely to be seen as highly energetic. The trait of industriousness tends to be linked to that of honesty. Someone who is a churchgoer is likely to be viewed as clean or neat. This phenomenon has come to be termed **implicit personality theory.** Simply stated, it is the tendency to perceive trait X in an individual given that trait Y exists. Because the consistency of clusterings of traits is not that substantial, assessments of others that are grounded in an implicit personality approach are likely to be in error.

Projection   We have a tendency to ascribe our own feelings and attributes to others. This is known as **projection.** It is a defense mechanism that helps us to protect ourselves from unpleasant or unacceptable truths. An individual's emotional state has been shown to influence his or her perception of that emotional state in others. In one study, fear was aroused in a group of subjects by telling them that they would later receive an electric shock.[18] Before any shock was administered, members of the group were asked to evaluate the fearfulness of other subjects. Compared to a control group, which had not been threatened with electric shock, the shock-threatened subjects tended to describe others as more fearful and aggressive.

In another study, individuals who were rated high on such unattractive traits as obstinacy, stinginess, and disorderliness tended to rate others as being higher on these same traits.[19] These results suggest the possibility of projecting one's own undesirable traits onto others. Consequently, it is easy to imagine a situation in which a manager who is fearful of organizational change and distrustful of others would project these attributes onto his coworkers, believing that they are fearful of change and cannot be trusted.

Perceptual Distortion   In addition to defending our egos by projecting feelings and attributes onto others, we may simply deny that something occurred or that we witnessed something. Similarly, we may modify or distort what we report in an attempt to avoid an unpleasant reality. Or we may deliberately pay attention only to what we want to see. These acts are forms of **perceptual distortion.**[†]

Illusions are another form of perceptual distortion. We are all familiar with the notion of an illusion, in which our perception of something does not reflect its reality. Consider for example, the well-known illusion of perceptual contrast shown in Figure 2.1. The grey area is of uniform color, yet when judged within a context, the grey ring appears to have differing tones. The context influences our perception and creates an illusion of difference that does not exist. So too in social relations, an individual may give a particular impression due to the context in which he or she is being judged. For example, an

---

[†]An interesting example of perceptual distortion is given by *occupational centrism,* the tendency to see one's own profession or work as more important than that of others. The concept is illustrated by a story attributed to football coach Knute Rockne of Notre Dame. After a particularly successful season, the question was asked as to who was responsible for the victories, the line or the backfield. After being put to a vote, the line won, not surprisingly, seven to four.[20]

FIGURE 2.1

Notice that the grey circle or ring is uniform in brightness. Now, place a pencil along the vertical line that is the border between the light and dark sections of the square. Has the apparent brightness of each half of the circle changed?

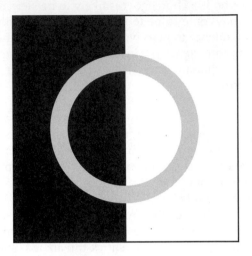

individual of moderate intelligence might be judged as being of substantially higher intelligence because of a prior belief that employees in his or her job classification are not typically very intelligent. This social misperception is based on an illusion influenced by context.

Subliminal Influences   Our perception of others may be affected by factors that we are not fully aware of. Influences that are below our threshold of awareness are called **subliminal influences.** Some degree of perceptual detection can occur even when people are unaware of having seen anything.[21] However, the effectiveness of attempts at deliberately designed subliminal influence appears to be overrated. Generally, stimuli of greater intensity have greater influence.

The existence of subliminal influences can be demonstrated by the successful use of posthypnotic suggestions. In such cases, a person is hypnotized and told that when awakened, he will respond in a specific way to a specific cue, such as whistling when hearing the word *bird*. The individual later responds to the cue when not hypnotized, but cannot recall the origin of the suggestion or the motive for the suggested action. Also, if two sharp pins are placed very near each other on the skin of a person's back, most individuals cannot consciously distinguish whether there are two pins or only one. Yet, when forced to guess, most subjects correctly guess the number of pins.

Selective Perception   Yet another obstacle to accurate perception arises from the tendency to be influenced by our own interests. As it is not possible to take in all stimuli we receive, we tend to select out certain elements. As an illustration of this, consider the experience that follows the purchase of a car. Suddenly you begin to notice that type of car on the street much more frequently. **Selective perception** occurs in organizations when managers tend to interpret problem situations in light of their own background and interest. For example, given an ambiguous problematic situation, a sales manager will be inclined to see sales issues as the underlying cause while a production manager will be inclined to see manufacturing-related issues.

Understanding Attributions

Within the area of perception, one of the more widely studied topics is the process of attribution. The term *attribution* is used to describe the process people go through to explain the causes of the behavior of others. Initially popularized by Fritz Heider, **attribution theory** examines the inference process used to deduce others' dispositions or traits from observations of their behavior.[22] Central to the theory is the proposal that people perceive behavior as being caused, either by the individual in question or by the environment. This is a distinction between internal causality and external causality—that is, whether people initiate actions or merely react to their environment. In addition, Heider proposed that the outcome of a particular action is perceived to be the result of environmental and personal forces, as well as the influences of personal power (ability) and effort (trying).

Consider the demolition of a building. Either an earthquake or a person with a wrecking ball could achieve the same result. The environmental force (the earthquake) could aid the personal force (the person with a wrecking ball), or either force could produce the same result with the other force absent. Personal and environmental forces conceivably can also work against each other and thereby cancel out one another.

The theory's components of personal power and effort are also important. If either of these components is absent, the strength of the personal force is reduced to zero. An observer of a set of actions must be able to take these various factors into account in order to make a correct attribution about a person.

Social status is often viewed as determining the extent to which an individual acts freely versus being controlled by the environment. In one study, student subjects were assigned the task of convincing either a high-status individual or a low-status individual that a choice of materials for a project was a good one.[23] The high- and low-status individuals were confederates of the investigators who accepted the subjects' attempts at influence and conceded the wisdom of each subject's choice of materials. When the subjects were later asked to rate the extent to which the compliance they received from their listeners was freely given, differences were observed that favored the high-status individual (that is, the compliance of the high-status individual was seen as more internally caused or freely given, relative to that of the low-status individual). Subjects also reported a greater amount of attraction for the high-status individual. High-status individuals, therefore, are viewed as acting more freely and, perhaps as a consequence, are more subject to praise as well as criticism.

Attribution research has also examined tendencies to distort one's view of behavior. One illustration is termed the **fundamental attribution error,** wherein we attribute the behaviors of others to internal factors. For example, you might conclude that another employee is doing poorly in meeting a sales quota because of a lack of ambition, when it may be that the other employee's sales territory does not provide much opportunity. The fundamental attribution error leads people to blame the victims of misfortune. For example, unemployed workers are viewed as lazy, and the homeless are seen as irresponsible. Women who are the victims of sexual harassment at work may be accused of being seductive.

The attributions that people make concerning the causes of their own behavior tend to be influenced by whether the outcome is positive or negative. This tendency to take credit for success (attributing it to personal traits or personal effort) and to blame failure on external, environmental causes is termed **self-serving bias.** Students sometimes manifest the self-serving bias when they attribute their success on tests to their intellectual prowess or having studied hard, and attribute their poor test performance to unfair test construction by the teacher. Self-serving bias is also manifest when people compare themselves to others on subjective and socially desirable dimensions. For example, most business managers view themselves as being more ethical than the average manager, and superior on performance dimensions.[24] Also, most managers see themselves as more open to innovation than do their subordinates or outside observers.‡

One popular approach to understanding the attribution process is given by **Kelley's theory of causal attribution.** In H.H. Kelley's view, judgments of another's behavior are influenced by three sources of information: *agreement, consistency,* and *distinctiveness.* Agreement refers to the degree that others' behaviors are similar to the observed person's behavior. Consistency defines the degree to which the observed person behaves in the same manner in other similar occasions. Distinctiveness refers to the degree the observed person behaves similarly in comparatively different settings. As an example of how these sources of information influence our judgments, consider a situation in which your colleague is complaining about his supervisor. If this colleague complains, but no one else complains, we would say that agreement is low. Plus, if this colleague always complains about the supervisor, then consistency is high. Finally, if your colleague complains about all of his past supervisors, then distinctiveness is low. The combination of low agreement, high consistency, and low distinctiveness would lead you to an internal attribution that the colleague is antagonistic to the supervisor because of a personal disposition that involves being generally antagonistic to authority figures. As a contrasting example, imagine that your colleague was not alone in complaining about the supervisor, as other coworkers also complained (i.e., agreement is now high). Further, the colleague frequently complains about the supervisor (i.e., consistency is again high). Finally, your colleague does not complain about any past supervisors (i.e., distinctiveness is now high). This second combination of the three sources of information would now lead to an external attribution of your colleague's complaining behavior, wherein we would conclude that the supervisor is, in fact, a difficult person.

Personality
• •

Thus far in this chapter, we have considered the difficulties of accurately perceiving others. Let us now turn our attention to how individuals differ. Such

---

‡As most academic administrators are aware, university faculty members are not exempt from the self-serving bias. One study found that 94 percent of the faculty at one institution, and 90 percent of the faculty members in a survey of 24 institutions, judged themselves to be superior to their average colleague.[25]

differences are what make social interaction stimulating and sometimes frustrating. First, we will consider the nature of personality and the determinants of personality. Next, we will examine the techniques used to measure differences in personality. And last, we will look at several important dimensions of individual differences.

Personality can be defined as the relatively enduring individual traits and dispositions that form a pattern distinguishing one person from all others. This is by no means a universally accepted definition. In fact, there are nearly as many definitions of personality as there are theories of personality. Nonetheless, for our purposes, this definition will suffice.[§]

The concept of personality represents stylistic differences in the behavior of people. Let us suppose, for example, that you have closely observed the behavior of one of your coworkers. This person rarely speaks in group meetings, has virtually no friends at work, and seems to prefer to be alone most of the time. From these observations, you would likely infer that this individual is introverted. This would help to explain the individual's past and present behavior and also predict behavior in future situations. Our definition of personality includes the notion that the traits are relatively enduring, which implies consistency of behavior across situations and over time. To be sure, people do change over time, but the rate of such change is typically very gradual. Normal maturation processes are sufficiently slow that we can usefully assess individual traits with a fair degree of certainty as to their stability.

The Determinants of Personality

There has been considerable debate about the origins of an individual's personality. One point of view argues that personality is largely determined at conception by each individual's unique assortment of genes. In essence, this perspective holds that personality traits, such as temperament and sociability, are determined in much the same way as hair color and facial features.

The counterpoint to the heredity position is an environmental argument. Environmentalists contend that the results of experience can shape and alter an individual's personality. For example, whether individuals are lethargic or industrious would be determined by whether they were rewarded or punished by parents, teachers, and friends for displaying related behaviors in the past. If the notion of the work ethic were ingrained in individuals at an early age and they repeatedly encountered situations in which hard work paid off, they would be inclined to espouse values that support the work ethic.

Some evidence shows that heredity can influence personality. Perhaps the most intriguing indication of the importance of genetic predisposition comes from studies of identical twins who have been separated at birth and raised apart. Even though many of the twins were raised by families from different

---

[§]It should be noted that some writers have questioned whether the notion of personality is even necessary. They contend that individual attributes can be easily explained by reducing the observations of an individual's "personality" to more basic concepts, such as habits, conditioned reflexes, attitudes, and so on. In other words, "personality" is something akin to the canals on Mars: It may be more in the eye of the beholder (as part of the observer's structuring of what is being observed) than it is an actual feature. There may be some truth to this criticism of the entire enterprise of studying personality. However, the consistency that we find within an individual's behavior suggests that it may well be worthwhile to infer the existence of traits and dispositions that can partially account for and thereby help explain employee behavior.

social classes, and sometimes in different countries, each set shared many common traits. For example, food and clothing preferences and such personal habits as smoking, fingernail biting, and the sporting of moustaches were often shared by the separately raised pairs.[26]

A considerable amount of evidence also suggests that the situations to which a person is exposed can shape and alter an individual's personality traits. The most striking illustration arises from cross-cultural comparisons. As many people have noted, the personality traits of Westerners are often distinct from traits of people raised in other cultures, such as Asians. Also, people who are raised in a new culture from an early age often reflect the influence of their experiences within that new culture.

One can also find evidence of a link between personality and more immediate environmental influences. For example, research on the relationship of birth order to personality has revealed some interesting findings. Firstborn children are more dependent, more influenced by social pressure, and more prone to schizophrenia than are later-born children.[27] Compared to later-borns, firstborns view the world as more predictable, rational, and orderly. In addition, firstborns are less likely to defy authority, and are more ambitious, more cooperative, and more concerned with being socially accepted. A disproportionate number of firstborns are listed in *Who's Who*.

The personality differences that have been identified between firstborn and later-born children are believed to result from the differing experiences to which the children are exposed. Firstborns are generally treated differently by parents. Compared to later-borns, they tend to receive more attention at first but are then expected to behave more responsibly in looking after younger children.

For most students of the topic, the heredity–environment debate is resolved by recognizing the importance of *both* heredity and environment as determinants of personality. Heredity may predispose an individual to certain patterns of behavior, while environmental forces may precipitate more specific patterns of action. Both sets of factors are necessary for a fuller accounting of individual behavior.

One of the most perplexing aspects of personality is its general resistance to modification. Studies of attempts to change an individual's personality typically show that it is very difficult, if not impossible, to do so for many individuals. This difficulty does not negate the possibility of personality change via environmental forces, but instead argues that the magnitude of such forces for change and the inclination of individuals to change are typically not sufficient. This resistance to change is significant because it suggests that managers must learn to deal with people's personality traits in the work setting. In short, a manager's hope of dramatically altering a worker's personality traits is not great. It may be more realistic to try to accept people as they are or to try for only modest accommodations between personality features and job requirements.**

**What follows is a review of the major techniques used for assessing traits. Omitted from discussion is the technique of graphology, or handwriting analysis. Oddly, and sadly, the technique is used by a sizable number of firms in the United States, Canada, and Western Europe. Although reliable scoring schemes have been developed for features of slant and height, there is no evidence of the validity of these measurements for predicting job performance or individual standing on more widely accepted measures of personality.[28]

Assessing Personality Traits

There are many techniques for measuring personality attributes. Among them are personality ratings, situational tests, inventories, and projective techniques.

Personality Ratings   A well-known device for assessing personality is the use of ratings. The most frequently used formats of such **personality ratings** are five-point and seven-point scales, with adjectives as endpoints, or anchors, for the scales. Such rating scales may not yield reliable assessments because the meanings associated with the endpoints and midpoints are not clearly defined. Thus, different raters may interpret the same scale differently.

This approach can be improved upon by using rating scales whose scale points are clearly defined by specific behavioral indicators. For example, consider the following example of a scale for measuring the trait of competitiveness.[29]

1 = Sensitive to the presence of competitive situations but becomes disorganized, let down, or unproductive, or flees from them. Discouraged about own abilities or appears to seek defeat compulsively.

2 = No real competitive interest; enjoys games for the fun of playing them but relatively unimportant who wins.

3 = Is stimulated by competitive situations and enjoys excelling, but can accept defeat without much strain. Periodic competitive sprees but not persistent and pervasive.

4 = Enjoys excelling competitors to the point of being upset when faced with a loss, takes failure very hard, or can't restrain an overt expression of satisfaction after winning. Competitive drive is very pronounced in several fields or has one field in which it is terribly important to excel.

5 = Extreme drive to excel competitors, won't play if can't win, always picks inferior opponents, or cheats to win. Beating competitors is primary or only satisfaction in work or play situations. Competitive drives extend to many situations that most individuals would not define as competitive.

As this example implies, it is important that a rater be in a position to observe the traits in question. The rater must also be unbiased and frank.[††] Typically, evaluators are reluctant to use the extreme negative positions on rating scales. As a consequence, ratings are often clustered toward the positive end of the scale, with the result that ratings do not discriminate among individuals and are, therefore, not informative.

Situational Tests   **Situational tests** (or behavioral tests) involve the direct observation of an individual's behavior in a setting that is designed to provide information about personality. The earliest situational tests were used to assess personality in children. For example, to assess the trait of honesty, students were asked to grade their own papers. A later check of the papers indicated how honest each student was. In an assessment of charitableness, children

---

[††]Unfortunately, raters are sometimes asked to perform evaluations without having an opportunity to observe the necessary traits. For example, university professors are often asked to provide evaluations of students who apply to MBA programs or law school. Many times these evaluations include ratings of such personality traits as maturity, social assertiveness, and dependability. Most faculty members, however, have only superficial contact with the students that they are asked to evaluate and oftentimes are very generous in their ratings.

were invited to anonymously donate small gifts, such as school supplies, to less fortunate children. Because the individual items were surreptitiously marked, it was possible to identify how much each child donated.

As part of a situational test of honesty in adults, soldiers were placed in isolation in a test situation in which a series of numerical problems were to be solved. The answer book was available in the room, but each individual was instructed to not open the book. By secretly observing the individual from behind a screen, the assessors were able to determine the individual's level of honesty.[30]

Another illustration of situational testing is provided by Toyota's screening program at its Georgetown, Kentucky, auto-assembly plant. As part of this program, the problem-solving ability of applicants is tested by putting them through a flawed mock-up of an assembly line and asking them to suggest improvements in the line's procedures.[31]

Situational tests offer many advantages. They are less subjective than rating scales, and the trait in question can sometimes be assessed in a fairly natural setting. This suggests that the results of the assessment will be more valid. Unfortunately, situational tests are very expensive to create and administer. Additionally, certain traits, such as self-esteem, do not readily lend themselves to situational assessment.

Personality Inventories **Personality inventories** are perhaps the most widely used method of assessing personality characteristics. Typically, inventories ask the respondent to indicate whether a statement pertains to or is true of himself or herself. A typical inventory question would be, "Do you find it easy to make friends?" The first concerted effort to use a personality inventory occurred when the U.S. Army attempted to identify men who were likely to have severe adverse emotional reactions to the rigors of warfare. Rather than screen the men with interviews, researchers devised a lengthy questionnaire, called the Personal Data Sheet, in which an individual would essentially interview himself.[32] Among the 116 items in the Personal Data Sheet were:

1. Have you ever had a vision?
2. Do you sometimes feel that you are being watched?
3. Have you ever had dizzy spells?
4. Do you feel that you have hurt yourself by taking drugs?
5. Did you have a happy childhood?

Individuals were screened out if they answered a specified number of questions in the "neurotic" direction.

Today, many devices are used to assess literally hundreds of personality characteristics. To find aids in determining whether a suitable inventory is available and whether the device has acceptable measurement characteristics, one can consult such reference sources as *Mental Measurements Yearbook* and *Tests in Print*.[33]

Although inventories have the clear advantage of ease of administration, there remains the problem of the possible "faking" of answers and the related issue of the "approval motive"—the respondent's tendency to answer in a socially desirable fashion.[34] Some of the more sophisticated inventories, however, provide checks for faking. Items are included in the inventory that do not measure personality traits per se but instead act as "flags" that a respondent is answering dishonestly.[‡‡]

Projective Techniques **Projective techniques** are designed to probe the more subtle aspects of an individual's personality. Projective techniques are based on the belief that a person will provide a highly individualistic interpretation of an ambiguous stimulus.[§§] Two of the more commonly used forms of projectives are storytelling devices and sentence completions.

Storytelling **Storytelling** devices have a fairly good track record in terms of standardized interpretation, reliability, and usefulness as a predictor of behavior. The most widely used storytelling technique is the **Thematic Apperception Test, or TAT.**[36] The TAT is composed of 20 pictures, each of which portrays a social setting of ambiguous meaning. For example, one picture shows a boy staring wistfully at a violin. For each picture, the respondent is asked to provide a story that contains the following elements: a description of the characters in the story, a statement about what is presently going on in the picture, and explanations of what led up to the current situation, as well as how the story is likely to conclude. The 20 stories are then analyzed for recurring themes. Assuming that people identify with the protagonist of their stories, it is possible to draw inferences about a respondent's attitudes, needs, aspirations, and self-perception.

Sentence Completions **Sentence completions** are another popular variety of projective technique in which respondents are asked to supply the endings for a series of partial sentences. The format of sentence completions is fairly straightforward. For example,

1. I wish my boss would _____.
2. I feel good about myself when _____.
3. The trouble with my coworkers is _____.

In some instances, standardized scoring schemes have been developed to aid in interpreting the responses. Because the intent of sentence completions is relatively transparent and respondents are usually given unlimited time to answer, this test format is best used when respondents have little to gain by faking their answers. Appropriate situations might include sensitivity-training sessions and team-building exercises. When people answer honestly, their responses to incomplete sentences can be very enlightening.

[‡‡]Faking scales are typically devised by paying people to fake their answers deliberately in a specific direction (either "fake good" or "fake bad"). Their responses to the questions are then analyzed to identify the items that discriminate between intentional fakers and others who are paid to answer honestly.

[§§]This tendency to interpret ambiguous stimuli in a unique, personalized manner was first noted by Leonardo da Vinci. As the story goes, one day during a playful moment, da Vinci threw a paint-soaked sponge at an apprentice. The apprentice ducked and the sponge struck a wall, leaving a smudge. Da Vinci noticed that the smudge, on various occasions, reminded him of different objects. More interesting was his observation that when visitors to his workshop were asked what they saw in the smudge, they reported seeing things that made sense in light of their occupations or past experiences.[35]

Important Dimensions of Personality

There is an enormous number of human traits. It has been estimated that there may be as many as 5,000 adjectives that could be used to describe personality traits. In terms of relevance to organizational behavior, however, the number of important personality traits is much smaller. Consequently, for now we will limit our discussion to four dimensions of personality: locus of control, the work ethic, cognitive style, and moral maturity. In organizational behavior research, these four dimensions have received much more attention than others. Throughout this text, however, we will consider other personality dimensions as they pertain to behavior in the workplace.

Locus of Control   Psychologist Julian Rotter proposed that the likelihood of an individual's engaging in a particular act is a function of (1) the person's expectancy that the act will yield rewards and (2) the personal value of those rewards to the individual.[37] In essence, Rotter's proposal rests on the notion of locus of control. **Locus of control** is the extent to which individuals believe that control over their lives lies within their own control or in environmental forces beyond their control. Someone who strongly believes that he or she controls events has a high *internal locus of control,* while someone who feels that he or she is at the mercy of fate has a high *external locus of control.*

Rotter developed a scale for measuring the extent to which an individual is internally or externally oriented. The Internal-External Control Scale asks the respondent to choose one of two possible interpretations as the cause of an event. The alternatives reflect internal versus external control. The following are sample items from the scale.[38]

1a. In the long run, people get the respect they deserve in this world.
 b. Unfortunately, an individual's worth often passes unrecognized, no matter how hard he tries.

2a. In my case, getting what I want has little or nothing to do with luck.
 b. Many times, we might just as well decide what to do by flipping a coin.

3a. By taking an active part in political and social affairs, people can control world events.
 b. Many times, I feel that I have little influence over the things that happen to me.

As you can see from these items, choice "a" in these examples indicates an internal response, while choice "b" exemplifies an external response.

It has been found, for example, that internally oriented individuals are less likely to respond to group pressures or persuasive communication.[39] Furthermore, a number of studies have observed that internal orientation is associated with success in school. For African-American students in particular, locus of control was a better predictor of academic achievement than was any other variable studied, including school location and quality.[40]

Social class and racial differences in locus of control have also been reported, in that upper-class individuals and whites tend to score as more internally oriented relative to lower-class individuals and blacks.[41] Because social class is correlated with race, it is difficult to say whether poverty or discrimination is a more important cause of an external locus of control. To be sure, the experience of powerlessness and the lack of personal evidence that hard work leads to success contribute to the external orientation that is found in certain segments of society.[42]

It is perhaps not surprising that compared to externally oriented individuals, internally oriented individuals have higher incomes, hold jobs of higher status, and advance more rapidly in their careers.[43] What perhaps is surprising is that scores on Rotter's scale have been shifting over the years with scores revealing that Americans appear to be becoming more externally oriented.[44]

Finally, it should be noted that internally and externally oriented individuals differ in the kinds of rewards they prefer. Externally oriented individuals, who believe that forces beyond their control are responsible for success, tend to prefer such extrinsic rewards as increased pay and job security. In contrast, internally oriented individuals usually prefer intrinsic (self-supplied) rewards such as a feeling of accomplishment and sense of achievement.[45] Internally oriented individuals, however, are not completely exempt from difficulties. It has been found that extreme internals may be maladjusted "controllers" who strive to have total control over their own and others' outcomes by being aggressive, intrusive, and domineering. For such individuals, frustration and anxiety are likely when they are in a subservient role or a setting where goal attainment is beyond their control.[46] The implication is fairly clear: Managers who understand their subordinates' loci of control can better tailor their reward systems to reflect individual needs.

The Work Ethic   The **work ethic** embodies a set of beliefs, including a belief in the dignity of all work, contempt for idleness and self-indulgence, and a belief that if you work hard, you will be rewarded. Personality research seems to indicate that a stable predisposition toward the work ethic can be identified. The measurement of this predisposition is typically done through inventories asking respondents to describe their own beliefs and behaviors. Individuals who subscribe to the work ethic have been found to be more accepting of authoritarian leadership.[47] They also tend to have an interest in jobs that can be characterized as concrete as opposed to abstract; for example, they may prefer carpentry to journalism. When asked to perform simple, dull, and repetitive tasks without financial incentive, endorsers of the work ethic are more persistent and productive.[48] When told that they are doing poorly on a boring task in comparison to other performers, endorsers of the work ethic respond by increasing their efforts, while others reduce their efforts.[49] In response to positive feedback, both endorsers and nonendorsers of the work ethic increase their effort.

Recent evidence suggests that the work ethic may be waning in the United States. For example, older workers are more prone to endorse the work ethic than are younger workers.[50] If we assume that the work ethic's belief system is learned early in life, this finding suggests the work ethic may be eroding. In a study of workers' desire to continue working even if they no longer had the financial need to do so, it was found that the number of people who would choose early retirement increased in the past decades.[51] From such evidence, we may conclude that adherence to the work ethic may be diminishing and that it may be gradually being replaced by a leisure ethic. The unprecedented current affluence of the United States in comparison to all other countries and all other times is a likely contributing factor to this shift. It should be noted, however, that such cultural value shifts are not new and that the present shift may reflect a more fundamental process of gradual cultural maturation.[52]

Another related topic is the question of whether the work ethic of a nation can be deliberately raised. For example, the workforces of the former Soviet Union and allied countries have not had a history of emphasizing individual initiative or competitiveness while under communist control. The specific mechanisms by which we might actually raise a culture's work ethic are not clear.***

Cognitive Style   Carl Gustav Jung, a famous European psychoanalyst, proposed a model of **cognitive styles,** or modes of problem solving. He suggested four dimensions of psychological functioning: Introverted versus Extroverted, Thinking versus Feeling, Sensing versus Intuiting, and Judging versus Perceiving. Introverts are oriented toward the inner world of ideas and feelings, while extroverts are oriented toward the outer world of people and objects. Thinkers desire to make decisions logically, while feelers base decisions on subjective grounds. Sensing individuals prefer to focus on details, while intuitive individuals prefer to focus on broad issues. Judging types desire to resolve issues, while perceiving types are comparatively flexible and seek additional information. By crossing the various types, 16 distinct personality types can be identified.

The measurement of these types has relied heavily on a paper-and-pencil test known as the Myers-Briggs Type Indicator, developed by the mother-daughter team of Katherine Briggs and Isabel Briggs-Myers. Table 2.1 summarizes some of the characteristics found to be associated with these different cognitive styles. The Myers-Briggs Type Indicator has become one of the more widely used personality tests in North America, within the nominally normal population. Typically, the test is given as part of management development programs to aid executives in understanding how they appear to others. Companies that have relied on the Myers-Briggs Type Indicator include Allied-Signal, Apple, AT&T, Exxon, General Electric, Honeywell, and 3M.

Research using the Myers-Briggs Type Indicator has generally supported the typology and shown that people of different cognitive styles prefer different occupations. For example, the ENTP individual is termed the "conceptualizer." This person loves new possibilities and hates routines. They are more likely to be an entrepreneur than a corporate executive. The ISTJ person is termed the "traditionalist," and often may be found in accounting and financial positions. The INTJ person is labeled the "visionary." Such individuals, although only a small proportion of the population, have a disproportionate representation among chief executives. One of the most common types in the general population, as well as among managers, is the ESTJ, termed the "organizer."[53]

Sometimes the test is used as an aid for improving work-team functioning. Following feedback and discussion, team members can gain insights to the orientations of coworkers and themselves, as well as to how their different orientations may help or hinder team dynamics. Skeptics might argue that it is the greater communication and discussion that generates positive results, rather than the feedback provided by the Myers-Briggs test itself.

***A further, fascinating issue is whether the entire notion of a work ethic has any relevance at all for some specific cultures. A friend of mine, who was working as a missionary for the Catholic Church on a small Polynesian island, once observed that the lack of an industrial base, coupled with a lack of marketable resources, may make the concept of a work ethic irrelevant for some cultures.

TABLE 2.1 ***The 16 Cognitive Styles of the Myers-Briggs Typology***

		Sensing Types (S)		Intuitive Types (N)	
		Thinking (T)	Feeling (F)	Feeling (F)	Thinking (T)
Introverts (I)	Judging (J)	ISTJ: Serious, quiet, practical, logical, dependable	ISFJ: Quiet, friendly, thorough, considerate	INFJ: Quietly forceful, succeeds by perseverance, conscientious	INTJ: Skeptical, critical, independent, determined, original
	Perceiving (P)	ISTP: Cool onlookers, quiet, reserved and analytical, flashes of original humor	ISFP: Retiring, sensitive, kind, modest, relaxed about getting things done	INFP: Cares about learning, ideas, and independent projects; undertakes too much, but gets it done	INTP: Quiet, reserved, impersonal, enjoys scientific subjects, little liking for parties or small talk
Extroverts (E)	Perceiving (P)	ESTP: Matter-of-fact, doesn't worry, may be blunt or insensitive	ESFP: Easy-going, accepting, friendly, likes sports and making things	ENFP: Warmly enthusiastic, high-spirited, imaginative, quick with solutions and help with problems	ENTP: Quick, ingenious, will argue either side of issue for fun, may neglect routine assignments
	Judging (J)	ESTJ: Practical, realistic, has a natural head for business or mechanics, likes to organize and run activities	ESFJ: Warm-hearted, talkative, popular, born cooperator, desires harmony, little interest in abstract subjects	ENFJ: Responsive and responsible, feels real concern for what others think or want, sociable, sensitive to praise and criticism	ENTJ: Hearty, frank, decisive, a leader, may be more positive than own experience in area warrants

Moral Maturity The topic of ethical decision making in organizations has received increasing attention in recent years. Managers who are lower in an organization's structure report more pressure to compromise their personal values in order to achieve company goals.[54] One *Wall Street Journal* survey revealed that 20 percent of executives reported having been asked to behave unethically.[55]

A popular model of moral judgment was developed and tested by Lawrence Kohlberg, a psychologist.[56] His **moral maturity** model emphasizes the cognitive, or reasoning, processes that can be used to characterize individuals when making ethical decisions. Kohlberg's research identified six stages of moral development. Moral development is reflected in movement from stage to stage in a fixed, or invariant, and irreversible sequence. Any individual's reasoning can be said to be operating in a manner characteristic of one of these stages. Table 2.2 outlines the six stages of Kohlberg's model. At stages one and two (termed the preconventional level), a person is focused on such concrete consequences as rewards and punishments, and personal interest. At stages three and four (the conventional level), correct behavior and judgment are defined by the expectations of good behavior of one's family and society. At stages five and six (the principled level), correct behavior or judgment is defined in terms of universal values and principles.

Kohlberg and his research associates have developed several tests for measuring a person's stage of moral maturity. Studies of behavior and decision making reveal that individuals of higher moral maturity are less likely to cheat in laboratory experiments and less likely to follow the orders of an authority figure if the directives are likely to injure another individual. Highly moral individuals are more likely to help another individual who is in need of assistance.[57] More highly morally mature individuals also are less likely to engage in padding an expense account.[58] Kohlberg's model of the stages of moral development has been found to be a reasonable representation of people in non-Western cultures as well.[59] However, Carol Gilligan has challenged Kohlberg's views as reflecting an abstract, impersonal concept of justice that is more characteristic of male than female moral judgment. Gilligan's research suggests that males may focus more on issues of justice, while females may emphasize caring and the fulfillment of human needs.[60]

The Big Five Model of Personality Five additional personality dimensions have been identified that have special relevance for the workplace: agreeableness, conscientiousness, emotional adjustment, extroversion, and inquisitiveness. Because these dimensions have been found in studies that have sought to identify the most basic dimensions of personality, they are popularly called the **"Big Five" dimensions** of personality.[61] The importance of the "Big Five" for employee behavior derives from their being related to other important work-related tendencies. For example, inquisitiveness is related to learning

TABLE 2.2 *Six Stages of Moral Development*

Stage	What is considered to be proper
Preconventional Level	
Stage One: Obedience and punishment orientation	Sticking to rules to avoid punishment. Obedience for its own sake.
Stage Two: Instrumental purpose and exchange	Following rules only when it is in one's immediate interest. Right is an equal exchange, a fair deal.
Conventional Level	
Stage Three: Interpersonal accord, conformity, mutual expectations	Stereotypical "good" behavior. Living up to what is expected by people close to you.
Stage Four: Social accord and system maintenance	Fulfilling duties and obligations to which one has agreed. Upholding laws except in extreme cases where they conflict with fixed social duties. Contributing to the society, group.
Principled Level	
Stage Five: Social contract and individual rights	Being aware that people hold a variety of values, that rules are relative to the group. Upholding rules because they are the social contract. Upholding nonrelative values and rights regardless of majority opinion.
Stage Six: Universal ethical principles	Following self-chosen ethical principles. When laws violate these principles, act in accord with principles.

Source: Adapted from L. Kohlberg, "Moral Stages and Moralizations: The Cognitive-Developmental Approach," in *Moral Development and Behavior: Theory, Research, and Social Issues*, ed. T. Lickona (New York: Holt, Rinehart and Winston, 1969): 34–35.

ability, while conscientiousness and emotional adjustment are related to work motivation, and agreeableness and extroversion may be related to task mastery. Of course, learning, work motivation, and task mastery are all ultimately components of employee job performance. Hence, the "Big Five" personality dimensions may be of importance because they are associated with antecedents of employee effectiveness.

SUMMARY

1. *Defend the notion that perception is a complex and active process.* Perception is the process by which an individual selects, organizes, and interprets information about the environment and thus gives it personal meaning. Because the environment and the individual's physiological and psychological systems are so complicated, perception is an extremely complex process. The individual takes an active role in screening out irrelevant stimuli and carefully structuring the relevant stimuli into meaningful messages that apply to the immediate situation. This is done in accordance with a prepared mental set based on previous experiences. In this way, the perceiver actually constructs his or her own version of the environment.

2. *Explain how facial expressions and other nonverbal cues affect the accuracy of our perceptions.* People's facial expressions and other nonverbal cues help us gauge the effects of our words and actions. When a person's words, facial expression, and nonverbal cues are all in agreement, they reinforce our perceptions. However, because people are masters of disguising their true intentions and feelings, it is important to watch for discrepancies between verbal and nonverbal cues. Nonverbal cues, such as amount of eye contact, frequency of smiling, and posture, can influence our perceptions of others.

3. *Identify the most common obstacles to accurate perception.* There are many barriers to precise perception, each a possible source of misleading or distorted information. Among the most common are stereotyping, the halo effect, projection, perceptual distortion, selective perception, and subliminal influences. A stereotype is a judgment of an individual based on certain characteristics attributed to a specific group. A person who has been thus categorized is expected to behave in fixed, preconceived ways, without regard to individual differences. The halo effect occurs when a perceiver's evaluation of specific traits is influenced by an overall impression, either favorable or unfavorable. Projection is the tendency to ascribe our own feelings and traits to others in order to protect ourselves from unpleasant or unacceptable truths. A related defense mechanism is perceptual distortion, the altering of a perception in order to avoid an unpleasant reality. Another obstacle arises from selective perception, or the tendency to be influenced by our own interests. Finally, our perception may be misled by subliminal influences, factors that are below our threshold of awareness. In such cases, an individual reacts without realizing the source of influence.

4. *Outline the basic principles of attribution theory.* According to attribution theory, when we observe an event, we try to understand its cause, assess responsibility for its outcome, and evaluate the personal qualities of the people involved. A key factor in attribution is whether the observer believes that the event is caused by an individual (internal causality) or by the environment (external causality). For example, a supervisor may attribute an employee's poor performance either to the worker's own laziness or to substandard working conditions. The cause that the supervisor infers will greatly influence his or her perception of the individual, the traits he or she attributes to the employee, and the steps taken to deal with the situation.

5. *Discuss the concept of personality and the factors that affect its development.* Personality is the relatively enduring pattern of individual traits and dispositions that distinguishes one person from all others. The origin of individual personality is the subject of considerable debate, with one point of view contending that personality is largely determined by heredity, and another holding that personality is primarily the product of environment. In fact, both heredity and environment are important determinants of personality. Heredity may predispose an individual to certain patterns of behavior, while environmental forces may cause more specific patterns of behavior.

6. *Describe the most commonly used techniques for measuring personality attributes.* Although there are many different techniques for measuring personality attributes, the most frequently used are ratings, situational tests, inventories, and projective techniques. Ratings usually take the form of five- or seven-point scales with adjectives describing personality traits as endpoints, or anchors. Some ratings include specific definitions for each point on the scale. In situational tests, an individual's behavior is directly observed in a setting that is specifically designed to reveal personality. Although they are expensive to create and administer, the results of situational tests are less subjective and, therefore, more valid than the results of ratings. Personality inventories, widely used to measure personality traits, ask individuals to respond to a series of statements by indicating whether the statements describe themselves. Projective techniques are designed to probe the more subtle aspects of personality by asking the individual to respond to deliberately ambiguous stimuli. Included in this category are storytelling and sentence completions.

7. *Specify and define several dimensions of personality that are especially relevant to organizational behavior.* Various dimensions of personality have received substantial attention in OB research: locus of control, the work ethic, cognitive style, and moral maturity. Locus of control identifies where individuals feel that control over their life lies: within their own control or in environmental forces beyond their control. Internally oriented persons differ from externally oriented individuals in terms of responsiveness to group pressures, success in school, income, job status, speed of career advancement, and preference for specific kinds of rewards. The work ethic embodies a cluster of beliefs, including respect for the dignity of all work, contempt for idleness and self-indulgence, and faith that hard work will be rewarded. Recent evidence suggests that the work ethic may be waning in the United States. Cognitive style refers to four modes of gathering and evaluating information: introversion-extroversion, thinking-feeling, sensing-intuiting, and judging-perceiving. Moral maturity refers to one's stage of ethical judgment. Much recent attention has focused on the "Big Five" dimensions of personality: agreeableness, conscientiousness, emotional adjustment, extroversion, and inquisitiveness.

KEY TERMS

Person perception
Nonverbal cues
Stereotypes
Halo effect
Implicit personality theory
Projection
Perceptual distortion
Subliminal influences
Selective perception
Attribution theory
Fundamental attribution error
Self-serving bias
Kelley's theory of causal attribution

Personality
Personality rating
Situational tests
Personality inventories
Projective techniques
Storytelling
Thematic Apperception Test (TAT)
Sentence completion
Locus of control
Work ethic
Cognitive style
Moral maturity
"Big Five" dimensions

CRITICAL INCIDENT

A Questionable "Fit"

Irene Long was recently promoted to department manager of accounting for the Badger Manufacturing Company. Badger produces metal toolboxes and related items under its own brand and for private labels. Irene has worked in the finance area and in accounting with Badger for twelve years. When the previous manager retired, she was asked to fill the position.

Several problems have arisen over the past two months between Irene and her manager Wayne, the vice president of finance and accounting. Wayne wants Irene to "run" the accounting department. This involves handling all the day-to-day issues, staying on top of what needs to be done, and so on. When you, the consultant, met with Wayne, he described Irene as too laid-back and not assertive enough in assuming her new responsibilities. Wayne provided you with some examples of Irene's failing to get things done on time, not following up on other people's duties to provide her with information, and always waiting to be told what to do instead of initiating action.

In meeting with Irene, you find that she feels that Wayne does not appreciate her and her abilities. She claims that she is willing to do whatever needs to be done but Wayne does not provide good direction. Irene says she wants to do a good job, but that she is not going to be a dictator. When you ask if she likes her new job, Irene replies that she thinks so, but she's not sure.

You decide that it would be helpful to assess Irene's personality type and you administer the Myers-Briggs Type Indicator. Irene's score indicates that she is more of a Sensing/Thinking type (ST). Giving Wayne the same test, you discover that he is an Intuiting/Thinking type (NT).

Using the type information, and what you know about the working relationship between Wayne and Irene, address each of the following questions:

1. What are the major difficulties Irene and Wayne have in trying to develop a working relationship?

2. What are the issues each must consider in trying to work together?

3. Using the Myers-Briggs information, what strategy would you propose for resolving the difficulties between Irene and Wayne?

3 Changing Employee Behavior through Consequences

Experience is what enables you to recognize a mistake when you make it again.

—Earl Wilson

Around here they use the "carrot-and-stick" approach— you know what the "stick" is, the "carrot" means that they won't use the "stick."

—An employee

Learning Objectives

After studying this chapter, you should be able to:

1. Explain what learning is and why managers need to understand the learning process.
2. Describe the process of classical conditioning and cite several examples of this form of learning in the workplace.
3. Tell what observational learning is and how it occurs in the workplace.
4. Discuss the nature of operant conditioning and cite four rules for applying operant conditioning principles to enhance employee performance.
5. Summarize the advantages and disadvantages of OB Mod.
6. Analyze the role of punishment in shaping employee behavior.

In Safety, Incentives Are the "Name of the Game"

A Business Case History

Safety involves two principles that are hardly seen as "fun"— warnings and repetition. Furthermore, the average employee believes that accidents happen to "other people, not me." So how can it be made interesting enough to improve results? Turner Bros. Trucking, based in Oklahoma City, tackled this problem for its 300 employees with remarkable results. Gary Ritzky, risk and human resources director of Turner Bros., created a comprehensive program disguised as a fun game that was built on behavioral principles:

- Immediate monetary rewards for safety
- Self-directed safety teams to increase ownership and investment in safety and productivity
- Peer observation of behavior and productivity bonuses tied to safety

Monthly awards were given to employees to monitor safety. Historical average losses were identified and employees were rewarded for a 30 percent reduction from that benchmark. The reward was relevant—one dozen work gloves, which saved each employee $30 per month on glove purchases. When the new level was lowered another 30 percent, employees saved an additional $70 per month. The results were that no teams lost gloves over four years, the additional money reduced employees' personal spending on work clothes, and safety became more interesting, rewarding, and fun. Peer pressure is integrated into the program in that either everybody or nobody receives a reward.

Any one person can keep the entire team from receiving the monthly safety bonus, which probably works better than discipline to encourage safety.

The results of this program had a direct impact on the bottom line. Over a five-year period, insurance premiums and the direct cost of losses dropped from more than 12 percent of gross revenue to 4.03 percent, injury losses were reduced by 99 percent, and the companywide trucking insurance policy was reduced by 75 percent, while labor relations improved over these years. Turner Bros. also reported that less money was paid to attorneys and adjusters. This company has no second thoughts about paying for safety; not only does it work, but it can also be fun.

Source: G. M. Ritzky, "Turner Bros. Wins Safety Game with Behavioral Incentives," *HR Magazine,* June 1998, 79–83.

Learning, one of the most fundamental processes, involves both the development and the modification of thoughts and behaviors. Other concepts of organizational behavior (for example, motivation and supervision) that will be discussed in later chapters can be more fully explained with the use of learning principles.

New employees bring with them a set of previously learned ways of behaving. They are then expected to learn additional information that applies to their jobs. Established employees continue to develop their job-related skills and abilities. Therefore, learning is a never-ending process for all employees. The process is also very complex. For example, an employee who has already learned one way to perform a job may have trouble learning a second, although better, way.

An employee's motivation to perform is closely linked to learning because it depends on the employee's knowing that he or she can do the job well. Therfore, a manager who understands the learning process can use the principles of learning to guide employee behavior and performance. To be successful, employee training and development programs must be based on sound learning principles.

The Nature of Learning

Learning is a fairly permanent change in behavior that occurs as a result of experience.[1] A distinctive feature of this definition is the term *change*. In order to say that learning has occurred, a change, or modification, of behavior must be evident. The change in behavior must also be more than temporary. It should also be possible to attribute this change to the occurrence of an event. Thus, while learning is a process that we cannot observe directly, we can infer that learning has occurred when we observe a fairly permanent change in behavior.

Only during the past century have people begun to systematically study the learning process. Their efforts have produced three approaches to the explanation of learning: classical conditioning; observational, or vicarious, learning; and operant, or instrumental, conditioning.

Classical Conditioning

Early in the 20th century, Ivan Pavlov, a Russian physiologist, conducted research on digestive glands. In the course of his work, Pavlov discovered that a laboratory dog's secretions of saliva were controlled by both learning processes and direct physiological stimulation. He noted that the sound of approaching footsteps, as well as the simple sight of food, would cause a dog to salivate.

FIGURE 3.1 *A Summary of Classical Conditioning*

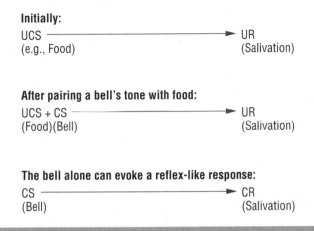

Initially:
UCS ——————————————→ UR
(e.g., Food)   (Salivation)

After pairing a bell's tone with food:
UCS + CS ————————————→ UR
(Food)(Bell)   (Salivation)

The bell alone can evoke a reflex-like response:
CS ——————————————→ CR
(Bell)   (Salivation)

In later research, Pavlov focused even more closely on how various stimuli could be used to produce a desired response. Specifically, he paired the ringing of a bell with the presentation of food to a dog. After a number of pairings, the sound of the bell alone (that is, without the food) was sufficient to produce salivation. Based on his experiments, Pavlov developed the notion of classical conditioning.

In **classical conditioning,** an **unconditioned stimulus (UCS)**—or stimulus that has the capacity to reliably evoke a naturally occurring reflexive or **unconditioned response (UR)**—is paired with the occurrence of a neutral stimulus, one that does not have an initial capacity to evoke the response of interest. Following a number of simultaneous presentations of the unconditioned stimulus and the neutral stimulus, the mere presence of the neutral stimulus will produce a reflexive response. This reflex-like response is termed the **conditioned response (CR).** When a neutral stimulus attains this capacity, it is termed a **conditioned stimulus (CS).** In Pavlov's experiments, the sight of food was the unconditioned stimulus that evoked the unconditioned response of salivation. The sound of the bell was the neutral stimulus that attained the power of a conditioned stimulus; that is, the bell gained power to evoke the conditioned, or learned, response of salivation. In classical conditioning, the initial relationship of UCS → UR is replaced by CS → CR (Figure 3.1).*

Many jobs require conditional responses. For example, driving a 40-foot tractor trailer or a forklift calls for reflexive behaviors. The driver's ability to apply the brakes quickly and firmly or otherwise react appropriately depends

———————————

*In an early demonstration of the power of classical conditioning, John Watson used Pavlovian techniques with an 11-month-old boy to condition a phobic (fearful) reaction to white furry objects.[2] The conditioning sequence consisted of pairing the presence of a white lab rat with a loud noise. After a number of pairings, the mere presence of sufficient white furry objects (such as a man's white beard) was sufficient to produce a fearful reaction in the boy. In a sense, the boy had developed a seemingly irrational fear of white furry objects. Before Watson could desensitize the boy (for instance, by pairing white furry objects with the presence of food), the boy's mother left town, taking the boy along. Whether the boy may have overcome the phobic reaction on his own is debatable. This case represents one of the first ethically questionable uses of conditioning techniques. After this experience, Watson abandoned research along these lines and went into advertising.

on conditioned responses to previously neutral stimuli, such as warning lights.[†] A manager's goal of training personnel to the point where they do not require continual monitoring and feedback also calls for classical conditioning.

Observational Learning

Much of the learning that occurs in organizations is based on observation. For example, new employees may observe a skilled employee performing a task. After simply observing the activities, the new employees are able to model their behavior after their observations. **Observational learning** occurs when a person witnesses the behavior of another and vicariously experiences the consequences of the other person's actions.[3] When tasks are fairly simple, observational learning can be immediate and complete; numerous trials and rehearsals are unnecessary. Furthermore, no apparent reward is administered in observational learning. Quick mastery of behavior and the lack of a visible reward for correct responses are unique to observational learning.

Some contend that the reward in observational learning is purely psychological. In essence, the individual engages in *self-rewarding,* perhaps by congratulating himself or herself each time a correct action occurs. If we accept this suggestion, then we must agree with the notion of a competency motive— that is, the desire to feel in control of one's surroundings and, therefore, self-sufficient.[4] Feelings of competency, or **self-efficacy,** can be said to arise from a sense of being able to master a task. In contrast to classical conditioning, in which the learner is totally dependent on someone else to set up the scheme for learning, observational learning is largely self-regulated. The choice of what to attend to, as well as how, when, and where to respond, is a matter of personal choice.

As previously noted, much of the learning that takes place in organizational settings is observational. In addition to informal observational learning, employees sometimes undergo formal training programs that rely on the same process. For example, the use of training films presumes that the observers will imitate the desirable forms of conduct portrayed on the screen. Training manuals and lectures are based on the premise that trainees will accept, retain, and enact the preferred forms of conduct in their jobs. At Xerox, for example, managerial training seminars often involve learning by watching films or videotapes of desired activities, as well as by role playing. These seminars cover such topics as interviewing, selling, listening, and reading effectively.[5] At a minimum, such training experiences can increase employee awareness of the existence of alternative ways of responding to problem situations.

Many advocates of observational learning contend that it is most successful when external rewards are provided.[6] Thus, they join observational learning principles with conditioning principles and recognize the importance of both individual cognition (that is, mental events) and external rewards.

[†]If you normally drive a car with a manual transmission but later switch to a car with an automatic transmission, you may notice your left foot reflexively stomping on a nonexistent clutch pedal. This is an example of a conditioned response encountered in everyday life.

Instrumental, or Operant, Conditioning

Much of human behavior in organizations is instrumental, in the sense that people act on their surroundings as well as deliberately move into and out of different situations. In other words, the behavior of employees is often instrumental in bringing about a desired outcome. When a desired outcome is obtained, the likelihood of that behavior recurring is enhanced. These principles are summarized in the **Law of Effect,** which states that responses that are followed by a desirable experience will be more likely to occur in the future, while responses that are followed by undesirable experiences will be less likely to occur.[7] More loosely stated, the law proposes that behavior that produces pleasant outcomes is less likely to recur.

In **operant conditioning,** reinforcement is used in conjunction with a response. There are two kinds of reinforcements: positive and negative. **Positive reinforcement** is any event used to increase the frequency of a response (for example, praise from a supervisor for the successful completion of a task). **Negative reinforcement** is any event that, when removed, increases the frequency of a response (for example, a loud buzzer that sounds when a worker fails to monitor a machine's operation and that shuts off only when the worker responds appropriately, or the criticism of a supervisor, which the worker can learn to avoid by performing a task correctly).

Both positive and negative reinforcement can increase the strength and frequency of the behaviors they follow.[8] However, these two types of reinforcement will create work environments with very different characteristics and behavioral dynamics. Positive reinforcement will lead to people performing in order to seek positive outcomes, while negative reinforcement will lead to people responding out of fear and anxiety.

Using Operant Principles in Organizational Settings

B.F. Skinner and his associates have elaborated on the principles of operant conditioning to the point where a systematic approach to the modification of human behavior has been developed.[9] Although Skinner did not deal with the topic of organizational behavior in his research, a number of OB researchers have adapted his principles to the field. The application of Skinner's principles to organizational settings is called organizational behavior modification, or **OB Mod.**

Acquiring Complex Behaviors: Shaping

One particularly powerful technique used to modify behavior is termed *shaping.* **Shaping** involves reinforcing small approximations of the final desired behavior. As shaping progresses, the reward is gradually withheld until larger portions of the complete task are performed. Many times, the desired worker behavior involves a set of responses so complex that the complete pattern of correct behavior is not likely to occur all at once. When shaping is used, the individual receives reinforcement for small, successive approximations of the desired behavior. For example, learning to operate a complex piece of machinery is likely to take a long period of time. In applying the principle of shaping, a trainer would praise a worker for each gradual improvement in operating the machine. Praise would then be withheld until more complex patterns of behavior were successfully performed.

Maintaining Desired Behavior

Because a manager cannot always be available to administer reinforcement, it is highly desirable that subordinates learn to perform at high levels without continual reward. To achieve this, the manager must increase the strength of the desired response to the point where it will not disappear if reinforcement is not provided. The elimination of a response due to the discontinuation of reinforcement is called **extinction.** For desired behaviors, extinction should be avoided, while for inappropriate behaviors, such as tardiness and insubordination, extinction may be actively sought.

A manager wants to increase a desired behavior's **resistance to extinction;** that is, he or she wants to ensure the response's persistence in the absence of reinforcement. Increased resistance to extinction can be achieved through **partial reinforcement.** When partial, or intermittent, reinforcement is used, a response is rewarded in a noncontinuous, or variable, manner. An alternative approach would be to praise a subordinate for every correct response, an approach termed **continuous reinforcement.** Behavior learned under a partial reinforcement scheme is more resistant to extinction than behavior learned under a continuous reinforcement scheme.

Schedules of Reinforcement   The scheduling of reinforcement is a particularly important aspect of OB Mod. There are four major kinds of partial reinforcement schedules: (1) fixed interval, (2) variable interval, (3) fixed ratio, and (4) variable ratio. **Interval schedules** reinforce behavior on the basis of time elapsed, while **ratio schedules** are based on the number of times the behavior is performed. In a **fixed schedule,** the amount of time or number of behaviors is specified in advance, while in a **variable schedule,** the amount of time or number of behaviors varies.

Fixed Interval Schedule   A **fixed interval schedule** reinforces individuals for their response after a predetermined period of time has elapsed. Although the response must meet minimal standards, performance beyond the minimum does not lead to greater rewards. Performance under a fixed interval schedule of reinforcement tends to be poor. As one might expect, the lack of a direct relationship between rewards and level of performance leads to only the minimal amount of effort necessary to meet the standard. In essence, a fixed interval scheme offers workers little incentive. Nonetheless, most organizations rely on such a schedule when they compensate employees on a weekly or hourly basis and ignore performance as long as it meets minimal standards. Also, responses learned under fixed interval schedules of reinforcement diminish or extinguish very rapidly when rewards are withheld.

Variable Interval Schedule   With a **variable interval schedule,** reinforcement is administered after varying periods of time have elapsed. Although the average period of time may be calculated, an individual cannot predict in advance how much time will elapse between reinforcements. (Recall that in a fixed interval scheme, the time period can be predicted precisely.)

As an example of such a scheme, consider a top-level manager's unannounced but fairly regular twice-monthly visits to a loading dock. Although the employees cannot say precisely when the manager will visit, they can nonetheless assume that *on the average* the manager will make an inspection every two weeks or so. Because of the controlling influence of the evaluative experience, it is possible that performance will drop somewhat after reinforcement is administered.

Fixed Ratio Schedule   In a **fixed ratio schedule,** reinforcement is given in exchange for a predetermined number of responses. The most common business use of a fixed ratio schedule is the piece-rate pay scheme. Under such a scheme, fruit pickers might be paid a set amount of money for every 10 pounds of fruit that they harvest. Performance tends to be higher under fixed ratio schedules than it is under interval schedules, but performance is likely to drop temporarily immediately after reinforcement. Thus, on the average, performance is high, but it tends to be variable. In such a scheme, employees are likely to exert effort in spurts in order to attain a given specified level of output.

Variable Ratio Schedule   Under a **variable ratio schedule,** reinforcement is provided after an individual has produced a number of desired responses. The desired number of responses, or standard, however, is not precisely stated, but instead varies around an average number. To receive reinforcement, an individual might have to correctly perform a behavior 18 times in one instance, 8 times the next, 15 times the next, and so on, with the average number being perhaps 12.

Although very few, if any, companies use a variable ratio schedule as their primary wage-payment method, many organizations use the scheme in other ways. For example, managers commonly praise employees via a variable ratio schedule. Thus, employees can rarely be certain beforehand that their actions will be rewarded. Other examples include the intermittent use of cash bonuses, public recognition, and other awards for good performance.

Comparing Schedules of Reinforcement   When these methods of reinforcement are compared, the variable ratio schedule is clearly the most effective in producing a consistently high level of performance. Behaviors rewarded under a variable ratio schedule are also the most resistant to extinction. As two illustrations, consider gambling and intimidating behavior. In gambling (say, playing slot machines or betting on horse races), one is rewarded on a variable ratio schedule in that one only wins occasionally. Despite the fact that in the long run gambling does not pay, the activity has an addictive quality in that it is always possible that the next play will be the lucky one that pays off.

An example of a negative behavior that is rewarded on a variable ratio schedule is a senior employee's threats and intimidating behavior. As most young managers find, it is difficult to ignore such posturing. By *occasionally* giving in to the angry senior employee, however, a manager is rewarding the employee on a variable ratio schedule. A likely consequence of such intermittent rewarding is that the employee will persist in his intimidating behaviors, given that he cannot be certain beforehand whether a particular instance will be the "lucky one" that pays off (in an analogous fashion to gambling). In general, a variable ratio reward schedule will enhance a response's resistance to extinction.

By contrast, the fixed interval schedule is the least effective scheme when judged against the criteria of performance enhancement and resistance to extinction. Perhaps because of their ease of administration, fixed interval schedules of reinforcement are the most commonly used in organizations. Relative to the fixed interval and variable ratio schedules, the two other schedules (fixed ratio and variable interval) can be judged as intermediate in effectiveness.

Rules for Applying Operant Principles

There are a number of useful rules for applying the principles of operant conditioning.[10] If a manager follows these rules in dealing with subordinates, their performance should be enhanced. With some modification, the rules can be summarized as follows:

1. *Use differential rewarding.* Many managers try to treat all subordinates alike. Although this sounds noble, it tends to encourage mediocrity. When all employees receive equal rewards, superior performers begin to feel that their efforts are unappreciated, while poorer performers recognize that they will not be penalized for minimal effort. In response, over time, most above-average performers will drop their performance to the minimal level. A few superior performers may, of course, persist, but most will lower their efforts to the level that they feel equals their rewards. When rewards are commensurate with performance, however, subordinates receive a quite different message. Superior performers get the signal that their efforts are valued, and potentially high performers are encouraged to try harder.

2. *Identify valued rewards for individuals.* If a manager hopes to influence an employee's behavior through the use of rewards, the rewards must have value to the employee. One of the best ways to obtain such information is simply to ask employees what rewards they would like to receive. Younger workers may prefer more paid vacation days or greater involvement in decision making, while older workers may choose better medical insurance or a larger contribution to their pension plan.

3. *Instruct subordinates on how rewards are tied to performance.* In order for operant conditioning principles to be maximally effective, employees must clearly understand how rewards and performance are connected. When specific information is lacking, subordinates may try to second-guess their manager's intentions by constructing their own imagined system of rewards. Thus, much confusion and counterproductivity can be avoided if a manager clearly states goals for performance and explains how rewards will be related to performance.

4. *Provide informative feedback on performance.* In order to meet their manager's standards of performance, employees must have instructive feedback. Their manager must evaluate and interpret their performance for them, indicating how well or how poorly they are doing and suggesting specific ways to improve. In addition to providing guidance, feedback can also serve as an additional form of reinforcement.[11]

Does OB Mod Work?

OB Mod programs constitute a useful approach to improving employee performance. In a review of OB Mod programs, ten organizations that had experimented with OB Mod were identified.[12] In nine of the ten cases, the introduction of OB Mod was judged as having had a positive effect. Many other recent examples (some involving control or comparison groups) also point to the success of OB Mod. Most instances in which OB Mod was applied shared several common characteristics. The typical OB Mod program attempts to improve either the performance or the attendance of blue-collar workers by providing immediate feedback about behavior and using praise or recognition from superiors as reinforcers. Interestingly, the programs do not commonly use money as a reinforcer of superior performance. More typically, such social rewards as praise and recognition are used. The use of these less costly rewards may be partially responsible for the appeal of OB Mod to many managers.

Controversies Surrounding OB Mod

Although much of the available evidence suggests that many OB Mod programs have been successful, there is a good deal of controversy surrounding the application of operant principles in organizations.[13]

Opponents of OB Mod accuse it of being manipulative, charging that OB Mod programs suggest a deliberate and calculated effort to control the behavior of others, sometimes at the cost of the individuals who are being controlled. Opponents argue that OB Mod smacks of a "Big Brother" approach to management, in which an all-knowing, all-powerful overseer attempts to maintain control and forced dependency by unilaterally defining the rules of the game. Further, there are ethical questions that can be raised.

Advocates of OB Mod acknowledge that the potential for misuse does exist, but they contend that good judgment is likely to prevail because deception and exploitation are apt to meet with worker resistance. Advocates of operant conditioning point out that, although the term *manipulation* may have negative connotations, it is ultimately a manager's responsibility to ensure that employee behavior contributes to the larger mission of an enterprise. Thus, managers must be aware of the factors that influence employee behavior and use them to fulfill their responsibilities to the company.

Another criticism of OB Mod is that it is not an original technique for managing employees. In some respects, OB Mod has much in common with traditional views of scientific management. For example, OB Mod programs require closer supervision of employees, more specific definitions of job activities, frequent evaluation and feedback, and the distribution of rewards based on output. The reliance of OB Mod on such rewards as praise and recognition can also be viewed as merely taking a page out of the human relations approach to management. At the least, it is fair to say that the OB Mod approach does borrow from other traditions in the field of organizational behavior.

An added criticism of OB Mod surrounds the faithfulness of OB Mod programs to operant principles. Many programs employ only a watered-down version of the principles of operant conditioning. For example, in programs relying heavily on self-feedback (in which employees maintain their own performance records), an alternative explanation of positive performance results—one based on the notion of self-reinforcement—can be offered.[14]

Conversely, in programs that are in closer conformity with operant principles, unpleasant questions arise as to whether an organization should be condoning such programs. For example, the following OB Mod program was designed to reduce high absenteeism in a manufacturing facility.[15] On every day an employee attended work, he or she drew a card from a deck of playing cards. After a week's time, each employee would have drawn five cards, a poker hand. The employee with the best hand received, say, a $50 bonus. This program employs the principle of intermittent rewards using a variable ratio schedule. The reward is both externally administered and contingent on behavior. In fact, such programs do reduce absenteeism rates. Unfortunately, they also raise two questions: (1) Should an organization endorse a form of gambling, the aim of which is to develop an addictive behavior in employees? and (2) should employees be enticed to work at a presumably distasteful job that most likely is responsible for the high absenteeism? In short, it might be more appropriate and more compassionate to first investigate the *causes* of high absenteeism and then remedy the causes by modifying the job, rather than focusing on the superficial manifestation of an underlying problem.

Operant conditioning has also been criticized for ignoring the importance of internally mediated rewards, for example, the motivation that results from the inherent enjoyment of performing certain attractive tasks. Some managers have suggested that the emphasis of OB Mod on externally administered, contingent rewards focuses attention on only one of the important features of motivation.[16] Furthermore, the use of such rewards for performing tasks that are intrinsically rewarding can undercut the motivation that a task may offer.

A final criticism of OB Mod is its lack of concern for mental processes. Because operant conditioning grew out of early work with animals and partly because of a reaction against early attempts to study mental events, advocates of OB Mod have downplayed the importance of dealing with thought processes. To be sure, such experiences are an important aspect of being human that cannot be totally ignored in any complete explanation of employee behavior.

The Role of Punishment

So far, we have focused primarily on the use of reward as a means of altering behavior, but the use of punishment must also be considered (Table 3.1). For purposes of discussion, we will define **punishment** as an undesirable event that follows a behavior it intends to eliminate. Punishment's role in shaping employee behavior is quite complex. Often, in response to its administration, an employee will not stop the undesirable behavior, but instead will seek other ways of engaging in the behavior as well as ways of getting even with the punisher. In most cases, punishment leads to only a temporary suppression of the punished behavior. Consequently, any proposal to use punishment must be carefully thought out.

TABLE 3.1   ***Frequently Used Rewards and Punishments***

Rewards	Punishments
Bonuses	Reprimands
Promotions	Oral warnings
Pay increases	Ostracism
Vacation time	Probation
Time off	Criticism from superiors
Use of company car	Suspension
Awards	Citations
Praise and recognition	Disciplinary hearing
Increase in formal	Written warning
responsibility	Pay cut
Increase in department	Demotion
budget	Reduced authority
Sense of accomplishment	Undesired transfer
Self-recognition	Termination

Alternatives to Punishment

Before using punishment to eliminate undesired behavior, managers should consider several other strategies. One alternative is to rearrange the work setting so that the undesired response cannot occur. For example, if unauthorized individuals are using a copying machine, the installation of a lock and a meter will prevent further misuse. Another example of preventing an undesired response is to install a filtering or screening program on computer terminals in order to prevent employees from using company equipment and time to "surf" pornographic Web sites.

A second strategy is extinction. As noted earlier, a response can be extinguished if the reward with which it is usually paired is eliminated. Identifying the reward that undesired behavior generates for an employee is often not too difficult. In some instances, the reward may actually be the satisfaction of knowing that a peer or supervisor has been annoyed. Extinction in such cases might consist of ignoring the irksome behavior, thereby reducing the probability that it will recur.

To be sure, ignoring undesirable behaviors is a form of inaction. However, many managers will attest that doing nothing about certain minor problem situations can sometimes be the best way to deal with them. For example, a problem may arise that seems to demand that some form of elaborate and detailed managerial action be taken (for example, an employee may frequently complain that a company policy is unfair). Sometimes, merely postponing discussion of the problem will coincide with the elimination of the origin of the problem (for instance, a problem employee may quit) or the diminution of its importance over time.

Effective Punishment

In some instances, none of these alternatives may be feasible. It may be too costly or physically impossible to change a situation to prevent the undesired behavior. Possibly the undesired behavior may provide its own reward and thus resist extinction. Or the undesired behavior may be so serious that it warrants some form of punishment. Advocates of the *reasoned* use of punishment contend that punishment can work under very specific conditions.[17] The features of effective punishment in the workplace are similar to those we have all encountered in daily life. For example, we have all learned to be careful in dealing with electricity and fire without personally resenting them. We accept the punishing aspects of natural forces due to certain common features: The punishment is impersonal, fairly immediate and strong, reliable over time, uniform from person to person, and specifically produced in response to an individual's own actions.

Effective punishment in an organizational setting should possess the same attributes. The recipient should recognize that the punishment is not directed toward his or her character or sense of self-worth. The punishment should be given as soon as possible after the undesired behavior. It should be sufficiently severe that it cannot be ignored. It should be administered with consistency across instances and across people. Finally, it should be extremely clear that the punishment was caused by the specific actions of the transgressor. As a result, the punishment is informative in that the recipient can see the connection between behavior and punishment.

In organizations, many factors undermine these principles and thereby reduce the effectiveness of punishment. For example, some managers may frequently ignore a transgression in the hopes of extinguishing it. But as a result, they may seem inconsistent in dealing with the undesired behavior, and the occasional attention that they do give may seem capricious. Some managers may delay administering punishment due to indecision. Others may feel guilty after punishing an employee. If a manager then responds to his or her guilt feelings by showering the employee with positive attention, the intended effects of the punishment may be greatly diluted.

Guidelines for Administering Discipline

Given that some situations require the use of discipline, the question is how to deliver it and in what form. The answer depends on several major considerations. An important one is a supervisor's personal style of leadership. Leadership style (see Chapter 7) influences both the preferred method of discipline and the practicality of other methods. For example, a manager who subscribes to the human relations approach may prefer to avoid punishment and in fact may be unable to enforce a strict approach.

Employees' backgrounds also determine which approaches to punishment will be most effective. Highly educated employees or professionals may object to a strict approach, while blue-collar workers might readily accept the same

An Inside Look
At Your Service

When human resource professionals try to attain the age-old goal of high employee motivation, convention may not be the rule-of-thumb to follow. The offering of time-saving perks to employees is gaining a high level of interest and may not be merely a new-age fad.

Today at Anderson Consulting in Boston, an on-site concierge arranges services for employees. A case in point was the birthday party that one employee threw for his wife at an inn on Cape Cod, all arranged through the concierge. Anderson Consulting also provides a weekly shoe shine service, while dry cleaning may be dropped off at the front desk each day. Such exotic conveniences, usually found only on the West Coast, are now working their way into even very conservative industries in all parts of the country.

This trend is driven by the demands of dual-income families and increasing workloads. To recruit and retain the best employees, management must offer not only competitive salaries but also a creative menu of unique and valuable perks.

Employees report that workplace perks are in their, as well as their employer's, best interest since saving time can boost productivity.

A recent *Compensation & Benefits Review* study reported that most respondents had some type of work-site convenience, including gift stores (30 percent) and on-site medical services (22 percent). The study also reported that larger firms typically offered a wider range of conveniences and gave higher ratings to the positive impact of perks on productivity. "All these services are an incredibly important phenomenon that recognizes couples and families in the workplace, but there is a line you have to draw in the sand," says Andrea Gabor, author of *Einstein's Wife,* a book on managing work and marriage. "They're great as long as they don't impinge on freedom." But, as Joan Lucas, of the Omaha-based food giant ConAgra, says, "We're trying to be the employer of choice. It's just gotten so competitive, but the services are exciting."

S. Armour, "Fringe Benefits on the Rise," *USA Today,* October 24, 1997.

approach. The size of an organization is another influence on the nature of discipline. Larger organizations have more formal systems of discipline. Given the difficulties inherent in coordinating larger enterprises, employees are often willing to accept a more formal system of discipline.

Progressive Discipline

Discipline should ultimately be a tool to improve performance. Its foremost goal should be to *change* behavior rather than simply to punish it. One very popular approach is **progressive discipline,** a system in which penalties are increased according to the frequency and severity of infractions. The rules are known in advance and are imposed objectively. Repeated transgressions ultimately lead to an employee's termination. A positive feature of progressive discipline is that it provides individuals with the opportunity to alter their own behavior; that is, it gives a person another chance if the infraction is not severe. Punishment is designed to be informative and to lead to a modification of the undesired behavior.

Progressive discipline programs consist of a series of steps that gradually impose increasingly severe penalties. For example, consider an employee who is repeatedly late to work by one or two hours. With a progressive discipline scheme, the employee would receive an informal verbal warning from the supervisor for the first offense. A second offense within a specified period of time would result in a meeting between the employee, the immediate supervisor, and a shift supervisor at which the employee would receive a formal oral warning. If the employee violated the same rule again, she would receive a formal written warning that would become part of her permanent record. A fourth infraction would lead to the employee being suspended without pay for the remainder of the workday. This fourth step might be coupled with the technique of mailing a letter to the employee's spouse. The letter would describe the seriousness of the situation (that is, the danger of the employee being ultimately terminated) and seek to enlist the spouse's cooperation in "turning around" the employee. If after all this, the employee was late to work on a fifth occasion, the employee would be terminated.

It should be noted that at every step in this process the employee is aware that a company policy is being enforced and that the superior's actions are not based on personal malice. Another benefit of such a program is that it provides guidance to supervisors about how to deal with infractions of company rules. A supervisor need not debate whether or how to discipline employees because the course of action is clearly spelled out. Unions are also more likely to accept the outcome of progressive discipline because union stewards often attend disciplinary meetings and are kept informed of the disciplinary actions.

Most progressive discipline programs can be tailored to the severity of the offense. For such serious offenses as gambling in the locker room or fighting, the discipline might begin at step four (suspension). For an unconscionable offense, such as theft of a large sum of money from the organization, discipline might skip to step five (termination).

Many companies post a list of how various infractions will be treated within a progressive discipline scheme (Table 3.2). For example, category A offenses might consist of such minor infractions as tardiness, category B offenses might cover such actions as sleeping on the job, and category C offenses might include major transgressions. All employees would understand that each category is associated with a different step in the progressive discipline program.

Conducting a Disciplinary Meeting

One of the most distasteful tasks a supervisor can face is conducting a meeting devoted to disciplining a subordinate. Given the emotions involved, and win/lose implications for both parties, it is easy to understand why some supervisors are reluctant to administer punishment.

From the reports of actual experiences of supervisors, there are certain ground rules that can make disciplinary meetings more effective.[18]

1. *Have a private meeting with the offender.* There's an old saying of managers, "Praise in public, punish in private." In the interests of protecting the individual's dignity, it is necessary that criticism and punishment be administered behind closed doors.

2. *Don't lose your cool.* Of course, this is more easily said than done. If it becomes impossible for the supervisor to control rage during a disciplinary meeting, it is perhaps best to break it off and set another time to complete the meeting. Words that are exchanged in anger are invariably regretted later on. If a subordinate displays anger, it is important not to respond in kind, but instead to remain calm.

TABLE 3.2   *Suggested Steps for Disciplinary Action*

A. *Offenses resulting in first, oral warning; second, written warning; and third, immediate discharge*

     1. Uncivil conduct

     2. Tardiness

     3. Foul language

     4. Unauthorized absence

B. *Offenses resulting in first, written warning; then, immediate discharge*

     1. Sleeping on the job

     2. Gambling

     3. Misuse of property

     4. Failing to report to work without notification

C. *Offenses resulting in immediate discharge*

     1. Theft or destruction of property

     2. Fighting

     3. Use of drugs

     4. Gross insubordination

     5. Actions that endanger the safety or well-being of others

3. *Be certain of your facts.* Some supervisors jump the gun when disciplining subordinates in that they are prepared to discipline an individual (for a variety of reasons) but do not have the facts to back up their charges. For example, imagine a supervisor who starts disciplinary action against an employee who is late returning from lunch. A subsequent investigation might reveal that the employee was late to work because she had to take her sick child to the hospital.

4. *Select an appropriate punishment.* The severity of the punishment should match the severity of the offense. It is perhaps best if a progressive discipline system has been previously worked out. Such a system can then be consulted when deciding on the most appropriate action.

5. *Accomplish the following three objectives: (a) state what is wrong, (b) state what you expect, and (c) state what happens if you don't get what you expect.* When stating the problem, your expectations, and the possible consequences, it is important to be very clear and specific. It is likely to be a mistake to diminish the seriousness of a problem in the mere hope of social harmony. During the course of the meeting, the employee should be asked to indicate that he or she understands your expectations and the possible consequences of further infractions.

6. *Keep records.* It is almost a cliché to say that employees are becoming more litigious. Because you may be required to present evidence in court or at a grievance hearing, it is essential that records be maintained on the nature

and content of all disciplinary meetings. One advantage to keeping records is that it will add strength to your case if your actions are ever contested. When keeping records, it is best to follow the rules of journalism: Answer the questions of who, what, when, where, and how as they pertain to a behavioral incident.

SUMMARY

1. *Explain what learning is and why managers need to understand the learning process.* Learning is a fairly permanent change in behavior that occurs as a result of experience. It is a complex and never-ending process for all employees that can greatly affect both performance and motivation. Consequently, a manager who understands the learning process can use its principles to guide employee behavior and achieve organizational goals.

2. *Describe the process of classical conditioning and cite several examples of this form of learning in the workplace.* In classical conditioning, an unconditional stimulus is repeatedly paired with a neutral stimulus until the neutral stimulus alone can elicit the same response that was evoked by the unconditioned stimulus. When this occurs, the neutral stimulus is termed a conditioned stimulus and the response, a conditioned response. Many jobs require conditional responses. For example, a truck driver's ability to apply the brakes quickly and firmly depends on a conditioned response to a conditioned stimulus, such as a warning light. A manager's attempt to train personnel to the point where they no longer require continual monitoring may also involve classical conditioning.

3. *Tell what observational learning is and how it occurs in the workplace.* Observational learning occurs when a person witnesses the behavior of another and vicariously experiences the consequence of that person's behavior. This form of learning is very common in organizations. For example, a new employee may observe an experienced employee performing a task and then model his or her own behavior on the observations. Employees who attend training programs also learn from observation by viewing films, reading manuals, and attending lectures.

4. *Discuss the nature of operant conditioning and cite four rules for applying operant conditioning principles to enhance employee performance.* Operant conditioning is based on the notion that behavior is a function of its outcomes. Thus, behavior that produces a pleasant outcome is more likely to be repeated, while behavior that produces an unpleasant outcome is likely not to recur. To use the principles of operant conditioning to encourage desired behavior in the workplace, managers should follow four basic rules: (1) Match the reward to the performance, so that superior performers receive greater rewards; (2) match the reward to the individual's preferences; (3) be sure that subordinates understand how rewards are tied to performance; (4) give employees informative feedback about their performance.

5. *Summarize the advantages and disadvantages of OB Mod.* Organizational behavior modification, or OB Mod, is the application of the principles of operant conditioning to organizational settings in the attempt to alter employee behavior. The typical OB Mod intervention seeks to improve either the performance or the attendance of blue-collar workers by providing immediate

feedback about behavior and by employing praise or recognition as reinforcers. Studies have indicated that such programs are generally quite effective. Nonetheless, OB Mod has many critics who contend that it is manipulative, unoriginal, and of questionable faithfulness to true operant conditioning principles, and that it ignores the role of mental processes in behavior.

6. Analyze the role of punishment in shaping employee behavior. Punishment is an undesirable event that follows a behavior it intends to eliminate. Its role in shaping employee behavior is quite complex and its administration often does not eliminate the undesirable behavior. Consequently, any proposal to use punishment should be carefully thought out in light of the available alternatives. For punishment to be effective, (1) the recipient must recognize that it is not directed at his or her character or self-worth, (2) it should be given as soon as possible after the undesired behavior, (3) it should be sufficiently severe that it cannot be ignored, (4) it should be administered consistently across instances and people, and (5) it should be extremely clear that the punishment was caused by the specific actions of the transgressor. Ultimately, punishment should be used as a tool to change behavior and improve performance rather than as an end in itself. A well-planned progressive discipline program, consisting of a series of steps imposing increasingly severe penalties, can often accomplish this purpose.

KEY TERMS

Learning
Classical conditioning
Unconditioned stimulus
Unconditioned response
Conditioned response
Conditioned stimulus
Observational learning
Self-efficacy
Law of Effect
Operant conditioning
Positive reinforcement
Negative reinforcement
OB Mod
Shaping

Extinction
Resistance to extinction
Partial reinforcement
Continuous reinforcement
Interval schedule
Ratio schedule
Fixed schedule
Variable schedule
Fixed interval schedule
Variable interval schedule
Fixed ratio schedule
Variable ratio schedule
Punishment
Progressive discipline

CRITICAL INCIDENT

The Wrong Reinforcement?

Royal Coach Corporation is a large manufacturer of school buses and related small vehicles that are used by tour groups, airport shuttle services, and so forth. A large warehouse operation is crucial to the success of the production process as many different parts are stored and then moved to the line as needed.

Charles Hodges has worked for Royal for almost four years. He is 26, single, and lives at home with his parents. His job in the warehouse involves moving raw materials to various assembly lines as they are needed. His work is steady and he uses both a forklift and motorized hand truck to transport parts.

Charles has had a history of sporadic absences from work over the past few years. These absences usually last two or three days at a time. Charles has also been late to work many times.

It is after 7:00 A.M. and Charles has not shown up for work. The warehouse crew is shorthanded once again. Charles's supervisor pulls his file while trying to decide what to do. This is the fourth supervisor for whom Charles has worked while at Royal. Each of the previous supervisors had placed written comments about Charles in the folder. Each had noted that after several periods of being absent, Charles would be called in for a meeting and promise to improve his attendance. Thereafter, he usually did.

Charles was generally a good worker. He did his job, but was not exceptional. He earned good wages and always seemed to have plenty of spending money. Two of his previous supervisors were fairly laid-back and permitted their employees to do their jobs with a minimum of supervision. A third was more autocratic and provided close supervision. He was the type who offered both help and criticism, and monitored everyone. According to the attendance record, Charles had missed more days under this supervisor than under any of the others.

It appeared to the present supervisor that Charles might be starting another period of absenteeism. He had already missed one day that week. The supervisor decided that something had to be done.

1. What principles of reinforcement have Charles's previous supervisors used? Why hasn't this reinforcement been effective?

2. What type of behavior modification program might the present supervisor try to use?

3. If a behavior modification approach does not seem to work, what should the supervisor do?

EXPERIENTIAL EXERCISE

Handling Discipline—A Role Play

I. Introduction   The text discussion focused on the importance of reinforcing appropriate behavior and recognizing the need to confront actions that are ill-suited to the workplace. It is often easier for a manager to reinforce or reward positive actions than it is to discipline or punish negative ones. This activity provides you with an opportunity to apply some of these concepts in a no-risk situation. What you learn from the experience will enable you to be more skillful when you must handle a real situation.

II. Procedure

1. Your instructor may assign individuals or ask for volunteers to play the three roles in this situation. All others in the class may function as observers.

2. Everyone should read the following description of the situation:
   Jim Turner and Bill Evans, mechanics in the service department, had been told to clean some large service equipment in the rear of the garage.

When their supervisor checked on them, they were tossing pennies at a line they had drawn on the floor, clearly gambling. This is the second problem this week with Turner, a new employee who has been with the company only eight months. On the other occasion, he was found sitting in the restroom looking at a comic book when he should have been putting away his tools and reading a manual he was asked to look over. Bill Evans has been with the company for seven years and is considered one of the most reliable and hard-working employees. He has never given any trouble.

3. The two persons playing the roles of Jim and Bill can begin to enact their parts (tossing pennies at a line, and so on). The individual who is playing the part of their supervisor should think of responses to the following questions. The supervisor should then begin the role play at the point of walking in and discovering the gambling. The supervisor's role play should demonstrate how he or she chose to answer these questions.

   a. How would you handle this situation?

   b. What penalties would you impose?

   c. Would you impose the same penalty for each employee?

4. Continue the role play until everyone understands what is going to occur in terms of any sanctions. When that point is reached, the activity can be terminated.

III. Discussion

1. How do the observers feel about the way the situation was handled?

2. Do the observers feel that a reasonable conclusion was reached?

3. Analyze any face-saving behaviors that were evidenced.

4. How did the supervisor feel in dealing with the situation? How did Jim and Bill feel?

5. Did the supervisor attempt to apply progressive discipline concepts in this situation? What were they?

6. Is a disciplinary meeting warranted? With whom and why? How should it be handled?

Source: Written by Bruce Kemelgor, University of Louisville; used by permission.

4 Motivation

Work is the price you pay for money.

—Anonymous

If hard work were such a wonderful thing, surely the rich would have kept it all to themselves.

—Lane Kirkland,
then AFL-CIO president

Be all that you can be.

—U.S. Army slogan

Learning Objectives

After studying this chapter, you should be able to:

1. Describe a technique for uncovering a person's dominant needs.
2. Describe Maslow's hierarchy of needs.
3. Compare the ways motivator factors and hygiene factors may influence employees.
4. Describe how expectations can influence an employee's efforts.
5. Explain how behavior modification affects behavior in organizations.
6. Explain how employees' sense of equity affects their motivation.
7. Describe how social learning influences behavior.
8. Identify steps managers can take to motivate employees.

What Motivates Workers Today? To Start With, Money and Control of Their Own Time

A recently completed nationwide telephone survey of 1,000 employees explored their level of satisfaction with employee benefits. To summarize, the findings showed that concerning time off from work, "employees want to do what they want, when they choose." For health care, "employees want employers to help them stay well." And when it comes to just about anything else, "they don't want employers poking into their personal business."

The study also looked into how employees value nontraditional benefits, which have grown dramatically in recent years. Respondents were asked to rate the importance of benefits on a one-to-ten scale with "10" being most important. Among nontraditional benefits, time-off banks (the ability to pool vacation, holiday, and sick days to be used whenever, with no questions asked) ranked first in importance (7.41)—ahead of flexible work schedules and working at home. Eileen Bove, director of human resources for Universal Health Services, Inc., says the value of the time-off bank is that "employees get to control their own destiny, and we get cost savings and productivity. The company likes the plan because employees now are more apt to schedule their time off, instead of just calling in sick."

Among traditional benefits, employees ranked preventive or wellness programs (8.25) and tax-free reimbursement for health-care expenses (7.87) slightly lower than they did medical insurance (9.59), employer-paid retirement plans (9.11), and vacation days (8.63). Even employees with dependents did not rank child-care or elder-care benefits as high as other benefits. The highest-ranked benefit for employees with dependents was tax-free accounts for child- or elder-care expenses. Money, however, is still a major concern, with only 65 percent reporting that they were satisfied with their pay.

This study, conducted by Goodwins Booke & Dickenson and HRStrategies, consulting unit of Aon Corp. in Chicago, concluded that employees' freedom to choose from an array of benefits tailored to their individual needs is very important. They also recommend that since employees were more satisfied with their vacation time than any other benefit, employers should offer workers the opportunity to exchange vacation time for more desirable benefits.

Nontraditional Benefits: How They Stack Up with Employees

BENEFIT	IMPORTANCE[a]	SATISFACTION[b]
Wellness coverage	8.25	7.19
Tax-free reimbursement for health-care expenses	7.87	6.95
Paid time-off banks	7.41	7.41
Flexible work schedules	7.15	7.44
Ability to work compressed work week	7.09	7.03
On-site or near-site day care for children	5.38	5.82
Day care for sick children	5.29	5.07

[a] 10-Absolutely must have benefit; 1-Do not need benefit at all [b] 10-Extremely satisfied; 1-Extremely dissatisfied
Source: Goodwins Booke & Dickenson/HRStrategies

Recently, I took a tour of a large manufacturing plant on the East Coast. My guide, a first-level supervisor, highlighted the size and capabilities of the facility. Since I was very much impressed by the large number of people who were employed in the plant, I asked my guide, "How many people work here?" Not knowing the intent of my question, he answered, "About half!"

This experience underscores one of the major concerns of all managers: How to motivate others to higher levels of performance. In one survey of over 4,000 adults, 57 percent reported that they could easily be more productive in their jobs if they wanted to.[1] As this evidence suggests, there is an untapped potential for greater productivity. The key to motivating others lies in somehow arousing and channeling their desire to produce.

The Nature of Motivation

Exactly how to motivate others is difficult to determine because motivation itself is such a complex phenomenon. For example, specific behavior may be the result of several motives, rather than a single motive. Furthermore, people who express essentially the same motive may engage in very different behaviors, while people who express very different motives may engage in very similar behavior.

Motives cannot be directly observed; they can only be inferred from the behavior of others. This difficulty can easily lead to errors in interpretation. In addition, motives are dynamic, or constantly changing. The changes result from the rise and fall of a motive's importance as it is variously satisfied or unsatisfied. To complicate things further, some motives do not decrease in importance when a desired goal is attained. Perhaps the best example of this is the reaction that may accompany a pay raise. Often, the raise increases, rather than decreases, an employee's desire for more money.

The complexity of motivational processes is perhaps matched by the complexity and variety of approaches that have been offered to explain motivation. In this chapter, we will review the major approaches to explaining worker behavior and consider a useful integration of these views.

Achievement Motivation Theory

The Thematic Apperception Test   One early approach to understanding motivation involved the use of story-telling' techniques to uncover dominant needs (that is, recurring concerns for goal attainment). Henry A. Murray created a test for establishing the presence and strength of various needs.[2] Specifically, Murray compiled a set of drawings cut out of stories in magazines. Even without their associated stories, the drawings were intriguing and provocative. For example, one drawing showed a man who was apparently outraged and about to run out of a room, while a woman attempted to restrain him from committing what might be a rash act.

Murray used a set of 20 drawings as a projective story-telling device (see Chapter 2 for a discussion of the story-telling technique). In administering his test, called the Thematic Apperception Test, or TAT, Murray would ask the respondent to look at each drawing and offer a story to explain it. Each story was to include a description of the main characters as well as summaries of what led up to the situation, what was currently going on, and what would be a likely outcome. Murray observed that people's stories tended to reflect their dominant needs. For example, the stories that people create when they are placed in need-heightening situations (such as when they are deprived of food, sleep, or social contact) typically contain themes devoted to the heightened need. Thus, in a food deprivation study, the stories may involve people going to a banquet or returning from a hamburger stand.

The McClelland Studies   David McClelland, a successor of Murray, continued to use story-telling techniques to understand dominant needs.[3] McClelland, however, focused on only a limited set of needs: the **need for achievement,** the **need for affiliation,** and the **need for power.**

McClelland's studies of the need for achievement have received great attention in the organizational behavior literature. In his studies, McClelland sought first to identify persons with a high need to achieve. He interpreted recurring themes of hard work and success in their stories as signs of a high need to achieve. He then studied these high-achievement individuals in a variety of natural and laboratory settings.

Using these studies, McClelland and his colleagues were able to identify some factors that showed a predisposition to strive for success.[4] In general, high performance levels and executive success appear to be correlated with a high need for achievement. Individuals with a relatively high need for achievement tend to prefer situations that involve moderate risk and personal responsibility for success rather than luck, and they desire specific feedback on their performance.

The need for achievement partly determines how employees will respond to challenging job assignments, because task persistence and the acceptance of challenge are closely related to this need. High achievers are driven by the prospect of performance-based satisfaction rather than by monetary gain. For these individuals, money is primarily a source of feedback on personal performance rather than an end in itself. Other evidence suggests that high-achievement individuals are more likely to set clocks and watches ahead by 10 or more minutes to avoid being late for appointments and that they doodle in a distinctive style (making clear symbols and filling up the bottom of a page, seldom retracing a line).

The need for achievement is an important explanation for individual success and failure, but it can be overemphasized. Though having the drive to succeed is desirable in many situations, it is not always appropriate to every job in every organization. Furthermore, individuals who are dominated by the need for achievement may have difficulties in getting along with coworkers.

In fact, a manager's effectiveness depends not on a single dimension but on a pattern of needs and the appropriateness of the pattern for a given work setting (for example, manufacturing versus social service). Managers should have a reasonably high need for power in order to function effectively as leaders.[5] A moderate level of need for affiliation can also be useful in many settings. In one study of the promotion histories of 237 managers at AT&T, McClelland found that a moderate-to-high need for power and a low need for affiliation were associated with managerial success for nontechnical (nonengineering) managers.[6] Also, high need for achievement was associated with career advancement, but only at lower-level positions, where individual contributions may be more important than the ability to influence others. The career success of technical managers with engineering responsibilities, however, could not be predicted from the same measures.

Individuals who have a high need for affiliation tend to be warm and friendly in their relationships. But unless their affiliation needs are balanced by the needs for achievement and power, they are likely to be seen as relatively ineffective in many settings.[7] Their ineffectiveness may stem from the fear of disrupting social relations by being direct and confrontational, even though a forthright approach may be the most appropriate.

McClelland's research on the need for achievement has moved into two further directions: the origins and the economic consequences of achievement motivation. The origin of achievement motivation appears to lie in one's socialization during childhood. Parents who encourage early self-reliance in their children (for example, by training a child to cross the street alone at a relatively early age) produce children who are more achievement-oriented later in life. However, early independence training must also be coupled with supportiveness. Warmth or supportiveness is crucial in that the self-reliant child must not feel that he or she has been abandoned.

McClelland proposed that a culture's growth is due to the level of need for achievement inherent in its population.[8] His research indicates that increases in the level of need for achievement precede increases in economic activity. An analysis of the literature of various cultures (including an analysis of popular themes in children's readers and the folklore of preliterate tribes) suggests that an increase in achievement themes may precede an increase in economic growth.

McClelland also proposed that achievement motivation can be enhanced in adults who otherwise lack a high level.[9] Training programs have been designed to heighten achievement motivation by having participants focus on goal setting and on thinking and acting in a high-achievement manner. The results of such programs have reportedly been successful; participants are likely to have greater subsequent success in their careers, as measured by rates of promotion, salary progress, and business expansion. One program, run by the Metropolitan Economic Development Association in Minneapolis-St. Paul for small-business owners and potential entrepreneurs, required participants to complete and interpret their responses to the Thematic Apperception Test as well as to engage in goal setting. Follow-up data revealed that participants experienced significant increases in personal income and expanded business activity.[10] However, because many participants in such training programs are selected for their entrepreneurial predisposition, it is difficult to say with certainty that the training program in itself was responsible for their later success. It is altogether possible that a placebo, or guinea pig, effect accounts for the reported enhancement in personal performance. More carefully controlled studies are needed in this area before we can firmly conclude that an individual's need for achievement can be substantially modified by training programs.

Maslow's Hierarchy of Needs

From his work as a clinical psychologist, Abraham Maslow devised a model for explaining the essential needs for healthy psychological development.[11] Maslow incorporated McClelland's emphasis on the importance of social acceptance, personal control, recognition, and achievement, but he went several steps further by proposing additional sets of needs and suggesting a rational order for them.

According to Maslow, needs can be classified into a hierarchy, with the needs that are lower in the hierarchy being more essential to survival. Maslow's **hierarchy of needs** is illustrated in Figure 4.1. Lower-order needs, called **deficiency needs,** must be satisfied to ensure an individual's very existence and security. Higher-order needs, or **growth needs,** are concerned with personal development and realization of one's potential. The specific needs under each general category are then arranged into a five-step hierarchy reflecting the increasingly psychological nature of each set.

Deficiency Needs

1. *Physiological needs.* This most basic level of Maslow's hierarchy includes the needs for food, water, sleep, oxygen, warmth, and freedom from pain. If these needs are unsatisfied, an individual's actions will be dominated by attempts to fulfill them. If these needs are sufficiently met, the second set of needs will emerge.

2. *Safety needs.* These needs relate to obtaining a secure environment in which an individual is free from threats. Society provides many devices for meeting these needs: insurance policies, job-tenure arrangements, savings accounts, and police and fire departments. If a person is reasonably safe and secure, a third set of needs will probably emerge.

3. *Social needs.* The third set includes the needs for affection, love, and sexual expression. The absence of friends or loved ones can lead to serious psychological maladjustment.

FIGURE 4.1   *Maslow's Hierarchy of Needs*

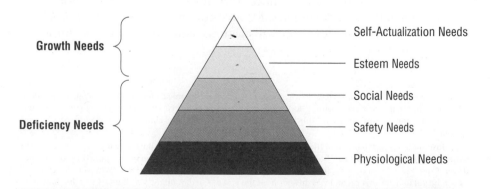

Growth Needs

4. *Esteem needs.* If the deficiency needs are reasonably satisfied, a concern for self-respect and the esteem of others may arise. Esteem needs include the desires for achievement, prestige, and recognition as well as appreciation and attention from others.

5. *Self-actualization needs.* This category includes the desire for self-fulfillment. Personal development may be expressed in many ways—for example, maternally, athletically, artistically, or occupationally. Some individuals may never experience the desire to develop their own potential. An individual who attains self-actualization will occasionally have peak experiences. A **peak experience** can best be described as a sense of euphoria that is not chemically induced.* It can be felt as a sense of completeness or of oneness with the universe.

One of Maslow's basic premises was that the five categories of needs followed a hierarchical ordering in terms of potency. By this he meant that if a deficiency arises, a lower-order need can supersede a higher-order need to demand its fulfillment. For instance, imagine that you are engaged in a pleasant conversation with a group of coworkers (you are satisfying your social needs) when suddenly your oxygen is cut off. It would, of course, be very difficult to think of anything else at that time except the restoration of oxygen, a lower-level need. This capacity of lower-order needs to assert themselves is termed **prepotency.**†

More typically, needs emerge gradually rather than suddenly. These unsatisfied needs produce an internal tension that must be reduced. Generally, needs are not 100 percent satisfied; partial satisfaction is more common. For example, physiological needs may be 95 percent satisfied, safety needs 65 percent, social 45 percent, and so on.

Most organizations probably do a fairly good job of satisfying employees' lower-order needs either directly (by opportunities to feel warm, safe, and part of a work group) or indirectly (by wages that can be used to purchase goods that will satisfy various needs). But organizations are not nearly so successful at providing opportunities to satisfy the higher-order needs for esteem and self-actualization.

Maslow believed that managers should strive to create the climate necessary to develop employees' potentials to their fullest. Ideal organizational climates would provide opportunities for independence, recognition, and responsibility. Poor work climates, Maslow contended, lead to high levels of employee frustration, low job satisfaction, and high rates of turnover.

---

*Drugs, however, do appear to be used to trigger peak experiences by some college students. In one survey, drug use ranked fourth in occurrence, behind "looking at the beauties of nature," "moments of quiet reflection," and "listening to music," and ahead of "physical exercise," "watching little children," "reading a novel," and "prayer."[12]

†An illustration of the dynamic and hierarchical nature of motives is given by the following anecdote. Going to work, I saw a sad, unkempt man holding a sign—"Will work for food." The man was picked up by another driver. Later, I saw the same man, now looking healthy and full, holding a new sign—"Will work for clothes." Again, he got into another car and was driven off. At the end of the day, on my way home, I saw the same man again, now wearing a new suit of clothes and holding yet another sign—"Will work for sex."

Maslow's theory, therefore, is of greatest importance in establishing organizational policies.

Findings on the validity of Maslow's hierarchy of needs have not always been supportive. For example, the proposed notion of prepotency has been difficult to verify. The measurement of various features of the model has also been problematic.[13] Because certain concepts that Maslow proposed (such as self-actualization) were derived from his work with neurotic clients in his practice as a psychologist, we cannot be certain to what extent the various principles can be generalized to the normal adult workforce. Although the notion of self-actualization may be important to a person who is struggling with his or her self-identity, it may have little meaning or importance to an unskilled laborer who has made a personal accommodation to the limits of his or her current position. As is generally true of the humanistic perspective, much of Maslow's writing also suffers from a degree of imprecision and fuzziness in terminology and conceptualization. Despite these problems, Maslow nonetheless deserves credit for being one of the first to espouse a humanistic approach to the treatment of employees.[14]

More recently, Mihaly Csikszentmihalyi, a professor at the University of Chicago, has proposed the notion of **flow.**[15] This concept refers to optimal experiences of joy and creativity in which an individual is so totally absorbed in an activity that little else seems to matter. The idea of flow is similar to Maslow's notion of peak experience, wherein there is a loss of self-consciousness. To be attained, flow experiences require great discipline, such as that required of a piano virtuoso, an experienced rock climber, or a craftsperson. To improve the quality of life through work, Csikszentmihalyi argues that jobs should be redesigned so that they resemble flow-producing activities by matching job challenges to individual skill level. Both Maslow and Csikszentmihalyi agree that certain childhood experiences and family life are required for a person to later experience personal fulfillment. Specifically, they argue that parents should provide a safe, nonthreatening, communicative environment that encourages, but does not push, children to try new and challenging activities. Additionally, parents should display trust toward children and encourage personal growth, rather than impose their own definitions of success on their children.

Two-Factor Theory

One of the most widely known and influential views of work motivation is Fred Herzberg's **two-factor theory.**[16] As part of a study of job satisfaction, Herzberg and his colleagues conducted in-depth interviews with 203 engineers and accountants. The researchers asked respondents to recall two separate job-related events in which their work satisfaction had improved or declined. The responses suggested that the work-related factors that led to feelings of satisfaction were different from those factors that led to dissatisfaction. The satisfiers usually pertained to the content of the job and included such factors as career advancement, recognition, sense of responsibility, and feelings of achievement. Herzberg called these **motivator factors.** The dissatisfiers more often stemmed from the context in which the job was performed. They related to job security, company policies, interpersonal relations, and working conditions. Herzberg called these **hygiene factors.**

Herzberg reasoned that motivator factors had the potential to motivate workers to higher levels of performance because they provided opportunities for personal satisfaction. Although the absence of these factors would not make employees *unhappy*, it would leave them feeling somewhat neutral toward their jobs.

Although they could not induce a worker to higher levels of performance, hygiene factors could create great dissatisfaction if they were not attended to. Hygiene factors could make a worker very unhappy, but they could not create more than a neutral feeling toward the job even if they were ideally modified.

Herzberg's argument is unique in that it differentiates the factors that motivate employees from those that lead to dissatisfaction. Furthermore, two-factor theory (or motivator–hygiene theory, as it is sometimes called) contends that improving physical working conditions may help to reduce worker discontent, but will not provide sufficient incentive for most workers to strive for superior performance. As a hypothetical illustration, consider the removal of your garbage from the front of your home every week. This issue is a hygiene factor in that it has the capacity to make one very unhappy if it is not attended to (imagine your unhappiness if the trash were not removed for a period of several weeks). Alternatively, if your trash is removed with complete regularity, you are not likely to turn cartwheels upon seeing that the garbage has been taken away sometime during the day. Trash removal, like poor working conditions, is something that we expect to have taken care of, but take little interest in once it is remedied. Motivator (or psychological) aspects of many jobs, in turn, tend to be neglected.

Critics of the two-factor theory argue that respondents in an interview setting may be providing answers in an ego-defensive manner. According to this argument, respondents are inclined to report that the good things that happen to them at work are related to their own efforts, while the bad things are due to external or environmental forces. It is easier to blame coworkers and company policy when things go poorly than it is to blame oneself. In addition, critics point out that many of the job factors that are rather neatly compartmentalized as motivators or hygienes within the theory are not exclusively members of one set or the other. For example, salary is certainly a potential source of dissatisfaction, and salary is externally administered (a hygiene factor). However, salary can be a source of personal pride and, therefore, serves as a source of psychological reward (a motivator factor).

Despite these shortcomings, two-factor theory has had a substantial influence on the field of management. It is probably safe to say that two-factor theory is one of the more widely known theories of motivation (rightly or wrongly) in managerial circles. The theory's influence continues through its prescriptions for job redesign.

Expectancy Theory

Expectancy theory represents an attempt to explain worker motivation in terms of anticipated rewards. The model assumes that people make rational decisions based on economic realities. Many researchers are attracted to expectancy theory because it brings together both personal and situational influences. Also, studies of the principles of expectancy theory generally have been supportive.

Although many variations of expectancy theory have been proposed, the most widely cited version was proposed by Victor Vroom of Yale University.[17] Vroom's model argues that the psychological force on an employee to exert effort is a function of his or her expectancies about the future and the attractiveness of specific future outcomes. Two kinds of expectations are important in the model: the expectation that effort will lead to performance and the expectation that performance will lead to rewards.

Fffort-Performance Expectancy (E→P)   In deciding on a course of action, employees will consider whether their effort will translate into a desired accomplishment. If the obstacles are such that they cannot reasonably expect their effort to lead to an acceptable level of performance, their motivation to perform will be diminished.

Performance–Outcome Expectancy (P→O)   Another consideration is whether a given level of performance will result in the obtainment of a particular outcome. The more strongly a person believes that performance will lead to a positive outcome (or the avoidance of a negative outcome), the more likely it is that he or she will be motivated to higher levels of performance.

Valence (V)   The outcomes that an employee receives can be evaluated in terms of their value or attractiveness. Expectancy theorists, however, prefer to use the special term **valence** to denote this attractiveness. The valence that an individual attaches to an outcome is a personal matter that cannot be accurately predicted by other people. Thus, it is essential to ask an individual about the valences that he or she attaches to anticipated outcomes. The valence of a given outcome may also vary in relation to how recently the individual has been rewarded.

The linkages of effort–performance expectancy and performance–outcome expectancy can be measured by questioning individuals on the subjective probabilities that they believe characterize the linkages. **Subjective probabilities** are estimates of the likelihood that one event will follow another. In this case, respondents would be asked to report their personal probability estimates that effort will lead to performance and that performance will lead to a given outcome. These probabilities can range from 0, indicating a belief that one event will definitely *not* follow the other, to 1.0, indicating complete confidence that one event *will* follow the other. The valence of an outcome is assessed by having respondents provide an associated value that can range from −1.0 (highly unattractive) to +1.0 (highly attractive).

The probability estimates can be multiplied together to yield an overall expectancy value. This value can then be multiplied by the associated valence to yield a summary index of the psychological force on an individual to exert effort. In summary, the mathematics involved are:

$$(E \rightarrow P) \times (P \rightarrow O) \times (V) = \text{Motivational Force}$$

As an example, consider a salesperson who is deciding whether to make additional sales calls. The salesperson believes that the additional calls (effort) will lead to additional sales (performance) and that the additional sales will lead to a bonus (outcome). The size, or magnitude, of the bonus (valence) must also be considered. For illustrative purposes, imagine that the salesperson's probability estimate of E→P is .8, and the estimate of P→O is .7. Also, the anticipated bonus has a valence of +.6. The motivational force that is exerted on the salesperson is given by $(.8) \times (.7) \times (.6) = .34$. If the salesperson had valued the bonus more highly, so that its valence were +.9, the motivational force would have been $(.8) \times (.7) \times (.9) = .50$. If he or she felt that the bonus was trivial, the valence portion of the equation would greatly reduce the motivational force.

Several clear implications for motivating others can be derived from expectancy theory. First, it is important for employees to recognize that effort and performance are closely related. A manager's job should include the establishment of conditions that help to translate effort into performance. This may involve the removal of obstacles and the creation of production systems that help employees see the link between effort and performance.

Managers also need to create linkages between rewards and performance. To establish this connection, the creation and maintenance of reward systems are necessary. Furthermore, the rewards that are offered should be tailored to the values of the individual employee. This may require surveying employees in order to determine individual preferences among reward options. Lastly, conflicting expectancies and rewards need to be eliminated. Conflicting influences may arise when coworkers attempt to restrict another's performance or when conflicting demands are made by different supervisors.

Reinforcement Theory

The principles of operant conditioning, presented in Chapter 3, can also be used to explain work motivation. The allocation of rewards in exchange for specific behaviors can have a powerful effect on subsequent behavior. The design of specific reward systems will be considered further in Chapter 5.

Operant conditioning, or **behavior modification** as its applied version is termed, is particularly influential in directing behavior if rewards are (1) substantial and highly desired, (2) administered intermittently, and (3) differentially distributed so that higher levels of performance lead to proportionally larger increases in reward.[18]

Proponents of organizational behavior modification (OB Mod) prefer to diagnose situations in terms of an "antecedent–behavior–consequence" or A–B–C framework. Antecedents are stimuli that precede behaviors. Consequences are the outcomes, or rewards and punishments, that follow from behaviors. These consequences, in turn, serve as antecedents for subsequent behavior. By managing the consequences of behavior, OB Mod specialists seek to modify later behavior.

Reinforcement theory and expectancy theory have a similar conceptual foundation. Both approaches derive from a simple hedonistic base. However, **reinforcement theory** focuses on the influence of past rewards in shaping present behavior, while expectancy theory focuses on the influence of anticipated rewards on present behavior. Reinforcement theory has been characterized as *hedonism of the past*, whereas expectancy theory has been described as *hedonism of the future*.[19] The historical emphasis on reinforcement theory partly stems from the approach's initial focus on studying nonverbal animals of limited mental ability (such as rats and pigeons). In contrast, expectancy theory has been devoted to studying the behavior of humans. Despite their differing origins, both expectancy and reinforcement theories generate essentially identical predictions for behavior in a variety of settings.

Equity Theory

Feelings of fairness, or equity, can serve as a powerful stimulus to increase or decrease effort. J. Stacy Adams proposed a theory that attempts to explain the influence of such feelings on employee behavior.[20] Adams' **equity theory** assumes that people will strive to restore equity if they feel an imbalance exists.

Basic to equity theory is the belief that employees monitor the degree of equity or inequity that exists in their working relations by comparing their own outcomes and inputs with those of another highly similar person. In the context of equity theory, *outcomes* are anything that employees view as being provided by their jobs or the organization. Outcomes include pay, an office with a window, access to the executive washroom, use of a company car, and so on. *Inputs* include all the contributions that a person makes to the

---

An Inside Look
Is the Laugh Track the Right Track to the Fast Track?

Should the workplace be fun? Can humor boost your career? Is there value to frivolity on company time? "No" you say? Well, you may change your mind after you read this.

A new wave of thinking in corporate corridors suggests that fun and games do have their place. Humor can motivate and relieve stress, as well as build stronger bonds between employees. As for the fast track, though, it works only if it can help produce superior results. Humor can be your ally in a host of everyday situations—to charm and disarm bosses, customers, and co-workers. But don't start buying whoopee cushions by the carload just yet. "Life does not become less serious because it's more fun," says Matt Weinstein, author of *Managing to Have Fun* and consultant to companies trying to put fun into the workplace. Start with the basics: Fun is good, but only if it is used in the right way at the right time.

Jeff Haines, president of Royce Medical in Camarillo, California, says, "The better managers are at providing this kind of leadership, the better results they get, and that's what they get rewarded for. That doesn't mean that this is not an intense place. There's accountability when we're not hitting goals." At McGuffey's Restaurants in the Southeast, employees evaluate managers on how much fun they are to work with,

and this can affect 20 percent of the manager's raise. "Results are still the primary goal, but how managers achieve their goals also counts. We're in a service business with high turnover; it's part of a manager's job to bring fun to the workplace," says McGuffey's president, Keith Dunn.

Here are guidelines to consider for bringing fun into the workplace:

Start small. Try putting jokes on the bulletin board and check reactions; but don't jeopardize your career for a laugh.

Make it meaningful. "You have to tie playfulness to productivity," says Mr. Weinstein. "Here's one I like because it tears down barriers: A top executive does your job for a day, with you supervising."

Keep it fresh. Nothing kills fun like the same old humor, over and over again.

Keep it inoffensive. The problem with humor is that someone or something is typically the butt of it. "Never do anything hurtful or anything that gets in the way of someone's personal values," says Diane Decker, a management consultant specializing in bringing fun into the workplace.

Source: H. Lancaster, "Your Career May Be a Laugh Track Away from the Fast Track," *The Wall Street Journal*, March 26, 1996.

employment relationship. Examples of inputs include personal effort, years and kind of education, prior work experience, training, and the like. Generally speaking, an input is anything that a person believes he or she should be compensated for (see Table 4.1).

The inputs and outputs that a person views as relevant are very personal choices. According to equity theory, it is essential to ask individuals their reactions to possible outcomes and inputs when attempting to assess the degree of equity or inequity that they feel exists.

Adams contends that an individual will estimate the ratio of outcomes to inputs, but this ratio is of only partial importance. Each person also calculates a similar ratio for a person whom he or she judges to be in a similar position. This second person is called the *comparison other*. Adams predicts that an employee will be relatively satisfied if his or her own ratio of outcomes to inputs is equivalent to the ratio for the comparison other. This condition may be summarized as follows:

$$\frac{\text{Outcomes A}}{\text{Inputs A}} = \frac{\text{Outcomes B}}{\text{Inputs B}} \tag{1}$$

If person A feels that his ratio is either higher or lower than person B's, he should experience a sense of inequity. The magnitude of this feeling will be proportional to the size of the gap between the ratios. Feelings of inequity produce a psychological tension that requires reduction.

$$\frac{\text{Outcomes A}}{\text{Inputs A}} < \frac{\text{Outcomes B}}{\text{Inputs B}} \tag{2}$$

If person A is undercompensated in comparison to person B (equation 2), he may attempt to restore equity by working on one of the four components in the two ratios:

TABLE 4.1   ***Examples of Inputs and Outcomes in Adams' Theory of Equity***

Inputs	Outcomes
Effort	Salary
Education	Fringe benefits
Training	Travel allowance
Experience	Number of subordinates
Loyalty	Autonomy
Age	Status symbols
	Time off
	Opportunities for overtime

---

1. He may increase his own outcomes by asking for a raise.

2. He may decrease his own inputs by being less productive.

3. He may decrease person B's outcomes by persuading his boss to alter B's pay.

4. He may increase B's inputs by pressuring her to work harder.

If person B is undercompensated in comparison to person A (equation 3), equity theory predicts that person A will experience guilt and will attempt to restore equity by altering one or more of the four components of the two ratios. For example, person A may attempt to reduce his own outcomes or increase person B's outcomes by appealing to his boss for an adjustment. Also, person A may increase his inputs by exerting greater effort on the job. Lastly, person A may help person B to decrease her input, perhaps by coaching her in how to work more efficiently.

$$\frac{\text{Outcomes A}}{\text{Inputs A}} > \frac{\text{Outcomes B}}{\text{Inputs B}} \tag{3}$$

If the four components of the ratios cannot be altered and if the magnitude of inequity is substantial, person A would be forced to choose another course of action. He might:

1. Alter his perception of the situation so that the inequity no longer seems unjustified, saying, for example, "I deserve to earn more money because I work harder than most people."

2. Leave the field by quitting or obtaining a transfer.

3. Choose a different comparison other, someone whose ratio provides a less uncomfortable contrast.

Evidence from studies of the condition of overcompensation in a piece-rate pay scheme has demonstrated that employees will, in fact, decrease the quantity of their output and increase the quality of their output relative to more equitably paid workers. This phenomenon is somewhat transitory, however, and diminishes over a period of several days.[21] The inability of expectancy theory or reinforcement theory to readily predict this result largely stems from the absence of employee comparison processes in these theories as originally formulated. Clearly, a consideration of employee comparison processes adds something to our ability to predict employee behavior.

Intuitively, it is difficult to accept the notion that people who are overpaid will not attempt to maximize quantity. In a study that sought to identify individual differences in the desire to restore equity versus maximization of reward, the performance of overpaid individuals and that of equitably paid individuals were compared under a piece-rate scheme.[22] Results suggested that actions of individuals who were measured as being more altruistic (that is, more morally mature) were more likely to follow the predictions of equity theory (decreasing quantity of output and increasing quality) than actions of individuals who were measured as being less altruistic. Therefore, equity theory may provide a better description of the behavior of less principled individuals.

Although equity theory has been criticized for not explicitly predicting which method an employee will select in order to restore equity,[23] the theory presents a unique perspective on a major facet of work motivation. The perception of fairness is an important determinant of the impact of any reward system.[24]

Social Learning Theory

Social learning theory offers another approach to understanding motivation.[25] The desire to imitate models can be powerful. Modeling first manifests itself in childhood, when children imitate adults and other siblings. In organizations, a desire to imitate superior performers or supervisors may be strong in some individuals. Certainly, the taking of roles and imitation of previously witnessed behavior illustrate the subtle influences of social learning.

Social learning theory contends that people develop expectancies about their capacity to behave in certain ways and the probability that such behavior will result in rewards. The first of these expectancies relates to how they perceive their own competence, while the second pertains to outcomes and is analogous to the concepts of expectancy theory. Therefore, organizational training programs that rely on films, lectures, and role-playing techniques (that is, the vast majority of organization-sponsored training programs) are using an approach based on social learning theory principles. The self-administration of rewards is also an important part of social learning theory. Modeling, or imitative behavior, serves as a standard for administering self-reinforcement in the form of increased personal satisfaction and enhanced self-image. The direct instruction of employees by peers, supervisors, or trainers on how to set personal standards for performance can also be used, but whether employees accept such direct instruction probably depends on the power and attractiveness of the instructors. The use of social learning theory principles in conjunction with extrinsic rewards for performance may provide a most effective combination of motivational approaches.

A Comprehensive Model of Motivation

So far we have examined a number of different perspectives on work motivation. Although each perspective takes a somewhat different approach to motivation, it is possible to identify similarities among them and to integrate them into a larger conceptual framework.

Each approach falls into one of two categories: content theories or process theories. **Content theories** focus on *what* motivates people to perform. They are concerned with identifying the different rewards that people seek in their work. The theories of Maslow, Herzberg, and McClelland are essentially content theories. The other theories that we have examined are more concerned with *how* rewards control behavior. These theories focus on the dynamics, or process aspects, of work motivation. Expectancy, equity, reinforcement, and social learning theories are examples of **process theories**.

The content and process theories can be integrated into a still broader conceptual framework. Figure 4.2 presents a well-known and accepted framework proposed by Lyman Porter and Edward E. Lawler.[26] In essence, they outlined a dynamic model of motivation—the **Porter-Lawler model**—that includes many of the aforementioned theories as components of a larger process.

Beginning on the left-hand side of the model, the expected value of a reward combines with the expectation that effort will result in a reward. These two influences determine the level of effort that an employee exerts. Effort, however, does not simply or easily convert into performance (or accomplishment). The employee's abilities and role perceptions interact in determining the level of accomplishment. Unless a person has a minimum level of ability and the correct understanding of just how to perform a job, his or her effort will not yield an acceptable level of performance.

Performance may or may not be linked to rewards in a given situation; hence, the wavy lines between rewards and performance. The employee's expectations of what is equitable in the way of rewards is influenced by the awareness of his or her own performance. Perceptions of equity or inequity interact with the rewards actually received to determine the level of satisfaction.

FIGURE 4.2   *The Porter-Lawler Model of Motivation*

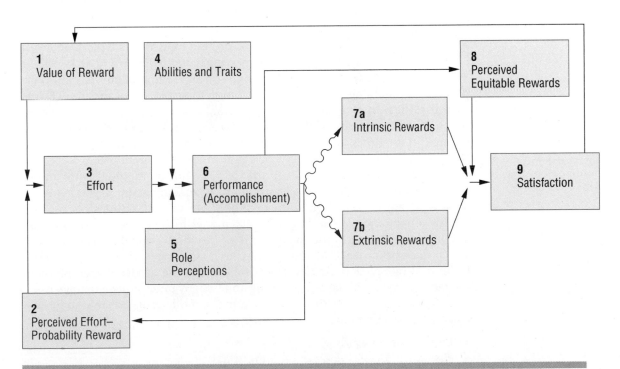

The model includes two feedback loops. The first links satisfaction to later estimates of the value of rewards. If an employee feels that rewards received for past performance are not particularly satisfying, he or she will diminish future efforts. The second feedback loop runs from the performance–rewards linkages to the expectation that future effort will result in rewards. Here again, the employee's future effort will be influenced by his or her experiences.

If we consider the various theories of motivation in light of the Porter-Lawler model, we see that each can be incorporated within this larger framework. Maslow's distinction between higher- and lower-order needs, as well as Herzberg's distinction between motivator factors (intrinsic factors) and hygiene factors (extrinsic factors), are represented by boxes 7a and 7b in the model. McClelland's principles regarding needs for achievement, affiliation, and power are contained in the intrinsic reward aspect of the model. Expectancy theory's principles are incorporated in the valence and expectancy features of the model, boxes 1 and 2. The concepts of equity theory are contained in box 8. Their influence is reflected in the interaction of equity perceptions and rewards in determining satisfaction.

The linkage between rewards and performance is a major theme in reinforcement theory. The conversion of the wavy lines that connect rewards to performance into straight lines is a goal of OB Mod advocates. The feedback loop from the performance–reward linkage to the expectancy estimate of box 2 incorporates a major operant conditioning principle (the importance of consequences for future behavior). Imitation and proper role conduct, important features of social learning theory, are implicit in box 5, role perceptions.

Several of the boxes in the model were not discussed in this chapter. However, job satisfaction (box 9) will be considered in Chapter 11. Abilities and traits (box 4) are in the province of human resources (or personnel) specialists, who attempt to select individuals who possess the requisite abilities and traits for successful job performance. Effort (box 3) is a topic that is typically considered by students of human factors engineering or work design.

The Porter-Lawler model does a good job of summarizing the major approaches to studying work behavior. From the perspective of the model, it is clear that the field of organizational behavior, which might appear fragmented because of the diversity of the topics it investigates, is not in disarray or segmented in its efforts to understand work behavior. Each of the various investigative lines of research can be viewed as examining different pieces of a larger puzzle. Although the Porter-Lawler model may not be the final word in describing work behavior, it nicely summarizes and integrates a good deal of what is already known about individual behavior in work settings.

The importance of the Porter-Lawler model for managers is substantial. The model underscores the many facets of the motivational process, each of which must be understood and attended to if a manager wishes to be successful in motivating subordinates. The complexity of the model also emphasizes the fact that many things can go wrong and thereby undermine a manager's efforts. The following checklist, derived from the model, suggests that to be successful managers should:

1. Offer valued rewards

2. Create perceptions that effort will lead to rewards

3. Design jobs so that effort leads to high performance

4. Hire qualified employees

5. Train employees in the correct manner for performing their tasks

6. Design tasks so that performance is measurable

7. Design reward systems so that rewards are tied to performance

8. Ensure that rewards are viewed as fair and equitable

SUMMARY

1. *Describe a technique for uncovering a person's dominant needs.* The Thematic Apperception Test uses drawings to uncover an individual's dominant needs. When a person tells stories about the drawings, a heightened need is likely to be revealed.

2. *Describe Maslow's hierarchy of needs.* Maslow grouped needs into deficiency (lower-order) and growth (higher-order) needs. From lowest to highest, deficiency needs are physiological needs, safety needs, and social needs; growth needs are esteem needs and self-actualization needs.

3. *Compare the ways motivator factors and hygiene factors may influence employees.* Motivator factors lead to feelings of satisfaction. These factors include career advancement, recognition, a sense of responsibility, and a feeling of achievement. The absence of hygiene factors leads to dissatisfaction. These factors involve job security, company policies, interpersonal relations, and working conditions. In theory, the absence of motivator factors does not make employees dissatisfied, nor do high levels of hygiene factors serve to increase employee satisfaction.

4. *Describe how expectations can influence an employee's efforts.* Employees consider whether their effort will translate into a desired accomplishment (effort–performance expectancy) and whether a given level of performance will result in obtaining a particular outcome (performance–outcome expectancy). Employees are predicted to make the greatest effort when these expectancies are high.

5. *Explain how behavior modification affects behavior in organizations.* Behavior modification interprets actions in terms of antecedents, behaviors, and consequences. Antecedents are stimuli that precede behaviors. Consequences are the rewards or punishments that follow from behaviors and become antecedents for subsequent behavior. Behavior modification involves managing the consequences of behavior, which can influence future behavior.

6. *Explain how employees' sense of equity affects their motivation.* Employees continuously monitor the degree of equity in their working relations. An employee will be relatively satisfied if his or her own ratio of outcomes to inputs is equivalent to the ratio for a comparison employee. Employees will strive to restore equity if they feel an imbalance exists.

7. *Describe how social learning influences behavior.* People develop expectations about their capacity to behave in certain ways and the probability that their behavior will result in rewards. When a person meets a standard of behavior, that person rewards himself or herself with increased personal satisfaction and enhanced self-image.

8. *Identify steps managers can take to motivate employees.* To motivate employees, managers should offer valued rewards, create perceptions that effort will lead to rewards, design jobs so that effort leads to high performance, hire qualified employees, train employees to do their tasks correctly, design tasks so that performance is measurable, design reward systems that tie rewards to performance, and ensure that rewards are seen as fair and equitable.

Key Terms

Need for achievement

Need for affiliation

Need for power

Hierarchy of needs

Deficiency needs

Growth needs

Peak experience

Prepotency

Flow

Two-factor theory

Motivator factors

Hygiene factors

Expectancy theory

Valence

Subjective probabilities

Behavior modification

Reinforcement theory

Equity theory

Social learning theory

Content theories

Process theories

Porter-Lawler model

CRITICAL INCIDENT

Salary versus Commission

Jerry Palmer was not an outstanding marketing student in college and felt very fortunate to have secured a sales position with a pharmaceutical firm. The pay appeared to be competitive and, best of all, he was going to be working with a fixed salary rather than on commission.

During the first year, Jerry had a hard time making sales. But as he kept working at improving his sales techniques, his sales began to rise. By the end of his third year, and based on discussions with other salespeople, Jerry believed he had become one of the top sales representatives in the company. However, since the company never revealed how its salespeople performed (no sales data and so forth), Jerry never knew if he was a top seller or not.

Last year was an excellent one for Jerry. His manager called him in for a brief meeting in October and praised him for his efforts. He was even told that if the company had ten more people like him, they would probably be number one in the industry. Jerry took these comments to mean he was an excellent sales representative. He had exceeded his sales goals by over 20 percent and was looking forward to another good year.

This year he is off to a good start and appears well on his way to exceeding the sales goal once again. However, Jerry has begun having some motivational problems. He has heard that competitors annually have sales contests and that they recognize top performers as salesperson of the month. He knows that they also give out awards and hold banquets. Jerry has begun to get upset with his company. He asked his manager about considering such incentives or even having a salary plus commission program. He was told "that's not how this company does things" and that he "shouldn't worry about it."

Jerry is starting to look around for another position with a competitor. He is convinced that pay should be tied to performance.

1. Why do you believe Jerry came to be dissatisfied with his company's fixed-salary payment policy?
2. In light of McClelland's notion of need for achievement, how would you characterize Jerry?
3. What is now motivating Jerry? What type of incentive program would probably be attractive to him?

EXPERIENTIAL EXERCISE

What Do Employees Want from Their Jobs?

This activity is designed to help you think about the above question and to help you better understand the factors that influence an employee to perform. Because it can be difficult to motivate, it is vital to recognize and understand the factors that employees seek on the job. By providing opportunities to have various needs satisfied, one can provide employees with a motivating environment.

1. Examine the following list of factors and think of how employees (that is, people you've worked with or supervised) would rank them. Remember, you are looking at this list from the employee's perspective. Your ranking should reflect what you think they would say they wanted from their jobs. Place a 1 after the factor you believe they would want most from their job, a 2 after the next most wanted factor, and so on.

Factors	Ranking	Supervisors' Rankings*	Employees' Rankings*
a. Interesting, challenging work			
b. A feeling of being "in" on things			
c. Job security			
d. Competent supervisor			
e. Good working conditions			
f. Tactful discipline			
g. Promotion and growth in organization			
h. Appreciation of work well done			
i. Sympathetic understanding of personal problems			
j. Good wages			
k. Involvement in plans or decisions			
l. Loyalty and support from management			
m. Relevant and timely feedback on performance			
n. Clear goals and objectives			

*Will be provided by your instructor.

2. After you have completed ranking these factors, your instructor will provide you with the supervisors' rankings from a study. Record these rankings in the appropriate column.

3. Looking at the supervisors' rankings compared to yours:
   a. Are you and the supervisors making similar assumptions about the workers' job satisfaction?
   b. Do you notice any areas or clusters of work factors to which there are similar rankings?
   c. (If asked to do by your instructor) Was the average class ranking on selected factors similar to that of the supervisors? How do you account for the differences?

4. Your instructor will now provide you with the employees' rankings. Given this information, the following discussion questions are of interest:
   a. Is there generally good agreement between the employees' rankings and those of their supervisors? And your ranking?
   b. On what factors or clusters of factors is there general agreement or disagreement?
   c. If there are some large differences, to what do you attribute them? What role might perception play?

5. Your instructor will ask you to form groups of four to six people. As a group, discuss the following questions:
   a. Why do you believe the supervisors and employees ranked the factors as they did?
   b. What are some implications of the data for managers?
   c. What should managers do to create motivating environments?

Source: Written by Bruce Kemelgor, University of Louisville; used by permission.

5 Enhancing Employee Motivation Using Rewards, Goals, Expectations, and Empowerment

Choose a job you love, and you will never have to work a day in your life.

—*Confucius*

People think we make $3 million and $4 million a year. They don't realize that most of us only make $500,000.

—*Pete Incaviglia, baseball player*

Work consists of whatever a body's obliged to do, and play consists of whatever a body's not obliged to do.

—*Mark Twain*

Learning Objectives:

After studying this chapter, you should be able to:

1. Distinguish between extrinsic and intrinsic rewards.
2. Explain why incentive plans have lost popularity.
3. Describe three attributes of goals that are important for improving performance.
4. Describe management by objectives and some of its advantages and possible problems.
5. Give some examples of the power of self-fulfilling prophecies.
6. Describe some ways of constructively managing self-fulfilling prophecies.
7. Describe methods of job redesign used to reduce worker discontent.
8. List the job characteristics that enhance a sense of the meaningfulness of one's work, a sense of responsibility, and knowledge of the results of one's work.
9. Describe the essential elements of quality circles.
10. Explain how self-directed work teams operate, and identify major consequences and problems of such teams.

Putting Executive Pay on the Line

The corporate trend of tying executive pay to performance is based on the attractive notion of basing reward on hard numbers. Take the case of Sears, whose pay-for-performance system, based on growth in net income, is also a pay-at-risk system: Level of compensation is directly tied to level of performance, and this can fluctuate from year to year. In the absolute, no performance means no bonus. At Sears, this is a major departure from a paternalistic company with steady paychecks and better-than-average benefits.

Arthur Martinez came to Sears as CEO to turn around the sagging retail giant, and was rewarded for his successes. His bonuses alone exceeded $1 million a year. In one year, he received a $1.9 million bonus on top of his $1.1 million salary. The following year, profits at Sears fell. Martinez, as well as thousands of Sears's managers, will have also seen a dramatic drop in bonuses. Martinez initiated this program and says, "That's the way bonuses should be. If it calculates to zero, it's zero. [The board] can't decide I tried hard and give me something. That's not going to happen."

Here's how it works at Sears. When Martinez started, approximately 250 executives received bonuses based on performance. Today, every one of the 19,000 salaried managers' bonuses is tied to performance. Officers in "business units," such as automotive or credit, receive bonus payouts based partly on corporate performance and partly on business unit performance. Bonuses are calculated on three criteria: (1) corporate performance, (2) business unit performance, and (3) attainment of personal goals. It's only at the department sales level that corporate performance does not affect bonus calculations. Here, bonuses are based on profits and customer satisfaction.

Says Martinez, "I wanted to move away from an entitlement mentality—put pay at risk and increase it over time to motivate and drive people." That was accomplished, and pay packages typically were larger than Sears managers have ever seen...in the boom years. Recently, Sears reported that net income fell 6.6 percent, to $1.19 billion, and earnings per share declined from $3.12 to $2.99. Top management, including Martinez, will likely receive no annual bonus. Another 250 executives could see bonuses drop by 50 percent from the previous year, while employees further down the ranks will only see small reductions. The potential impact on morale is clear, but Martinez feels "employee enthusiasm and dedication won't suffer because the pay-for-performance notion is now firmly embedded in Sears' new risk-taking management culture. Nobody should have trouble understanding we missed our plan this year. No one has any illusions."

Source: S. Chandler; "Sears's system of rewards has ups and downs," *The Chicago Tribune*, February 15, 1998.

In Chapter 4, we considered a variety of perspectives on the topic of work motivation. As shown by the Porter-Lawler model at the conclusion of the chapter, each of these perspectives offers insights into the process by which employees are motivated to perform. In this chapter, we will examine four ways to apply our knowledge of the motivational process in order to enhance employee performance: through reward systems, goal setting, management of expectations, and employee empowerment.

Reward Systems

Motivational specialists often distinguish between extrinsic and intrinsic rewards. **Extrinsic rewards** come from sources that are outside of, or external to, the individual, while **intrinsic rewards** may be more accurately characterized as self-administered (i.e., arising from within the person). Examples of extrinsic rewards include pay, fringe benefits, promotions, and perquisites. Examples of intrinsic rewards are feelings of competence, accomplishment, responsibility, and personal growth.

Although we typically think of extrinsic rewards as the primary means by which managers attempt to influence subordinates to perform well, intrinsics can also be used. In particular, the design of a job plays an important role in creating opportunities for intrinsic rewards. We will consider the redesign of work later in this chapter and, for the moment, will focus only on extrinsic reward systems.

The Role of Compensation

Edward E. Lawler III is one of the strongest advocates of tying rewards to performance. Although Lawler has studied the use of a number of different types of rewards, he is perhaps best known for his writings on how to use pay as a means of motivating employees.[1] Although organizations can use a variety of rewards, they tend to rely on only a few. Pay is used most frequently because it possesses certain useful characteristics.

First, a good reward should be valued by its recipient—and there is no question that pay is highly important to most people. Second, the size of a reward should be flexible. Some rewards, such as promotions, cannot be divided into various-sized portions, but the size of a pay raise can be easily manipulated. Third, the value of a reward should remain relatively constant. Some rewards, such as verbal praise, may lose their value if used repeatedly, but pay can be given frequently without diminishing its worth. Finally, for a reward to be effective (as noted in our discussion of expectancy theory in Chapter 4), the relationship of a reward to performance must be obvious. Because pay is so visible, employees can easily see the relationship between it and their performance. Thus, if we compare pay with other major organizational rewards on the dimensions of importance, flexibility, frequency, and visibility, pay is easily one of the strongest resources available for improving performance.

As noted several times in this text, the linking of rewards to performance is critical. Many managers think that performance and pay are closely linked in the units that they administer. However, in one survey, Lawler found that only 22 percent of workers in the United States believe that there is a direct link between how hard they work and how much they are paid.[2] There are a number of reasons for this disturbing perception. How hard one works, of course, may not be related to one's level of accomplishment. Intervening forces, such as uncooperative coworkers, unanticipated interruptions, and faulty equipment, can all conspire to undercut an employee's best intentions. Determining an employee's level of accomplishment is also an imprecise technology. Performance appraisal systems need to be designed to foster the perception that the measurement of performance is both objective and fair.

Attempts to relate pay and performance vary widely across organizations. These pay-for-performance schemes differ on three major dimensions: (1) the organizational unit, (2) the method of measuring performance, and (3) the form of monetary reward. One of three organizational units usually serves as the basis for comparing performance: the individual, the work group, or the total organization. The methods of measuring performance are more diverse and vary in terms of subjectivity. Ratings by supervisors are clearly the most widely used, but most subjective, device. Hard productivity data, such as sales figures and the number of units a person produces, are very objective. Other indexes of cost effectiveness and profitability (for example, number of errors and wastage) are also sometimes used. The two most common forms of monetary rewards are the bonus, which is a one-time, lump-sum reward, and the salary increment, which is a cumulative reward. Some organizations, for example Lincoln Electric, pay employees on a piecework system with an annual bonus based on the quality of output.[3]

Lawler has examined the combinations of the three dimensions of unit, performance, and pay, and offered an assessment of the effectiveness of each. The perception that pay is tied to performance is enhanced when rewards are administered on the basis of individual performance. Bonus schemes receive higher ratings on this dimension than do salary schemes. Objective measures of performance (productivity, cost effectiveness) also elicit higher ratings. The most successful pay schemes are, therefore, likely to be individually based bonus plans that rely on objective measures of performance. Such schemes do have some negative side effects. For example, social ostracism of superior performers and falsification of performance reports are more likely to occur with individually based bonus schemes.

Cooperation among group members tends to be greater with group and organizationwide pay plans. Such schemes foster the desire to help coworkers because of the perception that success is mutually beneficial. Individual schemes, on the other hand, encourage a greater sense of competitiveness.

On the dimension of employee acceptance, most of the pay plans rated moderately well. Individually based bonus plans, however, received a somewhat lower rating, possibly because the increased competition and the potential for falsification of performance reports produce the belief that the scheme is unfair.

In general, Lawler's analysis suggests that there is no single best pay incentive plan. Instead, each situation must be examined in terms of its unique characteristics. It is also important to note that these pay plans are not mutually exclusive. It is entirely possible to set up multiple or overlapping pay plans.

How Effective Are Incentive Plans? Although available research indicates that incentive pay plans can increase productivity by 15 to 35 percent, the popularity of such plans has declined in recent decades.[4] Piece-rate schemes in particular have lost their appeal. Incentive plans have run into problems because of a variety of factors, including adversarial relationships, class consciousness, and societal changes.

Adversarial Relationships When faced with incentive pay schemes, employees may use a number of ploys to lower production rates. When being observed, workers may produce at a very slow rate in order to deceive time-study consultants. And they may be reluctant to suggest improved methods for performing a task. Furthermore, informal norms will sometimes overpower individual initiative. As an additional tactic for dealing with the establishment of incentive schemes, employees may turn to collective bargaining by electing a union to negotiate on their behalf.

Class Consciousness Because the tasks involved in higher-level jobs (such as administrative and supervisory positions) do not lend themselves to easy quantification, incentive schemes are used more often for workers than for managers. This distinction can lead to a sense of "us versus them" within an organization's workforce. The sense of being discriminated against can, in turn, feed otherwise latent hostilities. The consciousness of class differences coupled with the adversarial tactics mentioned above may produce protectionism, little sharing of information, a narrow definition of loyalty, and little trust. In general, an unhealthy organizational culture can be expected to emerge.

Societal Changes The nature of work has changed significantly over the past 100 years. At present, many jobs involve service or information delivery. High technology has gained increasing importance in many otherwise simple jobs. The stand-alone jobs that involved simple manufacturing are being replaced by interdependent jobs that require the use of more complex equipment in more continuous operations.

In addition, there has been a movement in some settings to redesign work to make it less simple and repetitive, and thus to increase worker satisfaction, reduce turnover, and improve the quality of output. These attempts to enrich the nature of the work experience by offering more meaningful, complex, and interdependent tasks often create situations in which it is extremely difficult to measure performance in a simple, accurate, and fair manner.

The Future As a strategy for the future, Lawler suggests some combination of profit sharing, stock ownership, and gain sharing. At present, the use of all three types of plans appears to be increasing. Profit sharing and stock ownership are more commonly used than gain sharing. As a motivator, the link between reward and performance may be too weak to be effective, since one's on-the-job efforts are not immediately and visibly tied to the organization's performance. However, profit sharing and stock ownership emphasize the long-term benefits of joint efforts, and therefore may be ideal for directing the behavior of higher-level employees in ways that are beneficial to the entire organization. These two incentive schemes also can have significant symbolic value for employees in that they may develop a greater sense of identification with the organization.

An Inside Look
Peer Review: Settling Disputes, Saving Money

A growing trend is to use small panels of employees' peers to review and settle disputes between employees and management. This is not just a new, upstart trend; even companies with the stature of TRW, Inc., Rockwell International, and Marriott International are adopting this method to limit employee lawsuits and ease workplace tension.

Darden Industries of Orlando, Florida, owner of the Olive Garden and Red Lobster chains and employer of 110,000 workers, recently initiated peer review. Clifford Whitehall, general counsel for Darden Industries, says, "The program has been tremendously successful in keeping valuable employees from unfair dismissal and cutting $1 million from annual legal expenses for employee disputes, which now total $3.5 million. Now, about 100 disputes end up in peer review yearly, with only 10 resulting in lawsuits." Peer review is very popular with lawyers because it channels the anger and pain that employees feel after being fired.

At Red Lobster, an employee who is fired or disciplined can appeal to a panel of co-workers. The panel members review the case, hear testimony, and can overturn a management decision and award damages. Instead of starting a lawsuit, employees feel there is a reasonable alternative action to consider first. Red Lobster employees and management feel peer review can significantly reduce racial tensions. "Peer review has, in some cases, reversed decisions by managers who overreacted to complaints from minority customers and employees," says one employee. Panel members must have peer-review training, and are paid regular wages and travel expenses when they do a peer review. One Red Lobster employee decided to use peer review to settle a dispute about being fired. Though she won reinstatement to her job, she was not awarded three weeks of lost wages. Yet she was pleased with the outcome: "The process worked. The panel took my claim seriously."

Source: M.A. Jacobs; "Red Lobster Tale: Peers Decide Fired Waitress's Fate," *The Wall Street Journal*, January 20, 1998.

The earliest **gain-sharing** plans were devised by union leader Joseph Scanlon. Essentially, gain sharing ties an individual's bonuses to the performance of a business unit. Specifically, such a plan might provide monthly bonuses to all members of a department or plant if a predetermined formula indicates that there has been a measurable decrease in the cost of materials, supplies, operations, or labor. For example, Herman Miller, a furniture manufacturer with a long involvement in gain sharing, offers a bonus system plus opportunities for employees to participate in decision making.[5] Similarly, such diverse organizations as Cummins Engine Company, TWA, and Beth Israel Hospital of Boston have gain-sharing plans.

The growing popularity of gain sharing appears to be due to several factors. Gain sharing is often introduced in a participative fashion, with employees being given a say in the design of the plan. Also, all employees—both managers and workers—are likely to be covered in the plan. In addition, because the setting of individual work standards and the calculation of individual compensation are not necessary in a gain-sharing plan, workers perceive the system as fairer.

One of the more recent innovations in the area of compensation management is a variable pay-for-performance plan that typically starts with a reduced base wage or salary, but offers attractive bonuses to employees for attaining specific performance targets or other goals. Although bonus plans are not a new concept, the new plans attempt to tie risk and reward closer together. As a result, employee pay may be reduced during lean times. Experience with these plans (at such firms as Corning, Du Pont, Monsanto, and Valvoline) shows that employees can earn as much as 120 percent of the average wages of comparable jobs—or as little as 90 percent. One survey revealed that 35 percent of the *Fortune* 500 companies are experimenting with some form of pay-for-performance plan. Generally, such variable-pay plans seem to fare better in service industries where employees are more accustomed to commissions or other forms of nonfixed compensation.[6]

Goal Setting

Managers and employees need to understand each other's goals. In addition, managers are responsible for helping employees in setting goals or objectives. With a clear understanding of explicit goals or objectives, managers and employees can work together to achieve specific outcomes. Several attributes of goals are especially important for improving performance: goal specificity, goal difficulty, and goal acceptance.[7]

Specificity

Goal specificity refers to the preciseness with which a goal or objective is stated. Increases in goal specificity are positively related to increases in performance. Specific goals that are quantifiable reduce ambiguity and thereby help to focus employees' efforts.[8] Therefore, it is generally a good idea to avoid developing or stating goals in broad or ambiguous terms.

Difficulty

Increasing **goal difficulty** can also result in superior performance. The more difficult the goal is, so the research results suggest, the more challenging the task is perceived as being. Greater task challenge, in turn, results in greater effort being put forth by an employee. One major limitation to this argument, however, is that the goals must be feasible. Setting outlandish goals or goals that are unquestionably out of the reach of the employee will more likely lead to frustration and rejection of the goal.

Acceptance

Employees must also accept the goals that are set. **Goal acceptance** is most likely to occur when assigned goals correspond with personal aspirations. Difficult, specific goals that are accepted by an employee will therefore result in superior performance. This line of reasoning suggests that managers must encourage employees to focus on measurable and challenging goals while trying to elicit employee commitment to the goals.

Management by Objectives

Management-by-objectives (MBO) is a practical application of the reasoning behind the notion of goal-setting theory. MBO is a process in which employees participate with management in the setting of goals, or objectives.[9] An essential feature of an MBO program is that it involves a one-on-one negotiation session between a supervisor and a subordinate in order to set concrete, objective goals for the employee's performance. During the session, a deadline is set for the measurement of accomplishment, and the paths to the desired goals and the removal of possible obstacles are discussed. After an established period of time has elapsed (typically six months or a year), the supervisor and subordinate meet again to review the subordinate's performance using the agreed-upon goals as a measuring tool. Figure 5.1 summarizes the essential steps in the MBO process.

A positive feature of an MBO system lies in its emphasis on establishing specific, measurable goals. In fact, a goal is unacceptable or inadmissible in an MBO system unless it is measurable. You may think that this is impossible for all goals, especially those of top-level executives. Although it is difficult to set measurable goals at the higher levels of an organization, it is nonetheless possible. For example, one such quantifiable goal might be that an institution will be ranked in the top ten by an annual polling of executives in the same industry. Or, the head coach of a college football team may set a goal of making the top 20 in the Associated Press's writers' poll within the next five years. Some more typical goals would be to increase market share from 45 to 55 percent by the end of the next fiscal year, to increase annual production by 10 percent, or to increase profits after taxes by 3 percent. Some goals can be measured in simple yes or no fashion. For example, the goal of establishing a training program for sales personnel or completing a feasibility study by a certain date can be judged in a simple success or failure fashion when the deadline arises. Either such a project has been completed or it has not.

Advocates of MBO believe that everyone in an organization could and should be involved in goal setting. This includes all personnel, from the chief executive officer (who may set goals in consultation with the board of directors) to the newest member of the clean-up crew. In practice, however, middle-level managers and first-line supervisors are more commonly involved in such goal-setting systems.

Proponents of MBO systems also believe that supervisors must play a special role in the goal-setting process. Supervisors should view themselves

FIGURE 5.1 *An Outline of the Steps in the MBO Process*

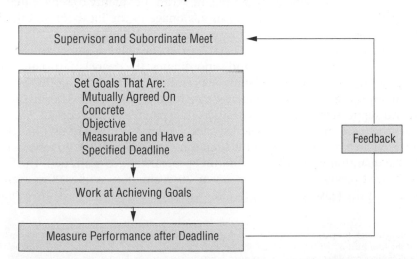

as coaches or counselors whose role is to aid their subordinates in goal attainment. This role of coach/counselor extends beyond merely helping to identify and remove obstacles to goal attainment (for example, using personal influence to expedite shipments from another department). It also implies that the supervisor will serve as a mentor—someone to whom subordinates can go with their work-related problems and assume that they will be treated with respect and support.

Do MBO Systems Work?   Research at such organizations as Black and Decker, Wells Fargo, and General Electric has shown that, on the whole, MBO programs can succeed.[10] Because MBO relies on the established principles of goal setting, it has great potential for improving performance. Real-world constraints, however, sometimes reduce the positive impact of a goal-setting system.

One major obstacle to the success of an MBO program can be lack of support from top-level executives. If key people in the organization—especially the president and vice presidents—do not fully endorse MBO, their lack of support will likely be felt and responded to at lower levels. The net effect will be a decided lack of enthusiasm for the program.

Problems may also arise if managers are not interested in having subordinates participate in the goal-setting process. Some managers prefer to retain an evaluative and superior posture and are uncomfortable with the notion of being a coach or counselor to their subordinates.

Personality conflicts between superiors and subordinates are another potential problem for goal-setting systems, as is competitiveness. A superior who feels threatened by talented subordinates may do little to help them be more successful and, consequently, more visible. In addition, subordinates may hesitate to set challenging goals for fear of failure and its consequences.

MBO systems also tend to emphasize the quantifiable aspects of performance while ignoring the more qualitative aspects. This is an understandable tendency, since participants in MBO systems are encouraged to focus on measurable dimensions in performance. Qualitative aspects of performance, which are often more difficult to identify and measure, are likely to be overlooked or de-emphasized. For example, how can the quality of service that an organization provides or an organization's image in the local community be defined and measured?

Because the success of an MBO system rests heavily on the quality of the relationship between supervisor and subordinates, the degree of trust and supportiveness that exists in a work unit is a central concern. For an MBO system to be highly successful, these elements are critical prerequisites. The absence of trust and supportiveness severely restricts the system's effectiveness.*

Despite these many potential obstacles, the track record of MBO has been fairly good. In a recent review of the literature devoted to MBO, 70 reports that included quantitative evaluations of MBO programs were examined. The findings showed productivity gains in 68 of 70 evaluation studies. The average productivity increase was 47 percent, while cost data showed an average

---

*This point prompts the paradoxical observation that MBO systems work best in situations where they may be needed the least (that is, where good supervisor–subordinate relations already exist), and MBO systems work least well in situations where they are needed most desperately (where divisiveness and conflict exist)!

savings of 26 percent. Employee attendance was also shown to improve by 24 percent. Follow-up surveys of the level of top-management support for the programs revealed that productivity increased by 57 percent when top-management commitment was high, 33 percent when commitment was average, and only 6 percent when commitment was low.[11]

MBO has passed through several phases since its introduction. Initially, MBO was greeted with much enthusiasm by managers and management scholars. Presently, MBO is viewed more objectively by scholars and practitioners as a tool that (like any tool) can be most effective under specific favorable conditions. It has become somewhat passé even to invoke the initials MBO. In fact, the principles and philosophies of MBO have become so emotion-laden in the minds of managers that an organization will often introduce an MBO system under a different label. For example, an organization may establish a program called START (an acronym for Set Targets and Reach Them) or GAP (Goal Acceptance Program). The mechanics of such programs are likely to borrow heavily, if not totally, from the MBO approach. In short, the trend is toward putting old wine into new bottles, with a recognition that mutual goal setting is not a panacea for all organizational problems under all possible circumstances.

Expectations

One of the more subtle approaches to influencing employee performance is through expectations.[12] People communicate their performance expectations both verbally and nonverbally. Often, we send cues revealing that we either approve or disapprove of another's conduct. This approach to influencing employee performance is often employed without deliberate intent in that few of us consciously try to influence others by our transmitted expectations. The use of expectations to change performance, however, is receiving increasing recognition in the field of organizational behavior as a powerful force in influencing employee effort and performance.

The Power of Self-Fulfilling Prophecies

Perhaps the clearest examples of the power of expectations can be seen in the responsiveness of children to the expectations of parents and teachers. All of us have seen children who are labeled as "little devils" or "star pupils" respond exactly as expected. It can be said more generally that an individual often responds to expectations in a manner that supports the beliefs of the person who transmits the cues.

Robert Rosenthal of Harvard University is the foremost researcher of the power of expectations. In one investigation, Rosenthal and Jacobson studied the influence of elementary school teachers' expectations on their pupils.[13] At the start of the school year, pupils were given an academic aptitude test. The investigators then provided false feedback to the teachers, identifying 20 percent of the children as likely to bloom academically during the coming school year. In fact, the likely "bloomers" had been selected by a random process. At the end of the school year, all pupils were again tested. The results showed that the so-called bloomers did in fact bloom, as evidenced by significant gains in IQ in comparison to their classmates. Because the teachers' expectations were the only deliberately manipulated aspect in this study, the investigators concluded that the changes in student performance were largely due to qualitative differences in how the teachers related to individual students.

In their report of this study, entitled *Pygmalion in the Classroom*, Rosenthal and Jacobson argued that the teachers probably conveyed messages of expected success and failure to individual students.[†] The students, in turn, responded by living up to the teachers' expectations. In essence, each teacher held a prophecy, or expectation, for each student, and each student then behaved to fulfill the expectation. This process is called a **self-fulfilling prophecy (SFP)**.

The relevance of the SFP phenomenon for organizations is straightforward. Employees, like all people, desire approval from their superiors. To some degree, supervisors transmit cues, or expectations, that an individual has the potential to succeed or, alternatively, will never succeed. Employers then typically respond by conforming to the communicated prophecy. An employee who receives positive cues can seemingly do no wrong, while an employee who receives negative cues can rarely do anything right. When faced with negative expectations, part of an employee's failure stems from the fear of being evaluated harshly by a supervisor. This obsession distracts the individual from performing well and encourages him or her to interpret ambiguous situations in a more negative light.

In a study that paralleled that of Rosenthal and Jacobson, King studied the performance of a group of hard-core unemployed men who were enrolled in a welding course.[14] Initially, King gave the men a test of mechanical aptitude. The classroom supervisors were then given false feedback about the students' test performances, with some of the men arbitrarily labeled as "high-aptitude" students. As in the Pygmalion study, the only real difference lay in the minds of the observers. At the end of the course, the men were given a comprehensive test of welding knowledge. The so-called high-aptitude individuals did in fact do better on the test than their classmates. In addition, these same individuals were absent fewer times during the course and completed many of the exercises ahead of their peers. A confidential poll of the men regarding the popularity of their classmates revealed that the "high-aptitude" men were the most popular members of the class (that is, they were rated "most preferred to be with" by their classmates).

A more controlled study of the SFP phenomenon was reported by Eden and Shani in a study entitled "Pygmalion Goes to Boot Camp."[15] In their study, Eden and Shani randomly labeled soldiers in the Israeli army as having "high command potential." These soldiers were then assigned to various instructors who were familiar with their alleged potential. Although the soldiers had different instructors, the results were much the same: Soldiers who had been randomly labeled as having high potential displayed superior performance during their training experience when compared to other trainees.

[†]Pygmalion, a character in Greek mythology, is said to have sculpted a stone statue of a lovely maiden. Because he fell in love with the statue and wished strongly for it to be a living person, the gods took pity on him and brought the statue to life, hence fulfilling his aspirations.

From these examples, it is clear that the SFP phenomenon is not limited to young children or animals.[‡] Other examples of the SFP effect can also be cited. A bank run, in which the depositors flock to a bank and demand their money, is a classic illustration of a self-fulfilling prophecy. In a bank run, the depositors act collectively on a rumor of insolvency and thereby convert the rumor into reality. To some extent, the national rate of inflation is partially due to an SFP. Consider a situation in which union bargaining representatives expect that inflation in the coming year will be around 2 percent. With this expectation, they will feel obligated to demand at least a 2 percent increase in wages in order to keep up with inflation. Manufacturing firms will, in turn, see their labor costs rising by at least 2 percent because of the workers' demands and will raise their prices accordingly. Thus, the expectation that the cost of everything will go up at least 2 percent in the coming year helps to create a situation in which the prophecy is fulfilled.

The Constructive Management of Self-Fulfilling Prophecies

All too often we are unwitting participants in self-fulfilling prophecies, either as the perpetrator (cue sender) or benefactor/victim (cue receiver). In organizations, the effects of this influence process can be substantial. Rather than lament the traps of SFPs, it is perhaps best to think about how we can control this process to positive ends. Since we cannot avoid influencing one another's actions, it is important to consider how we can use SFP to encourage optimal performance from all organizational members.

A primary consideration in using SFP for benevolent purposes is to be more sensitive to how others perceive us. That is to say, we should strive to be more aware of how subtle aspects of our own behavior and speech communicate our thoughts to others. Small factors, such as amount of eye contact, tone of voice, phrasing of sentences, and so on, can speak volumes about how we truly feel. Thus, we must pay greater attention to controlling our own actions in order to communicate positive expectations to all individuals.

Many times, managers honestly feel that they treat all subordinates equally, but they communicate personal biases nonetheless. Workers rarely feel that their supervisors treat all subordinates alike. Most commonly, they claim that some subordinates are members of the boss's inner circle, while others are viewed as outsiders.

Managers can also use SFP to foster motivation. One technique for doing so is to display enthusiasm for the work unit's mission. Such enthusiasm will usually be contagious and spread to subordinates. A contagious enthusiasm that focuses on task accomplishment also draws attention away from interpersonal concerns of relative likes and dislikes.

SFPs may also play a role when performance appraisal schemes rely too heavily on subjective appraisals. In such cases, personal bias can be introduced.

[‡]As an example of how humans and animals communicate expectations, consider how a dog typically reacts when we convey cues of fear versus confidence: Fear typically evokes an aggressive response, while confidence and relaxation elicit acceptance. In a dramatic illustration of the potential for subtle communication between humans and animals, Rosenthal and Fode told college students that individual lab rats they were asked to train in a maze were "bright" (allegedly based on past maze performance) or "dull."[16] The "bright" rats in fact outperformed the "dull" rats when the college students actually trained them to run a maze. Without knowing it, the college students had related to the rats in ways that conveyed positive or negative performance expectations. The rats were able to sense and respond to the students' cues.

One common safeguard against this potential problem is the use of more objective indexes of performance. Sales figures or widgets produced per day should provide less biased measures of performance. Yet, even the perception of seemingly simple objective indexes such as these can sometimes be influenced by strong prior expectations.

In summary, our expectations influence both our perception of others and the behavior of others. In order to optimize the performance of every subordinate, it is essential that managers pay great attention to their prior expectations and the transmission of those expectations. This is not to advocate the manipulation of others by conveying deceptive cues. Rather, it is to advocate bringing out the best in others by treating them supportively and optimistically. The principle of using expectations to maximize performance may be summarized as follows: "Do not treat others as you may believe they are—treat them as if they are already what you hope they will become."

Employee Empowerment

In addition to reward systems, goal setting, and the management of expectations, employee motivation can be enhanced by increasing an individual's sense of self-control at work. This notion of increasing employee self-determination is sometimes termed *employee involvement* or *employee participation.* However, a broader term that encompasses a number of specific techniques is **employee empowerment.** Employee empowerment refers to a set of motivational techniques that are designed to improve employee performance through increased levels of employee participation and self-determination. A major feature of employee empowerment is the deliberate merging of organizational and individual goals. In this section, we will examine three specific techniques: job redesign, quality circles, and self-directed work teams. Job redesign has traditionally focused on improved individual productivity, while quality circles and self-directed work teams are more group focused.

Job Redesign

A portion of the material wealth of our culture stems from the application of the principle of division of labor. The division of labor was recognized as an important factor in increasing productivity during the Industrial Revolution, when mechanization and job fragmentation began to emerge most strongly. Although Adam Smith, in his book *An Inquiry into the Nature and Causes of the Wealth of Nations*, identified division of labor as an important factor in improving productivity, he also suggested it had the potential to "corrupt" the worker through repetition and drudgery.[17] Karl Marx also observed that the trend toward industrialization in the West was creating a less than ideal set of circumstances for workers. As a solution, Marx advocated the overthrow of the capitalist system and the creation of a state in which factories and products were owned collectively by the workers.[§]

[§]Another solution was offered by an eccentric, Ned Lud, who feared that the Industrial Revolution would eliminate the means of livelihood of many peasants. Lud and his later followers, called Luddites, deliberately destroyed spinning and farming machinery in the early 1800s, not realizing that the Industrial Revolution actually helped to create many new jobs.

Despite these concerns, job specialization and greater division of labor continued. The productivity gains of job specialization resulted from decreased time spent changing tasks, decreased training time for employees, and increased skill due to repetition. Labor was also less able to claim that important skills were involved in the tasks and, therefore, was less able to demand higher wages. The early decades of the 20th century witnessed a continuing drive toward job simplification, helping to spur on the trend.**

More recently, management scholars have recognized that job simplification can improve productivity *up to a point.* Beyond that point, worker dissatisfaction can set in. Workers then become hostile toward the task and the employer, and consequently reduce their efforts or increase labor costs through absenteeism or turnover. The challenge, as many managers see it, is to find the ideal level of simplification that maximizes productivity without risking worker discontent. In practice, most managers have been more likely to focus on increasing productivity at some cost to worker satisfaction. To be sure, a level of worker discontent that risks causing a wildcat strike or serious insubordination is to be avoided. But levels short of that extreme may be incurred in order to increase short-run production.

For numerous reasons, working conditions continue to improve. Since the emergence of the organized labor movement, management has rarely used work speed-ups—a tactic in which the pace of an assembly line is drastically increased for a short period of time. Workers (especially younger, better educated workers) are also more likely to express a desire for more challenging work. And due to larger societal trends respecting individual rights and liberties, a movement toward the enrichment, or humanization, of work is gaining strength. This movement represents something akin to the return swing of the pendulum.[18] For many centuries, craftsperson-type jobs (where job simplification is low) were prevalent. Then, the trend moved toward more simplified work, and now the trend appears to be heading back toward jobs with less simplification (although the era of the craftsperson may not fully return). In a sense, the world of work has been passing through a period of relative dehumanization. More recently, the trend is toward the rehumanization of work.

Methods of Job Redesign   The first serious attempt to break from the principles of job simplification occurred during the 1950s. This approach, called **job enlargement,** involves an increase in the variety of an employee's activities. In essence, a job is extended to include additional elements without really altering its content. For example, a worker may solder the red wires as well as the black wires. On the whole, job enlargement tends to improve worker satisfaction and the quality of production. The quantity of production, however, does not appear to be clearly or directly affected.

Job rotation is a related notion in the area of job redesign. In job rotation, the task stays the same, but the personnel who perform the task are systematically changed. Many organizations use job rotation as a training device to

---

**One of the dullest and most repetitive jobs with which I am familiar is that of bottle capper in a perfume factory. The job entails screwing on small perfume bottle caps for eight hours a day. These workers cannot leave their workstation unless a relief person is present. Also, if a worker is running out of caps, it is a different person's sole responsibility to see that the bin of bottle caps is replenished. For the record, the longest substantiated industrial career in a single job was that of Polly Gadsby, who began working at the age of 9 and wrapped elastic for the same company until her death at the age of 95.

improve workers' flexibility. Nonetheless, job rotation may be the only available means for introducing variety into jobs that cannot be redesigned to make them more meaningful or challenging.

Fred Herzberg was one of the first people to make an important observation about job-redesign efforts.[19] He noted that many redesign efforts focused on changing the *variety* of activities without changing their content. Also, the new designs did not give workers control over their jobs. Often, workers' efforts were paced by the rate of an assembly-line process instead of being self-paced. Herzberg proposed that autonomy and self-regulation are important causes of positive changes in worker behavior. He also felt that job-redesign efforts should focus on giving more decision-making responsibility to workers, rather than merely expanding the number of tasks performed. A distinction can thus be made between vertical and horizontal expansions of a job. Vertical expansion represents **job enrichment,** while horizontal expansion represents job enlargement. The specific job factors that have the potential to enrich work are drawn from the list of motivators that Herzberg proposed in his two-factor theory of work motivation (see Chapter 4).

Studies of job enrichment processes have tended to be success stories. One of the more widely known examples of job enrichment programs is provided by Volvo's experiences at the Kalmar and Uddevalla plants in Sweden. The program changed the conventional assembly-line method of manufacturing to a more employee-centered system of controlling the assembly process. The assembly system relied on computer-controlled trolleys that carried partially assembled automobiles through the plant. However, reports of this experience and other job enrichment programs (such as those at Texas Instruments, General Foods, and Polaroid) have tended to be informal and lacking in rigor, so drawing a conclusive assessment of the value of job enrichment efforts is difficult.[20] Also, the Volvo plants at Kalmar and Uddevalla were eventually closed because of high absenteeism and low productivity (despite high employee satisfaction and high quality of output). Still more recently, Volvo sold its passenger car division to Ford.

In what may be viewed as something of a backlash to the job enrichment movement, it has been argued that not everyone is interested in an enriched job.[21] This position has been presented with several variations.[22] The most extreme statement is that people are very adaptable and will adjust to most situations.

A more moderate view is that only certain people desire enriched work, while others actually prefer the freedom from hassles resulting from an unchallenging job. Similarly, some claim that the high walls created by being "in a rut" offer a certain degree of insulation and security from potentially threatening surroundings.

Although the consideration of individual differences seems to be intuitively reasonable, and one can easily imagine situations in which specific individuals may prefer nonchallenging work, evidence from a national sample suggests that the magnitude of the differences among workers is not that great.[23] These data suggest that the vast majority of people respond positively to jobs of increasing quality (that is, greater challenge, autonomy, and responsibility), but that the strength of this desire is greater in some segments of the population. Thus, it appears that workers rarely report negative reactions to increases in job quality.[24]

Job Characteristics Theory   J. Richard Hackman and Greg Oldham have proposed a comprehensive theory of job enrichment that attempts to explain how various job dimensions affect worker behavior.[25] Their **job characteristics theory** also accounts for the possible influence of individual differences on the desire for enriched work. To their credit, Hackman and Oldham have tried to establish empirically the accuracy of their model and have designed measures of key concepts.

The main components of their model and the links among them are portrayed in Figure 5.2. According to the model, a number of work outcomes, such as desire to perform well (that is, high internal work motivation) and satisfaction, are influenced by the experience of three critical psychological states. These three states—the meaningfulness of work, felt responsibility, and knowledge of results of job—are all "critical" in the sense that the absence of any one of them will not foster the desired outcomes. Each of the three states is influenced in turn by the various core job characteristics. Specifically, a sense of the meaningfulness of work is enhanced by the presence of

1. *Skill variety*, or the extent to which a job requires that different duties be performed involving a number of different skills,
2. *Task identity*, or the extent to which a person is permitted to complete a "whole" or identifiable piece of work from start to finish, and
3. *Task significance*, or the extent to which a job affects the lives of others (that is, is the job of some value to others in the organization or the world?).

Responsibility is enhanced by the presence of

4. *Autonomy*, or the extent to which a job offers independence and self-determination for the scheduling of work and the performance of associated tasks.
5. *Feedback from the job*, or the extent to which the conduct of the job provides clear and direct information on the effectiveness of the worker's performance.

FIGURE 5.2   *The Job Characteristics Model of Job Enrichment*

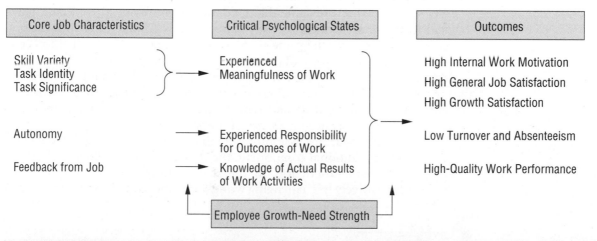

To assess the degree to which a job is enriched, Hackman and Oldham developed a series of questions that determine the extent to which a worker views his or her job as possessing each of the five job characteristics. Responses to the **job diagnostic survey** can then be combined in accordance with a formula for assessing a job's overall potential for motivating an individual. The Motivating Potential Score, or MPS, is given by:

$$\text{Motivating Potential Score (MPS)} = \left(\frac{\text{Skill Variety} + \text{Task Identity} + \text{Task Significance}}{3} \right) \times \text{Autonomy} \times \text{Feedback}$$

Because the formula involves the multiplication of terms, it suggests that a low or near-zero value on the job characteristics that define a critical psychological state will also lead to a total MPS value of near zero. The MPS formula is particularly useful for comparing different jobs and for assessing the same job over time (as might be done in a study of the effects of a job enrichment effort).

To illustrate the importance of the core job characteristics, consider almost any recreational activity in which people engage. The game of golf provides a particularly useful example. Golf involves a variety of skills and requires the use of personal judgment, as in deciding which club to use. A player completes the entire course, as opposed to only a portion. The game also possesses a form of significance, in that players keep a tally of the number of strokes they take to move the ball from the tee to the cup. This tally permits players to compare their performance against several standards: their own past performance on the hole, the par (or standard) for the hole, and the performance of their competitors. Autonomy is involved in that players are personally responsible for their performance. They are in charge of their own conduct and, consequently, their own success or failure. Finally, feedback is immediate. A player learns instantly if his or her shot hooks, slices, or lands in the sand. Clearly, the game of golf is highly "enriched," which explains why many people spend much of their spare time on the links.

It is interesting to consider what the game of golf would be like with any of the core characteristics removed. Suppose that feedback were eliminated, so that a player could not watch the flight of the ball to see how far it went or where it landed. Or imagine that autonomy were removed, so that a player had to follow someone else's directions on how to play each shot. In both cases, a great deal of the game's interest would be lost. If we failed to keep a tally of strokes (or a score of performance) and simply hit the ball around the course, we would also make the game less meaningful. In short, the removal of any of the critical psychological states would diminish the experience of enrichment or fulfillment and tend to make the activities seem more like "work" (in the most negative sense of the word).[††]

To complete our discussion of the job characteristics model, we need to consider one additional component: the strength of an employee's desire for personal growth experiences in the work setting. Clearly, not everyone responds positively to challenging work. Some individuals prefer to be given

---

[††]Another good illustration is given by video games. Objectively, the activity involved in playing video games is often highly repetitive. However, the sense of feedback, personal autonomy, and meaningfulness produced by a form of scoring provide a strong intrinsic appeal that can lead to an almost addictive involvement.

assignments that are very clear-cut and offer little challenge. An attempt to enrich such people's jobs may be futile. In recognition of this fact, Hackman and Oldham have incorporated the notion of individual differences into their model. **Employee growth-need strength** enters the enrichment experience in two places: (1) it influences the experience of psychological states in reaction to job characteristics (that is, individuals who are higher on growth-need strength tend to experience the states more fully), and (2) it influences the relationship between the psychological states and worker outcomes (that is, individuals who are higher on growth-need strength tend to have more positive outcomes in response to the psychological states). In short, the job characteristics model holds that the enrichment process will succeed only with individuals who are predisposed to benefit from the enrichment experience.

Evidence on the Validity of the Job Characteristics Model   The job characteristics model has been tested extensively in recent years. By and large, the results support the model's predictions.[26] The model predicts internal work motivation and job satisfaction quite well, and absenteeism less well. Predicting performance has proven to be more problematic. Quality enhancement is somewhat more certain, while quantity enhancement is not very reliable. It seems that the further one moves from psychological variables to job behaviors, the less successful the model is as a predictor.

Other Job Redesign Approaches   In addition to job enrichment, three other work redesign techniques are also growing in popularity: flextime, the modified workweek, and telecommuting.

Flextime refers to a work schedule that gives employees some discretion in arranging their working hours. Most frequently, the employer specifies a period of time during the day when all employees must be present—the core time. Employees may then schedule the rest of their work hours according to their own preferences. In most cases, the earliest starting time and latest stopping time are prescribed, as is the total number of hours that an employee must complete every week. Many flextime plans also hold an employee to a two-hour maximum time limit for lunch. But within these constraints, employees are free to select starting and finishing times each day. To be sure, flextime does not redesign the actual tasks that workers perform, but it does offer each employee a means of balancing work and home life.

Research on flextime has yielded generally positive results. For example, it has found that absenteeism and turnover were lowered, while performance increased following the introduction of flextime.[27] Significant increases in productivity were also reported in one study.[28] Other experiments have also tended to find positive effects, especially in reduced absenteeism and turnover.[29] Furthermore, the allowance of some scheduling flexibility has been growing in the United Sates from the early through late 1990s, such that 25 million employees (27.6 percent of full-time workers) had schedules that permitted variance in arrival and departure times.

Modified workweek plans attempt to design alternatives for the currently prevalent 8-hour day, 5-day workweek. The most commonly adopted design is the 4-day, 10 hours per day workweek, or 4-40 scheme. Because the rest of the business world still follows a 5-day workweek (and therefore expects to communicate and send goods on a 5-day schedule), many experimenting organizations have had to stagger their 4-day plans so that part of the company will be open on any given workday.

The impact of the 4-40 schedule has been mixed. Although employees can enjoy longer stretches of uninterrupted leisure time and less commuting, they are more likely to be fatigued from working longer shifts. Absenteeism, however, is often reduced due to the potentially greater cost that a lost workday has for the individual employee. Informal evidence of the productivity gains of 4-40 programs, such as surveys based on managers' impressions, has tended to be positive.[30] But other evidence suggests that while performance and satisfaction increased following the introduction of a 4-40 scheme, both outcomes returned to original levels after about two years.[31] Another survey suggests that some companies that have experimented with 4-40 schemes are returning to a traditional workweek.[32] Despite such mixed findings, many social forecasters still predict that a 4-40 workweek lies in our future. So the reasoning goes, substantial start-up and heating/cooling costs for manufacturing and office facilities, as well as reduced commuting costs, could be realized by the widespread adoption of a 4-40 workweek.

Telecommuting refers to the use of computer links with one's employer that permit the completion of all or part of one's job at home. Several million employees in the industrialized nations are currently involved in telecommuting, and projections indicate that this number will increase in the coming years. Telecommuting tends to be used most in information-intensive and information-processing industries, such as insurance, banking, financial services, and market research. Firms with successful telecommuting experiences include American Express, Mountain Bell, Hanover Trust, J.C. Penney, Beneficial Finance Corporation, Apple Computer, and Travelers Insurance.

Telecommuting offers some clear advantages to both the employer and employee. For example, there is a reduced need for work space at the employer's site, and the employee is spared the cost and time of commuting. In addition to being free from distractions at the workplace, employees are able to spend more time with family members. This can be of great importance to employees who must provide care for the young or elderly. Research on the impact of telecommuting on employee productivity suggests that gains of 15 to 30 percent are not uncommon, most probably as a result of employees being free from workplace interruptions.[33] Also, telecommuters report higher job satisfaction levels, perhaps because of fewer work-related frustrations.

On the downside, telecommuters are "out of the loop" in terms of being part of the workplace political network. Because of such isolation, they may be bypassed for promotions or receive smaller raises. Also, they may feel a greater sense of social isolation than other employees. These potential drawbacks suggest that employers should screen individuals who are interested in telecommuting. Such screening would identify those who can handle the negative aspects of telecommuting and who can be productive without immediate supervision. Also, telecommuters might be required to come to the office site periodically to talk with their supervisors and specific individuals, as well as to socialize with other employees. Often, telecommuters do not devote 100 percent of their time to working off-site. More typically, employees may telecommute two or three days a week.

Quality Circles

Quality circles are employee committees of six to ten workers who meet once or twice a week (usually on company time) to discuss production problems and problems with product quality. Although the notion of quality circles originated in the United States, it took root in Japan after World War II (after being introduced in Japan by American consultants). The use of quality circles was reintroduced to the United States, partly due to a fascination with Japan's business success.

In a quality circle program (1) membership is voluntary (employees must not be coerced into participating), (2) circle members are trained in problem-solving techniques, (3) members develop solutions to problems that they submit to management through formal presentations, and (4) members monitor the outcome of their solutions.

It has been estimated that from 12 to 25 percent of the Japanese workforce participates in quality circles. Although the proportion of the workforce in other industrialized nations that participates in quality circles is still relatively modest, it has been growing rapidly during the 1990s. Most of this growth has been in the manufacturing sector, and the firms that have implemented quality circles have experienced impressive success. For example, at Honeywell, a high-technology electronics firm, several hundred quality circles are in use; in addition to improving productivity, they have reduced absenteeism. Other large U.S. companies that have successfully introduced quality circles include American Airlines, General Motors, Ford Motor Company, Hughes Aircraft, International Harvester, Texas Instruments, Westinghouse, and Northrop Grumman. Many smaller firms have experimented with quality circles, too, as have such service-oriented institutions as hospitals and YMCAs.

Although all quality circles share certain common elements, programs may vary on a number of features. While there is little hard evidence to indicate exactly which details are critical to a quality circle's effectiveness, certain traits are characteristic of successful programs.[34] Chief among these is *commitment by top-level management* to the program. If top management does not fully endorse and support a circle program, the lack of enthusiasm will be detected and duplicated by others. As a result, the circle program will probably not receive the serious support it needs from lower-level supervisors. Second, successful programs are more likely to have *group facilitators*—usually senior workers rather than supervisors—*who have been specially trained* in both group relations and problem-solving strategies. Third, members of circles must be assured that they *will not lose their jobs or have their responsibilities reduced as a result of their suggestions*. Fourth, *recognition must be given* to individuals and circles for suggesting workable solutions to operational problems. At one organization, for example, a quality circle is awarded 10 percent of any dollar savings that result from its suggestions. Such monetary rewards are uncommon, however, as most organizations prefer to rely on psychological rewards to motivate participation.

The quality circle concept is not without its critics, however. Some critics question the real cost effectiveness of quality circles. They contend that since employees are not performing their normal duties while they meet in circles (most circles meet on company time) and since most circle suggestions generate only minor savings, it is difficult to prove that the savings gained from the groups' suggested improvements justify the time lost from work. Union representatives in particular have had mixed reactions to the quality circle concept. For example, leaders of the United Auto Workers are favorably inclined toward quality circles as long as the programs do not produce layoffs or increase the work pace. They look less favorably on the fact that most circles are not compensated for generating cost-saving solutions.

In addition, the motives of people who volunteer for quality circles are not fully understood. Some people who volunteer for the program may do so in order to get away from the assembly line and gain a sanctioned work break. Others may join merely to voice their frustrations and complain about their jobs rather than to offer constructive suggestions. Research that has focused on the attributes of quality circle volunteers suggests that circle participants are likely to be more highly educated, younger, in jobs of greater responsibility, and more satisfied with their jobs than are employees who show no interest in membership.[35] One study of the level of job satisfaction of quality circle members found an increase over several years. However, the level of member job satisfaction returned to the earlier, pre-circle level after three years.[36]

Because they are by definition voluntary, it is not possible to study circles in a rigorous scientific fashion. Some quality circle improvements may be due to nothing more than a Hawthorne effect (see Chapter 1). An additional concern relates to the longevity of quality circle programs. One review reported that nearly 75 percent of initially successful circle programs in the United States were no longer operating after only a few years.[37] Continuing interest in and support for circles may be difficult to sustain in many organizations. It is also possible that some of the attractiveness that has surrounded quality circles may be wearing off as firms recognize the limitations of the programs.

Self-Directed Work Teams

Perhaps one of the most exciting new developments in the area of employee motivation in recent years has been the emergence of self-directed work teams. In essence, a **self-directed work team (SDWT)** is a highly trained group of 6 to 18 employees that is fully responsible for creating a specified product.[38] Unlike the traditional view of an employee who has a narrowly defined set of responsibilities, each member of a team shares responsibility for performance. Team members are trained to perform a variety of cross-functional tasks in order to be interchangeable within the unit and provide assistance to others. Additionally, team members share information openly and participate in decision making. Team decisions typically cover domains once reserved for supervisors, such as setting priorities, production planning, and assigning work. Even interpersonal problems, such as excessive absenteeism or poor performance by a team member, are fair subjects for discussions at team meetings. It should be emphasized that SDWTs are truly "revolutionary" in their approach and go far beyond conventional work groups in terms of their role within an organization.

The allure of SDWTs stems from success stories that recount improved productivity coupled with reduced costs. One estimate is that a well-functioning system based on SDWT, compared to a traditionally run organization, can produce twice the output in one-quarter of the work space with one-third the workforce. Xerox Corporation plants that use SDWTs report 30 percent greater productivity than their conventionally run plants; productivity gains of 20 to 40 percent have been reported at General Motors plants; and Shenandoah Life reports a 50 percent increase in processing customer services with SDWTs while employing 10 percent fewer people.[39]

Although the notion of work groups certainly is not new, the beginnings of SDWTs can be traced to the early 1970s when several organizational "experiments" were undertaken. One of the first was at the Gaines Pet Food Facility in Topeka, Kansas. To combat "blue-collar blues" (the notion of worker alienation in manufacturing firms), General Foods established the pet foods facility based on the team concept. At the Topeka facility, employees rotated job assignments and met frequently to make joint, work-related decisions. The facility was highly successful and became a "showcase plant" visited by managers from around the globe.

At much the same time, Procter and Gamble (P&G) began a series of studies on new manufacturing techniques at its plants in Lima, Ohio, and Augusta, Georgia (where diaper and soap products were produced). Although the team-based studies were deliberately surrounded by a great deal of corporate secrecy, word eventually spread that significant, high levels of output were being achieved while producing costs were being reduced. Eventually, SDWTs spread to 18 P&G plants. Later, other large firms (such as Boeing, Caterpillar, and General Electric) adopted the SDWT approach. The 1990s witnessed the spread of the SDWT concept to firms outside the manufacturing sector. Because of the globe-spanning nature of corporate ownership and the sharing of information, SDWTs have become a worldwide phenomenon, with reports of SDWTs being installed in Russia, Eastern Europe, and Saudi Arabia.

The essential defining elements of SDWTs consist of team meetings, mandatory job rotation, skill-based pay, and increased training opportunities. At regular team meetings, members make decisions on performance-related issues as well as self-discipline issues (for example, dealing with a poor performer or a member who is frequently late to work). Leadership at these meetings is sometimes shared or rotated. In some instances, a team member is elected leader for a fixed period of time. The team leader does not make unilateral decisions, but instead facilitates discussion and consensus.

Mandatory job rotation is a key element of SDWTs. By rotating assignments, members gain knowledge of a broader range of tasks and are able to help out other team members who may need assistance. The team thus gains in versatility and flexibility. Because members become, in a sense, interchangeable as a result of shared knowledge, there is less "downtime" due to a single member lacking the know-how to remedy problems. Mandatory job rotation, which usually occurs at 6- or 12-month intervals, has the added advantage of eliminating "turf wars" that sometimes develop in work units. That is, no one "owns" a particularly enjoyable or cushy job, and everyone eventually spends some time doing the least enjoyable job in the unit. Because of rotation, no employee can obtain a permanent position that is removed from the work flow or that would provide a form of "early retirement with pay."

The compensation scheme for SDWTs also differs from traditional forms. Pay is skill-based in such systems. Employees move up the hourly- or salary-rate compensation ladder by demonstrating proficiency in a given task.

Employees thus have an incentive to learn a greater variety of tasks or skills in their work units. The employee benefits by gaining more marketable job skills and a sense of competency, while the organization gains by having a more flexible and more talented workforce. Because of the skill-based nature of the compensation system, employees welcome the opportunities provided by job rotation. In some SDWT systems, a gain-sharing program also provides bonuses to members of a department or plant for increased productivity.

In order to learn new skills, employees must spend more time in on-the-job training. When a person rotates into a new assignment, he or she must spend some time learning the ropes (often looking over the shoulder of another individual, asking questions, and trying out equipment). This added training requires that some additional slack be built into the unit to accommodate needed learning time. Typically, however, the gains in increased output and reduced costs more than compensate for the time lost by employees in a training phase. In addition, the opportunity to learn new skills tends to have a positive motivational effect, which also helps to make up for time lost due to training.

SDWTs are often introduced as part of a broader shift in organizational philosophy toward enhancing the quality of output or services. Because of global competition and a perception that levels of quality are not sufficient, some organizations have embraced the Total Quality Management perspective. **Total Quality Management (TQM)** is a set of principles that embodies a strong emphasis on establishing and maintaining a high level of quality. The key principles associated with TQM involve (1) getting it right the first time (that is, reducing errors by improved techniques and processes), (2) focusing on the customer or client (that is, being close to and understanding the needs of one's constituencies), (3) emphasizing continuous improvement (that is, making an emphasis on quality part of "the way we do things around here"), and (4) fostering mutual respect among coworkers (that is, eliminating fear based on hierarchical organizational designs and replacing that fear with autonomy and participation based on power-sharing).[40] SDWTs are seen as a vehicle for advancing a TQM philosophy in an organization. As the above points suggest, SDWTs are relevant to TQM as a device for instilling mutual respect through power sharing.

Consequences of SDWTs   Although the potential payoff for successfully implementing SDWTs is highly attractive, there are also some downside features to SDWTs. However, these potential problems can sometimes be ameliorated. Also, it should be understood that for every success story involving SDWTs, there may be a failed attempt at implementation. Sometimes even successful introductions of SDWTs did not occur on the first attempt, and the notion of learning from one's mistakes especially applied to introducing SDWTs.

A necessary consequence of implementing SDWTs is the elimination of the need for a number of supervisory positions. As noted earlier in the discussion on job redesign, fewer supervisors are required as employees take on more responsibility. Supervisors sense this likelihood and often offer resistance to the proposed introduction of SDWTs. Generally, after SDWTs are introduced supervisors are given different responsibilities. For example, they may become more involved in coordinating and integrating communications.[41] Also, former supervisors, who are retained as higher-level area managers whose jobs now entail coordinating team efforts, need to learn the new skills required for being facilitators and resource personnel, rather than acting as overseers who assign work, monitor production, and administer discipline. For some former supervisors, the transition can be difficult as it involves abandoning a set of hierarchical values for a set of more egalitarian values. It must be emphasized that SDWTs are rarely totally autonomous (that is, there is still a need for a level of supervision). However, the manager who oversees a set of teams and interacts with the teams' leaders does have a challenging task of balancing the need to give the team members sufficient autonomy, while being prepared to intervene if a team does not accept its responsibilities or conform to the organization's goals.

Another consequence of SDWTs is that the emerging, transformed organization is likely to be much "flatter," with fewer levels of administration and far fewer job titles. In some plants, the term *technician* is used in place of job titles. This term reflects the technical orientation of many jobs and the continual skill-learning aspect of these positions. Except for hat colors or other minor distinguishing features, differences among employees tend to be minimized (for example, there are often a common entrance and parking lot as well as a common cafeteria, rather than separate facilities for supervisors or managers).

A further necessary consequence of the introduction of SDWTs is the requirement of a sizable investment in training. Additional training staff and facilities are likely to be needed. Also, more attention to individual limitations in learning abilities may be warranted. Skills that are deficient in some individuals (for example, problem-solving techniques and interpersonal skills) may need to be taught by the firm in order to have the teams work efficiently. As a result, human resources development staff take on a more important role in firms that are committed to SDWTs.

Potential Problems and Criticisms of SDWTs   One of the more troubling problems for members of SDWTs occurs when they have learned all the tasks in their work units. An employee who has been in the unit for a relatively long time (more than six to ten years) may have learned, through job rotation, all of the jobs in the unit, and may have reached the maximum level of pay that is possible (sometimes termed *plant rate*). For employees who have "topped-out" by reaching plant rate, there are no new mountains to climb, and the psychological lift that came from relatively frequent pay boosts is no longer visible on the horizon. For such individuals, firms might suggest changing to a significantly different work unit, working on special projects, or pursuing formal education that would lead to a different career path. Often firms will offer to underwrite part of the educational expenses of employees who wish to seek additional formal education that may lead to another job. However, the preference is to support educational pursuits that may translate into a skill desired by the employer (for example, computer or office-related skills). As noted earlier, the introduction of a gain-sharing program can also help to maintain a sense of financial incentive.[42]

Another potential problem for SDWTs involves the unionized workforce. SDWTs have been introduced in unionized settings (with labor's agreement, of course). Although hard evidence is not available, it appears that SDWTs in unionized settings are far less productive than those in nonunionized settings. However, this may not be a fair comparison (SDWTs in unionized settings should probably be compared with those in other unionized settings). Despite the obstacles posed by being unionized, firms continue to **retrofit**—that is, to introduce SDWTs to existing workforces. A more common practice in recent years has been to begin afresh by establishing a new facility in a new location with a new work force. In such a setting, successful introduction of SDWTs has been reported to be far more likely (the Topeka Gaines Pet Food facility provides an example). This technique is termed establishing a **green-field site**—from, often literally, starting in an open field to build a brand-new facility based on SDWT principles.

It should be mentioned that even organizations that have successfully established SDWTs are not immune from being driven out of business. One firm, although operating quite successfully with SDWTs, went bankrupt because of a change in the price of raw materials and the inability to pay off a bank loan. In another instance, a high-level strategic decision was made to shift to a different market, and one extremely successful "showcase" SDWT was simply closed down. In short, a highly successful SDWT implementation, even when profitable, offers no guarantee of continued employment (although firms using SDWTs do strive to reduce layoffs in order to enhance employee loyalty and commitment).

Organized labor, understandably, has criticized the SDWT concept on the grounds that it eliminates long-established principles of seniority-based job assignments, puts supervisory responsibility on the shoulders of employees without paying supervisory wages, makes employees expendable by making them interchangeable, and reduces the size of needed workforces. Michael Parker and Jane Slaughter have drawn comparisons between SDWTs and traditional industrial supervision.[43] In their assessment, the labels may have changed, but the reality is still hierarchical and exploitive. For example, in traditional industrialist terminology:

> The foreman holds a meeting of his group and announces the week's productivity and scrap figures or discusses the latest safety memo. The foreman's "go-fer" takes care of vacation schedules and work gloves.

while in the more modern terminology:

> Hourly workers are organized into teams which meet with their adviser to discuss quality and work procedures. A team leader takes care of vacation scheduling and supplies.

Critics of the SDWT approach would also question whether it is ethical to try to build employee commitment in a calculated and deliberate manner.

Proponents of SDWTs would counter these arguments by pointing out that a fundamental difference in power-sharing exists in the SDWT-based system. The traditional industrialist view is based on a simple top-down, parent-to-child relationship, while the SDWT view is based on a cooperative, adult-to-adult relationship oriented toward collaborative problem solving. Moreover, SDWTs combine a pay-for-knowledge compensation scheme with ongoing opportunities for retraining. Additionally, the environment in which organizations must now operate requires that new forms of management–labor relations be devised, as the traditional form of confrontation-based management–labor relations no longer provides a sufficient base for global competition.

The ethical issue surrounding the deliberateness of efforts to build employee commitment is very much open to debate. Organizations that have workforces with high levels of commitment and loyalty have an advantage in competitive settings. Perhaps the key point lies in determining whether a given management is seeking to exploit its employees or to attain a level of organizational effectiveness that is mutually beneficial.

The Future of SDWTs   For the future, SDWTs are likely to spread to a greater variety of organizations (for example, not-for-profit and small firms). Many of the principles of SDWTs are easily transferable to nonmanufacturing settings. Also, it is likely that SDWTs will make the jump from rank-and-file operatives to office workers. At the Topeka pet food facility, for example, lower-level office positions have been rotated since the plant's creation. Upper-level positions, which require highly specialized training (for example, accounting and computer programming), are exempted from rotation.

Many observers of the SDWT movement predict that such programs will continue to gain acceptance and that SDWTs will likely replace quality circles at many firms. Viewed from an evolutionary perspective, quality circles may be seen as a transitional form of employee participation that will be supplanted by the stronger form of employee empowerment represented by SDWTs.[‡‡] Present estimates from surveys of the largest firms in North America and Europe show that 66 percent use quality circles, and 67 percent use SDWTs. It is interesting to speculate on what may be the next phase in the evolution of labor-management relations, or the next fad in employee motivation. Certainly, the trend through the 20th century and into the 21st century has been toward greater employee empowerment. Whether the future will take us toward a form of still greater organizational democracy (that is, greater power sharing and greater autonomy) or a return to a more hierarchical form is not as yet foreseeable.

SUMMARY

1. *Distinguish between extrinsic and intrinsic rewards.* Extrinsic rewards come from sources outside of the individual, while intrinsic rewards are self-administered.

2. *Explain why incentive plans have lost popularity.* Incentive plans have run into problems because they may foster an adversarial attitude in employees; because they can lead to a sense of class distinctions between workers and managers; and because of the impact of societal changes, such as the increasingly interdependent nature of jobs and workers' desires for more challenging and meaningful work.

[‡‡]Work teams in Western industrialized nations have tended to emphasize power sharing and active participation in decision making, whereas teams in East Asia (for example, Japan) have retained a more deferential, or obedient, posture with respect to management ranks. Some observers have suggested that this difference has the potential to produce greater innovation, more creative solutions, and stronger commitment in Western teams, where the best ideas must stand on their own merits, regardless of their source. As yet, there is little firm evidence that clearly demonstrates the superiority of either approach.

3. *Describe three attributes of goals that are important for improving performance.* Three goal attributes that are especially important for improving performance are (a) the specificity of the goal, or the preciseness with which a goal or objective is stated; (2) the difficulty of the goal; and (3) the acceptance of the goal by employees.

4. *Describe management-by-objectives and some of its advantages and possible problems.* MBO is a process in which employees participate with management in setting goals for the employee's performance. After an established period of time, employee and supervisor meet again to review the employee's performance based on the goals. Advantages are that goals are specific and measurable and that MBO programs have the potential to improve performance. However, problems can arise from lack of top-level support, management's discomfort with employee participation, personality conflicts between employee and manager, and the potential for neglect of the qualitative aspects of performance.

5. *Give some examples of the power of self-fulfilling prophecies.* Children develop in response to the expectations of parents and teachers. In one study, children performed in school according to their teachers' beliefs about their aptitude. Similarly, a group of men in a welding course performed in accordance with their teacher's expectations. Soldiers labeled as having high potential displayed superior performance. In all these studies, the labels were assigned randomly. A bank run is another example of the power of expectations.

6. *Describe some ways of constructively managing self-fulfilling prophecies.* People can manage SFPs by being more sensitive to how others perceive their behavior. They can also pay more attention to controlling their behavior and speech so as to communicate positive expectations to everyone. Displaying enthusiasm for the group's goals is another way to manage SFPs constructively, as is attempting to help poorer performers.

7. *Describe methods of job redesign used to reduce worker discontent.* Some methods of job redesign are job enlargement, which increases the variety of an employee's activities; job rotation, which rotates personnel in various tasks; and job enrichment, which is an expansion of an employee's autonomy and self-regulation in a job. Other methods include flextime, modified workweeks, and telecommuting.

8. *List the job characteristics that enhance a sense of the meaningfulness of one's work, a sense of responsibility, and knowledge of the results of one's work.* The job characteristics that enhance a sense of meaningfulness are skill variety, task identity, and task significance. A sense of responsibility is enhanced by autonomy, while knowledge of results is enhanced by feedback from the job.

9. *Describe the essential elements of quality circles.* Quality circles are employee committees that meet regularly to discuss production and service-related problems. Members, who volunteer for quality circles, are given training in problem-solving techniques and encouraged to offer solutions and monitor their outcomes. For quality circles to be effective, there must be (1) support from top-level management, (2) group facilitator support, (3) guarantees of job stability, and (4) recognition for quality circle contributions.

10. *Explain how self-directed work teams operate, and identify major consequences and problems of such teams.* Self-directed work teams are groups of 6 to 18 employees who have a significant responsibility for delivery of a product or services. In addition to frequent meetings to discuss a range of work-related issues, teams engage in mandatory job rotation and frequent retraining. Compensation in such teams is based on pay-for-knowledge. SDWTs require fewer supervisors and produce flatter organization structures. In order to produce a multiskilled workforce, greater investment is required in human resources training. Potential problems include "topping-out" on compensation ladders; and resistance from continuing, especially unionized, employees and first-line supervisors.

KEY TERMS

Extrinsic reward
Intrinsic reward
Gain sharing
Goal specificity
Goal difficulty
Goal acceptance
Management-by-objectives (MBO)
Self-fulfilling prophecy (SFP)
Employee empowerment
Job enlargement
Job rotation
Job enrichment

Job characteristics theory
Job diagnostic survey
Employee growth-need strength
Flextime
Modified workweek
Telecommuting
Quality Circles
Self-directed work team (SDWT)
Total Quality Management (TQM)
Retrofit
Green-field site

CRITICAL INCIDENT

Is Job Redesign Needed?

Healthcare America, Inc., is a large health insurance company that operates in 46 states. At its corporate headquarters, there is a great deal of reliance on a word processing department. There are 22 people working in this department, with one supervisor and an assistant supervisor. They type a wide variety of documents that are supplied by the various departments. Some of the work involves forms and letters, while other work centers on lengthy manuscripts. Most of the work is performed against a deadline.

The work is given to the individual typist by the supervisor. The supervisor attempts to equally distribute the work and monitor progress. The supervisor also checks to make sure everything is in order before giving it to the typist. If it is not, it is sent back to the originator.

Because of the importance surrounding the exactness of the work, completed documents are sent to proofreaders for review. These people then forward the documents or return them for corrections. However, many complaints are still received about an excessive amount of errors and deadlines not being met. In addition, the department has experienced high absenteeism and turnover.

As a consultant, you have been asked to analyze this situation and offer some recommendations.

1. What do you believe is causing the problems in this department? Why?
2. Consider redesigning the job of the word processor/typist according to the principles of job enlargement and job enrichment.
3. What are the advantages and disadvantages of each approach?

Source: Written by Bruce Kemelgor, University of Louisville; used by permission.

EXPERIENTIAL EXERCISE

Goal Setting and Performance

This activity is designed to help you understand and examine the relationship between the process of setting goals and the resulting performance of an individual in an organization. To the extent that the process of goal setting contributes to organizational behavior, this activity seeks to have you analyze the methods used by your manager to use objectives in relation to your job.

1. Think of your present job or a job you held recently. If you have not been employed, use your "job" as a student and consider one of your instructors as the manager. The following statements refer to that job and to the objectives associated with it. Please read each statement carefully and then circle the appropriate number indicating how true or untrue you believe each statement to be.

	Definitely Not True	Generally Not True	Slightly Not True	Uncertain	Slightly True	Generally True	Definitely True
1. Management encourages employees to define job objectives.	−3	−2	−1	0	1	2	3
2. If I achieve my objectives, I receive adequate recognition from my supervisor.	−3	−2	−1	0	1	2	3
3. My objectives are clearly stated with respect to the results expected.	−3	−2−	−1	0	1	2	3
4. I have the support I need to accomplish my objectives.	−3	−2	−1	0	1	2	3
5. Achieving my objectives increases my chances for promotion.	−3	−2	−1	0	1	2	3
6. My supervisor dictates my job objectives to me.	−3	−2	−1	0	1	2	3
7. I need more feedback on whether I'm achieving my objectives.	−3	−2	−1	0	1	2	3
8. My supervisor will "get on my back" if I fail to achieve my objectives.	−3	−2	−1	0	1	2	3
9. My job objectives are very challenging.	−3	−2	−1	0	1	2	3
10. Management wants to know whether I set objectives for my job.	−3	−2	−1	0	1	2	3
11. My supervisor will compliment me if I achieve my job objectives.	−3	−2	−1	0	1	2	3

12. My objectives are very ambiguous and unclear.	−3	−2	−1	0	1	2	3
13. I lack the authority to accomplish my objectives.	−3	−2	−1	0	1	2	3
14. Achievement of objectives is rewarded with higher pay.	−3	−2	−1	0	1	2	3
15. My supervisor encourages me to establish my own objectives.	−3	−2	−1	0	1	2	3
16. I always have knowledge of my progress toward my objectives.	−3	−2	−1	0	1	2	3
17. My supervisor will reprimand me if I'm not making progress toward my objectives.							
18. My objectives seldom require my full interest and effort.	−3	−2	−1	0	1	2	3
19. Management makes it clear that defining job objectives is favorably regarded.	−3	−2	−1	0	1	2	3
20. My supervisor gives me more recognition when I achieve my objectives.	−3	−2	−1	0	1	2	3
21. My objectives are very concrete.	−3	−2	−1	0	1	2	3
22. I have sufficient resources to achieve my objectives.	−3	−2	−1	0	1	2	3
23. My pay is more likely to be increased if I achieve my objectives.	−3	−2	−1	0	1	2	3
24. My supervisor has more influence than I do in setting my objectives.	−3	−2	−1	0	1	2	3
25. I wish I had better knowledge of whether I'm achieving my objectives.	−3	−2	−1	0	1	2	3
26. If I fail to meet my objectives, my supervisor will reprimand me.	−3	−2	−1	0	1	2	3
27. Attaining my objectives requires all my skills and know-how.	−3	−2	−1	0	1	2	3

2. For each of the nine subscales (A through I), compute a total score by summing the answers to the appropriate questions. Be sure to subtract minus scores.

A. Question	B. Question	C. Question
1. + ( )	3. + ( )	6. + ( )
10. + ( )	12. + ( )	15. + ( )
19. + ( )	21. + ( )	24. + ( )
Total	Total	Total

D. Question	E. Question	F. Question
4. + ( )	7. + ( )	9. + ( )
13. + ( )	16. + ( )	18. + ( )
22. + ( )	25. + ( )	27. + ( )
Total	Total	Total

G. Question	H. Question	I. Question
5. + ( )	2. + ( )	8. + ( )
14. + ( )	11. + ( )	17. + ( )
23. + ( )	20. + ( )	26. + ( )
Total	Total	Total

3. Plot the score from each of the subscales on the graph below. Use an X to indicate the appropriate scale value. Next, connect the nine subscale values by drawing a line from value A to value I. This provides you with a profile of your responses.

Subscale

A	−9	−7	−5	−3	−1	+1	+3	+5	+7	+9
B	−9	−7	−5	−3	−1	+1	+3	+5	+7	+9
C	−9	−7	−5	−3	−1	+1	+3	+5	+7	+9
D	−9	−7	−5	−3	−1	+1	+3	+5	+7	+9
E	−9	−7	−5	−3	−1	+1	+3	+5	+7	+9
F	−9	−7	−5	−3	−1	+1	+3	+5	+7	+9
G	−9	−7	−5	−3	−1	+1	+3	+5	+7	+9
H	−9	−7	−5	−3	−1	+1	+3	+5	+7	+9
I	−9	−7	−5	−3	−1	+1	+3	+5	+7	+9

4. Answer the following question: How satisfied are you with this job?
   a. Highly satisfied
   b. Satisfied
   c. It's OK
   d. Somewhat dissatisfied
   e. Very dissatisfied

5. Form small groups based on your (honest) response to this question. As a group, address the following questions:
   a. Is there a common pattern in your questionnaire responses?
   b. Do certain subscale values (A through I) suggest appropriate managerial use of objectives? Which one(s)?
   c. Are certain subscales representative of the characteristics of objectives? Which one(s)?

6. Remain in your small group. Your instructor will ask each group for a representative to describe its predominate profile. Look for similarities among and differences between the group responses.

7. What do you believe accounts for these differences? What characteristics of objectives and the managerial use of objectives contribute to satisfaction within organizations?

Source: Based in part on P. Lorenzi, H.P. Sims, Jr., and E.A. Slusher, "Goal Setting, Performance and Satisfaction: A Behavioral Demonstration," *Exchange: The Organizational Behavior Teaching Journal* 7, no. 1 (1982): 38–42.

PART TWO
Interpersonal Processes

6 Power and Politics

The secret of success is sincerity. Once you can fake that, you've got it made.

—Jean Giraudoux

To be clever enough to gain real power over others, one must be dumb enough to want it.

—G.K. Chesterton

I don't want any yes-men around me. I want everyone to tell me the truth, even if it costs them their jobs.

—Samuel Goldwyn

Learning Objectives

After studying this chapter, you should be able to:

1. Define and distinguish power, authority, influence, and politics.
2. Identify and describe three primary influence processes.
3. List and define five bases of power.
4. Describe some differences between formal and informal power.
5. Identify several political tactics, including devious political tactics and political blunders.
6. Explain several techniques for coping with organizational politics.
7. Cite evidence that the predisposition to obey authority is strong.

Pals with the Boss: Hazardous to Your Career?

Consider the case of Allison P. Burns, a 42-year-old, $140,000-a-year executive for a large midwestern consumer products company. "No one likes the teacher's pet. My colleagues turned against me because I had special ties with the boss." Ms. Burns and her husband often dined with the CEO and his wife. She also played golf with him and his friends. Colleagues and subordinates stopped trusting her. Coworkers tried to sabotage her projects and showed little support for her initiatives. Colleagues did not share crucial data with her for fear she would prematurely pass it on to the CEO.

"It became impossible for me to perform my job. Nearly everyone dreams of being friends with the boss. But my reality turned out to be a nightmare," says Ms. Burns. She still reports to her old boss even though she was transferred to another division, but she no longer brags about socializing with him. The moral of this story, and numerous ones similar to it, is clearly, "Being your boss's pal may be hazardous to your career."

In the past, friendships with bosses could move managers to the top corporate ranks and onto the executive floors of corporations. But in those days, management ranks were larger, companies were more paternalistic, and managers typically were less suspicious and anxious about their future. In the downsized, right-sized cutthroat business environment, one can not succeed by alienating the survivors. Good relationships are critical to success, but are not to be flaunted or exploited. According to Ingrid Murro, president of Murro Consulting, a Phoenix-based outplacement and career-strategy firm, "It's equally important to build solid relationships with your peers and people who directly report to you. In a team environment, you can't be effective if no one trusts or respects you."

Other problems can occur. Take the case of a 25-year-old manager in a high-tech firm who decided to become friendlier with her boss, so she spent time joking around with him. She lost promotions and professional stature because the boss saw her as "just a friend and not a capable employee."

"What happens if your boss gets laid off?" asks Leonard Felder, a Los Angeles psychologist and career counselor. "You're left with no one to support you." If your friendship with the boss falters, it may be difficult to repair the damage done to your reputation.

If you are in a friendship with your boss, remember that there are boundaries you may be over-stepping. You run the risk of losing the respect of your colleagues, as well as that of your boss. Anything that compromises your professional relationships probably will damage your career. Always keep in mind that a career, just like a reputation, takes a lot of careful effort to build, but can be destroyed in the blink of an eye, or more than likely, by poor judgment.

Source: J. Lopez, "Being Your Boss's Pal Can Be Hazardous to Your Career," Managing Your Career, *The Wall Street Journal*, June 8, 1994.

At one time or another, all of us have resisted attempts to be controlled or influenced by others. Likewise, each of us has attempted to control or influence those around us. Control—by others and of others—lies at the very heart of organizational relationships. This give-and-take among people is responsible for much of what is actually accomplished in a work unit, as well as for a fair amount of social friction.

Distinguishing Power and Influence

Power is an essential feature of a manager's role. Without some degree of power, a manager would find it difficult to direct the efforts of subordinates. Thus, power underlies a manager's effectiveness. Subordinates also possess forms and degrees of power. For example, subordinates can control the work flow or withhold support from their manager. Therefore, to some extent, each member of an organization possesses power.

Because power is intangible, it is very difficult to define clearly and precisely. Also, our language has several similar terms that we tend to confuse with *power*, such as *authority* and *influence*. In the interest of clarity, we shall define **power** as the ability to change the behavior of others. It is the ability to cause others to perform actions that they might not otherwise perform.[1]

Power is not always legitimate. Therefore, we speak of **authority** as the *right* to try to change or direct others. Authority includes the notion of legitimacy. It is the right to influence others in the pursuit of common goals that are agreed upon by various parties. Power, in contrast, does not always pursue common goals and may, at times, be clearly directed to pursuing only a single individual's goals.

Another term, **influence,** is also frequently used when discussing the notion of power. Influence tends to be subtler, broader, and more general than power. Although both influence and power can be defined as the ability to change the behavior of others, power embodies the ability to do so with regularity and ease. Influence is weaker and less reliable than power. Also, power rests on a number of specific sources or foundations, which will be examined in a subsequent section of this chapter. Influence relies on particular tactics and often employs face-to-face interactions. Thus, the exercise of influence tends to be more subtle than the exercise of power.

Interpersonal Influence Processes

In an important article, Kelman distinguished among three primary reasons for an individual to yield to another person's attempt to be directive.[2] If an employee accepts a manager's influence attempt because the employee believes he will be rewarded or avoid being punished, this response is one of

compliance. For example, an employee may skip lunch in order to finish typing a report for a supervisor. The employee may actually hope to receive an expression of appreciation from the supervisor or may merely wish to avoid the hard feelings that will result if the report is not finished on time. The employee's behavior is strictly motivated by concern with rewards and punishments. Supervisors who strive for consistent compliance must (1) be certain that they can in fact deliver rewards or punishments and (2) be in a position to frequently monitor their subordinates' behavior.

A second influence process, **identification,** occurs when one person follows another's direction because of a desire to establish or maintain a personally satisfying relationship. When a subordinate admires his manager, seeks his approval, and perhaps tries to imitate him, we infer that the subordinate has a strong desire to identify with the manager. One example of this process occurs when a junior executive who greatly admires the CEO of his organization espouses the CEO's philosophy and beliefs when addressing the employees in his own work unit.

In both compliance and identification, the performance of an action in itself is not necessarily personally satisfying. Rather, the action may be due to a desire for specific outcomes (compliance) or an attraction to the source of influence (identification).

Sometimes employees' actions stem from a third reason; the belief that the behavior is congruent with their value systems. **Internalization** occurs when an employee accepts an influence attempt because he or she believes that the resulting behavior is correct and appropriate. For instance, assume that a high-level executive announces that the organization is participating in a charitable fund-raising campaign. Some of the divisional managers may actively encourage subordinates to contribute to the fund because they strongly believe in the goals of the charity. These managers are not motivated by threats or rewards or admiration for their superior but rather by a personal commitment to a set of values.

The Five Bases of Power

Who gets what, when, and how are important concerns for every member of an organization. People at all levels are interested in and affected by the acquisition and distribution of rewards and resources. Of course, power plays a central role in such allocation processes. To explain how power operates, we will first examine the five distinct sources of power proposed by John French and Bertram Raven: reward power, coercive power, legitimate power, referent power, and expert power.[3]

Reward Power   **Reward power** is the ability to determine who will receive particular rewards. As long as the rewards are valued, a person who is able to distribute or withhold them can enjoy strong power over others' behavior. Granting promotions, giving raises, and conferring preferred job assignments are some typical rewards most managers can control. Unfortunately, this is not always the case. For example, when a workforce is unionized, salary increases and job assignments are based more on seniority and the specifics of a labor contract than on the judgment of a manager or supervisor. As noted in our discussion of motivation (Chapter 4), the relationship between performance and rewards should always be clear. When a manager lacks the ability to administer both extrinsic and intrinsic rewards, it becomes extremely difficult to direct a subordinate's behavior. Reward power gives a manager a distinct advantage in obtaining desired ends from his or her work group.

Coercive Power   If reward power can be termed "the carrot," then coercive power is "the stick." **Coercive power** stems from the capacity to produce fear in others. The threat of punishment can be a strong means of invoking compliance. The most obvious examples of punishments are demotions, salary cuts, suspension, removal of such perquisites as a company car or an expense account, and dismissal. However, coercive power can also be more subtle. For example, criticism and the denial of emotional support and friendship may also be effective forms of coercion.

The application of coercive power requires good social judgment. In some instances, a manager is actually expected to be coercive—as when a subordinate is extremely unproductive or interferes with the productivity of others. In such a situation, other employees and managers will rightly expect the supervisor to take firm action.

On the other hand, a manager must be careful when applying coercive power. If he or she is too heavy-handed and indiscriminately inflicts punishment on all employees, morale and productivity are likely to suffer. Such a manager may find that the unit's turnover rate is very high as people seek employment elsewhere. In addition, injured employees may retaliate by sabotaging the unit's operations or withholding useful suggestions for improving the unit's performance.

Despite its potentially negative effects, coercive power underlies much of the routine compliance that occurs in organizations. Decisions to arrive at work on time, meet deadlines, and so forth are often largely due to fear of being fired, ridiculed, or reprimanded. Rightly or wrongly, coercive power is frequently used in most organizations.

Legitimate Power   **Legitimate power** stems from the willingness of others to accept an individual's direction. They feel an obligation to follow the individual's lead and submit to his authority. There are two sources of legitimate power. The first is social conditioning: From early childhood, people are conditioned to accept the direction of authority figures. They learn that teachers and crossing guards, as well as foremen and managers, have the right to lead or direct others. The second source of legitimate power is designation: A person can gain power by being designated an authority figure by someone who already possesses legitimate authority. For example, the president of a company may assign a vice president the authority to make important decisions on the company's behalf. The president thus gives the vice president legitimate power to act as his representative and exercise authority accordingly.

Legitimate power can be effective only if it is accepted by the people it is intended to control. If the people withdraw their support from the system that is the basis of power, the power ceases to exist. Such withdrawals of support occur in revolutions, when ruling classes and their social systems are overthrown, and in riots, when a spontaneous but limited rebellion is made against authority.

Referent Power   People with attractive personalities or other special qualities possess a form of power. Their appearance, poise, interpersonal style, or values can inspire admiration and cause others to identify with them. The resulting ability to influence behavior is called **referent power.** It is often easy to identify an individual who possesses such power. For example, most people would agree that popular athletes and entertainers—such as Michael Jordan, John Travolta, and Oprah Winfrey—have this attribute. However, it is extremely difficult to define exactly what gives these people their charisma. Usually, vigor and the appearance of success play important roles. But other characteristics that contribute to referent power can be very difficult to pinpoint (consider, for example, that Adolf Hitler was judged to be charismatic in the eyes of his countrymen).

Referent power derives from people's desire to identify with the qualities of an attractive individual. Advertising that uses a celebrity to endorse a product is based on referent power, since the sponsor hopes that the audience will buy the product in an attempt to imitate the celebrity's behavior and attitudes.

Expert Power   Individuals with **expert power** are able to direct others because they are perceived as knowledgeable or talented in a given area. Most of us readily seek and follow the advice of experts, such as our family physician or athletic coach. So too are we likely to follow the directions of a coworker who is seen as having expertise in our field of work. This form of power is usually limited to a fairly narrow and specific realm, however, and does not spread to other areas of social interaction.

Most subordinates presume that their superiors possess expert power in the form of understanding all jobs in the work unit. Generally, greater levels of experience and job-relevant knowledge do give a manager an edge in expertise. However, in highly technical job settings, it may happen that some subordinates have more expert knowledge about certain aspects of their jobs than do their managers. In fact, some managers may be highly dependent on the technical expertise of their subordinates in order to successfully manage their work units. In such a situation, expert power can lead to an atypical reversal of the usual manager–subordinate relationship.

Interplay among the Power Bases

A manager can possess each of the five sources of power to varying degrees, and his or her use of one power base can affect the strength of another. For example, a person can gain greater legitimacy by being promoted to a higher-level position. Of course, a position of greater legitimate power usually entails more opportunities to use rewards and coercion. The exercise of coercion, however, could reduce the manager's referent power because coercion tends to produce immediate compliance but may have negative side effects.

Above all, the manager should bear in mind that the tendency to use power can lead to greater effectiveness, while the failure to use power can have the opposite effect. Managers who exercise power with some frequency can be counted on to continue such behavior in future settings and are, therefore, given greater deference by subordinates. More passive managers may have difficulty if they suddenly decide to use their power because their subordinates will have become accustomed to their lack of assertiveness.

TABLE 6.1   *A Comparison of Two Major Views of Power and Influence*

Interpersonal Influence Processes of Kelman		Power Bases of French and Raven
Compliance (reward-based)	is related to	Reward Power
Compliance (punishment-based)	is related to	Coercive Power
Identification	is related to	Referent Power
Internalization	is related to	Legitimate Power and Referent Power

Distinctions can be drawn among the five power bases. Expert and referent power bases are more informal in nature, while legitimate, reward, and coercive power bases are more formal. The informal power bases have a greater capacity to affect overall employee satisfaction and performance. The formal power bases, in contrast, have potentially greater impact on immediate behavior. Although formal power can elicit a quick response from an employee, it will not necessarily produce agreement and commitment. For example, a worker may comply with a manager's order but still resent having been coerced.

Many centuries ago, the Italian philosopher Machiavelli contended that people who have formal power tend to remain in their positions of authority longer than people who rely on informal power. This observation makes some sense in that the informal bases of power can be more easily eroded, since they depend on people's perceptions. For example, a manager may lose his expertise due to changes in technology or his appeal may diminish following a series of unpopular actions or personnel changes. While expert power can be regained through technical training, there are no surefire ways of increasing referent power.

In general, informal power resides in the personal characteristics of the manager, whereas formal power resides in the position itself. It can be forcefully argued, however, that all sources of power can really be reduced to a single category: control over reinforcers. As shown in Chapter 3, the most effective way to control others' behavior is to control when and how they receive reinforcement.

Politics: The Facts of Organizational Life

The terms *politics* and *power* are sometimes used interchangeably. Though they are related, they are nonetheless distinct notions. **Organizational politics** can be defined as "those activities taken within organizations to acquire, develop, and use power and other resources to obtain one's preferred outcomes in a situation in which there is uncertainty or [disagreement] about choices."[4] In a sense, the study of organizational politics constitutes the study of power in action. It may also be said that politics involves the playing out of power and influence.

The word *politics* has a somewhat negative connotation. It suggests that someone is attempting to use means or to gain ends that are not sanctioned by the organization. Actually, political behavior, as we've defined it, is quite neutral. Similarly, power is not inherently negative. Whether a person views power and politics as unsavory depends on a number of considerations, most important perhaps being where the individual stands on a specific issue in a given situation. Nonetheless, most managers are reluctant to admit to the political character of their own work settings.

A further point is that all members of an organization may exhibit political behavior. In our previous discussion of power, we took a fairly formal and traditional approach to the topic of influence. Thus, we looked at power from the perspective of a supervisor or manager who directs others. Yet, in the area of politics, everyone is a player. Subordinates, as well as their managers, can engage in the give-and-take of organizational politics.

Political Tactics

Several authors have identified a variety of political tactics used by employees at virtually all levels.[5] In this section, we will examine a number of these activities.

Ingratiation   This tactic involves giving compliments to or doing favors for superiors or coworkers. Most people have a difficult time rejecting the positive advances of others. Ingratiation usually works as a tactic insofar as the target often feels positive toward the source even if the ingratiation attempt is fairly blatant and transparent (see Table 6.2).

In the behavioral sciences, the notion of "social reciprocity" has been offered to help explain the process of ingratiation. In social reciprocity, there is a feeling of a social obligation to repay the positive actions of others with similar actions. For example, if someone pays you a compliment, there is a strong expectation that you should respond with a compliment of your own. If you fail to do so, you may be judged as being rude. Similarly, ingratiation involves giving positive strokes to a person with the expectation that he or she will feel obligated to return them in some form.

Forming Coalitions and Networks   Another political tactic consists of befriending important people. These people may not be in positions of any obvious political value. However, their jobs may provide them with information that could be useful to have. Some people find that forming friendships with people in upper-level management can help them gain access to important information. They may also find that by being on good terms with their boss's secretary, they can sometimes gain inside information and easier access to the boss.

Impression Management   A simple tactic that virtually everyone uses from time to time is the management of their outward appearance and style. Generally, most organizations prefer a particular image that consists of being loyal, attentive, honest, neatly groomed, sociable, and so forth. By deliberately trying to exhibit this preferred image, an individual can make a positive impression on influential members of the organization.

TABLE 6.2   *How Ingratiating Are You?*

Indicate whether you often engage in each of the following behaviors:

Yes	No	
____	____	1. Express admiration to your boss on his/her achievements, no matter how little you really care about them.
____	____	2. Go out of your way to do favors (e.g., run errands) for your boss.
____	____	3. Laugh heartily at your boss's jokes, even though you don't find them to be funny.
____	____	4. Compliment your boss on his/her appearance.
____	____	5. Smile frequently, and express enthusiasm and interest about your boss's ideas.
____	____	6. Praise your boss to others when he/she is present.
____	____	7. Only disagree with your boss on trivial issues, and always agree on critical issues.

The greater your agreement with the above items (and the more your peers agree that the items describe you), the more likely you are to be engaging in the political tactic of ingratiation.

Source: Based on items developed by K. Kumar and M. Beyerlein in "Construction and Validation of an Instrument for Measuring Ingratiatory Behaviors in Organizational Settings." *Journal of Applied Psychology 76* (1991): 619–627.

Information Management   A further tactic consists of managing the information that is shared with others. The nature, as well as the timing, of information given out can have strong effects on others' conduct. Releasing good or bad news when it is likely to have its fullest impact can greatly promote one person's self-interest or defeat the hopes of others. Similarly, an individual can ask for information (such as sales data or a production report) when it is most likely to make things appear particularly good or bad. People who play the information management game are not likely to lie or spread misinformation, however, because their future credibility would be jeopardized. Instead, they rely on the carefully planned release of valid information to obtain their ends.

Promote the Opposition   It may sound strange, but one way to eliminate opposition is to aid political rivals. For example, it is possible to eliminate a political rival by helping that person become so successful that he or she is transferred to a desirable position someplace else in the organization. Recommending a rival for a new assignment or even a promotion within another division of the organization can make one's own work life easier.

Pursue Line Responsibility   Within virtually every organization, some positions are more closely tied to the primary mission of the organization; these jobs are called line positions. They are at the very heart of the organization. People who occupy support positions include engineering, manufacturing, and sales in a customer-oriented firm. People in departments such as public relations, market research, and personnel are usually in staff positions. While staff people may come to wield great power within their own territories, it is the line people who usually "call the shots" on major issues. Line people not only make the more important decisions within the organization, they are also more likely to be promoted to top-level executive positions. In many organizations, there is a preferred department of origin and career path for top-level managers. These are usually line positions. Therefore, one way to gain influence within an organization is to be assigned initially to, or be transferred to, a line position. It will often provide more visibility, influence, and upward mobility.

Devious Political Tactics

Some political tactics are quite honest in nature. For example, accumulating seniority, providing copies of your accomplishments to your boss, and hitching your wagon to yourself are respectable means for gaining influence.* Some other tactics, however, are difficult to defend on moral grounds. In the interest of self-defense, it is worth examining several of these devious political tactics.[6]

Take No Prisoners   Sometimes it is necessary to do something unpopular or distasteful, such as demote or transfer someone or announce pay cuts. During corporate takeovers, many unpopular actions may be necessary. As a result, political enemies are likely to be made. One tactic for dealing with this potential problem is to ruthlessly eliminate *all* individuals who may resent your past actions by having them fired or transferred.

Divide and Conquer   This tactic involves creating a feud among two or more people so that they will be continually off balance and thus unable to mount an attack against you. This is a very old idea that is still practiced in some work settings. An unscrupulous individual who employs this tactic usually encourages bickering between possible rivals by spreading rumors or promoting competition between subordinates or factions. This is a risky tactic, however, as the opponents may eventually compare notes and conclude that someone else is really responsible for creating and maintaining their bad feelings.

Exclude the Opposition   Another devious tactic involves keeping rivals away from important meetings and social occasions. This can be done simply by scheduling important affairs when the opposition is out of town (on vacation or a business trip) or attending another meeting. With the opposition absent, it is possible to influence decision making or to take credit for a rival's efforts.

Political Blunders

Although certain tactics can promote desired ends, others can be costly political mistakes. Among the most common are violating the chain of command, losing your cool, saying no to top management, upstaging your supervisor, and challenging cherished beliefs. These activities constitute serious political blunders or mistakes.

---

*Pure and simple performance remains an essential ingredient of a successful career in virtually all fields of endeavor.

Violating Chain of Command   Occasionally, a person will feel that it is his duty to see his boss's boss, either to complain about his treatment at the hands of his own boss or to serve as an informant. A person may even feel that such an "end run" is justified because he is fervently convinced of the rightness of his position. However, going over the boss's head is often a very strong organizational taboo. Generally, it is expected that an employee will ask the boss's permission before seeing his superior on any matter.

Losing Your Cool   Throwing temper tantrums and acting aggressively toward others are often seen as acceptable and sometimes effective tactics in settings such as sports events. But in office settings, these tactics do not work well at all. Fist pounding and snide remarks usually earn a person a reputation for being hard to deal with, a label that can be extremely difficult to overcome. One devious twist on this tactic is to goad a person who tends to be acerbic and aggressive into displaying these tendencies at the wrong times. In this way, such a person's peers help him or her to commit political suicide.

Saying No to Top Management   One of the surest ways to stop your own career progress is to reject a request from top-level management. Instead of feeling fortunate to be selected for an assignment, some individuals believe that they are overburdened and that they are being "dumped on," or that they can afford to defy top management because they are indispensable. This represents poor judgment on two counts. First, people in the lower ranks of an organization are rarely indispensable. Second, if workers are overburdened, they should explain the situation to the manager and try to arrange for additional help.

Upstaging Your Supervisor   Generally speaking, one should avoid publicly criticizing others. For example, it is not considered appropriate for a supervisor to criticize a subordinate in public view. However, the reverse is also true. A subordinate should refrain from implicitly criticizing the boss by upstaging him or her. Upstaging often takes the form of bragging about one's own accomplishments or claiming credit for a unit's success.

Challenging Cherished Beliefs   In many firms, there are a number of cherished beliefs about the nature of the organization, and it is generally considered "poor form" to criticize or challenge such folklore within earshot of company loyalists. Examples of such fond beliefs include "This organization is the best in its field," "Our founder was (or is) an outstanding individual," and "People who leave our organization are people that we are better off without." To be sure, all people are entitled to their own opinions, but it can be politically foolish to engage in an open debate about the truth of certain widely held beliefs.

Coping with Organizational Politics

Political gamesmanship, when carried to the extreme, has many dysfunctional effects: Morale is weakened, victors and victims are created, and energy and time are spent on planning attacks and counterattacks instead of on productivity. Thus, combating politics must be part of a manager's job.

An Inside Look
The Subversive Subordinate

Just when you've survived attacks from the executive suite and dodged salvos at your career from your rivals, a new threat to your upward corporate mobility rears its head: the "subversive subordinate." Learning to recognize these employees and knowing how to deal with them are "must have" skills to protect your career.

Subversive subordinates can run the range from fairly obvious to virtually invisible. The obvious ones may be those people who sought an executive's job (or your job) and did not get it, or are extremely loyal to a losing candidate. These people must be identified quickly and tracked to determine their allegiance.

The virtually invisible ones may be the bigger risk; not only do you not know who they are, the damage they do may never overtly surface. Says New York executive coach Dee Soder, "Managers should regularly size up employees by asking: Does this worker respect me and come to me for advice on big and little matters? Does he or she ask whether my name should be on certain work, or give a 'heads up' on things I might want to know about? If you consis-

tently answer 'no,' that person might be working against your best interests."

A third subversive to your career might just be you! It is easy for managers to misinterpret transgressions in office etiquette as a conspiracy. And some managers can inadvertently (or overtly) encourage subversion by mistreating their employees.

To head off bigger problems, address subversive acts quickly, clearly, and consistently before they grow and become unmanageable. If a subordinate desires your job, identify the skills that made you the obvious choice and offer to mentor the person to possibly become your successor, but on one condition—the subordinate must support you. You can also groom him or her for a job in another department or division. "By helping a subordinate move on, a manager can turn an enemy into an ally. A manager's job is more secure when he or she treats people as partners and allies," says Wayne Baker, a professor of business policy at the University of Chicago.

Source: I. Rigden, "Look Out Below for Deadly Hits on Your Career," Managing Your Career, *The Wall Street Journal*, May 25, 1994.

Set an Example   When a manager plays political games, such as distorting the facts or manipulating people, he or she conveys to subordinates a message that such conduct is acceptable. A manager can create a climate either tolerant or intolerant of dirty tricks. Clearly, a department is better served by a manager who provides a positive role model by encouraging truthfulness and the even-handed treatment of others.

Give Clear Job Assignments   Politics seem to be more prevalent when overall purposes are unclear and it is difficult to assess the performance of individual employees.[†] One way to counter political activities is to give well-defined, discrete work assignments. When expectations are clear and subordinates understand how they will be assessed, game playing becomes less necessary as a device for gaining personal recognition.

Eliminate Coalitions and Cliques   Coalitions and cliques that are detrimental to unit performance can often be reduced in influence or eliminated. Although dismissal and transfer are two possible solutions, individuals may also be rotated through different job assignments. Job rotation encourages an

---

[†]The attributes of an open-ended purpose and difficulty in measuring individual performance are especially relevant to academic departments.

employee's perception of the larger enterprise and helps to counter an us–them view of other departments.

Confront Game Players   Even in a climate of trust and openness, individuals may make suggestive comments or offer information that has an ulterior motive. A good response in such a situation is simply to ask, "Why are you telling me this about Sam?" or "Why don't you and I go to see Sam's boss about this right now? I think you should tell her what you've just told me." Another useful response is to offer to discuss questionable information in a public forum. A manager may say, for example, "I think I understand your concerns on this issue. Let's bring it up for discussion at our next department meeting." Using a public forum to discuss and choose a course of action is an excellent defense to most dubious suggestions. As a rule, a manager should not get involved in any scheme that he or she is unwilling to have discussed in public. Knowing that all suggestions are subject to open discussion invariably discourages people who hope to engage a manager in political games.

Machiavellianism

Niccolò Machiavelli, a Renaissance Italian philosopher and statesman, was one of the earliest writers on the topic of political behavior. In his works, Machiavelli examined political effectiveness without regard for ethics or morality. Machiavelli simply ignored moral considerations in exploring not how people *should* behave, but how they actually *do* behave. Because of his uncompromising view of political reality, Machiavelli has sometimes been called the ultimate pragmatist. In recent years, his name has come to be synonymous with the use of political treachery and maneuvering. Thus, to say that someone is Machiavellian is a serious insult.[‡]

Christie and Geis have tried to assess the extent to which an individual's personal style is Machiavellian in nature.[7] To do so, they converted certain basic tenets of Machiavelli's writings into an attitude scale that can be used to measure the extent to which an individual agrees with Machiavelli's views. The statements of the Machiavellian scale (or **Mach Scale** for short) focus on several factors. Chief among them are (1) the use of manipulative interpersonal tactics ("It is wise to flatter important people" and "Never tell anyone the real reason you did something unless it is useful to do so") and (2) an unfavorable view of human nature ("Generally speaking, people won't work hard unless they are forced to do so" and "Anyone who completely trusts anyone else is asking for trouble").

A good deal is known about people who score high in agreement with Machiavelli's views.[8] Generally, they are able to control social interactions and effectively manipulate others. They are also especially effective in using their skills in face-to-face settings. A series of studies among college students found that highly Machiavellian students were more likely to be involved in medicine as a career and were more critical of their fellow students.[9] They also ad-

---

[‡]Other world cultures have also had their own version of Niccolò Machiavelli. About 300 B.C., both Lord Shang of China and Koutilya, a prime minister in the south of India, wrote much the same philosophy as Machiavelli. All three writers shared several common themes: Humankind is basically weak, fallible, and gullible; therefore, a rational person takes advantage of situations and protects himself or herself from the implicit untrustworthiness of others.

mitted to having strong feelings of hostility. In one contrived study, when students were induced to cheat and then accused of doing so, highly Machiavellian individuals looked their accuser in the eye and denied cheating longer than did less Machiavellian individuals.

Still other research indicates that Machiavellianism is positively correlated with occupational attainment (that is, job prestige and income) for individuals with above-average education, while for individuals with below-average education Machiavellianism is inversely related to occupational attainment. These results make sense in that highly Machiavellian individuals require situations that offer considerable latitude for improvisation and interpersonal manipulation (as is characteristic of white-collar jobs). Individuals in blue-collar jobs, where standards of performance are more objective and disciplinary measures are relatively coercive, may be penalized in proportion to their degree of Machiavellianism.[10]

In general, Machiavellian individuals are thought to be socially domineering and manipulative, and they are assumed to engage in political behavior more often than other organizational participants. They are lacking in (1) emotional display in interpersonal relations (that is, they remain cool and distant, and treat others as objects to be manipulated), (2) concern for traditional morality (that is, they find deceit useful rather than reprehensible), and (3) ideological commitments (that is, they prefer to maintain personal power in situations, rather than adhere to relatively inflexible ideals).

Consequences of Using Influence Tactics

The study of attempts to influence others has begun to focus on the specific techniques people use at work. After conversations with employees, David Kipnis and Stuart Schmidt developed a questionnaire for measuring six tactics for influencing others.[11] These tactics include:

1. Reason: relies on using data, logic, and discussion
2. Friendliness: interest, goodwill, and esteem are demonstrated to create a favorable impression
3. Coalition formation: other people in the organization are mobilized to support requests
4. Bargaining: relies on negotiation and exchanging favors
5. Assertiveness: relies on directness and forcefulness in communication
6. Appeal to higher authority: the influence of those higher in the organization is invoked to back up a request.

From responses to their questionnaire, Kipnis and Schmidt grouped employees into four influence styles:

1. Shotguns: people who refuse to take "no" for an answer and who use all of the preceding tactics to achieve their ends
2. Tacticians: people who try to influence others through reason and logic
3. Ingratiators: people who rely on ingratiation and flattery
4. Bystanders: people who watch the action rather than attempt to influence it.[12]

Comparisons of performance evaluations for the four types of employees revealed that people who assertively attempted to influence their supervisors (Shotguns) were viewed less favorably. Both male and female Shotguns received equally low evaluations from their supervisors. Male supervisors tended to give the highest ratings to male Tacticians, who relied on reason and logic. Women who received the highest ratings were likely to be Ingratiators and Bystanders. In responding to these findings, male supervisors explained that both male Tacticians and female Ingratiators were seen as deferential and thoughtful.

Salary was also found to be associated with influence style. In a comparison of the income of 108 male managers, Tacticians earned the most ($73,240), followed by Bystanders ($60,270), Shotguns ($56,480), and Ingratiators ($52,700). Based on both evaluations and income, it seems that Tacticians are valued more than their peers who use other styles. Also, Shotgun-style individuals reported more job tension and personal stress than their counterparts.

Kipnis and Schmidt argue, from these and other findings, that books and training programs that are designed to "put people in charge" (in essence, teach a Shotgun style) are questionable. They contend that people should not be taught to be overly assertive as the best tactic for achieving their desires. Instead, training programs should emphasize less vigorous influence styles that rely on reason and logic.[13] Also, it is interesting to contrast managers' preferred styles when trying to influence superiors versus subordinates. Kipnis and Schmidt report that reason is preferred for trying to influence both superiors and subordinates. However, assertiveness is far more likely to be used with subordinates than with superiors, while coalition formation is more likely to be used to influence superiors than to influence subordinates.

Other Influence Techniques

Beyond the influence tactics discussed thus far are several other, more subtle, mechanisms by which people can be influenced. One effective technique is to create the appearance of higher *status*. Research has shown that people who merely appear to have higher status by virtue of their manner of dress or the use of titles can exert greater influence. For example, in one study, a man violated the traffic light when crossing the street. In half the instances, the man was dressed in a well-tailored business suit, while in the remaining instances, he wore a work shirt and trousers. Of interest was the number of pedestrians who would cross the street with the man. As would be predicted from a status influence view, the well-dressed jaywalker influenced 3½ times as many people to cross the street with him.[14] Another way to create the appearance of higher status is to employ humor. Generally, higher status individuals tell jokes to lower status coworkers. Also, lower status individuals are more commonly the butt of jokes.[15]

A second subtle form of influence is to create the appearance that a behavior is *normative*. For example, bartenders often place a few dollars into a tip glass to create the appearance that tipping is a proper action, and that greenbacks, not change, are commonly given. Also, "ringers" are sometimes planted in the audiences of preachers, with instructions to come forward on cue with donations or "cures."§ The apparent popularity of an action generally tends to induce compliance. For example, in one study, several individuals stared upward at the sky over New York City for a prolonged period of time. Within a short while, most passersby were also gazing at the empty sky.[16]

Lastly, people can sometimes be influenced to comply with a request for a sizable favor that they would otherwise not agree to, if they are first asked to do a small favor. This **foot-in-the-door principle** was once demonstrated in a study in which researchers asked people to install a large "Drive Carefully" sign in their front yards. Only 17 percent agreed to post a large sign. However, individuals who were initially asked to display a small 3-inch sign in their windows (which nearly all agreed to do) yielded 76 percent of the time when asked two weeks later to post the large sign.[17]

The Ethics of Organizational Politics

Business ethicists Gerald Cavanagh, Dennis Moberg, and Manuel Velasquez have offered guidelines on whether a political behavior, or course of action, should be followed in a particular situation.[18] From their perspective, a political behavior is ethical and appropriate only if (1) the behavior respects the rights of all affected parties and (2) the behavior respects the canons of justice—a self-evidently correct judgment of what is equitable and fair. In essence, the model encourages the adoption of nonpolitical behaviors (where such alternatives exist), and the rejection of behaviors that interfere with the canons of justice.

To illustrate their logic, Cavanagh and his associates suggest a case in which two research scientists, Sam and Bill, are in competition in a new-product development lab. Each has prepared a proposal to win a significant cash award for the best new-product idea. Blind reviews of the proposals by other scientists indicate that both are equally meritorious. Sam inquires periodically about the outcome of the bidding process, while Bill wages an open campaign in support of his proposal. Specifically, Bill seizes every opportunity to point out the relative advantages of his proposal to individuals who may have some impact on the final decision. He does this after freely admitting his intention to Sam and others. His campaign of informal pressure is effective and his proposal is funded, while Sam's is not.

Using their logic, we first ask whether the outcome, in terms of the broad interests of society and the company, will be optimal. Since both proposals were judged to be equivalent in the blind reviews, we must answer yes to the first question. The second question focuses on whether Bill's behavior respected the rights of Sam. Because Bill told Sam he intended to campaign actively for his proposal, Bill cannot be accused of deceit. Also, Sam's inaction may be viewed as implied consent. A further question highlights the suspect nature of Bill's actions in pointing out irrelevant differences between the proposals. Given the equivalent merit of the proposals, other considerations (for

§The use of ringers to induce behavior in others in a calculated fashion dates from Parisian opera houses in the 1800s, where members of the audience were paid to applaud or cheer on cue during the performance. The modern descendent of this practice is the television laugh track.

example, which scientist was most qualified to implement the proposal, or other evidence of past performance) should be incorporated in the funding decision.

Responding to Authority: Obedience

For managers to meet their goals, they must rely on their subordinates to obey their directions. Obedience to authority is a strongly ingrained predisposition for most people. Without this predisposition, society would not be able to function. Usually, the depth of our predisposition to obey orders can only be guessed at. Occasionally, we hear of instances of blind obedience to authority, as in the war-crime trials of Adolf Eichmann and Lieutenant William Calley, but we tend to discount such cases as extreme and unusual.

In the early 1960s, Stanley Milgram of Yale University conducted a series of studies to examine the extent to which people would obey, even if the demands of authority violated their moral responsibilities.[19] As part of this research, 40 men from a wide variety of occupations were paid to serve as subjects in a learning experiment. Each subject was told that he was participating in a study of the effects of punishment on learning. The subject was then asked to help another adult (actually the researcher's confederate) learn a lengthy list of word pairs by using electric shock as a penalty for each incorrect answer.

The subject (teacher) met with the alleged learner and then watched as the learner was strapped into an apparatus that looked like an electric chair. The experimenter then took the subject into the next room and showed him how to communicate with the learner through an intercom system. The experimenter also explained how to administer the punishment for any errors the learner might make in responding to stimulus words in the list of word pairs. The shock generator contained 30 switches, one for each of 30 voltage levels ranging from 15 to 450 volts. The switches were also labeled in terms of the increasing strength of the voltage: slight shock, moderate shock, strong shock, very strong shock, intense shock, extreme intensity shock, danger: severe shock, and XXX.

After reading the list of word pairs to the learner, the teacher was to begin quizzing the learner. For each incorrect response, the teacher was to administer an electric shock, and for each additional incorrect response, the teacher was to apply the next higher voltage level on the generator.

The trials passed uneventfully until the learner began to make numerous mistakes. Then, in short order, the teacher found himself administering fairly high levels of voltage to the learner. At that point, the learner would begin to protest, saying that he wanted to drop out of the experiment because his heart was bothering him and the pain of the shocks was too much for him. If the teacher hesitated, the experimenter would encourage him to proceed, saying, for example, "Please go on" or "It is essential that you continue." If the teacher refused to proceed after four verbal encouragements, the experiment was discontinued.

As the voltage levels increased, the confederate (in accord with the experiment's protocol) would voice even stronger objections: He would pound on the wall and, at one point, scream loudly. Beyond a certain voltage level, the learner would no longer answer any of the teacher's questions, giving the impression that he was injured or dead. When this silence occurred, the experimenter would tell the teacher to treat the learner's failure to respond as an incorrect response, to administer the punishment, and to continue on with the next word pair.

Given these conditions, you would probably assume that very few subjects would obey the experimenter. But the actual results revealed that a majority of the subjects administered the maximum voltage on the shock generator and continued their participation in the experiment despite the learner's objections.

The results revealed that 26 out of 40, or 65 percent, of the participants administered the maximum level of electric shock. We should note, however, that although most subjects gave the maximum level of shock to the learner, they did not enjoy doing so. Typically, the subjects displayed strong signs of nervous tension, such as nail biting, trembling, and groaning. Many of them also laughed nervously whenever the learner protested or pleaded. However, the constraints of the situation compelled the subjects to continue their participation.**

The high level of obedience displayed by Milgram's subjects suggests that the predisposition to follow authority is very strong. In this case, the experimenter relied on his expertise and legitimacy to give the subject orders. Despite the fact that all subjects received their pay in advance and participated voluntarily, most felt a strong desire to avoid disobeying authority, even in light of the suffering they inflicted on another person.

These results suggest that society may be too successful at socializing its members to obey authority. When people take on roles that prescribe obedience (such as those of research subject, student, soldier, or employee), the sense of responsibility for the outcomes of their own conduct is likely to be diminished. The evidence from Milgram's work implies that human conscience cannot be relied on to step in and halt activities that are injurious to others. It can be inferred that organizational members generally will carry out orders given by those in authority, regardless of the content or consequences of the actions. This suggests that forms of socialization that emphasize personal responsibility to others may be lacking in our society.

Milgram's findings have raised a number of questions. One of the more intriguing is whether there are cultural differences in the predisposition to obey authority. For example, considering the Holocaust—the persecution and extermination of European Jews by Nazi Germany—one might hypothesize that the level of obedience would be higher in Germany than in other countries. To test this motion, the conditions of Milgram's original study were re-created in several countries: Canada, England, Jordan, and the former West Germany. The results yielded essentially similar findings, suggesting that the level of obedience to authority in the Milgram condition is fairly constant across different societies.[20] By inference, the atrocities that occurred in Nazi Germany could happen elsewhere in the world.††

**When each subject completed the experiment, he met with the learner and discovered that in fact no shocks had been given. The true purpose of the study was then explained to each subject.

††Such mass atrocities have in fact happened again—witness Cambodia, Serbia, Uganda, Mao's China, Rwanda, and Stalin's Russia. In an interview with Morley Safer for the news program *Sixty Minutes*, Milgram stated that "if a system of death camps were set up in the United States of the sort we had seen in Nazi Germany, one would be able to find sufficient personnel for those camps in any medium-sized American town.[21] However, other evidence from crossnational studies is somewhat suggestive of cultural differences. In a less well publicized self-decision condition (wherein the "teacher" was allowed to choose the shock level in each trial), various studies found extremely low levels of total shock administered by all national samples. However, the levels administered for German and Jordanian samples were somewhat higher than those observed for Australian and U.S. samples.[22]

In addition, the level of obedience in the Milgram study may have been near the "baseline" for injurious behavior. The victim (learner) in Milgram's original study was an innocent 47-year-old man. If the victim had been someone whom the subject disliked for any number of possible reasons (race, religion, or politics) or had the subject possessed a strong commitment to the purpose of the study in which he was involved, or expected to be continually involved with persons in the study, the level of obedience might well have been much higher.

Since the time of Milgram's studies, greater concern has arisen over research ethics and specifically the need to protect subjects from traumatic experiences. Because of these concerns about the rights of subjects, it has become exceedingly difficult to obtain peer approval to conduct and publish similar research. Therefore, something of a moratorium exists on conducting studies such as Milgram's that may involve unpleasant experiences for the subject. As a result, it cannot be determined whether the present level of obedience is lower than in the past. Some national experiences, such as the Watergate scandal and the Vietnam War protests, have certainly made it more socially acceptable to oppose authority. It is probably safe to say that it is now somewhat more difficult to extract conformity in a variety of settings (including work, school, and government) than it has been in the past.

In summary, Milgram's research suggests that people placed in a conflict situation pitting moral values against authority will tend to follow the dictates of authority. Perhaps the most sobering aspect of this discovery lies in how little real power an authority figure needs in order to succeed in directing others. Of course, opportunities for the abuse of authority also occur in business organizations. Because of this reality, it is essential that managers recognize the magnitude of their power over others and act in accordance with the responsibility that such power entails.

SUMMARY

1. *Define and distinguish power, authority, influence, and politics.* Power is the ability to change the behavior of others; it may be legitimate or illegitimate, used to attain common goals or personal gain. Authority is the legitimate use of power in the pursuit of common goals. Influence is defined as the ability to change other people's behavior, but in subtler, more specific, and less reliable ways. Politics constitutes the actions taken to obtain, develop and use power.

2. *Identify and describe three primary influence processes.* Kelman identified three reasons a person yields to another's influence: compliance, identification, and internalization. Compliance entails yielding to influence in the hope of receiving a reward or avoiding a punishment. Identification arises out of the desire to establish or maintain a satisfying relationship with the person exercising the influence. With internalization, the person being influenced believes the behavior is correct and appropriate.

3. *List and define five bases of power.* According to French and Raven, five bases of power are reward power, coercive power, legitimate power, referent power, and expert power. Reward power is the ability to determine who will re-

ceive particular rewards. Coercive power is the ability to punish or produce fear in others. Legitimate power arises from willingness to accept an individual's direction because of social conditioning or designation. Referent power is the ability to influence others because of one's attractiveness or ability to inspire. Expert power is the power that arises from being perceived as knowledgeable or talented in some area.

4. *Describe some differences between formal and informal power.* Managers with informal power—expert and referent power—have greater capacity to affect the satisfaction and performance of employees, whereas formal power—legitimate, reward, and coercive power—potentially has more impact on immediate behavior. Formal power will not necessarily produce agreement and commitment. Informal power bases are more easily eroded and can be harder to control. In general, informal power resides in the manager's personal characteristics, while formal power resides in the position itself.

5. *Identify several political tactics, including devious political tactics and political blunders.* Political tactics include ingratiation, forming coalitions and networks, impression management, information management, promoting the opposition, and pursuing line responsibility. Political tactics considered devious include eliminating all enemies, creating a feud between potential rivals, and excluding the opposition. Common political blunders are violating the organization's chain of command, losing one's cool, rejecting a request from top management, upstaging one's boss, and challenging cherished beliefs of the organization.

6. *Explain several techniques for coping with organizational politics.* A manager can create a positive climate for subordinates by setting an example of truthfulness and even-handed treatment. A manager can make expectations for performance clear by giving well-defined, discrete work assignments. Coalitions and cliques that interfere with group performance can be eliminated through dismissal, transfer, or job rotation. Managers can bring game playing into the open by confronting the players or offering to discuss the situation in a public forum.

7. *Cite evidence that the predisposition to obey authority is strong.* In a study conducted by Stanley Milgram, subjects obeyed the authority of the researcher, even though the researcher's authority was limited and the subjects were aware that they were severely hurting an innocent person. This research suggests that the predisposition to follow authority is very strong and that when people take on roles that prescribe obedience, their sense of responsibility for the outcome of their conduct is diminished.

KEY TERMS

Power	Coercive power
Authority	Legitimate power
Influence	Referent power
Compliance	Expert power
Identification	Organizational politics
Internalization	Mach Scale
Reward power	Foot-in-the-door principle

CRITICAL INCIDENT

Warner Memorial Hospital

Warner Memorial Hospital is located in a moderate-sized community, approximately 45 miles from a major metropolitan area. It is a 240-bed facility that employs about 300 people. During the past year, there have been wide fluctuations in the patient census. The chief negotiator for the Allied Health Workers Union, Betty Gordon, was visibly concerned about the new labor contract negotiations that were to begin in two days. She was afraid that the union would be asked to agree to wage and benefit concessions. Remembering the last contract negotiations, which resulted in a 41-day strike, did little to ease her concern. At those negotiations three years ago, few of the more critical issues separating labor and management were really settled.

The head of labor relations for the hospital, Bill Lenox, was also thinking about the upcoming negotiations. He recalled the last contract negotiations and some of the unrealistic demands that were presented by the union. Given that this was a health care service and delivery organization, Bill was convinced that the workers, especially the nurses and technicians, would be better off without the union.

The union holds a very strong position at Warner Memorial. Most of the eligible workers belong, which affects all aspects of hospital operations. The hospital could not easily replace these employees during a strike. Betty firmly believes that the union members are seeking improvements in wages and benefits. She is not convinced that management wishes to reach an equitable contract agreement. The union members also believe that if management really wanted to attract more patients, they would be investing in newer equipment and initiating a marketing program.

Bill and his staff have been spending weeks getting ready for the negotiations. They have pages of data in support of the need for concessions or at least a wage freeze. Bill is convinced that the union will adamantly oppose any request for concessions and that volatile, emotional arguments are inevitable. The hospital is not in a position to grant meaningful increases in wages and benefits and can ill afford a strike. Perhaps some patients as well as workers would be lost forever to the hospital's market-intensive competitors in the nearby city, 45 miles north.

1. What bases of power are evident in this case for Betty? For Bill?
2. What political tactics or games can be identified in this case?
3. What do you predict is likely to happen? What do you propose as a possible solution?

Source: Written by Bruce Kemelgor, University of Louisville, used by permission.

EXPERIENTIAL EXERCISE

Who Has Power?

In organizational settings, there are usually five types of power: legitimate, reward, coercive, referent, and expert. An individual may have one or more of these kinds of power; also, the person who possesses power is not necessarily considered a manager or leader.

This exercise examines power across several sets of individuals or occupations. For example, set 1 considers the power your professor, as the focal person, has over a student, the significant other. Thus, you should check which kind of power the professor has over students. But also in set 1, you should consider another possibility; that is, in the reverse sense, what power might the student as the focal person possess over the professor as the significant other? Complete the table for the eight sets, indicating on the first line the power of the focal person over the significant other and on the second line the power of the significant other over the focal person.

1. On balance, which person—the focal person or the significant other—has the most power? Make this judgment for each set.

2. Indicate, for each set, which of the five types of power is the most significant.

3. Can you identify instances in which a power base is equally divided between the focal person and the significant other? If so, can you explain why this occurs?

Set	Focal Person	Significant Other	Power				
			Legitimate	Reward	Coercive	Referent	Expert
1	Professor Student	Student Professor					
2	Manager—grocery store Cashier/checker	Cashier/checker Manager—grocery store					
3	President of the U.S. U.S. citizens	U.S. citizens President of the U.S.					
4	Secretary Executive	Executive Secretary					
5	Audit supervisor, IRS Agents for IRS	Agents for IRS Audit supervisor, IRS					
6	Mentor Mentee	Mentee Mentor					
7	University president Deans	Deans University president					
8	Car salesperson Customer	Customer Car salesperson					

Source: Ricky W. Griffin and Thomas C. Head, *Practicing Management*, 2nd ed. (Boston: Houghton Mifflin, 1987). Used with permission.

7 Leadership

By working faithfully 8 hours a day, you may eventually get to be a boss and work 12 hours a day.

—Robert Frost

Nearly all men can stand adversity, but if you want to test a man's character, give him power.

—Abe Lincoln

Charlatanism is to some degree indispensable to effective leadership.

—Eric Hoffer

We have, I fear, confused power with greatness.

—Stewart Udall

Learning Objectives

After studying this chapter, you should be able to:

1. Define leadership.
2. Describe ways in which leader behavior is related to employee attitudes and performance.
3. Explain the importance of leadership.
4. Identify the factors underlying situational favorableness and explain how they influence a leader's effectiveness.
5. Explain how leaders can clarify paths to goals to motivate employees.
6. Describe the components of subordinate maturity and the relevance of subordinate maturity to leadership style.
7. Describe the decision-making styles of the Vroom–Yetton model and explain how you would select an appropriate style.
8. Describe a way to evaluate leadership style taking into account managers' views of different employees.
9. Define leadership substitute and leadership neutralizer and give examples of each.
10. Offer some major reasons why managers fail.

So You Want to Be a Manager?

A growing trend among employees is the notion that a position in corporate management is *not* the ultimate career goal. Fear of management responsibility is running rampant, and here is what is being said about it:

"You're a backstop, caught in the middle between upper management and the workforce," complained a Portland, Oregon, cost accountant who left a managerial post.

"I hated the meetings. And I found the more you did for people that worked for you, the more they expected. I felt like I was coming in every day and people were expecting me to meet their needs. I was a counselor, motivator, financial advisor, and psychologist," said an award-winning real estate office manager in Jackson, Michigan.

"You can never slack off if you are on the technical side. It's a rare person who can manage to keep up on the technical side and handle a management job, too," commented a 28-year-old Chicago computer technician.

"There wasn't a single day where I could say I enjoyed myself. I didn't feel comfortable touting the company line on organizational policies and technical decisions I disagreed with. I found it very difficult to fire my team up on something I wasn't fired up about. It was very hard asking folks to do things I wouldn't like to do myself, like put in gobs of overtime or travel at the drop of a hat," said a 34-year-old computer-software designer who served in management for six months.

This change in attitude has been caused, in part, by recent changes in business practices. Restructuring and layoffs have eliminated the layers of management that typically offered steady and automatic climbs up the corporate ladder. Many of the traditional executive perks are gone or severely limited. Managerial positions demand more hours and deliver more headaches than ever before, and the financial rewards and perks are minimal. Today, managers supervise larger numbers of people spread over more locations, even continents, and they must manage across different functions, such as design, production, and marketing. They must be change-agents who support the latest reengineering or reorganization, even if they did not plan it or if they disagree with it. And then

there is Dilbert (the very popular Scott Adams cartoon) and television sitcoms, investigative news, and movies all frequently portraying managers as morons or the enemy.

With increasing numbers of employees cautious about moving into management, one wonders if companies are concerned about developing future leaders. The fact is, many are not concerned. Though companies have dismissed large numbers of managers, top executives believe there is still a surplus of interested people. Robert Kelly, a business professor at Carnegie Mellon University, says, "Another reason companies aren't short of managers is that so many workers today are self-managed, either individually or via teams, you don't need a manager." Brian Bass, a former advertising and public relations manager, adds, "Employers are looking for people who can do things, not for people who make other people do things." The American Management Association also supports this: "Who's being hired? The people who can develop and sell products: computer programmers, engineers, and sales people."

Source: T. Schellhardt, "Off the Ladder: Want to Be a Manager? Many People Say No, Calling Job Miserable," *The Wall Street Journal*, April 4, 1997.

What makes a manager an effective leader? What personal attributes distinguish effective leaders from ineffective leaders? And what situational factors can help a person be more effective as a leader? These are the questions asked by both managers and the people who study organizational behavior. In an effort to answer these questions, managers have at times participated as subjects in studies of leadership. The results of these investigations of leadership have produced an enormous body of knowledge.

In the most recent edition of the *Handbook of Leadership*, a fairly complete review of research on the topic identified over 5,000 studies and treatises dealing with the behavioral aspects of leadership.[1] Trying to make sense of such a mass of information is no simple task. Nonetheless, certain themes and consistencies can be identified. In this chapter, we will begin by examining the nature of leadership and its defining characteristics. We will then consider a variety of approaches to understanding the leadership process by examining the roles of individual differences and behavioral issues, as well as the role of situational influences in determining leader effectiveness.

The Nature of Leadership

Although many definitions have been offered for *leadership*, most contain certain common elements. A distillation of these elements suggests that **leadership** can be defined as a process through which a person tries to get organizational members to do something that the person desires. This definition overlaps, to a great extent, with the way in which we defined influence in the previous chapter. Therefore, leadership must be viewed as an influence process.

Typically, we think of leadership as being associated with the role of manager. However, *leader* and *manager* are not equivalent terms. Someone may be an outstanding manager without in fact being a work group's leader. Although the group's manager performs planning, organizing, and controlling activities, a real leader may actually be one of the subordinates. So, too, a work group's nominal head may be a great leader, while requiring that others handle the functional duties of planning, organizing, and controlling for the unit.

Leadership thus implies something more than mere supervisory responsibility or formal authority. It consists of influence that extends beyond the usual influence that accompanies legitimacy as a supervisor. Therefore, it can be said that leadership is the *incremental influence*, or additional influence, that a person has beyond his or her formal authority. Incremental influence can exist to varying degrees in every member of a work group. As a result, it is not uncommon to find situations in which a subordinate who lacks formal authority actually possesses substantial incremental influence. We would call such an individual an **informal leader.** Informal leaders are often invaluable to their groups because they can aid coworkers in a number of different ways.

For example, an informal leader may possess technical expertise that even the formal leader lacks. Or an informal leader may have special social skills (such as the ability to make people feel good about themselves or their accomplishments) that can maintain or improve group morale.

The presence of an informal leader (or leaders) may sound like a distinct plus for a manager. However, this is not always the case. Occasionally, an informal leader's values may not coincide with those of the formal leader. Sometimes the informal leader may encourage his or her peers to be less productive or more demanding in order to extract greater rewards from the formal leader. In so doing, an informal leader may become a political opponent. Clearly, the presence of an informal leader is not inherently a good or bad thing. The ultimate value of an informal leader depends on whether he or she supports or opposes the goals of the organization.

Thus, the differences between leadership and headship can be quite distinct, and leadership may exist on both formal and informal levels. While it might not be technically correct to use the terms *leader* and *manager* interchangeably, we will do so throughout the remainder of this chapter, because most views on the topic of leadership refer primarily to formal leaders, or managers, and do not maintain the distinction between leadership and headship.

Does Leadership Make a Difference?

One can make a good argument that leadership should have only a modest impact on group performance because work-unit accomplishments result more from the efforts of the unit's members than of one individual. For example, the players on a sports team would seem to be more important than the head coach in terms of final points on the scoreboard. Also, organizations have rules and policies that govern member behaviors. Yet, one also has a sense that a leader, under the right circumstances, can have a powerful impact on unit performance.

One interesting way to learn whether leaders can have an impact is to study the effects of leader succession. That is, what are the results of changing leaders for work units that are performing well or poorly? In most units, change of leadership is precipitated by poor performance by the group. Occasionally, the group's leadership is truly to blame, but in some instances, the leader is a scapegoat for other problems. By and large, financial problems do predict changes in organizational leadership.[2] Also, rates of executive succession tend to be higher in larger organizations.[3] Research on the consequences of leader succession suggests that group performance can be either enhanced or impaired by succession. For well-performing groups, succession can be disruptive and lead to greater personnel turnover. However, for poorly performing groups, succession offers an opportunity for performance enhancement. In studies that have examined such diverse positions as baseball coaches, mayors, and board chairpersons, evidence suggests that succession (hence leadership) can have strong effects on measurable performance outcomes.[4] A frequent change of leaders (that is, a high rate of succession), however, is associated with declines in performance.

What Do Managers Actually Do?

Before examining the major studies of leadership, it is instructive to consider what managers do during a typical day. By considering what managers actually do, we can develop an appreciation of what such jobs are like.

Studies of actual on-the-job behavior reveal that most managers perform a large number of brief, highly varied, and fragmented activities. The results of these studies, which are usually obtained through direct observation or by having a manager maintain a daily log of activities, suggest that the popular notion of the harried executive is fairly accurate. One such study found that on only nine occasions during a 4-week period did a manager remain uninterrupted for 30 minutes or longer.[5] In another study, it was found that CEOs averaged over 50 written and verbal contacts per day, with half of these activities taking less than 9 minutes and only one-tenth taking more than an hour.[6] Other researchers also have argued that most of a manager's time is devoted to face-to-face or telephone communications. The recurring nature of the problems tackled by a manager over a period of time is difficult to describe succinctly. However, one colorful summarization is that "the manager's job can usefully be pictured as a stranded rope made up of fibers of different lengths— where length represents time—each fiber coming to the surface one or more times in observable 'episodes' and each representing a single issue."[7]

Given the nonroutine nature of managerial work, it is reasonable to ask where managers find time to communicate with their people on a personal level or to attempt to motivate them. Often, there is truly little time for such activities. More typically, managers are involved in "putting out fires" and managing problems than in developing the human resources within their work units.

The Trait Approach

During the first half of the 20th century, researchers sought to understand leadership by comparing leaders with followers and effective leaders with ineffective leaders. This search for features of leaders, or leader traits, was prompted by a belief that leaders somehow possessed distinguishing traits that set them apart from other people. The logic of this approach is simple: To understand what makes some individuals more effective as leaders, merely measure such people on a large number of psychological, social, and physical attributes and note how they differ from most others.

As the research progressed, the number of traits of suspected importance began to grow.[8] Moreover, the results became increasingly mixed and did not follow a clear pattern.[9] By and large, the trait studies did not show any simple pattern of traits that was both strongly and consistently related to leadership.[10] At first glance, this seems surprising. Based on personal experience and observations, we might expect to find consistent differences between effective and ineffective leaders. However, if we consider a large number of effective leaders, we reach a different conclusion. For example, observations and experience may lead one to believe that effective leaders are likely to be outgoing and socially assertive. Yet, there have been outstanding leaders who were relatively shy and withdrawn, such as Abraham Lincoln and Mahatma Gandhi.

The search for leader traits, however, was not a total failure. Several traits do appear to be very modestly but inconsistently associated with leadership. Chief among these traits is intelligence. It appears that people who hold leadership positions tend to be somewhat more intelligent. On the other hand, there is good reason to believe that highly intelligent people are not likely to attain or maintain leadership in many settings.[11] According to this line of reasoning, individuals who are much brighter than their potential followers may have difficulty in communicating and relating to them.* In essence, there may be an optimal level of intelligence for a leader in a given situation.

Although intelligence has been shown to correlate only modestly with leadership, leader intelligence and other cognitive attributes can be highly correlated with effectiveness under special circumstances.[12] In particular, it has been found that in situations combining a leader's ability to be directive and a stress-free environment, intelligence can be used to predict work-unit performance with a fairly high degree of accuracy. Called **cognitive resource theory,** this view argues that directive leaders who are intelligent and possess relevant job experience will be more effective if they are in stress-free settings with subordinates who are supportive.[13] This fairly straightforward perspective of what makes for effective leadership is, in fact, the logic that underlies much of the hiring of managers. That is to say, when selecting supervisors, it is common to search for experienced managers possessing a fair degree of intelligence plus social skills that can be used to build supportiveness and reduce interpersonal stress. Research on the validity of cognitive resource theory has tended to be conducted primarily by the theory's originator. However, an independent test of the proposed processes further confirmed the critical notion that leader intelligence is related to group performance as stress in the work setting is diminished.[14]

Recent research by Robert Sternberg of Harvard has suggested that intelligence may be better conceptualized as comprising several major components (rather than being a single, unitary factor). In Sternberg's **triarchic model of intelligence,** intellectual functioning is viewed as consisting of analytical reasoning ability, social intelligence, and creativity.[15] Analytical reasoning refers to the ability to solve problems that have an abstract element. Problem solving that seeks to identify a single, correct answer exemplifies this ability. An individual who easily solves math problems can be said to have a high level of analytical reasoning ability. Analytical reasoning also includes the ability to use deductive thinking. Social intelligence refers to the ability to understand the motives and actions of others and to interact effectively with others. Individuals who possess relatively more social intelligence are expected to be capable of understanding and influencing others. Social intelligence is akin to what most of us refer to as "street smarts." Creativity refers to the ability to identify many possible solutions to a given problem. What is particularly novel about Sternberg's model is its suggestion that individuals who are especially able on any one dimension may not be regarded as effective if the setting in which they operate does not call for a specific cognitive ability. Hence, people who

---

*This argument is sometimes raised in political commentary to explain why the candidates for the presidency of the United States are usually not terribly intellectual (that is, a majority of the voting populace would have a difficult time identifying with a highly intellectual president).

may be especially competent at analytical reasoning may be quite unsuccessful if they lack social intelligence in a setting that requires competency on this dimension. Sternberg's model further implies that managerial jobs can be analyzed in terms of their requirements on the dimensions of analytical reasoning, social intelligence, and creativity, and that individuals can be assessed on these dimensions and "matched" to job requirements. For example, some jobs could require high levels of creativity and social intelligence and little analytical ability (for example, R&D and marketing research), while others might require high levels of analytical reasoning (for example, financial analysis). Managers could then be selected and developed based on their abilities across the three dimensions. To date, Sternberg has developed some reasonable measures of all three components, and these measures are available to industry. However, research on the optimal matching strategy has not yet been conducted. As suggested by many observers, Sternberg's work offers a promising new direction for understanding the role of managerial intelligence.[16]

Several other traits have also been linked to successful leaders. For example, leaders can be characterized by task persistence, self-confidence, tolerance of interpersonal stress, and the ability to influence others' behavior.[17] One somewhat surprising finding is a low but positive correlation between leadership status and height, which suggests that taller individuals have something of an advantage in gaining leadership positions. This may reflect a desire on the part of many people to "look up" to their leaders.

Gender Issues

Most views of leadership have ignored the possibility that men and women may display different traits, values, or behaviors. As more women enter leadership positions, interest has increased regarding whether female managers are at a disadvantage relative to male managers. A comprehensive review of the available literature on male-female differences revealed that men and women tend to differ in their leadership styles.[18] Women are somewhat more democratic in their orientation, while men are somewhat more directive in their styles. The overlap between the two groups, however, is substantial, rendering the magnitude of these differences small. Also, comparisons of men and women on other leadership dimensions have not substantiated reliable and meaningful differences. In one review of the evidence, it was concluded that there is little reason to believe that either women or men will be superior in the role of manager, or that either group offers a distinctive type of management.[19] In short, both groups can produce superior, mediocre, and poor managerial performers, and the constructs that determine the success and failure of any manager are the same for both genders.†

It is important to note, however, that because of their relatively recent entry in sizable numbers to managerial ranks, and because of certain social dynamics,

---

†Despite the limited evidence of male-female differences on leadership dimensions, it should not, of course, be inferred that there is no evidence whatsoever of sex differences in behavior. For some time, men have been found to be, in the aggregate, somewhat more aggressive, self-assertive, and rough in their manner and language than women, while females have been found to be more expressive of compassion and emotion than men.[20] However, the relevance of these differences to job behavior is minimal.

female managers do not often experience the same ease of entry and advancement afforded to men. For example, it has been observed that mentoring (a practice in which a senior manager helps a younger manager by offering advice and other forms of support) can be a significant aid in the advancement of a manager's career. Because many senior managers are male, and female managers tend to be younger, there is little opportunity for young female managers to find same-sex mentors. Crossing the "gender barrier" to find a mentor can be a problem for younger managers as there is a good deal of sensitivity surrounding the situation (both female and male managers fear appearing to have a sexual relationship, which would compromise their credibility).[21] As an alternative to traditional senior–junior mentoring, it has been suggested that young female managers use peer relationships as the basis for career development.[22]

The Behavioral Approach

As interest in the early trait approach to leadership began to decline, researchers focused their attention on leaders' actions rather than on their attributes. These studies of leader behavior tried to identify specific styles of leader conduct and attempted to discover whether leader behavior was associated with employee attitudes and performance.

An Inside Look
"Other" Leadership Styles

All employees want bosses who are coaches, mentors, and nurturers, who know that their own success comes through the success of their employees. But we all too often find that our boss may not be quite this way. Dr. Val Arnold, an organizational psychologist with Personnel Decisions, Inc., in Minneapolis, has identified several problem personality types that employees may encounter.

Abrasives are rude, curt, and insensitive, but oblivious to it. These bosses are results oriented; the only thing that counts is the bottom line. Subordinates fear them. Most people complain about them and take pains to avoid them. The **Field Marshals** are the control freaks, operating through intimidation, humiliation, and public verbal attacks on peers and subordinates who do not perform to their standards of excellence. The most intensely competitive are the **Street Fighters.** Only two types of people comprise their world, winners and losers; and they firmly believe that no one likes a loser. Attacking their opponent's weakest point is their preferred mode of operation. **Rebels** see themselves as the exception to the rule and prize being out of step with the norm. Since they are often extremely talented and highly successful, they get away with this behavior. **Jekyll and Hydes** are the polished business professionals who work extremely well with the next higher level of management, but not anyone else. To their boss, they are exemplary employees, but to peers and subordinates they are seen as manipulators who use people for their own gain.

All of these types can be stellar in their own sordid way—but they are not team players. The emerging trend is to reward stars for their cooperative talents rather than solely for their competitive talents. Teamwork is the goal, and relationships are fundamental to success in most organizational settings.

T. Lee, "Are You More of a Street Fighter or a Jekyll and Hyde?" *Managing Your Career, The Wall Street Journal*, June 11, 1996.

T. Schellhardt, "To Be a Star among Equals, Be a Team Player," *Managing Your Career, The Wall Street Journal*, April 20, 1994.

University of Iowa Leadership Studies   Some of the earliest studies of leader behavior, conducted at the University of Iowa, addressed the question of whether a democratic style of leadership is more effective than an authoritarian or a laissez-faire style. To compare these styles of leadership in a controlled situation, researchers randomly assigned 10-year-old boys to one of three groups involved in hobby activities after school hours.[23] In these groups, the boys did such things as make toy boats and papier-maché masks. Each group was under the direction of an adult who behaved in either a democratic, an authoritarian, or a laissez-faire style.

In the authoritarian condition, the adult leader assigned specific tasks to each individual, decided what was to be done without consulting the boys, assigned work partners, was subjective in his praise, and remained aloof from the group's activities. In contrast, the democratic leader allowed the group to decide who was to perform which task, permitted the boys to pick their own work partners, gave specific feedback on how to improve craftsmanship, and tried to be an involved member of the group. The laissez-faire leader was very detached from the group's activities. He gave the group members complete freedom to do what they wished and provided information only when he was specifically asked.

The boys' reactions were greatly influenced by the style of leadership to which they were subjected. Boys in the democratically led group were more satisfied and displayed less aggression toward one another than did boys in the autocratically led group. Although there was a slight tendency for the boys in the authoritarian setting to produce more items, judges rated the quality of output to be highest in the democratically led group. Another interesting finding from this study was that boys in the autocratically led group tended to stop working and engage in horseplay whenever the leader left the room.

It is possible to argue, however, that an autocratic style of leadership may not always be inappropriate. Sometimes a situation may call for urgent action, and in these cases an autocratic style of leadership may be best.[24] In addition, most people are familiar with autocratic leadership and, therefore, have less difficulty adopting that style. Furthermore, in some situations, subordinates may actually prefer an autocratic style. For example, a group of truckers may have difficulty respecting a truck dispatcher who tries to be participative rather than authoritarian in decision making.[25]

The Interaction Process Analysis System   During the 1950s, attention turned to the behaviors that members exhibit in groups. Researchers developed a system for coding the social interaction that occurs in groups. This system consists of 12 content categories within which the behaviors of group members are coded[26] (see Table 7.1). In using the system, two or more coders listen to a group discussion and code each individual's remarks into one of the categories. For example, member A might ask a question ("What do you think will happen if we don't complete this task in the time allotted?"), member B might offer an opinion ("It probably doesn't matter"), and member C might crack a joke (which would be coded as "tension release"). Although it may seem remarkable, all group discussion can be broken down into these 12 categories.

The use of this system for groups that lacked a designated leader revealed some interesting findings. For example, some members tended to take on

TABLE 7.1   *The 12 Categories of the Interaction Process Analysis Systems*

1. Shows solidarity; raises others' status; gives help, rewards

2. Shows tension release; jokes; laughs; shows satisfaction

3. Agrees; shows passive acceptance; understands; is concerned; complies

4. Disagrees; shows passive rejection; shows formality; withholds help

5. Shows tension; asks for help; withdraws out of field

6. Shows antagonism; deflates others' status; defends or asserts self

7. Gives suggestion or direction, implying autonomy for others

8. Gives opinion, evaluation, analysis; expresses feeling, wishes

9. Gives orientation, information; repeats; clarifies; confirms

10. Asks for orientation, information, repetition, confirmation

11. Asks for opinions, evaluation, analysis, expression of feeling

12. Asks for suggestion, direction, possible ways of action

specific, identifiable roles within a group. That is, one member tended to make comments and show behaviors that fit mostly into the first six categories listed in Table 7.1, while another member tended to make comments and show behaviors that fit mostly into the last six categories. Still other members might be categorized as relatively unresponsive—they contributed little to the group discussion. The first six categories are concerned with socio-emotional issues, while the second six are largely concerned with accomplishing the group's given task. From these results, it was concluded that groups have two roles that must be fulfilled for effective functioning: a task-oriented role and a socio-emotional role. In other words, groups need members to attend both to social relations maintenance issues and to task accomplishment issues. Of special interest is the finding that different members tend to emerge as socio-emotional leaders and task leaders. That is, a single individual rarely rises to occupy both roles. Such findings suggest that, for groups to be effective, they must have some attention shown to getting the job accomplished and helping to steer the group to meet its goals, as well as some attention to concerns for the feelings and welfare of members, and the social atmosphere within the group. In work groups, we would expect to find leaders expressing concern for both **task orientation** issues and **employee orientation** issues.[‡]

Ohio State Leadership Studies   Although many researchers have studied these dimensions of leadership, one group of researchers at Ohio State University came to be noted for its efforts. These researchers proposed that consideration and initiating structure are two primary dimensions of leadership that parallel the styles of employee and task orientations. **Consideration** is defined as the extent to which the leader has job relationships that rely on

---

[‡]The pervasiveness of this need for groups to attend to the dual function of social issues and task issues has been suggested in cross-cultural research. Also, it has been suggested that one of the most basic social groups, the family, embodies these two functions in the traditional role definitions of mother (that is, the socio-emotional leader) and father (that is, the task leader).

mutual trust, respect for subordinates, and sensitivity to subordinates' feelings. **Initiating structure** is the extent to which a leader defines and structures the work that subordinates perform, with an eye toward successful task accomplishment.

These two dimensions of leader behavior are assumed to be independent of each other, so that a leader may possess either a high or a low predisposition toward each dimension. The combination of the two dimensions for an individual suggests that several different types of managers can be identified (Figure 7.1). Manager A in Figure 7.1 would be described as highly considerate of subordinates, while lacking a concern for employee production. Manager B, on the other hand, lacks concern for the feelings of employees but is moderately concerned with unit output. Manager C is apparently devoted to maximizing both production and employee well-being. This third case exemplifies what some see as an ideal style, in that it combines the best of both dimensions.

Research on the Ohio State dimensions of consideration and initiating structure has generated some interesting findings. Questionnaires completed by both subordinates and leaders showed that high consideration was related to lower rates of grievance filings and lower turnover. However, beyond a certain point, increases in supervisory considerateness did not appear to decrease turnover and grievances further. In addition, the study found that highly considerate leaders could structure work more without risking an increase in grievances and that supervisors can, to some extent, compensate for displaying a high degree of structure if they increase their considerateness. In contrast, supervisors who are low on considerateness cannot eliminate their negative impact by being less concerned with the creation of structure. Low considerateness apparently has a strong and persistent negative effect on relations with subordinates.[27] In addition, other research has rather consistently found that low considerateness is associated with employee dissatisfaction with supervisors.[28]

FIGURE 7.1   *The Ohio State Leadership Dimensions*

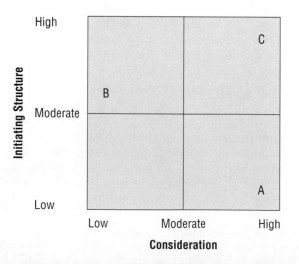

TABLE 7.2 ***Variables Found to Influence the Relationship Between Leader Behavior and Outcome***

Subordinate Characteristics	Supervisor Characteristics	Task Characteristics
Expertise	Influence with superiors	Time urgency
Experience	Attitude similarity with superior	Physical danger
Competence	Similarity of behavior with higher management	External stress
Knowledge of job		Autonomy
Job level		Ambiguity
Expectations of the leader		Meaningfulness of task

Source: Adapted from F. Landy and D. Trumbo, *Psychology of Work Behavior* (Homewood, Ill.: Dorsey, 1980).

Although early results suggested that the combination of high consideration and high initiating structure constitutes the most successful managerial style, other studies have not corroborated this finding.[29]§ Some researchers attempted to state the conditions under which consideration and structure are related to employee satisfaction and performance.[30] Their efforts suggest that many variables can affect the relationship between leader style and subordinate reactions. Table 7.2 lists a number of important subordinate, supervisor, and task variables that can have an influence on this relationship.

The Managerial Grid Practicing managers have found the Ohio State dimensions of leadership to be an appealing concept. In fact, Robert Blake and Jane Mouton have adapted the Ohio State approach to a managerial training program that explains leadership styles in the context of a grid.[31] In their Managerial Grid, the various combinations of a concern for people and a concern for production define five major leadership styles (Figure 7.2) as follows:

1. *Authority/obedience management,* or a 9,1 style, emphasizes efficiency in operations that results from arranging work conditions in such a way that human elements can interfere only to a small degree.

2. *Country-club management,* or a 1,9 style, involves thoughtful attention to the needs of people, because such satisfying relationships are expected to lead to a comfortable, friendly organizational atmosphere.

3. *Laissez-faire or impoverished management,* or a 1,1 style, is characterized by minimal effort to get the required work done and sustain organization membership.

4. *Organization man management,* or a 5,5 style, is concerned with balancing the necessity to get the work out while maintaining morale at a satisfactory level. The goal is adequate performance.

---

§In fact, the early assumption that the high-consideration/high-structuring combination was optimal has come to be known as the "hi-hi myth."

FIGURE 7.2   *The Managerial Grid*

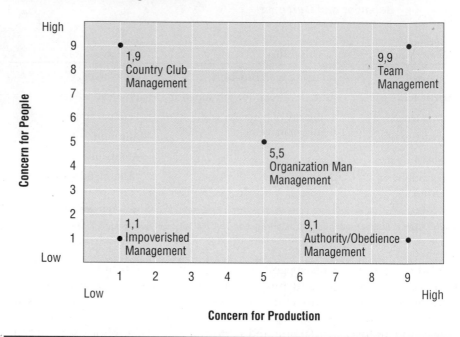

Source: R. Blake and J. Mouton, "A Comparative Analysis of Situationalism and 9,9 Management," *Organizational Dynamics* 21 (1982).

5. *Team management*, or a 9,9 style, relies on interdependence through a common stake in the organization's purpose. This interdependence leads to relationships based on trust and respect, and work accomplishment from committed employees.

The Managerial Grid model assumes that there is one best or most effective style of management—the team management, or 9,9 style. Managers who emphasize both concern for people and productivity are presumed to be more successful. As mentioned earlier, however, the evidence for a single best style of management is not strong.**

Charismatic Leadership   Some of the most fascinating research in the behavioral vein is being done on the quality of charisma. *Charisma* is a Greek word that refers to a divinely inspired gift (for example, being able to perform miracles or to predict the future). In the area of leadership, it refers to a type of social influence based on follower perceptions of the leader rather than on the leader's formal authority. **Charismatic leadership** is closest in meaning to the notion of referent power (see Chapter 6).

It is generally agreed that charismatic leaders exude self-confidence and a sense of purpose, and have the ability to articulate a view that subordinates are already likely to accept. Studies of identifiable charismatic individuals indicate that charismatic types often are rejecting of formal authority and willing to

---

**In response to such evidence, however, Blake and Mouton offer conceptual rather than empirical arguments as to why the 9,9 style *should* work when conditions are favorable.[32]

take personal risks because of their strong convictions.[33] Hence, charismatic leaders in formal organizational settings must be willing to accept the organization's primary norms, or face expulsion.

Although many researchers have assumed that charismatic leadership is exceedingly rare and not amenable to study, recent investigations have revealed that charismatic leadership can be found in all varieties of organizations (not-for-profit, large, small, volunteer, entrepreneurial, and so on) and at all levels within organizations.[34]

More recently, the distinction between transactional leadership and transformational leadership has been introduced.[35] **Transactional leadership** refers to the everyday exchanges that take place between leaders and subordinates as they routinely perform their duties. Such exchanges are based on the offer of contingent rewards for specific performance. **Transformational leadership,** a broader concept than charisma, implies reshaping entire strategies of an organization (although the terms *charisma* and *transformational leadership* overlap to a great extent in highlighting the influence of a leader's personal attributes and the trust of followers). Transformational leadership elevates the goals of subordinates and enhances their self-confidence to strive for higher goals. Transformational leadership is potentially strongest at the highest levels of management. This view underscores the importance of vision, intellectual stimulation, and individualized consideration in leadership, and the major role that leadership can have during times of change and crisis.

The phenomenon of charismatic leadership also has its "dark side." Although we can identify instances of positive charismatic leadership (for example, Franklin Roosevelt, John F. Kennedy, Lee Iacocca, and Mahatma Gandhi), we can also identify instances of charismatic leadership that were clearly negative in their consequences (for example, Adolf Hitler, Reverend Jim Jones, and David Koresh). One suggested measure for determining whether charismatic leadership is positive or negative is to examine whether charismatic leaders intentionally try to create devotion to themselves among their followers, rather than commitment to ideological principles.[36] The "dark side" of charisma is typically revealed by efforts that encourage devotion to self. In such cases, ideological principles eventually become vehicles for enhancing personal devotion and power. Positive charismatics focus on enhancing follower commitment to ideological principles, and sometimes actively avoid excessive limelight. Because of the difference in these basic goals, the two types of charismatic leadership have differing consequences for followers (follower enhancement versus follower destruction). Furthermore, it is possible that some negative charismatics begin as positive charismatics (initially placing ideology ahead of personal goals), but eventually are seduced by the experience of self-glorification.

There is reason to believe that early childhood experiences may predispose people to be negative charismatics.[37] Specifically, people whose parents were rejecting and emotionally unresponsive may develop beliefs that others cannot be depended upon for support. As a consequence of such emotional deprivation, these individuals develop narcissistic preoccupations concerning the attainment of prestige and success, along with an exaggerated sense of self-worth. Human relationships are simplified into good/bad or friend/enemy dichotomies, and real or imagined slights are interpreted as evidence of serious disloyalty. The narcissistic personality base serves as the foundation for undertaking self-glorifying projects in which personal credit is accumulated for any positive accomplishments and blame is fixed on others for any shortcomings.

The Situational Approach

Over time, there was a growing recognition that leadership could not be explained solely in terms of leader behavior, and that features of the context in which leadership occurred (for example, subordinate and task attributes) also needed to be examined in order to gain a more complete and accurate understanding of leadership. In this section, we will examine a number of different leadership models that explicitly consider situational attributes.

Fiedler's Contingency Model

Fred Fiedler was one of the earliest proponents of a leadership model that explicitly incorporated situational features. The underlying assumption of his **contingency model of leadership effectiveness** is that group performance is a function of the combination of a leader's style and several relevant features of the situation.[38]

Within the model, leadership style and the situation are defined with a high degree of precision. Leadership style is assessed with a rating scale that measures esteem for the **least preferred coworker,** or **LPC**. The scale asks that a person describe the coworker, past or present, with whom he or she has had the most difficulty working. Sample items from the scale are:

Pleasant : ____ : ____ : ____ : ____ : ____ : ____ : ____ : ____ : Unpleasant
              8   7   6   5   4   3   2   1

Helpful : ____ : ____ : ____ : ____ : ____ : ____ : ____ : ____ : Frustrating
              8   7   6   5   4   3   2   1

Warm   : ____ : ____ : ____ : ____ : ____ : ____ : ____ : ____ : Cold
              8   7   6   5   4   3   2   1

A person who completes the LPC scale by giving relatively lenient responses receives a fairly high total score, while a person who gives harsh marks will obtain a relatively low score. Fiedler infers that people who attain high LPC scores are motivated to achieve positive social relations in their work groups. People with low LPC scores are judged to be less relationship-oriented and more satisfied by task accomplishment. In short, high-LPC individuals are more relationship-motivated, while low-LPC types are more task-motivated. Clearly, Fiedler's LPC notion borrows heavily from the behavioral approach to leadership.

Actual work situations are multifaceted. To describe them, Fiedler proposed a single, broad definition of a critical situational dimension (favorableness) and several specific underlying attributes that define this larger dimension. According to his model, situations differ in terms of how favorable they are for a leader. **Situational favorableness,** therefore, is a broad notion of how easy or difficult a setting might seem to be for a manager.

Three factors are believed to underlie situational favorableness. In order of relative importance, they are (1) leader–member relations, (2) task structure, and (3) position power.

Leader–member relations reflect the extent to which a leader is accepted and generates positive emotional reactions from his or her subordinates. A situation in which leader–member relations are relatively good is potentially much easier to manage than a situation in which such relations are strained.

Task structure is the degree to which the job at hand can be clearly specified. Such structure is evident in rules, job descriptions, and policies. When tasks are relatively structured, there is little ambiguity about how they should be approached. In addition, goals are clear, performance measures are understood, and multiple solutions or approaches to a problem are unlikely to exist. With low task structure, the opposite holds true.

Position power is the extent to which a leader has recourse to formal sanctions. That is, can a leader control the fate of subordinates by offering rewards or threatening punishment? Other things being equal, situations in which a leader has position power are considered easier to manage than situations in which such power is lacking.

If we combine these three situational attributes, we obtain eight possible combinations, or octants, representing a range of situations (Figure 7.3). Situations to the left side of this arrangement are highly favorable (that is, they possess attributes that should make it easy to lead), while situations to the right side are highly unfavorable (possessing attributes that make it difficult to lead).

To illustrate these situations, consider octant 1. This is a situation in which all lights are "green." The subordinates and leader get along, the task is clearly structured so that all know what they should be doing, and the leader can fall back on his or her position power if need be. Such a situation might be enjoyed by a foreman in a nonunionized manufacturing setting who is admired by his subordinates. Octant 8, in contrast, has many obstacles to group performance. Here, the leader and the group's members have poor interpersonal relations, the task in which they are engaged is ambiguous, and the leader lacks any real base of power to reward or coerce. Such a situation might arise when an unpopular individual is asked to chair an ad hoc committee to prepare a report on how to ensure the quality of work life in the 21st century. In this situation, all lights are "red."

Fiedler applied his contingency model to a large variety of work groups (service station crews, basketball teams, laboratory groups, bomber crews, and others). The results of this data gathering suggested that high-LPC (interpersonally oriented) leaders were more effective than low-LPC (task-oriented) leaders only in certain octants. Low-LPC leaders were found to be more effective in the remaining octants. Generally, low-LPC leaders were

FIGURE 7.3 *Fiedler's Contingency Model*

	Most Favorable							Least Favorable
Leader–Member Relations	Good	Good	Good	Good	Poor	Poor	Poor	Poor
Task Structure	Strd.	Strd.	Unstrd.	Unstrd.	Strd.	Strd.	Unstrd.	Unstrd.
Position Power	Strong	Weak	Strong	Weak	Strong	Weak	Strong	Weak
Octant	1	2	3	4	5	6	7	8

FIGURE 7.4   *Summary of Fiedler's Original Findings*

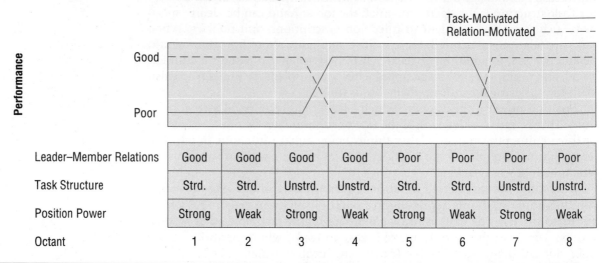

Leader–Member Relations	Good	Good	Good	Good	Poor	Poor	Poor	Poor
Task Structure	Strd.	Strd.	Unstrd.	Unstrd.	Strd.	Strd.	Unstrd.	Unstrd.
Position Power	Strong	Weak	Strong	Weak	Strong	Weak	Strong	Weak
Octant	1	2	3	4	5	6	7	8

determined to be more effective than high-LPC leaders in extremely favorable and unfavorable situations, while high-LPC leaders were relatively more effective in octants of moderate favorability. Figure 7.4 summarizes Fiedler's original findings.[††]

An important question remains: *Why* should high-LPC leaders be more effective in moderately favorable situations, while low-LPC leaders are more effective in the remaining situations? Presently, there is no satisfactory answer to this question. Even Fiedler admits that the model is still largely a "black box" in that no one has a fully satisfying explanation as to why the observed relationships should be as they were reported.[39] Perhaps the most popular explanation is still the original one offered by Fiedler when he first proposed the model. At the time, he contended that leaders who are task oriented will be successful in favorable situations because they will emphasize task accomplishment in a situation that merely requires persistence. So, too, in extremely difficult situations (octants 7 and 8) what is needed is firm, task-oriented leadership. In these unfavorable situations, if anything at all is going to be accomplished, the leader must have a strong desire to see results. Interpersonally oriented leaders, however, may have an advantage in settings that emit "mixed" signals. In these situations, such leaders can apply their social skills to overcoming the more manageable obstacles to performance.

Because the model was induced from findings on group performance, other explanations can be offered for the pretzel-shaped relationship portrayed in Figure 7.4. One alternative interpretation is that the findings reflect a "matching" of leader complexity with situational complexity. This line of reasoning holds that high-LPC individuals are cognitively complex: They are able to perceive people and events in shades of gray, rather than in simple black-and-white terms. This is reflected by their tendency to give some positive

---

[††]Although Figure 7.4 illustrates the essential points of the contingency model, it is not, strictly speaking, accurate in that levels of performance are not compared between octants, only within octants.

ratings in addition to negative ratings to their least preferred coworker. Low-LPC leaders, on the other hand, may be more cognitively simple in that they judge people and objects in a fairly simplistic fashion (good-bad, black-white) without seeing or accepting complexities and nuances. So, too, we can conceptualize situations as being relatively simple versus complex. Simple situations would be those in which the major attributes are largely congruent—that is, all good or all bad. Examples of such simple situations would be the highly favorable and highly unfavorable octants of the contingency model. Complex situations are those in which the signals are mixed, as in the middle octants.

According to this complexity interpretation, cognitively complex people are better as leaders in relatively complex settings, while cognitively simple people do better as leaders in relatively simple settings. As yet, no one has offered any evidence that clearly refutes a complexity-matching interpretation of Fiedler's original findings.

Critics point out that the lack of a strong explanation for the dynamics of the model means that the model is still little more than a "black box." Also, Fiedler's initial results were gathered from a large survey of a variety of work groups. Because of the possibility that these early results may reflect chance, it is necessary that other researchers replicate Fiedler's findings with a different set of work groups. Such efforts have generated very mixed results, so that considerable controversy still surrounds the validity of the contingency model.[40]

Implications of the Contingency Model   Perhaps the most basic conclusion to be drawn from Fiedler's model is that a leader who is effective in one situation may be ineffective in another. Managers need to recognize this fact and understand the limitations that a situation may place on them.

Fiedler suggests that leaders should attempt to engineer facets of their work setting in order to enhance their personal effectiveness rather than try to change their leadership style.[41] He contends that personal style is fairly difficult to change, even for an individual who strongly desires to do so. Therefore, it can sometimes be easier to change the situational attributes to fit one's own style. This may mean deliberately trying to change situational favorableness by enhancing relations with subordinates, changing the amount of structure in a task, or gaining more formal power with the goal of achieving a more conducive work setting based on personal leadership style.

Finally, there is reason to believe that performance actually declines across octants as we move toward the unfavorable end of situational favorability.[42] Within each octant, we might hope to find the predicted orderings of group performance based on leader LPC. However, groups in octant 1, led by low-LPC leaders, would likely do better than groups under other leaders in all other octants. From this reasoning, the notion of engineering situations for optimal performance leads to the unusual prediction that we should try to make all settings into octant 1 (that is, good leader–member relations, structured task, and strong position power), with low-LPC individuals as leaders. Changes in any of the octant parameters or changes in leadership style should produce relatively poorer performance. As yet, this notion has not been formally tested.

Path–Goal Theory

Path–goal theory suggests that leaders can influence the satisfaction, motivation, and performance of group members in several ways.[43] A primary means is by making rewards contingent on the accomplishment of performance *goals*. (This notion is similar to the notion of transactional leadership, discussed earlier.) In addition, a leader can aid group members in obtaining valued rewards by clarifying the *paths* to these performance goals and by removing obstacles to performance.

In order to accomplish these ends, a leader may be required to adopt different styles of leadership behavior as the situation dictates. Four distinct types of leader behavior have been identified:[44]

1. **Directive leadership** involves giving specific guidance to subordinates and asking them to follow standard rules. It is similar to the high-structure/low-consideration style in the Ohio State scheme, which was discussed earlier.

2. **Supportive leadership** includes being friendly to subordinates and sensitive to their needs. It is similar to the low-structure/high-consideration style.

3. **Participative leadership** involves sharing information with subordinates and consulting with them before making decisions. It is much like the high-structure/high-consideration style.

4. **Achievement-oriented leadership** entails setting challenging goals and emphasizing excellence, while simultaneously showing confidence that subordinates will perform well. It is not really equivalent to any of the Ohio State styles of management.

All four styles can be, and often are, used by a single leader in varying situations.

A number of propositions have been generated from path–goal theory regarding the impact of certain leader behaviors on subordinate performance and satisfaction. Chief among these are:

- In ambiguous situations, subordinates will be more satisfied with leaders who exhibit directive behavior. This satisfaction results from the subordinates' appreciation of the supervisor's help in increasing the probability of their obtaining a desired reward. In situations with greater task or goal clarity, such directive behavior will be of less value to subordinates.

- In stressful environments, supportive leader behavior will ameliorate subordinate dissatisfaction.

- Leaders who possess influence with their own superiors (upward influence) can enhance unit performance and satisfaction. With upward influence, a leader is better able to help subordinates be successful and receive appropriate rewards.

Thus far, there has been little research on path–goal theory. Available evidence suggests that when subordinates are involved with ambiguous tasks, directive leadership can increase satisfaction and motivation. With fairly unambiguous tasks, however, directive leadership can decrease satisfaction and motivation.[45] Also, supportive leader behavior typically is associated with increased subordinate satisfaction. When subordinates are employed on tasks that are inherently distasteful or frustrating, supportive leader behavior can enhance subordinate satisfaction.[46] Although path–goal theory remains as yet largely untested, its greatest theoretical strength seems to lie in its integration of leader behavior with such expectancy theory notions (Chapter 4) as providing contingent, valued rewards for performance.

Situational Leadership Theory

Of the various contextual views to leadership, **situational leadership theory** has been the least researched.[47] Yet it is widely used in management training programs. The theory is closely based on the leadership styles generated by the Ohio State model. The unique contribution of the model lies in its emphasis on matching a particular leadership style to the "maturity" of the followers.

Subordinate maturity is defined as the capacity to set high but attainable goals, the willingness to take on responsibility, and the possession of relevant education and/or experience. Maturity is judged in relation to a given task. Therefore, a particular subordinate may be quite mature in relation to one task and immature in relation to another. Subordinate maturity contains two components: **job maturity,** or technical knowledge and task-relevant skills, and **psychological maturity,** or feelings of self-confidence and the willingness and ability to accept responsibility. A subordinate who is highly mature possesses both technical competence and self-confidence for a given task. A subordinate who is low on maturity for a task lacks both ability and confidence. Although the theory acknowledges other variables as potentially important (for example, time pressure), it focuses primarily on follower maturity as the critical situational attribute.

The central thesis of the model is that as follower maturity increases, a leader should rely more on relationship-oriented behavior and less on task-oriented behavior. Beyond a certain point on this maturity dimension, however, the leader should rely less on both task-oriented and relationship-oriented behaviors. This pattern is depicted in Figure 7.5. With subordinates who are highly immature (situation M1), the leader should emphasize task-oriented behavior and be very directive and autocratic. In essence, this is a style of leadership that involves *telling* subordinates what to do. For situation M2, subordinates who are still on the somewhat low side of maturity, a leader should focus on being more relationship-oriented. Such a leader works on *selling* his or her ideas to the subordinates. Subordinates who are somewhat high in maturity (M3) will also need a fair degree of support and considerate treatment. The appropriate style in this case is one of *participating* with subordinates. Lastly, subordinates who are highly mature (M4) are self-motivated and can be trusted to rely on their own self-direction. In fact, highly mature employees may actually expect to be given a great deal of autonomy. The preferred style of leadership with such subordinates is one of *delegating.*

The theory was originally offered with little empirical evidence of its validity. Available research suggests that the model may only be partially correct in that less experienced (that is, less mature) subordinates may be somewhat more responsive to greater direction. Furthermore, the theoretical aspects of the model have been criticized for not giving a coherent or precise rationale for the proposed relationships.[48] Nonetheless, this model possesses an intuitive appeal that makes it an attractive instructional device for practicing managers. It also emphasizes the need for flexible, adaptable leader behaviors. But until more evidence is available, it is not possible to claim that situational leadership theory is superior to other perspectives.

The Vroom–Yetton Leadership Model

Victor Vroom and Philip Yetton developed a very promising model that deals with one specific facet of leadership: how to select a leadership style for making a decision.[49] The **Vroom–Yetton model** suggests that there are five decision-making styles, ranging from highly autocratic to highly participative. In order of increasing participation, the five styles are:

- *Autocratic I (AI)*—A manager solves a problem using the information that is already available.

- *Autocratic II (AII)*—A manager obtains additional information from subordinates and then solves the problem.

- *Consultative I (CI)*—A manager shares the problem with subordinates on an individual basis and obtains their ideas and suggestions. Again, the manager chooses a solution to the problem at hand.

FIGURE 7.5   *The Situational Leadership Model*

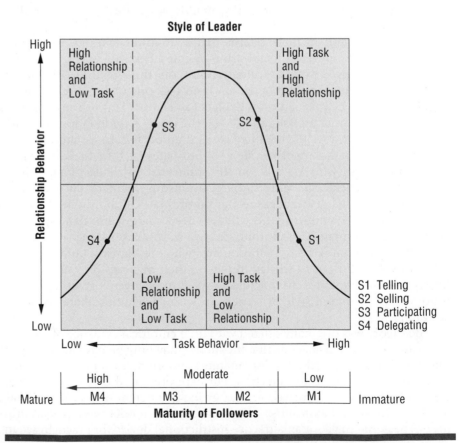

Source: P. Hersey and K. Blanchard, *Management of Organizational Behavior* (Englewood Cliffs, N.J.: Prentice-Hall, 1982), 152.

- *Consultative II (CII)*—A manager shares the problem with subordinates as a group. The final decision may or may not reflect subordinate input.
- *Group (G)*—A manager meets with subordinates as a group. However, the manager acts as a chairperson who focuses and directs discussion, but does not impose his or her will on the group. True subordinate participation, in a democratic sense, is sought.

Which of these five styles is most appropriate for a given situation depends on a number of important considerations. In total, Vroom and Yetton identify seven questions that must be answered to determine the appropriate style. These underlying contingencies (or decision rules) focus on such issues as whether sufficient information is available to make a good decision and whether subordinates can be trusted to approach the problem from a perspective that is congruent with organizational goals. The seven questions can be arranged in a sequential fashion that permits us to follow a logical path in matching a single, preferred leader style to a given situation.

Figure 7.6 shows the decision tree that Vroom and Yetton devised for selecting a best or most appropriate style. The seven decision rules are listed across the top of the model. For each question, a manager is to provide a yes or no response. At the end of each branch in the tree is a designated style, denoted by AI, AII, CI, CII, or G.

To see how a manager would use the decision tree, imagine a case in which a manager must deal with an order processor who is not inputting enough purchase orders each day (the answer to question A is yes). If the manager has a clear understanding of why the employee is a poor performer (B = yes), if the subordinate must accept the manager's decision in order for the solution to work (D = yes), and if the manager is also certain that the decision will be accepted by the subordinate (E = yes), then the manager should take a nonparticipative approach to dealing with the problem (AI).

As another example, consider a manager who is contemplating the introduction of flexible work schedules (Chapter 5). For such a decision to be successfully implemented, it is worthwhile to consider what the Vroom–Yetton model suggests. In this situation, one solution is likely to be more rational than another (A = yes), but the manager does not know the extent of individual preferences and job-related obstacles (B = no). The problem is relatively unstructured (C = no), while acceptance by subordinates is critical to implementation (D = yes). As the manager cannot be reasonably certain that an imposed solution will be accepted by subordinates (E = no), the final choice of style depends on whether subordinates are judged to share the organization's goals. If the manager believes that the subordinates share the organization's goals, then a highly participative approach is in order (G). Otherwise, a less participative strategy (CII) is appropriate.

The Vroom–Yetton model provides a useful device for diagnosing a situation. It prescribes a specific type of behavior for a leader who is confronted with a specific problem. As such, it is much more precise and somewhat more practical than the other models we have examined.

Further studies have tended to support the validity of the Vroom–Yetton model. Work by the original researchers as well as by independent investigators indicates that the model closely describes the actual decision process of most managers.[50] Also, the model is widely used by organizations that specialize in managerial training (for example, Kepner Tregoe).[51]

FIGURE 7.6   *The Vroom–Yetton Model*

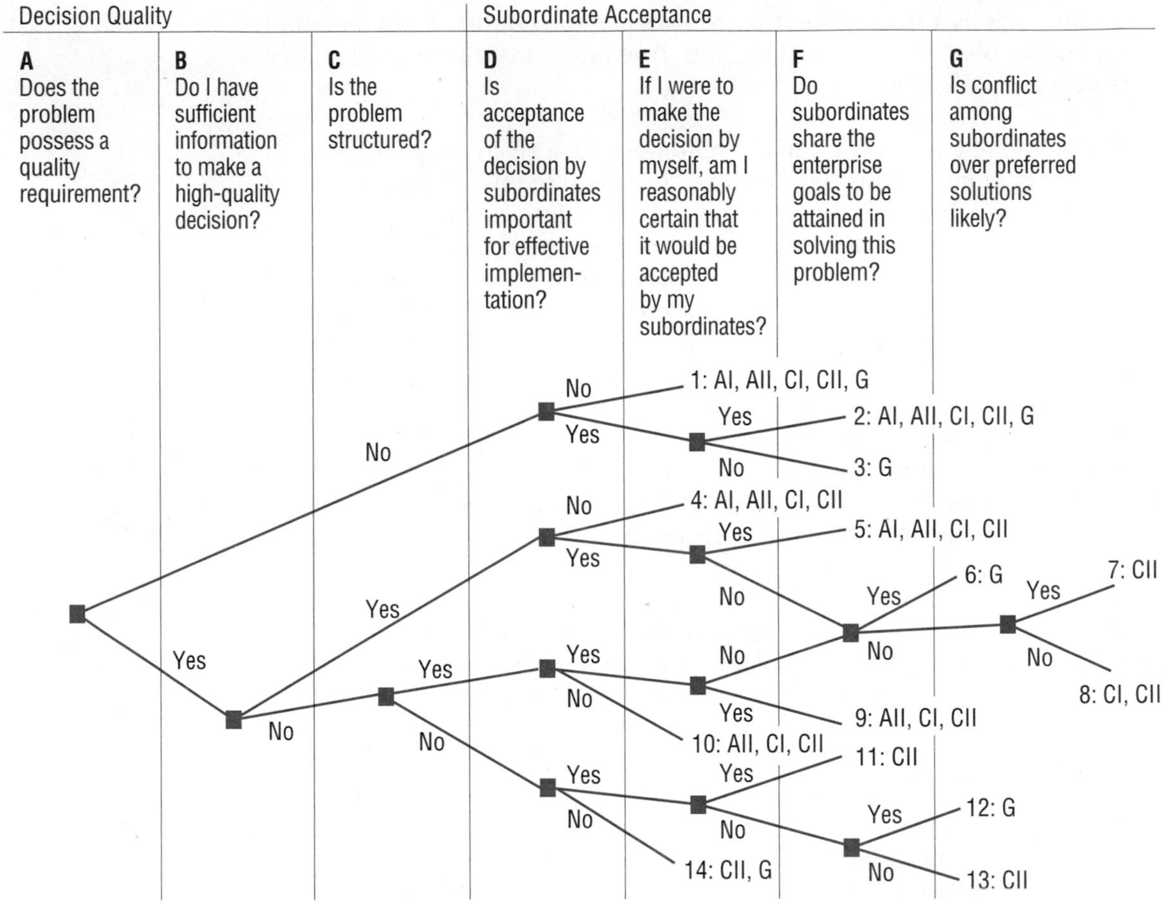

| Decision Quality | | | Subordinate Acceptance | | | |

| **A** Does the problem possess a quality requirement? | **B** Do I have sufficient information to make a high-quality decision? | **C** Is the problem structured? | **D** Is acceptance of the decision by subordinates important for effective implementation? | **E** If I were to make the decision by myself, am I reasonably certain that it would be accepted by my subordinates? | **F** Do subordinates share the enterprise goals to be attained in solving this problem? | **G** Is conflict among subordinates over preferred solutions likely? |

Decision-tree branches:

1: AI, AII, CI, CII, G
2: AI, AII, CI, CII, G
3: G
4: AI, AII, CI, CII
5: AI, AII, CI, CII
6: G
7: CII
8: CI, CII
9: AII, CI, CII
10: AII, CI, CII
11: CII
12: G
13: CII
14: CII, G

Decision-Making Methods
  AI = Autocratic decision without subordinates' input
 AII = Autocratic decision using information gathered from subordinates
  CI = Consultative decision with problem discussed individually with each subordinate
 CII = Consultative decision with problem discussed with subordinates as a group
  G = Group decision
Note: The numbers 1–14 denote Problem Types.

Source: Victor H. Vroom and Philip W. Yetton, *Leadership and Decision Making* (University of Pittsburgh Press, 1973), 41–42. Used with permission.

More recently, Victor Vroom and Art Jago have attempted to address several shortcomings of the model.[52] For example, it can be very difficult to always answer the seven decision rules with a simple yes or no response. Often, a manager has only a sense of what is likely to occur. In such cases, the manager may be able to give probability estimates but not simple, firm answers. To address this and other problems, Vroom and Jago have made a number of modifications, such as permitting probabilistic responses. As a result, the model is evolving into a very complex and unwieldy set of mathematical equations.

Nonetheless, managers who are not particularly interested in precise mathematical advice, perhaps because they lack the time or a computer program to work out the equations, will probably continue to use the decision tree presented in Figure 7.6 as a quick guide to selecting a leadership style.

The Vertical Dyad Linkage Model

A further perspective on the leadership process is provided by the **vertical dyad linkage model** (sometimes termed the leader–member exchange model[53] of leadership). In some respects, this model is similar to the other approaches we have considered in that it focuses on the influence of subordinates on leader behavior and the topic of subordinate participation in decision making. In all other ways, however, the model is unique.[54]

The model contends that much of the past theorizing on the leadership process presumes the existence of an *average* leadership style that a manager exhibits toward all members of a work group. But careful considerations reveals that leaders do not typically display a uniform style of leadership or set of behaviors toward all group members. Instead, they behave somewhat differently toward each subordinate. The model contends that each *linkage*, or relationship, that exists between the leader and a subordinate is likely to differ in quality. Thus, the same supervisor may have poor interpersonal relations with some subordinates and fairly open and trusting relations with others. In each work unit, these pairs of relations, or *dyads*, can be judged in terms of whether an individual is relatively "in" or "out" with the supervisor. Members of the in-group (or, more correctly, in-subgroup) are invited to share in decision making and are given added responsibility. Members of the out-group, however, are supervised within the narrow terms of their formal employment contract. In essence, an in-group member is elevated to the unofficial role of "trusted assistant," while an out-group member is assigned the role of "hired hand." In-group members, in many respects, enjoy the benefits of enriched jobs with many opportunities to participate in decision making. Out-group members are not given these opportunities. Further, it is expected that in-group members will display greater job satisfaction, superior performance, higher commitment, and lower turnover.

Panel *a* in Figure 7.7 portrays the traditional view of how leaders and subordinates are perceived, in that all subordinates are seen as being treated equally by a supervisor—that is, they have equal access to the leader, equal influence in decision making, equal information exchange, and equal social distance from the leader. Panel *b*, however, reflects the vertical dyad linkage perspective, wherein a subset of the subordinates (the in-group) has better working relations with the leader than another subset (the out-group). The differing distances of the individual subordinates from the leader reflect differences in the equality of the working relationships, and, therefore, differences in influence, authority, and information access.

How people come to be members of the in-group or the out-group is not as yet fully understood. Preliminary evidence suggests, however, that the leader's initial impression of an employee's competency plays an important role. Certainly, leaders and in-group members strongly believe that competency is the distinguishing characteristic between in-group members and out-group members. Out-group members, however, are just as firmly convinced

FIGURE 7.7   *Contrasting Views of Leader-Subordinate Relations*

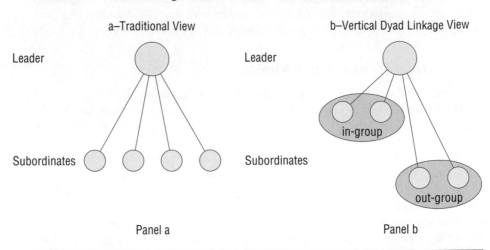

Panel a   Panel b

that ingratiation, favoritism, and politics are more important than competency in the selection of in-group members. In fact, interpersonal attraction probably does play some role in the selection process. However, it is likely that perceived competence plays a much larger and complementary role in most instances.

The existence of in-groups and out-groups is easy to demonstrate. In the original studies on the vertical dyad linkage (VDL) model, employees and their superiors were asked to identify who in each unit was relatively more or less trusted by the superior. Generally, people had little difficulty identifying such a hierarchy. Overall, the membership status of a particular individual (in versus out) is understood by all group members, especially the individual in question.

The original and validating studies on the VDL model generally have provided support for the model's central predictions, which are that in-group members are more satisfied and are judged to be superior performers. That in-group and out-group status may be related to employee turnover, however, has received far less consistent support.[55] An additional finding is that in-group members tend to see job-related problems in much the same way as their superiors. For example, in-group members' reports of job problems correlate more closely with their superior's perceptions than do the reports of out-group members.[56]

In summary, it seems that leaders do distinguish among their subordinates by inviting some to join an inner cadre, while excluding others. Initial impressions of the competency of subordinates can lead to categorization as in- or out-group members, which may affect their subsequent performance and promotion or turnover.

Substitutes for Leadership

It has been suggested, somewhat controversially, that leader behavior may sometimes be unnecessary or superfluous because factors in the situation offer sufficient aid to subordinates.[57] Such factors might include subordinate ability, training, or experience. The notion that leaders may not play a crucial role in all settings can help to explain why some work groups do quite well despite the presence of a poor leader. In other words, there can be situations in which leadership is unimportant or redundant.

Two types of variables can account for cases in which leadership may be redundant or unimportant: leadership substitutes and leadership neutralizers. The presence of a **leadership substitute** will make leadership redundant or unnecessary, while the presence of a **leadership neutralizer** prevents a leader from taking action in some fashion. Table 7.3 lists some possible leadership substitutes and neutralizers for two styles of leader behavior.

The essence of the "substitutes for leadership" proposal is that leadership is only one factor in successful work-group performance. The notions of substitutes and neutralizers help us keep a proper perspective on the role of leadership in work groups. Although leadership can be critical to unit performance, certain preconditions are necessary. In addition, the idea of leadership substitutes and neutralizers helps to account for the largely mixed results of studies on leadership. Studies of leadership that ignore the effect of neutralizers and substitutes may fail to uncover expected relationships because the particular leadership process is irrelevant, rather than because the theory is invalid.

TABLE 7.3   *Substitutes and Neutralizers for Supportive and Instrumental Leadership*

Factor	Supportive Leadership	Instrumental Leadership
Subordinate Characteristics		
1. Experience, ability, training		Substitute
2. "Professional" orientation	Substitute	Substitute
3. Indifference toward organizational rewards	Neutralizer	Neutralizer
Task Characteristics		
1. Structured, routine task		Substitute
2. Task feedback		Substitute
3. Intrinsically satisfying task	Substitute	
Organizational Characteristics		
1. Cohesive work group	Substitute	Substitute
2. Leader lacks position power	Neutralizer	Neutralizer
3. Formalization of goals and plans		Substitute
4. Rigid rules and procedures		Neutralizer
5. Physical distance between leader and subordinates	Neutralizer	Neutralizer

Note: Supportive and instrumental leadership are analogous to leader consideration and leader structuring.

Source: G. Yukl, *Leadership in Organizations* (Upper Saddle River, N.J.: Prentice-Hall, 1998).

Obstacles to Personal Effectiveness in Leadership and Managerial Positions

As noted earlier, leadership can sometimes be irrelevant to a given situation because of subordinate, task, or organizational characteristics. Leaders in such settings may find their assignments particularly difficult because of such realities. Leaders can also face a rough road for reasons beyond their control or for failing to follow some widely accepted management wisdom. J.K. Van Fleet has compiled a list of the biggest mistakes that managers make.[58] Any one of these mistakes can be fatal to a manager's career, and many of these principles are not readily deducible from any theory. Following is a selected list of the top ten mistakes:

1. Failing to stay abreast of developments in your field and limiting yourself to your own specialty area
2. Refusing to seek higher responsibility or to take responsibility for your own actions
3. Failing to make sure that assignments are understood, supervised, and accomplished
4. Refusing to assess your own performance and abilities realistically
5. Using your position for personal gain or failing to tell the truth
6. Not setting a positive, personal example for subordinates
7. Trying to be liked rather than respected
8. Emphasizing rules rather than skill
9. Failing to keep criticism in a constructive vein
10. Not attending to employee gripes and complaints

Additional research on why managers fail has been conducted by the Center for Creative Leadership in Greensboro, North Carolina.[59] From detailed interviews with managers who were initially successful in their careers but eventually failed (that is, they plateaued, retired early, or were dismissed), it was learned that failure was sometimes influenced by external factors, such as economic downturns or uncontrollable events. Four sets of individual factors, however, also were associated with failure:

1. Defensiveness: trying to hide mistakes or fix blame on others, rather than taking responsibility and seeking to remedy errors
2. Emotional instability: engaging in emotional outbursts or displaying moodiness, rather than projecting confidence and a calm demeanor
3. Poor interpersonal skills: lacking sensitivity and tact, and being arrogant or abrasive
4. Weak technical and cognitive skills: lacking technical know-how for upper-level jobs, possessing a narrow perspective based on a single specialty, or trying to micromanage the work of subordinates who possess substantial technical competence.

It is difficult to state precisely the level of flawed leadership in organizational positions. However, it has been estimated that the base rate for seriously flawed leadership exceeds 50 percent.[60] This suggests that the majority of employed adults work for someone who is not capable of exercising adequate leadership skills. The downside consequence of this state of affairs is that employees often retaliate against their supervisors in subtle ways (such as withholding loyalty, reducing output or customer service, and engaging in theft, sabotage, and vandalism).

SUMMARY

1. *Define leadership.* Leadership is a process through which a person tries to get organizational members to do something the person desires. The leader's influence extends beyond supervisory responsibility and formal authority.

2. *Describe ways in which leader behavior is related to employee attitudes and performance.* A democratic leadership style may lead to greater employee satisfaction and higher-quality output. Autocratic leadership may lead to a greater quantity of output, accompanied by decreased quality and employee satisfaction. Up to a point, high consideration for the employee may be related to employee satisfaction, and low consideration may lead to employee dissatisfaction. Both the Ohio State and the Managerial Grid models presume that the most successful managers emphasize concern for both people and productivity.

3. *Explain the importance of leadership.* Leadership has been shown to make a difference in the performance of groups and organizations. Studies of the impact of changing leaders reveal that the performance of poorly performing groups can be enhanced. Excessive turnover of leaders, however, can be detrimental to unit performance.

4. *Identify the factors underlying situational favorableness and explain how they influence a leader's effectiveness.* A favorable situation exists when leader–member relations are good, task structure (the degree to which the job can be clearly specified) is high, and the leader's position power (the extent to which the leader has recourse to formal sanctions) is high. Interpersonally oriented leaders are more effective in moderately favorable situations, whereas task-oriented leaders are more effective in situations that are extremely favorable or unfavorable.

5. *Explain how leaders can clarify paths to goals to motivate employees.* Path–goal theory suggests that leaders can affect satisfaction, motivation, and performance by basing rewards on the accomplishment of performance goals and by clarifying the paths to these goals and removing obstacles to performance. Depending on the situation, the leader does this by choosing one of four types of leader behavior: directive leadership, supportive leadership, participative leadership, or achievement-oriented leadership.

6. *Describe the components of subordinate maturity and the relevance of subordinate maturity to leadership style.* Subordinate maturity consists of job maturity (technical knowledge and task-relevant skills) and psychological maturity (feelings of self-confidence and self-respect). Situational leadership theory proposes that the leader should change his or her style to match the employee's level of maturity.

7. *Describe the decision-making styles of the Vroom–Yetton model and explain how you would select an appropriate style.* A manager can solve a problem by (1) using already available information; (2) obtaining additional information from subordinates and then making an individual decision; (3) sharing the

problem with subordinates individually, obtaining their ideas, and making an individual decision; (4) sharing the problem with subordinates as a group and possibly using subordinates' ideas in reaching a solution; or (5) meeting with subordinates as a group, focusing and directing discussion, but not imposing his or her will. To use the Vroom–Yetton decision tree in a particular situation, the manager answers the questions from left to right, moving along a branch of the tree. At the end of each branch is the style designated appropriate for the particular decision.

8. *Describe a way to evaluate leadership style taking into account managers' views of different employees.* In the vertical dyad linkage model, employees are members of an in-group or an out-group in the eyes of the manager. In-group members are invited to share in decision making and are given added responsibility, whereas out-group members are supervised within the narrow terms of their employment contract.

9. *Define substitute and leadership neutralizer and give examples of each.* A leadership substitute is a factor that makes leadership redundant or unnecessary; one example would be an extremely cohesive work group. A leadership neutralizer is a factor that prevents a leader from being effective; one such factor would be subordinates who are indifferent to organizational rewards. Other examples of each factor are shown in Table 7.3.

10. *Offer some major reasons why managers fail.* Managers fail for a variety of reasons. Along with external influences, failure can arise from such personal factors as defensiveness, emotional instability, poor interpersonal skills, and weak technical and cognitive skills.

KEY TERMS

Leadership
Informal leader
Cognitive resource theory
Triarchic model of intelligence
Task orientation
Employee orientation
Consideration
Initiating structure
Charismatic leadership
Transactional leadership
Transformational leadership
Contingency model of leadership effectiveness
Least preferred coworker (LPC)
Situational favorableness
Leader–member relations

Task structure
Position power
Path–goal theory
Directive leadership
Supportive leadership
Participative leadership
Achievement-oriented leadership
Situational leadership theory
Subordinate maturity
Job maturity
Psychological maturity
Vroom–Yetton model
Vertical dyad linkage model
Leadership substitute
Leadership neutralizer

CRITICAL INCIDENT

Hal's Halo

Hal Baines has been employed by IFP Financial Services Corporation for more than ten years. Two years ago, he was promoted to unit supervisor. Hal has always been a very loyal employee and has worked hard to follow and support the company's policies and procedures. In talking with any of Hal's superiors, one gets the impression that he is well liked and viewed as an asset to the organization.

Because employee dissatisfaction has become more pronounced in Hal's unit, you have been asked to assess the situation. In private talks with his employees, you discover that they think Hal is consumed with the desire to please upper-level management. They don't feel he "goes to bat" for the unit. For example, at each of the past two budget hearings, their department has received little or no increase. Also, whenever new ideas or suggestions from one of the employees are given to Hal to pass on, nothing ever comes of them. This has resulted in frustration and a general feeling of being unappreciated. Finally, whenever a request is made of Hal's department, regardless of whatever else is being done, Hal always promises to get it done immediately. This has meant additional work and long hours without compensation or recognition for many employees.

As the consultant, how would you address the following questions?

1. In terms of the leadership theories discussed in this chapter, how would you portray Hal's leadership style?

2. If you met with Hal right now, what advice or suggestions would you offer to alter his style of leadership?

3. Do you think a leadership skills training program would be helpful to Hal? If so, what should it consist of?

Source: Written by Bruce Kemelgor.

EXPERIENTIAL EXERCISE

*Leadership Style Profile**

According to situational leadership theory, there is no one best way to influence people. Most of the research on leadership indicates that leader behavior is a combination of task and relationship orientations. Task behavior is the extent to which a leader provides direction. Telling people what to do and/or setting goals for them and defining their roles is indicative of a task orientation. Providing support, being open, and being a good communicator are some of the behaviors of a relationship-oriented leader.

One's leadership style is, therefore, a combination of task and relationship behaviors. This exercise is designed to provide you with a profile of your leadership style.

Assume you are involved in each of the following 12 situations. Read each item and then circle the letter of the alternative that would most closely describe your behavior in the situations presented.

Situation 1

The employees in your program appear to be having serious problems getting the job done. Their performance has been going downhill rapidly. They have

---

*This exercise is adapted from the Managerial Skills Profile, Federal Government Publication 79-141P. It is based, in part, on Hersey and Blanchard's "Leader Effectiveness and Adoptability Description," University Associates, San Diego.

not responded to your efforts to be friendly or to your expressions of concern for their welfare.

a. Reestablish the need for following program procedures and meeting the expectations for task accomplishment.

b. Be sure that staff members know you are available for discussion, but don't pressure them.

c. Talk with your employees and then set performance goals.

d. Wait and see what happens.

Situation 2

During the past few months, the quality of work done by staff members has been increasing. Record keeping is accurate and up-to-date. You have made sure that all staff members are aware of your performance expectations.

a. Stay uninvolved.

b. Continue to emphasize the importance of completing tasks and meeting deadlines.

c. Be supportive and provide clear feedback. Continue to make sure that staff members are aware of performance expectations.

d. Make every effort to let staff members feel important and involved in the decision-making process.

Situation 3

Performance and interpersonal relations among your staff have been good. You have normally left them alone. However, a new situation has developed, and it appears that the staff members are unable to solve the problem themselves.

a. Bring the group together and work as a team to solve the problem.

b. Continue to leave them alone to work it out.

c. Act quickly and firmly to identify the problem and establish procedures to correct it.

d. Encourage the staff to work on the problem, letting them know you are available as a resource and for discussion if they need you.

Situation 4

You are considering a major change in your program. Your staff has a fine record of accomplishment and a strong commitment to excellence. They are supportive of the need for change and have been involved in the planning.

a. Continue to involve the staff in the planning, but you direct the change.

b. Announce the changes and then implement them with close supervision.

c. Allow the group to be involved in developing the change, but don't push the process.

d. Let the staff manage the change process.

Situation 5

You are aware that staff performance has been going down during the past several months. They need continual reminding to get tasks done on time and seem unconcerned about meeting objectives. In the past, redefining procedures and role expectations has helped.

a. Allow your staff to set their own direction.

b. Get suggestions from the staff, but see that the objectives are met.

c. Redefine goals and expectations and supervise carefully.

d. Allow the staff to be involved in setting goals, but don't pressure them.

Situation 6

You have just been appointed director of a program that had been running smoothly under the previous director. She had the reputation of "running a tight ship." You want to maintain the quality of the program and the service delivery, but you would like to begin humanizing the environment.

a. Do nothing at the present time.

b. Continue with the administrative pattern set by the previous director, monitoring the staff and emphasizing the importance of task accomplishment.

c. Get the staff involved in decision making and planning, but continue to see that objectives are met and quality is maintained.

d. Reach out to staff members to let them feel important and involved.

Situation 7

You are considering expanding your unit's responsibilities. Your staff members have made suggestions about the proposed change and are enthusiastic. They operate effectively day to day and are willing to assume responsibility.

a. Outline the changes and monitor carefully.

b. Reach consensus with the staff on the proposed changes and allow the staff members to organize the implementation.

c. Solicit input from the staff on proposed changes, but maintain control of the implementation.

d. Let the staff handle it.

Situation 8

Staff members have been working well. Interpersonal relations and morale are good. The quality of service delivery is excellent. You are somewhat uncomfortable with your apparent lack of direction of the group.

a. Be careful not to hurt your relationship with the staff by becoming too directive.

b. Take steps to ensure that staff members are working in a well-defined manner.

c. Leave the staff alone to work as they have been.

d. Discuss the situation with the staff, and then initiate the necessary changes.

Situation 9

You have been appointed to replace the chairman of a task force that is long overdue in making requested recommendations for certification requirements. The group is not clear on its goal. Attendance at meetings has been poor. Frequently, the meetings are more social than task oriented. Potentially, task force members have the knowledge and experience to complete the task.

a. Let the group members work out their problems.

b. Solicit recommendations from the group, but see that the objectives are met.

c. Redefine and clarify the goals, tasks, and expectations, and carefully supervise progress toward task completion.

d. Allow group involvement in setting goals, but don't push.

Situation 10

Your employees are usually able to take responsibility. However, they are not responding well to your recent redefinition of performance standards.

a. Supervise carefully to ensure that standards are met.

b. Solicit input from the staff on performance standards. Incorporate their suggestions and monitor their progress toward meeting the standards.

c. Allow staff involvement in the redefinition of performance standards, but don't push.

d. Avoid confrontation. Apply no pressure and see what happens.

Situation 11

You have been promoted to the position of manager. The previous manager appeared to be uninvolved in the affairs of the staff. They have adequately handled their tasks and responsibilities. Their morale is high.

a. Become active in directing the staff toward working in a clearly defined manner.

b. Involve your staff in decision making and consistently reinforce good contributions.

c. Discuss past performance with your staff and then examine the need for new procedures.

d. Continue to leave the staff alone.

Situation 12

You have recently become aware of some internal difficulties on your staff. They had been working well together for the past year. The staff has an excellent record of accomplishment and staff members have consistently met their performance goals. All are well qualified for their roles in the program.

a. Allow your staff members to deal with the new problem themselves.

b. Tell the staff how you propose to deal with the situation and discuss the necessity for these procedures.

c. Make yourself available for discussion, but don't jeopardize your relationship with the staff by forcing the issue.

d. Act quickly and firmly to nip the problem in the bud.

Scoring

1. Circle the letter you chose for each situation in both the following charts, labeled Flexibility and Effectiveness. For example, if you answered alternative C for situation 1, circle the C in row 1 of the Flexibility chart and the C in row 1 of the Effectiveness chart.

Flexibility

Situation Number	S1	S2	S3	S4
1	A	C	B	D
2	B	C	D	A
3	C	A	D	B
4	B	A	C	D
5	C	B	D	A
6	B	C	D	A
7	A	C	B	D
8	B	D	A	C
9	C	B	D	A
10	A	B	C	D
11	A	C	B	D
12	D	B	C	A

☐ S1   ☐ S2   ☐ S3   ☐ S4

Effectiveness

−2	−1	+1	+2	Situation Number
D	B	C	A	1
A	B	D	C	2
C	B	A	D	3
B	A	C	D	4
A	D	B	C	5
A	D	B	C	6
A	C	D	B	7
B	D	A	C	8
A	D	B	C	9
A	D	C	B	10
A	C	D	B	11
D	B	C	A	12

☐ × −2   ☐ × −1   ☐ × +1   ☐ × +2

‖   ‖   ‖   ‖

☐ + ☐ + ☐ + ☐ = ☐

Total

2. Add the total number of letters you circled in each column of the Flexibility chart on this page and enter these totals in the boxes labeled S1, S2, S3, and S4.

3. Still focusing on the Flexibility chart, place the total of each column in the corresponding quadrant of the following style matrix. That is, the S1 score

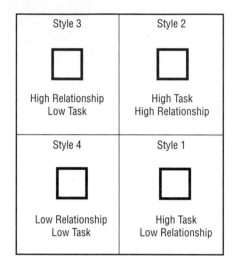

goes in the Style 1 box (high task, low relationship), the S2 score goes in the Style 2 box (High task, high relationship), the S3 score goes in the Style 3 box, and the S4 goes in the Style 4 box.

4. Add the total number of letters you circled in each column of the Effectiveness chart and enter these totals in the boxes below each column.

5. Multiply each number in the boxes by the number directly under it (be sure to indicate + or – as appropriate). Put the answer in the next box below that.

6. Add the four numbers and enter the total in the box labeled Total. Again, be sure to indicate the + or – sign.

7. On the following Effectiveness Scale, find the number in the Total box and mark it with an arrow.

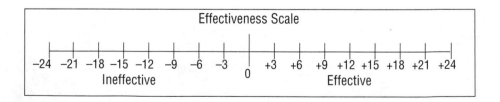

8. What does your style matrix tell you? How balanced are your scores? Do you have one predominant quadrant (this is not uncommon)? Do you have the potential flexibility to use all four leadership behaviors?

9. In terms of Effectiveness, how well did you do? The most appropriate behavior in each situation is indicated in the +2 column of the Effectiveness
   chart. You may want to go back to each situation and attempt to discover
   why that leadership behavior was best.

   Your instructor may choose to discuss the results and implications of this
exercise for leadership effectiveness.

8 Decision Making

If you come to a fork in the road, take it.

—*Yogi Berra*

When it is necessary to make a decision, sometimes it is necessary to not make a decision.

—*Lord Falkland*

Originality is the art of remembering what you hear but forgetting where you heard it.

—*Not sure who said this*

It isn't what you know that counts, it's what you think of in time.

—*Anonymous*

Learning Objectives

After studying this chapter, you should be able to:

1. Describe the types of decisions managers make.
2. List the steps of a highly rational decision-making process.
3. Describe some constraints on the decision-making process.
4. Identify obstacles to effective decision making.
5. Define groupthink and list its symptoms.
6. Describe techniques to improve decision making.
7. Identify characteristics of creative organization members.
8. Describe the steps in the creative process.
9. Identify ways that groups and individuals can enhance creativity.
10. Explain how ethics training is being used in larger corporations.

Learning Decision Making in the Line of Fire

Managers are paid to make decisions, but the vast majority of decisions are not the mergers, acquisitions, and mega-deals that make news headlines. The typical decisions that managers make concern fairly routine, day-to-day issues that require solid judgment based on good business experience. Though the decision-making style may vary from manager to manager, the issues they face are often universal; and their decisions affect both the situation and the decision-maker. Consider the case of Alan Robbins.

Ten years ago, Alan Robbins established the Plastic Lumber Company in Akron, Ohio, to convert recycled plastic soda bottles and milk containers into fake lumber. The toughest problems Alan faced were not in product development, technology improvement, or locating investors, but with employees. His list of problems included absenteeism, substance abuse, lawsuits, injury claims, allegations of discrimination, unemployment-compensation claims, abusive phone calls from an employee's wife, as well as government regulations and taxes. The well-intentioned Mr. Robbins used to put a lot of faith in his people and tried to create a freewheeling work environment where people could work hard and enjoy working. Cold beer and joking with employees at the end of a shift was his preference, rather than creating the rigid environment typically found on the shop floor of a factory.

His ideal of a boss being a friend, confidant, and one to whom employees could turn with personal problems actually eroded his ability to make effective business decisions. Robbins felt that much of the problem was his own doing, specifically wrong decisions in the work environment. Previously, he asked employees for input into decisions; now he makes them himself. He has implemented a zero-tolerance policy toward alcohol in the workplace, no longer works with employees on the plant floor, and has become "strictly business." His focus is on product development, and building the business, rather than building employee morale by throwing a party.

Often, a crisis will provoke a change in one's decision-making style. This is what happened with Alan Robbins. A fight on the floor between two employees forced Robbins to fire them both, which resulted in unemployment compensation claims and a racial discrimination complaint against Robbins. This discrimination case was dropped after an investigation, but one employee was awarded unemployment compensation. This was the point at which Robbins decided to be "the boss" and to change his decision style. He distanced himself from employees and addressed problems by instituting management systems for personnel issues. He approached decision-making with a top-down authoritarian approach. Robbins also made the decision to shift the running of his business from the position of his personal preferences and comfortable habits to that of an organizational approach with formalized policies and procedures in place. For his own protection, he developed a formal policy manual for the company by himself, with input from his attorney.

What was best for Robbins personally was not best for the business, so Robbins decided to introduce many changes. He also, out of necessity, changed his decision-making style.

Source: T. Aeppel, "Losing Faith—Personnel Disorders Sap a Factory Owner of His Early Idealism," *The Wall Street Journal*, January 14, 1998.

It can be reasonably argued that decision making is the most central activity of management, that it is the very essence of a manager's job. The nature of a manager's decisions, of course, is quite varied. They can range from such major issues as deciding whether to create a new product line to such seemingly minor issues as deciding where to take a client to lunch. In a given day, a manager will make a great number of decisions. The quality of these decisions can have a powerful impact on unit performance and, perhaps ultimately, on the performance of the entire organization.

Types of Organizational Decisions

Before considering the major models of decision making, let us first examine the variety of decisions a manager may make. Two useful classifications focus on whether decisions are (1) personal versus organizational and (2) programmed versus nonprogrammed.

Personal versus Organizational Decisions

Every day we engage in **personal decision making.** Such decisions directly affect ourselves, rather than others. For example, each of us decides what clothes to wear on a given day and whether to ride our bike, take a bus, or drive a car to work. Although personal decisions are often fairly trivial, they can sometimes be quite important. Selecting a college or a field in which to major, as well as applying for a particular job, are personal decisions that can have profound effects on the course of a person's life.

In contrast, **organizational decision making** involves decisions that pertain to the problems and practices of a given organization. Like personal decisions, some organizational decisions can be fairly trivial, such as deciding which brand of paper clips to order. But others may have a major impact on the organization, such as choosing an advertising campaign or deciding whether to acquire a competing firm. The essential distinction between personal and organizational decision making lies in the object of the process. Personal decision making focuses on the actions and life of an individual, while organizational decision making focuses on the practices and performance of an organization.

Programmed versus Nonprogrammed Decisions

Another useful way to distinguish among decisions has been proposed by Herbert Simon, who contends that decisions can be characterized in terms of whether they are fairly routine and well structured, or novel and poorly structured.[1] Well-structured decisions are termed **programmed decisions,** while poorly structured decisions are termed **nonprogrammed decisions.**

A good example of a programmed decision is when a clerk checks the on-hand inventory against a pre-established minimum standard. If the on-hand inventory falls below that standard, the clerk knows that it is time to order more stock.

With decisions that are unique and nonroutine, taking a preprogrammed approach becomes difficult. For example, the leaders of a nation may have trouble deciding how much to spend on military armaments for national defense, because of the uniqueness of political relations with neighboring countries and the difficulty of predicting the intentions of other world leaders. Not surprisingly, such nonprogrammed decision making may rely more on an individual's intuition and experience in similar situations.

By combining these two types of decisions (personal versus organizational and programmed versus nonprogrammed), we can create four classes or varieties of decisions (Figure 8.1). Personal programmed decisions involve simple, repetitive personal matters. Most people devote very little time to such decisions, and tend to rely on habits or simple decision rules. For example, an employee may usually park her car in the same spot in a parking lot, but on days that it rains, she may park in a different spot.

Personal nonprogrammed decisions arise during rare but significant events in an individual's personal life. For example, choosing which company to work for or whom to marry are personal decisions that people make only rarely. While some personal nonprogrammed decisions can be directly job-related, as when a person decides to quit one firm in hopes of finding a better position with another, others that are not so obviously job-related can also affect workplace behavior. For example, a person's choice of a marriage partner may mean having to relocate to be with him or her.

Organizational programmed decisions are typically handled according to established guidelines, rules, or procedures. Many simple problem situations can be dealt with by merely referring to a manual or rulebook that outlines the appropriate solution. In most organizations, lower-level personnel are responsible for handling organizational preprogrammed decisions. For example, a worker may be responsible for monitoring a control panel that provides information on the temperature and pressure within a vat. If the readings indicate that these valves are outside of a predetermined range, the worker is instructed to adjust the necessary mechanisms in order to maintain control of the process.

Organizational nonprogrammed decisions pertain to rare and unique situations that have potentially significant impact on the organization. Major planning issues and problems are often the topic of such decision making.

FIGURE 8.1   *Types of Decisions*

	Personal	Organizational
Programmed	Daily Routines Habits	Standard Operating Procedures Rulebooks and Manuals
Nonprogrammed	Job Choice Career Selection	Strategic Planning Issues Crisis Management

How to acquire capital, whether to sell off unprofitable corporate divisions, and whether to launch a new product line are examples of organizational nonprogrammed decision issues. Because of the critical nature of such decisions for the very well-being of the organization, they are more typically handled by high-level personnel. Organizational nonprogrammed decision making affords the greatest opportunities for creativity.

Classical Decision Theory

The traditional approach to understanding decision making, often called **classical decision theory,** assumes that decision making is, and should be, a highly rational process. The classical theory of decision making is often referred to as the **rational-economic model,** because of the model's presumption that decision makers are rational and because of its strong ties to the classical economic view of behavior. The process can be described in terms of a sequence of steps that a decision maker should follow in order to enhance the probability of attaining a desired goal. Figure 8.2 illustrates the steps in classical decision theory.[2]

As the figure shows, a situation must exist that triggers the decision-making process. A set of circumstances leads the decision maker to recognize the existence of the problem or opportunity that demands action. Recognition is an essential early step in decision making because unless a person believes a problem or opportunity exists, the decision-making process will not occur. Following recognition, the decision maker defines the nature of the situation. This definition leads to the generation of alternative approaches to coping with the situation. The manner in which the situation is defined will dictate the nature and variety of alternatives. The next steps in the process entail gathering information about each alternative (such as its relative cost and likelihood of success) and evaluating its desirability by weighting and combining the obtained information. From this evaluation, a single best course of action will emerge. This course of action is the one that will be implemented and subsequently evaluated in terms of its effectiveness in eliminating the problem or taking advantage of the opportunity. By monitoring the effectiveness of the solution, the decision maker can judge the extent to which it was appropriate and determine whether further action can or should be taken. It may be that the problem or opportunity will need to be redefined in light of the results. In essence, this step in the model provides feedback about how well the decision-making process was carried out.

The classical view is in fact popular with many scholars.* It does a fairly good job of describing how a decision *should* be made; in particular, the view points to the features managers should focus on when trying to improve the caliber of the decision-making process. Yet, the classical view is largely inaccurate as a description of *how* managers typically make decisions. Furthermore, its prescriptions for making better decisions are often in error.

---

*Most economists subscribe to the classical view of decision making.

FIGURE 8.2   *Steps in the Decision-Making Process:*
The Classical View

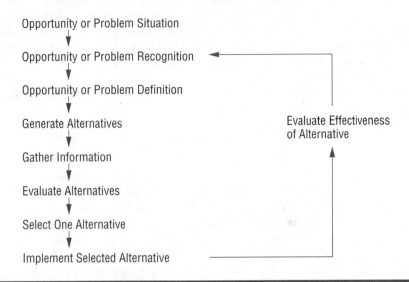

Opportunity or Problem Situation

Opportunity or Problem Recognition

Opportunity or Problem Definition

Generate Alternatives

Gather Information

Evaluate Alternatives

Select One Alternative

Implement Selected Alternative

Evaluate Effectiveness
of Alternative

One major set of deficiencies in the classical approach lies in its assumptions that all alternatives will be considered, that the consequences of each alternative will be considered, that accurate information is available at no cost, and that decision makers are totally rational beings.

In reality, a manager rarely considers all possible alternatives, since there often are too many to list. Additionally, many alternatives may not even occur to the decision maker. The assumption that the consequences of each alternative are considered is similarly impractical. In many circumstances, it may be impossible to estimate all the consequences. But even when full consideration is possible, examining all alternatives may require too much time and effort.

Rarely, if ever, is a manager's information perfectly accurate. More typically, the available information is often dated (because it takes time to gather, distill, and digest information) and only partially relevant to the question at hand (because information is often gathered for purposes other than a manager's specific needs). Also, information is not a free good. The cost of generating or purchasing needed data adds another constraint to the decision-making process. As a consequence, a manager is often forced to make decisions based on incomplete or insufficient information.

Furthermore, studies show that decision makers do not have the mental ability needed to store and process all of the data required to select the single best alternative. Available evidence suggests that people are simply not capable of performing the mental calculations that the classical view requires.[3]

Finally, there are a number of real-world constraints on a manager's decision making. For example, a manager may not have sufficient time to devote to making a decision. Despite a decision's importance, the need for prompt action may rule out a formal analysis of the situation.

A Behavioral Theory of Decision Making

Given the shortcomings of the rational-economic model, an alternative perspective has emerged that provides a more descriptive view of managerial behavior. This approach is termed a **behavioral theory of decision making**, sometimes called the **administrative model**.[4] Figure 8.3 illustrates the essential steps in the administrative model of decision making.

The administrative model explicitly acknowledges the real-world limitations on managers' decision making. Specifically, it holds that decision makers must work within conditions that provide a **bounded rationality.** Bounded rationality means that managers are restricted in their decision-making processes and must, therefore, settle for something short of an ideal or optimal solution. Bounded rationality recognizes that (1) all possible alternatives and their associated consequences cannot be generated, (2) both the available information and the definition of the situation are likely to be incomplete and inadequate to some degree, and (3) the final decision may be based on criteria other than simple optimization or outcome maximization.[†]

Due to the personal and situational limitations on managerial decision making, managers tend to make decisions that are "good enough" for the situation at hand. When managers seek solutions that are "good enough" rather than "ideal," they **satisfice** rather than **maximize.** When maximizing, a manager attempts to find the best or optimal solution. In contrast, when satisficing, a decision maker considers each alternative until one arises that is reasonably acceptable. Such an alternative meets all necessary requirements for a solution, but may not be the very best choice. March and Simon have provided a very useful illustration of the essential difference between satisficing and maximizing: Maximizing (or optimizing) is analogous to searching through a haystack for the sharpest needle to be found, whereas satisficing is much like searching through a haystack until a needle can be found that is sharp enough to sew with.[5]

Also included in the administrative model is the notion of **bounded discretion,** which suggests that optimal solutions are sometimes not feasible courses of action because they are ethically improper. In some circumstances, the best or optimal solution may actually involve morally questionable behavior. A retailer, for example, may reason that one way out of a difficult financial situation is to set her store on fire in order to collect the insurance. Or a food processor may have the option of significantly reducing product quality (perhaps by decreasing the amount of meat and increasing the proportion of filler in a hamburger patty) as a means of lowering costs and thereby raising profits. Most managers (but, of course, not all) prefer to avoid such unethical behavior. Therefore, bounded discretion represents a further constraint on the decision-making process.

In addition, managers often follow rules of thumb, or **heuristics,** when making decisions.[6] Because of the volume, variety, and complexity of business

---

[†]It is interesting to consider what an organization would be like if it were staffed with totally rational beings. In point of fact, it is because organizations are not staffed with collections of individuals like Mr. Spock (*Star Trek*'s science officer) that organizations pose many intriguing problems for the field of organizational behavior (in addition to making organizational life much more exciting).

FIGURE 8.3   *Steps in the Decision-Making Process: The Administrative View*

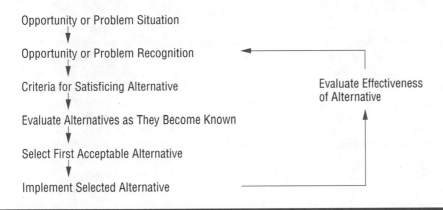

decisions, managers frequently use simplified decision rules to achieve satisficing solutions. For example, a heuristic for some investors is that if a stock drops 10 percent or more below its purchase price, they will decide to sell. These investors use this heuristic with great consistency, and regardless of other circumstances, to avoid holding on to a potentially disastrous, but previously attractive, stock.

The administrative model provides an interesting comparison to the rational-economic model. The two differ, most fundamentally, in their approaches to how decisions *should be* and *are* made. Each is successful in its own domain: The rational-economic model provides a useful summary of how decisions *should be made*, while the administrative model gives a good description of how decisions typically *are made*.

The Influence of Judgmental Strategies

It is now recognized that decision makers frequently go beyond the information they are given when making inferences. Daniel Kahneman and Amos Tversky have identified two judgmental strategies (sometimes termed judgmental heuristics) on which people frequently rely.[7] The strategies, unfortunately, oftentimes mislead people into making erroneous inferences.

The first judgmental strategy, termed the **availability heuristic,** reflects the influence of the relative availability of objects or events (that is, their accessibility through memory, perception, or imagination). Occasionally, the availability heuristic can be misleading. Consider a pollster who asks adults to estimate the current level of national unemployment. It is likely that a bias will be reflected in these estimates such that unemployed individuals will tend to overestimate the rate of unemployment, while employed individuals will underestimate it. Many people would not recall newspaper or television accounts of estimates of unemployment, or attempt to compensate for their possible bias by deliberately considering the impact of their own experiences on their beliefs.

The second judgmental strategy proposed by Kahneman and Tversky, termed the **representativeness heuristic,** involves the application of one's

An Inside Look
Ethics in Decision Making

A recent survey of over 400 managers concluded that "a typical executive" is a male in his mid-forties who frequently travels on business, says he values "self-respect," and may commit financial fraud. Of the participants, 47 percent of top executives, 41 percent of controllers, and 76 percent of MBA students were willing to understate write-offs that reduced profits. Additionally, 14 percent of the CEOs and 8 percent of the controllers indicated that they were willing to inflate sales figures to meet expectations. The Securities and Exchange Commission concurs with these findings: The most common type of fraud they investigate is improper reporting of write-offs.

Ignorance of what constitutes improper behavior is the primary factor leading to the commitment of fraud. Study coauthor Janet Dukerich of the University of Texas at Austin says that's especially true among MBA students. "The group most familiar with accounting procedures, the controllers, were the least likely to engage in fraud. In fact, [the results] . . . may well be conservative. After all, study participants didn't really have their job on the line."

Before the study, says lead author Arthur Brief of Tulane University, he believed people's "individual values" could make a difference in workplace behav-

ior. "But now I'm not convinced that they do." Stuart Greenbaum, dean of the Olin School of Business at Washington University in St. Louis, commented, "On its face, it's incredible (that values can disappear so quickly in the workplace). Values are deeply held beliefs. I don't see anything so fundamental to warrant the change (from somebody's home to their place of business)." But Michael Metzger, professor of business at Indiana University, was not surprised. "(If people) are in an environment where there are strong incentives to cheat, most people will."

For companies to instill a sense of ethics in their employees, a code of ethics must be clearly communicated. The business climate must reinforce and reward ethical behavior and punish unethical behavior, at all levels. Ethics training must be a part of employee development programs. Some organizations have a staff ethicist or ombudsman for employees to consult with on ethical issues, but the most critical element is having the CEO and top-level management set a good example.

Source: D. Blalock, "For Many Executives, Ethics Appear to Be a Write-Off," *The Wall Street Journal*, March 26, 1996.

---

sense of resemblance between objects or event. In applying this heuristic, a person assesses the extent to which an object or event possesses features that would enable that person to categorize the object or event appropriately. As an illustration of this tendency, consider the following: I have a friend who is a professor. He likes to write poetry, is rather shy, and is small in stature. Which of the following is his field of expertise—Chinese studies or psychology?

If you are inclined to answer "Chinese studies," you have been seduced by the representativeness heuristic. That is to say, you judged the personality profile to be a better fit for the stereotype of a sinologist than a psychologist. However, the odds are that any person is more likely to know psychologists, and psychologists are far more numerous than sinologists. In light of this more critical base-rate information, the better answer (from a statistical standpoint) would be "psychology." Stated a different way, the representativeness heuristic involves estimating the likelihood of something by how much it resembles our stereotype.

Numerous decision-making tasks, of course, rely on accurate estimation and categorization. Therefore, both the availability heuristic and the representativeness heuristic are important tools in drawing inferences. Although they often may lead us to correct inferences, they have the potential to lead to erroneous judgments as well. It should also be understood that Kahneman and Tversky's notions of availability and representativeness are not, strictly speaking, heuristics, in the sense of being explicit and fixed devices or formulae for making decisions. Rather, they represent automatic and nonconscious processes that are frequently involved in judgment and decision-making processes.

Obstacles to Effective Decision Making

A number of potential obstacles to effective decision making have been identified. In this section, we will examine four of the most common: judgmental biases, escalation of commitment, groupthink, and the willingness of groups to take risks.

Judgmental Biases

When the availability heuristic and the representativeness heuristic lead us to erroneous conclusions, they may be termed *biases*. Along with the availability bias and the representativeness bias are a number of common biases that have been found to influence decision making. These include:

1. **Implicit favorite bias:** The tendency of a decision maker to have a preferred alternative and, though not fully aware of this preference, to engage in a process of considering alternatives that merely confirms the initial prejudice.[8]

2. **Loss-aversion bias:** The tendency of a decision maker to treat potential losses as more important than potential gains, even though the objective values of both losses and gains are truly equal.[9]

3. **Selective perception bias:** The tendency of a decision maker to be influenced by prior expectations to interpret only certain, selected information (for example, a supervisor who believes strongly in a particular subordinate may interpret information on that worker's performance in only favorable terms).

4. **Personal experience bias:** The tendency of a decision maker to be so influenced by strong personal experiences that he or she ignores other information (for example, a manager who has had a bad experience in a unionized setting might believe all employees are hostile to their employers).

Escalation of Commitment

Barry Staw, of the University of California at Berkeley, has suggested that people are sometimes unwilling to change a course of action despite unequivocal evidence showing that their decision was incorrect.[10] In essence, a person may decide to "stay the course" because he or she has already invested substantial time, effort, and/or money in the existing situation. All the more remarkable is the tendency of people to invest still more resources in a course of action that appears doomed to failure. As examples of escalating commitment, Staw cites the following:

Imagine a person who has purchased a stock at $50 a share. Yet, when the stock drops in price to $20, he buys more shares at the lower price. When the price drops still further, the individual must decide whether to buy more, sell out, or hold on to what he has purchased.

Consider a person who spends several years working toward an academic degree in a field which offers minimal job prospects (for example, in the humanities). Yet, the person invests still more time and money in completing the degree (rather than changing fields). Ultimately, the person is faced with the choice of being unemployed, underemployed (that is, working in a job which is below his capabilities), or starting over in another field or career path.

During the early phase of U.S. involvement in the Vietnam War, the Undersecretary of State (George Ball) wrote to President Johnson: "The decision you face now is crucial. Once large members of U.S. troops are committed to direct combat, they will begin to take heavy casualties in a war they are ill-equipped to fight in a noncooperative, if not downright hostile, countryside. Once we suffer large casualties, we will have started a well-nigh irreversible process. Our involvement will be so great that we cannot—without national humiliation—stop short of achieving our complete objectives. Of the two possibilities, I think humiliation would be more likely than the achievement of our objectives." (Memo dated July 1, 1965.) [11]

We have all seen situations in which people stay committed to a specific course of action despite negative feedback. By committing additional resources to a losing strategy, they in essence throw good money after bad. There are several explanations of this phenomenon. One is that people pursue a course of action *in spite* of negative feedback largely *because of* negative feedback. This argument suggests that people value tenacity, or stick-to-it-iveness. They feel that a "damn the torpedoes, full speed ahead" stance has a certain social value. Because people generally admire those who stick to their principles, a decision maker may adopt a persistent approach in response to perceived social pressure. A second explanation suggests the people will forsake a more rational approach to difficult decision situations out of concern for establishing consistency.

To test the notion that social norms explain managerial consistency, Staw used practicing managers, college business majors, and other undergraduate students as subjects in a study. [12] Each subject was presented with a case study summary of a manager's behavior. The case portrayed the manager as being either consistent or experimenting (less consistent) in following a course of action. In addition, the manager's behavior was described as ultimately leading to either success or failure. In the consistency condition, the manager adhered to a single course of action despite a series of negative results. In the experimenting condition, the manager initially tried one course of action, then shifted to a second and a third course when negative results were obtained.

The subjects responded most favorably to the managers who followed a consistent course of action and were successful in the end. In addition, the hypothetical manager who persisted to an ultimately successful outcome was judged more highly than would be predicted from the separate effects of the variables of consistency and outcome success. In essence, Staw found a form of "hero effect" in which a manager who remained committed despite two setbacks *and* succeeded in the end was regarded quite positively. Furthermore, the subjects' reactions to consistency varied across groups of raters. Practicing managers showed the strongest appreciation, followed by college business majors and then other undergraduates. This suggests that consistency is viewed as important to effective management and that this perception may be acquired through participation in business roles.‡

Escalation of commitment is most likely to occur in certain predictable settings. Among these are situations in which a person feels a strong sense of personal responsibility, as when selecting a career or setting a policy with which the individual will be publicly associated. To counter the escalation of tendency, Staw suggests employing outside advisers who do not feel personal responsibility for previous losses or gains.[14] It may also be wise to rotate decision-making responsibility across managers if there is a history of losses due to the tendency to escalate commitment.

Groupthink

Irving Janis has identified a fascinating phenomenon that can lead groups to commit serious errors in decision making. In describing this situation, which he called **groupthink**, Janis proposed that highly cohesive working groups (that is, groups whose members enjoy a high degree of interpersonal attraction) are in danger of taking a distorted view of situations that confront them.[15]§ As a result, the group's decision-making processes may be slanted toward seeking *consensus* rather than exploring alternative courses of action. Because dissent and critical analysis are not encouraged in discussion sessions, the group may select a course of action that ignores potential dangers and pitfalls.

Janis has provided a number of illustrations of groupthink, including the Watergate cover-up by the Nixon administration, the escalation of U.S. military involvement in Vietnam, the failure of the Roosevelt administration to prepare for the Japanese raid on Pearl Harbor, the space shuttle *Challenger* disaster, Nazi Germany's decision to invade the Soviet Union, Ford Motor Company's decision to market the Edsel, and—perhaps the most clear-cut example—the Bay of Pigs incident during the presidency of John Kennedy (the incident in which President Kennedy and his top advisers unanimously decided to adopt a CIA proposal to invade Cuba and overthrow Fidel Castro).[16] None of Kennedy's advisers voiced opposition to the proposal. The operation was spearheaded by 1,400 Cuban exiles who were given air and naval support by the U.S. military and the CIA. The invasion, which occurred at the Bay of Pigs on the south coast of Cuba, was a total failure within a few days of the invasion, with a majority of the invaders being taken prisoner by the Cuban army.**

In retrospect, Kennedy and his advisers appear to have been victims of groupthink. Their decision to proceed with the invasion was based on a certain amount of wishful thinking in that the plan relied heavily on a popular

---

‡Research on the escalation of commitment phenomenon has been criticized for not yet employing decision-making situations in which the continued commitment of resources is explicitly inadvisable on economic grounds.[13]

§Janis selected the term *groupthink* to label this phenomenon because it had Orwellian overtones (cf. *newspeak* in George Orwell's novel *1984*).

**To the credit of Kennedy and his policy advisers, they recognized the mistakes they made during the Bay of Pigs invasion and tried to compensate by having open and frank discussions when coping with the Cuban Missile Crisis.

uprising by the Cuban people in support of the invaders. Kennedy and his advisers assumed that the invasion would be a simple operation that could not fail and would quickly lead to Castro's overthrow. They also gave no advance consideration to the possible adverse consequences of a failed invasion—the most significant of which were the anger of normally friendly Latin American and European countries, and the growth of closer military ties between the Soviet Union and Cuba. Later, Castro's concern for defense led to the installation of Soviet-built nuclear missiles in Cuba, within 90 miles of the United States. This defensive move precipitated a further problem for the Kennedy administration—the Cuban Missile Crisis.

Following the Bay of Pigs invasion, the confidence of Kennedy and his top advisers (such people as Robert McNamara, Robert Kennedy, Dean Rusk, and Arthur Schlesinger, Jr.) was deeply shaken as they came to realize their own tendencies toward self-deception. In writing about the decision process, Schlesinger observed that

> Had one advisor opposed the adventure, I believe Kennedy would have canceled it. No one spoke against it....Our meetings took place in a curious atmosphere of assumed consensus....In the months after the Bay of Pigs, I bitterly reproached myself for having kept so silent...though my feelings of guilt were tempered by the knowledge that a course of objection would have accomplished little save to gain me a name as a nuisance. I can only explain...that one's impulse to blow the whistle on this nonsense was simply undone by the circumstances of the discussion (Janis, 1972, pp. 39–40).

Janis has proposed eight main symptoms or signs of groupthink:

1. *An illusion of invulnerability.* Group members may develop a sense of powerfulness that leads them to ignore obvious danger signals. They may take extreme risks as a result of being overly optimistic.

2. *Rationalization.* The members may discredit or ignore evidence that contradicts the group's consensus. Sources of disagreeable information may be attacked, or elaborate rationalization may be offered to explain away the information.

3. *An assumption of morality.* Group members may view themselves as highly ethical and above reproach. The views of outsiders are then defined as intrinsically immoral or evil. Adopting a stance of self-righteousness makes it easier for the group to follow a course of action that is morally questionable because the members view themselves as pursuing a higher morality.

4. *Negative stereotyping.* Groups that suffer from groupthink may come to view opponents and people outside the group in simple negative stereotypic terms. By casting outsiders in negative terms, the group makes them easier to ignore because their opposition is to be expected.

5. *Pressure to conform.* The expression of dissent is suppressed by the group's members. Persons who voice objections or express doubts may be ostracized or expelled.

6. *Self-censorship.* Each member of the group may carefully monitor his or her own thoughts and suppress personal objectives, in essence withholding dissent.

7. *An illusion of unanimity.* As a result of self-censorship, no reservations are expressed. The consequence of this lack of dissent is the apparent unanimous endorsement of proposals.

8. *Mindguards.* Certain individuals in the group may take it upon themselves to serve as mindguards, guarding a manager's thoughts in the same way a bodyguard protects a leader's personal safety. These mindguards will act against sources of information or dissenters by deflecting them or their objections.

As this discussion of groupthink suggests, the existence of an apparently admirable condition—group cohesion—can have detrimental effects on the quality of decision making. Janis suggests that several steps be taken if a highly cohesive decision-making body is disposed to groupthink. Specifically, group members should be encouraged to voice criticisms, doubts, and objections. To promote open debate, managers should avoid stating their preferred positions during the early stages of group discussion. It may also be valuable for the group to invite outside experts to sit in on their sessions occasionally and offer suggestions.

Another tactic for countering groupthink is to assign several group members to teams that will investigate the advisability of alternative courses of action. After gathering evidence in support of an assigned position, the teams can present their arguments and participate in a directed debate. Such a confrontation of alternative points of view can lead to new insights on the issues underlying a decision-making situation.

A somewhat related technique is to appoint a group member to serve as a devil's advocate at each group meeting.[††] This person's responsibilities would include actively criticizing the proposals raised by all group members.

Another suggested technique is the scheduling of a **last-chance meeting** at which all group members are encouraged to raise any nagging doubts or hesitations they may have.

Last, and perhaps most important, a manager can help to overcome groupthink through a willingness to accept criticism. Setting an example of openness to criticism, as opposed to resentment or fear of subordinates' objections, can help to promote serious discussion of the pros and cons of alternative courses of action.[17]

Risk Taking within Groups

Imagine that you are a manager who must make a decision that entails a fair amount of risk—for example, deciding whether to expand your production facilities into a politically unstable country in Latin America. The risks are great in that your entire investment could be lost if the country is taken over by extremists who intend to nationalize all industry. However, the potential profits will be substantial if the country does not experience a revolution. Would you make the final decision on such an investment by yourself or would you turn it over to a committee?

[††]The procedure of appointing a "devil's advocate" originated with a Catholic church practice of assigning someone the role of arguing against the canonization of a candidate for sainthood.

Most people would argue that committee decisions tend to be conservative and that individuals, in comparison, are not constrained by the dynamics of debate or the doubts that might be raised within a committee. Boldness and initiative are more typically associated with individuals than with committees.‡‡

James Stoner, while a graduate student at MIT, was one of the first people to investigate whether groups are more cautious than individuals in decision making that involves risky propositions.[18] In his research, he devised a series of cases involving the propensity (or willingness) to take risks. The cases dealt with such diverse topics as (1) choosing between a secure though modest-paying job with one employer versus taking a high-paying job with a newly founded but financially less sound firm in a highly competitive field, and (2) choosing between calling a football play that would likely result in a tie versus calling a play that is riskier but could result in a victory.

In his research, Stoner found that individuals tended to take a less risky route, while groups favored riskier actions. When the individuals were placed in a group setting, they shifted their endorsement to a riskier position. This phenomenon, in which a group endorses a riskier position than would its individual members, is called the **risky shift.**

A number of explanations have been offered to account for the risky shift. One of the more popular is the concept of **diffusion of responsibility.** This line of reasoning holds that when individuals are in groups, they may feel less personal responsibility for the consequences of their actions. The diffusion of responsibility concept has also been used to account for the failure of an individual to come to the aid of an injured person if a large number of people are nearby. Thus, a mugging victim who is lying on the floor of a subway station is less likely to receive aid as the size of the crowd increases. Similarly, group decision making may sometimes reflect this sense of personal anonymity in endorsing a course of action. From studies of incidents similar to the subway station mugging, it appears that risky shifts can even occur in the absence of group discussion.[19]

Although the shift toward endorsing risk within groups has been found in a variety of settings,[20] there have been occasions where groups opted for the more cautious alternative action. For example, in one study, groups of housewives and students were asked whether a married couple should abort a pregnancy when future complications in the pregnancy could endanger the life of the mother. In this decision scenario, groups endorsed a more cautious course (abortion) than did the members acting alone.[21] In another study, groups were again more cautious than individuals in recommending that a couple not go ahead with their plan to be married when the couple expressed disagreement on a number of issues.[22] The tendency of groups to move in a more conservative direction than would individuals is called the **cautious shift.**

Clearly, the risky shift and the cautious shift are contradictory in their predictions of how groups will behave when faced with a decision that involves an element of risk. A close examination of the studies that have identified both risky and cautious shifts suggests that the prior inclination of the group's members (that is, when they make their premeeting judgment of their

---

‡‡As an illustration of the belief that committees tend to be conservative, consider the old saying, "A camel is a horse that was designed by a committee."

preferences) is an important factor in determining whether a shift will occur in a cautious or a risky direction. If the premeeting inclination is toward caution, the group's decision tends to go to the extreme of the cautious direction. If the premeeting inclination is toward risk, however, the group's decision is likely to go toward the risky extreme. For example, a group that is meeting to determine the level of punishment a student should receive for cheating is likely to opt for a more severe penalty than the members in isolation would have selected. Yet, a group that is betting on horses will be more conservative than its members acting alone.[23]

The tendency of groups to move toward extremes has been termed **group polarization**.[24] This phenomenon is most probably the result of several factors. First, the premeeting inclinations of the group's members encourage a certain bias during discussions that leads the group to explore and endorse arguments and information that support the members' initial positions. Throughout discussions, the group's members will voice, and thereby encourage, additional rationales for being either conservative or risky, depending on their original bias.

Techniques for Improving Decision Making

Individual versus Group Decision Making

In the previous discussion of individual versus group decision making, it was noted that groups tend to endorse extreme positions when confronted with decisions involving an element of risk. In situations where risk is not great or where achieving a high-quality solution is the primary goal, the question of the relative advantages of group versus individual decision making can be raised. A good deal of attention has been devoted to the issue of whether solutions generated by decision-making groups are superior, inferior, or equal to the solutions generated by individuals working alone on the same problem.

Studies of individual versus group decision making have typically relied on one of two approaches: (1) individuals initially work alone on a problem and subsequently work on similar problems in groups (and vice versa), or (2) some individuals work alone on several problems, while other individuals simultaneously work in groups on the same problems. The problems studied ranged from simple puzzles to complex reasoning tasks. Performance has frequently been measured in terms of quality of solution, time required to reach a solution, and sheer number of problems solved.

Despite variations in their designs and samples, these studies overall have yielded quite similar results. By and large, groups will outperform individuals working in isolation. That is, the group's solutions to problems are typically of higher quality than the average of the individual's solutions. One interesting additional finding is that the best solitary worker may often outperform the group. But in general, and for a variety of tasks, groups can be expected to outperform the vast majority of individuals who work alone.

Precisely why groups have an advantage over individuals has also been the subject of much inquiry. One self-evident explanation is that groups can pool information and abilities. By pooling these resources, the group gains access to a collection of knowledge that is greater than any single individual's. This knowledge enables the group to reject obviously incorrect approaches and provides a check on the possibility of committing errors.

Being in a group also tends to motivate and inspire group members. The stimulation of being in a social setting can enhance an individual's level of contribution. In addition, there are social rewards for making a significant contribution to a group's efforts. For example, praise, admiration, and feeling valuable to the group can be strong incentives for an individual to exert greater effort.

Finally, depending on the situation, it may be possible to divide a group's general assignment into smaller, more manageable tasks that can then be delegated to individual group members. Thus, groups have the potential for employing division of labor.

Despite these advantages, problems may arise. As we noted earlier, highly cohesive groups sometimes encourage a restricted view of alternatives (groupthink). Groups may also polarize toward extreme points of view if an appreciable element of risk is involved (risky and cautious shifts). Although it has not been formally studied yet, it is possible that groups may be successful in exerting social pressure on a manager to escalate commitment to a losing course of action because of the manager's desire to appear consistent in the eyes of the group's members.

In addition to these potential disadvantages, group decision making has other likely drawbacks. For example, group decision making tends to be much more costly than individual decision making. Given the time and energy that meetings can consume, it is usually best to reserve group decision making for more important decisions that require high-quality solutions. Group discussions can also give rise to hostility and conflict. This is especially likely when group members have divergent and strongly held opinions on alternative courses of action. In addition, decision making in groups tends to be influenced by the relative status of group members. Thus, when a group member who possesses relatively little status offers an objectively good suggestion, it may be rejected. But if the same suggestion is offered by a group member with high status, the likelihood of its being adopted is greatly increased.[25]

As Table 8.1 illustrates, there are many advantages and disadvantages to entrusting decision making to groups rather than to individuals. Before choosing

TABLE 8.1 *Advantages and Disadvantages of Group Decision Making*

Advantages	Disadvantages
Pooling of information	Groupthink
Social arousal of participants	Endorsement of extreme positions
Social rewards for participation	Escalation of commitment
Division of labor	Greater cost in time and energy
Higher-quality solution	Split positions that generate conflict
Sharing of resources	Status biases in member involvement

a format for decision making, a manager should examine the points outlined in the table to determine if any specific conditions strongly advise for or against the use of groups.

The Nominal Group Technique

One approach that attempts to capitalize on the positive feature of group decision making, while avoiding many of the potential pitfalls, is the **nominal group technique (NGT).** In this technique, seven to ten individuals are brought together to participate in a structured exercise that includes the following steps:

1. The members silently and independently record their ideas about how to tackle a problem.
2. In turn, each member presents one of his or her ideas to the group. As each idea is offered, it is summarized and recorded on a chalkboard or wall chart, without discussion of its merits.
3. A discussion is held in which all ideas are clarified and evaluated.
4. Individuals silently and independently vote on each idea. This voting may involve a rating of the proposals or a rank ordering. The group's decision is then derived by pooling the votes or rankings into a single preferred alternative.[26]

The nominal group technique is a quite popular means of reaching a group decision because it avoids many of the potential problems of group decision making outlined in Table 8.1. For example, a decision can be reached in a reasonable amount of time without being greatly influenced by the leader's preferred position. Also, the technique can be used effectively in a variety of organizations (for example, General Electric, ARA Services, government agencies, and universities have employed the technique). Perhaps the strongest drawback of NGT is its high degree of structure. As a result, the group may tend to limit its discussion to a single and often highly focused issue.

The Delphi Technique

Another technique for capitalizing on a group's resources while avoiding several possible disadvantages of relying on group decision-making processes was developed by the Rand Corporation.[27] This approach, called the **Delphi technique,** is similar to NGT in several respects, but also differs significantly in that the decision makers never actually meet. The steps in the Delphi technique are:

1. Select a group of individuals who possess expertise in a given problem area, for example, forecasting social trends or technical breakthroughs.
2. Survey the experts for their opinions via a mailed questionnaire or via e-mail.
3. Analyze and distill the experts' responses.
4. Mail the summarized results of the survey to the experts and request that they respond once again to a questionnaire. If one expert's opinion differs sharply from the rest, he or she may be asked to provide a rationale. This rationale could then be forwarded to the other participants.

5. After this process is repeated several times, the experts usually achieve a consensus. If not, the responses can be pooled to determine a most preferred view.

The Delphi technique has a number of advantages and disadvantages. Its greatest advantage is that it avoids many of the biases and obstacles associated with interacting groups (that is, groups where the members meet face-to-face). It has also been shown to generate fairly useful information and high-quality solutions.[28] A strong disadvantage stems from the amount of time it takes to complete the entire Delphi process—rarely less than several weeks, and often as long as five months. Clearly, urgent problems cannot be solved in this manner. Finally, like NGT, the Delphi technique follows a highly structured format. As a result, it does not offer much flexibility if conditions change. And, obviously, since respondents never meet face-to-face, social interaction and free dialogue are lost.

In an interesting comparison of three approaches to group decision making—interacting groups, NGT, and Delphi technique—an identical problem was given to 60 seven-person groups.[29] Twenty of the groups tackled the problem in an interacting format, while the remaining groups were assigned to either NGT or Delphi approaches. In terms of effectiveness, the NGT groups were somewhat more productive, followed in turn by the Delphi and interacting groups. Members of NGT groups also reported higher satisfaction than did members of the other groups. These results suggest that the presence and increased involvement of others can sometimes diminish the quality of decision making.[§§]

Social Loafing and the Stepladder Technique

In one well-known set of studies, the performance of individuals working alone was compared with the performance of the same individuals working in a group.[30] It was observed that some of the group members produced at less than their maximum capability when working in the group setting. This phenomenon, whereby a member of a group slacks off because of the experience of being in a group, is termed **social loafing.** There is some evidence that social loafing is greater in larger groups.[31] This is probably because members of larger groups believe that they are less noticeable, have less likelihood of affecting results, and are less likely to share in any rewards.

A problem-solving structure recently proposed as a solution to social loafing is termed the **stepladder technique.** The technique is intended to improve group decision making by structuring the entry of group members into a core group. Initially, a small core group of, for example, two members work together on a problem. Then, a third member joins the core group and presents his or her preliminary suggestions for solving the same problem. Next, the member's presentation is followed by a three-person discussion. Each additional member—fourth, fifth, and so on—joins the expanding core group and presents his or her preliminary solutions. At each step, there is a discussion. The technique has four

---

[§§]Following a discussion of decision-making techniques, it must be noted that effective decision making is not equivalent to effective decision implementation. Simply being able to decide on the best course of action does not ensure a particular outcome. Decision implementation is actually the concern of much of the field of OB in that effective implementation involves influencing others, managing group meetings, and building consensus.

requirements. First, each member is given sufficient time to think about the task before entering the core group. Second, the new member must make a preliminary solution presentation before hearing the core group's ideas. Third, sufficient time is allocated to discuss the problem as each member is added. Fourth, the final decision occurs only after the entire group has been formed. These steps make it difficult for a member to "loaf," or hide in the group. Research on the effectiveness of the stepladder technique has shown that stepladdered groups produce higher-quality decisions than conventional groups.[32]

Creativity and Decision Making

Many problems, especially nonprogrammed decisions that are broad in scope and consequences, require creative solutions. Given the competitive nature of business, it can be argued that those firms that can generate creative strategies for coping with decisions may enjoy an important competitive edge.

Creativity can enter the decision-making process at any step. The way in which a problem situation is defined, the generation of alternatives, the perception of opportunities, and the actual implementation of a solution can all be enhanced by creative perspectives.

In this section, we will discuss several aspects of creativity. Initially, we will consider the characteristics of creative individuals and how individual creativity can be measured. Then we will examine the steps in the creative process and some methods for enhancing creativity.

Characteristics of Creative Individuals

People vary in the extent to which they are creative. Although one widely held belief is that highly creative individuals are the products of peculiar childhoods, the available evidence does not support such a view.

The impact of age on creativity has also been heavily researched, with more conclusive results. A study of professionals in a variety of fields, including both the arts and the sciences, found that most individuals tended to be most creative between the ages of 30 and 40.[33] The peak period of creative productivity, however, seems to vary somewhat by discipline. In the field of music and other arts, creative accomplishment peaks during the period from age 35 to 39, while in the sciences the peak creativity period appears to be from age 30 to 34. It should be pointed out, of course, that people can still make creative contributions later in life (that is, they may continue to take out patents or compose symphonies). However, the frequency of creative productivity tends to decrease for most people as they age.

In terms of personality, creative individuals typically have a wide range of interests, value independence, and enjoy aesthetic impressions.[34] In analyzing creative executives, it has been found that some of their more salient characteristics include:

- A willingness to give up immediate gain to reach long-range goals
- A great amount of energy
- An irritation with the status quo
- Perseverance

- A pursuit of hobbies and specialized interests
- A belief that fantasy and daydreaming are not a waste of time[35]

Other studies of creative individuals have offered further insights. One study found that highly creative engineers did not identify as strongly with their employing organization as did their less creative coworkers.[36] In addition, highly creative people are more likely to change jobs frequently, although the precise reasons for this higher turnover are not yet understood.[37]

Measuring Individual Creativity

Especially in occupations related to research and development, advertising, and mass media, individual creativity is an important resource. To optimize the creative resources of their employees, managers must understand how to measure individual creativity.

One simple device for assessing the creative potential of employees is to observe their actions in situations that call for creative responses. For example, a manager may give an employee a challenging assignment, such as designing the cover of a newsletter, and then carefully monitor both the employee's problem-solving process and the final product. A more direct approach is to administer a paper-and-pencil test of creativity. Organizations that are strongly interested in creativity are more likely to use standardized creativity tests or devise their own. For example, the AC Spark Plug Division of General Motors has developed its own test of creativity for engineers and supervisors.[38]

Numerous tests of creativity are available. Although they appear to identify the general ability to be creative, they may not be particularly relevant to a given occupation. To illustrate this point, consider these sample items from some typical tests of creativity:

- Write a four-word sentence in which each word begins with the following letters: K . . . U . . . Y . . . I . . .
- In the next 30 seconds, name fluids that will burn.
- During the next 60 seconds, write words beginning with the letter J.

Another test asks a person to envision the consequences of various situations. For example:

- In a two-minute period, write down as many answers as you can to the question "What would happen if people no longer needed or wanted to sleep?"

Steps in the Creative Process

Most students of the creative process divide it into five stages.[39]

1. *Opportunities or problem recognition.* In this phase, an individual becomes aware of the existence of a problem or opportunity that needs attention. For example, an employee may remark, "There must be a better way of doing this."
2. *Immersion.* At this stage, the individual collects and recalls information that is relevant to the situation. He or she also generates hypotheses without

appraising their value, for example, "I think I recall reading somewhere that some firms use a different set of procedures."

3. *Incubation.* At this point, the information simmers in the person's subconscious. The individual does not appear to be actively focusing on the problem, yet is subconsciously rearranging the available information into new patterns.

4. *Insight.* While a person is engaged in a unrelated activity, an integrative idea will come to mind—for example, "A new reporting system that keeps both departments simultaneously apprised of our needs should do the trick!" Many people report that at this stage it is usually a good idea to jot down the creative insight, as it may quickly be forgotten.

5. *Verification.* Finally, the individual tests out the solution by logic or actual experimentation. At this point, tenacity may be critical, because other people often resist innovative ideas or quickly reject them as impractical.

Although this list of steps suggests that the creative process follows a certain order, creative insight does not happen in such an orderly or neat fashion. For example, incubation may occur during verification. Furthermore, the process is often repetitive because initial ideas may be unsatisfactory and require further revision.

Enhancing Creativity

Several methods are suggested for enhancing or "freeing up" individual creativity. Studies show that attempts to improve creative ability through training techniques are frequently successful. In fact, one review of 40 studies in the area of increasing creativity found that 90 percent of such efforts succeeded.[40]

We have already considered two of the more popular ways of maximizing group output: the nominal group technique and the Delphi technique. In the area of creativity enhancement, both of these techniques have applicability.

Brainstorming may also be used to train individuals to be more creative and to tackle complex problems. In a brainstorming session, a group of people is encouraged to exchange ideas freely in an atmosphere that is nonjudgmental and noncritical. When presented with a problem, group members try to generate as many ideas or solutions as they can. At this point, the quality of the ideas is not important. Instead, sheer quantity is emphasized. Outlandish ideas are especially encouraged because they may serve as springboards to useful solutions. Later, the recorded proposals are refined and evaluated.

A study of the effectiveness of having individuals brainstorm in isolation versus in groups found that individuals in isolation produce more and better ideas than do an equivalent number of people in groups.[41] These results suggest that the presence of others, despite any possible instructions of group leaders to the contrary, inhibits personal creativity and reduces the range of ideas that are generated.

Another technique in the creativity arsenal is called **grid analysis.** In this technique, ideas or materials of possible relevance to a problem are listed on the sides of a two-dimensional grid. Then each possible combination of ideas is created and examined for its usefulness as a solution. For example, a marketing firm may be interested in promoting alternative uses for its current products. To uncover such novel uses, they may list their products on a horizontal dimension and target audiences or other products that they do not manufacture on the vertical axis. The resulting combinations may suggest new markets for their products, or the possible conversion of their equipment or goods to the manufacture of other products.

Andrew DuBrin has suggested a number of techniques that individuals can use to increase their creativity.[42] Although these techniques do not offer formal guidance for solving specific problems, they can be valuable aids to personal development.

Don't Be Afraid to Try and Fail   Many people find it intimidating that a large proportion of their attempts at creativity are likely to fail. In fact, it is the *absolute number* of successful new ideas that counts and not the *percentage*. Roger Von Oech summarizes this point by saying, "We learn by trial and error, not by trial and rightness."[43]

Let Your Playful Side Come Out   One way to get into a creative state of mind is to think humorously. Approaching a problem with humor can generate novel perspectives and insights.

Identify Your Creative Time Period   Some people have a specific time of day when they are most likely to be creative. By recognizing this and scheduling work sessions accordingly, they can capitalize on peak periods. Some people find they are most creative while exercising or traveling. Others feel most creative shortly after a rest. Most people, however, report that one of their most creative periods occurs just before falling asleep.

Borrow Ideas   Studying ideas already in use in related fields can suggest new approaches to one's work problems. Reading books, magazines, and newspapers and contacting people who have related interests may give rise to ideas that, if appropriately modified, can be converted into workable solutions.

Maintain an Idea Notebook   Because many novel ideas are generated and lost in the course of daily activities, a notebook can be a practical means of recording flashes of insight for future reference. Some executives keep a separate "idea file" for storing bits of information that are useful in themselves or that may serve as the basis for other useful ideas.

Ethics in Decision Making

In recent years, there has been a growing recognition of the need to explicitly consider ethical issues when engaging in decision making. It has been estimated that over two-thirds of larger firms have a code of ethics and 44 percent of larger firms provide some form of ethics training for their managers.*** This interest in being ethical stems partly from a desire to avoid legal action and the resulting adverse public reaction, as well as from a desire to satisfy concerns of personal conscience.[44] Moreover, ethical conduct is believed to offer a strategic

---

***Interest in, and support of, ethical training seems to be characteristic of mostly larger firms. Smaller firms, which have fewer surplus resources to devote to managerial training, are far less involved in ethical training. Unfortunately, it is widely believed that smaller organizations are responsible for a sizable proportion of unethical conduct.

advantage over competitors. Ethical training is intended to aid decision making by helping people recognize ethical aspects of decisions, by clarifying rules and norms, by reducing confusion concerning issues of responsibility, and by providing decision-making frameworks for analyzing ethical options.[45]

Most ethics training programs include statements from the top officer emphasizing the importance of ethical decision making, discussion of the corporation's code of ethics, and discussion of specific procedures for reporting unethical conduct. Many programs, such as those in use at Chase Manhattan, General Electric, and Allied, incorporate case discussion, exercises for developing higher levels of ethical maturity, and discussion of ethical frameworks for analyzing decisions. The cases that are discussed are often created from actual corporate-specific instances of difficult decision making. Efforts to raise the ethical maturity level of managers have often relied on Kohlberg's theory of moral development (see Chapter 2). Although evidence is limited, there is some suggestion that individuals exposed to ethical training (especially when couched in Kohlbergian terminology) may show evidence of higher moral reasoning as measured within the context of Kohlberg's theory.[46]

SUMMARY

1. *Describe the types of decisions managers make.* Personal programmed decisions involve simple, repetitive personal matters. Personal nonprogrammed decisions arise during rare but significant events in an individual's personal life. Organizational programmed decisions pertain to relatively simple problem situations in an organization and are handled according to established guidelines or procedures. Organizational nonprogrammed decisions pertain to rare or unique situations that have a potentially significant impact on the organization.

2. *List the steps of a highly rational decision-making process.* When a situation triggers the decision-making process, recognize the existence of a problem or opportunity that demands action. Define the nature of the situation. Generate alternative ways to cope with the situation. Gather information about each alternative and evaluate its desirability. From this evaluation, arrive at a single best course of action. Implement this alternative. Evaluate the decision's effectiveness.

3. *Describe some constraints on the decision-making process.* Constraints on the decision-making process include inability to generate all possible alternatives and their associated consequences, unavailability of accurate information, ethical restrictions on otherwise optimal solutions, and managers' tendency to use heuristics and to satisfice (consider alternative actions only until a reasonably acceptable one is found).

4. *Identify obstacles to effective decision making.* Obstacles to effective decision making include judgmental biases, escalation of commitment, groupthink, and the tendency of groups to endorse extreme positions when confronted with decisions involving an element of risk.

5. *Define groupthink and list its symptoms.* Groupthink is the tendency of highly cohesive groups to take a distorted view of situations. Symptoms of groupthink include an illusion of invulnerability, rationalization, an assumption of morality, negative stereotyping of outsiders, pressure to conform, self-censorship, an illusion of unanimity, and the presence of mindguards (who deflect critics and criticisms).

6. *Describe techniques to improve decision making.* Weigh the advantages and disadvantages of group versus individual decision making when choosing a format for making a decision. To take advantage of the positive features of group decision making, use the nominal group technique, and the Delphi technique.

7. *Identify characteristics of creative organization members.* Characteristics of creative people include willingness to forgo immediate gain in favor of long-term goals, high energy, irritation with the status quo, perseverance, pursuit of hobbies and specialized interests, belief that fantasy and daydreaming are not a waste of time, relatively weak identification with their employing organization, and greater likelihood of changing jobs.

8. *Describe the steps in the creative process.* The first step is opportunity or problem recognition, during which an individual becomes aware that a problem or opportunity needs attention. Next comes immersion, during which the individual collects and recalls relevant information and generates hypotheses. Next is the incubation stage, when the individual subconsciously rearranges the available information. In the insight stage, while a person is engaged in an unrelated activity, an integrative idea will come into his or her consciousness. Finally, in the verification stage, the individual tests the solution with logic or experimentation.

9. *Identify ways that groups and individuals can enhance creativity.* Groups can improve creativity with brainstorming and grid analysis. People can enhance their own creativity by being unafraid of failure, permitting playfulness, identifying creative time periods in each day, borrowing ideas, and maintaining an idea notebook.

10. *Explain how ethics training is being used in larger corporations.* It is considered "good business practice" to follow ethical guidelines when making decisions. A majority of large firms have codes of ethics, and may require training in ethical decision making. Training programs typically consist of case discussion, exercises designed to enhance ethical awareness, and discussion of ethical frameworks for analyzing decisions.

KEY TERMS

Personal decision making
Organizational decision making
Programmed decision
Nonprogrammed decision
Classical decision theory
Rational-economic model
Behavioral theory of decision making
Administrative model
Bounded rationality
Satisfice
Maximize
Bounded discretion
Heuristics
Availability heuristic
Representativeness heuristic
Implicit favorite bias

Loss-aversion bias
Selective perception bias
Personal experience bias
Groupthink
Last-chance meeting
Risky shift
Diffusion of responsibility
Cautious shift
Group polarization
Nominal group technique (NGT)
Delphi technique
Social loafing
Stepladder technique
Brainstorming
Grid analysis

The Root of All Evil

The Ajax Toy Corporation is a medium-sized firm located in southern Michigan. The firm designs and manufactures toys and games. The wage and salary program of the company operates on a low-profile basis; that is, no information on salary ranges in regard to grade classification is given to employees, and they are not given minimum, medium, or maximum pay ranges attainable in their present job levels. When employees are formally evaluated each year, a merit increase, when given, is usually a small percentage increase, with management retaining any information as to how much money is available for merit increases. When management was asked by employees why merit increases and salaries were handled in this manner, the standard answer was, "It is company policy that this information cannot be given to employees. Only staff personnel have knowledge of this information."

The employees of the Research and Development Department for new products are due for a performance appraisal. Their current minimum and maximum levels of wages are $50,000 and $88,000 per year. These salaries are average for the industry. Last year, the company's conservative wage and salary policies resulted in two of the best people in the department being pirated by Ajax's largest competitor, hurting the performance of the Research and Development Department this year. Pirating of employees in other departments has also been a problem for the past two years.

A new director of Research and Development has recently been hired, and management has charged her with proposing recommendations to reduce the pirating of people from her department, while also conducting the department's individual performance appraisals and merit distribution. The manager of Human Resources will later review her ideas against the present system to determine what changes, if any, the department may wish to make.

Additional information about the Research and Development Department and its employees is as follows:

Roger Ballard: 60 years of age; 20 years' experience with Ajax; has not designed any new products during the past year, but works well with others to develop their ideas. Current salary: $88,000 (top of his salary range).

John Connelly: 45 years of age; 10 years with Ajax; is seldom late for work, but doesn't work well with others in the department; was a very good friend of the previous manager; has designed only one new product this year. Current salary: $78,000.

David Browing: 32 years of age; 4 years with Ajax; has designed two new products this year, one of which has been completed; past evaluations have shown him as an average performer, but this year his work has been very good. Current salary: $62,000.

Karen Harding: 24 years of age; was hired 10 months ago to replace one of the pirated employees; has designed two new products that have been completed and are doing very well; has ideas for three more new products; is currently working on these three new ideas with help from Roger; has not received a raise since joining Ajax. Current salary: $50,000.

The director of Research and Development was confidentially informed by the company that she has $24,000 to distribute for use as merit increases. Her recommendation for distribution of the merit dollars requires your approval. As Human Resources manager, you have just received the following merit increase recommendations from the director of Research and Development:

1. Roger Ballard…$4,000
2. John Connelly…$2,000
3. David Browing…$9,500
4. Karen Harding…$8,500

1. As Human Resources manager, would you agree with the distribution of the merit money among the four employees?
2. Defend and explain your decision.

Source: From Jack L. Simonetti, *Experiential Exercises and Cases for Human Resource Management* (New York: Allyn and Bacon, 1987).

EXPERIENTIAL EXERCISE

How Creative Are You?

In recent years, several tests have been developed to measure creative abilities and behavior. Although certainly useful, they do not adequately tap the complex network of behaviors—the particular personality traits, attitudes, motivations, values, interests, and other variables—that predispose a person to think creatively.

To arrive at assessment measures that would cover a broader range of creative attributes, one organization developed an inventory type of test. Part of this instrument is featured below.

After each statement, indicate with a letter the degree or extent with which you agree or disagree:

A = Strongly agree

B = Agree

C = In between or don't know

D = Disagree

E = Strongly disagree

Mark your answers as accurately and frankly as possible. Try not to "second guess" how a creative person might respond to each statement.

1. I always work with a great deal of certainty that I'm following the correct procedures for solving a particular problem.   _____
2. It would be a waste of time for me to ask questions if I had no hope of obtaining answers.   _____
3. I feel that a logical step-by-step method is best for solving problems.   _____
4. I occasionally voice opinions in groups that seem to turn some people off.   _____
5. I spend a great deal of time thinking about what others think of me.   _____

6. I feel that I may have a special contribution to give to the world. _____

7. It is more important for me to do what I believe to be right than to try to win the approval of others. _____

8. People who seem unsure and uncertain about things lose my respect. _____

9. I am able to stick with difficult problems over extended periods of time. _____

10. On occasion I get overly enthusiastic about things. _____

11. I often get my best ideas when doing nothing in particular. _____

12. I rely on intuitive hunches and the feeling of "rightness" or "wrongness" when moving toward the solution of a problem. _____

13. When problem solving, I work faster when analyzing the problem and slower when synthesizing the information I've gathered. _____

14. I like hobbies that involve collecting things. _____

15. Daydreaming has provided the impetus for many of my more important projects. _____

16. If I had to choose from two occupations other than the one I now have, I would rather be a physician than an explorer. _____

17. I can get along more easily with people if they belong to about the same social and business class as myself. _____

18. I have a high degree of aesthetic sensitivity. _____

19. Intuitive hunches are unreliable guides in problem solving. _____

20. I am much more interested in coming up with new ideas than I am in trying to sell them to others. _____

21. I tend to avoid situations in which I might feel inferior. _____

22. In evaluating information, the source of it is more important to me than the content. _____

23. I like people who follow the rule "business before pleasure." _____

24. One's self-respect is much more important than the respect of others. _____

25. I feel that people who strive for perfection are unwise. _____

26. I like work in which I must influence others. _____

27. It is important for me to have a place for everything and everything in its place. _____

28. People who are willing to entertain "crackpot" ideas are impractical. _____

29. I rather enjoy fooling around with new ideas, even if there is no practical payoff. _____

30. When a certain approach to a problem doesn't work, I can quickly reorient my thinking. _____

31. I don't like to ask questions that show ignorance. _____

32. I am able to more easily change my interests to pursue a job or career than I can change a job to pursue my interests. _____

33. Inability to solve a problem is frequently due to asking the wrong question. _____

34. I can frequently anticipate the solution to my problems. _____

35. It is a waste of time to analyze one's failures. _____

36. Only fuzzy thinkers resort to metaphors and analogies. _____

37. At times I have so enjoyed the ingenuity of a crook that I hoped he or she would go scot-free. _____

38. I frequently begin work on a problem that I can only dimly sense and not yet express. _____

39. I frequently tend to forget things, such as names of people, streets, highways, or small towns. _____

40. I feel that hard work is the basic factor in success. _____

41. To be regarded as a good team member is important to me. _____

42. I know how to keep my inner impulses in check. _____

43. I am a thoroughly dependable and responsible person. _____

44. I resent things being uncertain and unpredictable. _____

45. I prefer to work with others in a team effort rather than solo. _____

46. The trouble with many people is that they take things too seriously. _____

47. I am frequently haunted by my problems and cannot let go of them. _____

48. I can easily give up immediate gain or comfort to reach the goals I have set. _____

49. If I were a college professor, I would rather teach factual courses than those involving theory. _____

50. I'm attracted to the mystery of life. _____

Scoring Instructions

To compute your score, circle the value assigned to your answer for each question, as indicated below, and then add all the values.

	Strongly Agree A	Agree B	In-between or Don't Know C	Disagree D	Strongly Disagree E
1.	−2	−1	0	+1	+2
2.	−2	−1	0	+1	+2
3.	−2	−1	0	+1	+2
4.	+2	+1	0	−1	−2
5.	−2	−1	0	+1	+2
6.	+2	+1	0	−1	−2
7.	+2	+1	0	−1	−2
8.	−2	−1	0	+1	+2
9.	+2	+1	0	−1	−2
10.	+2	+1	0	−1	−2
11.	+2	+1	0	−1	−2

12.	+2	+1	0	−1	−2
13.	−2	−1	0	+1	+2
14.	−2	−1	0	+1	+2
15.	+2	+1	0	−1	−2
16.	−2	−1	0	+1	+2
17.	−2	−1	0	+1	+2
18.	+2	+1	0	−1	−2
19.	−2	−1	0	+1	+2
20.	+2	+1	0	−1	−2
21.	−2	−1	0	+1	+2
22.	−2	−1	0	+1	+2
23.	−2	−1	0	+1	+2
24.	+2	+1	0	−1	−2
25.	−2	−1	0	+1	+2
26.	−2	−1	0	+1	+2
27.	−2	−1	0	+1	+2
28.	−2	−1	0	+1	+2
29.	+2	+1	0	−1	−2
30.	+2	+1	0	−1	−2
31.	−2	−1	0	+1	+2
32.	−2	−1	0	+1	+2
33.	+2	+1	0	−1	−2
34.	+2	+1	0	−1	−2
35.	−2	−1	0	+1	+2
36.	−2	−1	0	+1	+2
37.	+2	+1	0	−1	−2
38.	+2	+1	0	−1	−2
39.	+2	+1	0	−1	−2
40.	+2	+1	0	−1	−2
41.	−2	−1	0	+1	+2
42.	−2	−1	0	+1	+2
43.	−2	−1	0	+1	+2
44.	−2	−1	0	+1	+2
45.	−2	−1	0	+1	+2
46.	+2	+1	0	−1	−2
47.	+2	+1	0	−1	−2
48.	+2	+1	0	−1	−2
49.	−2	−1	0	+1	+2
50.	+2	+1	0	−1	−2

Very creative	80 to 100	Below average	20 to 39
Above average	60 to 79	Noncreative	−100 to 19
Average	40 to 59		

Source: E. Raudsepp, *Personnel Journal*, April 1979. Further information about this test is available from Princeton Creative Research, Inc. P.O. Box 122, Princeton, NJ 08542.

9 Group Dynamics

A committee is a group that keeps minutes but squanders hours.

—*Anonymous*

To get along—go along.
—*Sam Rayburn*

There is no monument dedicated to the memory of a committee.

—*Lester J. Pourciau*

Learning Objectives

After studying this chapter, you should be able to:

1. Contrast formal and informal groups, and open and closed groups.
2. List some reasons people form groups.
3. Describe influences on the degree to which people are attracted to one another.
4. Describe stages of group formation and development.
5. List some important group properties that affect performance
6. List factors that induce and sustain cohesiveness in a group.

Group Dynamics: What's Your Type?

Today, levels of management are disappearing due to the downsizing, re-engineering, and flattening of corporate America. A distinctive trend in organizations is the increasing reliance on workgroups to complete the tasks that traditionally resided in the hands of managers. These days, group success means organizational success, and ensuring group success means going back to the basics of configuring a group: considering the types of people who are placed into each group. Group conflict occurs when members working toward a common goal have clashing personality types.

In 1998, Shell Oil Company completed a study of 1,123 randomly selected adult American workers. From this representative sample, they identified six worker-personality types. Each type had a unique set of motivations for working and work style. The **Risk Taker** (typically a young, well-educated, successful male) was motivated by money and had a history of job-hopping in pursuit of better positions. In this group, 40 percent had incomes of over $50,000. **High**

Achievers (primarily highly educated males) planned their careers from an early age. These earned the most money with 25 percent earning over $75,000 annually. **Ladder Climbers** (typically females with an average education) were team players loyal to the company, who typically stayed with one employer for a long time. They valued a stable income more than a high income, with 48 percent earning more than $50,000. **Fulfillment Seekers** (mostly white and married) had an intense desire to improve the world. They typically had high levels of satisfaction with their work, and saw themselves as team players but not leaders. **Paycheck Cashers** (typically young minority males with no college degree) desired good income and benefits but had no interest in learning skills to expand their capabilities. **Clock Punchers** (typically females with a high school diploma or less) were the most discontented. They were in their current job because it was the only available work. It is easy to imagine the potential conflict that could arise by putting, for example, High Achievers and

Clock Punchers in the same group, or having Risk Takers and Ladder Climbers working together to resolve a pressing problem. Thus, a sound strategy in developing groups is first to define the task, then to identify the best worker-personality types to address it, and finally to select individuals who best fit those types. For example, if the problem were to develop a more employee-centered work environment, Fulfillment Seekers and Ladder Climbers would be most attuned to these issues because of their job interests. Risk Takers and High Achievers would probably see this problem as mundane, and it would be a low priority relative to their own interests. However, Risk Takers and High Achievers would flourish with the assigned problem of identifying new profit centers or firms for possible acquisition.

Correctly configuring any group is crucial to the success of the project, as well as the individual team members in the group. Ultimately, group success translates into organizational success.

Source: C.G. Wagner, "Study Reveals Six Types of Workers," Demography, *The Futurist*, February 1999: 10–11.

Managers spend a sizable proportion of their day working in groups and dealing with groups. As a member of a work group and as a representative of a firm who interacts with various groups both inside and outside the organization, a manager must understand the dynamics of groups.

Groups constitute an essential part of organizations and can strongly influence the total level of accomplishment. They can also satisfy the social needs of their members. Thus, it is fair to say that groups have the potential to satisfy the needs of both individuals and organizations. The extent to which these needs are met, and the processes by which they can be met, are the concerns of this chapter. We will examine the nature of groups, the reasons for joining groups, group formation and development, the major variables that affect group performance, and the various kinds of groups that are typically found in modern organizations. Managers who understand the basic principles of group dynamics often find it easier to direct the efforts of a group in a desired direction.

The Nature of Groups

People are social animals—they seek the company of others both to satisfy social needs and to pool resources for improved effectiveness. The presence of others can satisfy a great variety of needs. Hence, people participate in groups. We can define a **group** as two or more people who interact with each other, share certain common beliefs, and view themselves as being members of a group. At a minimum, to be considered a group, at least two people must deal with one another on a continuing basis. Before they interact with each other, they are likely to share common beliefs that impel them to band together. Over time, other shared values may emerge and be solidified. As a consequence of continuing interaction and awareness of shared beliefs, the individuals will come to see themselves as belonging to a distinct entity—the group.

Formal versus Informal Groups

In organizations, people are frequently assigned to work groups. These teams, which are essentially task oriented, are classified as **formal groups.** For example, employees are typically assigned to departments or work crews. A committee is another example of a formal group. It can be said that every organizational member must belong to at least one formal organizational group—that is, every employee must have at least one formal role. Some organizational members may hold two or more formal group memberships (for example, by being on several committees). Such multiple members can serve as "linking pins" within the organization who can enhance integration by sharing information across groups and passing on directives to lower levels.[1]

Informal groups arise from social interaction among organizational members. Membership in such groups is voluntary and more heavily based on interpersonal attraction. Sometimes the activities or goals of an informal group are attractive to prospective members. For example, department softball and bowling teams are informal groups whose activities attract interested individuals. Not all informal groups, however, have a specific set of activities. Often, they are simply composed of coworkers who share common concerns. For example, a department head may informally meet with other managers to share information (or rumors) about an impending merger.

Informal groups are not inherently good or bad for an organization. When the informal group's goals are congruent with the organization's—such as when both seek to maximize customer satisfaction and produce a high-quality product—then all is well and good. In other instances, however, an informal group may oppose the organization's goals, as when employees decide to restrict daily output. In fact, informal groups are often sources of resistance to organizational change. They sometimes oppose approaches to job redesign and organizational restructuring. Because of the status and personal satisfaction they derive from their affiliation, members of informal groups can be counted on to resist attempts to disrupt or disband their social arrangement.

Open versus Closed Groups

Groups in organizational settings can also be classified in terms of whether they are open or closed. An **open group** frequently changes its membership, with people constantly moving in and out of the group. In contrast, a **closed group** has a relatively stable membership. In addition, most closed groups have well-established status relationships among their members, whereas open groups tend to fluctuate on dimensions of individual power and status. Open groups are also more subject to disruption because of their changing membership and are less able to focus on long-term issues because of their relative instability. Nonetheless, open groups have certain advantages. For example, their high rate of turnover permits the infusion of "new blood," and therefore new ideas and talents. They are also more adaptable to changes in their surrounding circumstances.

Certain types of activities are better performed by each type of group. For example, for long-range planning, a closed group is likely to be more effective because it has a stronger commitment to dealing with the future. For developing new ideas or new products, an open group is likely to be more effective because of its more fluid and change-oriented atmosphere. Closed groups possess a stronger historical perspective, while open groups are more tolerant of developing and implementing new perspectives.

Reasons for Forming Groups

By and large, people join groups for two reasons: to accomplish a task or goal and to satisfy their social needs. These two reasons are not perfectly distinct, however, because many group activities satisfy both task and social needs. In fact, a review of the various needs that were considered in Chapter 4—such as those in Maslow's hierarchy—would reveal that to some extent, nearly all needs can be satisfied by joining a group.

Security and Protection   Group membership can give an individual a sense of security and a real degree of protection. Being one member of a large organization can generate feelings of insecurity and anxiety, but belonging to a small group can reduce such fears by providing a sense of unity with others. During times of stress, such as when an organization is changing direction or leadership, belonging to a stable and supportive work unit can reduce individual anxieties.

By virtue of sheer numbers, groups afford a degree of protection that an individual might not otherwise enjoy. This principle is embodied in the union movement, which attempts to give members a sense of protection through highly organized collective strength.

Affiliation   An individual's need for affiliation and emotional support can be directly satisfied by membership in a group. Acceptance by others is an important social need. Feeling accepted by others at work can help to enhance one's feeling of self-worth.

Esteem and Identity   Groups also provide opportunities for an individual to feel important. They can give a person status and provide opportunities for praise and recognition. Many work-related achievements may not be appreciated or understood by people unfamiliar with the nature of the job. But in joining a group that does understand the job (either within organizations or through professional associations), people gain opportunities to receive recognition and esteem for their accomplishments.

Membership in a group also helps people to define who they are in the social scheme of things. Seeing oneself as a salesperson, an economist, or a teamster helps foster a feeling of identification with a larger purpose. Through membership in a work group, a person gains a formal title and a sense of purpose.

Task Accomplishment   A primary reason that groups are created is to facilitate task accomplishment. A group can often accomplish more through joint effort than can an equal number of individuals working separately. In fact, many goals are attainable only through cooperative group effort. By sharing ideas, pooling resources, and providing feedback to members, a group can be an effective mechanism for attaining otherwise difficult goals.*

Interpersonal Attraction

People sometimes join and remain in groups because of interpersonal attraction. Three key determinants of interpersonal attraction are physical distance, psychological distance, and similarity.

---

*It has been suggested that early in their history, humans recognized that group members benefited from cooperative effort. For example, members of a primitive tribe would work together in relays to wear out a game animal that the tribe would then share as a meal. No individual alone could defeat the animal, but together it was easy (and even something of a sport).

Physical and Psychological Distance

Having an opportunity to interact is an important determinant of attraction to others, especially for informal groups. Generally, people who are physically closer to one another develop closer relationships than those who are farther apart. This principle of proximity has been found to hold not only in work settings but also in relationships among neighbors.[2]

In addition to actual physical distance, psychological distance is important. Figure 9.1 shows how two sets of offices can be arranged either to facilitate social interaction or to discourage it. The top office arrangement (A) encourages social interaction by providing a common access to elevators and a shared secretarial-reception area. The lower office layout (B) discourages interaction by offering two avenues of entry and exit that reduce overlapping traffic patterns. People on each side of the layout would tend to use only the nearer elevator. In addition, the placement of the office doors does not encourage eye contact as people enter and leave their work spaces. Although the physical distance separating the office workers in both layouts is not great, the psychological

FIGURE 9.1   *Two Office Layouts*

A is designed to encourage social interaction, while B is arranged to discourage it.

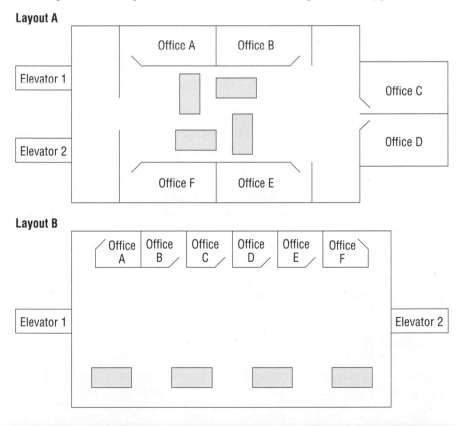

Source: H.J. Reitz, *Behavior in Organizations* (New York: Irwin, 1981).

distance is greatly increased in layout B because of the impact that the physical arrangements will have on social relations. As a result, the office workers in layout B would *feel* farther apart than those in layout A. Therefore, managers can consciously structure work settings, depending on whether the goal is to create camaraderie and group spirit, or to reduce informal contacts.

Similarity

There has been a fair amount of debate on the issue of whether "opposites attract" or "birds of a feather flock together." That is, do people who are dissimilar in terms of sex, race, income, age, religion, and the like find each other's company more satisfying than people who are highly similar on these dimensions? Although much of the research on this topic points to the potential for both processes, attraction among similar people appears to be somewhat more common and more easily produced in formal studies.

One particularly powerful and reliable finding in this area deals with similarity of attitudes. The proportion of similar attitudes that two people have in common (that is, whether they share a small, moderate, or high percentage of similar attitudes) appears to be a very strong determinant of interpersonal attraction. The greater the proportion, the greater the degree of attraction.[3] In fact, this finding has been found with such a high degree of reliability that it is sometimes termed the **law of attraction.**[†]

Although the notions of "opposites attract" and "birds of a feather flock together" may seem contradictory, one does not necessarily exclude the other. Most social scientists agree that individuals who possess similar *attitudes* and complementary *needs* and *abilities* will be highly attracted to one another. People often find each other's needs and abilities highly attractive because, by joining forces, they can achieve a form of need-completion or personal fulfillment. For example, in a successful business partnership, two partners may share common goals and values, yet one of them will be skilled at managing the financial aspect of their enterprise, while the other excels at marketing, public relations, and innovation.

According to **social exchange theory,** *reward* is any satisfaction that is derived from a relationship.[4] Investments (such as time and energy) as well as social problems (such as embarrassment and conflict) that are associated with a relationship are considered *costs*. According to this theory, a person is continuously monitoring rewards, costs, and the differences between rewards and costs—or *outcomes*. If rewards exceed costs, so that a person greatly benefits from a relationship, we would expect the relationship to continue. But if costs greatly exceed rewards, we would intuitively expect the relationship to cease.

Stages in Group Development

Groups are not static, but change and develop over time. In the earliest stage of a group's development, members are concerned with testing each other's reac-

---

[†]Most social scientists believe that these and other findings in the area of social attraction can be explained in terms of reinforcement or reward principles—that is, we like those who reaffirm our beliefs and are likely to reward us for holding a particular point of view.

FIGURE 9.2 *Stages of Group Formation and Development*

Stages	Concerns
Forming	Testing and Dependency
Storming	Division of Power
Norming	Rule Making
Performing	Accomplishing Goals

tion to determine which actions are acceptable and unacceptable.[5] In addition, the members depend on each other for cues about what is expected in the way of contribution and personal conduct. Problems associated with starting a group (for example, scheduling, finding a location, and obtaining resources) are also a significant part of this stage. This initial stage is called **forming.**

The second stage, **storming,** involves intragroup conflict. Hostility and disagreement arise as the group's members wrestle with how power and status will be divided. Members may resist the formation of a group structure and ignore the desires of the group's leader.

During the third stage, **norming,** feelings of cohesiveness develop. New standards and roles are adopted, and opinions about task accomplishment are freely voiced. The members' attraction to the group is strengthened, and job satisfaction grows as the level of cohesiveness increases. Cooperation and a sense of shared responsibility are primary themes of this stage.

In the final stage, **performing,** the group has established a flexible network of relationships that aids task accomplishment. Internal hostility is at a low point as the group directs its energies toward the successful performance of valued tasks.

Of course, not every group goes through these four stages in a fixed sequence. For more formal groups, for example, in which the division of power may be less subject to debate, storming may be virtually eliminated. Also, as a group experiences change, it may return to an earlier stage. For example, if an established group receives a new leader, it may temporarily give up performing and return to storming or norming. Figure 9.2 outlines the sequence of group development.

Impact of Group Properties on Performance

The Mere Presence of Others

Perhaps the most fundamental feature of groups is the presence of other people. Some interesting research has focused on the effects of the mere presence of others on an individual's task performance. In these studies, an individual is asked to perform a task without interacting with others who are present. Results of such studies indicate that having others nearby tends to facilitate performance on relatively simple and well-rehearsed tasks.[6] However, for fairly complex tasks, the presence of others can have a detrimental effect. The positive effect of others being present is called the **social facilitation effect,** while the detrimental effect is termed the **social inhibition effect.**

You may have noticed such effects greatly magnified if you have ever been asked to perform in front of an audience. If your assigned task was relatively simple, such as spelling your name or reciting other well-rehearsed information, you probably had little difficulty. But if you were asked to solve a problem that you had never encountered before, you probably did poorly.[‡] The reasons for these effects are twofold. First, when we expect others to evaluate us, we feel apprehensive (regardless of whether we are actually being judged). Second, the presence of others can increase arousal because of greater self-evaluation of performance. Such self-evaluation can aid performance of a simple task, but impair performance of a difficult task.[7] The implications of this line of research are fairly direct: For tasks that are simple and repetitive, the presence of coworkers can have positive effects, while for complex and novel tasks, working in isolation is preferable.

Size

Group size has detectable effects on group performance. In larger groups, the potential impact and contribution of each individual are somewhat diminished, but the total resources of the group are increased. Administering a larger group also creates unique problems for managers.

Although most organizations settle on groups of five to seven persons to handle most problem-solving tasks, some organizations use much larger "spans of control" for simple tasks. Hard evidence about an ideal size for groups is sparse, yet several conclusions seem possible.

First, members appear to become more tolerant of authoritarian and directive leadership as group size increases. Apparently, group members recognize and concede the administrative difficulties that can arise in a larger work unit. In addition, as unit size increases, it becomes more difficult for a handful of subordinates to be influential, and members may feel inhibited about participating in group activities.

Second, larger groups are more likely to have formalized rules and set procedures for dealing with problems. Despite this greater formality, larger groups require more time to reach decisions than smaller groups. Additionally, subgroups are not committed to the full group's formal goals and prefer instead to pursue the more selfish interests of a few members.

Third, a review of research on group size suggests that job satisfaction is lower in larger groups.[8] This probably occurs because people receive less personal attention and fewer opportunities to participate. It is also likely that employees in smaller work units feel that their presence is more crucial to the group and therefore are inclined to be more involved. For blue-collar workers, absenteeism and turnover also increase in larger work units. Cohesion and communication diminish with increased group size, making a job inher-

---

[‡]An illustration of the facilitation effect is reported by people who jog. Most joggers report feeling energized when running with another person, even though they are not truly competing with one another. Perhaps one of the more intriguing aspects of the social facilitation effect has been the pervasiveness of the phenomenon across species. It appears that even ants, cockroaches, and chickens demonstrate a social facilitation effect with well-rehearsed behaviors when in the presence of other members of their species!

ently less attractive and lessening the worker's desire to attend. In white-collar jobs, on the other hand, employees may have other sources of satisfaction to draw on.

Fourth, as group size increases, productivity reaches a point of diminishing returns because of the rising difficulties of coordination and member involvement. This may be a primary reason that five-member groups are so popular. Groups of five have several advantages. The group size is not intimidating, so that a member who disagrees with the majority is less inclined to remain silent. Having an odd number of members means that a tie or split decision can be avoided when voting. Members of such a group also have less difficulty in shifting roles within the group.

An interesting problem that tends to arise in larger groups is *social loafing.* In a famous study of this phenomenon, Ringelmann, a German psychologist, had workers pull as hard as they could on a rope. Each subject performed this task first alone and then with others in groups of varying sizes while a meter measured the strength of each pull. Although the total amount of force tended to increase as the size of the work group increased, the amount of effort exerted by each person actually decreased. In other words, the average productivity per group member decreased as the size of the work group increased. Researchers who later replicated Ringlemann's finding have argued that such social loafing occurs because each individual feels that the needed effort will be shared by the group's members and that he or she can count on others to take up necessary slack.[9] The social loafing phenomenon suggests that under some circumstances, a group's effort may actually be less than the expected sum of individual contributions.

Composition

How well a group performs a task depends in large part on the task-relevant resources of its members. The diversity versus redundancy of members' traits and abilities, then, is an important factor in explaining group performance. Groups composed of highly similar individuals who hold common beliefs and have much the same abilities are likely to view a task from a single perspective. Such solidarity can be productive, but it may also mean that members will lack a critical ingredient for unraveling certain kinds of problems. As we saw in our discussion of individual versus group problem solving (Chapter 8), one of a group's greatest assets in comparison to individuals acting alone is the likelihood of achieving higher-quality solutions. Carrying this logic a step further, we can reasonably expect that diversified groups tend to do better on many problem-solving tasks than do homogeneous groups of highly similar individuals.

The diverse abilities and experiences of the members of a heterogeneous group offer an advantage for generating innovative solutions, provided the skills and experiences are *relevant* to the task. Thus, merely adding more people to a problem-solving group to broaden the pool of skills and experience will not guarantee a better job. Attention must be paid to the relevance of the members' attributes and the mix of these attributes within the group. Additionally, the more *competent* members of a work group must also be the most *influential* members. If the people who are the least informed are the most influential group members, the quality of the decision will be diminished.[10]

One interesting finding about group composition is that members are more socially conforming in mixed-sex groups than in same-sex groups.[11] This suggests that members of mixed-sex groups focus more on interpersonal relations and, therefore, conform more than members of same-sex groups. Members of same-sex groups tend to be more concerned with accomplishing the task at hand.[§]

Roles

Every member of a group has a differentiated set of activities to perform. The set of expected behaviors relating to an individual's position within a group is called a **role.** Although the term *role* seems familiar enough (we can each easily define the roles of schoolteachers, managers, students, and others), it can be viewed in several different ways.

A person's **expected role** is the formal role that is defined in a job description or manual. This role may be conveyed through both a written job description and the signals that other members of a work unit send as they teach newcomers how to perform their jobs. An individual's expected role, however, may differ from his or her perceived role. A **perceived role** is the set of activities that an individual believes he or she is expected to perform. The perceived role may or may not greatly overlap with the expected role that originates with other members of the organization. Finally, an **enacted role** is a person's actual conduct in his or her position. It is more likely to reflect the individual's perceived role than the expected role.

Figure 9.3 illustrates how individuals receive information about their role and adjust their behavior accordingly. As this figure suggests, the process generally begins with the standards that are held by evaluators, such as managers, supervisors, peers, and subordinates. These standards or expectations are then communicated to the individual. Because communication is often imprecise, the expected (or sent) role may not be identical to the perceived (or received) role. Furthermore, due to constraints on actual behavior, the enacted role is observed by the evaluators, who then compare it to the standards they have set. This feedback then completes a single **role episode.** If the individual's behavior does not come sufficiently close to the standards, another role episode may be initiated.

The figure also suggests that many things can go wrong in a role episode. Sometimes the evaluators do not send consistent signals. For example, your superior may assign you a task, while his or her superior, in turn, may later tell you that you should not perform that duty, perhaps because it is not your responsibility or not included in your job description. Different groups sometimes send different signals, as when a supervisor's subordinates indicate that they would like less pressure for production, while his or her superiors simultaneously insist on higher levels of output. Differing signals from evaluating groups and individuals result in **role conflict.** On occasion, the messages that evaluators send are not clear, or they give incomplete information, which leads to **role ambiguity.** At each step in the role episode depicted in Figure 9.3, poor communication and other obstacles may interfere with the process.

Although role conflict and role ambiguity seem to be undesirable, there are some indications that in modest amounts and under the right conditions, they may actually have positive effects. In fact, a work setting that is totally devoid

---

[§]Although this finding suggests that managers should segregate the sexes or mix them depending on whether task accomplishment or social conformity is a major goal, it is difficult to defend any contention that espouses segregating the sexes within work settings.

FIGURE 9.3   *A Representation of a Role Episode*

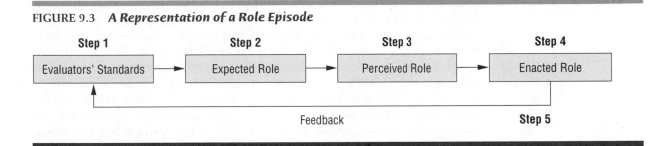

of conflict and ambiguity can be dull and uninspiring. Thus, in order to avoid stagnation and encourage innovation, managers should perhaps seek to create a productive level of conflict and ambiguity.

There is a variety of roles that employees can assume in a work group.[12] Although these categories do not fit into a workable model of role episodes, they do provide an insightful view of the ways in which individual group members tend to behave:

- *Task-oriented employees:* Those who can be counted on to "get the job done" and "deliver the goods"
- *People-oriented employees:* Those who are the Good Samaritans and social leaders
- *Nay-sayers:* Those who oppose most proposals, have thick skins, and find fault with nearly everything
- *Yea-sayers:* Those who counter the nay-sayers and help to circumvent the opposition
- *Regulars:* Those who are "in," accept the group's values, and are accepted by the group
- *Deviants:* Those who depart from the group's values—the mavericks
- *Isolates:* The "lone wolves" who depart further from the group than the deviants
- *Newcomers:* Those who know little and need to be taken care of by others; people who are expected to be "seen but not heard"
- *Old-timers:* Those who have been around a long time and "know the ropes"
- *Climbers:* Those who are expected to get ahead, often on the basis of potential rather than ability
- *Cosmopolitans:* Those who view themselves as members of a larger professional or cultural community
- *Locals:* Those who are firmly rooted in the organization and the local community

Status

Status is the social ranking or social worth accorded an individual because of the position he or she occupies in a group. Although we typically speak of status as a single notion, it is in fact made up of numerous factors, such as salary, title, seniority, and power. However, a difference on only one of these dimensions is often sufficient to confer status. For example, a group of tool-and-die makers may all have equivalent job titles, but the oldest member of the department, due to seniority, may enjoy higher status and, as a result, greater deference. Of course, status must exist in the eyes of those who confer it. If the other tool-and-die makers in the work unit do not respect seniority, then the oldest individual will not in fact enjoy high status (although he may still feel that he deserves it).

Although status is often conferred on the basis of achievement, personal characteristics, and the ability to administer rewards, it is perhaps most frequently associated with formal authority. Symbols of status, such as titles and perquisites, are designed to communicate difference and distinction, and serve several purposes. Status symbols *provide stability* to the social order, which helps to reduce uncertainty about the appropriateness of conduct and role expectations. In addition, they can *provide incentives* for people to strive for superior performance. Finally, status symbols *provide a sense of identification* by giving individuals information about group membership and reminding them of the group's values.

If all attributes of a high-status individual are greater than those of low-status individuals, the high-status individual is said to be congruent on all dimensions of status. For example, if the highest-level executive is also the oldest, most expert, most experienced, best educated, and best paid member of that organization, then he is similar, or congruent, on all aspects of status. If, however, that executive holds the highest level on all attributes except pay (that is, if another member of the organization were highest paid but lacked equal standing on the other dimensions), the executive would experience **status incongruence.**

Status incongruence can have an unsettling effect on group relations. In progressive organizations, people are more likely to be promoted for personal achievement than for length of service. In such organizations, status incongruence can be prevalent as younger, talented managers are promoted over their more senior colleagues. A situation in which a subordinate is substantially older than his or her superiors can be uncomfortable for both an older person and a fast-track manager. As a consequence, some amount of jealousy and hostility can be expected in group situations involving status incongruence.**

Status differences may also have undue influence on group decision making. In one well-known study, bomber crews were assigned a task that could not be easily completed.[13] After struggling with the task for some time, the men took a break during which one member of each crew (either the pilot or the tail gunner) was given a clue to the problem's solution. In crews where the clue was planted with the pilot, the suggestion was frequently adopted. But in crews where the tail gunner offered the new approach, the suggestion was adopted much more rarely. Pilots and tail gunners differ sharply on a number of status-related dimensions: pilots are older, more highly educated, hold higher military rank, have greater responsibility, and have more flying time than tail gunners. Thus, it is safe to conclude that the crew showed a bias toward favoring high-status individuals, rather than objectively assessing the quality of the proposal.

Norms

Norms are rules of conduct that are established to maintain the behavioral consistency of group members. They may be written (as in a code of professional ethics) or unwritten. Deviation from norms is frequently punished by

---

**In order to appreciate how uncomfortable a person can be in situations involving status incongruence, imagine taking a high-level math course that is taught by a professor who is 17 years old.

ostracism and verbal attacks. Other more formal sanctions may also be used, as when an unethical lawyer is disbarred. Work-group norms can be a powerful determinant of output.[14]

Norms have two primary purposes: (1) they give members a useful frame of reference for explaining and comprehending their group, and (2) they identify appropriate and inappropriate conduct. In addition, norms ensure that group members will focus their efforts in a common direction. This uniformity of purpose improves the group's chances of attaining its goals. J.R. Hackman has identified five major characteristics of norms:[15]

1. *They represent the structural characteristics of the group.* Group norms are analogous to individual personalities in that they reveal the underlying processes that regulate behavior.

2. *They apply strictly to behavior and not to private thoughts and feelings.* Private acceptance of group norms is not necessary. What really matters is public compliance.

3. *They are developed only for behaviors that are judged to be important by the majority of group members.*

4. *Although they usually develop slowly, norms can be developed rapidly if the need arises.*

5. *Not all norms apply to all members.* High-status individuals may be exempted from certain norms, but new group members may be expected to comply closely with all norms. Often it is expected that distasteful tasks will be handled by initiates.

As is true of many social phenomena in isolation, group norms are neither good nor bad. Their value to an organization depends on whether they are directed to enhancing, rather than restricting, productivity. If norms lead a work group to produce a high-quality product or to be the best in its industry, they are highly desirable. But norms that encourage workers to reduce productivity are clearly undesirable because they undercut management's goals.

As a manager, you may find yourself enforcing group norms when they are congruent with your own goals or opposing them when they are incongruent. Below is a set of guidelines for achieving both ends.[16] If you wish to enforce group norms, these guidelines should be followed:

1. Show a group member that the difference between the group's wishes and his or her wishes is not great, and that there is little need to resist group pressures.

2. Develop methods for rewarding employees who conform to group standards, such as bonuses, honor rolls, public recognition, and trophies.

3. Help members to understand how their contributions help the group accomplish its purposes.

4. Give participants a say in establishing standards, since standards are more closely followed by those who set them.

5. Make it known that members who do not conform to the group's standards will be removed from the team (while also helping anyone who is removed to overcome the resulting guilt and loss of self-esteem).

If the work group's standards are in opposition to your own, the following guidelines should be employed:

1. Recognize like-minded members and ally yourself with them.

2. Try to establish joint opposition with like-minded members by discussing your views and plans with them.

3. Do not give up legitimate professional preferences in order to prevent disharmony.

4. Hold out against social pressures by concealing from others what you do or think.

5. Attempt to publicize the value of cooperation and resultant rewards.

Cohesiveness

Cohesiveness is the extent to which members are attracted to a group and desire to remain in it. Cohesiveness is sometimes described as the sum of all forces acting on individuals to remain in the group. As the term implies, cohesiveness pertains to how group members "stick together." Listed below are the factors that induce and sustain cohesiveness in groups, and the effects of cohesiveness on group members and the organization.

Factors That Induce and Sustain Group Cohesiveness

1. *Similarity of attitudes and goals.* As mentioned in the discussion of interpersonal attraction, when group members have similar attitudes, they find each other's company pleasurable. So, too, individual members will be attracted to a group whose goals and ambitions are similar to their own.

2. *Threats.* The presence of external threats can help to increase group cohesion in that sharing a mutual fate can lead to greater awareness of interdependence. Competition from sources outside the group can also enhance cohesiveness, whereas competition among group members will tend to decrease cohesion.

3. *Unit size.* Smaller groups tend to be more cohesive than larger groups because smaller groups offer greater opportunities to interact with all members. Since diversity (and, therefore, dissimilarity of attitudes and values) tends to increase with group size, larger groups are likely to be less cohesive. In addition, in large units, the need for more rigid work rules and procedures reduces the informal nature of relations and communication among group members.

4. *Reward systems.* Cohesiveness can also be enhanced by offering rewards on a group, rather than an individual, basis. Group incentives, such as bonuses based on team performance, encourage a perception of a common fate and enhance cooperation. In contrast, reward schemes that encourage competition among group members—such as a winner-take-all bonus system for the single best performer in a unit—tend to diminish group cohesiveness.

5. *Work unit assignments.* The deliberate composition of work units based on interpersonal attraction, similarity of values, and common goals can facilitate cohesion. In a classic study, carpenters and bricklayers were assigned to teams based on a prior secret balloting of preferred workmates.[17] The work teams that were formed on the basis of personal preferences had higher

levels of job satisfaction than did the randomly assigned work units that served as a control group.

6. *Isolation.* Generally, groups that are isolated from others are more likely to be cohesive. Groups in isolation come to view themselves as unique and different. Isolation also helps to foster group members' sense of a common fate and need for defense against outside threats.

The Effects of Cohesiveness

1. *Satisfaction.* Members of highly cohesive groups are generally much more satisfied than members of less cohesive groups. This is, of course, to be expected, since the very definition of group cohesion implies a strong attraction among group members.

2. *Communication.* Communication among group members is significantly greater in highly cohesive groups than in less cohesive groups. Because members of cohesive groups are likely to share common values and goals and to find their own company satisfying, they are inclined to greater communicativeness. This communication in turn tends to foster greater personal revelation and depth of understanding, which cements positive social relations.

3. *Hostility.* Hostile and aggressive acts are more frequent in highly cohesive groups, but such hostility is usually directed toward people who are not members of the group.[18] Cohesion apparently creates a sense of superiority among group members, which can result in hostility toward, and rejection of, outsiders.

4. *Productivity.* Some researchers have found cohesive groups to be very productive, while others have found that highly cohesive groups are not as productive as less cohesive groups. Still other researchers have reported no relationship between productivity and group cohesion.[19] It appears that a primary determinant of the effect of cohesion on productivity is whether the group's goals are congruent with those of the organization. If the goals of a cohesive group include high performance, then high performance can be reasonably expected. Conversely, if a highly cohesive group values reduced productivity, then a relatively low level of productivity can be expected. In short, cohesive groups are more likely to attain their goals than are less cohesive groups. In a study of over two hundred small work groups in a manufacturing setting, cohesive groups were found to be less variable in their performance regardless of their absolute level of output.[20] This occurred because cohesive groups tend to emphasize compliance with work norms. Whether its norms endorse high or low productivity, a group will probably produce within its own relatively narrow but prescribed range of output. Despite evidence of less variance for highly cohesive groups, one recent review of the relationship between cohesiveness and performance did find that, on average, highly cohesive groups outperformed less cohesive groups.[21]

5. *Resistance to change.* Although it is less well documented, highly cohesive groups are believed to be more resistant to change than are less cohesive groups. Changes that disrupt the status quo threaten a group's networks and social supports and are, therefore, likely to be resisted. Attempts at job

An Inside Look
Making Meetings Less Miserable

The most fundamental example of group dynamics in corporate America is the corporate meeting. Here are some of the common endearments one typically hears about this most venerable of corporate institutions.

- "They're too long."
- "They're pointless."
- "They're dominated by windbags and suck-ups."

The reality is that meetings are a fact of corporate life, and they are here to stay. Morris Schectman, chairman of the Schectman Institute, a leadership training firm, offers several key observations about the corporate meeting: "Meetings are career-critical. They are a prime tool for developing staff through giving and getting feedback, identifying barriers to performance, and deciding how to remove those barriers. If you can't orchestrate a meeting, you're of little use to a corporation." He offers these tips for orchestrating meetings:

Be prepared. Never wing it. Don't be sloppy, for it will show. Plan your meeting, prepare an agenda, and distribute it to participants with ample time for them to review it and think about the issues prior to the meeting.

Keep the agenda simple. If you merely need to distribute information, use e-mail. Meetings are a place to generate and hone ideas, solve problems, and define what actions will be taken and by whom.

Make participants comfortable. Relaxed people are more willing to participate. Be welcoming and use friendly gestures to draw people into conversations. Making eye contact shows interest in what people are saying. Hold meetings in neutral or off-site settings to enhance the comfort level.

Judge not, lest ye be judged. The leader must minimize fear of reprisal or rejection of ideas to keep members involved. Never attack a poor idea; this is akin to attacking the person presenting the idea. Instead, encourage the contributor to take ownership of the idea and develop it more fully. Create a proper atmosphere for honest and open discussion.

Get everyone involved. It is the responsibility of the leader to encourage equal participation. Some will talk too much and try to dominate, while some will not talk at all. To bring in nonparticipants, open the topic up to the group or ask people to write down their thoughts for you to read to the group.

Take risks. If people are not encouraged to talk openly and honestly, they will not get to the true issues. Foster an environment where employees can feel free to speak their minds.

Source: Hal Lancaster, "Learning Some Ways to Make Meetings Slightly Less Awful," Managing Your Career, *The Wall Street Journal*, May 26, 1998.

redesign that ignore the existing social relations among employees run a greater risk of failing.[22]

SUMMARY

1. *Contrast formal and informal groups and open and closed groups.* Formal groups are task-oriented groups to which people are assigned; informal groups arise from voluntary social interaction among members of the organization. Open groups frequently change their membership; closed groups have a relatively stable membership.

2. *List some reasons people form groups.* People join groups for security and protection, for affiliation and emotional support, for esteem and a sense of identity, and to accomplish tasks.

3. *Describe influences on the degree to which people are attracted to one another.* The less the distance between people, the greater their interpersonal

attraction. Distance can be either physical or psychological. People with similar attitudes or complementary needs and abilities feel greater attraction.

4. *Describe stages of group formation and development.* A popular view is that groups pass through four stages as they develop: (1) forming, during which group members look to each other for clues about what actions are acceptable and expected; (2) storming, a stage of intragroup conflict during which power and status are allocated; (3) norming, the development of feelings of cohesiveness; and (4) performing, the accomplishment of valued tasks.

5. *List some important group properties that affect performance.* Performance is affected by the mere presence of others, the size and composition of the group, the roles and status of group members, the norms of the group, and the degree of cohesiveness of the group.

6. *List factors that induce and sustain cohesiveness in a group.* These factors include similarity of attitudes and goals, the presence of external threats, small group size, reward systems based on group performance, work unit assignments based on personal preferences, and isolation from other groups.

KEY TERMS

Group
Formal group
Informal group
Open group
Closed group
Law of attraction
Social exchange theory
Forming
Storming
Norming
Performing
Social facilitation effect

Social inhibition effect
Role
Expected role
Perceived role
Enacted role
Role episode
Role conflict
Role ambiguity
Status
Status incongruence
Norms
Cohesiveness

CRITICAL INCIDENT

The Bread II Team

By early 1999, the five-member team at Wilson Appliance, a small appliance manufacturer in Youngstown, Ohio, had been working for more than 12 months on "Bread II," a new electric breadmaker. The self-managed interdisciplinary work team was a first for the company. If it operated successfully, the teamwork concept would spread throughout the company. Julia Kendall, leader of the Bread II team, knew a lot was riding on the team's success.

Electric breadmakers had become a hot consumer item the past few years, and Wilson's Bread I machine, introduced in 1994, had been a popular model, but sales had recently leveled off. Wilson executives decided to adopt a team approach to developing a new breadmaker. The team, representing employees from marketing, engineering, manufacturing, and finance, was given a blank slate and a mission to create a new breadmaker that would be different from those already on the market.

Although Julia was the team's leader, as manager of the household appliance division, she had extensive responsibilities beyond the Bread II project. Her role with regard to Bread II was to keep the team on track and intervene when there were problems.

The team members worked interdependently, making important marketing, design, and product decisions by consensus. In addition to Julia, the team consisted of Linda Killington and Michael Delcamp from marketing; Henry Kichner, Wilson's engineering genius; Maggie Dresser from finance; and Jim Summers from manufacturing.

Focus groups with current owners of breadmakers and potential customers had revealed customers were universally dissatisfied with one aspect of currently available breadmakers. The process of electronic breadmaking, although it merely required the user to accurately measure ingredients and turn the appliance on, took nearly three hours from start to finish for each loaf. Families with children found one loaf of bread was consumed within two days. To produce enough bread for a family of four, the breadmaker would have to be in use two or three times per week. With this information, the team decided to introduce a breadmaker that would simultaneously bake two loaves of bread (hence the name Bread II) without compromising taste or quality.

Over the past year, the group had worked very well together. Despite some initial difficulties with the team format, the Bread II team had made substantial progress toward their September 1999 goal to introduce the Bread II to the market in time for holiday sales.

Following a meeting last week, Henry and Jim began a spirited discussion of the political changes that had occurred in recent years. Henry was very outspoken about his disapproval of women holding important political positions. Linda, Michael, and Maggie joined the discussion, intrigued by Henry's perspective. Before long the conversation got out of hand, and Henry and Linda became embroiled in a heated confrontation. Four days later the two were still not speaking to one another. With Bread II on a tight deadline, Julia knew she would have to intervene to return cohesion to the group. She was not sure how to handle the situation, particularly because she, too, felt Henry's comments were out of line. Realizing the conflict would grow deeper with each passing day, she headed for the conference room in which the Bread II team was about to meet.

1. What stage was the group in before the conflict erupted? After?

2. What factors have sustained the group's cohesiveness? What factors have fractured the group's cohesiveness?

3. What should Julia do?

Source: "The Bread II Team," written by Melissa Waite, State University of New York, University at Buffalo; and Susan Stites-Doe, State University of New York, College at Brockport.

EXPERIENTIAL EXERCISE

Group Effectiveness Checklist

The ability to work in groups is a skill increasingly called upon in today's businesses. Working effectively in groups will be an important skill to develop in both your personal and professional lives. The following 20 items provide a checklist for you to use in describing the effectiveness of a group or groups to which you belong. If you have been using groups to do role plays, cases, or other exercises in your Organizational Behavior class, use one of these groups as your point of reference.

	Mostly Yes	Mostly No
1. The atmosphere is relaxed and comfortable.	_____	_____
2. Group discussion is frequent and usually pertinent to the task at hand.	_____	_____
3. Group members understand what they are trying to accomplish.	_____	_____
4. People listen to each other's suggestions and ideas.	_____	_____
5. Disagreements are tolerated and an attempt is made to resolve them.	_____	_____
6. There is general agreement on most courses of action taken.	_____	_____
7. The group welcomes frank criticism from inside and outside sources.	_____	_____
8. When the group takes action, clear assignments are made and accepted.	_____	_____
9. There is a well-established, relaxed working relationship among the members.	_____	_____
10. There is a high degree of trust and confidence among the leader and subordinates.	_____	_____
11. The group members strive to help the group achieve its goal.	_____	_____
12. Suggestions and criticisms are offered and received with a helpful spirit.	_____	_____
13. There is a cooperative rather than a competitive relationship among group members.	_____	_____
14. The group's goals are set high, but not so high as to create anxieties or fear of failure.	_____	_____
15. The leaders and members hold a high opinion of the group's capabilities.	_____	_____
16. Creativity is stimulated within the group.	_____	_____
17. There is ample communication within the group of topics relevant to getting the work accomplished.	_____	_____
18. Group members feel confident in making decisions.	_____	_____
19. People are kept busy, but not overloaded.	_____	_____
20. The leader of the group is well suited for the job.	_____	_____

Scoring Guidelines: This checklist is designed to help you assess a group's effectiveness. The greater the number of statements to which you answered "Mostly Yes," the more likely the group is productive and its members are satisfied. You can also use this checklist as a development tool. If you want to improve a group's effectiveness, emphasize achieving the 20 qualities described in the checklist.

Source: "Group Effectiveness Checklist," A. J. DuBrin, *Contemporary Applied Management* (Plano, Texas: Business Publications, Inc., 1985), 169–170. Used by permission of the publisher.

10 Managing Conflict

Let us never negotiate out of fear; but let us never fear to negotiate.

—*John F. Kennedy*

If compromise continues, the revolution will disappear.

—*Lenin*

The secret of managing a club is to keep the five guys who hate you away from the five who are undecided.

—*Casey Stengel*

Learning Objectives

After studying this chapter, you should be able to:

1. Define conflict.
2. Contrast competition and conflict.
3. Explain how the understanding of conflict has changed.
4. List some sources of conflict.
5. Describe strategies for managing conflict in an organization.
6. List ways a manager can induce desirable conflict.

Balancing Work and Home with Employer Assistance

One of the most worrisome conflicts an employee faces is balancing the demands of the job with the demands of a life outside of the workplace. To remain employed requires a commitment to working. To develop a successful career track and move up the corporate ladder requires an even greater commitment to work, oftentimes at the expense of a life outside of work.

With greater demands on employees to produce and reduced employee morale due to downsizing and cost-cutting strategies, employees feel that to gain any sense of job security they must go along with company policy. But some companies are developing a sense of responsibility to help employees balance work and personal life. In fact, some see it as a solid business strategy to deal with the threats from competition.

Consider the cases of Marquette Electronics and Aetna Life & Casualty Company, two firms that have taken a position on bringing balance between work and personal life. At Marquette Electronics in Milwaukee, the 2,200 employees can personalize their work space, set their own work schedules, and dress as down as they wish. The company's sponsored on-site day care center helps "take the sharp edge of corporate coldness out of the place," according to Michael Cudahy, chairman of Marquette. Aetna Life & Casualty Co. of Hartford, Connecticut, is a strong believer in flexible scheduling. Even through five years of downsizing, flex-time remained in place on the belief that it strengthens employee commitment and gives workers a feeling of control over their work, while increasing productivity and reducing turnover.

Many companies are starting to replace the idea that employees are a line-item expense with the view that employees should be treated as valued assets to the viability of the organization. Improving employee attitudes can benefit the firm, not only through loyalty and productivity, but as the word spreads, in attracting the best employees. Employee attitudes, positive or negative, reach everyone that employees come in contact with, including customers, suppliers, vendors, and service providers. Each of these contacts can help the company maintain a competitive edge or—if relationships are less than positive—reduce a competitive position.

Management must understand that satisfied employees can benefit the organization, while less-contented employees can quickly erode the work environment and drive up operating costs. Discontent causes turnover, and any manager can understand the cost implications this presents. But it is more difficult to comprehend the potential costs of an unhappy employee complaining to a customer or supplier. As the reputation of the company is at stake, there are long-term ramifications for future sales, profits, and the company's competitive position. Savvy managers know the value of employees and invest in them, just as they would in any revenue-generating corporate asset. As for the others, just hope that they are your competition.

Source: S. Shellenbarger, "How Some Companies Help Their Employees Get a Life," Work & Family, *The Wall Street Journal*, November 16, 1994.

Conflict may well be an inevitable product of organizational life. Although most of us think of conflict as a negative experience to be avoided, it actually has the potential to produce positive organizational outcomes if properly managed. To increase understanding of how conflict can affect performance, we will examine the nature and origins of this phenomenon and some techniques for managing it.

Conflict

Conflict is the process that results when one person (or a group of people) perceives that another person or group is frustrating, or about to frustrate, an important concern.[1] Conflict involves incompatible differences between parties that result in interference or opposition.

It is important to distinguish between conflict and competition. Conflict is directed against another party, whereas competition is directed toward obtaining a desired goal without interference from another party. For example, competition may exist between two salespeople who vie for an annual performance award, but conflict (that is, incompatible differences) may not exist so long as the two do not interfere with or oppose each other. Students also compete for grades, yet they are not usually placed in a competitive system that induces conflict. To be sure, *intense competition* can sometimes lead to conflict. But conflict can result without the existence of competition.

If two parties can both gain from their competitive efforts, then competition is less likely to lead to conflict. For example, if two faculty members are trying to obtain a promotion, the efforts of one person need not block the other's success. In such a case, the promotion of both individuals is possible and, therefore, direct conflict is not likely to arise. In essence, the difference between competition and conflict lies in whether actions are taken to interfere with another's goal attainment. This difference suggests that eliminating opportunities for interference is a useful management tactic for preventing the escalation of competition into conflict.

Changing Views of Conflict

How we view the topic of conflict has changed over the years.[2] The earlier view was to consider conflict as harmful and unnecessary. The existence of conflict was regarded as a sign that something was wrong and required correction. According to this *traditional view*, conflict serves no useful purpose because it distracts managers' attention and saps energy and resources. Thus, conflict should be avoided. In addition, conflict was seen as the result of poor management and the efforts of troublemakers. Through proper management techniques and the removal of troublemakers, conflict could be eliminated and optimal performance could be achieved.

In recent years, management scholars have shifted their view of conflict. Today, conflict is seen as inevitable in every organization and oftentimes necessary to ensure high performance. That conflict can be harmful in some instances is not denied, but emphasis is placed on recognizing that some forms of conflict can be useful in achieving desired goals. According to this perspective, conflict can encourage a search for new tactics and strategies, and help overcome stagnation and complacency. Conflict as a device for directing effort is, therefore, sometimes a desirable state. The focus of this *contemporary view* is on the successful management of conflict rather than its total elimination.

The successful management of conflict involves both sustaining a target level of conflict and selecting a conflict-reduction strategy. In addition, managers may purposely create conflict. In situations that call for creativity and when frank discussions of alternatives are needed (as when resisting a tendency toward groupthink), the stimulation of conflict is advisable.[3]

In itself, conflict is neither desirable nor undesirable. It is only in terms of its effects on performance that the value of conflict can be judged. Figure 10.1 illustrates this notion, which suggests that an optimal level of conflict exists for any given situation. Carried to a high extreme, conflict can lead to chaos and disorder. In contrast, an extremely low level of conflict can result in complacency and poor performance due to lack of innovation.

Identifying the optimal level of conflict for a specific situation is not a simple matter. It requires a good understanding of the individuals involved and the nature of their assignments. Also, a manager needs a degree of creativity to determine strategies and tactics for reducing or, if necessary, increasing the level of conflict. Furthermore, simply increasing conflict when it appears necessary is not in itself sufficient: For conflict to foster creativity, it must be channeled and directed. Maintaining conflict at an optimal, or "Goldilocks," point

FIGURE 10.1   *Contemporary View of the Relationship Between Conflict and Performance*

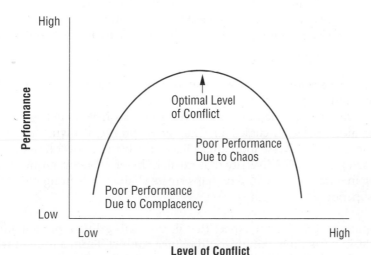

is also a difficult managerial challenge.* In the succeeding sections of this chapter, we will consider techniques for reducing as well as for intentionally stimulating conflict.

Sources of Conflict

Conflict can spring from a variety of sources. These sources can be grouped into three general categories: communication, structural, and personal behavior factors.[4]

Communication Factors

Managers typically attribute a sizable proportion of the conflicts that arise in organizations to poor communication. If we define true communication as creating a mental picture in the mind of a receiver in exactly the same detail as intended by the sender, then true or perfect communication is certainly rare. Given this inherent imperfection, there are many opportunities for misunderstanding to develop in the communication process. To be sure, conflict stemming from such unsuccessful communication is not the same as conflict based on substantive differences, yet it can still have powerful effects.

Incorrect, distorted, or ambiguous information can create hostility. For example, a manager may fail to communicate clearly to subordinates regarding who will be responsible for performing a distasteful task while she is away on vacation. Upon her return, she may find that the subordinates are "at each other's throats" and that the task remains to be done.

Structural Factors

Size   There is fairly consistent evidence suggesting that conflict is greater in larger organizations. It is likely that increases in size are associated with less goal clarity, greater formality, increased specialization, more supervisory levels, and increased opportunities for information to become distorted as it passes through more levels.

Staff Heterogeneity   It appears that differences among staff members in terms of authority, longevity, and values may also be sources of conflict. Differences among staff members, however, can also have beneficial effects on performance. As we discussed in Chapter 8, problem-solving groups composed of relatively diverse individuals have an advantage over homogeneously composed groups. The diversity that exists in heterogeneous groups can serve to bring in different ideas and perhaps create challenges among members that foster superior achievement.

Participation   One might expect that greater subordinate participation (for example, in decision making) would reduce conflict. From a human relations

---

*The Goldilocks point is the point on a curve where the conditions are "just right."

An Inside Look
A Primer on Employee Conflict Management

Personalities can clash and tempers can flare at any time and in any place, but in the corporate environment where the stakes are often great, efforts at conflict management are on the rise.

According to Max Messmer, chairman of Accountemps, executives spend about 18 percent of their time resolving employee personality clashes. This amounts to over nine weeks per year, and has doubled over the past ten years. Says Messmer, "Increased market competition and a more rapid business pace are contributing to conflict in the workplace. Company mergers and restructurings have created a more volatile environment that can increase employee competitiveness and insecurity."

Ultimately, each employee is responsible for his or her own behavior, especially in the workplace. Dr. Redford Williams, a behavior management expert, provides several suggestions for controlling hostility and aggressive behavior. When employees find they are becoming angry, they should distract themselves by doing other tasks or try to focus on something positive or soothing. Humor works well, too. Try to minimize situations that create anger. Since better relationships make one less angry, strive to improve relationships, both personal and professional.

Reducing conflict creates healthier workplaces as well as healthier employees. Anger can injure one's health and can cause heart function to deteriorate. People who are stressed have higher cholesterol levels, which can lead to heart attack or stroke.

Encouraging employees to resolve conflicts on their own can help to reduce workplace conflict. Ownership of a conflict resolution effort has greater impact than a delegated solution. Management should foster a "problem-solving attitude" with employees as the focus of any resolution. Employees should be directed to take issues to management only when other approaches fail. Since teams tend to resolve conflict better than individuals, teams should be used when possible. The power of peer pressure is a remarkable tool for generating consensus. Employees need to be coached in the sensitivities and dynamics of verbal communication, and taught that how one says something is just as important as what one says. In employee-focused problem solving, there needs to be a distinction between management and subordinate responsibilities. This avoids confusion and directs the process to a more favorable conclusion.

Sources: N. Hellmich, "Learn to Lighten Up and Live Longer," *USA Today,* February 9, 1994, 5D; E. McShulskis, "Managing Employee Conflicts," *HRMagazine,* September 1996, 16.

---

perspective, one might even argue that inviting subordinates to participate can satisfy a possible drive to be fully involved. Research on this topic, however, has shown that just the opposite is true: When subordinate participation is greater, levels of conflict tend to be higher. This somewhat unexpected result may occur because increased participation leads to greater awareness of individual differences. Also, simply participating in decision making does not ensure that an individual's point of view will prevail, since a subordinate can be involved in decision making but lack the authority to have his or her preferences put into action. However, as mentioned earlier, the increased conflict associated with greater participation is not necessarily undesirable. If the results of subordinate participation, and the subsequent conflict, enhance the overall performance of a work unit, then the existence of conflict can be productive.

Line-Staff Distinctions   In surveys of managers, one of the most frequently mentioned sources of conflict is the distinction between line and staff units within organizations. Line units perform jobs that are directly related to core activities of the organization. In a manufacturing setting, the production

department would be a line unit, while in a customer-oriented setting, the marketing or sales department might be considered line. Staff units perform jobs that support the line function. Examples of staff departments include research and development, public relations, personnel, and marketing research.

Conflict occurs between many line and staff divisions because of the functions they perform, their differing goals, and the values and backgrounds of their members. Line divisions are generally more operations oriented, while staff divisions are more removed from central operating activities. Line personnel are often very loyal to their firm, while staff personnel tend to be (and feel that it is their duty to be) critical of company practices. In fact, staff people frequently identify more strongly with a professional group or discipline than with the organization in which they are employed. For example, personnel officers and marketing researchers may belong to national associations that give them a sense of professional identification. Thus, a staff person may see himself primarily as a public relations specialist who happens to be working at Inland Steel, while a line person's strongest identification is likely to be with his employer. Lastly, the two groups' time horizons often differ—staff people more typically think in terms of long-range issues, while line people are more involved with short-term or day-to-day concerns. Given these differences in orientation, it is not too surprising that line and staff personnel experience a fair degree of conflict.

Reward Systems   If one party obtains rewards at the expense of another party, conflict can be easily generated. This form of conflict can arise among individuals and groups as well as among entire organizations. How mutually exclusive reward systems operate is not always obvious. For example, staff people are generally rewarded for being innovative and identifying the need for change. By suggesting and attempting to induce change, they are able to demonstrate their usefulness to the larger organization. On the other hand, most line people strongly prefer to avoid change because for them, it is both disruptive and inconvenient. In fact, line people are generally rewarded for productivity that results from uninterrupted activity.

Resource Interdependence   Typically, groups must compete for the resources of their organization. With a growing supply of money and other resources, such as space, equipment, and materials, conflicts may not arise. However, such bountifulness is not the norm for organizations. As a result, conflict and the resulting lack of coordination and cooperation between divisions exist.

Power   The distribution of power within an organization can also be a source of conflict. If a group feels that it possesses far less power than it should, or if it believes that an excessive amount of power is held by another group, it is likely to challenge the existing order. If departments are ostensibly equal when in fact they hold differing amounts of power, serious discontent can arise. For example, in many companies, staff people must continually justify their need to exist, be understanding of problems in line departments, and make constant efforts to get along with the line personnel. Similar expectations do not exist for line personnel, however, because the line usually wields greater authority than the staff. Such asymmetry of power distribution can add further tension to an already difficult situation.

Personal Behavior Factors

Another source of conflict lies in differences among individuals. Some people's values or perceptions of situations are particularly likely to generate conflict with others. For example, a manager may highly value the idea that all employees must "pay their dues." His argument might be that he spent much of his early career in an unglamorous lower-level position and that others would benefit from a similar experience. Of course, the imposition of this value on ambitious young subordinates could create serious conflict. Similarly, if a manager tends to perceive people in a certain way (for example, if she is quick to infer laziness or incompetence from only limited evidence), her responses to certain situations can be a source for conflict. In addition, some people simply enjoy being argumentative and combative. For such individuals, whose personal style is especially conflict-prone, life is a continuing series of escalating hostilities and battles.

Studies show that conflict-prone individuals are likely to possess certain traits. For example, highly authoritarian individuals are prone to antagonize their coworkers by escalating otherwise trivial differences. Also, individuals with low self-esteem may more readily feel threatened by others and therefore overreact. Both authoritarianism and low self-esteem can predispose people to feel the need to "defend their turf" against (objectively) trivial threats.[5]

Interpersonal Conflict

Researchers have created a number of situations in laboratory settings to study the tendencies to compete or cooperate when conflict exists. One such contrived conflict scenario is called the Prisoners' Dilemma:

> Two suspected criminals are taken into custody and separated. The district attorney is certain that they are guilty of a specific crime, but he does not have adequate evidence to convict them at a trial. He points out to each prisoner that each has two alternatives: to confess to the crime the police are sure they have done or not to confess. If they both do not confess, then the district attorney will book them on some very minor, trumped-up charge . . . ; if they both confess, they will be prosecuted, [and] he will recommend [a rather severe] sentence; but if one confesses and the other does not, then the confessor will receive rather lenient treatment for turning state's evidence, whereas the latter will get the "book" slapped at him.[6]

This situation is designed to create mixed motives for the prisoners. If each chooses what is best for him personally and ignores the other's circumstances, he will decide not to confess. However, if one prisoner does not confess and the other does, the holdout will suffer severely (by receiving a longer sentence). The best option for both prisoners, therefore, is to resist the divide-and-conquer strategy of the attorney and stick to their pleas of innocence. Of course, the question is whether they can really trust their partner in crime not to confess. Figure 10.2 shows the outcomes of the various choices for each prisoner. The outcome for each individual depends on the actions of the other participant.[†]

In role-playing studies using college students as subjects and substituting monetary rewards and penalties for threatened jail sentences, it has been found that the tendency of the participants to compete versus cooperate with

---

[†]In actuality, the practice of separating suspected criminals and offering these alternatives is effective in extracting confessions.

FIGURE 10.2   *Outcomes of Choices Available in a Prisoners'*
Dilemma Scenario

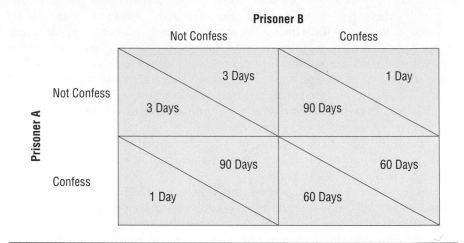

each other can be influenced by a variety of forces. Chief among these is the penalty–reward structure for cooperating and competing. By altering the rewards and penalties for various actions, it is possible to induce more or fewer choices of competition or cooperation.

As a real-world illustration of how the size of penalties and rewards can influence the choice of a competitive strategy, consider the payoff matrix for the United States and the former Soviet Union with respect to the use of nuclear weapons during most of the Cold War. If both countries had attacked each other, the magnitude of total annihilation would have been enormous (this is analogous to the values in the lower right-hand cell of Figure 10.2 being the electric chair). If one country had tried to preemptively (or sneak) attack the other with confidence that the other would strive to be cooperative, the attacker would have gained a clear advantage. However, the retaliatory capability of the attacked country could not be ruled out. Therefore, each found it to its advantage to avoid taking the competitive option of "pushing the button" because the costs were too high. In short, excessive penalties can force a form of cooperativeness (or at least reduced aggression) between otherwise contentious parties.

Other research on situations like the Prisoners' Dilemma also points to the importance of communication between parties as a means of inducing cooperation. This evidence suggests that the availability of "hot lines" between potentially antagonistic parties can help to reduce tension and conflict.

Strategies for Reducing Conflict

Superordinate Goals

Providing higher-level, or superordinate, goals to antagonistic parties can help to reduce the level of conflict. When people share a common superordinate goal, they must cooperate to achieve a degree of success or avoid disaster.

In a demonstration of the conflict-reducing power of superordinate goals, Sherif conducted a field experiment with groups of 12-year-old boys attending neighboring summer camps.[7] Initially, he established two independent groups of boys who were unaware of the other group's existence. These boys engaged in the usual summer fun and developed norms of behavior within their groups. Sherif then created a degree of conflict by informing both groups that the other camp would be using certain equipment, such as canoes, and that, as a result, they would be unable to engage in that activity. (In essence, he created win-lose situations for the groups.) As a result, the two groups came to resent each other strongly.

As the situation approached open warfare, Sherif experimented with several techniques to induce harmony between the camps. Initially, Sherif tried to give each group some favorable information about the other. This effort failed because the boys' negative impressions led them to reject the information. Next, Sherif had the boys eat their meals and attend movies together. This also failed to work, since hostility (such as name calling) erupted when the camp members were near each other. Then Sherif asked the group leaders to negotiate and share favorable information about their groups that could later be conveyed to their respective camps. Once again, the strategy failed because the leaders feared being "dethroned" by their constituents if they were seen to be too friendly to the out group.

Finally, Sherif attempted to create superordinate goals for the camps by staging situations in which both groups needed to participate in order to benefit their members. These planned situations involved a breakdown of the camps' food truck (boys from *both* camps were needed to push the truck in order to get it started), a disruption of the camps' water supply, and a cooperative effort to obtain funds to rent a desired film.

Because of the need to meet a common threat, the boys of the two camps eventually adopted friendly and cooperative behaviors. For example, near the end of their stays, when one group had excess funds, it used them to purchase refreshments for both camps, rather than solely for its own members.

The implementation of this strategy in organizational settings, however, is not always easy. For example, General Motors once attempted to use superordinate goals to unite management and labor in a battle against the threat of foreign competition.[8] The Chevrolet Vega, GM's intended answer to imported subcompacts, was to be manufactured in new production facilities in Lordstown, Ohio. Despite management's efforts to unite workers with managers through an attitude-change campaign focusing on the need to counter the foreign threat, a strike and open violence occurred not long after the plant opened. This experience suggests that a superordinate approach may need to be highly credible if it is to be effective.[9]

Structural Approaches

A number of options exist for managers who wish to reduce conflict via structural change. One technique is to transfer conflict-prone individuals to other units. Of course, this apparently simple approach cannot always be used, since some employees are nearly indispensable to their unit's performance. In some instances, it is the recognition of their value to the unit that gives such individuals the confidence to engage in battles over what they see as important issues.

One way to overcome line–staff conflict is to appoint one person to serve as moderator (and mediator) at line–staff meetings. This person tries to manage the interaction between the two factions to ensure that relations between the two groups remain constructive. For example, before a meeting takes place, an effective moderator may try to help both groups better understand the nature of their counterparts so that they will be more tolerant of each other. To ensure that the meeting goes smoothly, the moderator may also encourage both sides to "do their homework" and prepare for questions that may arise and encourage staff people to consult with line people as they develop their proposals.

The moderator is expected to serve as a buffer between the units and encourage understanding by both sides. However, because higher management often selects a moderator from among the line people, staff people may question that person's real loyalty and biases. Being the moderator of such conflict, therefore, can pose a serious challenge for anyone asked to serve in such a role. Furthermore, many organizational members perceive moderators as having only limited positive impact on line–staff relations.

Conflict management methods can be customized to match specific situations. A common technique is to create an appeals procedure (for example, a grievance system or arbitration) that provides a higher authority for resolving conflicts and a set of specific steps to follow when filing an appeal. One major shortcoming of an appeals procedure, however, is that the losing party often has difficulty in accepting the verdict. Although obliged to go along with the decision in principle, the person may feel compelled to "even the score" at a later time by a subtle, but vengeful, action or inaction. Thus, for an appeals process to succeed, the losing party must be made to bring the two parties closer together.

Another increasingly common technique for managing line-versus-staff conflict is to use cross-training assignments. This technique involves rotating the appointments of staff people through line units and line people through staff units. The forced rotation is designed to help employees understand alternative perspectives and develop working relationships with members of different units.

Styles of Conflict Management

Managers differ in their ways of dealing with conflict. Ken Thomas has suggested five major styles of conflict management that managers can adopt: forcing, collaborating, compromising, avoiding, and accommodating.[10] Table 10.1 summarizes the characteristics of these styles.

Forcing   In addition to defining the five basic styles of conflict management, Thomas has suggested a two-dimensional framework for comparing them (Figure 10.3). According to this framework, the **forcing** style attempts to overwhelm an opponent with formal authority, threats, or the use of power. Its underlying features are assertiveness and uncooperativeness.

Collaborating   The **collaborating** style represents a combination of assertiveness and cooperativeness. Collaborating involves an attempt to satisfy the concerns of both sides through honest discussion. Creative approaches to conflict reduction—for example, the sharing of resources—may actually lead to both

TABLE 10.1   *Five Conflict-Handling Styles*

Conflict-Handling Style	Related Term	Proverb
Forcing	Competing Conflictful Moving against the other	Put your foot down where you mean to stand.
Collaborating	Problem solving Integrating Confronting	Come let us reason together.
Accommodating	Yielding–losing Friendly–helping Moving toward the other	It is better to give than to receive.
Avoiding	Moving away from the other Withdrawing Losing–leaving	Let sleeping dogs lie.
Compromising	Splitting the difference Sharing Horse-trading	You have to give some to get some.

parties' being materially better off. For this style to be successful, trust and openness are required of all participants.

Accommodating   An **accommodating** style combines unassertiveness and cooperativeness. At its simplest level, this style may merely involve giving in to another's wishes. Accommodating behavior may be motivated by a desire to be altruistic or prosocial, but sometimes no other approach is feasible for someone in a truly weak position.

Avoiding   The combination of unassertiveness and uncooperativeness leads to an **avoiding** style, in which a person implies that he or she will either improve a difficult situation or attempt to appear neutral. In some cases, it may not be possible to adopt a truly neutral position, but a manager may nonetheless prefer to avoid the situation. Although a manager who avoids difficult issues is likely to be resented by subordinates, this strategy may be effective under certain circumstances. For example, a manager may initially stay out of a disagreement to avoid escalating the conflict during a particular phase of its development. Later, when she judges the time is right, she may take a more active role in finding a productive solution.

Experienced managers also recognize that action is not always necessary because some problems dissipate over time or are resolved by other organizational processes. For example, an intense conflict between two subordinates may seem to require intervention by their manager. But if the manager knows that one of the individuals will soon be transferred to another department or

FIGURE 10.3   *Thomas's Two-Dimensional Model of Conflict Behavior*

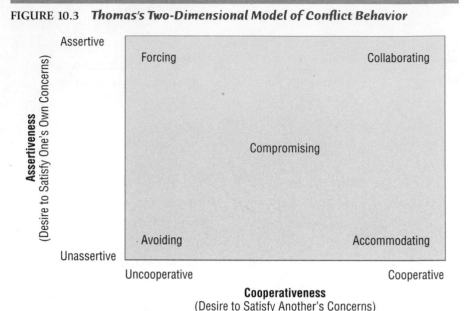

promoted to another position, it may be advisable to ignore the situation and let the impending changes resolve the difficulty.

Compromising   The fifth style, **compromising,** involves intermediate levels of assertiveness and cooperativeness and strives for partial satisfaction of both parties' desire by seeking a middle ground. To succeed at compromising, both parties must be willing to give up something.

Although people may be tempted to consider some styles of conflict management more effective than others (for example, collaborating versus avoiding), there is good reason to believe that each style works best in only certain situations.

Managing Intergroup Conflict

Conflict between groups can result from a variety of causes. Competition for resources, differences in goals, and interpersonal conflict can serve as the basis for conflict among groups or departments. Line and staff conflict, discussed earlier in this chapter, is a prime example of intergroup conflict. The management of conflict between groups or departments can be achieved through a variety of strategies.[11] Table 10.3 lists specific techniques for managing intergroup conflict.

Rules and Procedures   A fairly direct approach to managing intergroup conflict is the establishment of rules and procedures. This approach is likely to work best if the rules and procedures are set up before conflict arises. However, as a way of managing differences even after conflict has emerged, it is still a potentially useful technique. As an example, consider two departments that need to use a specific piece of equipment that can only accommodate

TABLE 10.2   *Uses of Five Styles of Conflict Handling*

Conflict-Handling Styles	Appropriate Situations
Competing	1. When quick, decisive action is vital, e.g., emergencies
	2. On important issues where unpopular actions need implementing, e.g., cost-cutting, enforcing unpopular rules, discipline
	3. On issues vital to company welfare when you know you're right
	4. Against people who take advantage of noncompetitive behavior
Collaborating	1. To find an integrative solution when both sides of concerns are too important to be compromised
	2. When your objective is to learn
	3. To merge insights from people with different perspectives
	4. To gain commitment by incorporating concerns into a consensus
Accommodating	1. When you find you are wrong—to allow a better position to be heard, to learn, and to show your reasonableness
	2. When issues are more important to others than to you—to satisfy others and maintain cooperation
	3. To build social credits for later issues and to minimize loss when you are outmatched and losing
	4. When harmony and stability are especially important
Avoiding	1. When an issue is trivial, or more important issues are pressing
	2. When you perceive no chance of satisfying your concerns
	3. When potential disruption outweighs the benefits of resolution and to let people cool down and regain perspective
	4. When others can resolve the conflict more effectively
Compromising	1. When goals are important but not worth the effort of potential disruption of more assertive modes
	2. When opponents with equal power are committed to mutually exclusive goals
	3. To achieve temporary settlements to complex issues
	4. To arrive at expedient solutions under time pressure

Adapted from: K.W. Thomas, "Toward Multi-Dimensional Values in Teaching: The Example of Conflict Behaviors."

one user at a time. To manage the potential conflict in this situation, certain times of day or certain days of the week can be reserved for each department to have exclusive use of the equipment. Rules and procedures often help to avert conflict or defuse tense situations by reducing the amount of contact between groups.

Appeal to Higher Authority   In circumstances where rules and procedures are not easily established, a higher authority may be relied on to decide how to best manage the needs of groups. For example, a supervisor may be assigned to make decisions about how each group will have its desires satisfied, with an eye toward satisfying the larger needs of the organization rather than just those of the immediate groups. This technique can also have drawbacks. For instance, group members may try to befriend the supervisor in an attempt to receive unwarranted, additional consideration in scheduling decisions. Also, the supervisor may find that continually trying to manage the interests of these groups is very time-consuming and detracts from time needed to perform other supervisory duties.

Boundary-Spanning Positions   When the coordination of the efforts and interests of departments becomes increasingly continuous and complex, it is sometimes desirable to assign a person on a full-time basis to manage relations between departments. Such a person's job entails spanning the boundaries, or crossing the divisional lines, between groups. In essence, a **boundary-spanning position** is one that requires a person to serve as a liaison, or communications link, between groups. Liaison, or boundary-spanning, positions can increase the frequency of contact between groups (through meetings and communiqués). Increased contact between groups can facilitate coordination and, ideally, foster cooperation. On the downside, employees who serve as go-betweens within organizations experience a good deal of job-related conflict and ambiguity concerning their actual role in the organization. This may, in part, account for the finding that boundary-spanners report somewhat lower job satisfaction.[12]

Negotiation   **Negotiation** is an interactive process wherein two or more groups discuss the allocation of resources. It is a commonly used technique for managing conflict. Negotiation typically follows one of two models: distributive bargaining or integrative bargaining. *Distributive bargaining* is an adversarial, win-lose approach to negotiation that focuses on the pool of resources as fixed. *Integrative bargaining* is a collaborative, problem-solving approach that seeks to create win-win outcomes for the parties. Although the integrative bargaining approach has a more attractive appeal, it is difficult to achieve. This difficulty stems partly from the unwillingness of parties to trust each other. For an integrative problem-solving approach to be effective, each party must also have a high degree of concern for the outcomes attained by the other party. In order to move groups from a distributive bargaining approach to an integrative

---

TABLE 10.3   *Techniques for Managing Intergroup Conflict*

Rules and Procedures

Higher Authority

Boundary-spanning Positions

Negotiation

Teams

bargaining approach, one should strive to create options that offer mutual gain. In addition, it helps to depersonalize the nature of the conflict and to focus on key interests of the parties.[13]

Teams   Teams are collections of employees who are assigned to manage intergroup relations. Teams may be created to manage long-term, continuous intergroup relations, or they may be established to examine a specific problem on a short-term basis. The primary purpose of teams is to tackle recurring problems resulting from intergroup conflict and to develop remedies for managing the conflict. Typically, such teams are made of employees who hold membership in the competing groups. However, the team members usually have a functional specialty that justifies their membership on the team. Such teams work best, of course, when the members take a problem-solving approach to the task and set aside competitive or antagonistic feelings toward members of the opposing group.

Stimulating Conflict

At the outset of this chapter, we suggested that there is an optimal level of conflict for any situation. Although the optimal level may sometimes be zero, in most cases a modest level of conflict actually encourages involvement and innovation. This indicates that some situations may in fact benefit from the creation of conflict. Some signs that a manager needs to stimulate conflict include an unusually low rate of employee turnover, a shortage of new ideas, strong resistance to change, and the belief that cooperativeness (the principle trait of a "yes-man") is more important than personal competence.[14]

Among the specific techniques that have been offered for inducing conflict are:

1. *Appointing managers who are open to change.* In some units, a highly authoritarian manager will tend to suppress opposing viewpoints. The resulting lethargy can be overcome to some extent by the appropriate selection and placement of change-oriented managers.

2. *Encouraging competition.* The use of individual and group incentives to performance, such as pay increases, bonuses, and recognition, tends to enhance competition. And competition, if managed properly, can result in creative conflict.

3. *Restructuring the work unit.* Changing members of work teams, rotating personnel, and altering lines of communication can do much to shake up an organization. Restructuring can also create new jobs to be filled by outsiders whose values and styles will contrast with the prevailing, but lethargic, norms.

SUMMARY

1. *Define conflict.*   Conflict is the process that results when a person or group perceives that another person or group is frustrating, or about to frustrate, an important concern.

2. *Contrast competition and conflict.* Conflict is directed against another party, whereas competition is directed toward obtaining a desired goal without interference from another party. The difference lies in whether one party takes actions to interfere with another's efforts to attain a goal.

3. *Explain how the understanding of conflict has changed.* The traditional view was that conflict is harmful and unnecessary. Today, conflict is considered to be inevitable in every organization and often necessary to ensure high performance. The value of conflict depends on how the conflict affects performance.

4. *List some sources of conflict.* Conflict can arise from poor communication, increased size of the organization, staff heterogeneity, greater subordinate participation, differences between line and staff personnel, mutually exclusive reward systems, competition for limited resources, unequal distribution of power, and differences among individuals.

5. *Describe strategies for managing conflict in an organization.* The manager can provide superordinate goals to antagonistic parties, so that they will cooperate to achieve the common goal. The manager can transfer conflict-prone individuals to other units, or institute an appeals procedure.

6. *List ways a manager can induce desirable conflict.* One can appoint managers who are open to change, encourage competition, and restructure the work unit to change lines of communication or to create new positions.

KEY TERMS

Conflict   Avoiding
Interpersonal conflict   Compromising
Forcing   Intergroup conflict
Collaborating   Boundary-spanning position
Accommodating   Negotiation

CRITICAL INCIDENT

A Manager's Nightmare

Wearever Tire has operated in Happyville, New York, for 45 years. Well known for its superior human relations policies and competitive benefits, Wearever has enjoyed good labor–management relations and has offered what is virtually lifetime employment to several generations of local families. The company has a reputation for being environmentally concerned and for providing strong community support.

Today, Wearever faces a serious threat. It has just learned that a "bread and butter" account will cut its orders this year due to foreign competition. Bob Stone, Industrial Division manager, has been advised that he must reduce his staff by 20 percent. A thorough plan drafted by the human resources department details his options. Some of the necessary labor cost reduction will come from attrition—that is, from normal levels of turnover and forecasted retirements. The bulk, however, will have to come from "forced" reductions—either early retirements or layoffs.

For those who will be laid off and are too young to retire, Wearever will offer a lump-sum service bonus intended to offset the emotional and financial costs of the layoff, and will offer each laid-off employee the opportunity to use out-placement services. The range of outplacement services provided will include career counseling, interviewing skills and job search training techniques, and clerical support for transmission of telephone messages, résumé preparation, cover letter generation, and so on. The placement firm also makes physical facilities available to clients, including desks, telephones, and conference areas.

To encourage early retirement among those close to retirement age, Wearever will offer a "5-5-4" package. Under this arrangement, employees will be given the opportunity to retire five years before normal retirement age; they may add five years to their length of service with the firm (thus increasing their retirement pay); and they get four weeks of pay for every year that they have been employed with the firm as a one-time, lump-sum bonus.

Bob dreads informing the staff at large of the cuts. A companywide assembly will be held at 2:00 to announce the details of the plans, but he wants to forewarn them, so he will call everyone into his office after lunch. He has already drafted a sketch in his mind of who will likely consider the 5-5-4 option. He knows that their decisions will not be easy ones to make. They will be enticed by the offer, yet he would like to make sure that they are acting out of prudent self-interest, and not because the offer is too good to pass up. He also has an idea whom he will target to be laid off. Some of the unfortunate few are his best employees, yet their positions can no longer be protected, and there's no place left in the organization for them to move to.

1. Why might employees in their late fifties face a personal conflict in their decision regarding early retirement?

2. Corporate downsizing causes considerable conflict among both workers who are laid off, and among remaining employees not laid off.

    a. What has Wearever done to mitigate the conflicts for employees targeted for layoff?

    b. List some possible forms of conflict that a remaining Wearever employee might perceive.

    c. What can Wearever do for the remaining employees at Wearever to reduce the conflicts that they might perceive?

Source: Susan Stites-Doe, State University of New York, College at Brockport.

EXPERIENTIAL EXERCISE

How Well Do You Manage Conflict?

Step 1

Listed below are 15 pairs of statements people use to describe why they behave the way they do in conflict situations. Allocate 3 points between the two alternative statements in each pair. Base your point allocation on your assessment of each alternative's relative importance to you as a means of handling conflict.

Allocate the points between the first and second statement as follows:

(a) __3__   (a) __2__   (a) __1__   (a) __0__
       or   or   or
(b) __0__   (b) __1__   (b) __2__   (b) __3__

There can be no tied allocations and each pair's numbers must add up to 3.

1. I am likely to give up something in order to get something.   (a) _____
   I am usually quite firm in pursuing my goals.   (b) _____

2. I usually work to soothe the other person's feelings to preserve our relationship.   (c) _____
   I try to get all of our concerns immediately out into the open.   (d) _____

3. I usually try to get the other person's help in working out a solution.   (e) _____
   I try to avoid taking a position that is likely to create a controversy.   (f) _____

4. I try to do what is necessary to avoid tensions.   (g) _____
   I sometimes give up my own wishes for the desires of the other person.   (h) _____

5. I usually press to get my points across.   (i) _____
   I usually let the other person have some of his or her wishes if he or she allows me to have some of mine.   (j) _____

6. I am usually quite firm in pursuing my goals.   (k) _____
   I usually try to get the other person's help in working out a solution.   (l) _____

7. I am likely to give up something in order to get something.   (m) _____
   I try to avoid taking a position that would create a controversy.   (n) _____

8. I usually work to soothe the other person's feelings to preserve our relationship.   (o) _____
   I usually let the other person have some of his or her wishes if he or she lets me have some of mine.   (p) _____

9. I usually press to get my points across.   (q) _____
   I sometimes give up my own wishes for the desires of the other person.   (r) _____

10. I am likely to give up something in order to get something.   (s) _____
    I try to get all of our concerns immediately out in the open.   (t) _____

11. I try to do what is necessary to avoid tensions.   (u) _____
    I usually let the other person have some of his or her wishes if he or she lets me have some of mine.   (v) _____

12. I usually work to soothe the other person's feelings to preserve our relationship.   (w) _____
    I am usually quite firm in pursuing my goals.   (x) _____

13. I try to avoid taking positions that would create a controversy.   (y) _____
    I usually press to get my points across.   (z) _____

14. I usually try to get the other person's help in working out a solution.   (aa) _____
    I sometimes give up my own wishes for the desires of the other person.   (bb) _____

15. I try to get all of our concerns immediately out in the open.   (cc) _____
    I try to do what is necessary to avoid tensions.   (dd) _____

Step 2

Score the survey by entering the score you have given to each of the statements and then total the scores for each column.

I	II	III	IV	V
(a) _____	(b) _____	(c) _____	(d) _____	(f) _____
(j) _____	(i) _____	(h) _____	(e) _____	(g) _____
(m) _____	(k) _____	(o) _____	(l) _____	(n) _____
(p) _____	(q) _____	(r) _____	(t) _____	(u) _____
(s) _____	(x) _____	(w) _____	(aa) _____	(y) _____
(v) _____	(z) _____	(bb) _____	(cc) _____	(dd) _____
=====	=====	=====	=====	=====

These scores reflect your perception of your use of various conflict-handling styles. Your highest total suggests a preferred style; however, we all have the potential to apply various conflict-management approaches depending on the situation. The various styles are labeled: I, compromising; II, forcing; III, accommodating; IV, collaborating; and V, avoiding.

The following steps are optional and may be used at the discretion of your instructor.

Step 3

Read the following brief incident, then join others in your class to discuss this situation and propose a plan of action to resolve it.

> Seville Electronics manufactures computer components to be used in industrial and military applications. All parts must be produced according to exacting standards.
>
> Stuart Van Ault was hired recently as vice president of production. Last week he toured the plant and was stopped by one of the production supervisors. This supervisor was visibly upset and shouted, "I'm glad you're here. We can't get anything done with the quality of materials we have to work with and the people personnel sends us!" Stuart was taken aback by this outburst. He asked the supervisor to visit him after work to discuss these problems.
>
> When they met, the supervisor explained that they were having to send more and more materials back to their suppliers because they didn't meet Seville's exacting quality standards. He felt that these standards were unrealistic and that quality control was messing up. The supervisor also complained about the lack of skilled, reliable help. Both absenteeism and turnover were running above industry norms. Finally, he pointed out that various production runs were halted in favor of some other components that, according to the sales department, had to be run immediately.

Step 4

Each group will be asked to report its plan of action. Select one member of your group to act as spokesperson. Be as specific as possible in describing what you would do and why. Look for the implications of these plans for conflict management.

Source: Written by Bruce Kemelgor, University of Louisville.

11 Managing Stress and Employee Job Satisfaction

Work is a four-letter word.
—Abbie Hoffman

Job satisfaction? I didn't know the two words went together!
—A steelworker

If my doctor told me I had only six months to live, I wouldn't brood—I'd type a little faster.
—Isaac Asimov

Learning Objectives

After studying this chapter, you should be able to:

1. Define stress.
2. Explain various views of job-related stress.
3. Identify personal causes of stress.
4. Explain interpersonal causes of stress.
5. List organizational causes of stress.
6. Describe typical reactions to stress.
7. List ways of managing stress.
8. Tell why management should take an interest in workers' job satisfaction.
9. Cite the most frequent sources of job satisfaction.
10. Describe some typical employee responses to low job satisfaction.

Controlling Anger in the Workplace

On any given day, newspaper and broadcast media report instances of violence in the workplace. These acts of assault, sabotage, or even murder are often the result of poor communication between management and labor. Workers who feel stressed, unappreciated, or overworked and act on those emotions can erode morale and affect productivity. Thus, managers are increasingly becoming attuned to the need to address hostility in the workplace before it results in violence. One method for confronting the problem is contingency planning—taking a proactive approach to potential crises rather than reacting after the fact.

It is important for employees to understand violence: what causes it and how to recognize a potentially violent employee. Employees also need to understand how to recognize anger or resentment within themselves before they strike out at others. A zero-tolerance policy for hostility and violence must be established, clearly communicated, and enforced.

How can managers recognize the signals of a potential problem? One sign is a change in someone's typical behavior patterns: A methodical employee suddenly becomes disorganized, or an outgoing person becomes withdrawn. Other stress indicators include a sudden life change, such as bankruptcy, divorce, or the unexpected death of a loved one. Behavior changes may be more difficult to recognize in a quiet, focused individual than in a more extroverted, emotional person. Managers, therefore, need to know their employees as individuals, wherever possible, in order to be alert to subtle signs of stress or anger.

If a manager recognizes any of these changes in an employee, it is best to approach the employee with an offer to air problems or concerns without fear of reprisal. The meeting should take place in a nonthreatening setting, and the manager or supervisor should not exhibit defensiveness or laugh off the person's concerns. While often a potential situation can be diffused at the managerial/supervisory level, it may be necessary to bring in a third party to instill trust and openness into the discussions. An individual or agency that specializes in employee–management relations may be useful in helping each person to see the other's point of view. In most cases, ignoring an employee grievance will only make the problem worse in the long run.

What should you do if confronted by an angry coworker? The best response is to remain cool. Do not allow yourself to be drawn into the person's hostility. Anger typically occurs when an individual feels misunderstood, ignored, or wronged. To prevent your coworker's anger from escalating, do not be aggressive or judgmental; listen as calmly as possible. If your coworker begins to lose control, walk away to protect yourself. Notify the proper personnel immediately, and let the professionals take it from there.

Source: C. Johnson, "Controlling Hostility," *HRMagazine*, August 1998: 65–70.

From our daily experiences, we all know that conflict-filled situations produce feelings of physical and psychological discomfort. When a person is confronted with a situation that poses a threat (as when extreme conflict arises), the form of physiological and emotional arousal he or she experiences is termed **stress**. Prolonged exposure to stressful situations is believed to produce serious dysfunctional influences that can affect job performance. In this chapter, we will examine the principal causes of stress, reactions to stress, and techniques for coping with stress. Then, we will explore the related topic of employee job satisfaction, an outcome that is influenced by job stress.

Views of Job-Related Stress

Dr. Hans Selye has identified three distinct stages of a person's response to stress: alarm, resistance, and exhaustion. These three stages define a **General Adaptation Syndrome** associated with stress.[1] In the alarm stage of the stress response, muscles tense, respiration rate increases, and blood pressure and heart rate increase. Following this stage, a person experiences anxiety, anger, and fatigue. These responses indicate that the person is resisting stress. During this resistance stage, the person may make poor decisions or experience illnesses. Because a person cannot sustain this resistance indefinitely, exhaustion occurs (see Figure 11.1). During this exhaustion stage, the individual develops such stress-induced illnesses as headaches and ulcers. Also, the capacity to respond to other work-related demands is greatly reduced. Although a person may be able to respond effectively to a threat during one of the earlier stages in this reaction, being unable to cope with a threat in the later stages can have serious detrimental effects for the individual. Selye's view suggests that all people go through the same pattern of response and that all people can tolerate only so much stress before a serious, debilitating condition of exhaustion occurs.

The preceding three-stage response to stress is sometimes termed the "fight or flight" response. It is an automatic response to threat that once served our species well when our primary concerns were finding food and protecting ourselves from wild animals. In ancient times, the powerful stress reaction was an aid in quickly responding by either fighting or swiftly fleeing from a predator. In the modern world, however, persistent forms of stress (for example, unresolved social problems) have a powerful effect on the well-being of an individual. Consider the lingering discomfort that results when an employee is harshly reprimanded by his or her supervisor. In such a situation, neither fighting with one's boss nor fleeing from the situation is an appropriate response. Nonetheless, the employee's physiological response prepares him or her to take some form of action when none may be possible. In essence, our physiological response to stress is no longer correct for many situations we currently face. Trapped in paleolithic bodies, we are not well suited for the stresses one finds in modern organizations.

FIGURE 11.1   *The General Adaptation Syndrome*

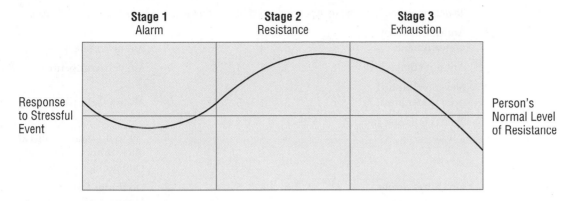

Despite the drawbacks of stress, its complete or near absence may be less than ideal for performance. In situations where stress is low or absent, employees may not be sufficiently aroused or involved in their tasks. Instead, to maximize performance, low levels of stress are preferable because, in modest amounts, stress can stimulate individuals to work harder and accomplish more. A certain amount of stress may thus be beneficial. Stress that has positive effects should be termed *eustress* (the prefix *eu-* is Greek for "good"). Eustress occurs when pressure for performance helps a person to achieve. When stress levels rise too high, however, employee performance is impaired. Extreme stress can leave workers feeling emotionally incapacitated, at least in the short run, and sap their energies and drive. The relationship between stress and employee performance follows the curve previously depicted in Figure 10.1.

Two experts in the area of job stress, John Ivancevich and Michael Matteson, have outlined the major causes of stress as well as reactions to it.[2] In the two sections that follow, we will consider their summary of the major causes and consequences of stress. Following these sections, we will consider techniques for coping with stress.

Causes of Stress

Personal Factors

Type A Personality   Some people are more stress-prone than others. Especially susceptible are individuals who display a cluster of traits known as **type A personality.** Type As tend to be impatient, competitive individuals who feel that they are constantly under time pressure. They also tend to be aggressive, try to accomplish several things at the same time, and have difficulty relaxing. In contrast, individuals with **type B personality** are relatively more mild-mannered, in less of a hurry, and far less competitive.[3]

In recent years, researchers have used personality tests to assess whether managers are type A or type B personalities. A simple example of one such test is presented in Table 11.1. When type A and type B managers were studied in

TABLE 11.1   *Self-Test for Type A or Type B Personality*

To determine your personality type, circle the number that best represents your own behavior.

Am casual about appointments	1	2	3	4	5	6	7	8	Am never late
Am not competitive	1	2	3	4	5	6	7	8	Am very competitive
Never feel rushed, even under pressure	1	2	3	4	5	6	7	8	Always feel rushed
Take things one at a time	1	2	3	4	5	6	7	8	Try to do many things at once, think about what I am going to do next
Do things slowly	1	2	3	4	5	6	7	8	Do things fast (eating, walking, etc.)
Express feelings	1	2	3	4	5	6	7	8	"Sit" on feelings
Have many interests	1	2	3	4	5	6	7	8	Have few interests outside work

Total points _____ multiplied by 3 = _____ Final Score

Final Score	*Personality Type*
120 or more	A+
106 to 119	A
100 to 105	A-
90 to 99	B+
Below 90	B

Source: Adapted from R.W. Bortner, "A Short Rating Scale as a Potential Measure of Patterns of Behavior."

terms of certain physical disorders, some interesting results appeared. For example, researchers have found that type A men are twice as prone to heart disease and fatal heart attacks as type B individuals.[4] Of 133 heart disease patients, 94 were classifiable as type A personalities.[5]

The same traits that predispose type A individuals to certain physical disorders also appear to predispose them to certain types of work. For example, 60 percent of a sample of managers could be clearly identified as type A while only 12 percent were clearly classifiable as type B.[6] Surprisingly, the characteristics that seem most helpful to type A individuals in their rise through managerial ranks (such as persistence, fanatic observance of deadlines, and the like) do not aid them in their performance as top-level managers. Rather, it appears that type B individuals have better performance records in top management positions. The relaxed and patient attitude of type B individuals appears to give them a better perspective on running large organizations. This evidence may seem to suggest that once people reach the top of their professions they should abandon type A behaviors and switch to type B. However, the tendency to display type A traits is fairly well ingrained in such individuals, and they find it very hard to adopt the type B behavior style.

Changes in One's Life   Another personal factor that can produce stress is both the magnitude and the frequency of changes in an individual's life. For example, a major change (such as being fired or the death of a spouse) can have a strong impact on a person's health. The frequent occurrence of many less dramatic changes over a short period of time can also have a negative effect. In studying this phenomenon, a weighting system was devised that reflects the relative severity of various stressful life changes (Table 11.2).[7] If a person experiences the equivalent of more than 150 points of stressfulness in one year, there is a better than 50 percent chance that he or she will suffer a serious physical disorder during the following year. The chance of illness increases to 80 percent for scores that exceed 300.

Demographic Attributes   As level of income increases, stress levels tend to decrease. People with higher income levels report less stress than those with lower earnings. Whites report less stress than minorities, and men have lower stress levels than women. However, minorities and women, in the aggregate, are in lower-quality positions that pay less and have greater demands. Hence, evidence of simple demographic differences in stress level is probably a reflection of differences in job attributes.

Interpersonal Factors

Jealousy and Envy   In recent years, there has been increasing recognition of the role of negative emotion at work. Two powerful and commonplace negative emotions are employee jealousy and employee envy. **Employee jealousy** can be defined as a pattern of thoughts, emotions, and behaviors that result from a loss of self-esteem and the loss of outcomes associated with a working relationship.[8] **Employee envy,** often confused with employee jealousy, can be defined as a pattern of thoughts, emotions, and behaviors that result from the loss of self-esteem in response to another individual obtaining outcomes that one personally desires.[*] Feelings of envy at work (that is, resenting the success of another) are generally regarded as petty and reflective of immaturity, while feelings of jealousy (that is, a protective reaction to a threat to a valued relationship) are widely sympathized with by others and more socially accepted. Also, it is not rare (and has probably become more common in recent years) for strong feelings of workplace jealousy and envy to result in extreme violence. Because loss of self-esteem plays a part in both jealousy and envy, it has been suggested that employees with low self-esteem may be more susceptible to these feelings.[9] Supervisors who wish to actively manage potential jealousy and envy should consider how decisions will affect the self-esteem of employees and should institute techniques that promote both cooperation and sharing of resources (for example, the introduction of self-directed work teams, as discussed in Chapter 5).[10] Preliminary research on employee jealousy and envy suggests that men express more workplace envy than women (perhaps because men are more attuned to competition), while women

---

[*]A simple way to distinguish jealousy from envy is to recall that jealousy involves three people, while envy only requires two.

TABLE 11.2   *Relative Weights of Life Changes*

Life Event	Scale Value
Death of spouse	100
Divorce	73
Marital separation	65
Jail term	63
Death of a close family member	63
Major personal injury or illness	53
Marriage	50
Fired from work	47
Marital reconciliation	45
Retirement	45
Major change in health of family member	44
Pregnancy	40
Sex difficulties	39
Gain of a new family member	39
Business readjustment	39
Change in financial state	38
Death of a close friend	37
Change to a different line of work	36
Change in number of arguments with spouse	35
Mortgage or loan for major purchase (home, etc.)	31
Foreclosure of mortgage or loan	30
Change in responsibilities at work	29
Son or daughter leaving home	29
Trouble with in-laws	29
Outstanding personal achievement	28
Spouse begins or stops work	26
Begin or end school	26
Change in living conditions	25
Revision of personal habits	24
Trouble with boss	23
Change in work hours or conditions	20
Change in residence	20
Change in schools	20
Change in recreation	19
Change in church activities	19
Change in social activities	18
Mortgage or loan for lesser purchase (car, etc.)	17
Change in sleeping habits	16
Change in number of family get-togethers	15
Change in eating habits	15
Vacation	13
Christmas	12
Minor violations of the law	11

Source: T.H. Holmes and L.O. Rahe, "Scaling of Life Change: Composition of Direct and Indirect Methods."

express more workplace jealousy than men (perhaps because women are more concerned with maintaining social relations). Additionally, employees who express greater jealousy and envy also express greater intent to quit and lower job satisfaction.[11]

Although we typically think of envy and jealousy as emotions rather than stressors, they are in fact stress inducers in that they arise from the perception of threats in the work environment. These threats imply a loss of self-esteem or social standing. As with other threats that we experience, we are aroused to remedy (that is, eliminate) the threat if possible.

Workplace Romance While it seems fairly self-evident that such negative emotions as envy and jealousy are related to stress reactions, it may seem odd to highlight workplace romance (a very positive interpersonal emotion) as a source of stress. However, stress reactions may result among observers of the romantic relationship who fear that favoritism might occur, or from the participants of the romance when the relationship turns sour. As the number of women in traditionally male occupations rises and people devote longer hours to work and work-related travel, the opportunities for romantic involvement among employees are expected to increase. At present, a sizable number of people date and ultimately marry individuals that they met through work. Surveys indicate that managers are not certain how to establish policies in this area (other than to transfer the spouse with less seniority to a different unit, if marriage results from a romantic relationship).[12]

Given the risk of possible charges of sexual harassment if intimate relations turn adversarial (especially between people of differing power or rank), managers can not afford to ignore a topic that has potential to be highly detrimental to work unit performance. At a minimum, **workplace romances** (definable as enduring, intense, and erotic attraction between employees) are known to stimulate gossip and to carry the potential for perceived exploitation. Nonetheless, a large majority of managers recognize that there is little that employers can do to dissuade romantic attraction among employees.[†]

On the plus side, it can, however, be argued that workplace romances may also have some interesting positive consequences for employers. For example, romantically involved employees may be less likely to quit, more open to communicating and working collaboratively, and may energize group morale (by contributing to a collective group sense that "love is in the air").[13]

Organizational Factors

Responsibility for Others Having responsibility, in general, can lead to greater stress.[14] Beyond that, having responsibility for *other people*, rather than responsibility for the other features of an enterprise, can be highly stressful.[‡]

[†]You are invited, at this point, to provide your own favorite example of a workplace romance that resulted in significant stress for both the participants and any observers.

[‡]In an experiment sometimes called the "executive monkey" study, two rhesus monkeys were strapped into electrified chairs. Five seconds after the illumination of a red warning light, both monkeys received mild electric shocks. After learning that the light served as a warning of the impending shock, an arm of one of the monkeys was released so that he could reach a lever, which would prevent both monkeys from being shocked. After a time, the monkey that had the opportunity to reach the lever came to control the occurrence of the shock reliably. The monkey with the responsibility (the "executive monkey") had to remain constantly vigilant. When the experiment was over, researchers examined the intestinal tracts of both monkeys. The "executive monkey" had begun to develop ulcers, while the companion monkey had not experienced intestinal distress.

For managers who deal with people, the stress associated with recognizing the impact of their actions on others' lives is more immediate and real than it is for managers who mostly deal with things and ideas.

Working Conditions   The work environment also plays a role in determining the amount of stress an employee experiences. Certain occupations are noted for the high levels of stress they entail. As you might imagine, it is truly difficult to prove conclusively that one occupation is more stressful than another. Nonetheless, in one fairly direct attempt to study the possible link of occupation to illness, the health records of more than 22,000 employees were examined for stress-related disorders. The results of comparisons for over 100 occupations revealed the existence of significant differences.[15] Stress was found to be generally greater in such jobs as construction laborer, secretary, inspector, office manager, foreman, waitress/waiter, mine operative, air traffic controller, and clinical lab technician. In contrast, stress was relatively low for craft workers, stock handlers, college professors, and heavy equipment operators. In addition, occupational status level was not found to be related to stress-related disorders; that is, both white-collar *and* blue-collar employees, and skilled *and* unskilled workers showed high and low incidences of disorders.

The repetitive and "dehumanizing" work environment created by assembly lines has been linked to health-related disorders. One study of industrial workers reported that employees in companies using assembly-line technology were more likely to show evidence of early coronary artery disease than were employees involved in other work technologies. Piecework systems have similarly been implicated. Such systems generally lead to higher productivity than do other pay systems, but the toll on the employee can be questioned. For example, the number of accidents is also higher under piece-rate systems than under salaried systems.[16]

The absence of intrinsically enjoyable and rewarding work is associated with feelings of stress, as is being overloaded. For example, a correlation has been found between tax deadlines and illness for accountants.[17]

Emotional Labor   An especially stressful aspect of some jobs involves the obligation to project specific emotions. For example, employees at vacation resorts, flight attendants, and salespeople are obliged to display an extremely positive demeanor when dealing with customers and clients, even when their true feelings are far from positive. The additional effort required to maintain these false feelings, or "face work," is termed **emotional labor**.[18] Learning to do one's job well when it requires emotional labor means learning proper affective tone, gestures, appearance, and language. To some extent, every job requires an occupational mask. Examples include supervisors who must enforce disciplinary rules that they don't genuinely believe in, and nurses who must display calm in the face of human suffering.

To cope with the stress caused by this high degree of self-control, employees in such jobs often find outlets for their true feelings. John Van Maanen, of the Massachusetts Institute of Technology, has provided some interesting behind-the-scenes insights on how employees cope with such stress.[19] Working as an amusement-ride operator at Disneyland, Maanen observed that the ride operators exercised norms for regulating their true feelings. Because ride operators are obliged to project a positive, upbeat, clean-cut image, they are not permitted to display animosity toward "guests," even if a guest is quite rude. Operators cope with such "ducks" (a derisive term used by operators to label unruly customers) by slapping seatbelts harshly across riders, squeezing seatbelts tightly, or arranging "near miss" collisions of ride vehicles that are designed to startle and intimidate guests. Ride operators also cope with the requirement of continuous emotion management by "going robot" or "checking out"—that is, willing emotional numbness while maintaining a smiling exterior.[§] At Disneyland, as well as in other public positions, employees cope with emotional labor by drawing together as cohesive, self-protecting units. Such cohesion helps employees work cooperatively in handling "ducks" and dealing with supervisors.

Role Conflict   **Role conflict** occurs when two or more sets of demands are made on an employee so that compliance with one set of demands makes it more difficult to comply with another.[20] In essence, an employee is expected to perform contradictory, or conflicting, activities. For example, a supervisor may find that his superior expects increased productivity from his department, while his subordinates expect his support in finding ways to reduce their daily quota. Likewise, a college faculty member may find that she is expected to devote significant amounts of time to preparing and delivering lectures, while at the same time she is expected to publish in highly competitive scholarly journals. If possible, one may resolve the conflict by devoting more time and energy to the most pressing demand in a given situation (for instance, by preparing a lecture as the time for a class approaches). It is well established that employee job satisfaction decreases as role conflict increases.[21] In addition, role conflict has been found to be connected with heart disease, high blood pressure, elevated cholesterol, and obesity.[22] Furthermore, abilities to make high-quality decisions and to be creative are likely to be impaired in situations containing a high degree of role conflict.

Role Ambiguity   **Role ambiguity** refers to the absence of clarity regarding how to perform one's job. Ambiguity or uncertainty may surround knowing what goals to set and how to best achieve them, and determining one's level of accomplishment. Initially, all newly hired employees experience some degree of role ambiguity when they are assigned to their tasks. However, some jobs are consistently more lacking in clarity concerning how to perform them. For example, managerial jobs generally lack a specific, well-defined set of activities that are to be routinely carried out. Project team managers are also likely to experience greater degrees of uncertainty, especially in the early stages of work.

Role ambiguity is closely associated with a variety of negative consequences. As with role conflict, decreased job satisfaction is thought to be a result of increased role ambiguity. In addition, lower levels of self-confidence, decreased satisfaction with life in general, and increased expression of intentions to quit have been found to be correlated with role ambiguity.[23]

Role Overload   In addition to conflict and ambiguity, role processes can play a part as a source of stress in yet a third fashion: role overload. **Role overload**

[§]Disneyland supervisors try to identify "malcontent" ride operators (the supervisors' term for undesirable operators) by posing as tourists and "ghostriding" various attractions to see if everything is up to snuff.

occurs when too many activities are expected of an employee, given the time available and the ability level of the employee. Indications of role overload include working in excess of sixty hours a week, holding down two jobs, and foregoing vacations. Being in a situation where one lacks the necessary time to perform required tasks has been found to be a possible cause of increased blood cholesterol levels.[24] Furthermore, overload has been found to be related to job dissatisfaction, lower self-esteem, increased heart rate, and increased cigarette consumption.[25]

Shift Work   Approximately 20 percent of the U.S. workforce (roughly 20 million people) is involved in rotating (afternoon and evening) work schedules as opposed to fixed daytime work schedules.[26] Shift work is unavoidable in a modern, technological society. Certain services must be available 24 hours a day, and hence require shifts. Firefighters, police officers, medical and military personnel, and utility operators, for example, must work in shifts around the clock. Because of the unpopularity of afternoon and evening shifts, many employers find it necessary to rotate staff through shifts.

Shift rotation, understandably, has an adverse influence on sleeping patterns and on opportunities for normal social activities. However, the range of adverse consequences of shift work is substantial. Table 11.3 lists a number of these problems.[27] Although there have been significant advances in the understanding of biological rhythms (that is, physiological functions that recur at regular

An Inside Look
Stress in the Executive Suite

Stress among CEOs can come from more than worrying about the bottom line. For today's CEOs, especially the more visible ones, fear of direct physical assault is a day-to-day reality of executive life. Attacks can range from the Bill Gates cream-pie-in-the-face incident to outright murder attempts by disgruntled employees or members of special interest groups.

Minimizing executive stress caused by concern for CEO safety is a serious issue at top corporate ranks in firms around the world. Bodyguard service (which can cost $500,000 or more a year) is no longer found solely with rock stars, celebrities, and public officials, but is becoming commonplace in the executive suites of the world's major corporations. "If a guard gives a CEO peace of mind and his attention is focused more on business than personal safety, then I'm all for it," says Charles Elson, an outside board member at Sunbeam and a Stetson University law professor.

Keeping executives safe around the clock is a formidable task that demands specialized skills, and graduates of Executive Security International, a bodyguard training firm in Aspen, Colorado, are some of the most sought after. Of the company's more than 2,000 graduates, its president, Bob Duggan, estimates that 10 percent to 15 percent protect CEOs (up from 1 percent to 2 percent five years earlier). Bodyguards are expert in defensive skills involving weapons and the martial arts. They can administer first aid, install and maintain home security, and detect surveillance and attempted intrusion. Many bodyguards, trained in evasive driving techniques, double as chauffeurs.

Clearly, reducing a CEO's concern for personal safety lowers some of the stress in a high-stress position and can assist the CEO in focusing on the job's demands and responsibilities. But having bodyguards on duty 24 hours a day can curtail privacy and change the way a CEO lives. One CEO commented, "A good security man keeps just close enough that he doesn't get in your hair."

Source: J. Lublin, "As Their Visibility Rises, More CEOs Hire Guards," *The Wall Street Journal*, February 11, 1998.

TABLE 11.3   *Stress Symptoms Associated with Shift Work*

Fatigue

Difficulty getting sleep

Disturbances in appetite, digestion, and elimination

Increased divorce rate

Increased incidence of sexual problems

Reduced involvement in social and religious organizations

Reduced contact with friends

Lowered productivity

Increased accidents

Reduced commitment to the organization

intervals), there have not been equivalent advances in the application of this knowledge in the form of interventions designed to ameliorate problems caused by shift work.

Reactions to Stress

Physical Problems

As suggested above, a high level of stress has been associated with a host of physical disorders, including heart disease, arthritis, ulcers, high blood pressure, and high levels of cholesterol.[28] There is also some suspicion that stress may be linked to cancer.[29]

Although it is impossible to quantify the personal cost of serious physical ailments for an individual, it is possible to estimate the cost of such problems for an organization. For example, Ivancevich and Matteson have created a worksheet for estimating the yearly costs associated with replacing employees lost to heart disease.[30] For a company that employs 4,000 people, the estimates would be:

1. Number of employees	4,000
2. Employees in age range 45 to 65 (0.25 × line 1)	1,000
3. Estimated deaths due to heart disease per year (0.006 × line 2)	6
4. Estimated premature retirement due to heart problems per year (0.003 × line 2)	3
5. Company's annual personnel losses due to heart disorders (sum of lines 3 and 4)	9
6. Annual replacement cost: the average cost of hiring and training replacements for experienced employees (line 5 × $9,600)	$86,400

As these figures suggest, heart disease can be a significant cost to an organization, and the absolute number of employees who are likely to die eventually of heart disease is not trivial. Furthermore, the additional costs of hospitalization coverage, lost wages, and lost performance are not included in the above estimate.

To be sure, a single organization cannot assume full responsibility for all employee deaths due to heart disease. In addition to work-related stress, many other factors play a role in the development of heart disease, including heredity, diet, and general state of well-being.

Alcoholism and Drug Abuse

The National Institute on Alcohol Abuse and Alcoholism estimates that between 6 and 10 percent of all employees are alcoholics. Although drug usage is not as widespread as alcohol abuse, it is nonetheless a serious problem. Both alcohol and drug abuse are linked to higher levels of stress among employees. In addition to threatening their own well-being, employees who attend work while under the influence of alcohol or drugs pose a serious threat to the well-being of their coworkers because they are more prone to on-the-job accidents.

Absenteeism, Turnover, and Dissatisfaction

Research generally has pointed to a relationship between stress and increases in such withdrawal behaviors as absenteeism and turnover.[31] A correlation has also been found between dissatisfaction and work-related stress.[32] Because these studies of stress as a predictor of turnover, absenteeism, and dissatisfaction have all been correlational in nature, it is difficult to state conclusively what factors are responsible for the relationship.

Workplace Violence

Although little solid evidence is available, it is widely believed that hostile actions in the workplace, such as violence and forms of sabotage directed against supervisors and workers, may result, at least indirectly, from stress. For example, stress associated with feelings of job insecurity (that is, plans to eliminate jobs) has been cited as a contributing cause to a number of shootings by U.S. Postal Service employees.[33] Recent efforts to understand workplace violence have revealed that a relatively small number of people are murdered on the job because of enraged coworkers who "go postal." While the vast majority of workplace homicides occur during robberies or other crimes (and typically have taxi drivers, police officers, hotel clerks, and gas-station attendants as the victims), former and current coworkers are responsible for roughly 5 percent of all workplace murders. More commonly, workplace violence tends to involve fairly petty expressions of aggressive behavior. Most workplace aggression can be characterized as covert (done anonymously to conceal the aggressor's identity), verbal (such as the use of offensive language or gossiping), or involving brief displays of intense anger (such as threats). Studies of the occurrence of **workplace aggression** (i.e., efforts to do harm to employees or organizations) reveal three forms or manifestations of the phenomenon.

Table 11.4 lists examples of these activities in descending order of frequency. As the listing suggests, most workplace aggression can be described as both indirect (rather than direct) and verbal (rather than physical) in nature.

Burnout—A Companion Problem

Like stress, **burnout** is a reaction to prolonged and energy-depleting difficulties. Its primary symptoms include feeling drained or used up. It typically

TABLE 11.4   *Three Major Forms of Workplace Aggression*

	Ranking
Expressions of Hostility	
Talking behind target's back/spreading rumors	1
Interrupting others when they are speaking/working	2
Flaunting status/acting in condescending manner	3
Giving someone the silent treatment	4
Verbal sexual harassment	5
Staring, dirty looks, or other negative eye-contact	6
Intentionally damning with faint praise	7
Leaving the work area when target enters	8
Failing to deny false rumors about target	9
Negative or obscene gestures toward the target	10
Holding target, or target's work, up to ridicule	11
Obstructionism	
Failure to return phone calls or respond to memos	12
Showing up late for meetings run by target	13
Causing others to delay action on important matters	14
Needlessly consuming resources needed by target	15
Intentional work slowdowns	16
Failing to warn target of impending danger	17
Overt Aggression	
Theft/destruction of target's personal property	18
Threats of physical violence	19
Physical attack/assault (e.g., pushing, shoving, hitting)	20
Destroying mail or messages needed by target	21
Attack with weapon	22

Note: The lower the ranking, the greater the reported frequency of occurrence.

Source: Adapted from J.H. Neuman and R.A. Baron, "Workplace Violence and Workplace Aggression: Evidence Concerning Specific Forms, Potential Causes, and Preferred Targets," *Journal of Management* 24 (1998): 391–419.

affects people who are highly conscientious and work in the helping professions, such as police officers, schoolteachers, social workers, and nurses. At some point, such employees may come to feel that they are not receiving the rewards that they expected for their efforts to help others. Their frustration leads to feelings of apathy and failure, which may result in physical symptoms such as high blood pressure and ulcers, and mental symptoms such as depression and irritability. In many respects, burnout and stress are highly similar reactions. A checklist for assessing burnout is presented in Table 11.5.

TABLE 11.5   *The Burnout Checklist*

	Mostly True	Mostly False
1. I feel tired more frequently than I used to.	_____	_____
2. I snap at people too often.	_____	_____
3. Trying to help other people often seems hopeless.	_____	_____
4. I seem to be working harder but accomplishing less.	_____	_____
5. I get down on myself too often.	_____	_____
6. My job is beginning to depress me.	_____	_____
7. I often feel I'm headed nowhere.	_____	_____
8. I've reached (or am fast reaching) a dead end in my job.	_____	_____
9. I've lost a lot of my zip lately.	_____	_____
10. It's hard for me to laugh at a joke about myself.	_____	_____
11. I'm not really physically ill, but I have a lot of aches and pains.	_____	_____
12. Lately I've kind of withdrawn from friends and family.	_____	_____
13. My enthusiasm for life is on the wane.	_____	_____
14. I'm running out of things to say to people.	_____	_____
15. My temper is much shorter than it used to be.	_____	_____
16. My job makes me feel sad.	_____	_____

Interpretation: The more of these questions you can honestly answer mostly true, the more likely it is that you are experiencing burnout. If you answered twelve or more of these statements mostly true, it is likely you are experiencing burnout or another form of mental depression. If so, discuss these feelings with a physical or mental health professional.

Source:"The Burnout Checklist," A.J. DuBrin, *Contemporary Applied Management* (Plano, Texas; Business Publications, 1982), 243. Reprinted with permission. The checklist is based in part on the questionnaire printed on the dust jacket of *Burn Out* by Freudenberger.

Coping with Stress

Helping a person maintain the level of stress that is best for him or her is the goal of various stress management techniques. By and large, the techniques we will consider focus primarily on the reduction, rather than the increase, of stress.

Flight or Fight

Flight and fight are two reactions that can serve as a primary means of successful coping. *Flight,* or leaving a distressing situation, is a perfectly reasonable response to stress if an avenue of flight is available. For example, some individuals try their hand at supervising others and find that they simply do not like it. This is not to say that they cannot handle the job, but rather that they prefer other types of assignments or activities. For such individuals, the recognition of this personal preference is an important and useful insight that can help them cope with the stress that may accompany supervisory responsibilities.

Fight, or confronting a threat or stressor, can also be an effective response. The desire to confront a threat may actually be the best way to bring about a change that will reduce the level of stress. For example, the urge to fight may lead an employee to confront her superior on an issue that has been bothering her for some time. The confrontation may then lead to a workable resolution.

Exercise

Physical exercise, including participation in sports, enables a person to develop resistance to the detrimental effects of stress. Exercise can both improve health and reduce fatigue. Fatigue plays a key role in stress-producing situations because people who are feeling fatigued are more apt to overreact to frustration. Therefore, tolerance for frustration can be increased by being in better physical health. Regular exercise is also thought to be of value in reducing the likelihood of coronary diseases. Some large organizations, such as Tenneco, Weyerhauser, Johns-Manville, and Exxon, provide a gymnasium at company headquarters to promote employee fitness.

Social Support

One means of resisting stress is to have a strong network of social supports. Studies indicate that the availability of sympathetic others (especially coworkers) can help a person deal with job-related stress.[34] The reassurance derived from knowing that others can be called on to help when needed can be invaluable.

Job Redesign

Jobs can be redesigned to minimize the creation of stress. One approach to job redesign that seeks to reduce assembly-line pressures and the dull, repetitive aspects of such work is job enrichment. As discussed in Chapter 5, one way in which job enrichment makes a task more attractive is by giving greater autonomy (usually self-pacing) to the individual worker. Such autonomy is critical to alleviating feelings of pressure and the resultant stress. Two other common ways of reducing stress are to provide employees with opportunities to participate in decision making and to improve communication, both of which can reduce workers' feelings of helplessness and dependence.

Relaxation Techniques

Relaxation techniques such as progressive relaxation, yoga, and Transcendental Meditation rely on the idea that relaxation of the major voluntary muscles reduces anxiety levels. The goal of these techniques is to achieve a state of physiological and psychological rest, and evidence suggests that such improvements can in fact result.[35] Although some corporations (such as New York Telephone Company and Metropolitan Life Insurance) are beginning to explore the sponsored use of relaxation techniques for their managers,[36] evidence of the effectiveness of these techniques within organizational settings is not yet available. Also, some large organizations, such as Apple Computer and Intel, allow managers to take sabbaticals (paid time off) to encourage "mental rejuvenation." Universities, for example, have a long tradition of permitting faculty time off to pursue alternative scholarly interests. AT&T, along with a growing number of firms, has adopted "stress-down days," when employees come to work wearing casual attire, including jeans and sweatshirts.

Time Management: A Practical Approach to Reducing Stress

One especially useful strategy for coping with job-related stress is effective **time management.** An inability to manage time can result in overcommitment, a lack of planning, and missed deadlines. Strictly speaking, one does not manage time as such, in that time moves at its own rate and is not subject to any effort to manipulate it. In truth, effective time management is really effective self-management. Time-management specialists have developed a number of useful techniques for gaining control over one's work life and, thereby, one's sanity.[37]

Time Log   The first step in trying to manage one's time is to develop a time log, or inventory. By jotting down the events that occur in a typical day with the time required for each activity, it is possible to learn where one's time is being spent. The results of a time log (which might be reviewed at the end of a week) can offer surprising insights. For example, some executives are amazed to find that a large percentage of each day is devoted to dealing with interruptions and pointless socializing. The results of such an inventory can help pinpoint sources of time wastage and thus help focus attention on using time more effectively.

Structuring Time   One can gain greater control over one's life by structuring the day so that time wasters are blocked or eliminated. For example, not being accessible by phone or to visitors for an hour or two in the morning provides a block of uninterrupted time during which mail can be read or writing can be done. Similarly, all visits can be arranged between 2:00 and 4:00 in the afternoon. Meetings can be strategically set one-half hour or an hour before lunch or quitting time to ensure that the participants will help complete the meeting on time.

Just Say No   Sometimes an employee is victimized by a desire to be accommodating to everyone. In such instances, others learn that their requests are seldom refused by such an employee and may take advantage of his or her good nature. For such individuals, an important step in gaining control of their lives is to learn how to say no to requests for their time and energy. Refusing the requests of others requires some delicacy, and should be done politely, but firmly. For people who are already heavily committed to their primary job duties, taking on the added responsibility of managing the office baseball team and the fund-raising drive will likely provide needless stress.

Make a List   One of the most useful techniques for managing time is to prepare a list of "things to do." Interviews with highly effective managers reveal that they invariably maintain a planning list of activities that aids their memories and focuses their attention and energy. A planning list contains such items as phone calls that must be returned, correspondence that must be prepared, meetings that need to be scheduled, and projects that must be monitored. In addition, the items on the list should be prioritized. The most critical items are labeled "category A," while the next most critical items are labeled "category B," and so on. Then, category A items are handled first, category B items are tackled if time permits, and lower-category items are put off until even later. In maintaining a "to-do" list, it is important to keep the list current, to never give in to the temptation to clean up the "small" or "easy" items first, and to scrutinize the list for items that can be reasonably delegated to subordinates.

Employee Job Satisfaction

Following a discussion of stress and its impact on employee well-being, it is fitting that we now focus our attention on the related topic of employee emotional reactions to work. Emotional reactions to employment experiences are inevitable. One's thinking and feeling (that is, one's attitude) toward work is termed **job satisfaction.** As is true of all attitudes, a person's level of job satisfaction is influenced by experience, especially stressful experiences. Although an employee's attitudes are formed by the job itself, communications from others can also play an important role. Furthermore, an employee's expectations about a job can greatly influence his or her interpretation and evaluation of work-related experiences.[38]

The Importance of Job Satisfaction

Modern managers recognize that an organization's performance should be measured in human dimensions as well as in terms of return on investment, market share, profit after taxes, and the like. A variety of reasons support the desirability of attending to workers' satisfaction. Perhaps the foremost reason is a moral one. Consider that working is a requirement for most people. The alternative, a subsistence-level existence based on government and charitable support, is unacceptable to most people. Given that most people must work, and that most people will spend the majority of their adult lives at work, it can be argued that employers have a *moral obligation* to make the experience personally rewarding (or, at a minimum, not painful or dehumanizing).**

Workers' *physical and mental well-being* appear to be correlated with job satisfaction in that more highly satisfied workers have better physical and mental health records.[39] This evidence, however, is strictly correlational in nature. As a consequence, it is difficult to say in what direction the "causal arrow" is pointing. It is also conceivable that other factors that may come into play (for example, educational level and income could be largely responsible for the observed correlations). Nonetheless, serious job dissatisfaction, as manifested by stress, can lead to a variety of physiological disorders, including ulcers and arterial disease.

Job satisfaction can also play an important role in a company's *ability to attract and retain qualified workers.* An organization's very survival rests heavily on this ability, and a company that is known to mistreat its personnel will have difficulty in drawing the best people to staff its positions.

Low levels of job satisfaction have been related to such problems as *turnover, absenteeism, union-organizing activity,* and the *filing of grievances.* Because such problems can be costly and disruptive to an organization, they cannot be lightly dismissed. Thus, job satisfaction is exceedingly important for the well-being of the organization as well as for the individual.

Sources of Job Satisfaction

More than 3,000 studies have been conducted on the topic of job satisfaction, or morale as it was more frequently termed in previous years.** Their results tend to point to much the same conclusions. For example, certain variables are consistently correlated with job satisfaction. One of the most important variables is job level. Satisfaction is higher among employees in higher-level positions, while satisfaction tends to be lowest among holders of jobs that can be characterized as hot, heavy, or dangerous, such as work in steel mills and unskilled jobs.

Length of service and race are also frequently correlated with job satisfaction. Individuals with less time on the job and African-American workers are, in the aggregate, somewhat more dissatisfied than "long-termers" and European-American workers. Of course, it is difficult to draw any firm conclusions from such correlational evidence because job level is also associated with length of service and race. Long-termers tend to be in higher-level jobs, and African-American workers tend to be less educated and are more likely to hold unskilled positions.

**It is an interesting exercise to calculate the proportion of one's life that is spent at work. Consider that the average adult will live to a predicted actuarial age. The number of years, in fact hours, of life that a person has left can then be determined. This finite number of hours can be further divided into unconscious time (spent sleeping), conscious but uninteresting and nonproductive time (when engaging in routine activities such as brushing teeth, dressing, and commuting), and conscious productive time. As a percentage, the majority of conscious productive time will be spent working.

**Perhaps the earliest report of a study of job satisfaction was a treatise by Rammizzini in Modeno, Italy, in the early 1600s. Having noted a look of disgust on the faces of cesspool cleaners, he decided to question them on their feelings about their work. In the mid-1800s, Karl Marx developed a satisfaction questionnaire. However, the early forms of surveys more often asked *supervisors* to state what they believed workers felt about their jobs, rather than asking the workers themselves.

Women are also more likely to be found in lower-level jobs. Historically, lower female expectations for employment opportunities have been fairly consistent with the lack of opportunities for women. Evidence of sex differences in job satisfaction levels has been mixed. It is likely, however, that rising expectations of women in the labor force will produce differences in job satisfaction between the sexes.

Finally, organizational size has been identified as a correlate of job satisfaction. Employees in smaller organizations tend to be more satisfied than employees in larger organizations. The size of an organization may not, in and of itself, affect job satisfaction, but size is associated with more specific sources of satisfaction.

Intrinsic versus Extrinsic Sources of Satisfaction All sources of job satisfaction fall into two categories: intrinsic and extrinsic. Intrinsic sources originate from within the individual and have psychological value. Such satisfactions are essentially self-administered. Autonomy (that is, independence, such as the ability to choose one's own work pace) is one source of intrinsic satisfaction.

Extrinsic sources of satisfaction originate from outside the individual; they come from his or her environment. Forces beyond the individual's control determine the frequency and magnitude of extrinsic sources of satisfaction. Working conditions and opportunities to interact with coworkers are sources of extrinsic satisfaction, as are job security and fringe benefits.

In addition, some sources of satisfaction serve a dual purpose in that they can be extrinsic, or tangible, in nature while having intrinsic, or psychological, value because of what they symbolize. Both a high salary and rapid career progress would offer dual sources of satisfaction.

Expectations Satisfaction is a very personal experience that depends heavily on an individual's expectations. For example, imagine that you have just been offered an executive position that pays $150,000 a year. It sounds attractive, of course. In the abstract, it's difficult to conceive of how someone could be dissatisfied with such a salary. Suppose, however, that you discover that other people who have much the same job are receiving $500,000 to $900,000 per year. What formerly seemed to be an attractive salary would suddenly become unsatisfactory.

Expectations can have a powerful influence on a person's level of satisfaction. For example, new employees often have unrealistically high expectations. In the time between being offered a job and the first day of work, new employees may fantasize about how rapidly they will rise in the new organization, what immediate working conditions will be like, and so on. Once on the job, however, they may experience a shock when confronted with a number of harsh realities. They may discover that no promotion ladder extends from their current position, that their coworkers are not very pleasant, or that the lunch room and restrooms are dilapidated. The unrealistic expectations of new employees may be generated partly by personal fantasy and by the media. But company recruiters may also play a role by deceiving prospective employees about the nature of their future employment.

Companies can counter the potential problem of unrealistic expectations by providing job-orientation programs that present a more realistic point of view. The effects of realistic job previews on individual's reactions to their work have been extensively studied. With minor exceptions, the results have generally shown that individuals who are told both the bad and the good features of their new jobs before they begin working have higher levels of job satisfaction, lower initial expectations about the job, and a lower rate of early turnover.[40‡‡] Some organizations (for example, Nissan Motor Manufacturing at its Smyrna, Tennessee, facility) modify the concept of providing realistic previews by having prospective employees participate in "preemployment" programs that are essentially "job tryouts." During a job tryout, an applicant completes a variety of exercises that simulate job-related tasks. Although the tryout is of value to the employer as it serves as both a screening and an indoctrination experience, the employee also gains an appreciation of what the actual job is likely to entail.[41]

Dispositional Influences   Although much work in the area of job satisfaction shows that external influences, such as job design, affect employee attitudes, some recent research suggests that individual job attitudes may be fairly consistent over time and jobs. In a nationwide longitudinal study of the job satisfaction of 5,000 middle-aged men, Staw and Ross found significant stability over a 5-year period. Even when individuals changed employers and/or occupations, prior attitudes continued to be a strong predictor of later job satisfaction. These findings suggest that individuals may be predisposed to feel good or bad about their employment situation, regardless of the actual specifics of the situation. These results help to explain why some people seem to be perpetually unhappy with their work or life, and others appear generally content and good-natured regardless of changes in their surroundings. In short, people may carry with them, across jobs, predispositions to feel good or bad about work. The term **negative affectivity** has been coined to describe this predisposition to feel dissatisfied with one's job or life in general. People who are relatively high on negative affectivity are comparatively introspective and tend to dwell on the negative side of themselves and the world. Such individuals tend to interpret ambiguous information more negatively and to provide negative evaluations of inherently neutral or innocuous objects common to everyday life (for example, one's telephone number, one's first name, or 8½-by-11 inch paper).[42]

A perhaps even more surprising finding in this area comes from research on the possible influence of genetics on job satisfaction. Specifically, researchers at the University of Minnesota studied the job satisfaction of identical twins who had been reared apart. These researchers found that part of the variance in job satisfaction responses could be attributed to genetics. Similarities across pairs of twins existed despite differences in jobs.[43] These findings suggest that organizations may have less control over employee satisfaction than previously thought. However, the likelihood that genetics is a contributing factor to job satisfaction does not mean that job satisfaction is not influenced by environmental factors.[44]

---

‡‡The importance of creating realistic expectations is increasingly being recognized. In addition to profit-oriented organizations, nonprofit organizations such as religious orders are using realistic job previews. One group of religious women provides a realistic preview to young women who are considering joining their convent. The preview is designed to show the drabness of the individual rooms and the hardships of daily chores. It is hoped that such previews will diminish attrition in the order by reducing the occasional expectation that life in the order will be a *Sound of Music*–type experience.

The Search for Trends in Job Satisfaction

Based on magazine articles, television, and movies, we might be tempted to conclude that most workers are dissatisfied with their jobs. However, available evidence indicates that such a conclusion would be in error. Surveys of workers in the United States show that the vast majority are fairly satisfied with their jobs. One set of surveys that spanned a 20-year period revealed that satisfied workers comprised 80 to 90 percent of the labor force in a given year.[45] Other representative samplings reveal much the same pattern.[46]

Despite this reassuring evidence, some alarmists argue that worker satisfaction is declining and that the resulting rise in worker alienation could lead to worker revolt. It is perhaps the implicit threat of a worker revolution that makes the prospect of declining satisfaction a topic of widespread concern.[§§]

Due to increasing levels of education, expectations in the work force are rising. If better educated workers do not obtain better jobs, it is conceivable that job satisfaction could decline over the coming years. The unprecedented affluence of recent decades may also contribute to the creation of a more defiant workforce that is less concerned with traditional extrinsic rewards and incentives, such as job security, and more concerned with intrinsic rewards, such as having a challenging and interesting job.[47]

Consequences of Job Dissatisfaction

Withdrawal Behaviors   Individuals are usually drawn to situations that are rewarding, while they tend to withdraw from situations that are unrewarding or painful. This principle of reward and punishment appears to underlie much of the evidence on the relationship between job satisfaction and employee behavior.

Absenteeism   Each year, more work time is lost due to absenteeism than to strikes and lockouts. Studies of absenteeism have often found that less satisfied employees are more likely to miss work.[48] When studying absenteeism, it is important to distinguish between avoidable (or voluntary) absenteeism and unavoidable (or involuntary) absenteeism. Unavoidable absenteeism—for example, that is due to illness or family emergency—is largely unrelated to level of job satisfaction.

To examine the relationship between satisfaction and absenteeism, the attendance rate of office employees at the Chicago headquarters of Sears, Roebuck was studied on the day of a severe blizzard.[49] As a comparison group, the attendance rate was examined for employees in a New York City office, where, on the same day, the weather was pleasant. By relating absenteeism to individual job satisfaction data, it was determined that absenteeism in Chicago was

---

[§§]The evidence of fairly high general job satisfaction should not be interpreted as indicating that working conditions (in factories, for example) are not in need of improvement. Such problems are overlooked when one examines aggregate data for the entire workforce. Also, people are remarkably adaptive to many unpleasant situations, and they often find alternative sources of satisfaction in otherwise adverse conditions. For example, social relations can be a major source of satisfaction in a dull and repetitive job. As evidence that many workers desire better positions, consider that only 24 percent of blue-collar employees report that they would choose the same type of work again. For white-collar employees, the figure only rises to 41 percent. Therefore, many people probably aspire to better conditions, although they are reasonably content with their present situation.

more variable—that is, highly satisfied employees were far more likely to make the extra effort to report to work despite the blizzard, while dissatisfied employees were more likely to remain home.

Tardiness   It is also generally believed that chronic tardiness tends to reflect employee dissatisfaction.[50] Of course, it cannot be assumed that chronic tardiness is invariably due to dissatisfaction, because intervening factors, such as car pooling or preparing a large family for school each morning, often play a role. Nonetheless, certain forms of employee tardiness, such as that caused by lingering in the parking lot or restroom, may be attributed to such attitudinal factors as dissatisfaction, low job involvement, or low professional commitment. Over and above attitudinal factors, the existence of formal organizational penalties and incentives related to tardiness, as well as social pressures, can play a role in an individual's decision to be tardy.

Turnover   Studies have shown, with a fair degree of consistency, that dissatisfied employees are more likely to quit. The specific influence of dissatisfaction on the decision to quit may be only moderate, however, because a variety of other factors are also involved. Perhaps of greatest influence is the availability of alternative employment opportunities. For example, general economic conditions and an employee's sense of confidence in the marketability of personal skills probably play major roles in the decision to seek a new job.[51] Fluctuations in quit rates, for example, are strongly associated with changes in job opportunities (as during periods of rising employment). In fact, the majority of the variation in quit rates may be explained by the simple factor of the business cycle.[52]

Although we might be tempted to think that managers should try to reduce employee turnover, it has been suggested that turnover may not be inherently undesirable. In fact, the desirability of turnover depends on who is leaving. If the people who are quitting are generally superior performers, turnover needs to be reduced or eliminated. But if turnover is great among poor performers, the change is actually in the best interests of the organization. The notion that high turnover among poor performers can benefit an organization is termed **functional turnover.**[53]

Union Activity   Increased interest in union activity has long been accepted as a consequence of employee dissatisfaction.[54] In an attitude survey of 62,000 employees, much of the variability in union activity could be predicted from job-satisfaction information.[55] The most important predictor of union activity was dissatisfaction with supervision. Although dissatisfaction with other facets of the job contributed to the level of union activity, dissatisfaction with pay had no significant relationship. Also, evidence shows that attitudes regarding job satisfaction and toward unions in general can predict voting behavior in union elections.[56] Pro-union voting was found to be associated with concern for economic issues (such as security and working conditions) rather than noneconomic issues (such as the desire for creativity and independence). In one study, information on job satisfaction permitted the prediction of employee voting with an accuracy rate of 75 percent. In addition to voting behavior, other forms of union activity (such as the frequency of strikes and grievance rates within departments) have been found to be correlated with job dissatisfaction.[57] Therefore, some organizations, such as Sears, Roebuck, deliberately use periodic attitude surveys as an early warning system to spot problems that may lead to union organizing activity.[58]

Hostile Actions   There is good reason to believe that extremely dissatisfied employees sometimes engage in hostile actions directed against their employers or coworkers. Hostile actions include sabotaging machinery or production, employee theft, vandalizing company property, unfairly criticizing the employer to customers or the public, and physical violence directed at coworkers and superiors. Other, more specific examples of hostile actions include deliberately destroying databases, placing work gloves into gears in order to halt assembly lines, tampering with company records, and overfilling or underfilling customer orders.[59]

To date, there has been little research on the relationship between dissatisfaction and hostile action. Such behavior is difficult to study because employees as well as employers are reluctant to discuss the topic with either insiders or outsiders.[60] Also, such actions do not commonly produce a discernible pattern for study, nor are such actions often easily attributable to a specific saboteur.*** Employees who engage in sabotage may, understandably, not be easily identifiable as they ordinarily appear content and compliant.[61] One confidential survey, however, did find that self-reports of hostile actions (theft, vandalism, deliberate destruction of work projects, and so on) were significantly correlated with employee dissatisfaction.[62] It may be that some employees engage in violent acts because of a desire to feel a sense of mastery or control over their work environment, which is not attainable through nonviolent means. In short, sabotage may represent an attempt to create the feeling that one is not at the mercy of one's employer.[63]

Job Satisfaction and Productivity

Most people believe that satisfied workers are more productive workers. They reason that satisfied employees are inclined to be more involved with their work and, therefore, are more productive. Research, however, has not identified much support for this proposal. In fact, the available evidence suggests that the relationship between job satisfaction and productivity is a very weak one.[64]

Because people tend to overestimate the influence of job satisfaction, they underestimate other factors that contribute to productivity. Among these other factors are informal work norms, task interdependence, and machine pacing of the production process. These forces often restrict the range of individual productivity. For example, coworkers usually will not allow an individual to work too fast or too slow (since a worker who is too productive will create a logjam at the next workstation, and one who is not productive enough will create a bottleneck for other workers who supply materials to the individual). Furthermore, machine pacing and production planning are designed to reduce uncertainty and maintain strong control over the production process. These factors limit employees' freedom to vary their performance to match their own personal desires.

Although these factors help explain the lack of support for a relationship between performance and satisfaction, they do not refute the proposition that such a relationship can exist. The belief that these variables are related, or at

---

***Our word *sabotage* is derived from the French word *sabot*, a hollowed-out wooden shoe worn by European peasants. During the Industrial Revolution, disgruntled factory workers were said to "sabotage" the production process by tossing their wooden shoes into the machinery.

least influence each other, is still widely held by the business community. Some researchers have suggested that the two dimensions will be correlated only when satisfaction can have a direct impact on performance.[65] For example, in situations in which there is little pressure to be productive, the two dimensions are more likely to be correlated. In situations with high pressure to produce (perhaps the majority of situations), employees will be fairly productive by necessity, and the two variables are unlikely to be related.

The Importance of Finding a Positive Association between Job Satisfaction and Productivity   If superior performers are receiving greater rewards than poor performers, satisfaction levels should be higher among superior performers. The consequence of such a state of affairs is that satisfaction and performance will be positively correlated. Therefore, the extent to which satisfaction and performance are positively correlated within an organization is an indication of the extent to which an organization is "healthy." Consider the converse situation of an organization in which satisfaction and performance are inversely related. Such a situation would be one in which poorer performers are more satisfied than higher performers and in which functional turnover is probably low. Clearly, this situation, as well as a situation in which satisfaction and performance are totally uncorrelated, is not in the best long-term interest of the organization. Managers should, therefore, strive to create linkages between performance and satisfaction by offering highly attractive, equitable rewards that are tied to performance.

SUMMARY

1. *Define stress.* Stress is the extreme physiological and emotional arousal a person experiences when confronted with a threatening situation.

2. *Explain various views of job-related stress.* Hans Selye has proposed three stages that characterize a person's response to stress: alarm, resistance, and exhaustion. These stages constitute the General Adaptation Syndrome. Another view holds that a certain degree of stress may be beneficial in that it may increase achievement.

3. *Identify personal causes of stress.* A major personal cause of stress is the possession of a type A personality. People with such a personality tend to be impatient and competitive. Another major personal cause of stress is change in one's life (for example, death of a spouse or loss of a job).

4. *Explain interpersonal causes of stress.* The negative emotions of jealousy (threats to self-esteem due to loss of a relationship) and envy (threats to self-esteem due to desired outcomes being allocated to another) can induce feelings of stress. Also, workplace romance can be a source of stress for both observers and participants.

5. *List organizational causes of stress.*   Organizational influences include having responsibility for others, being involved in shift work, and working in a stress-inducing occupation or one that requires emotional labor. Role conflict, role ambiguity, and role overload also contribute to the experience of stress.

6. *Describe typical reactions to stress.* High levels of stress are associated with physical disorders, including heart disease, arthritis, ulcers, high blood pressure,

high levels of cholesterol, and, possibly, cancer. Stress is linked to poor job performance, abuse of alcohol and other drugs, absenteeism, job turnover, worker dissatisfaction, workplace aggression, and burnout.

7. *List ways of managing stress.* People can manage stress by weighing the merits of fighting or fleeing a particular situation. Physical exercise and a strong network of social supports help people resist stress. Managers can redesign jobs to minimize the creation of stress. People can reduce stress by using time-management and relaxation techniques.

8. *Tell why management should take an interest in workers' job satisfaction.* Job satisfaction is the product of an individual's thoughts, feelings, and attitudes toward work. Because organizational performance should be measured in human as well as financial terms, management cannot ignore the significance of job satisfaction. Some might argue that because most people must work and consequently spend much of their adult lives doing so, companies have a moral obligation to make work rewarding. The company also benefits, however, because studies show that satisfied workers enjoy better physical and mental health and that job satisfaction plays a significant role in a firm's ability to attract and retain qualified workers. Furthermore, low levels of job satisfaction have been related to such problems as turnover, absenteeism, union organizing, and the filing of grievances. Thus, job satisfaction is a crucial issue for both individuals and organizations.

9. *Cite the most frequent sources of job satisfaction.* The results of numerous studies indicate that certain variables are consistently correlated with job satisfaction, among them job level, length of service, and size of organization. In addition, satisfaction strongly depends on the individual's expectations and personal disposition. Although surveys of the U.S. workforce indicate that the vast majority of workers are fairly satisfied with their jobs, recent trends indicate that, in the future, managers may well be challenged by a workforce that is more demanding, more educated, and less interested in work as an end in itself.

10. *Describe some typical employee responses to low job satisfaction.* Among the most common reactions to low job satisfaction are withdrawal behaviors, such as absenteeism, tardiness, and turnover. Employees may also express their dissatisfaction through increased union activity and hostile actions. Although numerous studies have investigated the relationship between job satisfaction and productivity, there is little empirical evidence to support the pervasive notion that satisfied workers are more productive.

KEY TERMS

Stress
General Adaptation Syndrome
Type A personality
Type B personality
Employee jealousy
Employee envy
Workplace romance
Emotional labor
Role conflict

Role ambiguity
Role overload
Workplace aggression
Burnout
Time management
Job satisfaction
Negative affectivity
Functional turnover

CRITICAL INCIDENT

No Response from Monitor 23

Loudspeaker: IGNITION MINUS 45 MINUTES.

Paul Keller tripped the sequence switches at control monitor 23 in accordance with the countdown instruction book just to his left. All hydraulic systems were functioning normally in the second stage of the spacecraft booster at checkpoint I minus 45. Keller automatically snapped his master control switch to GREEN and knew that his electronic impulse along with hundreds of others from similar consoles within the Cape Kennedy complex signaled continuation of the countdown.

It used to be an incredible challenge, fantastically interesting work at the very fringe of knowledge about the universe. Keller recalled his first day in Brevard County, Florida, with his wife and young daughter. How happy they were that day. Here was the future, the good life . . . forever. And Keller was going to be part of that fantastic, utopian future.

Loudspeaker: IGNITION MINUS 35 MINUTES.

Keller panicked! His mind had wandered momentarily, and he lost his place in the countdown instructions. Seconds later, he found the correct place and tripped the proper sequence of switches for checkpoint I minus 35. No problem. Keller snapped the master control to GREEN and wiped his brow. He knew he was late reporting and would hear about it later.

Loudspeaker: IGNITION MINUS 30 MINUTES.

Keller completed the reporting sequence for checkpoint I minus 30 and took one long last drag on his cigarette. Utopia? Hell! It was one big rat race and getting bigger all the time. Keller recalled how he once naively felt that his problems with Naomi would disappear after they left Minneapolis and came to the Cape with the space program. Now, 10,000 arguments later, Keller knew there was no escape.

> *Only one can of beer left, Naomi? One stinking lousy can of beer, cold lunchmeat, and potato salad? Leftovers after 12 hours of mental exhaustion?*
>
> *Oh, shut up, Paul! I'm so sick of you playing Mr. Important. You get leftovers because I never know when you're coming home . . . your daughter hardly knows you . . . and you treat us like nobodies . . . incidental to your great Space Program.*
>
> *Don't knock it, Naomi. That job is plenty important to me, to the Team, and it gets you everything you've ever wanted . . . more! Between this house and the boat, we're up to our ears in debt.*
>
> *Now don't try to pin our money problems on me. You're the one who has to have all the same goodies as the scientists earning twice your salary. Face it, Paul. You're just a button-pushing technician regardless of how fancy a title they give you.*

Loudspeaker: IGNITION MINUS 25 MINUTES.

A red light blinked ominously indicating a potential hydraulic fluid leak in subsystem seven of stage two. Keller felt his heartbeat and pulse rate increase. Rule 1 . . . report malfunction immediately and stop the count. Keller punched POTENTIAL ABORT on the master control.

Loudspeaker: THE COUNT IS STOPPED AT IGNITION MINUS 24 MINUTES 17 SECONDS.

Keller fumbled with the countdown instructions. Any POTENTIAL ABORT required a cross-check to separate an actual malfunction from sporadic signal error. Keller began to perspire nervously as he initiated standard cross-check procedures.

"Monitor 23, this is Control. Have you got an actual abort, Paul?" The voice in the headset was cool, but impatient. "Decision required in 30 seconds."

"I know, I know," Keller mumbled, "I'm cross-checking right now."

Cross-check one proved inconclusive. Keller automatically followed detailed instructions for cross-check two.

"Do you need help, Keller?" asked the voice in the headset.

"No, I'm O.K."

"Decision required," demanded the voice in the headset. "Dependent systems must be deactivated in 15 seconds."

Keller read and reread the console data. It looked like a sporadic error signal.

"Decision required," demanded the voice in the headset.

"Continue count," blurted Keller at last. "Subsystem seven fully operational." Keller slumped back in his chair.

Loudspeaker: THE COUNT IS RESUMED AT IGNITION MINUS 24 MINUTES 17 SECONDS.

Keller knew that within an hour after lift-off, Barksdale would call him in for a personal conference. "What's wrong lately, Paul?" he would say. "Is there anything I can help with? You seem so tense lately." But he wouldn't really want to listen. Barksdale was the kind of person who read weakness into any personal problems and demanded that they be purged from one's mind.

More likely Barksdale would demand that Keller make endless practice runs on cross-check procedures while he stood nearby . . . watching and noting any errors . . . while the pressure grew and grew.

Loudspeaker: IGNITION MINUS 20 MINUTES.

The monitor lights at console 23 blinked routinely.

"Keller," said the voice in the earphone. "Report, please."

"Control, this is Wallace at monitor 24. I don't believe Keller is feeling well. Better send someone to cover fast!"

Loudspeaker: THE COUNT IS STOPPED AT 19 MINUTES 33 SECONDS.

"This is Control, Wallace. Assistance has been dispatched and the count is on temporary hold. What seems to be wrong with Keller?"

"Control, this is Wallace, I don't know. His eyes are open and fixed on the monitor, but he won't respond to my questions. It could be a seizure or . . . a stroke."

1. Is there any way of avoiding the more serious manifestations (as with Paul Keller) of pressure on the job? Explain.

2. Are there any early warning signs given by employees under stress? If so, what are they?

3. What is the proper role of the supervisor here? Should he attempt counseling?

Source: Adapted with permission from Robert D. Joyce, *Encounters in Organizational Behavior*, pp. 168–172. Copyright 1972, Pergamon Press PLC.

EXPERIENTIAL EXERCISE I

Health Risk Appraisal

The Health Risk Appraisal form was developed by the Department of Health and Welfare of the Canadian government. Their initial testing program indicated that approximately one person out of every three who completed the form would modify some unhealthy aspects of his or her lifestyle for at least a while. Figuring the potential payoff was worth it, the government mailed out over 3 million copies of the questionnaire to Canadians who were on social security. Subsequent checking indicated that initial projections of the number of recipients altering their behavior was correct. Perhaps you will be among the one-third.

Choose from the three answers for each question the one answer that most nearly applies to you. Note that a few items may have only two alternatives.

Exercise

_____ 1. Physical effort expended during the workday: mostly?
  (a) heavy labor, walking, or housework
  (b) —
  (c) deskwork

_____ 2. Participation in physical activities—skiing, golf, swimming, etc., or lawn mowing, gardening, etc.?
  (a) daily
  (b) weekly
  (c) seldom

_____ 3. Participation in vigorous exercise program?
  (a) three times weekly
  (b) weekly
  (c) seldom

_____ 4. Average miles walked or jogged per day?
  (a) one or more
  (b) less than one
  (c) none

_____ 5. Flights of stairs climbed per day?
  (a) more than 10
  (b) 10 or fewer
  (c) —

Nutrition

_____ 6. Are you overweight?
  (a) no
  (b) 5 to 19 lbs.
  (c) 20 or more lbs.

_____ 7. Do you eat a wide variety of foods, something from each of the following five food groups: (1) meat, fish, poultry, dried legumes, eggs, or nuts; (2) milk or milk products; (3) bread or cereals; (4) fruits; (5) vegetables?
  (a) each day
  (b) three times weekly
  (c) —

Alcohol

_____ 8. Average number of bottles (12 oz.) of beer per week?
  (a) 0 to 7
  (b) 8 to 15
  (c) 16 or more
_____ 9. Average number of hard liquor (1½ oz.) drinks per week?
  (a) 0 to 7
  (b) 8 to 15
  (c) 16 or more
_____10. Average number of glasses (5 oz.) of wine or cider per week?
  (a) 0 to 7
  (b) 8 to 15
  (c) 16 or more
_____11. Total number of drinks per week including beer, liquor, or wine?
  (a) 0 to 7
  (b) 8 to 15
  (c) 16 or more

Drugs

_____12. Do you take illegal drugs?
  (a) no
  (b) —
  (c) yes
_____13. Do you consume alcoholic beverages together with certain drugs (tranquilizers, barbiturates, illegal drugs)?
  (a) no
  (b) —
  (c) yes
_____14. Do you use painkillers improperly or excessively?
  (a) no
  (b) —
  (c) yes

Tobacco

_____15. Cigarettes smoked per day?
  (a) none
  (b) less than 10
  (c) 10 or more
_____16. Cigars smoked per day?
  (a) none
  (b) less than 5
  (c) 5 or more
_____17. Pipe tobacco pouches per week?
  (a) none
  (b) 1
  (c) 2 or more

Personal Health

_____18. Do you experience periods of depression?
  (a) seldom

(b) occasionally
(c) frequently

_____19. Does anxiety interfere with your daily activities?
(a) seldom
(b) occasionally
(c) frequently

_____20. Do you get enough satisfying sleep?
(a) yes
(b) no
(c) —

_____21. Are you aware of the causes and dangers of VD?
(a) yes
(b) no
(c) —

_____22. Breast self-examination? (if not applicable, do not score)
(a) monthly
(b) occasionally
(c) —

Road and Water Safety

_____23. Mileage per year as a driver or passenger?
(a) less than 10,000
(b) 10,000 or more
(c) —

_____24. Do you often exceed the speed limit?
(a) no
(b) by 10 mph
(c) by 20 mph or more

_____25. Do you wear a seat belt?
(a) always
(b) occasionally
(c) never

_____26. Do you drive a motorcycle, moped, or snowmobile?
(a) no
(b) yes
(c) —

_____27. If yes to the above, do you always wear a regulation helmet?
(a) yes
(b) —
(c) no

_____28. Do you ever drive under the influence of alcohol?
(a) never
(b) —
(c) occasionally

_____29. Do you ever drive when your ability may be affected by drugs?
(a) never
(b) —
(c) occasionally

_____30. Are you aware of water safety rules?
(a) yes

(b) no

(c) —

_____31. If you participate in water sports or boating, do you wear a life
jacket?

(a) yes

(b) no

(c) —

General

_____32. Average time watching TV per day (in hours)?

(a) 0 to 1

(b) 1 to 4

(c) 4 or more

_____33. Are you familiar with first-aid procedures?

(a) yes

(b) no

(c) —

_____34. Do you ever smoke in bed?

(a) no

(b) occasionally

(c) regularly

_____35. Do you always make use of equipment provided for your safety at
work?

(a) yes

(b) occasionally

(c) no

To Score: Give yourself 1 point for each *a* answer; 3 points for each *b* answer; 5
points for each *c* answer. *Total Score:* _____

- A total score of 35–45 is *excellent*. You have a commendable life-style based
  on sensible habits and a lively awareness of personal health.

- A total score of 45–55 is *good*. With some minor change, you can develop an
  excellent life-style.

- A total score of 56–65 is *risky*. You are taking unnecessary risks with your
  health. Several of your habits should be changed if potential health problems are to be avoided.

- A total score of 66 and over is *hazardous*. Either you have little personal
  awareness of good health habits or you are choosing to ignore them. This is
  a danger zone.

Source: Dept. of Health and Welfare of Canada as found in J.M. Ivancevich and M.T. Matteson, *Organizational
Behavior and Management,* 2d ed. (Homewood, Ill.: BPI/Irwin, 1990), 250. Used with permission of the publisher.

EXPERIENTIAL EXERCISE II

Assessing Your Job Satisfaction

As discussed in this chapter, job satisfaction is an extremely important factor
for the well-being of both the individual and the organization. In this exercise,

you are asked to assess your feelings of job satisfaction in terms of your present job or in the kind of job you think you will have when you complete this aspect of your education.

If you are currently employed, either part-time or full-time, respond in terms of your current job. If you are not currently employed, describe your last job. If you have never worked, respond in terms of the kind of job you realistically think you will have when you start working.

Step 1   Below are 20 statements concerning characteristics or attributes of your job. For each statement, provide two ratings:

a. How much of the characteristic *is there now* associated with your job?

b. How much of the characteristic *should there be* associated with your job?

Circle the number on the scale that represents the amount of the characteristic being rated. That is, low numbers represent minimum amounts and high numbers represent maximum amounts. Thus, if you think there is very little of the characteristic associated with your job, circle 1. If you think there's a little, circle 2. If you think there is a lot of the characteristic, circle 4, and so on. For each scale, circle only one number. Please do all the scales.

1. The extent to which my job is challenging:
   a. How much is there now?   (min)   1 2 3 4 5   (max)
   b. How much should there be?   1 2 3 4 5

2. The feeling of personal accomplishment one gets from being in my job position:
   a. How much is there now?   (min)   1 2 3 4 5   (max)
   b. How much should there be?   1 2 3 4 5

3. The extent to which the pay associated with my job is appropriate:
   a. How much is there now?   (min)   1 2 3 4 5   (max)
   b. How much should there be?   1 2 3 4 5

4. The feeling of security one has in my job:
   a. How much is there now?   (min)   1 2 3 4 5   (max)
   b. How much should there be?   1 2 3 4 5

5. The opportunity one has to work closely with others and develop close friendships:
   a. How much is there now?   (min)   1 2 3 4 5   (max)
   b. How much should there be?   1 2 3 4 5

6. The extent to which one is recognized for achievements in performing my job:
   a. How much is there now?   (min)   1 2 3 4 5   (max)
   b. How much should there be?   1 2 3 4 5

7. The extent to which my job gives me prestige and status in the company:
   a. How much is there now?   (min)   1 2 3 4 5   (max)
   b. How much should there be?   1 2 3 4 5

8. The opportunity my job provides for developing a sense of responsibility:
   a. How much is there now?   (min)   1 2 3 4 5   (max)
   b. How much should there be?   1 2 3 4 5

9. The extent to which my job provides an appropriate set of fringe benefits:
   a. How much is there now? (min) 1 2 3 4 5 (max)
   b. How much should there be?   1 2 3 4 5

10. The opportunity my job provides for being involved in making decisions:
    a. How much is there now? (min) 1 2 3 4 5 (max)
    b. How much should there be?   1 2 3 4 5

11. The extent to which my job provides appropriate working conditions:
    a. How much is there now? (min) 1 2 3 4 5 (max)
    b. How much should there be?   1 2 3 4 5

12. The opportunity for autonomy (that is, independent thought and action) in my job:
    a. How much is there now? (min) 1 2 3 4 5 (max)
    b. How much should there be?   1 2 3 4 5

13. The feeling of being "in the know"—that is, having access to important or useful information in my job:
    a. How much is there now? (min) 1 2 3 4 5 (max)
    b. How much should there be?   1 2 3 4 5

14. The opportunity for participating in establishing goals and objectives for my job:
    a. How much is there now? (min) 1 2 3 4 5 (max)
    b. How much should there be?   1 2 3 4 5

15. The extent to which my job is governed by appropriate rules and procedures:
    a. How much is there now? (min) 1 2 3 4 5 (max)
    b. How much should there be?   1 2 3 4 5

16. The opportunity my job provides for meeting challenges and solving problems:
    a. How much is there now? (min) 1 2 3 4 5 (max)
    b. How much should there be?   1 2 3 4 5

17. The opportunity to earn additional income (for example, bonus, overtime) in my job beyond the normal wages:
    a. How much is there now? (min) 1 2 3 4 5 (max)
    b. How much should there be?   1 2 3 4 5

18. The feeling of being able to use my unique abilities in performing my job:
    a. How much is there now? (min) 1 2 3 4 5 (max)
    b. How much should there be?   1 2 3 4 5

19. The extent to which policies and procedures governing advancement are appropriate in my job:
    a. How much is there now? (min) 1 2 3 4 5 (max)
    b. How much should there be?   1 2 3 4 5

20. The extent to which my supervisor sees to it that every person does a fair day's work:
    a. How much is there now? (min) 1 2 3 4 5 (max)
    b. How much should there be?   1 2 3 4 5

Step 2   Compute your satisfaction/dissatisfaction score for each of the items using the table below. The extent of your satisfaction/dissatisfaction with each job characteristic is scored as the rating for (b) minus the rating for (a); that is, "how much should there be" minus "how much is there now."

1. For each question, subtract part (a)'s rating from part (b)'s rating—that is, (b) − (a).

2. Enter the (b) − (a) value for each question in the space next to the number of that question in the following columns. If (a) is greater than (b), be sure to retain the minus sign for the difference.

3. Next, add the numbers in each column to obtain a total for each category. Again, be sure to retain any minus signs.

4. Divide this total by the number of questions used to measure each category.

Remember, this adjusted score is a measure of dissatisfaction. The lower it is, the more satisfied you are. The higher it is, the more dissatisfied you are.

Intrinsic Factors		Extrinsic Factors	
1b − 1a = _____		3b − 3a = _____	
2b − 2a = _____		4b − 4a = _____	
6b − 6a = _____		5b − 5a = _____	
7b − 7a = _____		9b − 9a = _____	
8b − 8a = _____		11b − 11a = _____	
10b − 10a = _____		15b − 15a = _____	
12b − 12a = _____		17b − 17a = _____	
13b − 13a = _____		19b − 19a = _____	
14b − 14a = _____		20b − 20a = _____	
16b − 16a = _____			
18b − 18a = _____			
Total: _____		Total: _____	
Divide by:	11	Divide by:	9
Adjusted Score: _____		Adjusted Score: _____	

Step 3   Your instructor will ask you to form groups of three to five people. Each group should discuss the members' satisfaction scores in terms of:

1. The features of the job that could be viewed as responsible for each person's high and low satisfaction scores.

2. What might be done to change each job so as to lessen the dissatisfaction.

3. What type of job, for each individual, might lead to improved job satisfaction.

Step 4   Be prepared to share your responses to the previous questions with the entire class. In addition, you could discuss the implications of these findings for career planning. That is, what attributes of your job are significant in terms of satisfaction/dissatisfaction? How can such information assist you in making career decisions?

PART THREE
Organizational Structure and Dynamics

12 Communication

If you don't agree with me, it means you haven't been listening.

—*Sam Markerich*

If you don't say anything, you won't be called upon to repeat it.

—*Calvin "Silent Cal" Coolidge*

Nothing travels faster than rumor.

—*Virgil*

Whoever gossips to you will gossip about you.

—*Spanish proverb*

Learning Objectives

After studying this chapter, you should be able to:

1. List the steps in the communication process and name some obstacles to communication.
2. Identify common forms of communication in organizations.
3. Explain how a group's pattern of communication affects its performance.
4. Describe the nature of downward, upward, and horizontal communication.
5. Identify roles a person fills in an organization's communication network.
6. Identify basic dimensions of nonverbal communication.
7. Describe individual barriers to communication.
8. Describe organizational barriers to communication.
9. List techniques for improving organizational communication.

The Formidable Ritual of the Annual Performance Review

In organizations around the world, the most fundamental form of communication between supervisors and their subordinates is the annual performance review. This exercise was designed to convey the strengths and weaknesses of employee performance, tie salary increases and promotions directly to performance, and set goals and objectives for the next year. Ideally, the review would provide both a series of benchmarks to evaluate employee progress and a time to coach employees on management's expectations. But when 90 percent of employees feel that the annual performance review is ineffective and 70 percent feel that they are more confused about expectations after the review, its value has to be seriously questioned. Even W. Edward Deming, the father of quality management, referred to the annual performance review as a "deadly disease" that all employees endure each year.

Some of the typical problems with performance evaluations are that people do not like to hear bad news and supervisors find it difficult to give negative feedback. Some supervisors feel compelled to point out something wrong or areas for improvement with even the best performers. When employees receive both good and bad comments, the tendency is to dwell on the negative and downplay the positive.

Psychologist Harry Levinson outlines several reasons why managers have a difficult time giving accurate performance evaluations. These include guilt (which can occur from reprimanding someone who has family and financial responsibilities), difficulty in giving praise, and embarrassment from not knowing a lot about a specific employee. A "halo" effect can also come into play: If an employee receives a high rating on one category like "quality of work," there is a tendency to rate all other categories nearly the same for the sake of consistency. Many companies are reluctant to do away with the annual review for solid, practical reasons, including fear of wrongful-discharge lawsuits. Such lawsuits are expensive and time-consuming even if the employer wins. Employers are advised by attorneys and human resource specialists to maintain detailed documents on critical incidents or unacceptable performance that may lead to discharge. Typically, what hurts the employer in court is when the employee is consistently rated high and given regular raises, but then suddenly receives a poor rating and is fired.

If done properly, the annual performance appraisal can benefit both the employee and employer. To the employee, it can offer honest and constructive feedback that can help provide direction for employee development. To the employer, it can provide objective tracking of employee performance that can assist in making reward or termination decisions while legally protecting the company.

Source: T.D. Schellhardt, "Annual Agony: It's Time to Evaluate Your Work, and All Involved Are Groaning," *The Wall Street Journal*, November 19, 1996.

A Model of the Communication Process

True **communication** is the creation of a mental image in the mind of a receiver in exactly the same detail as intended by the sender. There are also many other definitions of communication. For example, communication can be defined as the "exchange of messages between persons for the purpose of constructing common meanings."[1] Both of these definitions suggest a view of communication that is interpersonal, involving the use of verbal and nonverbal signs and symbols to create understanding.

True, or accurate, communication is often difficult to achieve because it requires a complex sequence of steps: idea generation, encoding, transmitting via various channels, receiving, decoding, understanding, and responding. As the diagram in Figure 12.1 suggests, potential obstacles to successful communication exist at every step. These obstacles, which can be described as noise, barriers, and filters, have the potential to disrupt or alter the communication process.

To illustrate the communication process, consider the example of an inventory control clerk who determines that the supply of labels needed for packaging a product is running low. The *generation of the idea* that labels must be ordered results in the clerk's *encoding* a message consisting of symbols that will convey the desired information. In this case, the clerk's encoded message is a printed form that is sent to the purchasing agent. Encoded messages may

FIGURE 12.1 *The Communication Cycle*

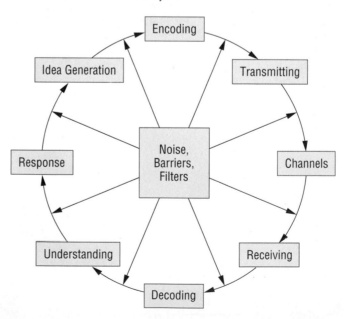

also be simple verbal instructions. The encoded message is then *transmitted* via one or more channels. For example, a memo might be transmitted by inter-office mail and a verbal instruction could be delivered personally or over the phone. In addition, several channels may be used simultaneously, as when a person verbally makes a statement and uses appropriate gestures and facial expressions to emphasize its meaning.

Receiving the message involves attending to and actually perceiving a written, spoken, or otherwise transmitted message. Reception is then followed by *decoding*, which involves deciphering the message. The receiver's personality, prior experience, and intellect may intervene at this stage. *Understanding* results from the decoding process. However, understanding is often imperfect. To the extent that the decoded message matches the encoded message, we can say that understanding has been achieved.

The final step in this cyclical process is the receiver's *response* to the communicative effort. This response may take the form of action or inaction. In our example, the purchasing agent may act by ordering more labels, or telling the clerk that labels will no longer be needed because of a change in the packaging process. This response, or action, serves as a form of feedback to the initiator of the process and determines the nature of any subsequent efforts at communication.

Because communication involves so many steps, numerous factors can intervene to confound the process. For example, the encoded message may not accurately correspond to the intended message because of the sender's poor choice of words, or the response may not accurately reflect the intent of the receiver as a result of forces outside of the receiver's control.

As this discussion implies, continually successful communication can be difficult to achieve. This fact contributes to the widespread belief that poor communication is responsible for many problems within organizations and that many larger problems would be resolved if only people tried to improve their communication skills. However, it has been pointed out that although communication may be at the root of many problems, it is possible to overestimate its role.[2] For example, *more* communication is not necessarily *better* communication. Furthermore, difficulties in communication may really be the symptom or outcome of another problem, rather than the cause of the target problem.

To keep the proper perspective, it is crucial to recognize that communication is a social process that includes both perception and influence. The accurate conveyance and reception of a message, plus the impact that the message has on the receiver, are equally important in explaining the phenomenon of communication.

Types of Communication

In organizations, there are several common forms of interpersonal communication. By far, the most frequently used form is the spoken word, since it is usually the quickest. In addition, oral communication is likely to be quite accurate because messages can be clarified through ongoing dialogue. Written communication is also important within organizations. Employees devote large portions of their workdays to expressing ideas in written form.[*] Memos, letters, reports, faxes, order forms, electronic mail, and the like can serve as permanent records, which enhance their precision and clarity in comparison to oral communication.

A third form of interpersonal communication, **nonverbal communication,** consists of unspoken cues that a communicator sends in conjunction with a spoken or written message. For example, through hand gestures, nodding, and posture, a speaker can underscore his or her spoken words. Sometimes, however, nonverbal cues may seem to contradict the content of the spoken word, as when a speaker smiles while announcing bad news. In such instances, sorting out the intended content can be a challenge for the receiver.

Nonverbal communication may also take the form of symbols. For example, the uniform a person wears or the specific form on which a message is written can convey additional information to the receiver. The topic of nonverbal communication will be examined more closely later in this chapter.

Communication Networks

The formal structure of relationships in an organization can affect various aspects of the communication process. Research on the impact of structure on communication has focused on how different kinds of **networks,** or patterns of relationships, influence communication. Of special interest has been the effect of a network's degree of centralization on the communication process. Figure 12.2 illustrates the amount of centralization in five different types of five-person communication networks that have been closely studied. The **centralized networks** are characterized by their members' differing abilities to obtain and pass on information. Note that in each centralized network, information must flow through a pivotal or *central* person (indicated by an X in Figure 12.2). In contrast, in a **decentralized network,** each member has an equal opportunity to participate in the communication process.

The formal study of networks has relied on the creation of experimental conditions in which subjects are placed in cubicles and permitted to communicate only with prespecified members of their group. From such studies, some fairly reliable results have emerged.[4]

Generally, members of decentralized networks report greater satisfaction, while the more centralized a structure is, the lower the satisfaction of its members. Wheel networks generate the lowest satisfaction ratings, while completely connected networks produce the highest ratings. Apparently, the more group members must depend on others for information and decision making, the less they enjoy their participation.

The networks also differ in their effectiveness in handling various kinds of problems. For relatively simple and routine tasks, when the goal is to finish a task quickly and make few mistakes, centralized networks are more efficient. But for complex tasks that require the sharing of information, decentralized networks have a relative advantage.

---

[*]In one review of the literature on managerial communication, it was concluded that managers generally overestimate the amount of time they spend reading and writing, and tend to underestimate the amount of time they spend talking.[3]

FIGURE 12.2   *Five Types of Group Communication Networks*

Centralized

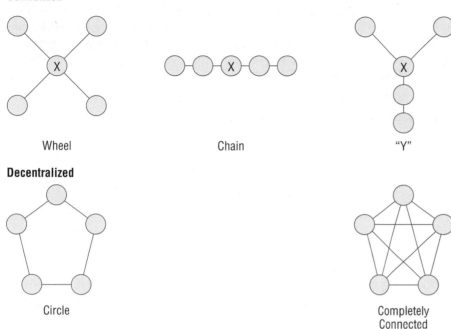

Wheel   Chain   "Y"

Decentralized

Circle   Completely
                                        Connected

Each circle represents a person, and an X indicates the most central position.

The nature of the task has also been found to influence the formation of a communication pattern. In one study, subjects were placed in completely connected networks and assigned several simple problems to solve.[5] Next, the subjects were asked to tackle a set of relatively complex tasks. When the groups worked on the simple tasks, they tended to adopt a centralized structure, converting into a wheel. However, as the tasks became more complex, the persons occupying the more central role felt that the demands on them were too great, and the groups reverted to their original, more decentralized structure.

The appearance of a single leader tends to occur more frequently in centralized networks due to the existence of a hub, or pivotal position. The greater availability of information to the hub occupant, plus the relative dependency of others on him or her for information and decision making, leads to the emergence of the hub occupant as a leader. By being such a critical link in the network, the person in the hub position comes to dominate group accomplishment. Furthermore, this person is typically the most satisfied of the group's members.

Centralized networks are also more prone to information overload. Members who occupy the more central positions experience greater requirements being placed on them to be effective. In a decentralized network, information and, ultimately, decision making are shared. As a result, no single position is easily overloaded.

The implications of these results are fairly direct. Communication patterns should be established to best serve the dual purposes of enhancing task accomplishment and group satisfaction. The nature of the task to be performed, to a large extent, dictates the appropriate network, but attention must also be paid to the social consequences of an assigned network or pattern of relationships. Below a certain level, group dissatisfaction can have serious negative effects, including lack of commitment to decisions and increased turnover. Therefore, when selecting a communication structure for a work group, a manager should consider both member morale and the goals of the task.

The Direction of Communication

In an organization, messages may travel in several directions: downward, upward, and laterally (horizontally).

Downward Communication

Downward communication travels from the upper levels of an organization to the lower levels. Traditionally, such downward flows of communication occur one step at a time, with no intermediate levels excluded. The primary kinds of messages that travel downward in organizations include job instructions and directives, explanations of tasks and their relationship to other tasks, feedback on individual performance, statements of organizational policies and practices, and statements of mission designed to indoctrinate the members with established goals.[6] Information sent downward often becomes condensed or distorted as it passes through various levels. Therefore, the originator of a downward message should check whether it was accurately received at its intended destination.

Another problem with downward communication is that its recipients tend to interpret it as a sign of dissatisfaction in the upper levels of the organization. This common perception reflects the belief that if upper management takes the time to send a memo, they must have detected an exception to the norm that needs correction.

Upward Communication

Upward communication travels from the lower levels of an organization to the upper levels. The most common kinds of information that flow upward in an organization include suggestions for improving work procedures, information on progress and goal attainment, requests for assistance, and individual reactions to work and nonwork issues.[7]

A number of obstacles may deter upward communication. For example, many employees feel that they will be rebuked if they speak up to their supervisors, and employees who hope to obtain promotions and other rewards are less likely to be outspoken. In addition, like downward communication, upward communication is subject to condensation and distortion.

Upward and downward communication are not simply reverse processes, however. Differences in authority between levels can alter the accuracy, frequency,

An Inside Look
Getting the Messages Across

In some ways, technology may make our lives easier, but not necessarily when it involves communication in the workplace. The telephone used to be the only way we could communicate electronically. Today, the list is much longer: voice mail, e-mail, cellular phones, pagers, and faxes. The traditional non-electronic forms of communication (such as mail) are still with us, but the emphasis is on faster delivery with overnight shipment. One study of 972 employees in major corporations showed that the average employee sends and receives an average of 178 messages per day. No doubt this number will increase as technology grows and develops.

Technology-based message overload can create new problems in the workplace. The instant electronic message can create a strong, but false, sense of urgency and immediacy. Since people are compelled to respond to each communication they receive, it can easily seem that one is continually putting out fires rather then addressing problems or projects that require attention, critical thinking, and analysis. Also, frustration results when one is continually pulled away from important tasks. Losing control creates anxiety that affects total job performance. To complicate the situation, instantaneous e-mail can be sent "High Priority," which elevates the urgency of the response. And, since e-mail systems can tell the sender if a message has been received and read, the feeling of a need to respond immediately is heightened.

One might think that e-mail is replacing other forms of communication, but it is not. A study sponsored by Pitney Bowes, Inc. discovered that often e-mail is "layered over existing messages, increasing the communications load." Many people routinely send an e-mail, then follow up with a voice-mail message: "I just sent you an e-mail."

Some business professionals feel that the phenomenon of "instant message/instant reply" can be a significant advantage. Being available to customers or clients 100 percent of the time can create a stronger sense of responsiveness. Performance and customer service may be judged not only by the quality of a response, but by the immediacy of the instantaneous response.

Source: A. Markels, "Memo 4/8/97, FYI: Messages Inundate Offices," *The Wall Street Journal*, April 8, 1997.

and effect of these two forms of communication. For instance, lower-level employees are expected to react quickly to communications from above, and high-level employees have the authority to monitor their reactions and issue follow-up orders. On the other hand, higher-level employees are not formally obligated to respond quickly, if at all, to communications from subordinates. In fact, an upper-level employee who is highly responsive to communications from below risks giving the appearance of "letting the tail wag the dog." Furthermore, a lower-level employee is not normally expected to remind superiors of previous messages or to monitor their final reaction to a message. Thus, employees who occupy lower-level positions receive less feedback about the impact of their upward communications than do higher-level employees about their downward communications.

Horizontal Communication

Horizontal communication consists of messages sent between employees who occupy the same level within an organization. Examples include communication between members of different departments or between coworkers in a single department. Because employees are grouped into departments, or sometimes work in relative isolation from others who occupy parallel positions, there is typically little opportunity for horizontal communication. Yet, coordination of actions sometimes necessitates that employees communicate quickly without going through the process of sending messages up the organizational hierarchy and then down the appropriate branch.

To address this problem, it has been suggested that a formal communication channel, or gangplank, should sometimes be laid between units to facilitate cooperation.[8] Figure 12.3 provides an example of how a gangplank would work. In this situation, units may communicate directly only if they share a linkage, as indicated by the solid lines. If unlinked units wish to communicate, they must send their messages through higher levels of the organization until a shared link is reached. For example, if unit 3 wanted to communicate with unit 11, it would have to route its message up to unit 6, which would then pass the message back down again. To increase speed and accuracy, one would open a new channel of communication directly between units 3 and 11, as shown by the dotted line.

Communication Roles

The specific functions a person serves in an organization's communication network may constitute his or her **communication role.** Four roles have been identified that organizational members may play: gatekeeper, liaison, isolate, and cosmopolite.[9]

Gatekeepers

A **gatekeeper** is an individual who passes information to others or controls messages. Common examples of gatekeepers are secretaries and assistants to upper-level managers. A gatekeeper who has the ability to control the sub-

FIGURE 12.3   *An Illustration of the Gangplank Principle*

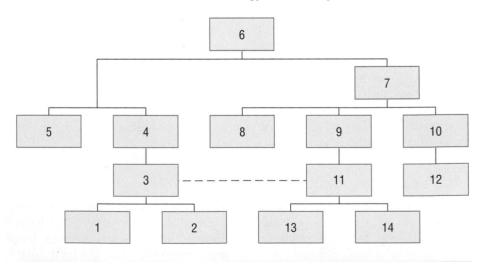

stance and/or the timing of the information that is given to a decision maker can actually influence the final decision.[10] Because the risk of information overload is greater at higher organizational levels, top-level managers come to rely heavily on gatekeepers to condense and edit incoming messages. As a result of this greater trust, gatekeepers tend to have increasing influence at higher levels in an organization.

Liaisons

An individual who serves as a communication link between groups, but is not a member of either group, is a **liaison.** This person serves as a bridge between groups that need to exchange messages. The gatekeeping function is implicit, to a degree, in the liaison role. Firms that use liaisons to link departments are relatively more effective than firms that do not.[11]

Isolates

An **isolate** is someone who has very little or no contact with other members of the organization. Certain jobs, such as night guard and messenger, are characterized by a lack of sustained contact with others in an organization. Yet some people whose jobs offer more opportunities for contact may still remain uninformed. They may consciously choose not to socialize with coworkers or participate in grapevines. Feelings of alienation tend to be associated with such social isolation. Evidence suggests that isolates are somewhat younger, less educated, less satisfied, and poorer performers.[12]

Cosmopolites

A **cosmopolite** is a person whose communication network frequently extends into the organization's external environment. By definition, cosmopolites have a greater interest in national, rather than local, affairs and tend to have stronger professional affiliations. They are also more likely to change jobs than are other employees. Like liaisons, cosmopolites can serve a gatekeeping function in that the organization's contact with and information from the outside world must be passed through them.

Nonverbal Communication

As mentioned at the outset of this chapter, two people can exchange information without the use of words. Through nonverbal communication, people use facial expressions, gestures, manner of dress, and the larger social context to convey silent messages. In popular terms, this type of communication is sometimes referred to as "body language." However, despite the suggestions of several best-selling books on this topic, there is not yet—nor is there likely to be—a "magical way to know employees' or customers' thoughts without having to ask them."[13] There is no precise key for translating nonverbal signals into consistently reliable messages. For example, while a clenched fist may indicate anger, many individuals also clench their fists when they are nervous.

Dimensions of Nonverbal Communication

Despite these limitations, it is possible to attribute limited meaning to certain general patterns of behavior in many situations. Nonverbal communication can be understood in terms of several fairly basic dimensions.[14]

Immediacy   Nonverbal signs may be interpreted in terms of their **immediacy.** Generally, people approach other people and objects that they like and desire, and withdraw from those that they evaluate negatively. This simple concept explains much of the hidden meaning in nonverbal messages. For example, we lean toward someone or ask many questions if we find them interesting or attractive, and we pull away or lean back (or even push our chair back) if we prefer to avoid involvement. When we wish to end a conversation, we often make abbreviated walking-away motions, for example, making little circles as we gradually walk farther away. Such motions are intended to convey the message that we are getting ready to leave (a message that may not be accepted, although it is usually understood, by the other person). Similarly, giving a very firm and long handshake to a person conveys a message of desired immediacy. Too prolonged a handshake, however, can make another person extremely nervous and uncomfortable, especially at a first meeting.

Total attraction toward another person can be understood in terms of the combined effects of the actual spoken words, the vocal expression of the message, and the facial expressions accompanying the message. Spoken words are the actual words in the message and their meaning is self-evident. Vocal expression involves the intonation and inflection in a spoken message.[†] Facial expressions refer to the clearly nonverbal aspects of the message. Mehrabian and Wiener have provided evidence suggesting that the total feeling or reaction one has to another's communication can be understood in accordance with the following approximate equation:[15]

Total feeling = 7% verbal feeling + 38% vocal feeling + 55% facial feeling.

Notice that facial expressions are far more important than verbal content in explaining how people react to a message. Therefore, it is not *what* is said but *how* it is said (that is, facial feeling plus vocal expression) that largely determines meaning. In short, whether the boss is smiling or grimacing while saying you're one of the most unusual employees he or she has ever known makes all the difference!

Power   A second dimension that enters into the interpretation of nonverbal communication is **power.**[16] Generally, the relative status of individuals can be inferred from how they relate to each other nonverbally. A person of higher status can assume a relaxed posture in the presence of others, but a person of lower status is expected to display a more tense body posture when superiors are present. Asymmetric postures, such as putting your feet on your desk or leaning your head on your arm, are considered acceptable for people of high

---

[†]Consider how changing the accent in the following sentence can dramatically alter the meaning:
The auditor will be HERE Tuesday.
The AUDITOR will be here Tuesday.
The auditor will be here TUESDAY.

status but are unacceptable when in the presence of people of higher status. The posture of people of lower status is expected to resemble the military posture of "attention." It has been suggested that the relatively more symmetric body postures of women reflect a lower-status position in society.[17]

Many of the preceding points can be used to explain why people dislike dealing with strangers. The uneasiness that commonly arises from dealing with strangers grows partly out of concern over how the other person will react to us. One study suggests that if a person wants to be liked by others, including strangers, it helps simply to smile more and be more positive in new situations.[18] People differ greatly in their predisposition to be positive or negative when meeting others. Such differences are significant because this predisposition tends to shade the quality of the relationships that later develop. Young people first entering the job market often fail to take advantage of nonverbal ways of conveying interest and positive emotion during job interviews. Many people who might otherwise be very good employees are not hired because they unwittingly convey negativism and dislike to an interviewer by avoiding eye contact and displaying "withdrawing" gestures (as a result of nervousness and self-consciousness). In essence, the greatest need of the "nonverbally handicapped" is an awareness of their own style and the impact that it has on those around them.

Proxemics

In his notion of **proxemics**, Edward Hall, an anthropologist, contends that physical space serves an important purpose in communication.[19] People tend to stand at a predictable distance from each other in accordance with the specific roles they occupy. For example, we tend to stand farther away from strangers than from people with whom we are intimate. When we find ourselves thrust together with strangers, as in elevators or on subway trains, we try very hard to avoid giving nonverbal signals that could be interpreted as inappropriate. For example, we do not smile or gaze for very long at a stranger when riding an elevator. If caught staring at someone, we are expected to smile (to show no mean intent) and then to avert our gaze (preferably to watching the elevator's floor indicator or our shoes).

Hall suggests that in North America there are definable **personal space zones:**

1. *Intimate zone (0 to 2 feet).* To be this close, we must have an intimate association with the other person or be socially domineering.
2. *Personal zone (2 to 4 feet).* Within this zone, we should be fairly well acquainted with the other individual.
3. *Social zone (4 to 12 feet).* In this zone, we are at least minimally acquainted with the other person and have a definite purpose for seeking to communicate. Most behavior in the business world occurs in this zone.
4. *Public zone (beyond 12 feet).* When people are more than 12 feet away, we treat them as if they did not exist. We may look at others from this distance, provided our gaze does not develop into a stare.[20]

Related to the notion of personal space is the concept of **territory.** Unlike personal space, which each of us carries with us, territory is assigned to a specific physical location. In terms of territory, there are many interesting analogies between human behavior in organizational settings and animal behavior. For example, more dominant animals have larger territories than less dominant animals.[21] Dominant animals visit the turf of lesser animals, but lesser animals do not visit the territories of their superiors. If a lesser animal does approach the territory of a dominant animal or the animal itself, it shows signs of nervousness and submission. Similarly, in organizational settings, employees of higher status have larger offices than employees of lower status; supervisors intrude on the work space of employees, but employees do not intrude on the work space of supervisors; and if an employee wants to enter a superior's office, he or she will usually stand at the doorway and ask, "Are you busy?"

In one famous study of behavior in work settings, the relations of kitchen workers and other restaurant employees were observed.[22] In the process, it was noted that the kitchen workers had a proprietary attitude (akin to a sense of territory) toward the kitchen area itself. If other employees entered the kitchen area, the routine pattern of social interaction was disrupted. Lower-status "invaders" were often openly blocked from entering, while higher-status invaders (who could not be blocked) were tolerated until their departure.

Spatial Arrangements

The arrangement of furniture, such as desks and chairs, affects the frequency and nature of interpersonal communication. The areas that drive people away from each other can be termed **sociofugal**, while those that bring people together can be termed **sociopetal**.[23] In several studies of hospital waiting areas, it was found that arranging furniture around the perimeter of a room was one of the surest ways to decrease social interaction.[‡]

However, simply restructuring the workplace to minimize social communication will not necessarily increase productivity.[25] As an example, consider the case of a young manager who attempted to increase worker productivity by decreasing the amount of time workers devoted to social interaction. To accomplish this, he rearranged the workers' equipment to make it difficult for them to speak to each other while they were at their posts. Although the amount of social communication on the job did decrease, so did the level of output.

Time

Although this form of nonverbal communication is more subtle in nature, status can be conveyed by the use of time. The way in which a request is phrased ("As soon as possible . . ." or "At your convenience . . .") implies how urgent the request is and how it should be approached. Arriving late for a social occasion, such as a business meeting or a dinner, may convey any number of different messages, including carelessness, lack of interest, and lack of ambition. Yet, the late arrival of a person of high status invariably reaffirms their relative social superiority. Their tardiness implies that they have a very busy schedule and that others will understand and forgive them. The same generosity does not extend to individuals of low status who are late. People who arrive 15 or

---

[‡]Intriguingly, the arrangement of furniture in many college dormitory lounges is similar to that of dayrooms in mental hospitals.[24]

so minutes *early* for an event are typically regarded as low in status and also as relatively lacking in sociability.[26]

Individual Barriers to Communication

Differences in Status

As we have seen throughout this text, status strongly influences people's behavior in organizations. Their willingness to listen to and react to an attempt at communication differs in response to the status of the communicator. Generally, employees are more responsive to, and even solicitous of, communication from people of equal or higher status. Moreover, managers report that they tend to find it more valuable and personally satisfying to communicate with superiors than with subordinates.[27] Given this bias, upward communication is often understandably less effective and less likely to elicit change.

The Credibility of the Source

The source of a communication can greatly influence whether the receiver accepts or rejects the message. For communication to be effective, its source should be credible. And a source who combines power and attractiveness with credibility is likely to be an especially effective communicator. People also respond better to sources who are similar to themselves. That is why politicians often emphasize the traits and experiences that they have in common with their audience.

Perceptual Biases

According to an old saying, people tend to hear what they want to hear. To be sure, this phenomenon is as common in organizations as it is in society in general. Employees may "tune out" what they do not wish to recognize, which is a form of selective perception keyed to their dominant needs and interests. When people are confronted with information that they find unsettling or distasteful, they are also likely to ignore it. This process is partly responsible for the failure of employees to accept critical comments during performance appraisal interviews.

Organizational Barriers to Communication

Information Overload

When an abundance of information is directed to a single position within an organization, decoding and interpreting the messages can become overwhelming. The primary result of such **information overload** is diminished effectiveness. In designing information channels, it is important to consider the amount and complexity of information that can be reasonably handled by one person. In addition, the amount of time it takes to examine and reach an understanding of messages must be taken into account. Two effective ways of eliminating information overload are to encourage employees to screen their messages and to encourage senders to condense their messages and send only essential information.

Time Pressures

The need to take quick action in response to a problem may require that information be sent out or requested on short notice. Such urgency can lead to superficiality and poor timing of communication. For example, data may not be detailed enough or they may arrive too late for employees to act on them. For communication to be effective, it must arrive at an appropriate time, as well as be accurate and complete.

Organizational Climate

The larger social system within an organization can be a barrier to effective communication. If the climate is one of openness and trust, then incomplete or controversial communications are more likely to be interpreted favorably. But when distrust is the norm, messages may be harshly scrutinized for "hidden meanings," and even good news may be greeted with suspicion and ridicule.

Technology

While we normally think of technology as a tremendous aid for speeding communication (e.g., via fax messages, voice mail, e-mail, teleconferencing, and the Internet), it is also true that the peculiarities of newer technologies can contribute to various forms of misunderstanding. For example, many novice users suffer from anxiety associated with using new technology. Some people may also be less responsive to electronic communications than they would be to person-to-person contact. Communication via these technologies is also likely to be less candid because of employee fear that messages are not fully confidential.[28] Also, telecommuters report that they feel greater social isolation because of their reduced contact with coworkers.

Informal Communication

Up to this point, we have focused on formal communication in organizational settings, but most organizations also have numerous pathways of informal communication. Because employees are generally free to exchange information with one another as part of their jobs, little can or should be done to directly control or eliminate such informal communication. Although informal networks may serve useful functions by cutting red tape and leading to greater loyalty through positive social relations, they may also give birth to pathways called **grapevines**.[§] Although organizational theorists generally regard grapevines as inevitable outgrowths of organizational structure,[30] most managers believe they have a negative impact on organizational functioning.

[§]The term *grapevine* is believed to have originated during the Civil War, when telegraph lines were sometimes strung from tree to tree, resembling grapevines. Because of their jerry-rigged nature, these telegraph systems often generated ambiguous and garbled messages. Hence, distorted messages were said to "come from the grapevine."[29]

Because they are flexible and personal, grapevines may be one of the most rapid communication systems that exist in most organizations. In one outstanding example of the speed of grapevines, it was determined that nearly half the managers in an organization knew within only 13 hours that another manager's wife had given birth to a baby (the birth had occurred at 11:00 P.M.).[31] The remarkable speed of grapevines can be attributed to the fact that their messages are oral rather than written. Moreover, people enjoy passing on timely information because it makes them appear in touch and well informed, and there is social value attached to bringing surprising news to others.

Figure 12.4 summarizes three types of grapevines that have been identified.[32] Some grapevines operate as a single-strand, chain system in which one member tells another, who in turn tells another, and so on. However, such grapevines are actually fairly uncommon. Most organizational grapevines operate as a cluster system in which a few individuals inform a cluster, or set, of other people. In one example, over three-quarters of the managers of a firm knew of an executive's plan to resign, but only 11 percent of those managers conveyed the rumor to another person. A third type of grapevine, the gossip system, occurs when a single member nonselectively communicates with everyone he or she meets. Most organizational grapevines are cluster systems, with occasional "gossips" rapidly accelerating the rate of spread.

Studies of grapevine behavior have yielded interesting results. One study of the accuracy of 30 rumors dealing with such topics as pay raises, profit sharing, promotions, and transfers found that 16 of the rumors were untrue, 9 were accurate, and 5 were only partly correct.[33] Other studies, however, have indicated that the accuracy of grapevines is usually quite high, especially when the information is noncontroversial.[34] With controversial information, the grapevine can be greatly in error. In light of these findings, it is perhaps not too surprising that a large proportion of employees view grapevines as their central source of information about events within their organizations.[35]

FIGURE 12.4 *Three Types of Grapevine Systems*

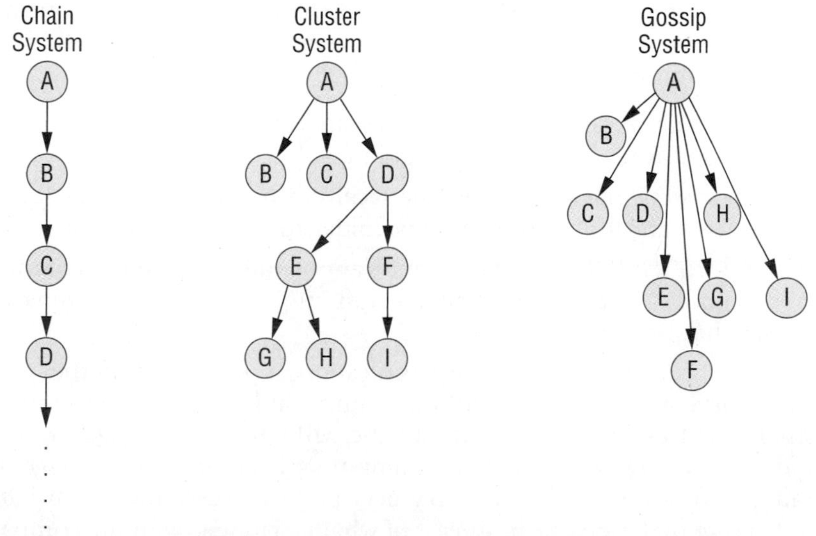

Of the varieties of information that are passed through grapevines, rumors are of special interest. **Rumors** are unverified beliefs that are transmitted from one person to another. Because rumors can harm both individuals and the organization itself, managers must consider how to control and eliminate rumor mills. For example, in one widespread rumor based on a misinterpretation of its corporate logo, which showed a moon and stars, Procter and Gamble was accused of promoting satanism. The company was finally forced to discontinue its use of the emblem. In another case, McDonald's was rumored to be selling hamburgers that contained worms, which forced the company to mount an advertising campaign emphasizing the purity and nutritiousness of its product. These rumors involve customer (rather than employee) perceptions, and show the potential harm that rumors can do to customer relations and possibly sales.

To cope with rumors, one should consider the following techniques:

1. Try to wait them out. Some rumors dissipate over time and do little actual harm.

2. If waiting does not work, publicly refute the rumor. Refuting and even ridiculing a rumor in public negates its "news value." This approach may also lead people to distrust those who later attempt to pass the rumor along.

3. Feed valid information into the grapevine to counteract the undesired message.[36]

This last point suggests a possible positive feature of grapevines. Managers can use grapevines to serve organizational purposes by "leaking" positive information to grapevine members. For example, through the grapevine, a manager may be able to influence employees' reactions to proposed changes in work procedures.

Improving Organizational Communication

Effective communication of all kinds is crucial to the success of every organization. Here are a number of suggestions for improving the effectiveness of organizational communication.[37]

1. *Use appropriate language.* Words, gestures, and symbols should be appropriate to the receiver's level of understanding.

2. *Practice empathic communication.* The receiver's frame of reference (that is, assumptions and attitudes) should be understood by the communicator.

3. *Encourage feedback.* Two-way communications can improve the communication process. Through feedback, a communicator can check whether a message has been accurately received.

4. *Develop a climate of trust.* Communication is enhanced if the participants have a trusting relationship. Gaining and maintaining the trust of others requires continual effort and the willingness to engage in honest and frank dialogue. At Tandem Computers headquarters, management and employees have regular Friday beer parties to exchange information and ensure that everyone is abreast of what is happening in the company.

5. *Use appropriate media.* Not all forms of organizational communication are equally appropriate for all purposes. Rather, the form of communication should match the situation. Oral communication is best for discussing employee problems, such as tardiness and poor performance. Written communication is best in matters that require future action, but it is too slow for issues that call for quick action, and too impersonal for discussing employee problems. A combination of oral communication followed by written communication is best for conveying information that requires quick action, job-specific directions, and procedural changes.

6. *Encourage effective listening.* Listening habits can also be improved. Among the techniques that encourage more effective listening are avoiding evaluative judgments, listening to the total meaning of the sender's message, and offering responsive feedback (sometimes called *active listening*) about the listener's degree of understanding. Active listening, which involves restating the speaker's remarks and reflecting on them, conveys the message that the listener is interested in the speaker as a person, and feels that what is being said is important.[38]

SUMMARY

1. *List the steps in the communication process and name some obstacles to communication.* The steps in the communication process are generation of an idea, encoding, transmitting, receiving, decoding, understanding, and responding. Obstacles to communication are noise, barriers, and filters.

2. *Identify common forms of communication in organizations.* Common forms of communication in organizations are oral communication, written communication, and nonverbal communication.

3. *Explain how a group's pattern of communication affects its performance.* The more group members must depend on others for information and decision making, the less satisfied they are. Centralized communication networks are most effective for quickly and accurately accomplishing simple and routine tasks. Decentralized networks are preferable for complex tasks that require the sharing of information. Centralized networks more often have a single leader. Members of centralized networks are more prone to information overload.

4. *Describe the nature of downward, upward, and horizontal communication.* Downward communication travels from the upper to the lower levels of an organization, ideally one step at a time. Upward communication travels from a lower level to upper levels of an organization. Horizontal communication travels between employees who occupy the same level of an organization. Often such communication is informal.

5. *Identify roles a person fills in an organization's communication network.* Communication roles consist of gatekeepers, liaisons, isolates, and cosmopolites. Gatekeepers pass information to others or control messages. Liaisons serve as communication links between groups but are not members of those groups. Isolates have little or no contact with other members of the organization. Cosmopolites have communication networks that extend into the organization's external environment.

6. *Identify basic dimensions of nonverbal communication.* Nonverbal signals may be interpreted in terms of their immediacy (the degree to which people approach or withdraw from others) and the relative status or power of the people in the transaction.

7. *Describe individual barriers to communication.* Differences in status inhibit the effectiveness of upward communication. A source that lacks credibility communicates less effectively. Perceptual biases also interfere with communication; specifically, people may tune out messages that are unsettling or distasteful.

8. *Describe organizational barriers to communication.* Organizational barriers include information overload (too much information directed to a single position), time pressures, technology, and an organizational climate of distrust.

9. *List techniques for improving organizational communication.* Techniques for improving communication in organizations are: using appropriate language, practicing empathic communication, encouraging feedback, developing a climate of trust, using appropriate media, and encouraging effective listening.

KEY TERMS

Communication
Nonverbal communication
Networks
Centralized networks
Decentralized networks
Downward communication
Upward communication
Horizontal communication
Communication role
Gatekeeper
Liaison
Isolate

Cosmopolite
Immediacy
Power
Proxemics
Personal space zones
Territory
Sociofugal areas
Sociopetal areas
Information overload
Grapevine
Rumors

CRITICAL INCIDENT

A Failure to Communicate

Jeff Williams, M.D., is head of surgery at a major urban hospital. Most of his time is spent in administrative duties such as handling budgets, coordinating facility use, working with staff and resident surgeons, meeting with hospital administrators, serving on hospital committees, and handling complaints.

Dr. Williams relies a great deal on his administrative assistant, Jackie Jones, to handle many of the day-to-day matters. Jackie has worked at the hospital for 12 years, the last 3 in surgery. Dr. Williams has been head of surgery for six months. Because of his position and the nature of surgery, Dr. Williams often works nontraditional hours. He therefore leaves work for Jackie on her desk with brief instructions.

Jackie arrived at work Thursday morning to find a small stack of papers with an accompanying note that read, "Please complete these as soon as possible." Among the papers were a request for transfer and some items concerning the budget. Jackie felt that these were the most important items so she addressed them first. After carefully checking them, she passed them on to a secretary for typing.

It was almost 4:00 and Jackie was preparing to leave. Dr. Williams hurried into her work area and asked for the budget information. Jackie explained that it was being typed and that they would have it sometime the next morning. Dr. Williams became rather agitated because he had a 7:00 A.M. breakfast meeting and needed that information immediately.

Jackie rushed over to the secretary, only to discover that she had not even started typing the budget proposal. Jackie felt there was no other recourse but to type it herself. She returned to her work area to find Dr. Williams waiting. "The budget isn't ready," she explained, "so I'm going to stay and prepare it myself." Dr. Williams was glad to hear that Jackie would have it ready, but he also was concerned that she did not have it available already.

Jackie became rather assertive and said, "Ready now? Nothing in your note said you needed it by this afternoon." Dr. Williams picked up his in-struction sheet and said, "It reads, right here, that they should be done as soon as possible."

1. What went wrong in the communication process?

2. Which person was in error in terms of failing to communicate?

3. How could this situation have been prevented?

Source: Written by Bruce Kemelgor, University of Louisville.

EXPERIENTIAL EXERCISE

Are You Really Listening?

Listening is probably one of the most important skills anyone can develop. It is used in all interpersonal verbal transactions and is essential for understanding to occur between sender and receiver. Effective listening is more than simply re-ceiving a message, however. Effective listening involves active participation in helping a speaker be understood. Thus, someone who has actively listened has an understanding of both what was said and what was meant.

The skill of active listening involves using responses that do not offer advice or opinion. The response simply captures the listener's understanding of what the speaker is saying and why. This opens up the communication process so that the speaker knows that the listener actually *heard* what was said. A more meaningful conversation, free of initial judgmental roadblocks, can then ensue.

Step 1   Below are some statements that were made by employees to their man-ager. Read each statement and select the response that best represents active listening by placing an X next to it.

1. Each day brings new problems. You solve one and here comes another. . . . What's the use?
   _____ a. I'm surprised to hear you say that.
   _____ b. That's the way it is. There's no use getting upset over it.
   _____ c. I know it's frustrating and sometimes discouraging to run into problem after problem.
   _____ d. Give me an example so I know what you're referring to.

2. At our meeting yesterday, I was counting on you for some support. All you did was sit there and you never said anything!

_____ a. I was expecting you to ask for my opinion.

_____ b. You're evidently upset with the way I handled things at the meeting.

_____ c. Hey, I said some things on your behalf. You must not have heard me.

_____ d. I had my reasons for being quiet.

3. I don't know when I'm going to get that report done. I'm already swamped with work.

_____ a. See if you can get someone to help you.

_____ b. All of us have been in that situation, believe me.

_____ c. What do you mean swamped?

_____ d. You sound concerned about your workload.

4. I've been scheduled to be out of town again on Friday. This is the third weekend in a row that's been messed up!

_____ a. Why don't you talk with someone higher up and get it changed?

_____ b. Going on the road must be a burden to you.

_____ c. Everyone has to be on the road—it's part of the job.

_____ d. I'm sure this is the last trip you'll have to make for a while.

5. It seems like other people are always getting the easy jobs. How come I always get the hard ones?

_____ a. You feel I'm picking on you and that I'm being unfair in assigning work.

_____ b. What evidence do you have for saying that?

_____ c. If you'd look at the work schedule, you'd see that everyone has hard and easy jobs.

_____ d. What about that job I gave you yesterday?

6. When I first joined this company, I thought there would be plenty of chances to move up. Here I am, four years later, still doing the same thing.

_____ a. Let's talk about some of the things you could do to be promoted.

_____ b. Maybe you just haven't worked hard enough.

_____ c. Don't worry, I'm sure your chance will come soon.

_____ d. Getting ahead must be important to you. You sound disappointed.

7. Performance evaluations are here again. I wish I could just give all my people good ratings—it sure would be easier.

_____ a. I know, but that's not possible.

_____ b. We all feel that way. Don't get upset over it.

_____ c. Performance evaluations seem to bother you.

_____ d. Just do the best you can.

8. It's the same old thing day in and day out. Any child could do this job!
   _____ a. Your work is evidently getting you down and making you feel useless.
   _____ b. I always thought you liked your job.
   _____ c. What good is complaining going to do?
   _____ d. If you've got some ideas on improving your job, I'll be happy to listen.

9. I really appreciate getting the promotion. I just hope I can do the job.
   _____ a. Don't worry. I'm sure you'll get better as you get more experience.
   _____ b. What makes you think you can't do the job?
   _____ c. Don't worry. Most people have those same feelings.
   _____ d. I'm sure you can do it, or you wouldn't have been promoted.

10. I'm tired. That last sale really wore me out. I don't think I can handle another customer.
    _____ a. Sure you can. Just rest a few minutes and you'll be fine.
    _____ b. What have you been doing that's gotten you so tired?
    _____ c. You sound like you're exhausted.
    _____ d. We all get to feeling that way; don't worry about it.

Step 2 Your instructor has information about the appropriate responses. You can verify your answers with this data.

13 Organizational Design

Properly organized, even crime pays.

—*Jim Fisk and Robert Barron*

Corporation: an ingenious device for obtaining individual profit without individual responsibility.

—*Ambrose Bierce*

No one can serve two masters.

—*Matt. 6:24*

Learning Objectives

After studying this chapter, you should be able to:

1. Define decentralization and identify strengths and weaknesses of a decentralized organization.
2. Contrast tall and flat organizations.
3. Describe unity of command and chain of command.
4. Describe the six systems in the behavioral approach to organizational design.
5. Describe the relationship between technological and social systems in an organization.
6. Describe modern organizational designs.
7. Discuss advantages and disadvantages of different organizational designs.

Going Global

"Going Global" may be the hottest trend in business today. The Ford purchase of Volvo and the merger of Chrysler and Daimler-Benz are just two recent examples. In 1998, AT&T and British Telecom announced the formation of a strategic alliance with estimated first year revenues of $11 billion. With companies such as Exxon generating 79 percent of their sales internationally, Coca-Cola 68 percent, and IBM 59 percent, the internationalization of business poses a formidable challenge for organizational design. To effectively manage commerce on a global scale, the right organizational structure is critical to global success.

Granted, every company going global will make modifications to existing corporate structure. But going global demands the development of a globally oriented organizational design. For example, CEOs and top managers now need to address issues of accommodating cultural differences, especially when foreign managers are incorporated into the ranks. The old idea that "our way is the right way" can negatively influence business practices across foreign borders. Protocol and etiquette vary from country to country, and they must be taken into account. To accommodate this fact may require a decentralized organizational structure with foreign managers in foreign countries having significant decision-making authority to quickly respond to market conditions.

Communication on a global scale presents another formidable design issue. Events in one part of the world sometimes affect other parts of the world almost instantaneously. Organizations must be designed to manage the flow of data, information, and communication as fast as it occurs, and globally. With business operations occurring in multiple countries and in multiple time zones, it is essential to have systems in place for managers to review activities on a real-time basis. This also means reducing the organizational layers to expedite information and communication, as well as having capabilities for language and currency conversion.

To manage these issues, a global organizational structure needs to integrate technology into its design. Real-time data access and communication needs to provide 24-hour access to managers in their offices as well as in their homes, hotel rooms, and remote offices. Remote access networks, providing links to business partners through e-mail, teleconferencing, and groupware, are growing in importance as the capability to provide real-time global communication increases.

Going global is part of the future of business. To tap these opportunities, the continual redesign of organizational structure is a necessity because of the demands and dynamics of global commerce. Astute managers will accept the realities of real-time decision making and its reliance on instant access to information for effective global control.

Sources: "Global Sales Force," *Sales & Field Force Automation*, April 1998: 1-22; G. Niak and S.N. Metha, "AT&T and BT to Form World-Wide Alliance," *The Wall Street Journal*, July 27, 1998.

In the previous chapters of this text, we examined concepts that apply to either individuals or small groups of individuals in organizational settings. In this chapter, we will turn our focus to the impact that the organization has on behavior. Thus, while the previous chapters emphasized the micro aspects of organizational behavior, this chapter will look at some macro influences. In this context, the terms *micro* and *macro* refer to different levels of analysis or conceptualization. The *micro level* examines conditions and processes from a more individually oriented perspective, while the *macro level* deals with conditions and processes involving organizations and the external environment.*

In this chapter, we will consider initially the major principles of organizing. Next, we will examine the classical, behavioral, and sociotechnical views of organizational design. Then, we will examine some contemporary notions of organizational design.

Principles of Organizing

Organizations can be described in terms of how their component parts are put together and operate. The concepts of organizational structure and function that are frequently used to describe organizations include several important dimensions: decentralization versus centralization, tall versus flat structure, unity of command, and chain of command.

Decentralization versus Centralization

Decentralization is the degree to which decision making occurs lower down in an institution's hierarchy. In a more centralized institution, there is relatively less participation by employees in a variety of decisions. Decentralized organizations are characterized by less monitoring or checking on decisions made by employees.

It is especially difficult to measure the extent of decentralization that exists in an organization. To be sure, we cannot rely on the statements of top management regarding the extent of decentralization present in their own corporation, since executives tend to endorse the value of decentralization and to perceive its existence. One particularly useful means of assessing the degree of decentralization is to examine the dollar amount of expenses employees are permitted to incur without prior approval by a superior. Generally, the larger the amount of latitude allowed employees on expenditures, the greater the extent of decentralization that may be inferred. In addition, the variety and magnitude of decisions made outside of the top or central office can provide an indication of the degree of decentralization.

---

*It has been humorously suggested that the micro approach to OB examines employees as if the organization did not matter, while the macro approach to OB examines organizations as if the employees did not matter.

Although the concept of decentralization has acquired a positive halo,[†] it is not reasonable to endorse the notion of decentralization for all organizations and all situations. Most organizational researchers believe that it is best to think in terms of an optimal level of decentralization for any given organization or its divisions. The identification of the specific forces that dictate the optimal level of decentralization has been a focus of much macro-level research.

There are several possible weaknesses associated with decentralized organizational structures:

1. Because of a lack of coordinated direction, there is a tendency to focus on current problems and functions, and to ignore opportunities for growth and innovation.

2. Shared resources (such as computer equipment, staff, and lab facilities) may pose problems because of the need to allocate their usage. Similarly, shared functions (such as research and development and purchasing departments) may create coordinating difficulties.

3. Internal disputes and conflicts may arise. These conflicts may not be easily resolved because each department or division operates with relative independence. Also, potential disputes between units are not as likely to be detected, averted, or well managed if the actions of units are not coordinated.[1]

As these points imply, extreme decentralization can lead to a lack of needed integration and coordination. Nonetheless, decentralization is often touted as a beneficial organizational attribute because of its anticipated enhancement of employee motivation, performance, satisfaction, and creativity. According to this popular line of reasoning, the greater level of autonomy that decentralization affords to employees leads to greater employee involvement and commitment. As a consequence, employees' attitudes and performance are enhanced. Many successful organizations have relied heavily on being decentralized. For example, Digital Equipment Corporation, following the philosophy of its founder, Kenneth H. Olsen, achieved significant growth in large part because of a decentralized organization structure that gave each senior manager substantial responsibility for an individual product line.[2] Evidence in the areas of job enrichment and self-directed work teams (see Chapter 5) generally confirms the positive impact of increasing employees' self-direction and sense of responsibility. Of course, studies in these areas have not typically attempted the sweeping changes that a radical decentralization of an entire organization implies. Therefore, the limits of decentralization (that is, the dysfunctional effects due to the lack of integration and coordination of efforts) have not been carefully studied.

Tall versus Flat Structures

Tall structure versus **flat structure** refers to the number of levels of authority and the width (or size) of each level. Tall organizations have more levels, while flat organizations have fewer levels. Figure 13.1 provides examples of

---

[†]One of the earliest "success stories" of the use of decentralization is reported in the Old Testament. In Exodus 18, Moses is reported to have been overburdened by judicial decision making. On the advice of his father-in-law, Jethro, Moses restructured the process so that a system of judges took responsibility for making many minor decisions.

both types of organization. Note that the tall organization has five levels of management, while the flat organization has three. Also, both organization structures used in the figure happen to involve the same number of units, 31. Thus, configuration rather than size determines the tallness or flatness of a structure.[‡]

Tall and flat structures also differ in terms of the span of control they employ. **Span of control** refers to the number of employees who report to a single supervisor and thus partially dictates the height of an organization. In the tall organization depicted in Figure 13.1, the span of control is two; in the flat organization, it is five. It can be said that the span of control partially dictates the tallness of the organization. Therefore, the question can be raised, "What is the ideal span of control?" The most widely used logic on this point argues that spans can be larger at lower levels in an organization than at higher levels. Because subordinates in lower-level positions are typically doing much more routine and uniform activities, more subordinates can be effectively supervised at lower levels. In fact, larger spans are often found at lower levels in organizations. However, there is a tendency in many organizations characterized by very large spans (for example, 20 or more subordinates) to employ informal team leaders within a unit. These informal team leaders report to the unit's supervisor. Yet, they may not be officially recognized as a layer of management within the organization. The informal team leader approach

FIGURE 13.1   *Examples of Tall and Flat Structures*

Flat Organization

Tall Organization

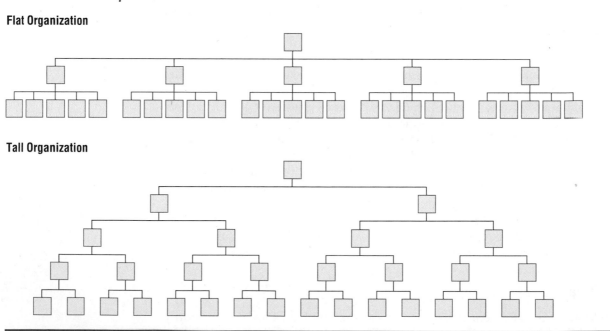

[‡]Noted management consultant Peter Drucker has recommended that seven layers of administration is the maximum necessary for any organization. Thomas Peters, another widely read consultant, insisted that five layers is the maximum for a large organization (based partly on the reasoning that five administrative layers are employed by the Catholic church to oversee 900 million members). For less sizable organizations, Peters recommends three administrative layers as the maximum.[3]

allows a supervisor to expand the number of subordinates he or she can effectively supervise and at the same time not create a cumbersome layer of management.

Generally, a taller organization, with its narrower spans of control, allows for closer control of subordinates in that supervisors have more time to devote to monitoring fewer individuals. Therefore, tall organizations tend to discourage decentralization, while flat organizations are more predisposed to use decentralized decision making.

In terms of overall performance, it had long been assumed that tall, tightly controlled organizations were superior to flat organizations. However, research, such as that conducted on Sears, Roebuck and Company, has challenged this assumption.[4] Sears stores using flat structures had relatively better sales, profitability, and employee job satisfaction than stores with taller structures. These results suggest that larger spans of control may produce positive advantages. The precise mechanism by which such gains can be achieved is not clearly understood as yet. However, it is likely that flatter structures possess greater decentralization, and decentralization serves as the driving force for improving employee performance and attitudes.

While flatter structures may have some unanticipated advantages, they also can be the source of disadvantages. When carried to an extreme, "flatness" can be dysfunctional. As an illustration, consider the following true story of a small, family-owned construction company. The firm initially did relatively simple repair jobs and modest home improvement projects. Soon business improved, and the founder needed to hire additional workers. These workers had to be supervised in teams, since the several groups were geographically dispersed when working on various projects. Eventually, a full-time accountant was needed to handle the financial side of the enterprise. Then, a sales manager was hired to prepare newspaper and radio ads, to meet with clients, and to close deals. Next, a full-time engineer was employed by the firm to draw up and modify construction plans. As business continued to improve, the owner discovered that it would be better to stock and maintain an inventory of needed materials rather than depend on other sources for supplies. The creation of the resulting warehouse operation afforded a new opportunity for revenues: People in the area came to the warehouse to purchase home repair and improvement materials (such as nails, siding, and lumber). As a result, the owner set up a successful outlet store as part of the warehouse operation.

At about this time, he came to recognize that running the firm was simply too burdensome for one individual. The structure of the organization was totally flat. All divisions of the enterprise reported to one person, the company's founder. Whenever a decision had to be made (regarding, for example, how much lumber to stock, whether to start a large project, or the hiring of construction workers), the owner felt obliged to make the decision. As a result, employees were continually approaching him with major, and many minor, issues. As his workweeks came to exceed 80 and 90 hours, the company's founder called in a consultant to recommend ways of improving efficiency and helping him to cope with the demands of the job.[§]

The consultant's recommendation was to redesign the organization so that it would be taller. Specifically, he recommended that two managers be

---

[§]In fact, the consultant was called in only after the founder had suffered a severe heart attack.

appointed, one to oversee warehouse/office operations and the other to oversee the construction/sales side of the firm. Figure 13.2 illustrates the original and the redesigned organizational structures for the firm. As the figure shows, the newer, taller structure affords greater control of each unit because of reduced spans of control. In addition, the founder no longer must coordinate the efforts of a large number of diverse units.

Alternatively, the founder could have tried delegating decision-making authority to the various units (that is, decentralizing the operations of the firm). Instead, he opted for the taller structure, which helped to increase rather than decrease his control of the firm. Given the high personal financial stakes involved in running a firm, it is not uncommon to find that founders are predisposed to seek greater personal control.

Unity and Chain of Command

Unity of command and chain of command are two further principles of organizing. **Unity of command** means that every subordinate should have one and only one supervisor—that is, each subordinate is accountable to and takes orders from a single supervisor. As you might imagine, this notion is intended to improve performance by reducing potential conflicts and ambiguities that might arise if a subordinate dealt with several superiors. By clearly assigning each subordinate to a specific superior, speed of response to problems and information flow should be optimum.

It has long been assumed that unity of command is a cornerstone of organizational efficiency. However, the notion that unity of command must not be violated has recently been challenged by the matrix system, a modern and innovative organizational structure that we will examine more closely later in this chapter.

Chain of command is concerned with the flow of information and authority within an organization. As a principle, chain of command means that information and authority should proceed from level to level in a strict hierarchical fashion without omitting an intermediate level. The need for downward flow of authority is, of course, easy to understand. The converse process, a bottom-up flow of authority, while still within the logic of chain of command, is generally not implied when the term *chain of command* is invoked. Flow of information, however, can be upward or downward within the chain of command. What is critical to the concept is that each succeeding level of management be completely informed.

The suspected advantages of strict adherence to the chain of command principle are that no higher level of management will be uninformed and that appropriate levels are involved in seeking common goals. By following a chain of command approach, coordination of effort and integration of activities should be more easily achieved. Although it is not widely invoked, a further reason for following chain of command involves simple courtesy to superiors and subordinates. Generally, it is best not to omit or "end-run" individuals within the chain of command, since they are likely to learn about it informally and be resentful of not having been informed or involved in the process.

Organizations differ in the extent to which chain of command is strictly followed. In organizations where uniformity of mission and purpose are

FIGURE 13.2   *Organizational Structures for a Construction Firm*

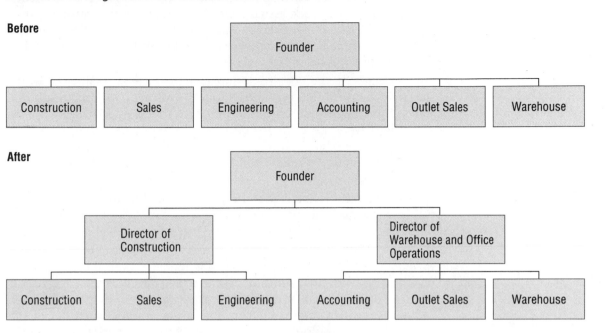

important (such as in maintaining orthodoxy in a religious organization), chain of command is likely to be more firmly ingrained as a practice. Similarly, in organizations where coordination of effort is highly valued, such as the military, chain of command is also closely followed. Less formally structured organizations (such as voluntary associations or social clubs) may have less serious need to follow the chain of command principle strictly.

The Classical Approach to Organizational Design

Max Weber, a German sociologist, has outlined a systematic view of organizations based on the notion of bureaucracy. Weber suggested that **bureaucracy** was the best administrative form for the rational and efficient pursuit of organizational goals.[5]

According to Weber, a perfect bureaucracy possesses:

1. *Rules and procedures.* Weber believed that a rational approach to managing tasks should be the dominant principle in organizations. In a bureaucracy, standard operating procedures provide greater certainty and aid in coordinating efforts.

2. *The principle of hierarchy.* In Weber's model, positions are arranged hierarchically, with the lower positions controlled and supervised by the higher ones. Such an arrangement helps to maintain control over the members of the organization and ensures order. In essence, Weber advocated a clear chain of command or hierarchy of authority.

3. *Division of labor and specialization.* Tasks should be broken down and assigned to employees. Each employee should have the expertise needed to master his or her work assignment. The obtainment of such expertise would be aided by making certain that each work assignment is highly specialized. In addition, each employee should be given the authority and resources to perform his or her duties.

4. *Impersonality.* In the idealized bureaucratic system, managers would maintain an air of impersonality toward employees, especially subordinates. This impersonal attitude would help to ensure that rational considerations were the basis for decision making, rather than favoritism or personal prejudice. Maintaining such a formal atmosphere would also make it easier to evaluate employees solely on the basis of actual performance.

5. *Competence.* Technical ability and expertise should be the basis for hiring, job assignments, and promotions. Possession of relevant qualifications and evidence of merit, rather than family ties or friendship, would determine the receipt of rewards.

6. *Record keeping.* People's memories enable them to recall the outcomes of past dealings with their surroundings and thereby adjust their future conduct in order to obtain advantages. Organizations can, in a sense, possess memories through the maintenance of written records. Such documents enable the organization's members to check on past performance and to record decisions and rules. Written records also aid in the creation of a base of information for training employees to perform specific tasks.

An Assessment of Weber's View

Weber advocated the bureaucratic form as an ideal approach to structuring organizations. Clearly, the widespread presence of bureaucracies throughout our nation and the world attests to the appeal of his principles. Yet the many positive aspects of the bureaucratic form are offset in practice by some negative features, as summarized in Table 13.1.[6]

One major drawback of bureaucracy stems from its *emphasis on authority.* Managers in bureaucratic organizations are often unwilling to surrender their authority and are typically interested in acquiring more power. They may also use their authority to preserve their own territory and eliminate challenges. For example, managers in a bureaucracy frequently resist proposed changes in rules and procedures. As a result, bureaucracies can be characterized as *conservative and inflexible,* characteristics that discourage innovation.

Reliance on rules and the maintenance of an impersonal attitude can lead to other dysfunctions, including the inability to cope with unique cases that do not "fit the mold" and for which the rule book does not dictate a solution. Impersonality can also lead to feelings of *frustration* for people who must work in or with a bureaucracy due to the system's lack of a "soft side" or "human face." In addition, the emphasis on rules and procedures can produce *excessive red tape.* The creation of new rules to cover emerging situations and new contingencies can make the official procedures, delays, and inaction of such systems virtually unbearable.

Highly specialized task assignments can lead to feelings of *alienation* or *estrangement* among employees, and the related lack of challenge and novelty

TABLE 13.1   **Pluses and Minuses of Bureaucracy**

Pluses	Minuses
Control	Barriers to change
Order	Reduced employee satisfaction
Efficiency	Reduced discretion
Memory	Red tape
Rule by reason	Power seeking

can lead to dissatisfaction and turnover. As discussed in Chapter 5, people generally prefer jobs that are not highly fragmented or specialized. Because competence can be difficult to measure in bureaucratic jobs and because a high degree of specialization enables employees to master their required tasks in little time, there is also a tendency to *base promotions on seniority and loyalty* rather than on competence and merit.

For many of us, the term *bureaucracy* has a negative connotation. It conjures up a vision of a large unfeeling institution that is frustrating to deal with. Among the organizations that fit this negative stereotype are agencies of the federal government, such as the Internal Revenue Service and the Defense Department, and state and local government agencies, such as boards of education.

But despite the problems they may create, bureaucratic characteristics have also been associated with positive measures of organizational performance. Specifically, it has been found that greater degrees of bureaucracy (when controlling for differences in the size of various organizations) are associated with higher levels of performance. Organizations that try to maintain a more informal structure do less well if they are relatively large. Smaller organizations of less than 2,000 members tend to have better performance records when they are less bureaucratic.[7]

Certain organizational attributes dictate that bureaucratic characteristics be avoided.[8] For example, smaller organizations should try to maintain informality by reducing rules and red tape, and they should use face-to-face interactions as the basis of supervision.[9] Professionals do not respond well to bureaucracies either. As a result of their training and the prevailing norms in their fields, researchers, technical specialists, consultants, and the like prefer freedom from rules and procedures. Finally, organizations that are experiencing a high rate of environmental change need to be more free flowing and flexible. A bureaucracy would be too slow moving for organizations that need to adapt frequently or quickly to meet constant changes in customer needs or innovations in technology.

In summary, bureaucracy offers many advantages for improving organizational performance. These benefits can be best realized in larger organizations that function in relatively stable environments and employ workers who are tolerant of the limitations of bureaucracy.**

**Resistance to bureaucracy may also stem from individual differences in the ability to adjust to the characteristics of bureaucracy. People who react to bureaucracy with strong suspicion due to their own immaturity may be termed *bureauotics;* those who suffer from "bureausis" rarely rise very far in an organization's hierarchy.[10]

The Behavioral Approach to Organizational Design

Given the speed of technological change, an increasing rate of innovation, and growing demands by a more highly educated work force, many scholars suggest that the classical view of organizations will become outdated. In response to the resulting frustration, bureaucracies will begin to fade away and will be replaced by more creative forms of organization. Rensis Likert, a proponent of a behavioral alternative to the bureaucratic approach, has proposed a multilevel classification of organizations (Figure 13.3).[11]

Each of the systems can be characterized in terms of a number of attributes. A System 0 organization is a permissive type of organization characterized by large spans of control and substantial confusion. It might best be characterized as an organization that is in an early, formative stage.

A System 1 organization relies mostly on fear and punishment to motivate employees. Distrust is likely to be high in such organizations, and employee satisfaction low. Because authoritarianism prevails, employees are not consulted before decisions are made.

In a System 2 organization, rewards are used to motivate employees and employees are permitted to comment on directives, but managers still control the decision-making process. Employees may have some freedom in how they conduct their jobs, yet their relations with superiors are guarded and cautious.

In a System 3 organization, subordinates are more readily consulted; however, major decisions are still made by upper management. Threats are avoided as a means of motivating employees, and there is a degree of trust between managers and subordinates. Employee performance and satisfaction are expected to be higher in this system than in Systems 1 and 2.

System 4 is viewed by Likert as an ideal state toward which managers should try to move their organizations. Trust is extremely high among System 4 members, and a variety of economic, ego, and social factors are used as incentives. Communication moves not only downward but also upward and horizontally. Most critically, decision making occurs at all levels and involves all members equally. In a sense, System 4 approaches a democratic, or highly participative, form in that the input of employees is fully incorporated in the decision-making process. As a consequence of these positive attributes, Likert predicted that both employee performance and satisfaction would be greatest in a System 4 organization.

System 4T is a somewhat idealized type of organization in which authority is based on intragroup relationships and overlapping group memberships instead of on a hierarchy. The *T* stands for *total* participation, and implies stable and strong working relationships among members.[12] Performance and employee satisfaction should be maximal in this type of organization.

FIGURE 13.3 *Likert's Six Systems of Organization*

System 0	System 1	System 2	System 3	System 4	System 4T
Permissive	Exploitative Authoritative	Benevolent Authoritative	Consultative	Participative	Total Participation

Evidence on the accuracy of Likert's model is sparse. In one review, it was suggested that the model may work best at the level of the work group, since it is largely stated in terms of work group processes.[13] Furthermore, the accuracy of the model probably depends on particular circumstances.[14] However, the model is not sufficiently specific to help a manager identify the appropriate circumstances in advance.

The Sociotechnical Systems Approach

Researchers at the Tavistock Institute in Great Britain are well known for conducting a series of studies that led to a new, insightful approach to understanding organizational functioning.[15] These studies, which focused on the coal-mining industry in Great Britain, examined the interaction of technological systems and social systems. At the beginning of the studies, coal was mined by a time-honored method known as shortwall mining. This method involved groups of two to eight miners working as teams to extract coal. In addition to being paid as teams for their output, the groups selected their own members and rotated the numerous tasks associated with mining a small section (or seam) of coal. Because of the dangers of working with explosives in dark, confined areas seldom more than three feet high, the men

An Inside Look
Big Brother Is Reading Your E-Mail

The aim of modern organizational design has been to increase performance efficiency and productivity. Corporate structures have been created to facilitate the flow of communication up and down the organizational chart, as well as to enhance it laterally. With increasing acceptance of telecommuting, and e-mail readily available to almost every employee, organizational structures are adapting to the demands of technology. However, new corporate responsibilities have arisen. Consider the case of e-mail.

E-mail provides everyone virtually instant access to everyone else, and at any corporate level. Granted, this is more the norm in smaller organizations than at one the size of IBM or Ford, but access is more readily available than ever before. There is an inherent destructuring effect with something as simple as e-mail. With the ability to quickly communicate information to large numbers of employees, the reliance on meetings tends to diminish, and a more informal environment is fostered. Informality also has the tendency to give employees a sense of privilege. With e-mail, there is a belief that it is the new

telephone, which can be used for one's own personal, as well as business, communication. But as organizations incorporate new technologies into organizational design, policy must also be put in place to ensure their proper use.

Legally, employers can monitor the use of e-mail, cell phone, and other technology without employee consent if it is within the course of daily business. In employee-centered organizations, it is in the company's best interest to establish and communicate a policy to all employees. This policy serves several functions. If employees are notified of the policy, it becomes more difficult to bring an invasion-of-privacy lawsuit against the employer. A formal policy lowers employees' expectations about privacy on the job. It may thwart an employee's willingness to engage in illegal activities at work. And it conveys a set of expectations about what behaviors will and will not be tolerated.

Source: R. Tadjer, "Boss as Big Brother," *Small Business Computing & Communications*, May 1998: 103–104.

came to develop strong emotional ties with group members. These social relations below ground were closely mirrored in social relations above ground.

As technology advanced, newly developed mining equipment dictated a radically different approach to coal mining. In this new longwall method, the miners were reorganized into large shifts of specialized workers. During the first shift of the day, all of the miners performed the same operation: cutting into the coal wall. The second shift was responsible for shoveling coal into a new type of conveyor. The miners on the third shift worked exclusively at advancing the face of the wall, enlarging gateways, and building roof supports (relatively low-prestige tasks).

In addition, the miners on each shift were spread out along the face of the coal wall at such distances that they could not easily communicate with one another. Similarly, the single supervisor of an entire shift group, consisting of 40 to 50 miners, was not able to monitor the activities of each miner because of the manner in which the men were dispersed.

Although the longwall method had promised to raise productivity, a norm of low productivity emerged. With reduced variety and challenge, the miners found the redesigned work to be unpleasant. They preferred to operate autonomously and to perform *all* the tasks rather than to be solely performing the tasks of cutting, shoveling, or filling.

Although the Tavistock researchers eventually helped to ameliorate the negative consequences of the longwall method, the message was clear: A technological change that appears quite rational from an engineering perspective can disrupt the existing social system so as to reduce greatly the anticipated benefits of the new technology. Of even greater importance is the insight gained by the Tavistock researchers on the interplay of technical and social systems. This notion of a **sociotechnical system** arose, therefore, from a consideration that any production-oriented organization involves both a technological system (equipment, task, and process design) and a social system (working relations). While the technological system places demands on the social organization, the social organization has properties of its own, quite independent of the technology, that have an impact on the technological system. Attempts to change the technological and/or social system must be mindful of the relationship between the two systems.

The sociotechnical approach has much to suggest to job redesign (see Chapter 5). In fact, the approach has been used in numerous job redesign efforts. Some of the better publicized redesign efforts have been attempted at General Foods, Rushton Mining, and General Motors. At the Kalmar plant of Volvo, automobile assembly procedures were radically altered from traditional methods in light of an approach that was sensitive to the interface of social and technological systems. By and large, the results of these efforts have netted reduced turnover and accident rates, and superior product quality.[16]

A Look at Some Modern Organization Designs

Far and away, the most prevalent organization designs in use today are of three varieties: functional, product, and a hybrid of functional and product. Each of the three varieties offers advantages for coping with various contingencies. However, each form also has potential weaknesses.

Functional Design

Organizations designed along functional lines group personnel and activities according to the resources that are essential to the production process. The contributions of the resulting functional departments aid in the total organizational mission. Figure 13.4 provides an organization chart for a hypothetical firm with a functional design.

A **functional design** is especially appropriate when the most important needs of an organization are collaboration and expertise within a defined set of operations, when the environment is stable, and when only one or a few products are produced. However, a functional design suffers from several weaknesses. It tends to be slow to respond to changes in the organization's environment. It may also result in less innovation and a restricted view of and allegiance to the organization's broader goals. A functional design may also have difficulty in coordinating activities among departments. The measurement of the contribution of each department is also problematic as the end product is a composite result of production, personnel, engineering, and marketing efforts. Last, the distinct advantage of a functional design (that is, greater coordination) may become a disadvantage as the organization becomes larger and more complex.

Product Design

An organization that selects a **product design** groups personnel and activities according to organizational output. Each product line is provided with its own production, marketing, and development resources as part of the structuring. The primary goals of a product structure are coordination within product lines and attention to customer desires. Figure 13.5 provides an organizational chart for a hypothetical firm with a product design.

A product design is better suited to adapt to changes in the organization's environment and is especially appropriate for organizations that produce

FIGURE 13.4   *Example of a Functional Design*

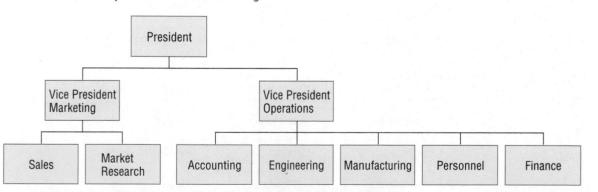

many diverse products or are highly consumer oriented. At the same time, a product design may lead to tremendous losses in economies of scale, redundancy of effort, and little cooperation across product lines. Sharing of competencies and technical advantages is also limited. Internal competition may arise as well. Although competition can be healthy up to a point, the structure of the organization may propel the initial competition into a full-blown power struggle.

Hybrid Design

As a consequence of either form's limitations, few firms use a pure functional or product structure. More typically, large modern organizations combine the advantages of both functional and product forms into a **hybrid design.** Some functions may be highly specialized and located at corporate headquarters, while other product or market units may be self-contained and located elsewhere. By striving for a balance between functional and product designs, an organization can have the best of both worlds. Hybrids typically provide product groups with the functional support they need within a product line, while also trying to maintain functional departments for activities that are required by all divisions of the organization. Figure 13.6 presents a sample organization chart of a hybrid organization involved in three distinct product areas.

Of course, an organization's structure is rarely static. More commonly, structure evolves over time as top-level managers attempt to better adapt their firm to the changing features of its surroundings.

FIGURE 13.5   *Example of a Product Design*

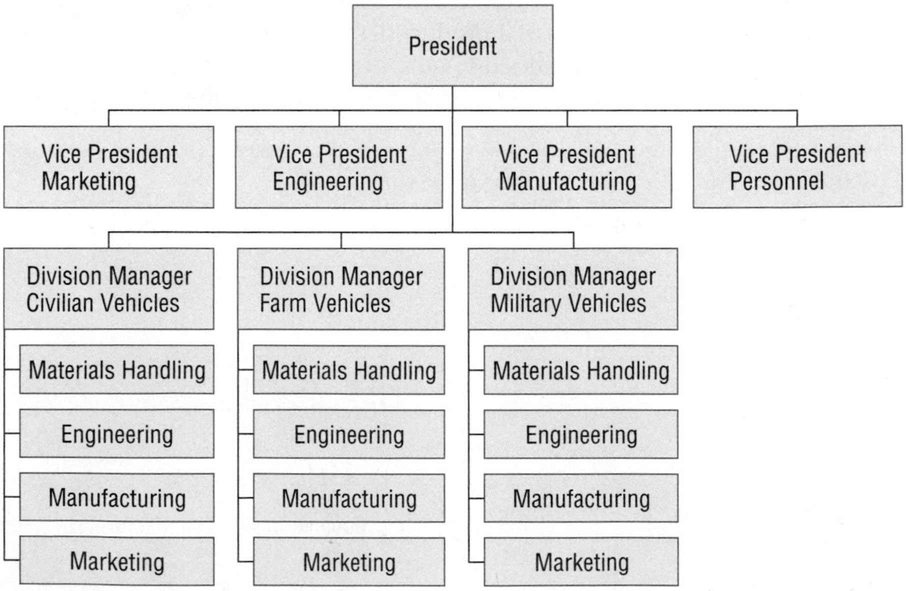

FIGURE 13.6 *Example of a Hybrid Design*

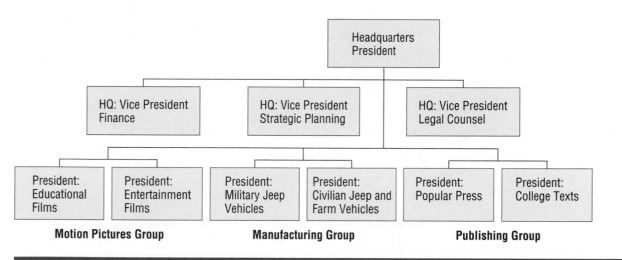

Matrix Design   In some situations, a refined balance between functional and product structures is required to give recognition to both functional and product-related issues. When continuous interchange between product and function is necessary, a matrix organizational design, a type of hybrid design, may be warranted. In a **matrix design**, the functional and product managers enjoy equal authority. Personnel are required to report to managers from both the functional and product divisions. In essence, a matrix design involves a dual hierarchy.

To illustrate more precisely what is meant by a matrix system, consider Figure 13.7. In this organization, a top-level manager oversees one manager whose responsibilities are functional and one manager whose responsibilities are product related. These two managers, in turn, oversee the single employee whose work relates to both their areas. Thus, in violation of the principle of unity of command, the employee is involved in a two-boss system.[††]

Carrying this illustration a step farther to include an entire management group, we could create the matrix design shown in Figure 13.8. At each intersection of the lines of authority and responsibility for the product and functional divisions, project groups would exist. As this figure suggests, personnel and resources would be grouped together to tackle product-specific problems.

In theory, everyone in an organization could be in the web of a matrix. However, most organizations that employ a matrix design limit its use to management-level personnel and maintain a traditional pyramid-shaped structure for the remainder of the firm.[17]

On the negative side, matrix systems can create significant frustration and confusion, especially for the employee who reports to two superiors. In addition, employees who are not adequately trained in how to adapt to a matrix

---

[††]Although the concept of a two-boss system may seem very strange, remember that people typically have had a good deal of experience being in a two-boss system: as a child dealing with a mother and a father.

FIGURE 13.7   *The Matrix Unit*

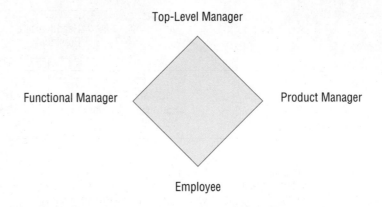

FIGURE 13.8   *Example of a Matrix Organization*

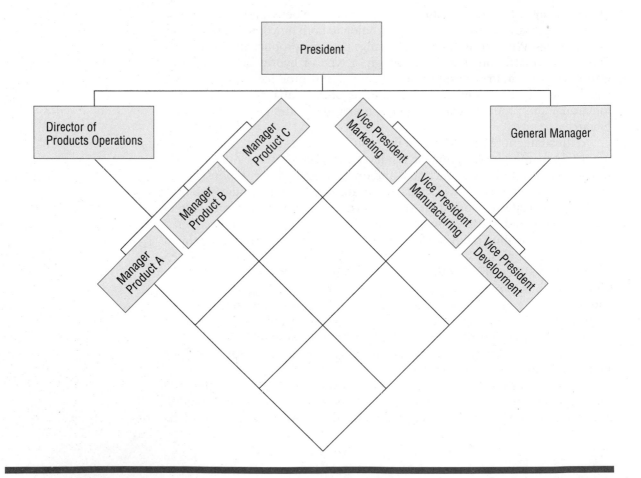

system may persist in behaving as if they were in a more traditional top-down, one-boss situation. Finally, the use of a matrix design is time-consuming. Frequent meetings and conflict-resolution sessions are likely to be necessary, and communications must often be duplicated for the benefit of both superiors. Performance evaluation may also become complicated because in appraising a single subordinate, the potentially conflicting views of two superiors must be resolved. In short, many of the problems that one would expect from violating the principle of unity of command will occur in a matrix system if people do not cooperate in resolving conflicts over the sharing of power and resources. A collaborative and collegial spirit is, therefore, necessary if a matrix form of organization is to succeed.[‡‡]

SUMMARY

1. *Define decentralization and identify strengths and weaknesses of a decentralized organization.* Decentralization is the degree to which decision making occurs lower down in an organization. A strength of decentralization is that it can enhance employee motivation, performance, satisfaction, creativity, involvement, and commitment. Weaknesses include a tendency to focus on immediate problems and ignore opportunities for future growth, difficulties in allocating shared resources and coordinating shared functions, and internal conflicts that are difficult to detect and resolve.

2. *Contrast tall and flat organizations.* Tall organizations have more levels and narrower spans of control than flat organizations. Generally, tall organizations allow for closer control of subordinates. Tall organizations tend to discourage decentralization, while flat organizations are more likely to be decentralized.

3. *Describe unity of command and chain of command.* Unity of command is the idea that every subordinate should have only one supervisor. Chain of command maintains that information and authority proceed from level to level in a hierarchical fashion without omitting any level.

4. *Describe the six systems in the behavioral approach to organizational design.* An organization in an early, formative stage may be characterized as permissive, with large spans of control and much confusion (System 0). An exploitative-authoritative organization (System 1) relies on fear and punishment to motivate employees. Decision makers do not consult employees. A benevolent-authoritative organization (System 2) uses rewards to motivate employees. Employees may comment on directives, but managers still make the decisions. In a consultative organization (System 3), managers consult subordinates more readily and avoid using threats, but upper management still makes the major decisions. In a participative organization (System 4), decision making occurs at all levels and involves all members equally. Trust is extremely high, and incentives include economic, ego, and social rewards. An idealized form of organization (System 4T) is based on intragroup relationships and overlapping group memberships.

[‡‡]Given the continual reshuffling of human and material resources, a good way of describing the dynamics of matrix design is with the three-dimensional analogy of a Rubik's cube.

5. *Describe the relationship between technological and social systems in an organization.* Every organization has both a technological system and a social system. The technological system (equipment, task, and process design) interacts with the social system (working relations), each influencing the nature of the other.

6. *Describe modern organizational designs.* A functional design of organization groups personnel and activities according to the resources that are essential to the production process. A product design groups personnel and activities according to organizational outputs. A hybrid design often combines functional and product designs. A matrix system is a hybrid design involving a dual hierarchy.

7. *Discuss advantages and disadvantages of different organizational designs.* A functional design is useful when collaboration and expertise are needed and the environment is stable. However, a functional design is slow to respond to environmental changes and is less likely to foster innovation. A product design offers greater attention to customer needs and is better suited to respond to environmental changes. A product design, however, incorporates redundancy of effort. A hybrid design strives to balance the functional and product designs. A hybrid design can be highly flexible and can coordinate responses to customer- and production-related pressures, plus offer a greater degree of responsiveness to environmental change. A hybrid design may create problems for evaluating employee performance, as well as generate confusion.

KEY TERMS

Decentralization	Bureaucracy
Tall structure	Sociotechnical system
Flat structure	Functional design
Span of control	Product design
Unity of command	Hybrid design
Chain of command	Matrix design

CRITICAL INCIDENT

The Horizontal Corporation

It was clear to Mike O'Reilly, president and CEO of Cambridge Lighting, that the organizational structure of Cambridge was no longer serving the needs of the company. Cambridge, a manufacturer of lamps and lighting fixtures, had developed a hierarchical structure over the years as sales grew and the work force expanded. The organization had been structured according to specialized functions, creating "silos of excellence." Cambridge had multiple layers of management and a formal chain of command. The organization's ability to adapt quickly to change was severely constrained because most key decisions required managerial approval. The hierarchy had become deeply entrenched.

Mike was concerned that the structure was no longer appropriate in the increasingly competitive lighting market. The past few years had seen major changes in the lighting industry. Inexpensive lamps and lighting fixtures were being imported from Pacific Rim countries, and energy-efficient halogen lighting was becoming an increasingly popular alternative. Mike knew that Cambridge would have to respond to these pressures if it wanted to remain a viable competitor in the lighting industry.

After studying the organization for several months, Mike realized that several functional departments had limited interactions. Friction between departments (for example, between marketing and sales and between engineering and manufacturing) had occasionally been intense and had kept the organization from operating smoothly. Mike wondered if a new organizational structure might be in order.

After reading several articles on horizontal corporations, a trend in organizational redesign, Mike and his executive team developed a plan to restructure the organization around key processes. In horizontal organizations, leaders identify the core competencies or key processes and design the organization around those. Key processes, such as new product development, sales, and customer support, were identified and specific performance goals defined for each. Because the lighting market had become very competitive, Mike and his team decided that Cambridge should adopt a customer orientation. Therefore, performance goals were defined in terms of customer satisfaction. According to the plan, teams of functional specialists would work on a given key process toward established performance goals.

Following the redesign, teams of employees from different functions would be responsible for every stage of their key process. The multidisciplinary teams would be empowered to make decisions without supervisor input, thereby reducing the chain of command and flattening the organization's hierarchy. To provide better service, teams would meet regularly with suppliers and customers to learn more about their needs and constraints.

The plan looked good on paper, but Mike was concerned about its implementation. On his desk was the 150-page plan book he and his executive team had prepared. They had nicknamed it the "roadmap" because it outlined how Cambridge would proceed from its present vertical structure to its desired horizontal structure. The restructuring process was to begin in about six weeks. But first, Mike and his executive team had to share the entire plan with everyone in the organization. The first meeting to unveil the new organizational structure to upper and middle management was about to begin. With a sigh of both excitement and hesitation, Mike grabbed his road map and headed for the conference room.

1. How are the managers at this meeting likely to respond?

2. How should Mike respond to managers' and employees' concerns?

3. What role should the human resources management department play in this reorganization?

4. What types of personnel policies should change to reflect the new organizational structure?

5. How does the horizontal structure implemented at Cambridge differ from a matrix organization?

Source: "The Horizontal Corporation," written by Melissa Waite, State University of New York, University at Buffalo; and Susan Stites-Doe, State University of New York, College at Brockport.

EXPERIENTIAL EXERCISE

Bureaucratic Orientation Test

Have you thought about what kind of organization you would like to work for when you finish your studies? The following checklist may help you define what type of organizational structure would be best for you.

Step 1   For each statement, check the response (either Mostly Agree or Mostly Disagree) that best represents your feelings.

	Mostly Agree	Mostly Disagree
1. I value stability in my job.	_____	_____
2. I like a predictable organization.	_____	_____
3. The best job for me would be one in which the future is uncertain.	_____	_____
4. The U.S. Army would be a nice place to work.	_____	_____
5. Rules, policies, and procedures tend to frustrate me.	_____	_____
6. I would enjoy working for a company that employed 85,000 people worldwide.	_____	_____
7. Being self-employed would involve more risk than I'm willing to take.	_____	_____
8. Before accepting a job, I would like to see an exact job description.	_____	_____
9. I would prefer a job as a freelance house painter to one as a clerk for the Department of Motor Vehicles.	_____	_____
10. Seniority should be as important as performance in determining pay increases and promotion.	_____	_____
11. It would give me a feeling of pride to work for the largest and most successful company in its field.	_____	_____
12. Given a choice, I would prefer to make $80,000 per year as a vice president in a small company to $100,000 as a staff specialist in a large company.	_____	_____
13. I would regard wearing an employee badge with a number on it as a degrading experience.	_____	_____
14. Parking spaces in a company lot should be assigned on the basis of job level.	_____	_____
15. If an accountant works for a large organization, he or she cannot be a true professional.	_____	_____
16. Before accepting a job (given a choice), I would want to make sure that the company had a very fine program of employee benefits.	_____	_____
17. A company will probably not be successful unless it establishes a clear set of rules and procedures.	_____	_____

18. Regular working hours and vacations are more
    important to me than finding thrills on the job.   _____   _____
19. You should respect people according to their rank.   _____   _____
20. Rules are meant to be broken.   _____   _____

Step 2   Give yourself one point for each statement for which you responded in the bureaucratic direction:

 1. Mostly agree   11. Mostly agree
 2. Mostly agree   12. Mostly disagree
 3. Mostly disagree   13. Mostly disagree
 4. Mostly agree   14. Mostly agree
 5. Mostly disagree   15. Mostly disagree
 6. Mostly disagree   16. Mostly agree
 7. Mostly agree   17. Mostly disagree
 8. Mostly agree   18. Mostly agree
 9. Mostly disagree   19. Mostly agree
10. Mostly agree   20. Mostly disagree

Step 3   Interpret your scores. A very high score (15 or over) would suggest that you would enjoy working in a bureaucracy. A very low score (5 or lower) would suggest that you would be frustrated working in a bureaucracy, especially a large one.

Step 4   Do you think your score is representative of most college students in your major? Discuss with students in your class.

Source: Andrew J. DuBrin, *Human Relations: A Job Oriented Approach,* 5th ed. (Englewood Cliffs, N.J.: Prentice-Hall, 1992), 434–435.

14 Environmental and Cultural Influences

The growth of a large business is merely a survival of the fittest.

—John D. Rockefeller, Sr.

Let's put our strength and minds together, Doing our best to promote production, Sending our goods to the people of the world.

—Matsushita workers' song

Every nation ridicules other nations, and all are right.

—Arthur Schopenhauer

Learning Objectives

After studying this chapter, you should be able to:

1. Identify three dimensions that describe an organization's external environment.
2. Explain how the environment influences whether organizations will succeed or fail.
3. Explain how organizations handle their dependency on their environment.
4. Describe two strategies organizations can use for managing the environment.
5. Identify an organization's structural dimensions and contextual dimensions.
6. Describe how an organization's structure complements its technology.
7. Define organizational culture and describe influences on its creation and maintenance.
8. Describe characteristics of typical managers in the United States.
9. Contrast Japanese and American management styles.
10. Give some examples of the differences in social customs and business practices in other cultures.

A Corporate Culture That Works

The world's largest closely held software company is not in Silicon Valley, but on the outskirts of Raleigh, North Carolina. The SAS Institute, founded by Dr. James H. Goodnight, is an $850 million company with a well-crafted corporate culture that offers an employee-centered environment. In the software industry, employee turnover typically exceeds 20 percent annually. At SAS, the rate is around 4 percent. SAS routinely receives hundreds of applicants for every job opening, at every level of the company.

Dr. Goodnight states very simply, "I like happy people," and this is the rationale for the country-club environment at corporate headquarters and the lavish array of perks provided for the 2,700 employees who work at the SAS Institute. Every employee has a private office. On staff are a full-time artist-in-residence and an ergonomics specialist, who advise employees about furniture and office décor in order to create the best work environment for each individual. SAS sponsors a free medical clinic for all employees; the staff of two doctors and six nurse-practitioners promises that the wait for medical service is no more than five minutes. Employees can make use of the 35,000-square-foot recreation center and enjoy a pianist who entertains each day in the company's subsidized lunchroom. Year-end bonuses and profit-sharing are available to all employees, in addition to the extra week of paid vacation between Christmas and New Year's. Each of the 20 buildings on the SAS campus has break rooms, providing free soda, fresh fruit, pastries, and candy. Employees purchasing a house in one of the subdivisions that Dr. Goodnight owns receive a 10 percent discount on the land. They also get a discount on membership fees at the country club owned by Dr. Goodnight.

In the intensely competitive software business, 60- to 80-hour work weeks are the norm—but not at SAS, where Dr. Goodnight advocates a 35-hour week. The flexible and family-centered policies, and the two day-care centers, are strongly favored by the women at SAS, who account for more than 50 percent of the workforce of the company.

Dr. Goodnight has constructed a corporate environment to create and bind employee loyalty to his company, but avoids perks that he feels may create autonomy in employees. He offers no stock options, which can create personal wealth that can be used as venture capital for employees to start their own company. There is no tuition reimbursement; says David Russo, SAS's human-resources chief, "Basically you're training someone for outplacement—they're going to leave." Sales people do not earn commissions because they may result in high-pressure sales tactics, of which Dr. Goodnight does not approve.

Many employees receive calls from headhunters offering higher salaries but refuse to leave the ambience of the work environment and employee-valued orientation of the company. Stanford University business professor Jeffery Pfeffer, who has studied SAS extensively, comments, "At first blush, you look at SAS and it seems like a very paternalistic organization. But if you look carefully, it's actually an enormously effective business model."

Source: T.D. Schellhardt, "An Idyllic Workplace under a Tycoon's Thumb," Management, *The Wall Street Journal*, November 23, 1998.

As we have seen throughout this text, employees' attitudes and behaviors are influenced by the immediate circumstances in their work units, such as their tasks, intragroup relations, and rules and policies. The circumstances that define these subenvironments within the work unit are, in turn, determined by diverse facets of the larger organizational structure.

In the previous chapter, we focused on the influence of the organization's structure, and we emphasized that effective management requires an understanding of how larger structural issues affect individuals. In this chapter, we will examine dimension of external environments and strategies for actually managing the external environment, with the ultimate goal of controlling the resulting structures and the subenvironments within these structures. This chapter also explores the notion of organizational culture, as well as some ways cultures are created and maintained. Finally, the chapter compares Western culture with the cultures of other parts of the world.

Dimensions of External Environments

An organization exists within a particular external environment that is composed of all the various factors (such as the government, legal system, labor pool, suppliers, customers, and state of existing technology) that can affect the organization's functioning. In analogous fashion to a living organism, an organization is influenced by and influences its surroundings. Similarly, the organization is highly dependent on environmental features and must quickly adapt to changes in the environment if it is to survive.

The number of features that constitute an organization's external environment is considerable. However, organizational scholars have attempted to reduce these features to a few critical dimensions. Chief among these schemes for analyzing external environments is one developed by Robert Duncan.[1] His theory suggests three important dimensions for understanding environments: simplicity–complexity, static–dynamic, and environmental uncertainty.

Simplicity–Complexity

Environments can be characterized in terms of their intricacy and relative diversity.[2] A simple environment contains few factors that affect the organization and tends to be relatively unvaried. In contrast, a complex environment contains many more elements of importance and is more diverse. As an illustration of a simple environment, consider the environment faced by a manufacturer of washboards at the turn of the century. In such a setting, the technology was relatively simple, and the market was unchanging. In comparison, consider a present-day drug manufacturer. The number of products produced is highly varied, and the customers are quite different (for example, hospitals, doctors, and over-the-counter drugstores). The manufacture, marketing, and distribution of drugs is also highly complex. In addition, government regulations cover the preparation and distribution of drugs.

Static-Dynamic

A second important dimension of environments is the degree of stability or dynamism that characterizes the organization's surroundings. Environments can be said to differ in terms of the rate at which change is occurring; hence, they can be said to differ in terms of predictability. In our example of the washboard manufacturer, we can say that the surrounding environment was relatively static during the beginning of the 20th century. (Washboards were widely used until washing machines became available and affordable later in the century.) Today's drug manufacturer functions in a highly dynamic and changing environment. New drugs are continually being developed and tested. There are continuing changes in the packaging of drugs in response to customer concerns over possible product tampering. In addition, the drug industry is responsive (quickly adapts) to innovations in the drug-manufacturing process.

Environmental Uncertainty

The degree of uncertainty that characterizes the environment is related to the descriptive dimensions of simplicity–complexity and static–dynamic.[3] According to Duncan, environmental uncertainty is a consequence of the inability to assign probabilities to environmental factors with a high degree of confidence, and a lack of information concerning both the factors that are important to decision making and the costs associated with poor decision making.[4]

The Population Ecology Perspective

In recent years, organizational theorists have offered a popular view of how organizations relate to their environments.[5] According to the **population ecology perspective,** organizations seek to find a niche in a highly competitive surrounding so that they will be able to survive. In this view, a niche is defined as a combination of environmental resources and needs that are capable of sustaining the organization. Initially, a niche may be fairly small. But as the organization grows, it may expand the size of its niche. The population ecology perspective borrows heavily from the notions of natural selection in biology. In both views, entities are seen as competing for survival in a difficult, sometimes predatory, and crowded environment.[*]

The population ecology view suggests that there are three stages in the change process: variation, selection, and retention.[6] **Variation** is analogous to the concept of genetic mutation in the theory of evolution. Organizations with unique attributes are continually being born. Often, these new organizations are deliberately designed to cope with a particular set of environmental constraints. If the new organization possesses adaptive variations, it will likely be successful. Those organizations that do not possess the needed organizational form will fail. Failure may be due to the organization's lack of skilled personnel, lack of sufficient capital, or chance factors (such as a takeover by another company). Consequently, a process of **selection** occurs. Over a long period, only a few organizations (out of the large number founded every year) can be

---

[*]Interestingly, the mortality rates of the young of many species and of young organizations are very high.

expected to survive and be reasonably prosperous. **Retention** refers to the institutionalization of certain adaptive organizational forms. As long as the organization's outputs are sought or endorsed by the larger society, the organization will be a critical component of the society. Examples of institutionalized organizational forms include state governments, educational institutions, and automobile manufacturers. In the long term, even these established institutionalized forms may disappear. The key determinants of the longevity of institutionalized organizational forms are the extent of change in the environment and the organization's ability to adapt to such change.

As an example, consider the process of change related to the roadside hamburger stand. In the past, independently owned and operated hamburger stands served an important societal need. As the public became more mobile, roadside dining became a more frequent activity for the average citizen. Over time, chains of franchised hamburger stands (McDonald's, Burger King, Wendy's) came to dominate the roadways by offering the customer a standardized product along with the convenience of fast service and drive-through windows.

At present, the original, independently owned hamburger stands must hold second place (in terms of appeal and sales) to the large institutionalized forms of fast-food restaurants. The clientele of the nonfranchised restaurants are now more likely to be repeat customers who live in the surrounding neighborhood than the traveling public. In this example, we see how the small, independent organizations are gradually being selected out of the environment. With time, it is, of course, possible that the current domination of fast-food restaurants will end. For this to occur: (a) the chains must be supplanted by a new (as yet unforeseen) organizational form that is superior in some fashion, (b) the desires of the public will have to change (for example, the public must lose its desire to eat beef, or its desire to eat out must be greatly diminished), and (c) the fast-food chains must fail to respond (or be incapable of responding) to the challenge.

The Resource Dependence Model

Another view of how organizations relate to their environments is termed the **resource dependence model.** This view contends that organizations are highly dependent on their external environments for raw resources and markets. The success of any organization is, therefore, a function of the extent to which the organization can manage its environment. Because organizations are vulnerable to their environments, they must take action to reduce or eliminate their dependency. One approach to this dependency is to purchase or control those forces that can exert influence. For example, a manufacturer who relies heavily on certain raw materials may try to purchase the operations of various suppliers. This represents an attempt to reach out and change the environment. Also, an organization may attempt an internal change in order to deal with its vulnerability. These internal changes include increases in structural complexity and the creation of boundary-spanning roles.

Increases in organizational complexity reflect the complexity of the external environment. For example, marketing departments are created and specialized in order to identify new markets and understand customer desires and needs. Legal departments interface with federal and state agencies in order to protect the firm from legal constraints. Purchasing agents focus on identifying suppliers and new sources of raw materials. As the complexity of the external environment increases, the complexity of the organization's structure will likely increase in order for the organization to more effectively cope with its surroundings.

An organization needs to have effective relationships with the major elements of its environment. To achieve this end, **boundary-spanning positions** are often created. Boundary spanners seek to understand the external environment and to represent the organization to various constituencies. Examples of boundary-spanning roles include positions in public relations, marketing research, college recruiting, and purchasing. However, the boundary-spanning function is not solely the province of specialized positions. Many employees whose jobs are primarily directed toward performing duties within the organization may occasionally engage in boundary-spanning activities. For example, someone in the finance department may call a friend who works for a supplier in order to learn more about the operations of the supplier, or someone in accounting may meet with a job candidate for a position in another department in order to persuade the candidate to join the organization.

Managing the External Environment

It is possible for organizations to change the external environment through two major strategies. The first consists of establishing favorable linkages with critical elements in the external environment. The second involves controlling the environmental domain. Each of these strategies can be accomplished through several different methods.

Establishing Favorable Linkages

To improve relations, linkages (or associations) can be set up with elements of the external environment. One useful way of establishing a linkage is to acquire another organization through a merger. Mergers can eliminate dependence on an external factor by gaining control over it. For example, uncertainty about a supplier's ability to deliver sufficient quantities of materials on time can be reduced by acquiring the supplier and thereby guaranteeing preferential treatment. Acquisition of one firm by another with the goal of controlling forces that affect the production process is termed **vertical integration.** Examples of vertical integration include an automobile manufacturer that acquires an auto radio and battery producer, and a food processor that purchases a poultry farm.

Hiring practices can also help to establish favorable linkages. In one approach, a firm may decide to recruit executives from other firms with which it wishes to have good relations. Thus, a defense contractor may hire retired military officers from the Department of Defense to join its contract-negotiating division. Another approach is to select board members who represent various constituencies, such as customers, suppliers, or community interest groups. Membership on a board of directors provides these individuals with an appreciation of, and a continuing interest in, the performance of the firm. A similar tactic involves placing board members of another corporation on your own board. This tactic creates **interlocking directorates.** As a result of sharing board memberships, the individuals experience a sense of common interests.

Last, a firm can attempt to establish favorable linkages by investing in advertising and public relations. Such efforts attempt to enhance the firm's image in the eyes of customers and the public and, as a result, influence the way in which these groups relate to the firm.

Controlling Environmental Domains

There are other means by which an organization can attempt to control the domains in which it operates. One direct approach is simply to buy or sell a product line. This involves seeking or avoiding different suppliers, competitors, government regulations, customer groups, and so on. Additionally, an organization may aggressively diversify into different business arenas, forming **conglomerates.** Conglomerates can sometimes provide built-in markets for products and easier access to supplies. In East Asia, conglomerates have grown to be comparatively large. In Japan, such an enormous corporation is called a *keiretsu.* One of the largest examples of a keiretsu is the Mitsubishi group, which includes such diverse industries as glass, banking, mining, electronics, automotive products, and cement.

A second device consists of joining with other similar organizations that have common goals and interests. For example, coal mine operators may join forces to form a trade association, with the aim of lobbying for their interests. The goals of such associations include encouraging regulators to pass or rescind laws that promote or restrict an industry's well-being. In some technologically advanced industries (for example, robotics and computers), an individual firm may lack the ability to single-handedly develop and market a new product. In such instances, firms may operate cooperatively, sometimes across national boundaries, to form **strategic alliances.**

The Contingency View of Organizational Design

Today, scholars of organizational design generally subscribe to a view that organizations are **open systems.** As an open system, an organization must deal with its environment by obtaining and consuming resources, and exporting finished goods or services. Organizations do not exist in a vacuum nor can they operate independently from their environment; that is, they cannot function as **closed systems.**

Given this view of organizations as open systems, it is useful to consider how an organization's internal characteristics are influenced by the larger features of the environment and the entire organization itself. These internal characteristics, called **structural dimensions,** include such features as specialization, hierarchy of authority, decentralization, and complexity. Characteristics of the entire organization and its environment, called **contextual dimensions,** include size, technology, and such external constituents as customers, suppliers, competitors, and the government. The goal of the contingency view is to explain how differences in the contextual and structural dimensions are related. As the term *contingency* implies, this approach does not seek simple universal principles that can be used for every situation, but instead seeks to explain how one attribute or characteristic depends upon

TABLE 14.1 *Features of Mechanistic and Organic Organizational Forms*

Mechanistic	Organic
Specialized tasks	Employee contributions to a common task
Hierarchy of authority	Less adherence to formal authority and control
Hierarchical communication	Network communication
Centralized knowledge and control	Decentralized knowledge and control
Insistence on loyalty and obedience to the organization	Loyalty and commitment given to the project or group
High degree of formality	High degree of flexibility and discretion

another. In the search for contingencies, two landmark research programs are worth noting.

Mechanistic and Organic Systems

In a study of 20 firms in England, researchers examined the relationships between external environments and the nature of internal organizational structure.[7] Relying on unstructured observations and interviews, they attempted to characterize the manner in which internal management operations were structured and the rate of change in the external environment. Their results indicated that firms in relatively stable or unchanging environments tend to have more highly structured and formal management operations. They termed such organizations **mechanistic** because of their emphasis on rules, procedures, and dominance by a hierarchy of authority. In contrast, firms in more unstable environments tend to have a free-flowing, decentralized, and more adaptive internal organization that they called **organic.** Table 14.1 summarizes the major differences between mechanistic and organic organizations.

Central to this view of organizational design is the notion that these two extreme forms of organizational system are most appropriate for different environments: Organic systems are more capable of adapting to change, while mechanistic systems are appropriate to relatively static settings.[†] For example, a computer software company must survive in a dynamic, rapidly changing environment characterized by constant technical innovations, so it needs a more organic form of organization. At the other extreme, a synthetic fabric firm operates in a relatively predictable and stable environment, so it would probably have a more mechanistic form of organization.

Woodward's Studies of Technology

Another contextual variable of importance in the structure of organizations is **technology,** the tools, techniques, and knowledge used to transform raw

---

[†]It should be noted that this research did not actually prove that effectiveness is greater when organic systems exist within unstable environments, and so on, but merely that an organic system was associated with environmental change. Nonetheless, the implication is straightforward: Mechanistic organizations are presumed to be limited in their adaptability as a result of their rigidity.

resources into finished goods. Some of the most important research on the impact of technology was conducted by Joan Woodward, a British industrial sociologist.[8]

In her studies, which focused on 100 firms in England, Woodward initially set out to determine what structural factors were associated with commercial success. The results, however, did not identify characteristics that were more strongly associated with effectiveness (for example, more bureaucratic organizations were not necessarily more or less successful than less bureaucratic organizations). In further analyses of these data, Woodward sought to uncover underlying factors that might help to explain the otherwise meaningless patterns in the data. By reclassifying organizations in terms of type of technology, a set of meaningful results began to emerge suggesting that organizational structure should complement technology. Specifically, Woodward classified the firms into one of three categories: unit (or small-batch) production, mass (or large-batch) production, and long-run process production.

Unit production firms manufacture small orders that are custom-made for the purchaser. Made-to-order products such as furniture, electronics, and specialized construction equipment characterize this type of enterprise. **Mass production** firms manufacture standardized articles that do not require much specialized or varied attention. For example, automobile and mobile home manufacturers employ mass production technology. **Long-run process production** requires mechanization of the entire manufacturing operation. From beginning to end, the process is highly controlled, so the quality of the final product can be very easily predicted. Among the users of long-run process production technology are oil refineries, chemical plants, and distilleries.

Based on this classification system, certain patterns of results suggested that structuring within the sampled firms was indeed related to type of technology. For example, the number of management levels increased from unit to long-run process production—that is, as technological complexity increased.

Woodward also observed several complex patterns in her results. For example, the amount of verbal communication tended to be lowest in mass production organizations, whereas the amount of written communication was greatest. In addition, mass production firms tended to be more highly centralized and to employ more formalized procedures than did the other types of

---

TABLE 14.2   *Major Findings of Woodward's Studies on Technology and Structure*

Structural Attribute	Unit Production	Mass Production	Long-run Process Production
Number of management levels	Low	Moderate	High
Formalization	Low	High	Low
Centralization	Low	High	Low
Verbal communication	High	Low	High
Written communication	Low	High	Low
Overall structure	Organic	Mechanistic	Organic

An Inside Look
Putting a Dollar Value on Employee Happiness

The days may soon be gone when management views employees as nothing more than a necessary expense that can be readily replaced. A growing trend with employers is to view employees as a resource capable of having an indirect, but valuable, effect on the bottom line. Commitment and loyalty are two words entering the lexicon of managers. This is not just the newest management fad. There is a growing body of research suggesting that if employee satisfaction is improved, this may carry over to improved customer satisfaction.

The trend in the new corporate environment is to measure employee satisfaction, and the results are striking. Sears Roebuck concluded from a comprehensive 800-store study that satisfaction with the work environment has a measurable association with customer satisfaction and revenue. Northern Telecom of Toronto, in a similar study, reached the same conclusions: that satisfied employees satisfy customers better, and the result may improve the financial position of the company.

Among the greatest costs directly attributed to employee dissatisfaction are costs related to turnover.

MCI learned that a new employee will produce only 60 percent as much as an experienced employee for the first three months. MCI also learned that while dissatisfaction reduces efficiency by only 5 percent, it can easily reduce revenues by several hundred million dollars.

Robert Kaplan, an accounting professor at the Harvard Business School, is a leader in the movement to measure intangible assets. He proposes that an employer's respect for work-life balance is an indicator of the soundness of the company. According to Kaplan, "If you are out of control on it, it's going to hurt performance . . . you don't even get a chance to implement your strategy because key people leave." When companies understand this and build it into their corporate culture, the result will be improved performance for the firm and a better life for the employees.

Source: S. Shellenbarger, "Companies Are Finding It Really Pays to Be Nice to Employees," Work & Family, *The Wall Street Journal*, July 22, 1998.

firms. Overall, the unit and long-run process production firms were relatively more organic, while the mass production firms were relatively more mechanistic. Table 14.2 summarizes these findings.

Further analyses by Woodward on the financial success of the same firms, as measured by market share, reputation, and the like, showed that successful firms tended to fit the pattern of structural attributes that was most typical for their technology grouping, as outlined in Table 14.2. For example, successful mass production firms tended to have mechanistic structures, while successful unit or long-run process, production firms tended to have organic structures. Other studies in the United States[9] and Japan[10] have corroborated Woodward's findings that technology is related to structure and that appropriateness of structure is related to organizational performance.

Cultural Influences

Every organization exists in an external culture and perpetuates its own internal culture. The study of cultural influences, a topic that is central to the field of anthropology, has existed for some time, but its application to business organizations is a recent phenomenon. In the remainder of this chapter, we will examine cultures within organizations. Then, we will turn our attention to the topic of cultural, or national, differences in employee attitudes and behaviors.

Organizational Culture

Although the notion of organizational culture is currently enjoying much popularity, a precise definition of it is difficult to offer. Edgar Schein suggests that organizational culture has been variously defined as a philosophy that underlies an organization's policy, the rules of the game for getting along, and the feeling or climate conveyed by the physical layout of the organization.[11] Ralph Kilmann proposes that organizational culture is largely a matter of norms.[12] Examples of some organizational norms include: Don't say what the boss doesn't want to hear; Don't be associated with an ugly event; Do cheat on your expense account; Don't criticize the company to outsiders; Don't be a bearer of bad news; and (perhaps the most ironic norm) Don't make norms explicit to anyone who inquires about them.[‡]

Although there is considerable variation in the suggested definitions of organizational culture, it appears that most contain several common elements. Based on these, we can define **organizational culture** as the shared values and norms that exist in an organization and that are taught to incoming employees.[§] This definition suggests that organizational culture involves common beliefs and feelings, regularities in behavior, and a historical process for transmitting values and norms. Despite its lack of precision, the concept of organizational culture is widely used in management circles, sometimes as a convenient catch-all explanation for why things happen or do not happen in a particular way in a firm, as in, "It's the way we do things here—it's part of our culture."

Rituals and Stories

Organizational rituals and stories (notions borrowed from cultural anthropology) play key roles in maintaining and building organizational cultures. For example, a number of ceremonial rituals may accompany the appointment of a new chief executive officer, including introductory announcements, banquets, meetings, and speeches. Similarly, the public awarding of a lapel pin can take on powerful meaning if employees believe that such an award symbolizes a significant achievement.

The function and origin of organizational stories or myths are often unclear.[13] Occasionally, a story will convey a theme that embodies the values of the corporation's founder or other major figures. Depending on its goal, its tone may be either positive or negative. For example, a positive story may recount how the president attended a company picnic and displayed great

---

[‡]Intriguingly, Kilmann reported that more than 90 percent of the norms cited by organizational members are negative in tone and connotation.

[§]Strictly speaking, the notion of values and norms already exist in the field of organizational behavior. Also, socialization of new members is a topic in itself. Therefore, the concept of organizational culture continues to be a rather fuzzy notion. In addition, organizations are themselves products of a culture, so it is confusing to speak of cultures existing within a cultural artifact.

personal warmth toward the spouses and children of the firm's employees. Such a story is meant to convey the underlying concern that the president has for the corporate family. Or a story may retell how all employees in the firm (from the CEO on down) agreed to a 10 percent wage cut during an economically difficult period in order to avoid any layoffs. On a more negative note, a story may be spread of how a former employee was ruthlessly dismissed and his career ruined by being blacklisted for the "crime" of disloyalty. The intent of such a story is, of course, to induce fear and control employees' behavior through intimidation.

The Measurement and Change of Organizational Culture

In order for the study of organizational culture to make a substantial contribution to the field of organizational behavior, it is necessary to have a set of methods for studying organizational culture. Unfortunately, the study of organizational culture presents unique challenges. Schein has observed that achieving an understanding of an organization's culture can be aided by locating a motivated insider within the organization, someone who is capable of deciphering the organization's culture and is motivated to discuss it.[14] Of course, a researcher is highly dependent on an insider's ability to provide reconstructions of events and the beliefs of others. Therefore, the direct observation of some facets of an organizational culture may not be possible (short of personal membership in an organization).

In addition to interviewing organizational members and joining the organization, surveys can be used to obtain data on insiders' perceptions of the organization's culture. However, the quality of the responses is likely to be limited because the investigator cannot interact with the respondent to probe issues. Furthermore, the use of the survey method presupposes that the investigator is already familiar enough with the culture to know what questions and issues need to be investigated.

Although surveys, interviews, and partial membership in an organization are all potentially useful for studying organizational culture, Schein and Kilmann advocate the use of group sessions by an investigator in order to check his or her emerging perceptions against actual members' views.[15] Kilmann also proposes that group members be asked to list a set of new norms that would facilitate organizational performance. With such lists, one can begin to discuss the changing of norms and, thereby, the changing of a major element of the organization's culture. Kilmann reports that the proposed norms that employees most frequently list include: Treat everyone with respect; Listen to other members' views even if you don't agree with them; Provide recognition to those who suggest new ideas and ways of doing things; and Speak with pride about your organization and department. Such lists of desired norms can serve as a useful starting point for altering an organization's culture. However, the commitment to changing cultural features must of necessity be obtained from top-level administrators if the desired change is to occur and be maintained.

The Creation and Maintenance of Organizational Culture

Since our knowledge of organizational culture is limited, it is difficult to state, with firm confidence, detailed prescriptions for creating and maintaining organizational cultures. Nonetheless, several observations and cautious suggestions can be made, based on the available understanding of organizational culture. It appears that there are at least four major influences on the origins of organizational culture.[16]

1. The *beliefs and values of the organization's founder* can be strong influences in the creation of organizational culture. During his or her tenure, these beliefs and values can become embedded in the organization's policies, programs, and informal statements perpetuated by continuing members of the organization (akin to the oral tradition of storytelling). For example, James Cash Penney infused his organization with "the Penney idea," consisting of such guiding principles as "Treat everyone as an individual" and "Value loyalty."

2. The *societal norms* of the firm's native or host country can also play a role in determining an organization's culture. That is, the culture of the surrounding society influences the culture of firms existing within it.

3. *Problems of external adaptation and survival* pose challenges for organizations that its members must meet via the creation of organizational culture (that is, norms). For example, the development of strategies and goals and the selection of methods to achieve goals require the creation of norms. At PepsiCo, competition with Coca-Cola has produced an internal atmosphere of extreme competition where careers are made or destroyed by slight fluctuations in market share.

4. *Problems of internal integration* can lead to the formation of organizational culture. For example, setting rules for social relations and the distribution of status, and establishing criteria for group and organizational membership require the development of norms and the acceptance of a set of beliefs.

The maintenance or reinforcement of an organization's culture can be best understood by knowing (1) what managers consider important (what they measure and control); (2) the manner in which top management reacts to crises and critical events; (3) what types of deliberate role modeling are provided by managers; (4) criteria for distributing rewards and status; and (5) criteria for hiring, firing, and promotion.[17] These five elements for understanding the maintenance of organizational culture also provide insights as to how to change an organization's culture. That is, culture may be best changed by altering what managers measure and control, changing the manner in which crises are handled, using different role models for new recruits and altering the socialization/orientation process, establishing different criteria for allocating rewards, and changing the criteria for promotion, hiring, and dismissal.

Studies of Organizational Culture

Research on organizational culture has moved beyond a purely descriptive stage and begun to develop and test predictions. One study developed a questionnaire for assessing long-time employees' perceptions of organizational values, and compared these organizational values with the value preferences of organizational newcomers.[18] Results showed that new employees whose values matched the organizational values on such dimensions as respect for people, team orientation, innovation, and so on had greater commitment and job satisfaction, and less turnover. This suggests that it may be possible to seek a match between an organization's values and new employees' values by screening job applicants for values–culture "fit" along with skill proficiency.

Organizations are now viewed as having a **dominant culture** that espouses the critical, core values shared by most employees. Also, organizations are acknowledged to have many **subcultures,** or sets of values and norms that are unique to a particular unit of the organization. These values and norms may or may not conform to the dominant culture of the organization. Another term often used in the area of corporate culture is **strong culture.** A strong (versus weak) culture is distinguished by whether the organization's values and norms are intensely held and widely endorsed. It is generally believed that a strong culture will provide advantages to an organization in terms of employee commitment and satisfaction. In a series of studies that examined the importance of congruence of values between employees and supervisors, researchers at the University of South Carolina found that employees are both more committed and more satisfied when their values are congruent with those of their supervisor.[19]

Cross-Cultural Studies

While the study of organizational culture focuses on the conduct of individuals within organizations, cross-cultural research explores the differences and similarities among members of different societal cultures. Defining what is meant by the term *culture* at this level of analysis is no less problematic. Most often, national boundaries are used as the basis for defining culture, but this is largely a matter of convenience, since the important dimensions of culture are sometimes difficult to specify. In the realm of organizational behavior, it may be more accurate to say that concern is with cross-*national* studies or comparative organizational behavior rather than with cross-*cultural* issues.

Even if we accept a label without the term *culture,* the results of studies comparing employees across different countries are still difficult to interpret. This difficulty stems from a lack of theoretical notions for explaining what culture or nationality is, and an inability to predict the effects of culture or nationality on other variables.[20] We are often left simply with results stating that a group of employees in Country A did or did not differ from a group of employees in Country B. Why these results occurred and how any differences were brought about are often unexplained. Additionally, much cross-cultural research may be limited by the use of "made in America" theories. That is, cross-cultural researchers often use concepts and measures of constructs that were originally designed in the West for studying Westerners. Although much theorizing on organizational behavior issues does originate in North America, it is probably incorrect to assume that the ideas that are relevant to explaining the behavior of North American workers are equally appropriate for explaining the behavior of workers in all other countries.

Cultural Differences

Studies of the differences between national groups have uncovered some interesting results. For example, researchers checked clock accuracy, walking speed, and the average time it took postal clerks to sell stamps in six countries.[21] Their results showed that Westerners tend to have fairly precise measures of time and a stronger concern for punctuality than have most other people. Anthropologists have distinguished two temporal styles: monochronic and polychronic.[22] People who display a monochronic style focus on one thing at a time, separating activities in time and space. People who display a polychronic style focus on several things at once (dovetailing or interspersing other activities). Northern European-derived nations (for example, the United States) tend to be monochronic, while Latin American nations tend to be polychronic. These different styles may underlie some misunderstandings and conflicts that arise when members of different nations interact. Table 14.3 displays a questionnaire developed for assessing one's temporal style.

Other research, based on interviews with roughly 1,000 people in each of five countries, identified strong differences in levels of interpersonal trust. Specifically, it was found that the percentage of respondents who agreed that "most people can be trusted" varied as follows:

United States	55%
England	49%
Mexico	30%
Germany	19%
Italy	7%

In a comparison of the values of 3,600 managers representing 14 countries, a number of similarities were observed on dimensions of leadership and attitudes.[23] Other research on the value systems of 2,600 managers in five countries also found many similarities, suggesting that managers often have common views on business-related activities regardless of national affiliation.[24]

Certain patterns and clusters of results have also been observed in these and similar cross-national studies. Specifically, it has been found that managers from the United States, Canada, Australia, and Britain tend to hold fairly similar attitudes; Japanese and Korean managers tend to have greater agreement on value issues; Central and South Americans tend to agree; and so on. These clusters of responses suggest that although many similarities may exist among managers worldwide, they can also be sorted into clusters based on historical, religious, linguistic, and racial similarities.

Reliable differences between clusters of countries are frequently reported. Across several studies, it has been found that various clusters of countries often differ on attitudes toward sharing information and the belief that individuals have the capacity for leadership and initiative.[25] By and large, these results suggest that Anglo-American managers are much more democratic in their orientation, while managers from other countries tend to be more autocratic.

Another attitudinal difference between the United States and other countries can be seen in the extent of gender bias. A failure to appreciate this continuing bias in attitudes toward women in other countries can lead to

TABLE 14.3 **A Measure of Polychronicity**

Please consider how you feel about the following statements. Circle your choice on the scale provided.

	Strongly disagree	Disagree	Neutral	Agree	Strongly agree
1. I do not like to juggle several activities at the same time.	5 pts	4 pts	3 pts	2 pts	1 pt
2. People should not try to do many things at once.	5 pts	4 pts	3 pts	2 pts	1 pt
3. When I sit down at my desk, I work on one project at a time.	5 pts	4 pts	3 pts	2 pts	1 pt
4. I am comfortable doing several things at the same time.	5 pts	4 pts	3 pts	2 pts	1 pt

Add up your points, and divide the total by 4. Then plot your score on the scale below.

```
   |     |     |     |     |     |     |     |     |     |
  1.0   1.5   2.0   2.5   3.0   3.5   4.0   4.5   5.0
```
monochronic   polychronic

The lower your score (below 3), the more monochronic your orientation; the higher your score, the more polychronic.

Source: A. Bluedorn, C. Felker-Kaufman, and P.M. Lane, "How Many Things Do You Like to Do at Once: An Introduction to Monochronic and Polychronic Time," *Academy of Management Executive* 6 (1992): 17–26.

difficulties for those who hope to conduct business in the international arena.** In addition, class consciousness and de facto caste systems are prevalent outside the United States. Even in some European countries, hirings and promotions are still based on social and academic origins rather than on objective merit. Fraternization across management levels and between managers and workers is frowned upon in many countries in the world. However, a limited degree of informal socializing of upper management with the "troops" is regarded quite favorably by most North Americans. By and large, North Americans object to elitist conduct and class distinctions, while the peoples of many other countries do not hesitate to invoke social rank.[26]

Dimensions of Cultural Differences

One of the most ambitious studies of cultural differences as they relate to organizational issues was undertaken by Geert Hofstede, a Dutch scholar.[27] This research involved data on more than 116,000 employees of IBM representing

---

**The United States was the first nation to legally recognize sex discrimination and sexual harassment. Only Australia, Canada, France, New Zealand, Spain, and Sweden also have specific statutes on harassment. In most countries, harassment is handled indirectly (if at all) as a by-product of other laws, such as those dealing with unfair dismissal.

40 countries. Based on his results and a review of evidence in the field of cultural differences, Hofstede deduced four useful criteria for comparing cultures: power-distance, the avoidance of uncertainty, individualism versus collectivism, and masculinity versus femininity.

Power-distance refers to the degree that the members of a culture accept the unequal distribution of power, and the appropriateness of maintaining distance between people.

Avoidance of uncertainty is the degree to which members of a culture are able to cope with ambiguous or anxiety-provoking situations.

Individualism versus collectivism refers to whether the members of a culture endorse a view that people are expected to take care of only their immediate lies (individualism) versus a view that people are expected to care for members of an extended family and offer loyalty to groups (collectivism).

TABLE 14.5   *Dimensions of Cultural Differences*

Power-Distance

Small Power-Distance	Large Power-Distance
Inequality among people should be reduced	There should be a degree of inequality, where everyone has a rightful place
Leaders and followers consider each other to be just like themselves	Leaders and followers view one another as being different
Those in power should try to appear less powerful	Those in power should try to appear powerful

Avoidance of Uncertainty

Weak Avoidance	Strong Avoidance
There should be few rules	There is a need for written rules
Competition can be used constructively	Competition can unleash aggression and should, therefore, be avoided
Authorities should serve citizens	Citizens lack competence compared to authorities

Individualism versus Collectivism

Individualist	Collectivist
"I" consciousness is dominant	"We" consciousness is dominant
People should strive for themselves and only immediate family	People belong to extended families or clans
Emphasis on initiative and leading	Emphasis on belonging and following

Masculinity versus Femininity

Feminine	Masculine
Men need not be assertive, but can be nurturing	Men should be assertive and women should be nurturing
Equality of sexes is ideal	Men should dominate in society
People and environment are valued	Wealth and goods are valued

Source: G. Hofstede, "Cultural Constraints in Management Theories," *Academy of Management Executive* 7 (1993): 81–93; G. Hofstede, *Culture's Consequences* (New York: Sage Publications, 1980), 122, 184, 235, 295.

Masculinity versus femininity is concerned with whether members of a culture value traits and attributes that are traditionally defined as masculine versus traits and attributes that are more characteristically feminine in nature. Table 14.5 summarizes the defining endpoints of these four dimensions.

In a comparison of managers from the United States to managers from 39 countries on these four dimensions, Hofstede found that the United States ranked 26th (below average) on power-distance, 32nd on avoidance of uncertainty (again, below average), 1st on individualism (that is, highly individualistic), and 13th on masculinity (above average). In their totality, these results suggest that U.S. managers (in the aggregate and relative to managers in other countries) prefer a small power-distance, feel capable of coping with ambiguity, are highly individualistic, and endorse traditionally masculine values.

Japanese Management

Much has been written about the alleged superiority of **Japanese management** techniques in comparison to the American style of management. The major characteristics of the Japanese approach to management (assuming that it is fair to speak in very general terms of a nation's system of management) have been identified by numerous writers.[28] Contrasting their descriptions with how American firms are structured or tackle similar problems produces some interesting differences.

A major stylistic difference between the two approaches lies in the extent to which consensus is sought when making decisions. Japanese firms involve many more workers in the decision-making process and try to work on a solution until all of those involved are reasonably satisfied. In the United States, decision making is more often an individual manager's prerogative.

A second major difference between the two styles of management lies in their amount of commitment to the worker. Some Japanese firms offer the equivalent of lifetime employment to their employees, thereby creating feelings of security and family membership. U.S. firms, in contrast, tend toward a short-term view of employment, releasing employees when the company finds it necessary.

Third, Japanese evaluation and promotion systems are designed to reward seniority more than merit. A consequence of this feature, coupled with a commitment to employment security, is that individuals must wait a long time to rise through management ranks. In the United States, young managers expect that they will rise rapidly within a firm, or, if they do not, they will seek employment elsewhere. Other less frequently cited features of Japanese management include intensive socialization of employees to create greater group cohesiveness, emphasis on quality and productivity, and reliance on an informal approach to controlling the behavior of employees.

While it is commonly suggested that the features of Japanese management contribute to Japanese productivity, it does not follow that Japanese industry is stronger or that the Japanese approach to management is better in any meaningful sense. The fact that differences exist is not in itself sufficient to explain Japan's economic output. Furthermore, Japan's relative economic advantage is only seen in certain areas, such as steel and iron production. The United States leads Japan in terms of quality and technology in aircraft, computers, and software, pharmaceuticals, medical equipment, telecommunications equipment and networking, farm equipment, pulp and paper, total energy production, truck production, synthetic fibers, plastics, and printing. In machine tools, steel, and automobiles, the United States is not a leader; but quality and efficiency are improving.[29]

If for the sake of argument we assume that Japanese management practices are superior to American practices, we must then consider whether it is feasible to adopt the Japanese approach in the United States. Many students of Japanese management feel that it is not reasonable to think in terms of transplanting many features of Japanese management.[30] For example, the notions of promoting slowly and rewarding heavily for seniority rather than merit would find little acceptance among U.S. employees. Other features, such as seeking consensus in decision making, may be more workable but may also be unnecessary. That is to say, frequent group meetings to achieve consensus may have evolved in Japan because of the difficulty of relying on written communication in the Japanese language. As a result, oral communication may have come to be preferred for business purposes.[31][††]

Finally, many of the positive features of Japanese management are not common in the country's larger companies. For example, it is estimated that only 30 percent of Japanese workers enjoy the security of a lifetime job guarantee.[32] Also, lifetime employment practices (left over from feudal times) appear to be eroding in recent years due to the difficulty of retaining a large workforce during an economic downturn.[33] Some Japanese firms, as a result, are turning to increased subcontracting, temporary help, and women (who can be fired more easily).[‡‡] In addition, there are few opportunities for women to enter management ranks. By and large, these and other shortcomings of Japanese business practices argue against a simple transplanting of Japanese management practices to the United States.[35] In addition, it has been suggested that young Japanese employees are less committed to their work than were their predecessors. One comparison found that only 14 percent of young Japanese were satisfied with the workplace versus 70 percent of their U.S. counterparts.[§§] A major source of dissatisfaction seems to be the Japanese practice of assigning employees to jobs without regard for their preferences. A cross-cultural comparison by the Aspen Institute for Humanistic Studies found that Japanese (and British) workers reported the greatest disparity between what they desired in a job and what they actually experienced. Although the touted Japanese commitment to work is not in danger of collapse, these and related findings suggest a growing sense of alienation among Japanese workers.[37]

In closing this discussion of differences among managers in various countries, it should be stated that many students of comparative management believe there is a general set of management practices that can be applied across all cultures. Thus, they contend that management can be practiced in a generic

---

[††]Gutenberg's invention of printing from movable type—a technique not readily adaptable to the enormous number of Japanese written characters—may, therefore, be responsible for the Western emphasis on written business communications.

[‡‡]Although the lifetime employment system in Japan is often cited by foreign observers as a positive attribute, critics point out that the system actually increases management's control of employees by forcing greater employee dependency upon managers.[34]

[§§]A survey of Japanese workers found that 40 percent fear that they may work themselves into an early grave. In fact, the Japanese have a term for death from overwork—*karoshi*.[36]

sense. One typically finds the major organizational functions (that is, marketing, production, and finance) existing in firms around the world. In short, the principles of effective management may be said to be fairly universal, or lacking a high degree of uniqueness, for various cultures.[38]

Doing Business Overseas

The increasing integration of the world economy has produced a growing demand for managers skilled in international business practices. The sophistication required to work effectively with people from other countries takes considerable time to develop. As a first step in learning to relate with people from other cultures, it is useful to consider how we are seen by others. Following are some observations made by visitors to the United States.[39]

- "Americans seem to be in a perpetual hurry. Just watch the way they walk down the street. They never allow themselves the leisure to enjoy life." (India)

- "Americans appear to us rather distant. They are not really as close to other people—even fellow Americans—as Americans overseas tend to portray. It's almost as if an American says, 'I won't let you get too close to me.' It's like building a wall." (Kenya)

- "Once we were out in a rural area in the middle of nowhere and saw an American come to a stop sign. Though he could see in both directions for miles and no traffic was coming, he still stopped!" (Turkey)

- "The tendency in the United States to think that life is only work hits you in the face. Work seems to be the one type of motivation." (Colombia)

- "In the United States, everything has to be talked about and analyzed. Even the littlest thing has to be, 'Why, Why, Why?' I get a headache from such persistent questions." (Indonesia)

- "The American is very explicit; he wants a 'yes' or 'no.' If someone tries to speak figuratively, the American is confused." (Ethiopa)

- "The first time . . . my (American) professor told me, 'I don't know the answer, I will have to look it up,' I was shocked. I asked myself, 'Why is he teaching me?' In my country, a professor would never admit ignorance." (Iran)

Functioning as a manager in another country requires an understanding of the traditions, customs, and business practices of the host country. Although there is little hard evidence of the precise requirements to be effective in doing business overseas, the collected wisdom of experienced overseas managers does give some insight on what works (and what doesn't) in specific countries.[40]

Latin America   Conducting business in Latin America takes time. Few people rush into business. Although some customs are changing, men and women still congregate into separate groups at social functions (until recently, having a chaperone was still an accepted practice). Latins also stand more closely together than do North Americans when in conversation. Instead of shaking hands, men may embrace. Guests invariably arrive late for functions (although North Americans are expected to be punctual). Several unique traits are the *mañana* concept (meaning a belief in an indefinite future, and, therefore, little need to worry about deadlines), *machismo* (an expectation that in business a man will display forcefulness, self-confidence, and leadership with a flourish), and *fatalism* (a resignation to the inevitable, or taking whatever comes, sometimes seen as heroic posture). As a rule for non-Latins, when in doubt, be formal.[41]

East Asia (Japan, the Chinas, South Korea)   Initially, business meetings are devoted to pleasantries—serving tea, engaging in friendly chitchat, and developing a relationship. Indirect and vague communication is considered acceptable. Sometimes statements are left unfinished so that the listener can reach the conclusion in his or her own mind. Forcing another to admit failure or impotency is to be avoided. Seniority and elderliness command respect. When confronted with a strange, unexpected, or emotionally powerful situation, East Asians may laugh or smile in a seemingly inappropriate manner (as a function of releasing tension rather than finding the circumstance humorous). In addition many Westerners are convinced that East Asians consciously use slow-down techniques as bargaining ploys in the belief that they can exploit a natural inclination of Westerners to be impatient. Finally, it is very much expected that business cards will have one side printed in English and the other in oriental characters (although the presentation of your business card may not always result in your being offered a business card by the other party).[42]

Russia   Notorious for being protocol conscious, Russians expect to do business with only the highest-ranking executives. To Westerners, they appear stiff and dull. When greeting foreigners for the first time, Russians sometimes use the stilted term *gospodin* (citizen). In private, however, Russians are far more expressive and sociable. Written agreements are essential as informal, quid pro quo understandings may not be honored. Unfortunately, writing a contract can be difficult as there are no Russian equivalents for many Western business terms. Contracts, therefore, must be back-translated (that is, translated from English into Russian and then translated from Russian back into English to determine if the exact meaning is retained).[43] In a land of chronic shortages and few choices, the Russians have virtually no advertising experience. The basic sales philosophy can be summarized in the words of a Russian citizen who was asked how he might go about attracting more customers to stay at his hotel. "Well," he responded, "I would hope that all the other hotels were full."

Middle East   Middle Easterners are known to occasionally prefer to act through trusted third parties rather than deal directly. Personal honor is given a high premium, and the avoidance of shame is very important. Fatalism influences the view of time. A favorite expression is "Burka insha Allah"—"Tomorrow if God wills." Compared with people of other societies (especially East Asians), Middle Easterners are far more emotionally expressive. They stand closer together, and eye contact is more intense. Also, occasional bodily contact during conversations (for example, gently tapping another's arm or knee) is not unusual. Guests should avoid discussing politics, religion, and the host's family and personal possessions (commenting on the host's female family members is a taboo, and praising a possession implies the host should offer the item as a gift). A signal that a meeting is concluded is given by the offer of coffee or tea.[44]

SUMMARY

1. *Identify three dimensions that describe an organization's external environment.* Environments can be relatively simple or complex; they can be static or dynamic; and they possess varying degrees of environmental uncertainty.

2. *Explain how the environment influences whether organizations will succeed or fail.* To maintain its existence, the organization must have an appropriate form, including goals, human resources, products, and technology. Chance, random forces, and continual change are also important elements in determining which organizations survive. Organizations with varying attributes are continually formed, and those that lack the needed organizational form will fail. A few adaptive forms will survive.

3. *Explain how organizations handle their dependency on their environment.* Organizations try to manage their environment. They might try to purchase or control influential forces. They might try to make internal changes that will make them less vulnerable. Such changes include increasing structural complexity and creating boundary-spanning roles.

4. *Describe two strategies organizations can use for managing the environment.* Organizations can change the external environment by establishing favorable linkages with critical elements in the environment and by controlling the environmental domain. Establishing favorable linkages includes vertical integration, hiring executives from companies the organization wants to link with, recruiting directors from targeted constituencies, creating interlocking directorates, and investing in advertising and public relations. Controlling environmental domains includes buying or selling a product line and joining with similar organizations having common goals or interests.

5. *Identify an organization's structural dimensions and contextual dimensions.* Structural dimensions are internal characteristics of the organization, such as specialization, hierarchy of authority, decentralization, and complexity. Contextual dimensions are characteristics of the organization and its surroundings, and include size of the organization, technology, and external constituents (for example, customers, suppliers, competitors, and the government).

6. *Describe how an organization's structure complements its technology.* In ascending order of technological complexity, manufacturers can be classified as unit production firms, mass production firms, or long-run process production firms. The number of management levels increases as technological complexity increases. Mass production firms tend to be more mechanistic in structure, while unit and long-run process production firms are relatively organic.

7. *Define organizational culture and describe influences on its creation and maintenance.* Organizational culture comprises the shared values and norms in an organization that are taught to incoming employees. Influences on the creation of cultures are: the beliefs and values of the organization's founder;

societal norms; problems of external adaptation and survival; and problems of internal integration. Maintaining an organizational culture depends on manager's priorities; top management's reactions to critical events; role modeling by managers; criteria for distributing rewards and status; and criteria for hiring, firing, and promotion.

8. **Describe characteristics of typical managers in the United States.** In the aggregate, U.S. managers prefer a small power-distance, feel capable of coping with ambiguity, are highly individualistic, and endorse values traditionally considered masculine.

9. **Contrast Japanese and American management styles.** Japanese firms involve many more workers in the decision-making process and try to achieve consensus, while in the United States managers more often make decisions individually. Japanese management places more emphasis on job security, whereas U.S. companies tend to take a more short-term view. Japanese systems tend to reward seniority more than merit; in the United States, young managers expect to rise rapidly within a company or they will leave it.

10. **Give some examples of the differences in social customs and business practices in other cultures.** In Latin America, there is less attention to punctuality but more physical contact. In East Africa, seniority is given great respect. Russians tend to be formal in public settings, but expressive and sociable in private. Middle Easterners value honor and tend to be emotionally more expressive.

KEY TERMS

Population ecology perspective	Contextual dimensions
Variation	Mechanistic organization
Selection	Organic organization
Retention	Technology
Resource dependence model	Unit production
Boundary-spanning positions	Mass production
Vertical integration	Long-run process production
Interlocking directorates	Organizational culture
Conglomerate	Dominant culture
Strategic alliance	Subculture
Open system	Strong culture
Closed system	Japanese management
Structural dimensions	

CRITICAL INCIDENT

The Culture at Continental Communications

Six years ago, Continental Communications was founded by two former telephone executives, Bill Schuman and Mark Willis. Their goal was to create a new long-distance telephone company that would compete with the larger long-distance carriers without imposing the bureaucratic culture associated with the larger phone companies. The company, with 400 employees, now provides long-distance service to the entire New England area, and is still owned and headed by its enterprising founders.

Both owners bring a lot of energy and spirit to the company and seek employees with similar levels of drive and determination. Continental recruits at several top business schools and hires many entry-level managers right out of school. "Newly minted graduates have no pre-established ideas about how communications companies should operate," says Bill. "They are like a blank slate onto which we transfer our company's values." Employees at Continental are youthful and energetic; the median age of the workforce is 34.

In an effort to turn Continental into a viable, nationwide long-distance carrier, employees are encouraged to seek innovative solutions, try risky alternatives, and work long hours. Most salaried employees work between 50 and 60 hours a week. From the start, Bill and Mark have maintained open lines of communication with all employees. The official policy states that any employee can discuss problems, issues, or ideas with any other employee at any time. According to Mark, "We're in the business to foster communications. We have an obligation to our customers to facilitate open communication both within and outside our corporate boundaries." Many inside Continental credit the open communications policy for allowing innovative ideas to circulate throughout the company. Employees bounce ideas off one another and proposals often develop into tangible services offered to customers. To maintain an invigorating climate, employees are eligible for a generous annual bonus based on individual and team performance and on company profit measures.

Both Bill and Mark are avid bicyclists, and the company biking team frequently competes in local races. Employees who share the owners' love of biking receive a 12-speed racing bike valued at $1,200 upon completing a continuous 100-mile ride on one of the biking team's regular outings. Many employees remember the time Mark and Bill unknowingly mismarked the route, and employees riding for the complimentary racing bike actually rode closer to 120 miles. Mark and Bill are reminded of the incident whenever their sales or revenue projections seem a little off the mark. To date, over 70 racing bikes have been awarded. Employees also receive a personalized decorative wall plaque denoting entrance into the "100 Mile Club." Similar plaques are awarded to employees who have ridden 50- and 75-mile distances. Through these and other acts, all employees at Continental are made aware of the importance of achieving difficult goals.

1. Describe the organizational culture at Continental Communications. What are its main features?

2. List examples of Continental's observable culture, shared values, and common assumptions.

3. Given what you know about its corporate culture, is Continental Communications the type of organization you would like to work for? Why or why not?

Source: "The Culture at Continental Communications," written by Melissa Waite, State University of New York, University at Buffalo; and Susan Stites-Doe, State University of New York, College at Brockport.

EXPERIENTIAL EXERCISE

Is Your Culture Gap Showing?

This activity is designed to help you better understand the culture at your college or university. There are no good or bad cultures per se. The cultural norms either help or hinder the organization in realizing its goals, mission, and purposes.

Following are several sets of paired statements concerning elements that constitute the college culture. Please work quickly and do not read too much into each statement.

Step 1   Complete the following cultural assessment instrument. Respond to each pair of statements in the following manner:

a. Choose the (A) or (B) item in each pair that is the *actual* norm right now. Mark that norm with an *A*.

b. Label the (A) or (B) norm that is the *desired* condition with a *D*. This may be the same or the opposite statement you labeled in part a. Thus, you could have one of the following configurations:

(A) A   (A) D   (A) AD   (A)
(B) D   (B) A   (B)   (B) AD

c. Using the following 7-point scale, indicate the importance of the choice (or issue) to you.
   7: This is a critical issue.
   6: This is very important.
   5: This is moderately important.
   4: This is a neutral issue.
   3: This is moderately unimportant.
   2: This is very unimportant.
   1: This is an extremely unimportant issue.

	Actual/Desired	Importance
1. (A) The professors go out of their way to help students.	_____	_____
(B) The professors just teach their classes.	_____	_____
2. (A) Channels for expressing student complaints are readily accessible.	_____	_____
(B) Few people pay serious attention to student complaints.	_____	_____
3. (A) Many students here develop a strong sense of responsibility about their roles in contemporary social and political life.	_____	_____
(B) The expression of strong personal belief or conviction is pretty rare around here.	_____	_____
4. (A) Students respect the rules.	_____	_____
(B) Students pay little attention to rules.	_____	_____
5. (A) Most of the professors are very thorough teachers and really probe into the fundamentals of their subjects.	_____	_____

(B) Most of the professors just cover the bare facts. _____ _____

6. (A) Students are conscientious about taking good care of school property. _____ _____

(B) Students are indifferent to or abuse school property. _____ _____

7. (A) Students set high standards of achievement for themselves. _____ _____

(B) Students do just enough to get by. _____ _____

8. (A) Many students play an active role in helping new students adjust to campus life. _____ _____

(B) Most students pay little attention to new students. _____ _____

9. (A) The administration and faculty make every effort to treat everyone equally. _____ _____

(B) Anyone who knows the right people among the faculty or administration can get a better break here. _____ _____

10. (A) The big college events draw a lot of student enthusiasm and support. _____ _____

(B) Major college events are usually greeted with indifference. _____ _____

11. (A) Academic advisors are knowledgeable and provide valuable advice. _____ _____

(B) The academic advisors provide little useful information. _____ _____

12. (A) Information of concern to students, such as the last date to drop a course, is readily available. _____ _____

(B) Information of concern to students is not well publicized. _____ _____

13. (A) The talk among people on campus is warm and friendly. _____ _____

(B) People are polite but reserved. _____ _____

14. (A) Many students get involved in clubs and organizations. _____ _____

(B) Only a small number of students seem to be involved in organizations. _____ _____

15. (A) Faculty members are available for conferences and meetings. _____ _____

(B) Faculty members are rarely available for meetings. _____ _____

16. (A) Students have a high regard for ethics and values. _____ _____

(B) Students do not seem interested in what's ethical. _____ _____

17. (A) Most faculty show warmth, interest, and
        helpfulness toward students.   _____   _____
    (B) Most faculty do not seem to care about the
        students as people.   _____   _____

18. (A) Students have a great deal of freedom and
        latitude concerning such things as
        class attendance.   _____   _____
    (B) Students have very few opportunities to
        express freedom of choice.   _____   _____

19. (A) Students respect the value of learning and
        do their own work.   _____   _____
    (B) Students resort to various forms of cheating
        to get by.   _____   _____

20. (A) Residence halls seem to be congenial, fun
        places to live.   _____   _____
    (B) Residence hall life is dull and sterile.   _____   _____

21. (A) The administration seems to really care
        about student welfare.   _____   _____
    (B) The administration seems to be indifferent
        toward students.   _____   _____

22. (A) Students help each other with course
        assignments and projects.   _____   _____
    (B) Students regard classwork as "everyone for
        himself or herself."   _____   _____

23. (A) Innovative courses or programs of study
        are introduced and tried.   _____   _____
    (B) The courses and programs seem to be
        always the same.   _____   _____

24. (A) Fraternities and sororities seem to have a
        major impact on the social atmosphere.   _____   _____
    (B) Fraternities and sororities exist but seem to
        have little impact on campus.   _____   _____

25. (A) Students seem to make extensive use of the
        library as a source of information.   _____   _____
    (B) Students do not seem to make use of the
        library resources.   _____   _____

26. (A) It is quite common to find students
        browsing through the bookstore.   _____   _____
    (B) The bookstore is only a place to buy your
        texts.   _____   _____

27. (A) Intramural athletic activities and other
        forms of reaction (bowling, ping pong) seem
        to be a significant part of student life.   _____   _____
    (B) Intramurals and other recreational pursuits
        are not part of the campus scene.   _____   _____

28. (A) The courses provide students with a basis for
        improving their social and economic status
        in life.   _____   _____

(B) The courses provide students with skills and
techniques applicable to a job.   _____   _____

Step 2   To score your answers, look for paired statements in which the A and
D labels are associated with different norms. Examples: (A) A, (B) D; or (A) D,
(B) A.

Using the table below, record the importance score for *only* those items in
which a difference exists between Actual and Desired.

Task	Social		Task	Social
1._____	3._____		17. _____	14. _____
2._____	4._____		18. _____	16. _____
5._____	6._____		21. _____	19. _____
9._____	7._____		23. _____	20. _____
11._____	8._____		25. _____	22. _____
12._____	10._____		26. _____	24. _____
15._____	13._____		28. _____	27. _____

Step 3   Either as a class or in small groups, examine the results and look for
one or two norms where a major difference exists. If the entire class is involved,
try to reach a consensus on the predominant area(s) of concern. If small
groups are used, each group should focus on a particular area of concern. In either case, develop a brief action plan to address what should be done to reduce
the culture gaps. Consider the following when developing your plan:

a. What are the current norms?
b. What would be some ideal norms?
c. Establish some new norms.
d. How can each individual contribute to altering the culture toward the new
norms?

Step 4   (For small group situations only) Each small group should be prepared to present its action plan. Comments and discussion are encouraged.

Source: Written by Bruce Kemelgor, University of Louisville.

15 Managing Organizational Change and Development

How many OD specialists does it take to change a light bulb? Ten: one to change the bulb and nine to relate to the experience.

—*Anonymous*

A consultant is someone who will take your watch off your wrist and tell you what time it is.

—*David Owen*

It if ain't broke, don't fix it— unless you are a consultant.

—*Winston G. Rossiter*

Consultant: Any ordinary guy more than fifty miles from home.

—*Eric Sevareid*

Learning Objectives

After studying this chapter, you should be able to:

1. Identify external and internal sources of change in an organization.
2. Describe the stages of organizational growth.
3. List causes of organizational decline.
4. Identify factors that lead to an organization's success or failure.
5. Describe the phases in the process of change in an organization.
6. Describe techniques that change agents use to help bring about change in organizations.
7. Identify the conditions that enhance the likelihood an OD effort will succeed.
8. Evaluate the track record of OD programs.

360 Degrees of Feedback

As organizations of all types strive to become flatter and move to team-based programs, bosses spend less time supervising and evaluating employee performance. Likewise, employees are spending more time with peers and customers than with their boss. With less and less manager-employee interaction, how can the manager judge performance? Enter the latest evaluation tool: 360-degree feedback. In addition to the traditional evaluation by a superior, this method uses comments by peers in the work team and by customers, along with a variety of direct reports.

In the 1990s, Saint Francis Medical Center in Peoria, Illinois, adopted the 360-degree feedback system. Changes in healthcare delivery, coupled with the center's staff cuts and shift to flattened management layers, created the need for a newer mode of employee evaluation. Put simply, managers needed better feedback.

In Saint Francis's program, 132 managers each select eight "feedback providers" among their employees and customers. Each feedback provider completes an evaluation form. These forms, along with other forms for the individual, are sent to Performance Systems in Dallas for tabulation of each of the peer and customer group feedback providers. Recipients are sent a confidential report with composite scores for each group. Managers are taught how to interpret their scores, and then an action plan is written to address ways to strengthen or develop areas of concern. The Education Department at the center receives the action plans and serves as a developmental resource for managers to implement their plans. Additionally, managers are able to get coaching and support from any employee they choose to assist them in improving their skills.

The issues of confidentiality and protecting the identity of feedback providers are critical to making 360-degree feedback work. Saint Francis used the program for attaining employee and organizational development goals. By addressing development issues, employees felt safer about being candid with their evaluations. Likewise, addressing development allows employees to feel that the organization is making a personal and professional investment in them.

From a management perspective, 360-degree feedback offers an opportunity to gain solid, honest, and accurate information on issues deemed important to the organization as a whole. It can offer a solid position from which to make decisions about training and development programs, as well as a clearer definition and understanding of issues relevant to the overall organization.

Though ineffective for short-term problems, the 360-degree feedback system works well when applied to attaining long-term organizational goals, such as managing a change of culture from within. Advocates of 360-degree feedback firmly believe that it will work best in an organization with a mission and a clear set of values already firmly in place.

Source: P. Brotherton, "Candid Feedback Spurs Changes in Culture," *HRMagazine,* May 1996: 47–52.

Organizations are not static, but continually change in response to a variety of influences coming from both inside and outside. For administrators, the challenge is to anticipate and direct change processes so that organizational performance is enhanced. In this chapter, we will examine what is meant by organizational change and how it occurs. Then, we will consider techniques for managing and evaluating organizational change.

Sources of Change

"The one unchanging principle of life is the principle of change." This old saying contains an important element of truth: Change is an inevitable feature in both the lives of individuals and the lives of organizations. For both people and organizations, some facets of change are slow and nearly imperceptible, while others occur quite rapidly. In addition, the impact of change processes can vary from quite minor to truly substantial. Among the most common and influential forces of organizational change are the emergence of new competitors, innovations in technology, new company leadership, and evolving attitudes toward work.

It is useful to classify the sources of change as either external or internal. *External sources of change* originate in the organization's environment. In addition to competitors and suppliers, the external environment includes customers, the prevailing economic climate, the labor force, and the legal environment. Changes in any of these features of the external environment can have profound positive or negative effects on an organization. The rise and fall of competitors has clear implications for organizational performance, as does the cooperativeness and competencies of suppliers. If the preferences of customers change as a result of changes in taste, the well-being of a product line can be affected. Recessions, periods of inflation, and upturns or downturns in the local or national economy can have both direct and indirect influences on organizations. The education, talents, and attitudes of potential employees also play an important role in an organization's well-being. Changes in these facets of the labor force can lead to a shortage or a surplus of qualified employees. Last, legislation can produce change. Federal legislation, such as the enforcement of the policies of the Equal Employment Opportunity Commission and the Federal Trade Commission, can alter the procedures an organization traditionally uses in its recruiting and marketing functions.

Internal sources of change exist within the organization itself. Examples of internal pressures for change include shifts in workers' attitudes toward their supervisor or their benefits package, declining productivity, and changes in key personnel, whose goals and values influence large populations of the organization. Changes in attitudes among employees (due to increased age or changes in job responsibility) can result in changes in job satisfaction, attendance behavior, and commitment. Changes in top-level and other key individuals in an organization can alter the internal character of the organization. For example, if an incoming president emphasizes corporate ethics and customer service to his or her staff, those concerns will come to be reflected in the creation of new programs, the restructuring of the organization, and the evolution of a different organizational culture.

Organizational Growth and Decline

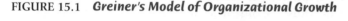

Organizational change often follows an evolutionary pattern of gradual growth and decline. The study of organizational change at the macro level of analysis reveals that forms of evolution and revolution occur as organizations grow.

In a popular model of organizational growth, Larry Greiner contends that every organization has an ideal structure that corresponds to its stage in the growth process.[1] For example, large organizations need more formalization of procedures and operations than do small, newly created organizations.

Greiner suggests that a series of stages characterize organizational growth. Each stage has a dominant theme or set of issues, and each new stage is preceded by a period of transition, which may be termed a *growth crisis*. Figure 15.1 depicts Greiner's model of organizational growth.

Growth through Creativity

At its birth, an organization is usually fairly informal and loose in structure. The control and moment-to-moment involvement of the organization's founders are likely to be strong. The creative energies of this founding group will help to carry the organization through its birth process. With the growth

FIGURE 15.1   *Greiner's Model of Organizational Growth*

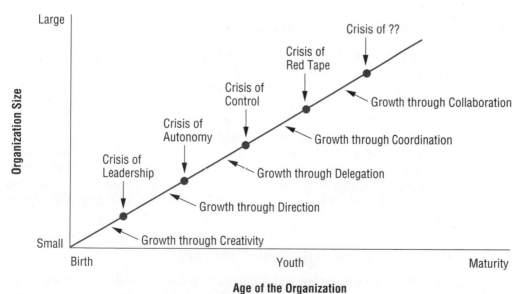

of the fledgling organization, the nature and variety of problems change. Personnel problems arise as the size of the workforce increases. Also, the organization's founders (whose first love may be closer to innovating and marketing than to management, operations, and personnel) may find themselves ill-equipped to lead their growing firm. This represents a *crisis of leadership*. This crisis can be overcome, most often, by acquiring professional managers to direct the organization.

Growth through Direction

Following resolution of the crisis of leadership, the organization enters a stage of growth through direction. Formalization is introduced by the professional managers. Greater bureaucratization takes place as departments and programs are established to help manage the organization. One result of this growth of bureaucracy is the creation of specialized divisions. Such specialization can lead to problems because as individuals within each division become increasingly skilled, they may seek greater control of their operations. These efforts at greater self-direction may be resisted by the same upper-level managers who originally introduced the specialization. The resulting tension can produce a *crisis of autonomy*.

Growth through Delegation

The next stage, delegation, follows the successful resolution of the crisis of autonomy. The crisis of autonomy is overcome by delegating greater decision-making power to middle- and lower-level managers; and top management begins to focus on long-range, strategic planning. However, middle- and lower-level managers eventually come to realize that the autonomous divisions sometimes pull in different directions and that performance may suffer due to a lack of control. Thus, the organization faces a *crisis of control.*

Growth through Coordination

The crisis of control can be resolved through increased coordination. For example, linkages may be created between members of different departments to enhance communication. Consultants may be hired to assess the extent of coordination needed and to suggest ways of improving efficiency and reducing redundancy. Project groups and task forces may be created to improve coordination, and matrix design concepts may be introduced. However, one consequence of creating these coordinating mechanisms is a profusion of managerial programs, and the resulting complexity may mean that more time and effort are spent on coordinating systems than on increasing actual productivity. The strangulation caused by such a proliferation of programs creates a *crisis of red tape.*

Continued Growth through Collaboration

Simplification of programs and systems and reliance on self-control and social norms may eventually replace more formal structures as an organization works its way through the red-tape crisis. Larger organizations often will bring

An Inside Look
The Buzzwords of Organizational Change

Building one's management vocabulary is just as formidable a task as reengineering the corporate culture in today's business environment. As corporate trends come and go, so does the accompanying vocabulary. Managers whose career goals are set on climbing to the loftiest ranks of corporate America must keep abreast of these trends and integrate the latest words and phrases into their own vocabulary to remain on the cutting edge. The hottest topic in corporate ranks today is "Change," and with change comes a new set of words.

Every employee should have "Core Competencies" to some degree. Desirable skills today include leadership skills, abilities to plan and strategize, effective communication skills in a variety of formats, and skills for working on a team, as well as a strong orientation to quality and service.

One who is "In Transition" is really unemployed. For executives in transition, this allows for a time of reflection on one's skills, core competencies, successes and failures. Often a transition leads to becoming a consultant or starting one's own business. For lower-level managers, it leads to employment counselors, headhunters, and job placement firms.

Today, firms "De-Layer," which typically occurs in middle management. Technology gathers information, which used to be a mid-management function,

so the logical choice is to de-layer at this level. "Derailment" can also affect the career climb. One who is derailed is knocked off of the fast track. A clue to a potential derailment or de-layerment is a "Disconnect"—when one is out of the communications loop.

To increase the odds of career success, establish "Face Time," which is the idea that time in the office is directly related to career success. "Thinking Out of the Box" is another way to bolster a career. Building new successes is a sure way to move one's career up the ranks, but do not do it as a challenge to your boss, for you might be disconnected. When faced with down-sizing decisions, companies keep employees who are "In Alignment" with their own attitudes and values. Team players are always in alignment.

Managers fight "Constant Whitewater" during the turbulent times of mergers, acquisitions, and re-engineering. Surviving the constant whitewater requires learning transition management skills. Successful managers learn "Empowerment," which pushes decision making to the lowest possible level. This gives lower-level managers the opportunity to grow, but it can also present a convenient scapegoat for a higher-level manager.

Source: "The Top 10 in Changespeak," *The Globe and Mail* , August 8, 1995.

in outside consultants to help them in their continued quest for collaboration. The goal of this stage is to teach managers how to cope with the organization's structure without giving in to the impulse to create additional structure.

Managing Organizational Decline

Just as organizations can be said to go through phases of birth, youth, and maturity, they also go through periods of decline.[*] **Organizational decline** can be defined as a "cutback in the size of an organization's work force, profits, budget, or clients."[2] This degeneration can occur in any industry and in any size organization.

---

[*]Organizations also experience death, although this topic has not received much serious study. Actually, approximately 90 percent of U.S. corporations do not survive more than 25 years. In taking a long-term perspective, it is interesting to note that very few formal organizations have survived since 1500. Among the survivors are the Catholic church, some European guilds, and some universities. Therefore, organizational death is not a rare phenomenon. Somewhat surprisingly, organizations that are dying (that is, being shut down) actually experience an increase in employee productivity, possibly a peculiar form of employee pride.

There are several specific factors that can lead to organizational decline. For example, within the organization itself, atrophy may occur. That is to say, the organization may simply become less efficient over time and lose its will to compete. Further problems may be created by self-complacency, loss of competitive drive, and a recalcitrant workforce.

An organization may also be in danger of declining if it is in a vulnerable state. Newly created organizations that are not yet fully established are especially vulnerable because they often lack cash reserves and managers who are experienced in handling crises. Economic downturns and vigorous competitors can also undo vulnerable organizations.

Changes in societal values and consumer tastes can lead to a loss of legitimacy and subsequent decline. For example, an organization that manufactures a product that the buying public no longer desires may well decline. An instance of these processes can be found in the reduced purchase of toy guns by parents during a time of war.

Last, organizations may decline because of insufficient external resources. Needed resources may become scarce, or uncertainty about a reliable supply may make it difficult to produce and deliver a finished good. Dependency on a supplier's ability to obtain and deliver resources can threaten the survival of many organizations.

Managing decline requires many of the same administrative skills as managing growth. The ability to seek creative solutions, the willingness to innovate, and the tactful management of conflict are necessary skills for managers of all organizations, declining or growing. "Toughing it out," minimizing losses, and making it to the next upswing, however, become management's top priorities during periods of decline.

Critical Determinants of Organizational Success and Failure

The features of organizations that make for success are not always the same ones that lead to failure.[3] Based on reports generated by professional consultants, it is possible to identify the specific factors that contribute most to success and failure. It is also possible to classify these factors as primarily environmental, structural, or management-oriented. Figure 15.2 summarizes this classification system.

Factors That Lead to Success

Although a successful organization need not possess all the positive attributes shown in Figure 15.2, most successful organizations show more positive than negative attributes. Successful organizations tend to focus on customers and their needs. They invest in ways to improve sales and provide superior service to clients, and they do not forget that their customers' needs underlie their organization's existence.

Successful organizations also adapt their structures to the needs of their missions. At the department level, controls may be simultaneously loose, in that managers have autonomy, and tight, insofar as specific performance goals may be set. Highly successful organizations often maintain a simple but appropriate structure that employs an adequate number of staff; they avoid

FIGURE 15.2   *Factors That Lead to Organizational Success and Failure*

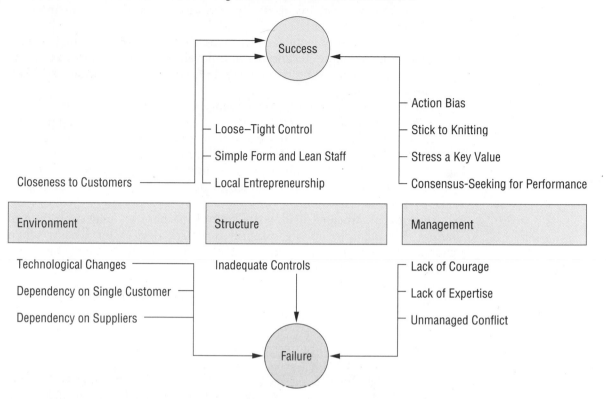

empire building and padding with surplus staff. Also, entrepreneurship is encouraged within the divisions of the organization by rewarding successful innovation and encouraging risk taking.

A major management feature that can lead to success is a deliberate bias toward implementing solutions to problems. Management discourages "paralysis through analysis" of alternatives, and, instead, emphasizes satisficing action that ensures goal attainment. Another management feature in successful firms is a commitment to the organization's original area of expertise. This is called "sticking to one's knitting." It involves staying close to what the organization knows how to do best and not being led down different paths in pursuit of attractive, but uncertain, alternative product lines.

Successful organizations also tend to stress a single value, such as delivering a quality product, reducing the cost of services to customers, or concern for each customer's unique needs. By emphasizing a single dominant value in their promotional materials and in their training of employees, the organization establishes a useful, distinct reputation for excellence in a specific area.

Finally, managers in successful companies often try to improve performance by achieving the agreement or consensus of employees. Thus, managers and workers may work together to set mutually agreeable performance goals. Employee suggestions are actively sought and a positive work group spirit, which will serve as a basis for enhanced motivation, is encouraged.

Factors That Lead to Failure

Different factors in an organization's environment, structure, and management may lead to its failure.

Among the environmental factors, changes in technology are a major cause of organizational failure. Technological innovations by competitors, as well as innovations that cannot be implemented within the organization itself, can lead to lost business.

Two forms of dependency—dependency on suppliers and dependency on a single customer—can also create problems. Difficulties in obtaining raw materials and financing from other institutions can prove fatal for an organization in a competitive environment. In addition, a customer that realizes that another organization is highly dependent on its business may use its resulting power to drive down prices or extract greater concessions by threatening to take its business elsewhere.

In terms of structure, inadequate control mechanisms may contribute to failure. For example, an organization may lack devices for sensing when changes occur that need to be corrected. As a result, product quality may suffer or changes in employee or customer satisfaction levels may be ignored.

Management factors may also contribute to failure. Courageous and decisive leadership can inspire an organization to overcome difficult situations or take quick action. In contrast, a tendency to overanalyze data or to take a "wait-and-see" attitude may cause a firm to lose ground to competitors and may exacerbate internal problems. The kinds of expertise that enable a young organization to thrive may become outdated as an organization matures. The need for professional managers to aid, or replace, the founding group may go unrecognized, and the importance of hiring new talent to revitalize the innovative process may be ignored.

Conflict can lead to serious dysfunction if it is not well managed. Conflicting groups often set their own goals for political and personal gain ahead of organizational goals. For this reason, conflict should be managed to ensure that it remains in desired forms and at desired levels. (Recall that a certain level of internal conflict is probably inevitable and even desirable.)

As Figure 15.2 suggests, success and failure factors are not evenly distributed across the three major sources. For example, more environmental factors may contribute to failure than to success. Conversely, more structural factors are potential sources of success than of failure. And an almost equal number of management factors seem to lead to both success and failure. This analysis, while somewhat simplistic, suggests a useful insight: Environmental factors are more likely to pose potential threats to an organization's well-being, while structural factors are an organization's major means of achieving success or, at least, coping with threats. It almost goes without saying that management-related factors are potential sources of both organizational success and organizational failure.

Organizational Development

Organizational development (OD) is a distinct area within the field of organizational science that focuses on the planned and controlled change of

Figure 15.3 *Interdependent Organizational Elements That May Be the Focus of Change in OD*

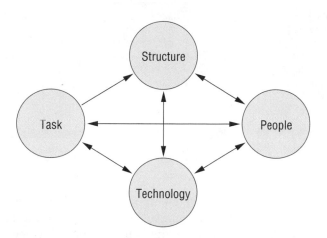

organizations in desired directions. In general, outside consultants, rather than organizational members, are usually responsible for managing the development process. In essence, OD attempts to change an organization as a totality by changing the organization's structure, technology, people, and/or tasks. Figure 15.3 presents one view of OD that emphasizes these four facets of an organization. In reality, any facet of an organization is a legitimate target of OD. In our discussion we will focus primarily on change efforts that are directed at people rather than at tasks, structure, or technology. A popular definition of OD, which we can use for discussing the people side of planned change, states that OD is a "long-range effort to improve an organization's problem-solving and renewal process . . . through a more effective . . . management of organization culture . . . with the assistance of a change agent . . . and the use of the theory and technology of applied behavioral science."[4]

Phases in the OD Process

All OD specialists, sometimes called change agents, recognize the difficulties inherent in bringing about successful, positive changes. Some years ago, Kurt Lewin, a famous behavioral scientist, argued that the process of change involves three basic phases (see Figure 15.4): unfreezing, changing, refreezing.[5] **Unfreezing** begins to occur when a situation is recognized as being deficient or inadequate in some way. The recognition that employees' attitudes or skills are insufficient, or that rules and procedures generate problems that hinder task completion, may trigger the unfreezing process. Sometimes a crisis must occur before a problem is given the attention it deserves. For example, unsafe working conditions may be allowed to continue until a wildcat strike or a life-threatening accident forces management to acknowledge the problem and take action. Unfreezing must occur before OD can succeed because an individual's failure to recognize or accept the existence of a problem can block any desire to change.

FIGURE 15.4   *Lewin's View of the Change Process*

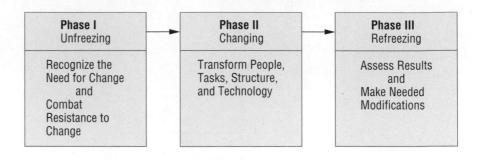

The second phase in the process, **changing,** occurs when a new plan or system is implemented in the organization. Such a plan may call for a new recruiting or orientation program, or the introduction of a new accounting system. It may affect the entire organization, as would a total restructuring, or it may focus on only a few key individuals, as would a values-clarification exercise involving the top-level management team.

Refreezing, the third phase in the change process, occurs as the newly created patterns of behavior and techniques become part of ongoing organizational processes. During the refreezing phase, change agents usually attempt to appraise the effectiveness of their intervention. If they believe that intervention has failed, they may redirect their efforts to compensate for their program's shortcomings.

Resistance to Change

Attempts at organizational development are often met with resistance.[†] Employees tend to fear change, partly from a desire for security and contentment with the status quo. Consequently, they may be quick to identify shortcomings in a proposed plan for change and use them to their advantage. If their objections are registered but not redressed, they may act to ensure that the identified problems actually do undercut the program for change.

Resistance to change, one of the most serious challenges for an OD specialist, may be overcome in a number of ways. One of the most common techniques is *education,* not in the formal sense but in terms of meeting with groups of employees to address their concerns and explain the planned changes. *Participation* in the development of plans for change is also an effective way of overcoming resistance. In one well-known study, it was observed that resistance to change can be significantly reduced by having the affected employees actually participate in the design of the change effort.[6] Programs for change that are, in a sense, "owned" by the people who are most affected are often more likely to

[†]As noted long ago by Machiavelli, "There is no more delicate matter than to introduce changes. For he who innovates will have for his enemies all those who are well off under the existing order of things, and only lukewarm supporters in those who might be better off under the new."

succeed.[7] Another means of overcoming resistance is *negotiation*. When dealing with employees who have taken a stand against change, this means obtaining statements in writing about trade-offs and concessions that both management and employees will make in order to accommodate change.

In practice, strong-arm tactics, despite their questionable ethical merit, are sometimes used. Chief among these methods are outright *coercion*, such as threatening people with dismissal if they resist the planned change, and *manipulation of opinion* through the careful selection and timing of the information released so as to ensure a favorable impact.

OD Techniques

Survey Feedback   One of the most widely used sources of information for OD specialists is **survey feedback.** To obtain the information they need, they administer written questionnaires or interview employees. The questions in these surveys typically touch on such topics as satisfaction, leadership, and decision making. The results are summarized and statistically analyzed before they are given back to top-level administrators. Once senior management has examined the results and considered their meaning, the data are fed back to the participants for their consideration and interpretation. In practice, such feedback is often intended to arouse awareness of the need for change. For example, through survey feedback, top management may discover that morale is especially low among members of a particular department, or a group of employees may begin to recognize that they all share a common view of a problem. Following recognition of the need for change, employees' suggestions for designing and implementing change programs are solicited.

Although the OD survey feedback technique may sound similar to the traditional notion of conducting a survey of employees, there are important distinctions between the two approaches.[8] In the traditional approach, data are usually collected only from lower-level employees, but in survey feedback, everyone in the organization is likely to be surveyed. Similarly, in the traditional approach, only top management is likely to see the results, but in the OD variation, everyone in the organization receives feedback at some point. Furthermore, the development of plans to deal with survey results is the prerogative of top management in the traditional approach, but everyone can have input in the survey feedback approach. Because of these essential differences, the survey feedback approach is more likely to achieve productive change.

Team Building   Another OD technique, **team building,** has been widely used by specialists in recent years at such diverse organizations as Trans Australia Airlines, Mead Corporation, and Tandem Computers. The hub of team building is existing work groups, called *family groups,* or newly formed groups of employees brought together for a particular purpose, called *special groups.* The goal in both existing work groups and special groups is to improve performance by tackling problems and obstacles.

In a typical team-building effort, a small group of people is brought together at a retreat-like location removed from their place of employment. By getting away from the workplace, they can avoid interruptions and fully concentrate on problem solving.

At their initial meeting, the work group might examine both "hard" and "soft" data that pertain to productivity problems, such as monthly sales figures and customer satisfaction reports. The purpose of examining these data is to encourage the group to enter the unfreezing phase of the OD process and get them to recognize the need for change. During subsequent meetings, the change agent attempts to facilitate the process by encouraging frank and open discussions of various aspects of the problem facing the group. Ultimately, the group will be encouraged to develop a specific plan for attaining a desired end state. At later meetings, the group will review the success of the plan and develop and implement refinements of its content.

Sensitivity Training   A third technique that has been widely used by change agents is **sensitivity training.** Sometimes called T-groups (for training groups), this approach originated at the National Training Laboratory in Bethel, Maine. Over the years, despite some changes in name to *encounter groups* and *laboratory training,* the technique has remained much the same. In a T-group, 8 to 12 individuals are brought together for a series of 2- to 3-hour sessions. The group's trainer does not take an active role in the group's discussions, but instead serves more as a guide or facilitator. The ostensible goal of the sessions is to increase self-awareness and sensitivity to others. To achieve this goal, members are expected to focus on behavior and on giving feedback about their perceptions of one another. Getting to the point at which personal and social learning occurs is sometimes difficult, and, in some cases, group members' reactions may get out of hand. For example, the group may turn on one particular member and severely criticize him or her without reaching a positive reconciliation by the end of the session. Because the group does not have an agenda, some members who are used to working in an ordered and goal-directed social system may become uncomfortable. Often, one member will strive to become group leader to fill the leadership vacuum created by the trainer's refusal to control discussions and behavior. Later, other group members may criticize and resent the individual who attempted to take the leadership role.

For some groups, a state of open and frank discussion is difficult to achieve. This is especially true for groups composed of people who work together in a naturally occurring work unit. To encourage freer discussions, some trainers prefer to work with stranger groups—groups whose members do not know one another—and cousin groups—groups whose members work within the same organization but do not report to one another.

In recent years, T-groups have been declining in popularity due to a variety of factors. One of the chief forces lies in a fear that people "may be taken apart like a clock and not put back together." Team building, with its focus on the enhancement of productivity instead of social skills, has been more widely adopted.

Confrontation Meetings   A further technique for bringing about desired change attempts to manage dysfunctional conflict (see Chapter 10) through **confrontation meetings.** In this approach, conflicting groups are brought together in a structured situation that is designed to enhance cooperation.[9]

Most confrontation meetings follow a predictable sequence. First, the conflicting groups' leaders discuss the need for change with the change agent. At this session, the leaders and the consultant draw up a specific plan for meetings between the two groups. Next, each group meets separately to create a list that summarizes their views of the other group's attitudes and behaviors. In addition, they attempt to develop a list of impressions that they believe the other group would devise in describing themselves. Next, at a formal joint meeting, a spokesperson for each group reads aloud his or her group's lists. No discussion or reaction is allowed. The groups then meet again in separate rooms to discuss what they have learned about themselves and the other group. Each also draws up a list of issues that need to be resolved.

At the second joint meeting, all members openly discuss the lists of issues that need resolution and develop a plan of action for reducing conflict and achieving cooperation. At subsequent meetings, groups discuss their progress toward implementing their plans and the removal of further obstacles to improved collaboration.

Quality of Work Life   In many Western industrialized countries, there has been a growing recognition of the importance of simultaneously enhancing both the value of employees' psychological experiences at work and employees' productivity. This philosophy is embodied in the **quality of work life (QWL)** approach to OD.[‡] QWL is not a set of specific techniques, but rather an approach that seeks to enhance the total work climate in an organization or its subsystems. QWL programs focus on such issues as conflict reduction, employee satisfaction, and work participation. In terms of actual techniques, QWL programs often encompass job redesign (Chapter 5), employee involvement in decision making (Chapter 8), redesign of pay systems (Chapter 5) and/or the creation of quality circles (Chapter 5). In essence, QWL represents a desired end state that emphasizes the importance of providing opportunities for employees to contribute to their jobs as well as to receive more from their jobs.[10] Successful QWL programs have been used in such firms as AT&T, IBM, Texas Instruments, Xerox, and Procter & Gamble.[11]

Conditions for the Successful Adoption of OD

From numerous successes and failures in implementing OD programs, practitioners have been able to generate a specific list of conditions that help to ensure that an OD effort will succeed. Among the most important are:

1. Recognition by top-level management that problems exist
2. Support and involvement in the program by top-level management, work group supervisors, and opinion leaders
3. Early successes in the OD program that suggest that the program is working and thereby encourage further cooperation
4. Respect for the managerial talents of those whose domain of responsibility is being improved
5. Cooperation and involvement on the part of human resource managers
6. Effective coordination and control of the OD program
7. Measurement of outcomes.[12]

[‡]QWL is often pronounced "quill" by change agents.

Does OD Work?

Despite the difficulty of measuring the effects of OD efforts, it is possible to draw some tentative conclusions about the general value of OD in enhancing organizational effectiveness.

A review of 29 studies determined that using employee participation in a change effort was associated with enhanced productivity in 14 studies, while reduced productivity was observed in only 2 studies (the remaining studies had ambiguous results).[13] Training programs were also found to have positive productivity effects. For example, one study found a 19 percent rise in productivity over a three-year period relative to firms that did not introduce training. A further study of *Forbes* 500 firms found that those with more progressive management style, organizational structure, and reward systems had higher rates of growth in profits, sales, and earnings per share over a five-year period.

Another review of 35 studies sorted the obtained results into outcome variables and process variables.[14] Outcome variables refer to measures of productivity, efficiency, absenteeism, profits, and so on (relatively "hard" measures), while process variables refer to measures of trust, perceptions of leadership, motivation, and decision making (relatively "soft" measures). In addition, the sample of studies was further divided into categories based on whether the OD efforts were directed at groups, organizations, individuals, or leaders. The analyses of these studies suggested that group outcome variables (for example, group productivity) were most likely to be enhanced following OD interventions. Individual process variables also showed relatively positive improvement (for example, individual job satisfaction increased in roughly 40 percent

TABLE 15.1   *Effects of OD Efforts on Outcome and Process Variables*

Outcome Variables	Examples	Number of Studies	Average Positive Change
Group	Performance, length of meetings	8	63%
Organization	Profit, return on investment	12	47%
Individual	Performance, satisfaction	14	42%
Leader	Performance	3	—
Total		22	51%

Process Variables	Examples	Number of Studies	Average Positive Change
Individual	Self-awareness, self-actualization	10	62%
Group	Trust, involvement	20	49%
Leader	Openness to influence, interaction facilitation	20	45%
Organization	Leadership, decision making	27	36%
Total		35	46%

of the OD studies in which it was measured). Table 15.1 summarizes these results in order of positive impact.

A further analysis was made of these studies in terms of the impact of various OD procedures. By and large, the most common OD techniques, such as team building and survey feedback, were reported to have positive effects, while T-groups were somewhat less effective.

Despite the methodological shortcomings of many OD-related studies and the tendency of OD specialists to report their results in the most positive light (OD failures are less frequently written up), these results suggest that the efforts are usually effective.[§] As these reviews suggest, the precise nature of OD's impact depends on the type of technique, its duration, and the measures chosen to evaluate the intervention.

OD in Perspective

Although various reviews point to positive conclusions, the value of OD as commonly conducted is often questioned by both managers and behavioral scientists. Some of this criticism derives from a healthy skepticism on the part of managers and behavioral scientists. However, other factors can partially account for this criticism.[16]

First of all, OD is not a cure-all for every difficulty an organization may face. Its successful use requires skill and expertise, and it is most applicable to interpersonal problems. When used by nonexperts and applied to inappropriate situations, OD cannot be expected to succeed.

Users may also be disappointed to find that OD often does not live up to its stated ideal as described in articles and texts, but the flaw may be traceable to the users' approach. For example, OD is often performed at the lower levels of an organization, following top management's endorsement. The attitude that OD is a task to be delegated to lower-level managers is likely to minimize the impact of most such programs. Yet high levels of participation, support, and concern for OD efforts from top-level management are fairly rare.

As discussed earlier, resistance to change is a significant obstacle to OD efforts. Although resistance on the individual level may be manageable, more difficult challenges arise when resistance stems from the total organizational system and its need to cope with its external environment. The external environment, of course, cannot be meaningfully changed by most OD efforts— and OD efforts are rarely intended to make such changes. Therefore, this larger constraint limits the progress that is possible within the organization.

In addition, organizations may be based on values that can significantly curtail certain forms of change. For example, religiously affiliated organizations typically adhere to specific sets of values, mission statements, and codes of conduct that set limits on what is feasible in the way of change. Thus, the perceived nature of an organization and what it stands for will dictate what changes are deemed permissible by both its members and its constituent groups in the larger society.

[§]A specific finding that should increase our caution in drawing inferences about the merits of OD is that the more methodologically rigorous a study is, the less likely it is to report that an OD effort has been successful.[15]

It has also been suggested that the chief values espoused by change agents—trust, openness, and power sharing—are not appropriate for some organizations. As part of their work, OD practitioners attempt to convert employees to their value system. Then, when the specific OD effort is completed, the employees must function within the larger, as yet unchanged, system of their organization. At this point, OD training may backfire because an employee who attempts to implement a philosophy of openness in a hostile environment may experience frustration and punishment rather than acceptance. In fact, people who adopt an open style of conduct may have problems competing with the more political and devious members of their organization.[17] In some instances, highly valued, competent, and successful employees may come to so fully embrace the values of openness and honesty that they reject their employment setting because it does not support their newfound values. As a result, the organization may actually lose valuable employees due to a shift in personal values induced by an OD effort. The irony, of course, is that the OD effort was intended to help such individuals perform better, rather than encouraging them to leave. In such cases, critics may contend that OD has made the employees less able to cope with the real world.

It has been suggested that change agents rely largely on "truth and love" as sources of influence.[18] OD is, of course, more appropriate under conditions of openness and collaboration. But, in practice, change agents may sometimes rely on the truth-love model when it is inappropriate—that is, in situations characterized by distrust and conflict. This, then, is the basic dilemma for change agents: How can they help people in situations of conflict to realize and affirm the values of trust and collaboration? The truth-love model is more typically endorsed by wealthy and powerful organizations, such as IBM, AT&T, and Union Carbide. But many "disadvantaged organizations" most in need of OD, such as local governments, smaller firms, and social action groups, are less likely to be involved in OD efforts.

In the future, organizations may need to rely more heavily on the services of change agents as they are forced to undergo planned change. This need for managed change will result from a variety of emerging forces. Rapid changes in technology, for example, will require organizations to adjust their structure and processes. Also, the environment for many organizations will become more turbulent and uncertain. Contributing to this pressure will be an increasingly global business environment and a shrinking qualified labor pool (caused by both a "baby bust" and continuing challenges for the American educational system to reliably produce highly competent individuals for the workforce). All these forces will require organizations to be more flexible and responsive. The ability to effectively implement planned change, therefore, will likely be of even greater importance in the years to come.

SUMMARY

1. *Identify external and internal sources of change in an organization.* External sources of change include competitors, suppliers, customers, the prevailing economic climate, the labor force, and the legal environment. Internal sources of change include shifts in workers' attitudes, declining productivity, and changes in key personnel.

2. *Describe the stages of organizational growth.* An organization begins with a loose structure and grows through creativity until a crisis of leadership develops. The organization hires professional managers and enters a phase of growth through direction. A more formal structure leads to tension among specialized divisions and a crisis of autonomy. During the next stage, growth through delegation, middle- and lower-level managers receive greater power to make decisions, and a crisis of control arises. In the next stage, growth through collaboration, programs to increase coordination resolve the crisis of control but create a crisis of red tape. To continue growth through collaboration, the organization simplifies programs and systems.

3. *List causes of organizational decline.* Organizations decline as a result of atrophy within the organization, self-complacency, loss of competitive drive, a recalcitrant work force, vulnerability because of low resources or inexperienced management, economic downturns, vigorous competition, changes in societal values, and lack of external resources.

4. *Identify factors that lead to an organization's success or failure.* Organizations that succeed emphasize customers and their needs, exercise loose control at the departmental level but tight control over specific goals, have a simple structure, encourage entrepreneurship within the organization, emphasize action, maintain a commitment to original areas of expertise, stress a key value, and seek consensus among employees. Factors leading to failure include technological changes, dependency on suppliers or a single customer, inadequate control mechanisms, hesitancy to make change, lack of expertise, and unmanaged conflict.

5. *Describe the phases in the process of change in an organization.* The first phase, unfreezing, begins with recognition that a situation is deficient. The second phase, changing, occurs with implementation of a new plan or system. The third phase, refreezing, occurs as the newly created patterns of behavior and techniques become part of ongoing organizational processes.

6. *Describe techniques that change agents use to help bring about change in organizations.* Change agents use feedback from surveys to obtain information and arouse awareness of the need for change. Another technique, team building, uses discussion of problems as a way to improve performance. Sensitivity training attempts to increase self-awareness and sensitivity to others. The goal of confrontation meetings is to manage dysfunctional intergroup conflict. Quality of work life programs use such techniques as job redesign, employee involvement in decision making, redesign of pay systems, and quality circles to enhance the total work climate.

7. *Identify the conditions that enhance the likelihood an OD effort will succeed.* Conditions favorable to success include top-level management recognition that problems exist, leader support of and involvement in the program, early successes in the OD program, respect for the talents of the affected managers, cooperation and involvement from human resources managers, effective coordination and control of the OD program, and measurement of outcomes.

8. *Evaluate the track record of OD programs.* The success of an OD program depends on the type of technique, its duration, and the way the results are measured. Overall, research suggests that OD programs are usually effective.

KEY TERMS

Organizational decline
Organizational development (OD)
Unfreezing
Changing
Refreezing

Survey feedback
Team building
Sensitivity training
Confrontation meetings
Quality of work life (QWL)

CRITICAL INCIDENT

Staunch Resistance at Metropolitan Police Department

Jerry Spore was disgusted. As commander of the 10th Division of the Metropolitan Police Department (MPD), he had just issued an ultimatum to Deputy Chief Robert Powell. All officers not in compliance with the new uniform standards within two weeks' time would be issued official reprimands that carry time-off-without-pay sanctions. He just couldn't understand what the problem was.

It all began two years ago, when a group of city officials responded to complaints from citizens about the Gestapo-like design of MPD officers' uniforms. Until that time, officers still donned the old-fashioned eight-pointed hat. Their other accessories were also traditional in style. Leather Sam Browne belts were worn over leather pants belts. Gun holsters, cuffs, and other equipment pertinent to the job were attached to the Sam Browne belts. City officials perceived citizens' comments to be reflective of the total MPD image, and they prompted Spore to work on improving that image by modifying the uniforms.

Spore took the task seriously. He formed a committee of local citizens and businesspeople to research and evaluate possible uniform modifications. Uniform suppliers called on the committee and encouraged them to adopt coordinated uniforms and accessories designed to maximize utility. The committee's conclusions were that they could get a lot of "bang for their buck" by simply changing key accessories in the uniform. They recommended that the city purchase new Sam Browne belts, new pants belts, and new rounded-top hats for the officers. The committee recommended that the uniforms be introduced in the police academy, and then adopted by the entire force over a period of six months, allowing for ample acquisition and distribution time.

All new recruits, therefore, were issued new belts and hats, as were all experienced officers. The hats were accepted almost without comment, but the belts met with resistance. The outside of the pants belt was Velcro as was the inside of the Sam Browne belt, thus allowing them to be conveniently attached. Belt closures were also Velcro. The belts required less maintenance and were slightly less expensive than the former standard belts.

Officers claimed that the rigid Velcro backing cut the pants loops. They also said that the belts were uncomfortable to wear. Spore observed that the problem probably related more to obesity than to the belt design. The more portly officers were accustomed to wearing their belts low, under their abdomens, and the backing material on the new belts did not cooperate. A few of the older officers also complained that the new belts were dangerous. They argued that each officer placed tools necessary for protection in a slightly different spot on the belts, and that this change could actually cost an officer's life in an emergency situation.

Most officers fresh out of the academy had replaced the issued Velcro-style belts, which they had discarded, with leather versions. Anyone seen with a Velcro belt was labeled as "green," or "nerdy." The change had been completely ignored by the other officers, and apparently Powell had been reprimanded by the now-disbanded committee about the waste of its time and money.

Meanwhile, Powell had been given the task to shape up these guys. Powell sensed that there was a lot more than logic behind the officers' resistance. Powell judged that Spore had made one key mistake in handling this whole uniform business, and that mistake was affecting the entire change process. He didn't blame the officers for their gripes, but he also knew that his own neck was on the line. Powell was only one year from retirement, and didn't want to blow things now.

1. What do you think Spore's key mistake was?

2. What were the forces for change behind the uniform issue?

3. Use Kurt Lewin's model of change to recommend an ideal plan for making the change to the new uniform.

Source: Adapted by Susan Stites-Doe, State University of New York, College at Brockport, from J.B. Ritchie and Paul R. Thompson, *Organization and People*, 4th ed. (San Francisco: West Publishing, 1988): 444–446. Used with permission.

EXPERIENTIAL EXERCISE

Introducing a Change—A Role Play

Most changes in organizations go far beyond the technical aspects of doing work; they usually involve alterations that influence the work satisfaction of the employees. In fact, change is often encountered on a personal level by most people. And frequently their reaction to change is one of resistance—not necessarily to the change itself but to what the change represents: the loss of known satisfaction.

As a manager, one might think of a continuum of approaches to introducing change, not unlike a leadership continuum (Chapter 7). At one end is telling/selling, where facts and arguments are presented showing the advantages of the change. In the middle is consultation, where the manager discusses the need for change with subordinates, solicits their ideas, and makes the decision. At the other end is collaboration, where the manager and the subordinates discuss the need for change and reach a consensus on a plan for implementing the change. The nature of the discussion that the manager initiates, plus the valence or attractiveness of what's at stake, will go a long way toward affecting the forces for and against change.

Step 1   This activity is a role play that concerns a change that must be introduced. The change affects everyone personally. Four volunteers will be selected for the roles. The remaining class members will serve as observers. Your instructor will provide each role player with a description of his or her role (the role descriptions are provided in the *Instructor's Manual*). If you are a role player, you should *not* let anyone else know the role situation you are in.

Step 2   The remaining class members will receive an observer's form from the instructor. It is very important for this activity that you fulfill your responsibilities as an observer. Having read and interpreted the roles, each role player should move to the front of the classroom. Four chairs arranged in a semicircle will represent the supervisor's office. On the instructor's signal, the group supervisor should begin the meeting.

Step 3   Once the role play has resulted in an acceptable outcome, the entire class can reconvene to discuss the observer's responses. The questions posed to the observers explore the dynamics of change in a manner that seeks recognition of the importance of power, influence, communication, motivation, and so forth. This activity will enable you to integrate most of the issues you have learned about in organizational behavior.

Source: Written by Bruce Kemelgor, University of Louisville.

Glossary*

Accommodating A style of conflict management involving giving in to another's wishes. (10)

Achievement-oriented leadership In path–goal theory, a leader behavior that entails setting challenging goals while simultaneously showing confidence in the subordinates' abilities. (7)

Administrative model A decision-making model recognizing that bounded rationality limits the making of optimally rational-economic decisions. (8)

Attribution theory A theory that suggests that we observe the behavior of others and then attribute internal or external causes to it. (2)

Authority Power based on the legitimate right to try to change others' behavior or tell them what to do. (6)

Availability heuristic A process used when an individual estimates the frequency or probability of an event or class of objects by the ease with which instances can be brought to mind. (8)

Avoiding A style of conflict management in which a person attempts to adopt a neutral stance. (10)

Behavior modification An approach to motivation that uses the principles of operant conditioning. (4)

Behavioral theory of decision making An approach to decision making that recognizes that bounded rationality limits the making of optimal decisions. (8)

"Big Five" dimensions Personality dimensions found to have special relevance to the workplace: agreeableness, conscientiousness, emotional adjustment, extroversion, and inquisitiveness. (2)

Boundary-spanning position A position within an organization that represents the organization to various constituencies in the external environment. (10)

Bounded discretion Limitations imposed on the decision-making process that result from moral and ethical constraints. (8)

Bounded rationality The assumption that organizational, social, and human limitations lead decision makers to settle on decisions that are "good enough" rather than optimal. (8)

Brainstorming A technique designed to generate creative solutions to problems by encouraging group members to express their ideas freely in a non-critical atmosphere. (8)

Bureaucracy An organizational structure proposed by Weber emphasizing rationality and including such features as adherence to formal rules, a hierarchy of authority, specialization, hiring based on qualifications, and promotion based on merit. (13)

Burnout Physical, emotional, and mental exhaustion resulting from prolonged exposure to stressful situations. (11)

Cautious shift A tendency for groups to make more conservative decisions than individuals. (8)

Centralized network A communication network in which members have unequal opportunities to obtain and pass on information. Information flows through a pivotal or central person. (12)

Chain of command A concept maintaining that information and authority proceed from level to level in a strict hierarchical fashion. (13)

Changing The second phase of Lewin's model of change, in which a new plan or system is implemented. (15)

Charismatic leadership Leadership based on referent power and characterized by self-confidence, sense of purpose, and an articulated vision. (7)

Classical conditioning An approach to learning in which an unconditioned stimulus is repeatedly paired with a neutral stimulus until the neutral stimulus alone can elicit the same response that was evoked by the unconditioned stimulus. When this occurs, the neutral stimulus is termed a conditioned stimulus and the response, a conditioned response. (3)

Classical decision theory An approach to decision making that assumes that decision makers are objective, have complete information, and consider all possible alternatives and their consequences before selecting the optimal solution. *See also* Rational–economic model (8)

Closed group A group in which the membership remains fairly stable. (9)

Closed system A system that does not interact with its external environment. (14)

Coercive power Power based on the extent to which an individual or organization has control over punishments. The opposite of reward power. (6)

Cognitive resource theory The view that directive leaders who are intelligent and possess relevant job experience will be more effective if they are in stress-free settings with subordinates who are supportive. (7)

Cognitive style Mode of gathering and evaluating information. Jung identified four types: sensing, intuiting, thinking, and feeling. (2)

Cohesiveness The sum of all forces acting on group members to remain a part of the group. (9)

Collaborating A style of conflict management that attempts to satisfy the concerns of both sides through honest discussion. (10)

Communication The creation of a mental image in the mind of a receiver in exactly the same detail as intended by the sender. (12)

Communication role The specific functions an individual serves in an organization's communication network. (12)

*The chapter in which a glossary term is initially discussed is given in parentheses.

G-1

Compliance   An individual's acceptance of an influence attempt in the belief that rewards will follow or punishment will be avoided. (10)

Compromising   A style of conflict management that strives for partial satisfaction of both sides' desires. (10)

Conditioned response   In classical conditioning, a reflexive response evoked by a conditioned stimulus. (3)

Conditioned stimulus   In classical conditioning, a neutral stimulus that has attained the capacity to evoke a conditioned response. (3)

Conflict   A form of interaction between individuals or groups in situations that occurs when one or both sides perceive that the other has thwarted or is about to thwart an important concern. (10)

Confrontation meetings   An organizational development technique in which conflicting groups are brought together in a structured situation designed to enhance cooperation. (15)

Conglomerate   An organizational firm that includes a broad range of diverse business units. (14)

Consideration   A factor referring to the extent to which a leader exhibits concern for the welfare of the group members. (7)

Content theories   Theories that focus on the specific factors that motivate people to perform. Examples are the theories of Maslow, Herzberg, and McClelland. (4)

Contextual dimensions   Characteristics of the entire organization and its external environment, such as size, technology, and external constituents (e.g., customers, suppliers, and competitors). (14)

Contingency approach   An approach to organizational behavior stating that there is no one best way to manage every situation, but that management must find different ways to deal with different situations. (1)

Contingency model of leadership effectiveness   A theory suggesting that leadership effectiveness is determined both by the characteristics of the leader and by the level of situational favorableness that exists. (7)

Continuous reinforcement   A schedule designed to reinforce correct behavior every time it is exhibited. (3)

Cosmopolite   An individual whose communication network extends into the organization's external environment. (12)

Culture-quality movement   A perspective emerging in the early 1980s that emphasized the importance of such organizational value issues as employee involvement and commitment in influencing the quality of production output. (1)

Decentralization   The degree to which decision making occurs lower down in an organization. (13)

Decentralized network   A communication network in which each member has an equal opportunity to obtain and pass on information. (12)

Deficiency needs   The lower-order needs (physiological, safety, and social) in Maslow's hierarchy that must be satisfied to ensure a person's existence. (4)

Delphi technique   A technique for improving group decision making in which the opinions of experts are solicited by a mailed questionnaire and then compiled. The consensus is used to make a decision. (8)

Diffusion of responsibility   A concept, often used to explain the risky shift, that holds that individual responsibility is shared among a group's members. (8)

Directive leadership   In path–goal theory, a leader behavior that involves giving specific guidance to subordinates and asking that they follow standard rules and regulations. (7)

Dominant culture   A set of core values that is shared by most employees. (14)

Downward communication   Communication that flows from higher to lower levels within an organization. (12)

Emotional labor   The active self-management of behaviors, affective tone, and moods by employees in order to maintain a positive self-presentation. (11)

Employee empowerment   A set of motivational techniques designed to improve employee performance through increased levels of employee participation and self-determination. (5)

Employee envy   A pattern of thoughts, emotions, and behaviors that results when an employee feels a loss of self-esteem in response to another obtaining personally desired outcomes. (11)

Employee growth-need strength   The strength of an employee's desire for personal growth experiences in the work setting. (5)

Employee jealousy   A pattern of thoughts, emotions, and behaviors that results from an employee's felt loss of self-esteem and the loss of outcomes associated with a working relationship. (11)

Employee orientation   A style of leadership referring to the extent a leader shows concern for the welfare of the group members. (7)

Enacted role   The actual set of behaviors exhibited by an individual in a position. (9)

Equity theory   A theory that suggests that a person will strive to maintain a ratio of input to outcome that is equal to the ratio of a comparison other. (4)

Expectancy theory   A theory suggesting that behavior is a function of a person's expectancies about the future and the value of future outcomes. (4)

Expected role   The formal set of behaviors conveyed both by a job description and by members of the work unit. (9)

Expert power   Individual power based on the possession of expert, job-relevant knowledge. (6)

Extinction   The decline in response rate that occurs when reinforcement is removed from behaviors that were previously rewarded. (3)

Extrinsic reward   A reward external to the job, such as pay or promotion. (5)

Fixed interval schedule   A schedule in which a reward is applied only after a fixed amount of time has passed since the last reward was given. (3)

Fixed ratio schedule   A schedule in which a set number of responses must be performed before a reward is applied. (3)

Fixed schedule   A reinforcement schedule in which the amount of time or number of behaviors performed is specified. (3)

Flat structure   Describes an organization with fewer levels of authority and larger spans of control. (13)

Flextime   A work schedule that gives employees some discretion in arranging their working hours, specifically their starting and ending times. (5)

Flow A totally absorbing experience in which one senses joy, fulfillment, and creativity. (4)

Foot-in-the-door principle The tendency to comply with a request for a sizable favor following a request for a small favor. (6)

Forcing A form of conflict management that attempts to overwhelm an opposing side with formal authority, threats, or the use of power. (10)

Formal group A group formed within an organization to accomplish the goals of the organization. (9)

Forming The earliest stage of group development, in which members determine behaviors that are acceptable and unacceptable. (9)

Functional design A basic type of organization design that groups personnel and activities according to resources that are essential to the production process. (13)

Functional turnover The assumption that high turnover among poor performers can benefit an organization. (11)

Fundamental attribution error The tendency to attribute the behavior of others to internal forces. (2)

Gain sharing An incentive scheme that ties an individual's bonuses to the performance of a business unit. (5)

Game playing Forms of patterned social interaction based on giving and getting "strokes" in the transactional analysis view. (12)

Gatekeeper An individual in an organization who controls the flow of information to others. (12)

General Adaptation Syndrome Refers to the three stages of stress identified by Selye: alarm, resistance, and exhaustion. (11)

Global approach An approach to studying job satisfaction taking into account an employee's overall reaction to a job. (11)

Goal acceptance The degree of a person's acceptance of the goal. (5)

Goal difficulty The degree of proficiency or level of job performance that is being sought by the goal. (5)

Goal specificity The degree of precision of the goal. (5)

Grapevine Informal channels of communication that exist within an orga-

nization and short-circuit the formal channels. (12)

Greenfield site A new facility with a new workforce, often established as part of an effort to introduce self-directed work teams. (5)

Grid analysis A technique for improving creativity in which ideas are listed on the sides of a two-dimensional grid and all possible combinations of ideas are examined. (8)

Group A collection of two or more individuals who interact with each other, share common beliefs, and perceive themselves as being in a group. (9)

Group polarization The tendency for members of a group to move to extreme positions (in the direction they originally favored) following group discussion. (8)

Groupthink The tendency for members of a highly cohesive group to seek consensus so strongly that they fail to explore alternative, possibly correcting, courses of action. (8)

Growth needs The higher-order needs (esteem and self-actualization) in Maslow's hierarchy that are concerned with the realization of one's potential. (4)

Halo effect An overall favorable or unfavorable impression of a person that is used as a basis for performance evaluation, regardless of the actual performance level. (2)

Hawthorne effect A phenomenon seen in test situations, in which enhanced employee performance largely results from the employees' awareness that they are being observed. (1)

Hawthorne Studies A series of studies of worker behavior conducted at the Hawthorne plant of Western Electric near Chicago from 1924 to 1934. The studies, which demonstrated the effect of social processes on job performance, provided the impetus for the human relations approach to organizations. (1)

Heuristics Simplified decision rules (rules of thumb) that are used to make quick decisions. (8)

Hierarchy of needs Maslow's theory that there are five sets of needs arranged in such a way that lower-level, more basic needs must be satisfied before higher-level needs can be fulfilled. The needs are physiolog-

ical, safety, social, esteem, and self-actualization. (4)

Hindsight bias The claim that one would have foreseen the relative inevitability of a known outcome. (1)

Horizontal communication Communication between individuals at the same level in an organization. (12)

Human relations approach An approach recognizing the importance of social factors and processes in explaining worker behavior. (1)

Human resources management A field of study that applies principles of behavioral sciences to design and implement ways of attracting, developing, and motivating individuals in an organization. (1)

Hybrid design A type of organization design that combines the functional and product forms. (13)

Hygiene factors In two-factor theory, the group of variables that pertains to the context in which a job is performed (e.g., job security, company policies, and working conditions). (4)

Identification An individual's acceptance of an influence attempt out of a desire to establish or maintain a satisfying relationship with the source of influence. (6)

Immediacy A concept used in interpreting nonverbal communication based on the fact that people physically approach people whom they evaluate positively and withdraw from those whom they evaluate negatively. (12)

Implicit favorite bias The tendency to have a preferred alternative in a decision-making exercise, and to engage in the review of alternatives so as to confirm the initial prejudice. (8)

Implicit personality theory The tendency to perceive a trait in a person because he or she exhibits a linked trait. (2)

Influence Efforts by individuals to change the behavior of others in situations in which they do not possess formal power or authority over their targets. (6)

Informal group A group in which membership is voluntary and based on interpersonal attraction. (9)

Informal leader An individual who lacks formal authority but possesses substantial influence in a group. (7)

Information overload A situation occurring when the information-processing capacities of a member of a communication network are saturated. (12)

Initiating structure   A factor referring to the extent to which a leader initiates activity in a group, organizes it, and defines the way that work is to be done. (7)

Intergroup conflict   Conflict that exists between groups. (10)

Interlocking directorates   A situation created when a company places board members of another corporation on its own board. (14)

Internalization   An individual's acceptance of an influence attempt in the belief that the resulting behavior is correct and appropriate. (6)

Interpersonal conflict   Conflict that exists between two individuals. (10)

Interval schedule   A schedule that reinforces behavior on the basis of time elapsed. (3)

Intrinsic reward   A reward that is a part of the job itself, such as degree of challenge or responsibility. (5)

Isolate   An individual in an organization who has very little or no contact with other members of the organization. (12)

Japanese management   A management approach incorporating informal control of employees, an emphasis on quality and productivity, intensive socialization, slow evaluation and promotion, commitment to the worker, and consensus seeking. (14)

Job characteristics theory   A model of job enrichment in which the presence of five job characteristics—skill variety, task identity, task significance, autonomy, and feedback—leads to three critical psychological states that in turn result in positive work-related outcomes. (5)

Job diagnostic survey   A series of questions designed to determine the extent to which workers view their jobs as possessing the five characteristics of job characteristics theory. (5)

Job enlargement   Expansion of a worker's job to include more and varied tasks at the same level; the horizontal expansion of a job. (5)

Job enrichment   Efforts to make jobs more satisfying by providing the workers that perform them with greater autonomy and decision-

making responsibility; the vertical expansion of a job. (5)

Job maturity   The component of subordinate maturity that is defined in terms of subordinates' technical knowledge and job-related skills. (7)

Job rotation   Systematically shifting workers from one job to another with the goal of increasing motivation and interest. (5)

Job satisfaction   An individual's attitude toward his or her job. One of the more widely studied aspects of the field of organizational behavior. (11)

Kelley's theory of causal attribution   A model based on observations of behavioral agreement, consistency, and distinctiveness that predicts internal versus external attributions. (2)

Last-chance meeting   A technique for countering groupthink in which a meeting is held where members are encouraged to voice any nagging doubts or hesitations about a decision. (8)

Law of attraction   A finding that the greater the proportion of similar attitudes that two people share, the greater the degree of interpersonal attraction. (9)

Law of Effect   A law that proposes that behavior that produces pleasant outcomes is more likely to recur, whereas behavior that produces unpleasant outcomes is less likely to recur. (3)

Leader–member relations   A factor in the contingency model referring to the degree of confidence, trust, and respect that the leader obtains from the group members. (7)

Leadership   The process through which leaders influence the attitudes, behavior, and values of others. (7)

Leadership neutralizer   Individual, task, or organizational characteristic that may prevent the leader from being effective. (7)

Leadership substitute   Individual, task, or organizational characteristic that may make leadership superfluous. (7)

Learning   A fairly permanent change in behavior that occurs as a result of experience. (3)

Least preferred coworker (LPC)   A questionnaire that measures how respondents characterize their feelings about a person with whom they work

least effectively. A high LPC score (favoring the least preferred coworker) is considered to indicate a relationship-oriented individual, while a low LPC score is considered to indicate a task-oriented individual. (7)

Legitimate power   Individual power based on the belief that the individual has a legitimate right to exert control over others. (6)

Liaison   An individual in an organization who serves as a communication link between groups, but is not a member of either group. (12)

Locus of control   The extent to which a person believes that his or her behavior has a direct impact on the consequences of that behavior. People with an internal locus of control believe they control their lives themselves. People with an external locus of control view their lives as guided by external factors. (2)

Long-run process production   A technology in which the entire manufacturing process is continuous and mechanized. (14)

Loss-aversion bias   A decision-making tendency wherein losses are treated as more important than gains, though their objective value is equal. (8)

Mach Scale   An attitude scale that measures the extent to which individuals agree with Machiavelli's views (and are thus assumed to be domineering and manipulative). (6)

Management by objectives (MBO)   A process in which superiors and their subordinates set goals for a specified time period, at the end of which they meet again to assess the subordinate's performance in terms of the previously designated goals. (5)

Mass production   A technology based on long runs of standardized parts or products. (14)

Matrix design   A form of organization design in which a product form is superimposed on a functional form, creating a dual system of authority. (13)

Maximize   The attempt to find the best or optimal solution to a problem. (8)

Mechanistic organization   An organization characterized by a high degree of formalization and centralization. (14)

Modified workweek   A shortened workweek. The most common form involves working 4 days a week, 10 hours each day (called a 4-40). (5)

Moral maturity   refers to one's stage of ethical judgment. Kohlberg identifies six stages of moral development, grouped into three categories: preconventional level, conventional level, and principled level. (2)

Motivator factors   In two-factor theory, the group of variables that pertains to the content of the job (e.g., career advancement, degree of responsibility, and feelings of achievement). (4)

Need for achievement   The need to excel or to accomplish a goal or task more efficiently than others. (4)

Need for affiliation   The need for human companionship. (4)

Need for power   The need to control or have an impact on others. (4)

Negative affectivity   The stable predisposition to feel dissatisfied with one's job or life in general in the absence of any objective source of stress. (11)

Negative reinforcement   The use of stimuli to weaken undesired responses, leading to their elimination. (3)

Negotiation   An interactive process, wherein two or more groups discuss the allocation of resources. (10)

Networks   Patterns of relationships. (12)

Nominal group technique (NGT)   A technique for improving group decision making in which a small group of individuals presents and discusses its ideas before privately voting on its preferred course of action. The group's decision is derived by pooling the votes into a single preferred alternative. (8)

Nonprogrammed decision   A decision made about a unique, complex situation for which there is no preestablished course of action. (8)

Nonverbal communication   The transmission of information through facial expressions, eye contact, body language, and the use of physical objects and space. (12)

Nonverbal cues   Messages sent with facial expressions, posture, shifts of tone or pitch of voice, and eye and head movements. (2)

Norming   The third stage of group development, in which group cohesiveness develops. (9)

Norms   Written or unwritten rules of conduct that guide group members' behavior. (9)

OB Mod   The application of operant conditioning principles to individuals in organizational settings, usually aimed at increasing desired behaviors through the use of positive reinforcement. (3)

Observational learning   The learning that occurs when an individual witnesses the behavior of another and vicariously experiences the outcomes of the other person's actions. (3)

Open group   A group that frequently changes its membership. (9)

Open system   A system that has some degree of interaction with its external environment. All organizations are open systems, though they vary in degree of environmental interaction. (14)

Operant conditioning   A form of learning in which behaviors that produce positive outcomes or eliminate negative ones are acquired or strengthened. (3)

Organic organization   An organization characterized by a relatively low degree of formalization and centralization. (14)

Organizational behavior (OB)   The study of human behavior within an organizational setting. OB borrows many concepts and methods from such fields as psychology, sociology, and cultural anthropology to explore (1) individual perceptions and values, (2) interpersonal and work-group processes, and (3) organizational and environmental forces. (1)

Organizational commitment   The degree to which an employee identifies with an organization and its goals, as well as the employee's desire to maintain membership. (11)

Organizational culture   The system of values, beliefs, and norms that exists in an organization and that is transmitted to new employees. (14)

Organizational decision making   Decisions that pertain to the problems and practices of organizations. (8)

Organizational decline   Cutbacks in the size of an organization's profits, budget, workforce, or clients. (15)

Organizational development (OD)   The process of introducing and managing changes in organizational settings. (1, 15)

Organizational politics   Activities used to acquire, develop, and use power to attain one's preferred (and usually selfish) outcome in situations in which there is uncertainty or disagreement. (6)

Organizational theory   A field of study focusing on the organization (and such attributes as goals, technology, and culture) as a unit of analysis. (1)

Partial reinforcement   A situation in which a response is rewarded in a noncontinuous or variable manner. Behavior acquired under partial reinforcement is usually more resistant to extinction than that acquired under continuous reinforcement. (3)

Participative leadership   In path–goal theory, a leader behavior in which the leader shares authority and responsibility with subordinates, encouraging their participation in decision making and on matters affecting their jobs. (7)

Path–goal theory   A theory based on the expectancy model of motivation suggesting that leaders can affect the satisfaction and performance of subordinates by basing rewards on the accomplishment of performance goals and by clarifying the path to these goals (7)

Peak experience   An intense, mystical experience in which a person exists in a state of joy, fulfillment, and wonderment. (4)

Perceived role   The set of behaviors that an individual believes he or she is expected to perform. (9)

Perceptual distortion   The act of altering perception to avoid an unpleasant reality. Forms include denying events, modifying or distorting reality, seeing only what we want to see, and accepting illusions. (2)

Performing   The fourth and final stage of group development, in which the group directs its energies toward performance of valued goals. (9)

Person Perception   The process by which the individual receives and interprets information about another individual. (2)

Personal decision making   Decisions that directly affect an individual rather than others. (8)

Personal experience bias   The tendency to be influenced by vivid, personal experiences rather than by valid and relevant objective information when making a decision. (8)

Personal space zones   Culturally defined distances that exist between people. (12)

Personality The set of traits and characteristics that form a pattern distinguishing one person from all others. (2)

Personality inventories A widely used method of assessing personality characteristics that asks respondents to indicate whether statements are applicable to themselves. (2)

Personality ratings A device for assessing personality in which respondents rate themselves on scales either with adjectives as endpoints or with specific definitions for each point in the scale. (2)

Population ecology perspective A view of how organizations relate to their environment contending that the success of an organization depends on its finding a niche in a highly competitive surrounding. (14)

Porter–Lawler model A conceptual framework that attempts to integrate the various approaches to motivation. (4)

Position power A factor in the contingency model referring to the power inherent in a position. (7)

Positive reinforcement The use of stimuli to strengthen desired responses, leading to their recurrence. (3)

Power The ability of a person or group to change the attitudes or behavior of others. (6, 12)

Prepotency In Maslow's hierarchy of needs, the capacity of lower-order needs to assert themselves over higher-order needs. (4)

Process theories Theories that focus on the process by which rewards control behavior. Examples are expectancy, equity, and reinforcement theories. (4)

Product design A basic type of organization design that groups personnel and activities according to a product line. (13)

Programmed decision A fairly routine decision that can be made according to preestablished procedures. (8)

Progressive discipline The use of a sequence of penalties for infractions of rules, in which each penalty is more severe than the preceding one. (3)

Projection The tendency to ascribe our emotions and attributes to others; a defense mechanism. (2)

Projective techniques Tests that are based on the idea that people will provide highly individualistic responses to ambiguous stimuli. Projective techniques include the Rorschach test, storytelling, and sentence completions. (2)

Proxemics The study of physical space as a form of nonverbal communication. (12)

Psychological maturity A component of subordinate maturity that is defined in terms of the subordinate's self-confidence, and willingness and ability to take on responsibility. (7)

Punishment The presentation of an unpleasant event that follows an undesirable behavior. It is a negative reinforcer that attempts to eliminate the undesired behavior. (3)

Quality circle A small group of workers who volunteer to meet regularly to identify, analyze, and solve quality and related problems pertaining to their work. (5)

Quality of work life (QWL) An organizational development approach that seeks to enhance the work climate of an organization. QWL programs are assumed to improve both productivity and employees' psychological experiences at work. (15)

Ratio schedule A schedule that reinforces behavior on the basis of the number of times a behavior is performed. (3)

Rational–economic model A model that assumes that decision making is and should be a rational process consisting of a sequence of steps that enhance the probability of attaining a desired goal. *See also* Classical decision theory. (8)

Referent power Individual power based on a high level of admiration or respect for the power holder. (6)

Refreezing The third phase of Lewin's model of change, in which newly created systems or behaviors become part of ongoing organizational processes. (15)

Reinforcement theory A theory using operant conditioning principles that views present behavior as a function of the consequences of past behavior. (4)

Relay Assembly Room study One of the Hawthorne Studies, which first suggested that increased productivity could be partially attributed to the employees' awareness that they are being observed (the Hawthorne effect). (1)

Representativeness heuristic An assessment made on the basis of the similarity between the specific attributes of a given event or object and the attributes of a class of such events or objects. (8)

Resistance to extinction The persistence of a behavior in the absence of reinforcement. (3)

Resource dependence model A view of how organizations relate to their environment contending that the success of an organization is a function of how well it manages its environment. (14)

Retention A stage in the population ecology perspective in which certain successful organizational forms are institutionalized. (14)

Retrofit To introduce self-directed work teams to an existing workforce. (5)

Reward power Individual power based on the extent to which one person controls rewards valued by another. The opposite of coercive power. (6)

Risky shift The tendency for groups to make riskier decisions than individuals. (8)

Role The set of expected behaviors associated with an individual's position in a group. (9)

Role ambiguity A situation occurring when an individual is uncertain about how he or she is expected to behave in a role. (9, 11)

Role conflict A situation occurring when an individual receives conflicting messages regarding appropriate role behavior. (9, 11)

Role episode The process by which individuals receive information about their role and adjust their behavior accordingly. (9)

Role overload A situation occurring when too many activities are expected of an employee given the time available and ability level of the employee. (11)

Rumors Unverified beliefs transmitted through informal channels within an organization. (12)

Satisfice A situation in which a decision maker considers alternatives only until one arises that is minimally acceptable and then looks no further. (8)

Scientific management One of the first approaches to managing worker behavior, developed by Frederick W. Taylor, an engineer. Scientific management sought to improve job performance by (1) measuring productivity, (2) emphasizing efficiency in job procedures, and (3) instituting incentive pay schemes. (1)

Selection A stage in the population ecology perspective in which only organizations that possess the needed form survive, and those that do not, fail. (14)

Selective perception The tendency to be influenced by our own interests. (2)

Selective perception bias The tendency to attend only to specific information because of strong prior expectations. (8)

Self-directed work team A highly trained group of employees, responsible for creating a product, sharing decision making, and rotating jobs, with pay based on skill proficiency. (5)

Self-efficacy Feelings of competency that are derived from a sense of being able to master a task. (3)

Self-fulfilling prophecy (SFP) A phenomenon in which ratees perform in accordance with a rater's prophecy, or expectations, for them. (5)

Self-serving bias The tendency to attribute success to internal factors and to attribute failure to external factors. (2)

Sensitivity training An organizational development technique that seeks to enhance employees' understanding of their own behavior and its impact on others. Such enhanced sensitivity is assumed to reduce interpersonal conflict in the organization. (15)

Sentence completion A projective technique for assessing personality in which respondents are asked to supply the endings for a series of incomplete sentences. (2)

Shaping A behavior modification technique in which the individual receives reinforcement for small successive approximations of the desired behavior. (3)

Situational favorableness In the contingency model, the notion of how easy or difficult a situation might be for a leader. Three factors—leader–member relations, task structure, and position power—combine to represent a range of possible situations. (7)

Situational leadership theory A theory proposing that optimal leader behavior is related to the maturity of subordinates. (7)

Situational tests A technique involving the direct observation of an individual's behavior in a test situation designed to provide information about personality. (2)

Social exchange theory A theory suggesting that in relationships people continually monitor the difference between rewards and costs, and judge the outcomes against two standards: a comparison level and a comparison level of alternatives. (9)

Social facilitation effect The tendency for the presence of others to enhance an individual's performance. (9)

Social inhibition effect The tendency for the presence of others to impair an individual's performance. (9)

Social learning theory An approach to motivation emphasizing the importance of modeling and self-regulatory processes in learning. (4)

Social loafing The tendency for group members to exert less individual effort on a task the larger the group size. (8)

Sociofugal areas Arrangements of physical space that drive people away from each other. (12)

Sociopetal areas Arrangements of physical space that bring people together. (12)

Sociotechnical system The view that every organization is simultaneously a technical and a social system and that attempts to change either system must take into account their interrelatedness. (13)

Span of control The number of people who report to a given supervisor. (13)

Status The social ranking or worth accorded to an individual because of the position he or she occupies in a group. (9)

Status incongruence A situation in which all dimensions of an individual's status are not congruent. (9)

Stepladder technique A decision-making structure for groups that begins with a small, core group and, through adding members one at a time, actively involves all members in making the final decision. (8)

Stereotypes Beliefs that all members of a group (e.g., a racial, ethnic, religious, or occupational group) share the same traits and behaviors. (2)

Storming The second stage of group development, in which members wrestle with the division of power and status. (9)

Storytelling A projective technique for assessing personality in which respondents supply stories about pictures they are shown. *See also* Thematic Apperception Test (2)

Strategic alliance A cooperative venture involving two or more firms within technically related areas. (4)

Stress Physical and psychological reactions experienced by an individual when confronted with a threatening or excessively demanding situation (such as extreme conflict). (11)

Strong culture A set of values and norms that is widely endorsed and intensely held. (14)

Structural dimensions An organization's internal characteristics, such as degree of specialization, hierarchy, and decentralization. (14)

Subculture A set of values and norms that is unique to a given organizational unit. (14)

Subjective probabilities Estimates of the likelihood that one event will follow another (e.g., that performance will lead to a given outcome). (4)

Subliminal influences Factors influencing perceptions that occur below the threshold of awareness. (2)

Subordinate maturity The critical situational attribute in the Hersey–Blanchard model. It consists of the job maturity and psychological maturity of the subordinate for a given task. (7)

Supportive leadership In path–goal theory, a leader behavior that entails being sensitive to and supportive of group members' needs. (7)

Survey feedback An organizational development technique in which questionnaires are used to obtain information on issues of concern, and the results are summarized and returned to employees for consideration and interpretation. (15)

Tall structure Describes an organization with more levels of authority and smaller spans of control. (13)

Task orientation A style of leadership referring to the extent to which a leader shows concern for getting a job done and helps steer the group to meet its goals. (7)

Task structure A factor in the contingency model referring to the degree to which a job can be clearly specified. (7)

Team building An organizational development program designed to help existing work groups or newly formed special groups improve performance by tackling obstacles and problems. (15)

Technology The knowledge, tools, and techniques used by organizations in performing their work. (14)

Telecommuting The use of a computer link to complete all or part of one's job at home. (5)

Territory A specific physical location toward which an individual has a proprietary attitude. (12)

Thematic Apperception Test A storytelling device for assessing personality composed of 20 pictures portraying situations of ambiguous meaning. The respondent constructs stories that are analyzed for recurrent themes. (2)

Time management A strategy for coping with job-related stress through effective self-management. (11)

Total Quality Management A set of principles that emphasizes establishing and maintaining high-quality output. (5)

Transactional leadership A leadership style based on exchanges of rewards for performance. (7)

Transformational leadership A leadership style that implies reshaping the entire strategy of an organization. (7)

Triarchic model of intelligence A view of general intelligence that argues for the notion of three fundamental components: analytical reasoning, social intelligence, and creativity. (7)

Two-factor theory Herzberg's theory of job satisfaction contending that satisfaction and dissatisfaction stem from different groups of variables, termed motivator and hygiene factors. (4)

Type A personality A personality type characterized by impatience, competitiveness, and the drive to succeed. (11)

Type B personality A personality type characterized by a relaxed, easygoing, noncompetitive attitude toward work and life. (11)

Unconditioned response In classical conditioning, a reflexive response evoked by the occurrence of an unconditioned stimulus. (3)

Unconditioned stimulus In classical conditioning, a stimulus that has the ability to evoke a natural reflexive response (an unconditioned response). (3)

Unfreezing The first phase in Lewin's model of change, in which people become aware of the need for change. (15)

Unit production A technology in which products are custom-made in response to specific customer orders. (14)

Unity of command A concept maintaining that employees are accountable to and take orders from only one superior. (13)

Upward communication Communication that flows from lower to higher levels within an organization. (12)

Valence The value a person places on rewards that he or she expects to receive. (4)

Variable interval schedule A schedule in which a reward is applied after a variable amount of time has passed since the last reward was given. (3)

Variable ratio schedule A schedule in which a reward is applied after a variable number of responses are performed. (3)

Variable schedule A schedule for reinforcement in which the amount of time or number of responses performed varies. (3)

Variation A stage in the population ecology perspective referring to the development of organizations with unique attributes. (14)

Vertical dyad linkage model A model stressing the importance of individual relationships between leader and subordinates. Each relationship is termed a vertical dyad. (7)

Vertical integration A situation that occurs when one organization acquires another with the goal of controlling forces that affect its production process. (14)

Vroom–Yetton model A model that focuses on selecting the appropriate leadership style for decision making, based on situational considerations. The model proposes five styles: two are autocratic (AI and AII), two are consultative (CI and CII), and one is oriented to a group decision (G). (7)

Work ethic A belief in the dignity of all work, especially the belief that hard work brings success. (2)

Workplace aggression Efforts to do harm to employees or organizations. (11)

Workplace romance Enduring, intense, and erotic attraction between employees. (11)

Notes

Chapter 1

1. S. Wilentz, "Speedy Fred's Revolution," *The New York Review*, Nov. 20, 1997, 32–37; J. Gies, "Automating the Worker," *Invention and Technology* (Winter, 1991): 56–63; F.J. Lundy, "Hugo Münsterberg: Victim or Visionary?" *Journal of Applied Psychology* 77 (1992): 787–802.

2. L.W. Fry, "The Maligned F.W. Taylor: A Reply to His Many Critics," *Academy of Management Review* 30 (1976): 124–139; E.A. Locke, "The Ideas of Frederick W. Taylor: An Evaluation," *Academy of Management Review* 7 (1982): 14–24.

3. C.D. Wrege and R.G. Greenwood, *Frederick Taylor: The Father of Scientific Management: Myth and Reality* (Homewood, Ill.: Irwin, 1991); J.M. Gotcher, "Assisting the Handicapped: The Pioneering Efforts of Frank and Lillian Gilbreth," *Journal of Management* 18 (1992): 5–13.

4. F.J. Roethlisberger and W.J. Dickson, *Management and the Worker: An Account of a Research Program Conducted by the Western Electric Company, Hawthorne Works, Chicago* (Cambridge, Mass.: Harvard University Press, 1939); "Hawthorne Revisited: The Legend and the Legacy," *Organizational Dynamics* 3 (1975): 67–68; A.H. Schulman, J.W. Gibson, and R.G. Greenwood, "The Hawthorne Studies: What Are We Teaching?" (Paper presented at the National Meeting of the Academy of Management, 1991); E. Mayo, *The Human Problems of an Industrial Civilization* (New York: Viking, 1933).

5. R.H. Franke, "The Hawthorne Experiments: Empirical Findings and Implications for Management," (Paper presented at the National Meeting of the Academy of Management, 1987); R.H. Franke and R.P. Urian, "Illumination and Productivity at Hawthorne," (Paper presented at the National Meeting of the Academy of Management, 1991).

6. S.R. Barley and G. Kunda, "Design and Devotion: Surges of Rational and Normative Ideologies of Control in Managerial Discourse," *Administrative Science Quarterly* 37 (1992): 363–399.

7. T.J. Peters and R.H. Waterman, Jr., *In Search of Excellence* (New York: Harper & Row, 1982); T.E. Deal and A.A. Kennedy, *Corporate Cultures* (Reading, Mass.: Addison-Wesley, 1982); W.G. Ouchi, *Theory Z: How American Business Can Meet the Japanese Challenge* (Reading, Mass.: Addison-Wesley, 1981).

8. S. Jackson, J. Brett, V. Sessa, D. Cooper, J. Julin, and K. Peyronnin, "Some Differences Make a Difference: Individual Dissimilarity and Group Heterogeneity as Correlates of Recruitment, Promotions, and Turnover," *Journal of Applied Psychology* 76 (1991): 675–689; R. Lattimer, "Managing Diversity for Competitive Advantage," *Textbook Authors Conference of American Association of Retired Persons* (Washington, D.C., 1992): 23–26; W. Watson, K. Kumar, and L. Michaelson, "Cultural Diversity's Impact on Interaction Process and Performance: Comparing Homogeneous and Diverse Task Groups," *Academy of Management Journal* 36 (1993): 590–602; A. Tsui, T. Egan, and C. O'Reilly, "Being Different: Relational Demography and Organizational Attachment," *Administrative Science Quarterly* 37 (1992): 549–579.

9. P. Stuart, "Perspectives on Murder at Work," *Personnel Journal*, February (1992).

10. C.M. Solomon, "Keeping Hate Out of the Workplace," *Personnel Journal*, July 1992: 30–36.

11. G.N. Powell and S. Foley, "Something to Talk about: Romantic Relationships in Organizational Settings," *Journal of Management* 24 (1997).

12. J.P. Dillard and K.I. Miller, "Intimate Relationships in Task Environments," in S.W. Duck (ed.), *Handbook of Personal Relationships* (New York: Wiley, 1988): 449–465.

13. P.F. Lazarsfeld, "The American Soldier—An Expository Review," *Public Opinion Quarterly* 13 (1949): 377–404; P. Slovic and B. Fischhoff, "On the Psychology of Experimental Surprises," *Journal of Experimental Psychology: Human Perception and Performance* 3 (1977): 544–551; J.J. Christensen-Szalanski and C. Fabian-Willham, "The Hindsight Bias: A Meta-Analysis," *Organizational Behavior and Human Decision Processes* 48 (1991): 147–168; C. Ofir and D. Mazursky, "Does a Surprising Outcome Reinforce or Reverse the Hindsight Bias?" *Organizational Behavior and Human Decision Processes* 69 (1997): 51–57.

14. R.P. Vecchio, "Some Popular (But Misguided) Criticisms of the Organizational Sciences," *Organizational Behavior Teaching Review* 11 (1987): 28–34; R. Sternberg, R.K. Wagner, W.M. Williams, and J.A. Horvath, "Testing Common Sense," *American Psychologist* 50 (1993): 912–927.

Chapter 2

1. R. Buck, *Nonverbal Behavior and the Communication of Effect* (New York: Guilford Press, 1983); P. Ekman, "Cross-cultural Studies of Facial Expression," in *Darwin and Facial Expression*, ed. P. Ekman (New York: Academic Press, 1973).

2. C. Darwin, *The Expression of the Emotions in Man and Animals* (London: Murray, 1872).

3. P. Ekman and W.V. Friesen, *Unmasking the Face* (Englewood Cliffs, N.J.: Prentice-Hall, 1975).

4. L.A. Streeter, R.M. Krauss, V. Galler, C. Olson, and W. Apple, "Pitch Changes During Attempted Deception," *Journal of Personality and Social Psychology* 35 (1977): 345–350.

5. R.E. Kraut, "Verbal and Nonverbal Cues in the Perception of Lying," *Journal of Personality and Social Psychology* 36 (1978): 388–391; S. Chollar, "In the Blink of an Eye," *Psychology Today* 22 (1988): 8–10.

6. A.S. Imada and M.D. Hakel, "Influence of Nonverbal Communication and Rater Proximity on Impressions and Decisions in Simulated Employment Interviews," *Journal of Applied Psychology* 62 (1977): 295–300.

7. L. Ulrich and D. Trumbo, "The Selection Interview since 1949," *Psychological Bulletin* 63 (1965): 100–116.

8. C.L. Kleinke, F.B. Meeker, and C. LaFong, "Effects of Gaze, Touch, and Use of Name on Evaluation of 'Engaged' Couples," *Journal of Research in Personality* 1 (1974): 368–373.

9. M.L. Knapp, *Nonverbal Communication in Human Interaction*, 2d ed. (New York: Holt, Rinehart and Winston, 1978).

10. P.C. Ellsworth and J.M. Carlsmith, "Eye Contact and Gaze Aversion in an Aggressive Encounter," *Journal of Personality and Social Psychology* 28 (1973): 280–292; P.C. Ellsworth and E.J. Langer, "Staring and Approach: An Interpretation of the Stare as a Nonspecific Activator," *Journal of Personality and Social Psychology* 33 (1976): 117–122.

11. I.H. Frieze, J.E. Olson, and J. Russell, "Attractiveness and Income for Men and Women in Management," *Journal of Applied Social Psychology* 21 (1991): 1039–1057; A. Feingold, "Good-Looking People Are Not What We Think," *Psychological Bulletin* 111 (1992): 304–341; L. Harper "Good Looks Can Mean a Pretty Penny on the Job, and 'Ugly' Men Are Affected More Than Women," *The Wall Street Journal*, Nov. 23, 1993, B-1.

12. L.J. Cronbach, "Processes Affecting Scores on 'understanding of others' and 'assumed similarity,'" *Psychological Bulletin* 52 (1955): 177–193.

13. R. Taft, "The Ability to Judge People," *Psychological Bulletin* 52 (1955): 1–23.

14. J.S. Wiggins, *Personality and Prediction: Principles of Personality Assessment* (Reading, Mass.: Addison-Wesley, 1973); B. Kleinmuntz, "Why We Still Use Our Heads Instead of Formulas: Toward an Integrative Approach," *Psychological Bulletin* (1990): 296–310.

15. H.C. Triandis and V. Vassiliou, "Frequency of Contact and Stereotyping," *Journal of Personality and Social Psychology* 7 (1967): 316–328.

16. S.S. Zalkind and T.W. Costello, "Perception: Some Recent Research and Implications for Administration," *Administrative Science Quarterly* 7 (1962): 218–235.

17. S.E. Asch, "Forming Impressions of Personality," *Journal of Abnormal and Social Psychology* 41 (1946): 258–290.

18. S. Feshback and R.D. Singer, "The Effects of Fear Arousal upon Social Perception," *Journal of Abnormal and Social Psychology* 55 (1957): 283–288.

19. S.S. Sears, "Experimental Studies of Perception, I. Attribution of Traits," *Journal of Social Psychology* 7 (1936): 151–163.

20. R. Jacobs and J. Farr, "Industrial and Organizational Psychology at the Pennsylvania State University," *The Industrial-Organizational Psychologist* 30 (1993): 75–79.

21. J.V. McConnell, R.L. Cutler, and E.B. McNeil, "Subliminal Stimulation: An Overview," *American Psychologist* 13 (1958): 229–242; J.V. McConnell, "Reinvention of Subliminal Perception," *Skeptical Inquirer* 13 (1989), 427–429; A.G. Greenwald, E.R. Spangenberg, A.R. Pratkanis, and J. Eskenazi, "Double-blind Tests of Subliminal Self-Help Audiotapes," *Psychological Science* 2 (1991): 119–122; B.C. Audley, "Subliminal Tapes: Controlled Tapes," *Skeptical Inquirer* 16 (1992): 349–350; P.M. Merikle and H.E. Skanes, "Subliminal Self-Help Audiotapes: A Search for Placebo Effects," *Journal of Applied Psychology* 77 (1992): 772–776.

22. F. Heider, "Social Perception and Phenomenal Causality," *Psychological Review* 51 (1944): 358–374; F. Heider, *The Psychology of Interpersonal Relations* (New York: Wiley, 1958); W. Ryan, *Blaming the Victim* (New York: Vintage Books, 1977); Y. Trope, "The Multiple Roles of Context in Dispositional Judgment," in *On-Line Cognition in Person Cognition*, ed. J.N. Bassil (Hillsdale, N.J.: Lawrence Erlbaum Assoc., 1989); R.S. Wyer, G.V. Bodenhausen, and R.W. Gorman, "Cognitive Mediators to Rape," *Journal of Personality and Social Psychology* 48 (1985): 324–338; J.M. Crant and T.S. Bateman, "Assignment of Credit and Blame for Performance Outcomes," *Academy of Management Journal* 36 (1993): 7–27.

23. J.W. Thibaut and H.W. Riecken, "Some Determinants and Consequences of the Perception of Social Causality," *Journal of Personality* 24 (1955): 113–133.

24. R. Baumhart, *An Honest Profit* (New York: Holt, Rinehart and Winston, 1968); S.N. Brenner and E.A. Molander, "Is the Ethics of Business Changing?" *Harvard Business Review* (1977): 57–71; J.S. French, "The Conceptualization and the Measurement of Mental Health in Terms of Self-Identity Theory," in *The Definition and Measurement of Mental Health*, ed. S.B. Sells (Washington, D.C.: Dept. of Health, Education, and Welfare, 1968); E.P. Hollander, "Leadership and Power," in *The Handbook of Social Psychology*, 3rd ed., ed. G. Lindzey and E. Aronson (New York: Random House, 1985); H.H. Kelley, "Attribution in Social Interactions." In eds. E.E. Jones, D.E. Kanous, H.H. Kelley, R.E. Nisbett, S. Valins, and B. Weiner, *Attribution: Perceiving*

the *Causes of Behavior* (Morristown, N.J.: General Learning Press, 1972).

25. P. Cross, "Not *Can* but *Will* College Teaching Be Improved?" *New Directions for Higher Education* (Spring 1977): 1–15; R.T. Blackburn, G.R. Pellino, A. Boberg, and C. O'Connell, "Are Instructional Improvement Programs Off Target?" *Current Issues in Higher Education* 1 (1980): 31–48.

26. C. Holden, "Identical Twins Reared Apart," *Science* (March 1980): 1323–1324.

27. J.R. Warren, "Birth Order and Social Behavior," *Psychological Bulletin* 65 (1966): 38–49.

28. A. Rafaeli and R.J. Klimoski, "Predicting Sales Success through Handwriting Analysis: An Evaluation of the Effects of Training and Handwriting Sample Content," *Journal of Applied Psychology* 68 (1983): 212–217; G. Ben-Shakkar, M. Bar-Hillel, Y. Bilu, E. Ben-Abba, and A. Flug, "Can Graphology Predict Occupational Success: Two Empirical Studies and Some Methodological Ruminations," *Journal of Applied Psychology* 71 (1986): 645–653; E. Neter and G. Ben-Shakur, "The Predictive Validity of Graphical Inferences: A Meta-analysis," *Personality and Individual Differences* 10 (1989): 737–745; S.F. Blinkhorn, "The Writing Is on the Wall," *Nature* 366 (1998): 208.

29. J.W. Macfarlane, L. Allen, and M.P. Honzik, "A Developmental Study of the Behavior Problems of Normal Children Between 21 Months and 14 Years," *University of California Publications in Child Development* 2 (1954): 483.

30. D.W. Mackinnon, "Violation of Prohibitions," in *Explorations in Personality*, ed. H. Murray (New York: Oxford University Press, 1938).

31. R. Koenig, "Toyota Takes Pains, and Time, Filling Jobs at Its Kentucky Plant," *The Wall Street Journal*, December 1, 1987, 1.

32. R.S. Woodworth, *Personal Data Sheet* (Chicago: Stoelting, 1918).

33. J.C. Nunnally, *Psychometric Theory* (New York: McGraw-Hill, 1994); O.K. Buros, ed., *Tests in Print III* (University of Nebraska, 1983); O.K. Buros, ed., *Mental Measurements Yearbook* (University of Nebraska, 1941).

34. D.P. Crowne and D. Marlowe, *The Approval Motive: Studies in Evaluative Dependence* (New York: Wiley, 1964).

35. A.I. Rabin, "Projective Methods: An Historical Introduction," in *Projective Techniques in Personality Assessment*, ed. A. Rabin (New York: Springer, 1958), 3.

36. C.D. Morgan and H.A. Murray, "A Method of Investigating Fantasies: The Thematic Apperception Test," *Archives of Neurological Psychiatry* 34 (1935): 289–306; W.D. Spangler, "Validity of Questionnaire and TAT Measures of Need for Achievement: Two Meta-analyses," *Psychological Bulletin* 112 (1992): 140–154.

37. J.B. Rotter, "Level of Aspiration as a Method of Studying Personality, III. Group Validity Studies," *Character and Personality* 11 (1943): 254–274; J.B. Rotter, "Generalized Expectancies for Internal versus External Control of Reinforcement," *Psychological Monographs* 80, no. 609 (1966).

38. Rotter, "Generalized Expectancies," 11–12.

39. H.M. Lefcourt, "Recent Developments in the Study of Locus of Control," in *Progress in Experimental Personality Research*, ed. B. Maher (New York: Academic Press, 1972), 1–39; R.W. Renn and R.J. Vandenberg, "Differences in Employee Attitudes and Behaviors Based on Rotter's (1966) Internal-External Locus of Control," *Human Relations* 44 (1991): 1161–1178.

40. J.S. Coleman, E.Q. Campbell, L.J. Hobson, J. McPartland, A.M. Mood, F.D. Weinfeld, and R.L. York, *Equality of Educational Opportunity* (Washington, D.C.: Government Printing Office, 1966).

41. R.P. Vecchio, "Workers' Belief in Internal versus External Determinants of Success," *Journal of Social Psychology* 114 (1981): 199–207.

42. M. Seeman, "On the Meaning of Alienation," *American Sociological Review* 24 (1959): 782–791; M. Seeman, "Alienation and Social Learning in a Reformatory," *American Sociological Review* 69 (1963): 270–284.

43. P.J. Andrisani and C. Nestel, "Internal-External Control as a Contributor to and Outcome of Work Experience," *Journal of Applied Psychology* 61 (1976): 156–165.

44. J.B. Rotter, "Some Problems and Misconceptions Related to the Construct of Internal versus External Control of Reinforcement," *Journal of Consulting and Clinical Psychology* 43 (1975): 56–67.

45. R.M. Baron and R.L. Ganz, "Effects of Locus of Control and Type of Feedback on the Task Performance of Lower-Class Black Children," *Journal of Personality and Social Psychology* 21 (1972): 124–130.

46. P.T. Wong and C.F. Sproule, "An Attribution Analysis of the Locus of Control Construct and the Trent Attribution Profile," in *Research with the Locus of Control Construct: Vol. 3, Extensions and Limitations*, ed. H.M. Lefcourt (New York: Academic Press, 1984): 309–360.

47. J.M. Minelo and J. Garrett, "The Protestant Ethic as a Personality Variable," *Journal of Counseling and Clinical Psychology* 36 (1971): 40–44.

48. M. Merrens and J. Garrett, "The Protestant Ethic Scale as a Predictor of Effective Work Performance," *Journal of Applied Psychology* 60 (1975): 125–127.

49. J. Greenberg, "The Protestant Work Ethic and Reactions to Negative Performance Evaluation on a Laboratory Task," *Journal of Applied Psychology* 62 (1977): 682–690.

50. O. Cherrington, "The Values of Younger Workers." *Business Horizons* 20 (1977): 18–20; R. Eisenberger, *Blue Monday: The Loss of the Work Ethic in America* (New York: Paragon House, 1989).

51. R.P. Vecchio, "The Function and Meaning of Work and the Job: Morse and Weiss (1955) Revisited," *Academy of Management Journal* 23 (1980): 361–367.

52. P.A. Sorokin, *The Crisis of Our Age: The Social and Cultural Outlook* (New York: Dutton, 1941).

53. I.B. Myers and K.C. Briggs, *Myers-Briggs Type Indicator* (Princeton, N.J.: Educational Testing Service, 1962); W. Taggert and D. Robey, "Minds and Managers: On the Dual Nature of Human Information Processing and Management," *Academy of Management Review* 6 (1981): 187–195; J.W. Slocum and D. Hellriegel, "A Look at How Managers' Minds Work," *Business Horizons* 26 (1983): 58–68; W. Woods, "Personality Tests Are Back," *Fortune,* March 30, 1987, 74–82.

54. A.B. Carroll, "Linking Business Ethics to Behavior in Organizations," *SAM Advanced Management Journal* 43 (1978): 4–11.

55. R. Ricklees, "Ethics in America," *The Wall Street Journal,* October 31, 1983, 33.

56. L. Kohlberg, "Stage and Sequence: The Cognitive-Developmental Approach to Socialization," in *Handbook of Socialization Theory and Research,* ed. D.A. Goslin (Chicago: Rand-McNally, 1969), 347–400.

57. L. Kohlberg and D. Candee, "The Relationship of Moral Judgment to Moral Action," in *Morality, Moral Behavior and Moral Development,* ed. W. Kurtines and J. Gerwitz (New York: Wiley, 1984), 52–73.

58. W.E. Stratton, W. Flynn, and G. Johnson, "Moral Development and Decision Making: A Study of Student Ethics," *Journal of Enterprise Management* 3 (1981): 35–41.

59. J.R. Snarey, "Cross-cultural Universality of Social-Moral Development: A Critical Review of Kohlbergian Research," *Psychological Bulletin* 97 (1985): 202–232.

60. C. Gilligan, *In a Different Voice: Psychological Theory and Women's Development* (Cambridge Mass.: Howard University Press, 1982); C. Gilligan and G. Wiggins, "The Origins of Morality in Early Childhood Relationships," in *The Emergence of Morality,* ed. J. Kagan and S. Lamb (Chicago, Ill.: University of Chicago Press, 1987). L.K. Trevino, "Ethical Decision Making in Organizations: A Person-Situation Interactionist Model," *Academy of Management Review* 11 (1986): 601–617; J. George, "The Role of Personality in Organizational Life: Issues and Evidence," *Journal of Management* 18 (1992): 185–213; R. Tett, D. Jackson, and M. Rothstein, "Personality Measures vs. Predictors of Job Performance: A Meta-analytic Review," *Personnel Psychology* 44 (1991): 703–742.

61. M.R. Barrick and M.R. Mount, "The Big Five Personality Dimensions and Job Performance: A Meta-analysis," *Personnel Psychology* 44 (1991): 1–26; J. Block, "A Contrarian View of the Five-Factor Approach to Personality Description," *Psychological Bulletin* 117 (1995): 187–215; J.A. Wagner and J.R. Hollenbeck, *Organizational Behavior* (Upper Saddle River, N.J.: Simon and Schuster, 1998); B. Barry and G.L. Stewart, "Composition Process, and Performance in Self-Managed Groups: The Role of Personality," *Journal of Applied Psychology* 82 (1997): 62–78; J.F. Salgado, "The Five-Factor Model of Personality and Job Performance in the European Community," *Journal of Applied Psychology* 82 (1997): 30–43; J.M. Crant, "The Proactive Personality Scale and Objective Job Performance among Real Estate Agents," *Journal of Applied Psychology* 80 (1995): 532–537; J.M. Crant, "The Proactive Personality Scale as a Predictor of Entrepreneurial Intentions," *Journal of Small Business Management,* July 1996: 42–49.

Chapter 3

1. G.H. Bower and E.R. Hilgard, *Theories of Learning* (Englewood Cliffs, N.J.: Prentice-Hall, 1981).

2. J.B. Watson and R. Rayner, "Conditioned Emotional Reactions," *Journal of Experimental Psychology* 3 (1920): 1–14.

3. A. Bandura, *Social Learning Theory* (Englewood Cliffs, N.J.: Prentice-Hall, 1977).

4. R.W. White, "Motivation Reconsidered: The Concept of Competence," *Psychological Review* 66 (1959): 297–333.

5. T.J. Peters and R.H. Waterman, Jr., *In Search of Excellence: Lessons from America's Best-Run Companies* (New York: Harper & Row, 1982).

6. A.P. Goldstein and M. Sorcher, *Changing Supervisor Behavior* (New York: Pergamon, 1974).

7. E.L. Thorndike, *Animal Intelligence* (New York: Macmillan, 1911).

8. N.E. Miller and B.R. Dvorkin, "Visceral Learning," in *Contemporary Trends in Cardiovascular Psychophysiology,* ed. P.A. Obrist et al. (Chicago: Aldine, 1973); B.T. Engel, "Operant Conditioning of Cardiac Function: A Status Report," *Psychophysiology* 9 (1972): 161–177.

9. B.F. Skinner, *The Behavior of Organisms* (New York: Appleton, 1938); L.W. Fredericksen, *Handbook of Organizational Behavior Management* (New York: Wiley, 1982); J.L. Komaki, "Applied Behavior Analysis and Organizational Behavior; Reciprocal Influence of the Two Fields," in *Research*

in Organizational Behavior, vol. 8, ed. B.M. Straw and L.I. Cummings (Greenwich, Conn.: JAI, 1986).

10. W.C. Hamner and E.P. Hamner, "Behavior Modification on the Bottom Line," *Organizational Dynamics* 4 (1976): 3–21.

11. W.C. Hamner, "Worker Motivation Programs: The Importance of Climate, Structure, and Performance Consequences," in *Contemporary Problems in Personnel*, ed. W.C. Hamner and F.L. Schmidt (Chicago: St. Clair Press, 1977); F. Luthans and R. Kreitner, *Organizational Behavior Modification* (Glenview, Ill.: Scott, Foresman, 1975).

12. Hamner and Hamner, "Behavior Modification on the Bottom Line."

13. E.A. Locke, "The Myths of Behavior Mod in Organizations," *Academy of Management Review* 2 (1977): 543–553.

14. F.H. Kanfer and P. Karoly, "Self-control: A Behavioristic Excursion into the Lion's Den," *Behavior Therapy* 3 (1972): 398–416.

15. E. Pedalino and V. Gamboa, "Behavior Modification and Absenteeism: Intervention in One Industrial Setting," *Journal of Applied Psychology* 59 (1974): 694–698.

16. E.L. Deci, "The Effects of Contingent and Noncontingent Rewards and Controls on Intrinsic Motivation," *Organizational Behavior and Human Performance* 8 (1972): 217–229; P.C. Jordan, "Effects of Extrinsic Reward on Intrinsic Motivation: A Field Experiment," *Academy of Management Journal* 29 (1986): 405–411; U.J. Wiersma, "The Effects of Extrinsic Rewards in Intrinsic Motivation: A Meta-analysis," *Journal of Occupational and Organizational Psychology* 65 (1992): 101–114; W.E. Scott, J.L. Farh, and P.M. Podsakoff, "The Effects of 'Intrinsic' and 'Extrinsic' Reinforcement Contingencies on Task Behavior," *Organizational Behavior and Human Decision Processes* 41 (1988): 405–425; A. Kohn, *Punished by Rewards* (New York: Houghton-Mifflin, 1993); R. Eisenberger and J. Cameron, "Detrimental Effects of Reward: Reality or Myth?" *American Psychologist* 51 (1996): 1153–1166.

17. R.L. Solomon, "Punishment," *American Psychologist* 19 (1964): 239–253.

18. J.A. Mello, "The Fine Art of the Reprimand: Using Criticism to Enhance Commitment, Motivation, and Performance," *Employment Relations Today* 22 (1995): 19–27; K. Tyler, "Careful Criticism Brings Better Performance," *HR Magazine* 42 (1997): 57.

Chapter 4

1. "America's Growing Anti-business Mood," *Business Week*, June 17, 1972, 101; R.A. Kovach, "Employee Motivation: Addressing a Crucial Factor in Your Organization's Performance," *Employment Relations Today* 22 (1995): 93–107.

2. H.A. Murray, *Explorations in Personality* (New York: Oxford University Press, 1938); H.A. Murray, *Thematic Apperception Test Manual* (Cambridge, Mass: Harvard University Press, 1943).

3. D.C. McClelland, *The Achieving Society* (Princeton: Van Nostrand, 1961); D.C. McClelland, "Toward a Theory of Motive Acquisition," *American Psychologist* 23 (1965): 321–333.

4. D.C. McClelland and D.G. Winter, *Motivating Economic Achievement* (New York: Free Press, 1969); G.A. Steiner and J.B. Miner, *Management Policy and Strategy* (New York: Macmillan, 1977).

5. H.A. Wainer and I.M. Rubin, "Motivation of Research and Development Entrepreneurs: Determinants of Company Success," *Journal of Applied Psychology* 53 (1969): 178–184.

6. D.C. McClelland and R.E. Boyatzis, "Leadership Motive Pattern and Long-Term Success in Management," *Journal of Applied Psychology* 67 (1967): 737–743.

7. D.A. Kolb and R. Boyatzis, "On the Dynamics of the Helping Relationship," *Journal of Applied Behavioral Science* 6 (1970): 230–237.

8. McClelland, *The Achieving Society*; R.P. Vecchio, "A Test of a Moderator of the Job Satisfaction–Job Quality Relationship: The Case of Religious Affiliation," *Journal of Applied Psychology* 65 (1980): 195–201.

9. McClelland, "Toward a Theory of Motive Acquisition"; R.L. Helmreich, L.L. Sawin, and A.L. Carsrud, "The Honeymoon Effect in Job Performance: Temporal Increases in Predictive Power of Achievement Motivation," *Journal of Applied Psychology* 71 (1986): 185–188.

10. D.E. Durand, "Effects of Achievement Motivation and Skill Training on the Entrepreneurial Behavior of Black Businessmen," *Organizational Behavior and Human Performance* 14 (1975): 76–90; J.A. Timmons, "Black is Beautiful—Is It Bountiful?" *Harvard Business Review* 49 (1971): 81–94; Metropolitan Economic Development Association, "Business Leadership Training—What's Happening," *MEDA Reports* 5, no. 1 (1977): 1–7.

11. A.H. Maslow, *Motivation and Personality* (New York: Harper, 1954); A.H. Maslow, *Toward a Psychology of Being* (New York: Van Nostrand, 1968).

12. C. Keutzer, "Whatever Turns You On: Triggers to Transcendent Experiences," *Journal of Humanistic Psychology* 8 (1978): 68–72.

13. M.A. Wahba and L.G. Bridwell, "Maslow Reconsidered: A Review of Research on the Need Hierarchy Theory," *Organizational Behavior and Human Performance* 15 (1976): 212–240; E.E. Lawler and J.L. Suttle, "A Causal Correlational Test of the Need Hierarchy Concept," *Organizational Behavior and Human Performance* 7 (1972): 265–287;

D.T. Hall and K.E. Nougaim, "An Examination of Maslow's Need Hierarchy in an Organizational Setting," *Organizational Behavior and Human Performance* 3 (1968): 12–35.

14. C.P. Alderfer, *Existence, Relatedness, and Growth* (New York: Free Press, 1972).

15. M. Csikszentmihalyi, *Flow: The Psychology of Optimal Experience* (New York: Harper & Row, 1990).

16. F. Herzberg, B. Mausner, and B. Synderman, *The Motivation to Work* (New York: Wiley, 1959).

17. L.W. Porter and E.E. Lawler, *Managerial Attitudes and Performance* (Homewood, Ill.: Irwin, 1968); J.P. Campbell, M.D. Dunnette, E.E. Lawler, and K.E. Weick, *Managerial Behavior, Performance, and Effectiveness* (New York: McGraw-Hill, 1970); M. Sussmann and R.P. Vecchio, "Conceptualizations of Valence and Instrumentality: A Fourfold Model," *Organizational Behavior and Human Performance* 36 (1985): 96–112; V.H. Vroom, *Work and Motivation* (New York: Wiley, 1964).

18. B.F. Skinner and W.F. Dowling, "Conversation with B.F. Skinner," *Organizational Dynamics* 1 (1973): 31–40; F. Luthans and R. Kreitner, *Organizational Behavior Modification* (Glenview, Ill.: Scott, Foresman, 1975); F. Luthans, *Organizational Behavior* (New York: McGraw-Hill, 1977).

19. Vroom, *Work and Motivation*.

20. J.S. Adams, "Injustice in Social Exchange," in *Advances in Experimental Social Psychology*, vol. 2, ed. L. Berkowitz (New York: Academic Press, 1965); P.S. Goodman and A. Friedman, "An Examination of Adams' Theory of Inequity," *Administrative Science Quarterly* 16 (1971): 217–288; J.S. Adams and S. Freedman, "Equity Theory Revisited: Comments and Annotated Bibliography," in *Advances in Experimental Social Psychology*, vol. 9, ed. L. Berkowitz and E. Walster (New York: Academic Press, 1976); Campbell and Pritchard, "Motivation Theory in Industrial and Organizational Psychology."

21. E.E. Lawler, C.A. Koplin, T.E. Young, and J.A. Faden, "Inequity Reduction over Time in an Induced Overpayment Situation," *Organizational Behavior and Human Performance* 3 (1968): 253–268; J.W. Harder, "Equity Theory versus Expectancy Theory: The Case of Major League Baseball Free Agents," *Journal of Applied Psychology* 76 (1991): 458–464; C. Kulik and M. Ambrose, "Personal and Situational Determinants of Referent Choice," *Academy of Management Review* 17 (1992): 212–237.

22. R.P. Vecchio, "An Individual Differences Interpretation of the Conflicting Predictions Generated by Equity Theory and Expectancy Theory," *Journal of Applied Psychology* 66 (1981): 470–481.

23. R. Mowday, "Equity Theory Predictions of Behavior in Organizations," in *Motivation and Work Behavior*, 2d ed., ed.

R.M. Steers and L.W. Porter (New York: McGraw-Hill, 1979); M.R. Carrell and J.E. Dittrich, "Equity Theory: The Recent Literature, Methodological Considerations and New Directions," *Academy of Management Review* 3 (1978): 202–210; R.W. Griffeth, R.P. Vecchio, and J.W. Logan, "Equity Theory and Interpersonal Attraction," *Journal of Applied Psychology* 74 (1989); 394–401; E.W. Miles, J.D. Hatfield, and R.C. Huseman, "Equity Sensitivity and Outcome Importance," *Journal of Organizational Behavior* 15 (1994): 585–596.

24. P.S. Goodman, "Social Comparison Processes in Organizations," in *New Directions in Organizational Behavior*, ed. B.M. Staw and G.R. Salancik (Chicago: St. Clair Press, 1976); R.P. Vecchio, "Predicting Worker Performance in Inequitable Settings," *Academy of Management Review* 7 (1982): 103–110; R.P. Vecchio, "Models of Psychological Inequity," *Organizational Behavior and Human Performance* 34 (1984): 266–282.

25. A. Bandura, *Social Learning Theory* (Englewood Cliffs, N.J.: Prentice-Hall, 1977); A.P. Goldstein and M. Sorcher, *Changing Supervisor Behavior* (New York: Pergamon, 1974).

26. Porter and Lawler, *Managerial Attitudes and Performance*.

Chapter 5

1. E.E. Lawler and G.D. Jenkins, "Strategic Reward Systems," in M.D. Dunnette and L.M. Hugh (eds.), *Handbook of Industrial and Organizational Psychology* (Palo Alto, Cal.: Consulting Psychologists Press, 1992); E.E. Lawler III, *Pay and Organizational Effectiveness* (New York: McGraw-Hill, 1971); E.E. Lawler III, "New Approaches to Pay: Innovations That Work," *Personnel* 53 (1976): 11–23; E.E. Lawler III, *Pay and Organization Development* (Reading, Mass.: Addison-Wesley, 1981); E.E. Lawler III, "Whatever Happened to Incentive Pay?" *New Management* 1 (1984): 37–41.

2. Lawler, "Whatever Happened to Incentive Pay?"

3. H.C. Handlin, "The Company Built upon the Golden Rule: Lincoln Electric," *Journal of Organizational Behavior Management* 12 (1992): 151–163; K.W. Chilton, "Lincoln Electric's Incentive System: A Reservoir of Trust," *Compensation and Benefits Review* 26 (1994): 29–34.

4. Lawler, "Whatever Happened to Incentive Pay?"; D.R. Spitzer, "Power Rewards: Rewards That Really Motivate," *Management Review* 85 (1996): 45–50; A. Mitra, N. Gupta, and G. Douglas, "A Drop in the Bucket: When Is a Pay Raise a Pay Raise?" *Journal of Organizational Behavior* 18 (1997): 117–137.

5. J. Ramquist, "Labor-Management Cooperation," *Sloan Management Review* 23 (1982): 49–55; E. Leefeldt, "Profit-Sharing Plans Reward Productivity," *The Wall Street Journal*, November 15, 1984, 1.

6. T. Curry and K. Jackson-Fallon, "Workers' Risks and Rewards," *Time*, April 15, 1991, 42–43.

7. G.P. Latham and G. Yukl, "A Review of Research on the Application of Goal-Setting in Organizations," *Academy of Management Journal* 18 (1975): 824–845; E.A. Locke, "Job Satisfaction and Job Performance: A Theoretical Analysis," *Organizational Behavior and Human Performance* 5 (1970): 484–500; J. Hollenbeck, C. Williams, and H. Klein, "An Empirical Examination of the Antecedents of Commitment to Difficult Goals," *Journal of Applied Psychology* 74 (1989): 18–23; P.C. Earley, T. Connolly, and G. Ekegren, "Goals, Strategy Development, and Task Performance," *Journal of Applied Psychology* 74 (1989): 24–33; M. Tubbs, "Goal Setting: A Meta-analytic Examination of the Empirical Evidence," *Journal of Applied Psychology* 71 (1986): 474–483; A.J. Mento, R.P. Steel, and R.J. Karren, "A Meta-analytic Study of the Effects of Goal Setting on Task Performance," *Organizational Behavior and Human Decision Processes* 39 (1987): 52–83; G.P. Latham and E. Locke, "Self-Regulation through Goal-Setting," *Organizational Behavior and Human Decision Processes* 50 (1991): 212–247.

8. S.E. White, T.R. Mitchell, and C.H. Bell, "Goal Setting, Evaluation Apprehension, and Social Cues as Determinants of Job Performance and Job Satisfaction in a Simulated Organization," *Journal of Applied Psychology* 62 (1977): 665–673.

9. H. Tosi, J.R. Rizzo, and S. Carroll, "Setting Goals in Management-by-Objectives," *California Management Review* 12 (1970): 70–78.

10. P.F. Drucker, *The Practice of Management* (New York: Harper, 1954); A.P. Raia, *Managing by Objectives* (Glenview, Ill.: Scott, Foresman, 1974); S.J. Carroll and H.L. Tosi, *Management by Objectives: Applications and Research* (New York: Macmillan, 1973); J. Kondrasuk, "Studies in MBO Effectiveness," *Academy of Management Review* 6 (1981): 419–430.

11. R. Rodgers and J.E. Hunter, "Impact of Management by Objectives on Organizational Productivity," *Journal of Applied Psychology* 76 (1991): 322–336; R. Rodgers, J.E. Hunter, and D.L. Rogers, "Influence of Top Management Commitment on Management Program Success," *Journal of Applied Psychology* 78 (1993): 151–155.

12. R.A. Jones, *Self-Fulfilling Prophecies: Social, Psychological, and Physiological Effects of Expectancies* (Hillsdale, N.J.: Erlbaum, 1977); J.S. Livingston, "Pygmalion in Management," *Harvard Business Review* 47 (1969): 81–89.

13. R. Rosenthal and L. Jacobson, *Pygmalion in the Classroom: Teachers' Expectations and Pupil Intellectual Development* (New York: Holt, Rinehart and Winston, 1968).

14. A.S. King, "Managerial Relations with Disadvantaged Work Groups: Supervisory Expectations of the Underprivileged Worker" (Ph.D. diss., Texas Tech University, 1970).

15. D. Eden and A.B. Shani, "Pygmalion Goes to Boot Camp: Expectancy, Leadership, and Trainee Performance," *Journal of Applied Psychology* 67 (1982): 194–199; D. Eden, "Pygmalion without Interpersonal Contrast Effects: Whole Groups Gain from Raising Manager Expectations," *Journal of Applied Psychology* 75 (1990): 394–400; S. Oz and D. Eden, "Restraining the Golem: Boosting Performance by Changing the Interpretation of Low Scores," *Journal of Applied Psychology* 79 (1994): 744–754; D. Eden, "Leadership and Expectations: Pygmalion Effects and Other Self-Fulfilling Prophecies in Organizations," *Leadership Quarterly* 3 (1992): 271–305; T. Dvir, D. Eden, and M. Lang-Bingo, "Self-Fulfilling Prophecy and Gender: Can Women Be Pygmalion and Galatea?" *Journal of Applied Psychology* 80 (1995): 253–270.

16. R. Rosenthal and K. Fode, "The Effect of Experimental Bias on the Performance of the Albino Rat," *Behavioral Science* 8 (1963): 183–189.

17. A. Smith, *An Inquiry into the Nature and Causes of the Wealth of Nations* (New York: Modern Library, 1937; first published in 1776).

18. A.C. Filley, R.J. House, and S. Kerr, *Managerial Process and Organizational Behavior* (Dallas: Scott, Foresman, 1987).

19. F. Herzberg, B. Mausner, and B. Snyderman, *The Motivation to Work* (New York: Wiley, 1959).

20. R.A. Guzzo, R.D. Jette, and R.A. Katzell, "The Effects of Psychologically Based Intervention Programs on Worker Productivity: A Meta-analysis," *Personnel Psychology* 38 (1985): 275–292; R.E. Kopelman, "Job Redesign and Productivity: A Review of the Evidence," *National Productivity Review* 4 (1985): 237–255; R.A. Melcher, "Volvo and Renault: Marriage May Be the Answer," *Business Week*, November 23, 1992, 50–51; S. Prokesch, "Edges Fray on Volvo's Brave New Humanistic World," *The New York Times*, July 7, 1991, C5.

21. C.L. Hulin and M.R. Blood, "Job Enlargement, Individual Differences, and Worker Responses," *Psychological Bulletin* 69 (1968): 41–55.

22. M.R. Blood and C.L. Hulin, "Alienation, Environmental Characteristics and Worker Responses," *Journal of Applied Psychology* 51 (1967): 284–290.

23. R.P. Vecchio, "Individual Differences as a Moderator of the Job Quality–Job Satisfaction Relationship: Evidence from a National Sample," *Organizational Behavior and Human Performance* 26 (1980): 305–325.

24. J.K. White, "Individual Differences and the Job Quality–Worker Response Relationship: Review, Integration, and

Comments," *Academy of Management Review* 3 (1978): 267–280.

25. J.R. Hackman and G.R. Oldham, "Motivation Through the Design of Work: Test of a Theory," *Organizational Behavior and Human Performance* 16 (1976): 250–279; J.R. Hackman and G.R. Oldham, *Work Redesign* (Reading, Mass.: Addison-Wesley, 1980).

26. J. Kelly, "Does Job Design Theory Explain Job Re-design Outcomes?" *Human Relations* 45 (1992): 753–774; Y. Fried and G.R. Ferris, "The Validity of the Job Characteristics Model: A Review and Meta-analysis," *Personnel Psychology* 40 (1987): 287–322; C.R. Berlinger, W.H. Glick, and R.C. Rodgers, "Job Enrichment and Performance Improvements," in *Productivity in Organizations,* eds. J.P. Campbell and R.J. Campbell (San Francisco: Jossey Bass, 1988); J.B. Miner, *Theories of Organizational Behavior* (Hinsdale, Ill.: The Dryden Press, 1980); T. Taber and E. Taylor, "A Review and Evaluation of the Psychometric Properties of the Job Diagnostic Survey," *Personnel Psychology* 43 (1990): 467–500; R.W. Renn and R.J. Vandenberg, "The Critical Psychological States: An Underrepresented Component in Job Characteristics Model Research," *Journal of Management* 21 (1995): 279–303.

27. A.R. Cohen and H. Gadon, *Alternative Work Schedules: Integrating Individual and Organizational Needs* (Reading, Mass.: Addison-Wesley, 1978).

28. V.E. Schein, E.H. Maurer, and J.F. Novak, "Impact of Flexible Working Hours on Productivity," *Journal of Applied Psychology* 62 (1977): 463–465.

29. R.T. Golembiewski and C.W. Proehl, "A Survey of the Empirical Literature on Flexible Workhours: Character and Consequences of a Major Innovation," *Academy of Management Review* 3 (1978): 837–855; D. Dalton and D. Mesch, "The Impact of Flexible Scheduling on Employee Attendance and Turnover," *Administrative Science Quarterly* 35 (1990): 225–257; "HR Update—Fourth of Full-Timers Enjoy Flexible Hours" *HRM Magazine* (June 1998): 26.

30. P. Dickson, *The Future of the Workplace* (New York: Wybright and Talley, 1975); J. Pierce and R. Dunham, "The 12-Hour Work Day: A 48-Hour, Eight-Day Week," *Academy of Management Journal* 35 (1992): 1086–1098.

31. J.M. Ivancevich and H.C. Lyon, "The Shortened Workweek: A Field Experiment," *Journal of Applied Psychology* 62 (1977): 34–37.

32. Cohen and Gadon, *Alternative Work Schedules.*

33. J.N. Goodrich, "Telecommuting in America," *Business Horizons* (1990): 31–37; A.J. Chapman, N.P. Sheely, S. Heywood, B. Dooley, and S. Collins, "The Organizational Implications of Teleworking," in C.L. Cooper and I.T. Robertson (eds.), *International Review of Industrial and Organizational Psychology* (Winchester, UK: John Wiley, 1995); L. Haddon and A. Lewis, "The Experience of Teleworking: A Review," *The International Journal of Human Resource Management* 5 (1994): 193–223.

34. J.D. Blair, S.L. Cohen, and J.V. Hurwitz, "Quality Circles: Practical Considerations for Public Managers," *Public Productivity Review* 10 (March 1982): 14.

35. R.P. Vecchio, "Employee Attributes and Interest in Quality Circles," *Proceedings of the Southeast Regional Meeting of the American Institute for Decision Sciences,* 1985, 106–108; S.A. Zahra, W.J. Lundstrom, and D.R. Latham, "An Empirical Investigation into the Dynamics of Volunteerism for Quality Circle Participants" (Paper presented at Southern Management Association, 1983); M. Marks, "The Question of Quality Circles," *Psychology Today* 20 (1986): 36–46; M. Marks, P. Miruis, E. Hackett, and J. Grady, "Employee Participation in a Quality Circle Program: Impact on Quality of Work Life, Productivity, and Absenteeism," *Journal of Applied Psychology* 71 (1986): 61–69; J. Brockner and T. Hess, "Self-Esteem and Task Performance in Quality Circles," *Academy of Management Journal* 29 (1986): 617–622; T. Wada and R.P. Vecchio, "Quality Circles at Mitsubishi," *Quality Circles Journal* 7 (1984): 33–34; R.W. Miller and F.N. Prichard, "Factors Associated with Workers' Inclination to Participate in an Employee Involvement Program," *Group and Organization Management* 17 (1992): 414–430.

36. R.W. Griffin, "Consequences of Quality Circles in an Industrial Setting: A Longitudinal Assessment," *Academy of Management Journal* 31 (1988): 338–358.

37. Blair, Cohen, and Hurwitz, "Quality Circles: Practical Considerations."

38. J.D. Osburn, L. Moran, E. Musselwhite, J.H. Zenger, and C. Perrin, *Self-directed Work Teams* (Homewood, Ill.: Irwin, 1990).

39. J. Hoerr, M. Pollock, and D. Whiteside, "Management Discovers the Human Side of Automatic," *Business Week,* September 1986, 70–76; A. Bernstein, "GM May Be Off the Hook," *Business Week,* September 1987, 26–27.

40. R. Rogers, *Implementation of Total Quality Management* (New York: International Business Press, 1996); A. Wilkinson and H. Willmott, *Making Quality Critical* (New York: Rutledge, 1995); E.E. Lawler, "Total Quality Management and Employee Involvement: Are They Compatible?" *Academy of Management Executive* 8 (1994): 68–76; M.A. Huselid, "The Impact of Human Resource Management Practices on Turnover, Productivity, and Corporate Financial Performance," *Academy of Management Journal,* in press.

41. E.L. Harrison, "The Impact of Employee Involvement on Supervisors," *National Productivity Review* (1992): 447–452.

42. R.W. Griffin, "Effects of Work Redesign on Employee Perceptions, Attitudes, and Behaviors: A Long-Term Investigation," *Academy of Management Journal* 34 (1991): 425–435; J. Cordery, W.S. Mueller, and L. Smith, "Attitudinal and Behavioral Effects of Autonomous Group Working: A Longitudinal Field Study," *Academy of Management Journal* 34 (1991): 464–476; R.J. Magjuka and T. Baldwin, "Team-based Employee Involvement Programs: Effects of Design and Administration," *Personnel Psychology* 44 (1991): 793–812; K. Thomas and B. Velthouse, "Cognitive Elements of Empowerment: An 'Interpretive' Model of Intrinsic Task Motivation," *Academy of Management Review* 15 (1990): 666–681; C. Leana, R. Ahlbrandt, and A. Murrell, "The Effects of Employee Involvement Programs on Unionized Workers' Attitudes, Perceptions, and Preferences in Decision Making," *Academy of Management Journal* 35 (1992): 861–873; N. Hayes, *Successful Team Management* (New York: International Business Press, 1997); R.D. Banker, J.M. Field, R.G. Schraeder, and K.K. Sinha, "Impact of Work Teams on Manufacturing Performance: A Longitudinal Field Study," *Academy of Management Journal* 39 (1996): 867–890; S. Cohen and G.E. Ledford, "The Effectiveness of Self-Managing Teams: A Quasi-Experiment," *Human Relations* 47 (1994): 13–43.

43. M. Parker and J. Slaughter, *Choosing Sides: Unions and the Team Concept* (New York: A Labor Notes–South End Press, 1988).

Chapter 6

1. D.C. McClelland, *Power: The Inner Experience* (New York: Irvington, 1975); D.C. McClelland, "Power Is the Great Motivation," *Harvard Business Review* 54 (1976): 100–110.

2. H.C. Kelman, "Processes of Opinion Change," *Public Opinion Quarterly* 25 (1961): 57–78.

3. J.R.P. French, Jr., and B.H. Raven, "The Bases of Social Power," in *Studies in Social Power,* ed. D. Cartwright (Ann Arbor: University of Michigan, Institute for Social Research, 1959); T. Hinkin and C. Schriesheim, "Development and Application of New Scales to Measure the French and Raven Bases of Social Power," *Journal of Applied Psychology* 74 (1989): 561–567; A. Etzioni, *A Comparative Analysis of Complex Organizations,* rev. ed. (New York: Free Press, 1975); R. Mayer, "Understanding Employee Motivation through Organizational Commitment" (Ph.D. diss., Purdue University, 1989); M. Sussmann and R.P. Vecchio, "A Social Influence Interpretation of Worker Motivation," *Academy of Management Review* 7 (1982): 177–186; R.P. Vecchio and M. Sussman, "Preference for Forms of Supervisory Social Influence," *Journal of Organizational Behavior* 10 (1989): 135–143; H. Aguinis, M.S. Nesler, B.M.

Quigley, S.J. Lee, and J.T. Tedeschi, "Power Bases of Faculty Supervisors and Educational Outcomes for Graduate Students," *Journal of Higher Education* 67 (1996): 267–297.

4. G.R. Ferris and K.M. Kacmar, "Perceptions of Organizational Politics," *Journal of Management* 10 (1992): 93–116; J. Pfeffer, *Power in Organizations* (Boston: Pitman Publishing Co., 1981).

5. R.W. Allen, D.L. Madison, L.W. Porter et al., "Organizational Politics: Tactics and Characteristics of Its Actors," *California Management Review* 12 (Fall 1979): 77–83; A.J. DuBrin, *Winning at Office Politics* (New York: Ballantine, 1978); R.H. Miles, *Macro Organizational Behavior* (Santa Monica, Cal.: Goodyear, 1980), 174–175; Pfeffer, *Power in Organizations.*

6. A.J. DuBrin, "Deadly Political Sins," *National Business Employment Weekly,* Fall 1993; 11–13; DuBrin, *Winning at Office Politics.*

7. R. Christie and F.L. Geis, eds., *Studies in Machiavellianism* (New York: Academic Press, 1970).

8. D.S. Wilson, D. Near, and R.R. Miller, "Machiavellianism: A Synthesis of the Evolutionary and Psychological Literatures," *Psychological Bulletin* 119 (1996): 285–299; G.R. Gemmil and W.J. Heisler, "Machiavellianism as a Factor in Managerial Job Strain, Job Satisfaction, and Upward Mobility," *Academy of Management Journal* 15 (1972): 53–67.

9. R.V. Exline, J. Thibaut, C.O. Hickey et al., "Visual Interaction in Relation to Machiavellianism and an Unethical Act," in *Studies in Machiavellianism,* eds. R. Christie and F.L. Geis (New York: Academic Press, 1970), 53–75; D. Kipnis and S.M. Schmidt, *Profiles of Organizational Influence Strategies* (San Diego: University Associates, 1982); S.M. Schmidt and D. Kipnis, "The Perils of Persistence," *Psychology Today,* November 1987, 32–34; D. Kipnis, *The Powerholders* (Chicago: University of Chicago Press, 1976); P. Block, *The Empowered Manager* (San Francisco: Jossey-Bass, 1988).

10. C.F. Turner and D.C. Martinez, "Socioeconomic Achievement and the Machiavellian Personality," *Sociometry* 40 (1977): 325–336.

11. Kipnis and Schmidt, *Profiles of Organizational Influence Strategies;* C. Schriesheim and T. Hinkin, "Influence Tactics Used by Subordinates: A Theoretical and Empirical Analysis and Refinement of the Kipnis, Schmidt, and Wilkinson Subscales," *Journal of Applied Psychology* 75 (1990): 246–252; G. Yukl and J.B. Tracey, "Consequences of Influence Tactics Used with Subordinates, Peers, and the Boss," *Journal of Applied Psychology* 76 (1992): 525–535; C. Falbe and G. Yukl, "Consequences for Managers of Using Single Influence Tactics and Combinations of

Tactics," *Academy of Management Journal* 35 (1992): 638–652; D. Brass and M. Burkhardt, "Potential Power and Power Use: An Investigation of Structure and Behaviors," *Academy of Management Journal* 36 (1993): 441–470.

12. Schmidt and Kipnis, "The Perils of Persistence."

13. Kipnis, *The Powerholders*; Block, *The Empowered Manager*; D. Kipnis, S.M. Schmidt, C. Swaffin-Smith, and I. Wilkenson, "Patterns of Managerial Influence: Shotgun Managers, Tacticians, and Bystanders," *Organizational Dynamics* (1984): 58–67; S.M. Farmer, D.B. Fedor, J.S. Goodman, and J.M. Maslyn, "Factors Affecting the Use of Upward Influence Strategies," *Proceedings of the Academy of Management* (1993): 64–68.

14. M. Lefkowitz, R.A. Blake, and J.S. Mouton, "Status Factors in Pedestrian Violation of Traffic Signals," *Journal of Abnormal and Social Psychology* 51 (1955): 704–706.

15. W. Duncan and J. Feisal, "No Laughing Matter: Humor in the Workplace," *Organizational Dynamics* 17 (1989): 18–30.

16. S. Milgram, L. Bickman, and L. Berkowitz, "Note on the Drawing Power of Crowds of Different Size," *Journal of Personality and Social Psychology* 13 (1969): 79–82.

17. J.C. Freedman and S.C. Fraser, "Compliance without Pressure: The Foot-in-the Door Technique," *Journal of Personality and Social Psychology* 4 (1966): 195–202.

18. G.F. Cavanagh, D.J. Moberg, and M. Velasquez, "The Ethics of Organizational Politics," *Academy of Management Review* 6 (1981): 363–374.

19. S. Milgram, "Behavioral Study of Obedience," *Journal of Abnormal and Social Psychology* 67 (1963): 371–378.

20. S. Milgram, *Obedience to Authority* (New York: Harper, 1974); M.E. Shanah and K.A. Yahya, "A Behavioral Study of Obedience in Children," *Journal of Personality and Social Psychology* 35 (1977): 530–536.

21. CBS News, Transcript of *Sixty Minutes* segment, "I Was Only Following Orders," (March 31, 1979): 2–8; D.M. Mantell, "The Potential for Violence in Germany," *Journal of Social Issues* 27 (1971): 101–112; M.E. Shanah and K.A. Yahya, "A Cross-Cultural Study of Obedience," *Bulletin of the Psychonomic Society* 11 (1978): 267–269; W. Kilham and L. Mann, "Level of Destructive Obedience as a Function of Transmitter and Executant Roles in the Milgram Obedience Paradigm," *Journal of Personality and Social Psychology* 29 (1974): 696–702; S.R. Shalala, "A Study of Various Communication Settings Which Produce Obedience by Subordinates to Unlawful Superior Orders" (Ph.D. diss, University of Kansas, 1974).

22. T. Blass, "Obedience to Authority: Some Issues and Significance," in *Perspectives on Stanley Milgram's Contributions to Social Psychology* (Symposium conducted at the Annual Meeting of the American Psychological Association, Boston, Mass., August 24, 1990).

Chapter 7

1. B.M. Bass, *Bass and Stogdill's Handbook of Leadership*, 3rd ed. (New York: Free Press, 1990).

2. W.G. Wagner, J. Pfeffer, and C.A. O'Reilly, "Organizational Demography and Turnover in Top-Management Groups," *Administrative Science Quarterly* 29 (1984): 74–92; K.B. Schwartz and K. Menon, "Executive Succession in Failing Firms," *Academy of Management Journal* 28 (1985): 680–686.

3. G.R. Salanci, B.M. Staw, and L.R. Pondy, "Administrative Turnover as a Response to Unmanaged Organizational Independence," *Academy of Management Journal* 10 (1980): 422–437.

4. R. Hogan, G.J. Curphy, and J. Hogan, "What We Know about Leadership," *American Psychologist* 49 (1994): 493–504; S. Lieberson and J.F. O'Connor, "Leadership and Organizational Performance: A Study of Large Corporations," *American Sociological Review* 37 (1972): 117–130; N. Weiner and T.A. Mahoney, "A Model of Corporate Performance as a Function of Environmental, Organizational, and Leadership Influences," *Academy of Management Journal* 24 (1981): 453–470; G.R. Salancik and J. Pfeffer, "Constraints on Administrator Discretion: The Limited Influence of Mayors on City Budgets," *Urban Affairs Quarterly* 12 (1977): 475–498; D. Miller, "Some Organizational Consequences of CEO Succession," *Academy of Management Journal* 36 (1993): 644–659; A. Cannella and M. Lubatkin, "Succession as a Sociopolitical Process: Internal Impediments to Outsider Selection," *Academy of Management Journal* 36 (1993): 763–793; S. Friedman and K. Saul, "A Leader's Wake: Organization Member Reactions to CEO Succession," *Journal of Management* 17 (1991): 619–642; D. Hambrick and G. Fukutomi, "The Seasons of a CEO's Tenure," *Academy of Management Review* 16 (1991): 719–742.

5. R. Stewart, *Managers and Their Jobs: A Study of the Similarities and Differences in the Ways Managers Spend Their Time* (London: Macmillan, 1967).

6. H. Mintzberg, "The Manager's Job: Folklore and Fact," *Harvard Business Review* 53 (July–August 1975): 49–61; H. Mintzberg, *The Nature of Managerial Work* (New York: Harper & Row, 1973).

7. D.L. Marples, "Studies of Managers—A Fresh Start," *Journal of Management Studies* 4 (1967): 282–299.

8. R.M. Stogdill, "Personal Factors Associated with Leadership: A Survey of the Literature," *Journal of Psychology* 25 (1948): 35–71.

9. D.L. Cawthon, "Leadership: The Great Man Theory Revisited," *Business Horizons* 39 (1996): 1–4.

10. R.M. Stogdill, *Handbook of Leadership* (Glencoe, Ill.: Free Press, 1975); Bass, *Handbook of Leadership*.

11. E. Ghiselli, *Exploration in Managerial Talent* (Santa Monica, Cal.: Goodyear, 1971).

12. F.E. Fiedler, "Cognitive Resources and Leadership Performance," *Applied Psychology: An International Review* 44 (1995): 5–28.

13. F.E. Fiedler and J.E. Garcia, *New Approaches to Effective Leadership* (New York: John Wiley and Sons, 1987); F.E. Fiedler, "The Contribution of Cognitive Resources and Behavior to Leadership Performance" (Paper presented at the Annual Meeting of the Academy of Management, Boston, Mass., 1984); F.E. Fiedler and A.F. Leister, "Leader Intelligence and Task Performance: A Test of a Multiple Screen Model," *Organizational Behavior and Human Performance* 20 (1977): 1–14; J. Blades, "The Influence of Intelligence, Task Ability, and Motivation on Group Performance" (Ph.D. diss., University of Washington, 1976); R.P. Vecchio, "Cognitive Resource Theory: Successor to the 'Black Box' Model of Leadership," *Contemporary Psychology* 33 (1988): 1030–1032.

14. R.P. Vecchio, "A Theoretical and Empirical Examination of Cognitive Resource Theory," *Journal of Applied Psychology* 75 (1990): 141–147.

15. R.K. Wagner and R.J. Sternberg, "Street Smarts," in *Measures of Leadership*, eds. K.E. Clark and M.B. Clark (West Orange, N.J.: Leadership Library of America, 1990).

16. Vecchio, "A Theoretical and Empirical Examination of Cognitive Resource Theory."

17. Stogdill, *Handbook of Leadership*.

18. A.H. Eagly and B.T. Johnson, "Gender and Leadership Style: A Meta-analysis," *Psychological Bulletin* 108 (1990): 233–256; A. Eagly, M. Makhijani, and B. Klonsky, "Gender and the Evaluation of Leaders: A Meta-analysis," *Psychological Bulletin* 111 (1992): 3–22; J.S. DeMatteo, G.H. Dobbins, S.D. Myers, and Carolyn L-Facteau, "Evaluations of Leadership in Preferential and Merit-Based Leader Selection Situations," *Leadership Quarterly* 7 (1996): 41–62; A. Eagly, S.J. Karau, and M.G. Makhijani, "Gender and the Effectiveness of Leaders: A Meta-analysis," *Psychological Bulletin* 117 (1995): 125–145; D. Park, "Androgynous Leadership Style," *Leadership and Organization Development Journal* 18 (1997): 166–171; J.A. Kolb, "Are We Still Stereotyping Leadership? A Look at Gender and Other Predictors of Leadership Emergence," *Small Group Research* 28 (1997): 370–393.

19. G.N. Powell, "One More Time: Do Female and Male Managers Differ?" *Academy of Management Executive* 4 (1990): 68–75.

20. L.M. Terman and C.C. Miles, *Sex and Personality: Studies on Masculinity and Femininity* (New York: McGraw-Hill, 1936); M.E. Shaw, *Group Dynamics* (New York: McGraw-Hill, 1971).

21. R.A. Noe, "Women and Mentoring: A Review and Research Agenda," *Academy of Management Review* 13 (1988): 65–78.

22. K.E. Kram and L.A. Isabella, "Alternatives to Mentoring: The Role of Peer Relationships in Career Development," *Academy of Management Journal* 28 (1985): 110–132.

23. K. Lewin, R. Lippitt, and R.K. White, "Patterns of Aggressive Behavior in Experimentally Created Social Climates," *Journal of Social Psychology* 10 (1939): 271–301.

24. B. Bass, *Leadership, Psychology, and Organizational Behavior* (New York: Harper & Row, 1960); C. Gibb, "Leadership," in *The Handbook of Social Psychology*, 2d ed., eds. G. Lindzey and E. Aronson, 5 vols. (Reading, Mass.: Addison-Wesley, 1969), 4:205–282.

25. V.H. Vroom and F.C. Mann, "Leader Authoritarianism and Employee Attitudes," *Personnel Psychology* 13 (1960): 125–140.

26. R.F. Bales, "The Equilibrium Problem in Small Groups," in *Working Papers on the Theory in Action*, ed. T. Parson, R.F. Bales, and E.A. Shills (Glencoe, Ill.: Free Press, 1953).

27. E.A. Fleishman and E.F. Harris, "Patterns of Leadership Behavior Related to Employee Grievance and Turnover," *Personnel Psychology* 15 (1962): 43–56.

28. Stogdill, *Handbook of Leadership*; Yukl, *Leadership in Organizations*.

29. L.L. Larson, J.G. Hunt, and R. Osburn, "The Great Hi-Hi Leader Behavior Myth: A Lesson from Occam's Razor," *Academy of Management Journal* 19 (1976): 628–641.

30. S. Kerr, C.A. Schriesheim, C.J. Murphy et al., "Toward a Contingency Theory of Leadership Based upon the Consideration and Initiating Structure Literature," *Organizational Behavior and Human Performance* 12 (1974): 62–82; Stogdill, *Handbook of Leadership*; Yukl, *Leadership in Organizations*.

31. R.R. Blake and J.S. Mouton, *The New Managerial Grid* (Houston: Gulf Publishing Co., 1978).

32. R.R. Blake and J.S. Mouton, "A Comparative Analysis of Situationalism and 9,9 Management by Principle," *Organizational Dynamics* 24 (Spring 1982): 21.

33. P.M. Podsakoff, S.B. MacKenzie, and W.H. Bommer, "Transformational Leader Behaviors as Determinants of Employee Satisfaction, Commitment, Trust, and Organizational Citizenship Behaviors," *Journal of Management* 22 (1996): 259–298. L.K. Hall, "Charisma: A Study of

Personality Characteristics of Charismatic Leaders." (Ph.D. diss., University of Georgia, Athens (1983); J.A. Conger and R.N. Kanungo, "Behavioral Dimensions of Charismatic Leadership," in *Charismatic Leadership: The Elusive Factor in Organizational Effectiveness,* eds. J.A. Conger and R.N. Kanungo (San Francisco: Jossey-Bass, 1988); J.A. Conger and R.N. Kanungo, "Toward a Behavioral Theory of Charismatic Leadership in Organizational Settings," *Academy of Management Journal* 12 (1987): 637–647; R. House, W.D. Spangler, and J. Woycke, "Personality and Charisma in the U.S. Presidency: A Psychological Theory of Leader Effectiveness," *Administrative Science Quarterly* 36 (1991): 364–396.

34. B.M. Bass, "Theory of Transformational Leadership Redux," *Leadership Quarterly* 6 (1995): 463–478; B.M. Bass, *The Multifactor Leadership Questionnaire—Form 5* (Binghamton: State University of New York, 1985); B.M. Bass and B.J. Avolio, "Phototypicality, Leniency, and Generalized Response Set in Rated and Ranked Transformational and Transactional Leadership Descriptions," Binghamton State University of New York Center for Leadership Studies, Report Series 88-2, (1988).

35. B.M. Bass, "Policy Implications of Transformational Leadership," in *Research in Organizational Change and Development,* eds. R.W. Woodman and W.A. Pasmore (Greenwich, Conn.: JAI Press, 1988); J.M. Burns, *Leadership* (New York: Harper & Row, 1978).

36. S.J. Musser, "The Determination of Positive and Negative Charismatic Leadership" (Unpublished paper, Grantham, Penn.: Messiah College); D. Sankowsky, "The Charismatic Leader as Narcissist: Understanding the Abuse of Power," *Organizational Dynamics* 23 (1995): 57–71; R.J. House and R.N. Aditya, "The Social Scientific Study of Leadership: Quo Vadis?" *Journal of Management* 23 (1997): 409–473.

37. M.R. Kets de Vries and D. Miller, *The Neurotic Organization: Diagnosing and Changing Counter-productive Styles of Management* (San Francisco: Jossey-Bass, 1984); M.R. Kets de Vries and D. Miller, "Narcissism and Leadership: An Object-relations Perspective," *Human Relations* 38 (1985): 583–601.

38. R. Ayman, M.M. Chemers, and F. Fiedler, "The Contingency Model of Leadership Effectiveness: Its Levels of Analysis," *Leadership Quarterly* 6 (1995): 147–167; F.E. Fiedler, *A Theory of Leadership Effectiveness* (New York: McGraw-Hill, 1967).

39. F.E. Fiedler, "The Contribution of Cognitive Resources and Behavior to Leadership Performance" (Paper presented at Annual Meeting of the Academy of Management, Boston, Mass., 1984).

40. R.P. Vecchio, "Cognitive Resource Theory: Successor to the 'Black Box' Model of Leadership," *Contemporary Psychology* 33 (1988): 1030–1032; R.P. Vecchio, "A Theoretical and Empirical Examination of Cognitive Resource Theory," *Journal of Applied Psychology* 75 (1990): 141–147. R.P. Vecchio, "An Empirical Investigation of the Validity of Fiedler's Model of Leadership Effectiveness," *Organizational Behavior and Human Performance* 19 (1977): 180–206; M.J. Strube and J.E. Garcia, "A Meta-analytic Investigation of Fiedler's Contingency Model of Leadership Effectiveness," *Psychological Bulletin* 90 (1981): 307–321; R.P. Vecchio, "Assessing the Validity of Fiedler's Contingency Model of Leadership Effectiveness: A Closer Look at Strube and Garcia (1981)," *Psychological Bulletin* 93 (1983): 404–408; M.J. Strube and J.E. Garcia, "On the Proper Interpretation of Empirical Findings: Strube and Garcia (1981) Revisited," *Psychological Bulletin* 93 (1983): 600–603; C.A. Schriesheim, B.J. Tepper, and L. Tetrault, "Least Preferred Co-Worker Score, Situational Control, and Leadership Effectiveness: A Meta-analysis," *Journal of Applied Psychology* 79 (1994): 561–573.

41. F.E. Fiedler, *The Leadership Game: Matching the Man to the Situation,*" Organizational Dynamics 4 (1976): 6–16.

42. Vecchio, "An Empirical Investigation of the Validity of Fiedler's Model."

43. M.G. Evans, "The Effects of Supervisory Behavior on the Path–Goal Relationship," *Organizational Behavior and Human Performance* 5 (1970): 277–298; M.G. Evans, "Extensions of a Path–Goal Theory of Motivation," *Journal of Applied Psychology* 59 (1974): 172–178.

44. R.J. House, "A Path–Goal Theory of Leader Effectiveness," *Administrative Science Quarterly* 16 (1971): 321–338.

45. A.D. Szilagyi and H.P. Sims, "An Exploration of the Path–Goal Theory of Leadership in a Health-Care Environment," *Academy of Management Journal* 17 (1974): 622–634; C.A. Schriesheim and A.S. DeNisi, "Task Dimensions as Moderators of the Effects of Instrumental Leadership: A Two-Sample Replicated Test of Path–Goal Leadership Theory," *Journal of Applied Psychology* 66 (1981): 589–597.

46. R.J. House and G. Dessler, "The Path–Goal Theory of Leadership: Some Post Hoc and A Priori Tests," in *Contingency Approaches to Leadership*, eds. J.G. Hunt and L.L. Larson (Carbondale, Ill.: Southern Illinois University Press, 1974); H.K. Downey, J.E. Sheridan, and J.W. Slocum, "Analysis of Relationships among Leader Behavior, Subordinate Job Performance, and Satisfaction: A Path–Goal Approach," *Academy of Management Journal* 18 (1975): 253–262.

47. K.H. Blanchard and P. Hersey, "Great Ideas Revisited," *Training and Development Journal* 50 (1996): 42–47; P. Hersey and K.H. Blanchard, *Management of Organizational Behavior*, 3d ed. (Englewood Cliffs, N.J.: Prentice-Hall, 1977).

48. C.L. Graeff, "The Situational Leadership Theory: A Critical Review," *Academy of Management Review* 7 (1983): 285–291; G. Yukl, *Leadership in Organizations* (Englewood Cliffs, N.J.: Prentice-Hall, 1981); R.P. Vecchio, "Situational Leadership Theory: An Examination of a Prescriptive Theory," *Journal of Applied Psychology* 72 (1987): 444–451; C.F. Fernandez and R.P. Vecchio, "Situational Leadership Theory Revisited: A Test of an Across-Jobs Perspective," *Leadership Quarterly* 8 (1997): 67–84; C.L. Graeff, "Evolution of Situational Leadership Theory: A Critical Review," *Leadership Quarterly* 8 (1997): 153–170.

49. V.H. Vroom and P.W. Yetton, *Leadership and Decision Making* (Pittsburgh: University of Pittsburgh Press, 1973).

50. V.H. Vroom, "Leadership Revisited," in *Man and Work in Society*, eds. E.L. Case and F.G. Zimmer (New York: Van Nostrand Reinhold, 1975); V.H. Vroom and A.G. Jago, "On the Validity of the Vroom-Yetton Model," *Journal of Applied Psychology* 63 (1978): 151–162; R.H. Field, "A Test of the Vroom–Yetton Normative Model of Leadership," *Journal of Applied Psychology* 67 (1982): 523–532; W.C. Wedley and R.H. Field, "The Vroom–Yetton Model: Are Feasible Set Choices Due to Chance? *Academy of Management Proceedings* (1982): 146–150; R.H. Field and R.J. House, "A Test of the Vroom–Yetton Model Using Manager and Subordinate Reports," *Journal of Applied Psychology* 75 (1990): 362–370.

51. B. Smith, "The TELOS Program and the Vroom–Yetton Model," in *Crosscurrents in Leadership*, eds. J.G. Hunt and L. Larson, (Carbondale, Ill.: Southern Illinois University Press, 1979): 39–40.

52. V.H. Vroom and A.G. Jago, "Leadership and Decision Making: A Revised Normative Model" (Paper presented at Annual Meeting of the Academy of Management, Boston, Mass., 1984).

53. G.B. Graen and M. Uhl-Bien, "Relationship Based Approach to Leadership: Development of Leader–Member Exchange Theory of Leadership," *Leadership Quarterly* 6 (1995): 219–247; R.M. Dienesch and R.C. Liden, "Leader–Member Exchange Model of Leadership: A Critique and Further Developments," *Academy of Management Review* 11 (1986): 118–134; D. Duchon, S. Green, and T. Tabor, "Vertical Dyad Linkage," *Journal of Applied Psychology* 71 (1986): 56–60.

54. F. Danserau, G. Graen, and W.J. Haga, "A Vertical Dyad Linkage Approach to Leadership within Formal Organizations: A Cognitudinal Investigation of the Role-Making Process," *Organizational Behavior and Human Performance* 15 (1975): 46–78; G. Graen and J.F. Cashman, "A Role-Making Model of Leadership in Formal Organizations: A Developmental Approach," in *Leadership Frontiers*, eds. J.G. Hunt and L.L. Larson (Kent, Ohio: Kent State University Press, 1975): 143–165; R.C. Liden and G. Graen, "Generalizability of the Vertical Dyad Linkage Model of Leadership," *Academy of Management Journal* 23 (1980): 451–465; R.P. Vecchio, "Are You IN or OUT with Your Boss?" *Business Horizons* 29 (1987): 76–78; R.P. Vecchio, "A Dyadic Interpretation of the Contingency Model of Leadership Effectiveness," *Academy of Management Journal* 22 (1979): 590–600; K. Dunegan, D. Duchon, and M. Uhl-Bien, "Examining the Link Between Leader–Member Exchange and Subordinate Performance: The Role of Task Analyzability and Variety as Moderators," *Journal of Management* 18 (1992): 59–76.

55. C.R. Gertsner and D.V. Day, "Meta-analytic Review of Leader–Member Exchange Correlates and Construct Issues," *Journal of Applied Psychology* 82 (1997): 827–844; J. Miner, *Theories of Organizational Behavior* (Hinsdale, Ill.: The Dryden Press, 1980); R.P. Vecchio, "Predicting Employee Turnover from Leader–Member Exchange," *Academy of Management Journal* 28 (1985): 478–485; G. Ferris, "Role of Leadership in the Employee Withdrawal Process: A Constructive Replication," *Journal of Applied Psychology* 70 (1985): 777–781.

56. G. Graen and W. Schiemann, "Leader–Member Agreement: A Vertical Dyad Linkage Approach," *Journal of Applied Psychology* 63 (1978): 206–212; R. Katerberg and P.W. Hom, "Effects of Within-Group and Between-Groups Variation in Leadership," *Journal of Applied Psychology* 66 (1981): 218–223; R.P. Vecchio, "A Further Test of Leadership Effects Due to Between-Group Variation and Within-Group Variation," *Journal of Applied Psychology* 67 (1982): 200–208; R.P. Vecchio, R.W. Griffeth, and P.W. Hom, "The Predictive Utility of the Vertical Dyad Linkage Approach," *Journal of Social Psychology* 126 (1987): 617–625; R.P. Vecchio and B.C. Gobdel, "The Vertical Dyad Linkage Model of Leadership: Problems and Prospects," *Organizational Behavior and Human Performance* 34 (1984): 5–20; R.P. Vecchio, "Effective Followership: Leadership Turned Upside Down," *Journal of Business Strategies* 4 (1987): 39–47.

57. S. Kerr and J.M. Jermier, "Substitutes for Leadership: Their Meaning and Measurement," *Organizational Behavior and Human Performance* 22 (1978): 375–403; S. Kerr, "Substitutes

for Leadership: Some Implications for Organization Design," *Organization and Administrative Sciences* 8 (1977): 135; P.M. Podsakoff, B. Niehoff, S. MacKenzie, and M.L. Williams, "Do Substitutes for Leadership Really Substitute for Leadership? An Empirical Examination of Kerr and Jermier's Situational Leadership Model," *Organizational Behavior and Human Decision Processes* 54 (1993): 1–44.

58. J.K. Van Fleet, *The 22 Biggest Mistakes Managers Make* (West Nyack, N.Y.: Parker, 1973).

59. M. McCall and M. Lombardo, *Off the Track: Why and How Successful Executives Get Derailed—Technical Report No. 21* (Greensboro, N.C.: Center for Creative Leadership, 1983).

60. A.H. Church, "From Both Sides Now: Leadership—So Close and Yet So Far," *The Industrial-Organizational Psychologist* 35 (1998): 57–69.

Chapter 8

1. H.A. Simon, *The New Science of Managerial Decision Making*, 2d ed. (Englewood Cliffs, N.J.: Prentice-Hall, 1977).

2. A. Ebling, *Behavioral Decisions in Organizations*, 2d ed. (Glenview, Ill.: Scott, Foresman, 1978).

3. H.A. Simon, *Administrative Behavior*, 3d ed. (New York: Free Press, 1976); K.R. MacCrimmon and R.N. Taylor, "Decision Making and Problem Solving," in *Handbook of Industrial and Organizational Psychology*, ed. M.D. Dunnette (Chicago: Rand-McNally, 1976).

4. H.A. Simon, *Models of Man* (New York: Wiley, 1957).

5. J.G. March and H.A. Simon, *Organizations* (New York: Wiley, 1958).

6. Simon, *Models of Man*.

7. I.P. Levin, S.L. Schneider, and G.J. Gaeth, "All Frames Are Not Created Equal: A Typology and Critical Analysis of Framing Effects," *Organizational Behavior and Human Decision Processes* 76 (1998): 149–188; D. Kahneman and A. Tversky, "Intuitive Prediction: Biases and Corrective Procedures," *Management Science* 62 (1980): 250–257.

8. P.O. Soelberg, "Unprogrammed Decision Making," *Industrial Management Review* (1987): 19–29; D.J. Power and R.J. Aldag, "Soelberg's Job Search and Choice Model: A Clarification, Review, and Critique," *Academy of Management Review* (1985): 48–58.

9. A. Tversky and D. Kahneman, "The Framing of Decisions and the Psychology of Choice," *Science* 211 (1981): 453–458.

10. B.M. Staw, "The Escalation of Commitment to a Course of Action," *Academy of Management Review* 6 (1981): 577–587.

11. Ibid., 577.

12. B.M. Staw and J. Ross, "Commitment in an Experimenting Society: An Experiment on the Attribution of Leadership from Administrative Scenarios," *Journal of Applied Psychology* 65 (1980): 249–260.

13. H. Garland, "Throwing Good Money after Bad: The Effect of Sunk Costs on the Decision to Escalate Commitment to an Ongoing Project," *Journal of Applied Psychology* 75 (1990): 728–731; J. Ross and B.M. Staw, "Organizational Escalation and Exit: Lessons from the Shoreham Nuclear Power Plant," *Academy of Management Journal* 36 (1993): 701–732; J. Brockner, "The Escalation of Commitment to a Failing Course of Action: Toward Theoretical Progress," *Academy of Management Review* 17 (1992): 39–61; H. Drummond, "Giving It a Week and Then Another Week: A Case of Escalation in Decision Making," *Personnel Review* 26 (1997): 99–113; B.M. Staw and H. Hoang, "Sunk Costs in the NBA," *Administrative Science Quarterly* 40 (1995): 474–494; G. Whyte, A.M. Saks, and S. Hook, "When Success Breeds Failure: The Role of Self-Efficacy in Escalating Commitment to a Losing Course of Action," *Journal of Organizational Behavior* 18 (1997): 415–432.

14. Staw, "The Escalation of Commitment."

15. I.L. Janis, *Victims of Groupthink* (Boston: Houghton-Mifflin, 1972); G. Whyte, "Groupthink Reconsidered," *Academy of Management Review* 14 (1989): 45–56; M.E. Turner and A.R. Pratkanis, "Twenty-Five Years of Groupthink Theory and Research: Lessons from the Evolution of a Theory." *Organizational Behavior and Human Decision Processes* 73 (1998): 105–115; J.K. Esser, "Alive and Well after 25 Years: A Review of Groupthink Research," *Organizational Behavior and Human Decision Processes* 73 (1998): 116–141.

16. I.L. Janis, "Sources of Error in Strategic Decision Making," in *Organizational Strategy and Change*, ed. J.M. Pennings (San Francisco: Jossey Bass, 1985).

17. M.E. Turner, A.R. Pratkanis, P. Probasco, and C. Leve, "Threat, Cohesion, and Group Effectiveness: Testing a Social Identity Maintenance Perspective on Groupthink," *Journal of Experimental and Social Psychology* 63 (1992): 781–796.

18. J.A.F. Stoner, "A Comparison of Individual and Group Decisions Involving Risk" (Master's thesis, Sloan School of Management, MIT, 1961).

19. A.F. Teger and D.G. Pruitt, "Components of Group Risk Taking," *Journal of Experimental Social Psychology* 3 (1967): 189–205.

20. N. Kogan and M.A. Wallach, "Group Risk Taking as a Function of Members' Anxiety and Defensiveness," *Journal of Personality* 35 (1967): 50–63.

21. J.A.F. Stoner, "Risky and Cautious Shifts in Group Decisions: The Influence of Widely Held Values," *Journal of Experimental Social Psychology* 4 (1968): 442–459.

22. N. Kogan and M.G. Wallach, *Risk Taking: A Study of Cognition and Personality* (New York: Holt, Rinehart and Winston, 1964).

23. R.E. Knox and R.K. Safford, "Group Caution at the Racetrack," *Journal of Experimental Social Psychology* 12 (1976): 317–324.

24. D.G. Myers and H. Lamm, "The Group Polarization Phenomenon," *Psychological Bulletin* 83 (1976): 602–627; M.F. Kaplan, "The Influencing Process in Group Decision Making," in *Group Processes,* ed. C. Hendrick (Newberry Park, Cal.: Sage, 1987).

25. M.L. Maznerski, "Understanding Our Differences: Performance in Decision-Making Groups with Diverse Members," *Human Relations* 47 (1994): 531–552; J.P. Wanous and M.A. Youtz, "Solution Diversity and the Quality of Group Decisions," *Academy of Management Journal* 29 (1986): 149–159; M.E. Shaw, *Group Dynamics,* 3d ed. (New York: McGraw-Hill, 1981).

26. A.H. Van de Ven and A.L. Delbecq, "The Effectiveness of Nominal, Delphi, and Interacting Group Decision-Making Processes," *Academy of Management Journal* 17 (1974): 605–621.

27. N. Dalkey, *The Delphi Method: An Experimental Study of Group Opinions* (Santa Monica, Cal: The Rand Corporation, 1969).

28. A.L. Delbecq, A.H. Van de Ven, and D.H. Gustafson, *Group Techniques for Program Planning* (Glenview, Ill.: Scott, Foresman, 1975).

29. Van de Ven and Delbecq, "The Effectiveness of Nominal, Delphi, and Interacting Group Processes."

30. S. Harkins, B. Latané, and K. Williams, "Social Loafing: Allocating Effort or 'Taking It Easy,'" *Journal of Experimental Social Psychology* 16 (1980): 457–465.

31. R. Albanese and D. Van Fleet, "Rational Behavior in Groups: The Free Riding Tendency," *Academy of Management Review* 10 (1985): 244–255; J. George, "Extrinsic and Intrinsic Origins of Perceived Social Loafing in Organizations," *Academy of Management Journal* 35 (1992): 191–202.

32. S.G. Rogelbert, J.L. Barnes-Farrel, and G.A. Lowe, "The Stepladder Technique: An Alternative Group Structure Facilitating Effective Group Decision Making," *Journal of Applied Psychology* 77 (1992): 730–737.

33. H.C. Lehman, *Age and Achievement* (Princeton, N.J.: Princeton University Press, 1953).

34. D.W. MacKinnon, "Assessing Creative Persons," *Journal of Creative Behavior* 1 (1967): 303–304.

35. E. Raudsepp, "Are You a Creative Manager?" *Management Review* 58 (1978): 15–16.

36. T. Rotondi, "Organizational Identification: Issues and Implications," *Organizational Behavior and Human Performance* 13 (1975): 95–109.

37. E.P. Torrance, "Is Bias Against Job Changing Bias against Giftedness?" *Gifted Child Quarterly* 15 (1971): 244–248.

38. R.M. Guion, *Personnel Testing* (New York: McGraw-Hill, 1965).

39. J.F. Mee, "The Creative Thinking Process," *Indiana Business Review* 3 (1956): 4–9; F.D. Randall, "Stimulate Your Executives to Think Creatively," *Harvard Business Review* (July–August 1955): 121–128.

40. S.J. Parnes and E.A. Brunelle, "The Literature of Creativity, Part I," *Journal of Creative Behavior* 1 (1967): 52–109; D.J. Treffinger and J.C. Gowan, "An Updated Representative List of Methods and Educational Programs for Stimulating Creativity," *Journal of Creative Behavior* 5 (1971): 127–139.

41. D.W. Taylor, R.C. Berry, and C.H. Black, "Does Group Participation When Using Brainstorming Techniques Facilitate or Inhibit Creative Thinking?" *Administrative Science Quarterly* 3 (1958): 23–47.

42. A.J. DuBrin, *Contemporary Applied Management* (Plano, Texas: Business Publications, Inc., 1985).

43. R. Von Oech, *A Whack on the Side of the Head: How to Unlock Your Mind for Innovation* (New York: Warner Books, 1984).

44. S. Harrington, "What Corporate America is Teaching about Ethics," *Academy of Management Executive* 5 (1991): 21–30.

45. E. Jansen and M.A. Von Glinow, "Ethical Ambivalence and Organizational Reward Systems," *Academy of Management Review* 10 (1985): 814–822; D.P. Rubin, R.E. Reidenbach, and P.J. Forrest, "The Perceived Importance of an Ethical Issue as an Influence on the Ethical Decision-Making of Ad Managers," *Journal of Business Research* 35 (1996): 17–28; L.K. Trevino and S.A. Youngblood, "Bad Apples in Bad Barrels: A Causal Analysis of Ethical Decision-Making Behavior," *Journal of Applied Psychology* 75 (1990): 378–385; L. Barton, *Ethics: The Enemy in the Workplace* (Cincinnati, Ohio: South-Western College Publishing, 1995).

46. B.D. Penn and B.D. Collier, "Current Research in Moral Development as a Decision Support System," *Journal of Business Ethics* 4 (1985): 131–136.

Chapter 9

1. J.R. Hackman, "Group Influences on Individuals in Organizations," In M.D. Dunnette and L.M. Hough (eds.), *Handbook of Industrial and Organizational Psychology* (Palo Alto, Cal.: Consulting Psychologists Press, 1992); R. Likert, *New Patterns in Management* (New York: McGraw-Hill, 1961).

2. S. Mazumdar, "How Birds of a Feather Flock Together in Organizations: The Phenomena of Socio-Physical Congregation and Distancing," *Journal of Architectural and Planning Research* 12 (1995): 1–10.

3. D. Bryne and G.L. Clore, "A Reinforcement Model of Evaluative Responses," *Personality: An International Journal* 1 (1970): 103–128; D. Bryne, *The Attraction Paradigm* (New York: Academic Press, 1971).

4. J.W. Thibaut and H.H. Kelley, *The Social Psychology of Groups* (New York: Wiley, 1959).

5. B.W. Tuckman, "Developmental Sequence in Small Groups," *Psychological Bulletin* 63 (1965): 384–399.

6. R.S. Baron, N.L. Kerr, and N. Miller, *Group Process, Group Decision, Group Action* (Pacific Grove, Cal.: Brooks-Cole Publishing, 1992); R.B. Zajonc, "Social Facilitation," *Science* 149 (1965): 269–274.

7. B. Guerin, "Mere Presence Effects in Humans: A Review," *Journal of Experimental Social Psychology* 22 (1986): 38–77; R.G. Green, "Alternative Conceptions of Social Facilitation," in *Psychology of Group Influences*, ed. P.B. Pavles (Hillsdale, N.J.: Erlbaum, 1989); J.M. Jackson, S. Buglione, and D.S. Glenwick, "Major League Baseball Performance as a Function of Being Traded: A Drive Theory Analysis," *Personality and Social Psychology Bulletin* 14 (1988): 46–56; K. Bettenhausen, "Five Years of Group Research: What We've Learned and What Needs to Be Addressed," *Journal of Management* 17 (1991): 345–382.

8. R.M. Steers, *An Introduction to Organizational Behavior* (Glenview, Ill.: Scott, Foresman, 1984).

9. R.S. Baron, N.L. Kerr, and N. Miller, *Group Process, Group Decision, Group Action*; B. Latane, K. Williams, and S. Harkins, "Many Hands Make Light the Work: The Causes and Consequences of Social Loafing," *Journal of Personality and Social Psychology* 37 (1979): 822–832.

10. N.R.F. Maier, *Problem Solving and Creativity in Individuals and Groups* (Belmont, Cal.: Brooks-Cole, 1970).

11. H.T. Reitan and M.E. Shaw, "Group Membership, Sex-Composition of the Group, and Conformity Behavior," *Journal of Social Psychology* 64 (1964): 45–51.

12. B.M. Gross, *Organizations and Their Managing* (New York: Free Press, 1968), 242–248.

13. E.P. Torrance, "Some Consequences of Power Differences on Decision Making in Permanent and Temporary Three-Man Groups," *Research Studies, Washington State College* 22 (1954): 130–140.

14. K. Bettenhausen and J.K. Murnighan, "The Emergence of Norms in Competitive Decision-Making Groups," *Administrative Science Quarterly* 10 (1985): 350–372.

15. J.R. Hackman, *Handbook of Industrial and Organizational Psychology*.

16. A. Zander, *Making Groups Effective* (San Francisco: Jossey-Bass, 1983), 55–56.

17. R.H. Van Zelst, "Validation of a Sociometric Regrouping Procedure," *Journal of Abnormal and Social Psychology* 47 (1952): 299–301.

18. K.L. Dion, "Cohesiveness as a Determinant of Ingroup-Outgroup Bias," *Journal of Personality and Social Psychology* 28 (1973): 163–171.

19. R.M. Stogdill, "Group Productivity, Drive, and Cohesiveness," *Organizational Behavior and Human Performance* 8 (1972): 26–43.

20. J.R. Hackman, *Handbook of Industrial and Organizational Psychology*; S.E. Seashore, *Group Cohesiveness in the Industrial Work Group* (Ann Arbor: University of Michigan Press, 1954).

21. C. Evans and K. Dion, "Group Cohesion and Performance: A Meta-analysis," *Small Group Research* 22 (1991): 175–186.

22. E. Trist and K. Bamforth, "Some Social and Psychological Consequences of the Long-Wall Method of Goal-Setting," *Human Relations* 4 (1951): 1–38.

Chapter 10

1. K.A. Jehn, "A Qualitative Analysis of Conflict Types and Dimensions in Organizational Groups," *Administrative Science Quarterly* 42 (1997): 530–557; J.A. Wall and R.R. Callister, "Conflict and Its Management," *Journal of Management* 21 (1995): 515–558. K.W. Thomas, "Organizational Conflict," in *Organizational Behavior*, ed. S. Kerr (Columbus, Ohio: Grid, 1979).

2. S.P. Robbins, *Managing Organizational Conflict* (Englewood Cliffs, N.J.: Prentice-Hall, 1974).

3. A.C. Amason, "Distinguishing the Effects of Functional and Dysfunctional Conflict on Strategic Decision Making: Resolving a Paradox for Top Management Teams," *Academy of Management Journal*, 39 (1996): 123–148.

4. Robbins, *Managing Organizational Conflict*.

5. J.M. Rabbie and F. Bekkers, "Threatened Leadership and Intergroup Competition," *European Journal of Social Psychology* 8 (1978): 19–20; V.S. Mouly and J.K. Sankaran, "On the Study of Settings Marked by Severe Superior–Subordinate Conflict," *Organization Studies* 18 (1997): 175–192.

6. R.D. Luce and H. Raiffa, *Games and Decisions* (New York: Wiley, 1957), 95.

7. M. Sherif, *In Common Predicament: Social Psychology of Intragroup Conflict and Cooperation* (Boston: Houghton Mifflin, 1966).

8. Robbins, *Managing Organizational Conflict*.

9. J. Lowell, "GMAD: Lowdown at Lordstown," *Ward's Auto World*, April 1972, 29.
10. Thomas, "Organizational Conflict"; D. Weider-Hatfield and J.D. Hatfield, "Superiors' Conflict Management Strategies and Subordinate Outcomes," *Management Communication Quarterly* 10 (1996): 189–208; C. Jarboe and H.R. Witteman, "Intragroup Conflict Management in Task-Oriented Groups," *Small Group Research* 27 (1996): 316–338; K.W. Thomas, "Toward Multi-Dimensional Values in Teaching: The Example of Conflict Behaviors," *Academy of Management Review* 2 (1977): 484–490.
11. J.W. Galbraith, *Designing Complex Organizations* (Reading, Mass.: Addison-Wesley, 1973); J.A. Wall and M.W. Blum, "Negotiations," *Journal of Management* 17 (1991): 273–304.
12. R.T. Keller and W.E. Holland, "Boundary-Spanning Activity and Research and Development Management: A Comparative Study," *IEEE Transactions and Engineering Management* (1975): 130–133.
13. J.P. Meyer, "The Pros and Cons of Mediation," *Dispute Resolution Journal* 52 (1997): 8–14; C. Watson and L.R. Hoffman, "Managers as Negotiators," *Leadership Quarterly* 7 (1996): 63–85; R. Adler, B. Rosen, and E. Silverstein, "Thrust and Parry: The Art of Tough Negotiating," *Training and Development Journal* 50 (1996): 42–48.
14. Robbins, *Managing Organizational Conflict*.

Chapter 11

1. H. Selye, *The Stress of Life* (New York: McGraw-Hill, 1976).
2. M.T. Matteson and J.M. Ivancevich, *Controlling Work Stress* (San Francisco: Jossey-Bass, 1987).
3. M. Friedman and R. Rosenman, *Type A Behavior and Your Heart* (New York: Knopf, 1974); D. Ganster, J. Schaubroeck, W. Sime, and B.T. Mayes, "The Nomological Validity of the Type A Personality among Employed Adults," *Journal of Applied Psychology* 76 (1991): 143–168; R.W. Bortner, "A Short Rating Scale as a Potential Measure of Patterns of Behavior," *Journal of Chronic Diseases* 22 (1966): 87–91.
4. R. Rosenman and M. Friedman, "The Central Nervous System and Coronary Heart Disease," *Hospital Practice* 6 (1971): 87–97.
5. C.D. Jenkins, "Psychologic and Social Precursors of Coronary Disease," *New England Journal of Medicine* 284 (1971): 244–255.
6. J.H. Howard, D.A. Cunningham, and P.A. Rechnitzer, "Health Patterns Associated with Type A Behavior: A Managerial Population," *Journal of Human Stress* 2 (1976): 24–31.

7. T.H. Holmes and R.H. Rahe, "Social Readjustment Rating Scale," *Journal of Psychosomatic Research* 11 (1967): 213–218; A. DeLongis, S. Folkman, and R. Lazarus, "The Impact of Daily Stress on Health and Mood: Psychological and Social Resources as Mediators," *Journal of Personality and Social Psychology* 54 (1988): 486–495.
8. R.P. Vecchio, "It's Not Easy Being Green: Jealousy and Envy in the Workplace," in *Research in Personnel and Human Resources Management*, ed. G.R. Ferris (Greenwich, Conn.: JAI Press, 1995).
9. Ibid.
10. Ibid.
11. R.P. Vecchio, "Employee Jealousy: Antecedents, Consequences, and Testable Hypotheses" (Paper presented at the 1993 Meeting of the Western Division of the Academy of Management, San José).
12. G.N. Powell and S. Foley, "Something to Talk About: Romantic Relationships in Organizational Settings," *Journal of Management* 24 (1998): 421–448; A.B. Fisher, "Getting Comfortable with Couples in the Workplace," *Fortune* 130 (Oct. 3, 1994): 138–144.
13. L.A. Mainero, "A Review and Analysis of Power Dynamics in Organizational Romances," *Academy of Management Review* 11 (1986): 750–762.
14. A.A. McLean, *Work Stress* (Reading, Mass.: Addison-Wesley, 1979); J.V. Brady, "Ulcers in Executive Monkeys," *Scientific American* 199 (1958): 89–95.
15. M.M. Smith, M. Colligan, R.W. Horning et al., *Occupational Comparison of Stress-Related Disease Incidence* (Cincinnati: National Institute for Occupational Safety and Health. 1978).
16. McLean, *Work Stress*, 80.
17. Ibid., 82.
18. E. Goffman, "On Face Work," *Psychiatry* 18 (1955): 215–236; A.R. Hochschild, "Emotion Work: Feeling Rules and Social Structure," *American Journal of Sociology* 85 (1979): 551–575; D.E. Gibson, "Constructing Emotional Maps: Structures in Organizations and Emotions" (Paper presented at the 1993 Meeting of the Western Division of the Academy of Management, San Jose).
19. J. Van Maanen and G. Kunda, "Real Feelings: Emotional Expression and Organizational Culture," in *Research in Organizational Behavior* 11, eds. B. Staw and L. Cummings (Greenwich, Conn.: JAI Press, 1989), 43–103.
20. R.L. Kahn et al., *Organizational Stress* (New York: Wiley, 1964).
21. Ibid.
22. J. Cassel, "Psychosocial Processes and Stress: Theoretical Formulation," *International Journal of Health Services* 4 (1974): 471–482; W.H. Hendrix, N.K. Ovalle, and R.G.

Troxler, "Behavioral and Physiological Consequences of Stress and Its Antecedent Factors," *Journal of Applied Psychology* 70 (1985): 188–201; W.H. Hendrix, "Factors Predictive of Stress, Organizational Effectiveness and Coronary Heart Disease Potential," *Aviation, Space, and Environmental Medicine* (July 1985): 654–659; J. Martocchio and A. O'Leary, "Sex Differences in Occupational Stress," *Journal of Applied Psychology* 74 (1989): 495–501.

23. B.L. Margolis, W.M. Kroes, and R.P. Quinn, "Job Stress: An Unlisted Occupational Hazard," *Journal of Occupational Medicine* 16 (1974): 659–661.

24. Friedman and Rosenman, *Type A Behavior and Your Heart.*

25. J.R.P. French and R.D. Caplan, "Organizational Stress and Individual Stress," in *Failure of Success* ed., A.J. Marrow (New York: AMACOM, 1972).

26. C.M. Winget, L. Hughes, and J. La Don, "Physiological Effects of Rotational Work Shifting: A Review," *Journal of Occupational Medicine* 20 (1978): 204–210.

27. A. Brief, R.S. Schuler, and M. Van Sell, *Managing Job Stress* (Boston: Little, Brown & Co., 1981).

28. T.G. Cummings and C.L. Cooper, "A Cybernetic Framework for Studying Occupational Stress," *Human Relations* (1979): 395–418.

29. K. Bammer and B.H. Newberry, eds., *Stress and Cancer* (Toronto: Hogrefe, 1982); D. Ganster and J. Schaubroeck, "Work Stress and Employee Health," *Journal of Management* 17 (1991): 235–271; D. Nelson and C. Sutton, "Chronic Work Stress and Coping: A Longitudinal Study and Suggested New Directions," *Journal of Applied Psychology* 33 (1990): 859–869.

30. J.M. Ivancevich and M.T. Matteson, *Stress and Work* (Glenview, Ill.: Scott, Foresman, 1980).

31. L.W. Porter and R.M. Steers, "Organizational, Work, and Personal Factors in Employee Turnover and Absenteeism," *Psychological Bulletin* 80 (1973): 151–176; R.M. Steers and S.R. Rhodes, "Major Influences on Employee Attendance: A Process Model," *Journal of Applied Psychology* 63 (1978): 391–407; W.H. Mobley, R.W. Griffeth, H.H. Hand, et al., "Review and Conceptual Analysis of the Employee Turnover Process," *Psychological Bulletin* 86 (1979): 493–522.

32. A. Kornhauser, *Mental Health of the Industrial Worker* (New York: Wiley, 1965); J. Schaubroeck, D.C. Ganster, and M.L. Fox, "Dispositional Affect and Work-Related Stress," *Journal of Applied Psychology* 77 (1992): 322–335; S. Sullivan and R.S. Bhagat, "Organizational Stress, Job Satisfaction, and Job Performance: Where Do We Go from Here?" *Journal of Management* 18 (1992): 353–374.

33. J.H. Neuman and R.A. Baron, "Workplace Violence and Workplace Aggression: Evidence Concerning Specific Forms, Potential Causes, and Preferred Targets," *Journal of Management* 24 (1998): 391–419.

34. McLean, *Work Stress;* V.J. Sutherland and C.L. Cooper, "Chief Executive Life Style Stress," *Leadership and Organization Development Journal* 16 (1995): 18–28.

35. R.K. Wallace and H. Benson, "The Physiology of Meditation," *Scientific American* (1972): 84–90; T. Schultz, "What Science Is Discovering about the Potential Benefits of Meditation," *Today's Health,* April 1972, 34–37.

36. A.J. DuBrin, *Fundamentals of Organizational Behavior* (New York: Pergamon Press, 1978), 142.

37. A. Lakien, *How to Gain Control of Your Time and Your Life* (New York: Peter Wyden, 1973); R.A. MacKenzie, *The Time Trap* (New York: McGraw-Hill, 1972).

38. R.P. Vecchio, "Worker Alienation as a Moderator of the Job Quality–Job Satisfaction Relationship: The Case of Racial Differences," *Academy of Management Journal* 23 (1980): 479–486; A. Dalessio, W.H. Silverman, and J.R. Schuck, "Paths to Turnover: A Reanalysis and Review of Existing Data on the Mobley, Horner, and Hollingsworth Turnover Model," *Human Relations* 39 (1986): 245–263.

39. S.M. Crow and S.J. Hartman, "Can't Get No Satisfaction," *Leadership and Organization Development Journal* 16 (1995): 34–38.

40. J. Wanous, T. Poland, S. Premack, and K. Shannon-Davis, "The Effects of Met Expectations on Newcomer Attitudes and Behaviors: A Review and Meta-analysis," *Journal of Applied Psychology* 76 (1991): 288–297.

41. J.P. Wanous, *Organizational Entry: Recruitment, Selection, Orientation, and Socialization of Newcomers* (Reading, Mass.: Addison-Wesley, 1992); J.P. Wanous and A. Colella, "Organizational Entry Research: Current Status and Future Directions," in *Research in Personnel and Human Resources Management;* vol. 7, ed. K. Rowland and G. Ferris (Greenwich, Conn.: JAI Press, 1989), 59–120; P.W. Hom, R.W. Griffeth, L.E. Palich, and J.S. Bracher, "Realistic Job Previews for New Professionals: A Two-Occupation Test of Mediating Processes" (Working paper, Arizona State University, 1993); R.J. Vandenberg and V. Scarpello, "The Matching Model: An Examination of the Processes Underlying Realistic Job Previews," *Journal of Applied Psychology* 75 (1990): 60–67.

42. B.M. Staw and J. Ross, "Stability in the Midst of Change: A Dispositional Approach to Job Attitudes," *Journal of Applied Psychology* 70 (1985): 469–480; B.M. Staw, N.E. Bell, and J.A. Clausen, "The Dispositional Approach to Job Attitudes: A Lifetime Longitudinal Test," *Administrative Science Quarterly* 31 (1986): 56–77; T.A. Judge and E.A. Locke, "Effect of Dysfunctional Thought Processes on Subjective Well-being and Job Satisfaction," *Journal of Applied Psychology* 78

(1993): 475–490; T.A. Judge, "The Dispositional Perspective in Human Resources Research," in *Research in Personnel and Human Resources Management,* 10th ed., ed. G.R. Ferris and K.M. Rowland (Greenwich, Conn.: JAI Press, 1992): 31–72; K.R. Parkes, "Coping, Negative Affectivity, and the Work Environment: Additive and Interactive Predictors of Mental Health," *Journal of Applied Psychology* 75 (1990): 399–409; P.Y. Chen and P.E. Spector, "Negative Affectivity as the Underlying Cause of Correlations Between Stressors and Strains," *Journal of Applied Psychology* 76 (1991): 398–407; T. Judge, "Does Affective Disposition Moderate the Relationship Between Job Satisfaction and Voluntary Turnover?" *Journal of Applied Psychology* 78 (1993): 395–401; J. George and A. Brief, "Feeling Good—Doing Good: A Conceptual Analysis of the Mood at Work–Organizational Spontaneity Relationship," *Psychological Bulletin* 132 (1992): 310–329; P. Moyle, "The Role of Negative Affectivity in the Stress Process," *Journal of Organizational Behavior* 16 (1995): 647–668.

43. R.D. Arvey, T.J. Bouchard, H.L. Segal, and L.M. Abraham, "Job Satisfaction: Environmental and Genetic Components," *Journal of Applied Psychology* 74 (1989): 187–192.

44. D.W. Organ, "The Happy Curve," *Business Horizon* 38 (1995): 1–3; J. Schaubroeck, D.C. Ganster, and B. Kemmerer, "Does Trait Affect Promote Job Attitude Stability?" *Journal of Organizational Behavior* 17 (1996): 191–196; A. Davis-Blake and J. Pfeffer, "Just a Mirage: The Search for Dispositional Effects in Organizational Research," *Academy of Management Review* 14 (1989): 385–400; I. Levin and J. Stokes, "Dispositional Approach to Job Satisfaction," *Journal of Applied Psychology* 74 (1989): 752–758; T.J. Bouchard, R.D. Arvey, L. Keller, and N. Segal, "Genetic Influences on Job Satisfaction: A Reply to Cropanzano and James," *Journal of Applied Psychology* 76 (1991): 89–93.

45. R.P. Quinn and G.L. Staines, *The 1977 Quality of Employment Survey* (Ann Arbor: Institute for Social Research, University of Michigan, 1979).

46. C.N. Weaver, "Job Satisfaction in the United States in the 1970s," *Journal of Applied Psychology* 65 (1980): 364–367.

47. H.L. Sheppard and N. Herrick, *Where Have All the Robots Gone?* (New York: Free Press, 1972); M.C. Morse and R.S. Weiss, "The Function and Meaning of Work and the Job," *American Sociological Review* 20 (1955): 191–198; R.P. Vecchio, "The Function and Meaning of Work and the Job: Morse and Weiss (1955) Revisited," *Academy of Management Journal* 23 (1980): 361–367.

48. G. Johns, "The Great Escape," *Psychology Today,* October 1987, 30–33; L.R. Waters and D. Roach, "Relationship between Job Attitudes and Two Forms of Withdrawal from the Work Situation," *Journal of Applied Psychology* 55

(1971): 92–94; R. Hackett and R.M. Guion, "A Reevaluation of the Absenteeism–Job Satisfaction Relationship," *Organizational Behavior and Human Decision Processes* (1985): 340–381; K.D. Scott and G.S. Taylor, "An Examination of Conflicting Findings on the Relationship Between Job Satisfaction and Absenteeism: A Meta-analysis," *Academy of Management Journal* 28 (1985): 588–612.

49. F.J. Smith, "Work Attitudes as Predictors of Attendance on a Specific Day," *Journal of Applied Psychology* 62 (1977): 16–19.

50. S. Adler and J. Golan, "Lateness as a Withdrawal Behavior," *Journal of Applied Psychology* 66 (1981): 544–554.

51. R.P. Vecchio, "Workers' Perceptions of Job Market Favorability and Job Insecurity," *Mid-Atlantic Journal of Business* 21 (1983): 9–16; J.M. Carsten and P.E. Spector, "Unemployment, Job Satisfaction, and Employee Turnover: A Meta-analytic Test of the Muchinsky Model, *Journal of Applied Psychology* 72 (1987): 374–381.

52. H. Wool, "What's Wrong with Work in America?: A Review Essay," *Monthly Labor Review* 96 (1973): 38–44.

53. D.R. Dalton, W.D. Todor, and D.M. Krachhardt, "Turnover Overstated: The Functional Taxonomy," *Academy of Management Review* 7 (1982): 117–123; M.B. Staw, "The Consequences of Turnover," *Journal of Occupational Behavior* (1980): 253–273.

54. M.E. Gordon and A.S. DeNisi, "A Re-examination of the Relationship Between Union Membership and Job Satisfaction," *Industrial and Labor Relations Review* 48 (1995): 222–236.

55. W.C. Hamner and F.J. Smith, "Work Attitudes as Predictors of Unionization Activity," *Journal of Applied Psychology* 63 (1978): 415–421.

56. J.G. Getman, S.B. Goldberg, and J.B. Herman, *Union Representation Elections: Law and Reality* (New York: Russell Sage Foundation, 1976); C.A. Schriesheim, "Job Satisfaction, Attitudes Toward Unions, and Voting in a Union Representation Election," *Journal of Applied Psychology* 63 (1978): 548–552; M.D. Zalesny, "Comparison of Economic and Noneconomic Factors in Predicting Faculty Vote Preference in a Union Representation Election," *Journal of Applied Psychology* 70 (1985): 243–256.

57. E.A. Fleishman and E.F. Harris, "Patterns of Leadership Behavior Related to Employee Grievances and Turnover," *Personnel Psychology* 15 (1962): 54–56; E.A. Fleishman, E.F. Harris, and H.E. Burtt, *Leadership and Supervision in Individuals* (Columbus: Ohio State University Personnel Research Board, 1955).

58. D. Buss, "Job Tryouts without Pay Get More Testing in U.S. Auto Plants," *The Wall Street Journal,* January 10, 1985, 31.

59. M. Sprouse, *Sabotage in the American Workplace: Anecdotes of Dissatisfaction, Mischief and Revenge* (San Francisco: Pressure Drop Press, 1992).

60. R.A. Giacolone and P. Rosenfeld, "Reasons for Employee Sabotage in the Workplace," *Journal of Business and Psychology* 1 (1987): 367–378.

61. M.D. Crino and T.L. Leap, "What HR Managers Must Know about Employee Sabotage," *Personnel* (1989): 31–37.

62. C.M. Staehle, *Job Dissatisfaction and Action Alternatives: A Study of the Relationship between Dissatisfaction and Behaviors in Work Organizations* (Honors thesis, College of Business and Management, University of Maryland, 1985).

63. V.L. Allen and D.B. Greenberger, "Destruction and Perceived Control," in *Advances in Experimental Psychology*, 2d ed., ed. A. Baum and J.E. Singer (N.J.: Erlbaum, 1980).

64. M.T. Iaffaldana and P.M. Muchinsky, "Job Satisfaction and Job Performance: A Meta-analysis," *Psychological Bulletin* 97 (1985): 251–273.

65. R.S. Bhagat, "Conditions Under Which Stronger Job Performance–Job Satisfaction Relationships May Be Observed: A Closer Look at Two Situational Contingencies," *Academy of Management Journal* 25 (1982): 772–789.

Chapter 12

1. J. Fulk and B. Boyd, "Emerging Theories of Communication in Organizations," *Journal of Management* 17 (1993): 407–446; M.M. Allen, J.M. Gotcher, and J.H. Seibert, "A Decade of Organizational Communication Research," in S. Deetz (ed.), *Communication Yearbook* (Newbury Park, Cal.: Sage, 1993); O.W. Baskin and C.E. Aronoff, *Interpersonal Communication in Organizations* (Glenview, Ill.: Scott, Foresman, 1980), 4.

2. G. Johns, *Organizational Behavior: Understanding Life at Work* (Glenview, Ill.: Scott, Foresman, 1983).

3. C.A. O'Reilly and L.R. Pondy, "Organizational Communication," in *Organizational Behavior*, ed. S. Kerr (Columbus, Ohio: Grid, 1979), 119–150.

4. M.E. Shaw, *Group Dynamics: The Psychology of Small Group Behavior* (New York: McGraw-Hill, 1976).

5. Ibid.

6. B.L. Hawkins and P. Preston, *Managerial Communication* (Santa Monica, Cal.: Goodyear, 1981).

7. L.W. Rue and L. Byars, *Communication in Organizations* (Homewood, Ill.: Irwin, 1980).

8. H. Fayol, *General and Industrial Management*, trans. Constance Storrs (London: Pitman, 1949).

9. E.M. Rogers and R.A. Rogers, *Communication in Organizations* (New York: Free Press, 1976).

10. A. Pettigrew, "Information Control as a Power Resource," *Sociology* 6 (1972): 187–204.

11. P.H. Lawrence and J.W. Lorsch, *Organization and Environment: Managing Differences and Integration* (Homewood, Ill.: Irwin, 1969).

12. K.H. Roberts and C.A. O'Reilly, "Some Correlates of Communication Roles in Organizations," *Academy of Management Journal* 22 (1979): 42–57.

13. S. Martin, "The Role of Nonverbal Communication in Quality Improvement," *National Productivity Review* 15 (1995): 27–39; Baskin and Aronoff, *Interpersonal Communication in Organizations*, 102.

14. A. Mehrabian, "Verbal and Nonverbal Interaction of Strangers in a Waiting Situation," *Journal of Experimental Research in Personality* 5 (1971): 127–138; A. Mehrabian, *Silent Messages* (Belmont, Cal.: Wadsworth, 1971).

15. Ibid.

16. Ibid.

17. A. Mehrabian, "Significance of Posture and Position in the Communication of Attitude and Status Relationships," *Psychological Bulletin* 71 (1971): 359–372; Mehrabian, "Decoding of Inconsistent Communications."

18. Ibid.

19. E.T. Hall, "A System for the Notation of Proxemic Behavior," *American Anthropologist* 5 (1963): 1003–1026.

20. E.T. Hall, *The Hidden Dimension* (Garden City, N.Y.: Doubleday, 1966).

21. R. Ardrey, *The Territorial Imperative* (New York: Atheneum, 1966).

22. Ibid.

23. H. Osmond, "Function as the Basis of Psychiatric Ward Design," *Mental Hospitals* 8 (1957): 23–32; H. Osmond, "The Relationship between Architect and Psychiatrist," in *Psychiatric Architecture*, ed. C. Goshen (Washington, D.C.: American Psychiatric Association, 1959).

24. S. Van der Ryn and M. Silverstein, *Dorms at Berkeley: An Environmental Analysis* (Berkeley: Center for Planning and Development Research, 1967).

25. Baskin and Aronoff, *Interpersonal Communication in Organizations*.

26. E.H. Marcus, "Neurolinguistic Programming." *Personnel Journal* 27 (1983): 972.

27. E.E. Lawler, L.W. Porter, and A. Tannenbaum, "Managerial Attitudes Toward Interaction Episodes," *Journal of Applied Psychology* 52 (1968): 432–439.

28. D. Synder, "Electronic Mail Privacy," *Journal of Individual Employment Rights* 3 (1996): 235–249; T.A. Daniel, "Electronic and Voice Mail Monitoring of Employees," *Employment Relations Today* 22 (1995): 1–10; T. Brady, "Avoid Privacy Collisions in the Information Highway," *Management Review* 86 (1997): 45–47; R.F. Federico and J.M. Bowley, "The Great E-Mail Debate," *HR Magazine* 41 (1996):

67; J. Schmitz and J. Fulk, "Organizational Colleagues, Media Richness, and Electronic Mail: A Test of the Social Influence Model of Technology Use," *Communication Research* 18 (1991): 487–523.

29. K.E. Davis, *Human Behavior at Work* (New York: McGraw-Hill, 1977).

30. Ibid.

31. K.E. Davis, "Management Communication and the Grapevine," *Harvard Business Review* 31 (1953): 43–49.

32. Ibid.

33. R. Hershey, "The Grapevine—Here to Stay But not Beyond Control," *Personnel* 20 (1966): 64.

34. M.K. Kennedy, "Who Pruned the Grapevine?" *Across the Board* 34 (1997): 55–56; B. Smith, "Care and Feeding of the Office Grapevine," *Management Review* 85 (1996): 6; J. Smythe, "Harvesting the Office Grapevine," *People Management* 1 (1995): 24–26; Davis, *Human Behavior at Work*; E. Rudolph, "A Study of Informal Communication Patterns within a Multi-Shift Public Utility Organization Unit" (Ph.D. diss., University of Denver, 1971).

35. W. St. John, "In-House Communication Guidelines," *Personnel Journal* (1981): 877.

36. A.J. DuBrin, *Foundations of Organizational Behavior* (Englewood Cliffs, N.J.: Prentice-Hall, 1984).

37. K.H. Chung and L.C. Megginson, *Organizational Behavior: Developing Managerial Skills* (New York: Harper & Row, 1981), 203–204.

38. D. Craib, "Allstate's Communication Strategy: It's a Tool for Growth," *Communication World*, May 1986, 24–26; R.M. Harris, "Turn Listening into a Powerful Presence," *Training and Development Journal* 51 (1997): 9–11.

Chapter 13

1. R. Duncan, "What Is the Right Organization Structure?" *Organizational Dynamics* 33 (1979): 66; H. Wilmott, "What Has Been Happening in Organizational Theory, and Does It Matter?" *Personnel Review* 24 (1995): 33–53; M.M. Lucio and M. Noon, "Organizational Change and the Tensions of Decentralization," *Human Resource Management Journal* 5 (1994): 65–78; L. Keen, "Organizational Decentralization and Budgetary Devolution in Local Government," *Human Resource Management Journal* 5 (1994): 79–98.

2. P. Petre, "America's Most Successful Entrepreneur," *Fortune*, October 27, 1986, 24–32.

3. T. Peters, *Thriving on Chaos* (New York: Harper & Row, 1987), 430.

4. J.C. Worthy, "Organizational Structure and Employee Morale," *American Sociological Review* 15 (1950): 169–179; R.P. Vecchio, "A Cross-National Comparison of Span of Control," *International Journal of Management*, 72 (1995): 261–270.

5. M. Weber, *The Theory of Social and Economic Organizations*, trans. A. Henderson and T. Parsons (New York: Free Press, 1947); K. Gergen and T.J. Thatchenkery, "Organization Science as Social Construction," *Journal of Applied Behavioral Science* 32 (1996): 356–377.

6. P.M. Blau, *On the Nature of Organizations* (New York: Wiley, 1974).

7. J. Child, "Managerial and Organizational Factors Associated with Company Performance, Part II. A Contingency Analysis," *Journal of Management Studies* 12 (1975): 12–27.

8. R.L. Daft, *Organizational Theory and Design* (New York: West, 1983).

9. Child, "Managerial and Organizational Factors Associated with Company Performance."

10. Blau, *On the Nature of Organizations*.

11. R. Likert and J.G. Likert, *New Ways of Managing Conflict* (New York: McGraw-Hill, 1976).

12. Likert and Likert, *New Ways of Managing Conflict*.

13. J.B. Miner, *Theories of Organizational Structure and Process* (Hinsdale, Ill.: The Dryden Press, 1982), 52.

14. J.B. Miner, "Limited Domain Theories of Organizational Energy," in *Middle Range Theory and the Study of Organizations*, eds. C.C. Pinder and L.F. Moore (Boston: Maritimes Nijhoff, 1980), 273–286; R.N. Stern, S.R. Barley, W.R. Scott, and J.R. Blau, "Organizations and Social Systems: Organization Theory's Neglected Mandate," *Administrative Science Quarterly* 41 (1996): 146–179.

15. M.W. Stebbins and B.R. Shani, "Organization Design and the Knowledge Worker," *Leadership and Organization Development Journal* 16 (1995): 23–30; E.L. Trist and K.W. Bamforth, "Some Social and Psychological Consequences of the Longwall Method of Goal Setting," *Human Relations* 4 (1951): 1–38.

16. R.E. Miles, H.J. Coleman, and W.E.D. Creed, "Keys to Success in Corporate Redesign," *California Management Review* 37 (1995): 128–145; D.S. Cohen, "The Quality-of-Worklife Movement," *Training HRD* 30 (January 1979): 24.

17. R.E. Anderson, "Matrix Redux," *Business Horizons* 37 (1994): 6–10; W.F. Joyce, "Matrix Organization: A Social Experiment," *Academy of Management Journal* 29 (1986): 536–561.

Chapter 14

1. R.B. Duncan, "The Characteristics of Organizational Environments and Perceived Environmental Uncertainty," *Administrative Science Quarterly* 17 (1972): 313–327; B. Boyd and J. Fulk, "Executive Scanning and Perceived Uncertainty," *Journal of Management* 22 (1996): 1–21.

2. Ibid.

3. P. Thompson and J. O'Connell-Davidson, "The Continuity of Discontinuity: Management and Rhetoric in Turbulent Times," *Personnel Review* 24 (1995): 17–33; J.B. Miner, *Theories of Organizational Structure and Process* (Hinsdale, Ill.: The Dryden Press, 1982); E. Gerloff, N. Kanoff-Muir, and W.D. Bodensteiner, "Three Components of Perceived Environmental Uncertainty: An Exploratory Analysis of the Effects of Aggregation," *Journal of Management* 17 (1991): 749–768.

4. M. Sharfman and J. Dean, "Conceptualizing and Measuring the Organizational Environment: A Multidimensional Approach," *Journal of Management* 17 (1991): 681–700.

5. D.B. Marin, M.C. White, and D.V. Brazeal, "Towards a Theory of Organizational Evolution," *International Journal of Management* 13 (1996): 523–530; J. Pfeffer and G. Salancik, *The External Control of Organizations* (New York: Harper & Row, 1978); D. Wholey and J. Brittain, "Organizational Ecology: Findings and Implications," *Academy of Management Review* 11 (1986): 513–533.

6. R.L. Daft, *Organizational Theory and Design* (St. Paul, Minn.: West, 1983).

7. T. Burns and G.M. Stalker, *The Management of Innovation* (London: Tavistock, 1961); T. Burns, "Industry in a New Age," *New Society* 31 (1963): 17–20; R.P. Vecchio and T.L. Keon, "Predicting Employee Satisfaction from Congruency among Individual Need, Job Design, and System Structure," *Journal of Occupational Behavior* 2 (1981): 283–292.

8. J. Woodward, *Industrial Organization* (London: Oxford University Press, 1965); R.M. Price, "Technology and Strategic Advantage," *California Management Review* 38 (1996): 38–56.

9. W.L. Zwerman, *New Perspectives on Organizational Theory* (Westport, Conn.: Greenwood, 1970).

10. R.M. Marsh and H. Mannari, "Technology and Size as Determinants of the Organizational Structure of Japanese Factories," *Administrative Science Quarterly* 26 (1981): 33–56.

11. E.H. Schein, *Organizational Culture and Leadership* (San Francisco: Jossey-Bass, 1985)

12. R.H. Kilmann, "Corporate Culture," *Psychology Today,* April 1985, 62–68.

13. Schein, *Organizational Culture and Leadership;* H.M. Trice and J.M. Beyer, *The Cultures of Work Organization* (Englewood Cliffs, N.J.: Prentice-Hall, 1993).

14. Ibid.

15. Ibid.; Kilmann, "Corporate Culture."

16. Schein, *Organizational Culture and Leadership.*

17. Ibid.; C.G. Smith and R.P. Vecchio, "Organizational Culture and Strategic Management: Issues in the Management of Strategic Change," *Journal of Managerial Issues* 5 (1993): 53–70; L.J. Mischel, "Revisiting the Porter, Lawler, and Hackman Congruency Model," Paper presented at the Society for Industrial and Organizational Psychology Meeting, May 1995.

18. C.A. O'Reilly, J. Chatman, and D.F. Caldwell, "People and Organizational Culture: A Profile Comparison Approach to Assessing Person-Organization Fit," *Academy of Management Journal* 34 (1991): 487–516.

19. B. M. Meglino, E.C. Ravlin, and C.L. Adkins, "Value Congruence and Satisfaction with a Leader: An Examination of the Role of Interaction," *Human Relations* 44 (1991): 481–495; E.C. Ravlin and B.M. Meglino, "The Transitivity of Work Values: Hierarchical Preference Ordering of Socially Desirable Stimuli," *Organizational Behavior and Human Decision Processes* 44 (1989): 494–508.

20. Meglino, Ravlin, and Adkins, "A Work Values Approach to Corporate Culture"; P.C. Earley, "East Meets West Meets Mideast: Further Explorations of Collectivistic and Individualistic Work Groups," *Academy of Management Journal* 36 (1993): 319–348; C.M. Fiol, "Managing Culture as a Competitive Resource: An Identity-based View of Sustainable Competitive Advantage," *Journal of Management* 17 (1991): 196–211; G. Hofstede, B. Neuijen, D. Ohayv, and G. Sanders, "Measuring Organizational Cultures: A Qualitative and Quantitative Study across Twenty Cases," *Administrative Science Quarterly* 35 (1990): 286–316; N. Boyacigiller and N. Adler, "The Parochial Dinosaur: Organizational Science in a Global Context," *Academy of Management Review* 16 (1991): 262–290.

21. R. Levine and E. Wolff, "Social Time: The Heartbeat of Culture," *Psychology Today,* March 1985, 28–35.

22. E.T. Hall, *The Dance of Life* (Garden City, N.Y.: Anchor-Doubleday, 1969).

23. M. Haire, E.E. Ghiselli, and L.W. Proter, *Managerial Thinking* (New York: Wiley, 1965).

24. G.W. England, *The Manager and His Values* (Cambridge, Mass.: Ballinger, 1975).

25. Haire, Ghiselli, and Porter, *Managerial Thinking;* R. Griffeth, P. Hom, A. DeNisi, et al., "A Multivariate Multinational Comparison of Managerial Attitudes," in *Proceedings of the 40th Annual Meeting of the Academy of Management* (1980): 63–67.

26. R. Vernon and L.T. Wells, *Manager in the International Economy* (Englewood Cliffs, N.J.: Prentice-Hall, 1981); W. Hardman and J. Heidelberg, "When Sexual Harassment Is a Foreign Affair," *Personnel Journal* 75 (1996): 91; V.E. Schein, R. Mueller, T. Lituchy, and J. Liu, "Think Manager—Think Male: A Global Phenomenon," *Journal of Organizational Behavior* 17 (1996): 33–41.

27. G. Hofstede, *Culture's Consequences* (New York: Sage Publications, 1980); G. Hofstede, "Cultural Constraints in Management Theories," *Academy of Management Executive* 7 (1993): 81–93.

28. W.G. Ouchi and M. Price, "Hierarchies, Clans and Theory Z: A New Perspective on Organization Development," *Organizational Dynamics* 32 (Autumn 1978): 24–44; K.H. Chung and M.A. Gray, "Can We Adopt the Japanese Methods of Human Resources Management?" *Personnel Administrator* 64 (May 1982): 43–47; R.R. Rehder, "Education and Training: Have the Japanese Beaten Us Again?" *Personnel Journal* 64 (January 1983): 42–47; W.G. Ouchi, *Theory Z: How American Business Can Meet the Japanese Challenge* (Reading, Mass.: Addison-Wesley, 1981).

29. D. Wallechinsky, "Are We Still Number One?" *Parade,* April 1997, 4–7.

30. L.S. Dillon, "Adopting Japanese Management: Some Cultural Stumbling Blocks," *Personnel* 32 (July 1983): 77–81.

31. Ibid.

32. Ibid.

33. H. Befu and C. Cernosia, "Demise of 'Permanent Employment' in Japan," *Human Resource Management* 29 (1990): 231–250.

34. J.J. Sullivan and R.B. Peterson, "A Test of Theories Underlying the Japanese Lifetime Employment System," *Journal of International Business Studies* (1991): 79–97.

35. S. Kamata, *Japan in the Passing Lane* (New York: Pantheon, 1983).

36. "Dying for a Living," *Time,* May 3, 1993, 19.

37. L. Smith, "Cracks in the Japanese Work Ethic," *Fortune,* May 14, 1984, 162–168.

38. R.N. Farmer, "International Management," in *Contemporary Management: Issues and Viewpoints,* ed. J.J. McGuire (Englewood Cliffs, N.J.: Prentice-Hall, 1974).

39. N.J. Adler, *International Dimensions of Organizational Behavior* (Boston: Kent, 1985).

40. P.R. Harris, and R.T. Moran, *Managing Cultural Differences* (Houston: Gulf, 1987); L.E. Palich, P.W. Hom, and R.W. Griffeth, "Managing in the International Context: Testing Cultural Generality of Sources of Commitment to Multinational Enterprises," *Journal of Management* 21 (1995): 671–690; J.S. Osland, "Working Abroad: A Hero's Adventure," *Training and Development Journal* 49 (1995): 47–51; R. Stewart, "German Management," *Business Horizons* 39 (1996): 52–54; J.S. Osland, "Working Abroad: A Hero's Adventure," *Training and Development Journal* 49 (1995); 47–51; R. Stewart, "German Management," *Business Horizons* 39 (1996): 52–54.

41. C.R. Greer and G.K. Stephens, "Employee Relations Issues for U.S. Companies in Mexico," *California Management Review* 38 (1996): 121–145.

42. B. Stening and E.F. Ngan, "The Cultural Context of Human Resource Management in East Asia," *Asia Pacific Journal of HRM* 35 (1997): 3–15; M. Johnson, "China: The Last True Business Frontier," *Management Review* 3 (1996): 39–43; E.D. Smith, "Doing Business in Vietnam: A Cultural Guide," *Business Horizons* 39 (1996): 47–51; C. Hebard, "Managing Effectively in Asia," *Training and Development Journal* 50 (1996): 35–39.

43. K. Rubens, "Changes in Russia," *HR Magazine* 40 (1995): 70–80.

44. H.C. Triandis, "The Psychological Measurement of Cultural Syndromes," *American Psychologist* 51 (1996): 407–415; S. H. Schwartz, "Beyond Individualism-Collectivism: New Cultural Dimensions of Values," in U. Kim, H. C. Triandis and G. Yoon (eds.) Individualism and Collectivism: Theoretical and Methodological Issues (BSF, 1993).

Chapter 15

1. C.L. Pearce and C.P. Osmond, "Metaphors for Change," *Organizational Dynamics* 24 (1996): 23–35; L.E. Greiner, "Evolution and Revolution as Organizations Grow," *Harvard Business Review* 50 (1972): 37–46.

2. D.A. Whetten, "Organizational Decline: A Neglected Topic in Organizational Science," *Academy of Management Review* 5 (1980): 557; E. Stark, "Surviving Organizational Death," *Psychology Today* , June 1989, 17; R. D'Aveni, "The Aftermath of Organizational Decline," *Academy of Journal* 32 (1989): 577–605.

3. J. Basaszewski, "Thirteen Ways to Get a Company in Trouble," *Inc.,* September 1981, 97–100; R.L. Daft, *Organization Theory and Design* (St. Paul, Minn.: West, 1983); T.J. Peters, "Putting Excellence into Management," *Business Week,* July 21, 1980, 196–205.

4. W.L. French and C.H. Bell, *Organization Development: Behavioral Science Interventions for Organization Improvement,* 2d ed. (Englewood Cliffs, N.J.: Prentice-Hall, 1978), 14; J.I. Porras, *Stream Analysis* (Reading, Mass.: Addison-Wesley, 1987).

5. B. Schneider, A.P. Brief, and R.A. Guzzo, "Creating a Climate and Culture for Sustainable Organizational Change," *Organizational Dynamics* 24 (1996): 7–19; C. Hardy and F. Redivo, "Power and Organizational Development: A Framework for Organizational Change," *Journal of General Management* 20 (1994): 29–41. K. Lewin, *Field Theory in Social Science* (New York: Harper and Row, 1951).

6. R.D. Iverson, "Employee Acceptance of Organizational Change," *International Journal of Human Resource*

Management 7 (1996): 122–149; K.E. Hultman, "Scaling the Wall of Resistance," *Training and Development Journal* 49 (1995): 15–18; R.J. Recardo, "Overcoming Resistance to Change," *National Productivity Review* 14 (1995): 5–12. L. Coch and J.R.P. French, "Overcoming Resistance to Change," *Human Relations* 1 (1948): 512–532.

7. P.R. Lawrence, "How to Deal with Resistance to Change," *Harvard Business Review* 47 (1969): 115–122; A. Armenakis, M. Harris, and K. Mossholder, "Creating Readiness for Large-Scale Change," *Human Relations* 46 (1993): 681–703.

8. French and Bell, *Organization Development.*

9. D. Lewis, "The Organizational Culture Saga," *Leadership and Organizational Development Journal* 17 (1996): 12–19.

10. M. Fields and J. Thacker, "Influence of Quality of Work Life on Company and Union Commitment," *Academy of Management Journal* 35 (1992): 439–450.

11. R. Golembiewski and B. Sun, "Positive-Findings Bias in QWL Studies: Rigor and Outcomes in a Large Sample," *Journal of Management* 16 (1990): 665–674.

12. French and Bell, *Organization Development.*

13. S.C. Marrinac, N.R. Jones, and M.W. Meyer, "Competitive Renewal Through Workplace Innovation: The Financial and Non-Financial Returns to Innovate Workplace Practices." A report prepared for the U.S. Department of Labor (Boston: Ernst and Young Center for Business Innovation, 1995).

14. J.I. Porras and R.C. Silvers, "Organization Development and Transformation," *Annual Review of Psychology* 42 (1991): 51–78. J.I. Porras and P.O. Berg, "The Impact of Organization Development," *Academy of Management Review* 3 (1978): 249–266; J.I. Porras, P.J. Robertson, and L. Goldman, "Organization Development: Theory, Practice, and Research," in *Handbook of Industrial/Organizational Psychology* , ed. M.D. Dunnette (Palo Alto, Cal.: Consulting Psychologists Press, 1992); G.A. Neuman, J. Edwards, and N. Raja, "Organizational Development Interventions: A Meta-analysis of Their Effects on Satisfaction and Other Attitudes," *Personnel Psychology* 42 (1989): 461–483; A.N. Kluger and A. DeNisi, "The Effect of Feedback Interventions on Performance," *Psychological Bulletin* 119 (1996): 254–284.

15. D. Terpstra, "Relationship between Methodological Rigor and Reported Outcomes in Organizational Development Evaluation Research," *Journal of Applied Psychology* (1981): 541–542.

16. A.J. DuBrin, *Foundations of Organizational Behavior* (Englewood Cliffs, N.J.: Prentice-Hall, 1984); P.J. Robertson, D.R. Roberts, and J.I. Porras, "Dynamics of Planned Organizational Change: Assessing Empirical Support for a Theoretical Model," *Academy of Management Journal* 36 (1993): 619–634.

17. Ibid., 471.

18. W.G. Bennis, *Organization Development: Its Nature, Origins, and Prospects* (Reading, Mass.: Addison-Wesley, 1969); J. Woodall, "Managing Culture Change: Can It Ever Be Ethical?" *Personnel Review* 25 (1996): 26–40.

Name Index

Subject Index